CH00687016

Also by Timothy Green:

The World of Gold (1968)
The Smugglers
The Adventurers
The World of Gold Today (1973)
How to Buy Gold
The World of Diamonds
The New World of Gold (1981 and 1985)
The Prospect for Gold: the view to the Year 2000
The World of Gold (1993, completely revised)
The Millennium in Gold and The Millennium in Silver

With Deborah Russell: The Gold Companion: the A-Z of Mining, Marketing, Trading & Technology

THE AGES OF
GOLD

MINES, MARKETS, MERCHANTS AND
GOLDSMITHS FROM EGYPT TO TROY,
ROME TO BYZANTIUM, AND VENICE TO
THE SPACE AGE

TIMOTHY GREEN

GFMS Limited
London

Copyright © 2007, Timothy Green

First published in Great Britain in 2007

GFMS Limited
Hedges House
153-155 Regent Street
London, W1B 4JE
Great Britain
www.gfms.co.uk

All rights reserved. No part of this publication may be reproduced, stored in a retrieval system or transmitted in any form or by any means without the prior written permission of the copyright owner. Brief extracts may be reproduced only for the purpose of criticism or review and provided that they are accompanied by a clear acknowledgement as to their source and the name of the copyright owner.

The right of Timothy Green to be identified as the author of this work has been asserted by him in accordance with the Copyright, Designs and Patents Act, 1988.

Cover design and page layout by Laurette Perrard
Maps by Gillian Tyson
Other contributor: Sapna Loknath

Printed in Great Britain by Park Communications, London

ISBN: 978-0-9555411-1-7

Contents

Preface   vii

Part One: The Ancient World 4000 – 1 BC

1.   Mesopotamia: The Land Between the Rivers   15
2.   Egypt: A gift from the Nile   35
3.   Troy: The Jewellery Emporium   61
4.   Minoan Crete: To the 'Wine-Dark Sea'   69
5.   Mycenæ: Heroes Ancient and Modern   77
6.   The Phoenicians: World Travellers   87
7.   The Etruscans: Virtuoso Goldsmiths   101
8.   Lydia/Persia:The coins of Croesus; The Persians' Challenge   109
9.   Athens Goes for Silver; Alexander for Gold   123
10. Black Sea Shores: Scythia: Nomad Warrior Meets Classical Goldsmith   141
11. On the Fringe: Celtic Craftsmanship   157

Part Two: Empires AD 1 – 1200

12. China: A serious player: Ancient and Modern   171
13. Rome: An Empire Built on Gold   187
14. Byzantium: The Thousand Year Gold Standard   207
15. The Rise of Islam: Cornering African Gold   225

Part Three: New Horizons 1200 – 1700

16. Italy: Venice: first gold 'fixing'   241
            Florence: Renaissance goldsmiths   253
17. Precolumbian Gold: A Unique Legacy   261
18. Spain: Squandered Treasure   281

Part Four: Gold standard: whence it came, where it went: 1700 – 2000

19. Britain and Brazil: The 'Accidental' Gold Standard   293
20. London: The 1810 Bullion Committee   307
21. 1848-1914: Gold Standard Triumphant   325
22. 1914-1933: Goodbye Gold Standard   351
23. 1934-1968: The Age of $35 Gold   365
24. The View from 2000: High Technology Gold   377

Notes to Chapters   387
Bibliography   421
Index   433

Preface

The history of gold is a moveable feast. Every year new treasures and coin hoards turn up under the plough or the archaeologist's trowel unveiling fresh insights. The dawn for gold as a revered metal was long regarded as being in Mesopotamia or Egypt around 3000 BC. That theory evaporated with the discovery in the 1970s of gold axe-sceptres, bracelets, necklaces and hundreds of beads fashioned by goldsmiths before 4000 BC in an ancient necropolis at Varna on the Black Sea coast of Bulgaria. That debut, in turn, was revised in 2004 when the British Museum put on show a simple gold wire bracelet, dated c. 4475 BC, that an expedition to Nubia had unearthed in a grave in the Wadi Allaqui, an early source for Egypt's gold. Other veils will undoubtedly rise on more 'wonderful things' (to quote Howard Carter when he first glimpsed the Tutankhamun treasure chamber), pushing back the origins of craftsmanship in gold even earlier.

In the meantime, this is the story of the miners, the goldsmiths, the coin-makers and the merchants who have created a unique legacy for gold over the last six thousand years in civilisations ancient and modern. In the hands of early metalworkers the soft slivers of gold that gleamed from the bed of streams could be hammered and fashioned easily into ornaments that shone like the sun, establishing an instant bond between the two. 'The sweat of the sun,' as the Precolumbian people of the Americas called it, became a symbol of wealth and power. It was exchanged as gifts or bartered in trade, with rings of electrum (the natural alloy of gold with silver) being used on the eastern shores of the Mediterranean before 3500 BC. Thus gold quickly assumed the dual role of ornament and standard of value, if not immediately as money. Merchants were even underwriting trading contracts in gold ingots in Mesopotamia before 2000 BC, although gold coins struck with the head of a ruler did not appear before Croesus in Lydia around 550 BC.

Gold's natural beauty and unique properties of conductivity, ductility, malleability and resistance to corrosion have meant it was valued in differing ways by successive ages. Its versatility has made it adaptable in the glowing tiles of Byzantine mosaics, the easily traded ducat of the Venetian merchant or, today, in electronics for the integrated circuits and connectors of iPods and space probes. The fact that it does not corrode enabled it to provide virtually a colour photograph of people and their age; witness the death mask of Tutankhamun, boy-king of Egypt in 1327 BC, and the golden panels in his tomb depicting the king and his queen hunting wildfowl in the marshes along the Nile. As Dr Paul Craddock of the British Museum's Department of Scientific Research pointed out, "In a Bronze Age barrow the organic material is gone, the bronze is a heap of corrosion, but the gold of antiquity is there grinning at you the way it went into the ground thousands of years ago". A sentiment echoed by the Mesopotamian scholar Dr Joan Oates when she remarked that archaeologists love gold "because it needs no cleaning".

The genesis of Ages of Gold was the research that I did on the modern market around the world for over thirty years for the successive editions of my book The World of Gold, and as a consultant on the annual surveys of Consolidated Gold Fields and Gold Fields Mineral Services (GFMS). My approach now is somewhat similar, except that, instead of analysing the current gold scene, I am tracking it since 4000 BC. Happily, too, much of gold's heritage is the glory of those uncorroded ornaments and artefacts rather than dry statistics.

The most moving moment in my new travels was stepping into the gloom of the restored subterranean tomb at Vergina west of Thessoloniki in Greece, where the burnished solid gold casket containing the ashes of Philip of Macedon, father of Alexander the Great, rests in a softly lit niche, surmounted by a gold wreath. We know that Alexander himself saw his father's assassination in 336 BC, supervised the funeral and probably placed his father's remains in the casket, where it lay undisturbed until 1977.

The reward along this trail was how much of gold's past is to be seen at ancient sites, such as Vergina, or in museums. The most famous, perhaps, is the Tutankhamun treasure in the Cairo Museum, but the collections of goldsmiths' achievements are legion. Do not miss the delicate Minoan ornaments (including a memorable bee) on show at Heraklion on Crete, or the two great finds of Heinrich Schliemann; the robust breastplate, masks and vases from Mycenæ in the National Museum in Athens and the golden treasures of Troy, now mercifully re-discovered after disappearing from Berlin in World War II, in a dedicated gallery of the Pushkin Museum in Moscow. The National Museum of Ireland displays golden lunulae, large crescent moons perfectly engraved with geometric patterns by a master craftsman around 1800 BC, while the Hermitage in St Petersburg offers Scythian treasures, including a magnificent comb crowned with a struggling jumble of lions, horses and warriors. The subtle creations of Precolumbian goldsmiths in South America are preserved in the Museo del Oro in Bogotá (in a wing of the Colombian Central Bank) and in the Museo de America in Madrid, where I found the Quimbaya treasure with its lime-flasks, in the form of human figures, among the most intriguing creations in gold. Benvenuto Cellini's famous golden salt cellar deserved the headlines it got when it was stolen from the Kunsthistorisches Museum in Vienna in 2003, and it was good to see it safely restored there in a new prime position after its recovery in 2006.

The British Museum is in itself a short walk through the history of gold. It begins with the treasures from the Royal Tombs at Ur, which astonish with the sheer mastery of detail achieved by the ancient goldsmiths of Mesopotamia. The collections proceed through delightful assortments of Minoan, Greek, Etruscan and Roman jewellery, not forgetting the Oxus treasure from Persia, where the highlight is a witty chariot of gold drawn by four small horses harnessed with gold wire.

The visual legacy is supported by all manner of ancient stories from Herodotus' account of Carthaginian sailors' technique for bartering for gold on the beaches of Africa to the Elder Pliny's descriptions of Roman mining techniques in Spain, with the added bonus of reasonable estimates of output. The fluctuating gold reserves of the Han dynasty in China up to AD 23 are recorded in contemporary records, as are the declining fortunes of successive Byzantine emperors in their wilting empire. The archives of Venice record a delightful 'recipe' for refining gold at the mint around 1340, which instructed that layers of thin gold sheet should be sprinkled with a 'flux' of sea-salt and crushed red tile "comme gittassi formaggio grattugiato sopra lasagne" – "like sprinkling grated cheese over lasagne".

A special tribute must be paid to the academics who have turned detective to ferret out long forgotten statistics. They have made an immense contribution in helping us to gain a correct perspective on the scale of the gold trade throughout the ages. I would like to acknowledge, in particular, the researches of Christopher Howgego and R. Duncan-Jones on Roman coinage, Frederick Lane and Reinhold Mueller on money and banking in medieval Venice, Eliyahu Asher on the Levant trade in the Middle Ages, Harry Miskiman on medieval France, Peter Spufford on medieval Europe, Earl J. Hamilton on gold and silver from the Americas to Spain, and K. H. Chaudhuri on the East India Company's precious metal shipments. Their books, and those of other researchers, are acknowledged in the bibliography.

One of the difficulties in gauging mine output, metal flows or coin fabrication is the diverse weights and currencies that are often quoted in sources. For simplicity, I have sought to convert every measure of gold into metric tonnes (m.t) or kilograms (kg) and troy ounces (t.oz) to provide a common denominator. Thus, a flow of 400,000 Spanish escudo coins to France in the 16th century is also shown as 1,350 kg/43,500 t.oz; a statistic that suggests a lot of coins, but they weighed only just over one tonne, a reminder how rare gold then was.

My thanks are due to many people who have helped me to understand the story of gold. Dr Henry Jarecki, then at Mocatta Metals in New York, got me going in the 1970s with a history of Mocatta & Goldsmid as the oldest members of the London gold market. Jessica Cross of Virtual Metals and John Lutley at The Gold Institute in Washington DC (now, sadly, closed) supported the research for my report Millennium in Gold, published in 1999, which convinced me that a full-scale history was worth embarking on. My knowledge was then amplified by the short essays on gold's history I wrote for the website www.gold.avenue at the request of my friend Mehdi Barkhordar of MKS SA, Geneva and Pamp SA, who had originally sponsored my A–Z on gold, The Gold Companion. Henry Harington at the World Gold Council's Gold magazine also encouraged me with assignments on the Hermitage in St Petersburg, Minoan Crete, the Venice gold market and the British Museum.

I have learned much on the early refining and fabrication of gold from Dr Paul Craddock, Susan La Niece and Nigel Meeks at the British Museum's Department of Scientific Research. And Ian McIntyre of the Conservation Department, busy restoring the splendid Mold Cape that belonged to a Celtic chieftain around 1800 BC, gave me a real insight into the skills of ancient goldsmiths when he remarked, "Gold is a forgiving metal … it talks to you, it is so easy to work". An equal cornerstone for research was the London Library with its knowledgeable staff and the great facility to browse the stacks and take home likely books for study. I am also grateful to Ms K. Begley at the Bank of England's Library and Information Centre, who helped me track down statistics on central bank holdings and gold flows since AD 1850.

In the gold business, the geologist Dr Tim Williams compared ancient African deposits with those he is now investigating, while the analyst Robert Weinberg, just back from a visit to Sardis in Turkey, former seat of King Croesus, shared his conclusions on production there 2,500 years ago. Dr Chris Corti and Dr Richard Halliday at the World Gold Council offered advice and searched for pertinent articles that have appeared in their Gold Bulletin over the last thirty years. In Russia, Dr Natalia Zubarava in Moscow gave me useful introductions, and in St Petersburg Elena Poliakova arranged and interpreted at a special visit to the Hermitage's unique jewellery galleries.

Special thanks also to my former colleagues on the Consolidated Gold Fields and, later, Gold Fields Mineral Services (GFMS) surveys. While we were analysing the current gold scene, visits to souks such as Fez in Morocco or the Bazaar in Bombay gave us a sense of how they were centuries ago. In Kalgoorlie, Western Australia, of course, the gold rush spirit was as alive in the 1990s as a century earlier when gold was first found. I am grateful to David Lloyd-Jacob who first assigned me a territory 'east of Venice up to and including Hong Kong'. Thereafter, Irena Podleska, Louise de Boulay, Deborah Russell, George Milling-Stanley, Philip Klapwijk, and Kevin Crisp joined me on the trail, while Steward Murray (now Chief Executive of the London Bullion Market Association) kept us at it. In Mumbai, Madhusudan Daga has been as full of suggestions as he always was in instructing me in the mysteries of the Indian gold market; although over eighty, he is actively proposing a translation of this book into Hindi.

Beyond that, it was Philip Klapwijk, now Executive Chairman of GFMS, who came up with the generous proposal that they should undertake the publication of this book, in part to mark the fortieth anniversary of their gold survey. I am most gratified that the organisation for which I was a consultant for three decades is shouldering this task.

My thanks also to Georgie Robins who, as always, has laboured long to transfer my portable typewriter's drafts to clean copy on her computer. Laurette Perrard at GFMS has also worked diligently to design and assemble the whole book. Finally, the great pleasure of researching the Ages of Gold has been that my wife,

Maureen, apart from her customary meticulous editing, has joined me in museums and ancient sites to admire gold's legacy. I shall always remember the morning, shortly after dawn, when we stood alone on the hill-top of the Palace of Knossos on Crete, looking out on the landscape of cypress trees and olive groves below, little changed since Minoan times 3,500 years ago. It has been an exceptional experience to link the modern world of gold with the ancient one.

T.S.G.
London, September 2007

Part One
The Ancient World (4000 - 1 BC)

CHAPTER 1

Mesopotamia:
The Land Between the Rivers

Like a butterfly emerging perfectly formed from its chrysalis, so the goldsmith's art blossomed between the rivers Euphrates and Tigris in Mesopotamia (modern Iraq) around 3000 BC. In Sumer, the first great civilisation of this 'land between the rivers', as the Greeks later called it, their work was already accomplished. "Sumerian jewellery fulfilled practically all the ornamental functions which were to occur during the course of history," wrote one jewellery critic. "In fact, there were more different types of jewellery than there are today."[1] The technology of filigree, lost-wax casting and granulation were all mastered, the skills of engraving and relief were impeccably executed.

The admiration comes through in Sir Leonard Woolley's description of the helmet of Prince Mes-kalam-dug, dating c. 2500 BC, which he unearthed in 1927 during his long excavations of the Royal Graves at Ur on the banks of the Euphrates. "It was a helmet of beaten gold … in the form of a wig, the locks of hair hammered up in relief, the individual hairs shown by delicate engraved lines," he reported. "Parted down the middle, the hair covers the head in flat wavy tresses and is bound round with a twisted fillet: behind it is tied into a little chignon, and below the fillet hangs in rows of formal curls about the ears, which are rendered in high relief … similar curls on the cheek-pieces represented whiskers." Woolley concluded, "As an example of the goldsmith's work this is the most beautiful thing we have found … and if there were nothing else by which the art of these ancient Sumerians could be judged, we should still, on the strength of it alone, accord them high rank in the roll of civilized races."[2] Strictly speaking, the helmet was of electrum, the natural alloy of gold and silver, and was 625 fine/15 carats, but that in no way detracted from its splendour. Indeed, Woolley noted that the gold was as clean as when it was first put into the grave, with no tarnish after almost 4,500 years underground.

The Royal Cemetery at Ur, encompassing a multitude of graves from the period c. 2800–2350 BC, revealed a mature goldsmiths' trade that became ever more diverse over the centuries. This is the dawn, not just of gold as a symbol of wealth and power in fine ornaments, but of stocks in temple treasuries, as a medium of exchange between merchants, as an investment in trading ventures and as a standard of value. The city of Babylon, flush with gold from Egypt, was effectively on a gold standard for a short while after 1400 BC; Babylon's temples pioneered gold loans. All this evolved in the constantly changing pattern of city-states making shifting alliances with each other to create the successive civilisations of Sumer, Babylonia and Assyria (with several interregnums of chaos on the way). They flourished and sometimes foundered to local and foreign immigration and invasions over a span of more than three thousand years. The first cities evolved before 4000 BC and the saga continued until the fall (not for the first time) of Babylon to the Persians in 539 BC. Thus, Mesopotamia was at the heart of the gold business for half the entire history of gold. No other country, not even Egypt, can claim such enduring importance.

Many individual cities had their moment of glory. In the north, which ultimately became Assyria, Tepe Gawra, Tell Brak, Ninevah, Assur and Nimrud set the pace at different times. In the south, the flat plains between the Tigris and Euphrates gave birth in succession to Tell al'Ubaid, Eridu, Uruk, Jemnat Nasr, Ur, Larsa, Umma, Nippur and Babylon. While the city of Mari, to the west up the Euphrates, became the staging post for trade with Syria and the Mediterranean coasts, including Egypt.

Links with its neighbours were vital to Mesopotamia's prosperity. Its initial wealth was founded on irrigation through the taming of the Euphrates and Tigris, and the digging of canals which gave the region an abundance of grain and other agricultural products. Yet Mesopotamia lacked the accessories of wealth – not just precious stones or ivory or fine timbers, but metals. All copper and tin (the essential mix for hard bronze), silver and gold had to be imported. The country became a trading forum. Brilliant blue lapis lazuli (the Mesopotamian jeweller's favourite companion to gold), semi-precious stones, gold, spices and probably copper came from Afghanistan, India and Persia (Iran) either by overland caravans or by sea up the Persian Gulf to the busy ports of Ur and Umma. From the west came gold, silver and tin from Anatolia (Turkey), and gold, ivory and ostrich eggs from Egypt by way of the cities of Byblos and Ugarat, which grew up on the shores of the Mediterranean after 2000 BC. The Euphrates and Tigris rivers were the thoroughfares both on their waters and along their banks (although the fast-flowing Tigris was difficult to navigate). Overland stretches to and from the Mediterranean or Anatolia were covered by caravans of up to 400 donkeys.

Merchants set up syndicates, sometimes financed by gold, for these operations. They profited not just from imports for domestic consumption, but the turn on re-exports. Silver, for instance, came from Anatolia and was, in part, sold on in the east, which even then paid a premium for the metal as it did until modern times. Gold, however, was absorbed, initially in temple treasuries for use as adornment of furnishings, or statues of deities and ornaments for rulers, who were usually revered as the living incarnation of the gods. Gold jewellery from the outset was primarily for religious or mystical purposes; its application for business really came only after 2000 BC. Initially, silver fulfilled the wider monetary role for the practical reason that it was in more abundant supply. Gold was a rare metal, a vital factor in establishing its credentials, especially its affinity with gods.

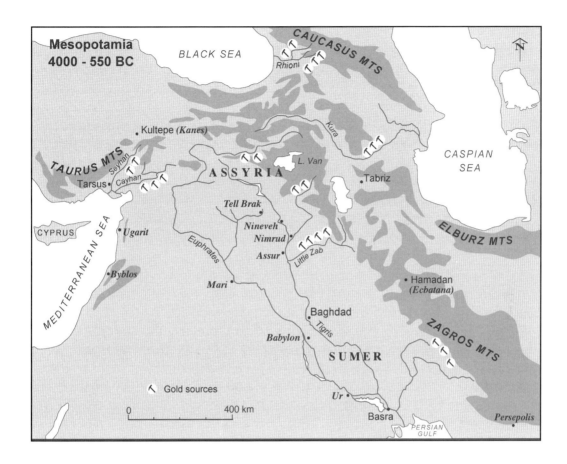

Mesopotamia 4000 - 550 BC

Written records are the indelible guide to all this activity. Even before 3000 BC, a wedge-shaped cuneiform script inscribed on clay or stone was devised and eventually recorded everything from inventories and business contracts, to letters, epic poems and stories, scientific notes and religious tracts. The earliest political records are from 2400 BC while, in Babylon, King Hammurapi (1792–1750 BC) drew up a written code of laws. Thus, we learn of gold and silver, not so much through the discoveries of ornaments, as in most early civilisations, but by dealings inscribed on tablets. Even a clerk's calculations of how much thin gold sheet or leaf will be required to adorn a new temple are set down.

The first goldsmiths

The roots of these urban societies lay in the shift to managed agriculture and animal husbandry during the Neolithic age from 10,000–6000 BC, leading to established villages. Craft industries emerged. In northern Mesopotamia the settlement of Maghzaliya was making and trading sharp tools of obsidian, a black volcanic glass, by 7000 BC. Shortly after, the Halaf culture was firing well-made pottery for distribution. The pace, however, was set in the south where, by 5000 BC, the communities of Tell al'Ubaid and Eridu on the Euphrates were cultivating wheat, barley and date palms, herding sheep and goats, and fishing. The territory there between the two rivers, the archaeologist Max Mallowan (husband of mystery writer Agatha Christie) once observed, was "a cradle geographically constructed for the growth of urban life".[3]

The prosperity of these nascent cities soon demanded luxuries for living and the adornment of their temples. We learn through a written Sumerian legend how Emmerkar, ruler and builder of Uruk (just across the Euphrates from al'Ubaid), bargained with the 'lord' of Aratta (somewhere in western Persia) for gold, silver, blue lapis lazuli and red carnelian to decorate his new temple. He would pay in grain.

Through such deals with neighbours the trade routes expanded. Overland trails were alive with caravans. Just catering for them created jobs in small towns. The archaeologist Joan Oates recounts how a "road-side café", as she put it, at Tell Brak on the road to Anatolia, dating from 3800 BC, had a courtyard with big ovens, open hearths and griddles. Mutton, beef, pig, gazelle and birds (the smallest baked intact in clay) were served on flat, cheap clay plates. The plates, in turn, kept potteries busy.[4] Other craftsmen at Tell Brak were already making beads of gold, silver, lapis lazuli and amethyst. Gold beads have also turned up at Tepe Gawra, near modern Mosul, dating from 4000 BC or even earlier.

At Tepe Gawra the goldsmiths' repertoire evolved. A rich burial, dated c. 3250 BC, revealed not just gold beads, but gold studs inlaid with semi-precious stones, gold bands, pendants of insects, hairpins and rosettes pierced for attachment to clothing. The prize was a dramatic wolf's head of electrum. The entire head was fashioned from a single piece of metal, except for the ears, lower jaw and the teeth, which were from electrum wire.[5] The goldsmiths had learned to appreciate the malleability of gold. They could hammer it into thin sheets, shape them into objects (cups and bowls soon appear) or cut thin strips and beat out wires from which chain could be made (the 'drawing' of gold into wire probably came later).

Sources of gold

Where did the gold come from? In the beginning, it must have been local alluvial deposits in the streams coming down from the mountains of the Mesopotamia/ Anatolia border. Tell Brak, for instance, is scarcely 150km/93 miles from the Murad Su river which feeds into the upper Euphrates and has been a source of alluvial gold into modern times. And the mountain of Hahhum, mentioned in Sumerian records for its gold, may be on the Elbistan plateau from which the Murad Su drains. Tepe Gawra was equally close to the Great and Lesser Zab rivers, which flow into the Tigris near Mosul, and to the Sasum mountains west of Lake Van in Anatolia, which are considered ancient gold sources.[6] Actually, much of the metal found was electrum, as the wolf's head from Tepe Gawra and the Ur helmet demonstrated, with silver comprising 20 to 50% of the natural alloy.

Modern assays of the finds show how erratic the gold content was, pointing to alluvial gold from a variety of sources which had not been subjected to any sophisticated refining. The goldsmiths worked with whatever natural alloy came to hand. A bead from Tepe Gawra was analysed as gold at 380 fine, silver 614 fine and copper 5.6 fine. A spear from the Royal Cemetery at Ur was rated gold 303 fine, silver 594 fine and copper 103. While the Ur helmet is 625 fine gold (the other metals have not been detailed), a dagger with a gold blade found near it assayed at 911 fine gold, 77 fine silver and 12 fine copper. By contrast, several hair ribbons and a gold cup all proved to be close to 750 fine, silver at ± 240 fine and copper the balance, suggesting perhaps the same source of gold or even some simple refining. A round bowl from the Cemetery, though, only managed 587 fine gold, 400 fine silver and 18 fine copper.[7] The diversity not only indicates erratic gold supply from different places – and always alluvial or 'native' gold, as early archaeologists tended to call it – but that colour was paramount. Gold was not yet made into coins, so a consistent fineness was not required. Grading of different qualities of gold appeared only during the 3rd Dynasty of Ur from 2100–2000 BC. Moreover, through much of antiquity, miners believed that all metals grew in the ground, with gold, like some exotic truffle, being the ultimate perfect state. They recognised, too, that metals varied slightly, depending on their location, so that gold found in Egypt differed slightly from that of Anatolia or Central Asia; actually, a rational observation because gold alloys contained differing amounts of silver, lead, copper or other metals. It was just that this had nothing to do with the surrounding soil, as with a vegetable, but with geological upheavals.

The search for gold widened with trade links. The Zagros mountains just to the east in Persia were a fresh source of metals. In Anatolia the Seyhan and Cayhan rivers draining from the Taurus mountains into the Mediterranean proved a reliable source, as did the Corun river which flows north into the Black Sea. From there it was but a step into Transcaucasia (Georgia) where the tributaries of the Rhioni river, coming down from the Caucasian mountains, are a source of gold to this day.[8] Transcaucasia was Jason's destination when, around 1100 BC, he set out to seek the Golden Fleece (the sheepskin spread across streams to trap particles of gold) (*see chapter 5*). A much earlier link with Sumerian goldsmiths has been proved by jewellery recovered from barrow graves at Trialeti, near Tbilisi, the Georgian capital, which bears close resemblance to styles from Uruk and Ur.[9] The implication is that Caucasian gold was traded with Ur, perhaps against jewellery, before 2200 BC.

Further afield, the tablets charting Sumer's history mention Dilmun, Magan and Meluhha as suppliers of gold dust or 'red' gold along with other metals. Dilmun was the island of Bahrain in the Persian Gulf, which was a trading port for metals, pearls, agate, corals and wood from more distant lands. One account of this trade tells of the *alik Telmun* or 'travellers to Dilmun' from Ur. They were financed by private investors, who apparently took none of the risk, but received a fixed return on the profits.[10] Through Dilmun came copper, ivory and gold dust from Magan (probably Oman) and copper, gold dust, timber and lapis lazuli from Meluhha, which is thought to be the Indus Valley of Pakistan. Both gold and lapis were brought down the Indus river from Afghanistan and beyond. An alternative route was a caravan link across northern Persia. Thus, Sumer and its successors were plugged into the substantial gold sources of central Asia. The full circle of gold supply was ultimately provided by Egypt, although not in significant quantity until after 1400 BC, when production there reached its peak.

The profit in sending gold to Mesopotamia, at least in later periods, is revealed by an intriguing analysis of the gold:silver ratio around 1300 BC as seen in the city of Ugarit on the Mediterranean, which was a transit point for the metals trade. In Egypt the gold:silver ratio was 1:2; in Ugarit it varied between 1:3 or 1:4, while in Mesopotamia it was 1:9. Gold was thus valued at over four times the Egyptian price in Mesopotamia.[11] No wonder all caravan routes led there. The gold dust and nuggets, we learn from an earlier Sumerian source, were carried on the backs of donkeys in leather pouches.[12] Each animal could carry a load of 90 kg and their daily march was up to 30km/18.6 miles.

The quantity of gold arriving is impossible to gauge. It must have been erratic, not least because alluvial deposits tend to be worked out relatively quickly. The most telling clue is that first in Sumer and later in both Babylonia and Assyria, silver, not gold, became firmly established as a standard of value and exchange, along with grain. "One of the most important functional distinctions between silver and gold in Mesopotamia (for in much else they were interchangeable) was the general role of silver, passing by weight, as a primary means of exchange and payment," the Oxford archaeologist P. R. S. Moorey argued.[13] In this pursuit, degrees of purity of silver were already being recorded by 2500 BC, indicating sufficient assaying ability to test it. Shortly after, in the Akkadian or Sargonic period between 2350–2100 BC, the word for silver came to mean money (as it did in French, millennia later). Thus, there was usually not enough gold around for it to fulfil a real monetary role, except in merchants' private dealings. The relative scarcity of gold, as late as 700 BC, is underlined by King Sargon II of Nimrud, admitting that in the treasure house of his Juniper palace he had 11 talents, 30 minas of gold, compared with 2,100 talents, 24 minas of silver, "which my hand captured from Pisiris, king of Carcemish". That translates into 310kg/9645 t.oz of gold against almost 47 m.t/1.8 million t.oz of silver.[14]

The invisible factor in all this is, of course, scrap, rather like the unseen part of an iceberg. The scrap gold came from the combination of looting the vanquished (as Sargon admitted), persistent grave-robbing and the long-standing custom throughout the region to trade in regularly old ornaments for new. Thus, goldsmiths or metal traders came to rely on scrap, not just in Mesopotamia, but throughout history. Today, scrap regularly accounts for at least 20% of world supply and, in countries such as Saudi Arabia, where ornaments are traded in frequently, can provide 50% of the gold annually. Modern Iraq became a consistent source of scrap to the international market from the 1970s due to distress sales of ornaments because of the privations created by Saddam Hussein.

In ancient Mesopotamia the constant meltdown left a somewhat limited legacy of actual ornaments. Written records and frescoes (the *Vogue* of the ancient world depicting the jewellery, fashions and hairstyles of Babylonia, Egypt and Minoan Crete) provide much of our knowledge. Fortunately, there are two great exhibitions, as it were, of the art of the Mesopotamian goldsmith: the finds from the Royal Cemetery at Ur covering over 450 years after 2800 BC, and the relatively recent discovery in 1988/9 at Nimrud of remarkable treasures assembled between 900 and 700 BC. Along the way there are wonderful individual necklaces and other ornaments, but Ur and Nimrud, two thousand years apart, leave us in no doubt of the skills achieved. To vary Mallowan's phrase, Mesopotamia was the 'cradle' of goldsmiths.

The Royal Graves at Ur

First, it was Sir Leonard Woolley spending twelve years at Ur digging patiently through over two thousand graves, of which eighteen were 'royal', that gave us a fully fledged goldsmith's repertoire. The helmet of Prince Mes-kalam-dug was unique, but there was much else. In the prince's tomb were two golden bowls and a lamp inscribed "Mes-kalam-dug. Hero of the Good Land". In a nearby tomb was a dagger with a blade of gold, its hilt of blue lapis lazuli decorated with gold studs and its sheath made of gold beautifully decorated with an open lattice-work design like plaited grass. No one is sure who Mes-kalam-dug was; not a king apparently, but perhaps a warrior prince (or war-lord in modern parlance). His grave was richer than the other 'royal graves', but with one distinctive feature: he was buried alone.

In the royal graves, by contrast, a king or queen was buried with a retinue of retainers, men and women, who died peacefully (probably by poisoning) as part of a ritual that honoured them as priest-kings or queens. The most spectacular finds in these 'death pits', as they are called, were in the graves of King A-bar-gi and Queen Pu-abi, dating c. 2600 BC. Actually, the king's tomb had been plundered, the queen's was untouched. Amid the cluttered remains of wagons and oxen, Woolley found the bodies of nine court ladies, each wearing a headdress of lapis and carnelian beads from which hung golden pendants shaped like willow leaves, lunate gold earrings and necklaces of lapis and gold. A soldier clasped four spears with heads of gold. Beside the courtiers lay four musicians with their instruments, including a boat-shaped harp of 13 strings with round gold-headed tuning pins. "On the remains of a wooden bier, lay the body of the Queen," Woolley wrote, "a gold cup near her hand; the upper part of the body was entirely hidden by a mass of beads of gold, silver, lapis lazuli … against the right arm were three long gold pins with lapis heads and three amulets in the form of fish, two of gold and one of lapis, and a fourth in the form of two seated gazelles, also of gold".[15]

Pu-abi was crowned with an ornate headdress, formed by a broad gold ribbon from which were suspended three gold wreaths of willow leaves and flowers, whose petals had gold and blue inlay.[16]   A "Spanish comb", as Woolley called it, was fixed to the back of her hair with seven rising points surmounted by gold flowers with lapis centres. Gold earrings hung to Pu-abi's shoulders and she wore ten rings of gold and lapis. The diversity of jewellery in the Queen's tomb was astonishing. A diadem of gold figures of animals, fruits and flowers was set against a contrasting background of blue lapis. Necklaces combined gold, silver, lapis and carnelian. Over twenty different types of beads, seven styles of hairpin, many amulets (charms) – including one of a hollow gold fly, and pendants of coiled gold wire were found.[17]

The queen's accessories included an exquisite pale gold oval-shaped bowl with wire handles, a gold strainer for filtering liquids and an elegant gold cup with thin, graceful spout that may have been used for feeding an invalid or a child. Confronted with such treasures, many of which are in the Sackler Galleries at the British Museum, the immediate impression is the sheer professionalism of the Ur goldsmiths, their absolute mastery of fine detail. Even a little double cone-shaped bead speckled with granulation is perfectly finished, while a small gold cylinder, like a lipstick case, contained a tiny toilet set of tweezers, scoop and applicator, fit for a chic handbag.

The Royal Cemetery, covering many generations, yielded other remarkable relics, such as the exotic figure of the 'ram in the thicket', dated c. 2600 BC. The ram (some prefer goat) carved of wood, with horns of lapis and face and legs covered with thick gold leaf, is entangled in a shrub covered with gold leaf. Graphic scenes of life in Ur were dramatised on the 'Standard of Ur', a hollow box inlaid with mosaics depicting, on one side, peaceful scenes of gifts being brought to a king who is banqueting while being entertained by a singer; the other side shows a Sumerian army with chariots (the earliest known representation of wheeled vehicles), an infantry charge and prisoners brought before the king. An inlaid board for the 'Royal Game of Ur', with gaming pieces and a four-sided dice also turned up; the game, dated c. 2400 BC, was apparently played like our children's Ludo.[18]

Thus did society amuse itself at Ur in the middle of the 3rd millennium BC. "It was an urban civilisation of a highly developed type," Sir Leonard Woolley summed up. "Its craftsmen in metal possessed a knowledge of metallurgy and a technical skill which few ancient peoples have ever rivalled … Sumer was the pioneer of the western world and to it we can trace much of the art and thought of the Egyptians and Babylonians, of the Assyrians, Phoenicians and Hebrews and, ultimately, the Greeks."[19]

The goldsmiths' trade

Written records flesh out the visual legacy. Goldsmiths usually worked for the temple authorities. During the 3rd Dynasty of Ur (2100–2000 BC) one official supervised eight different workshops, embracing blacksmiths, carpenters, fetters, goldsmiths, leatherworkers, metalworkers, reedworkers and stone cutters. Their task was to service all the temple's needs. Originally, in Sumerian, gold was known as *guškin*, but after 2350 BC the word became *hurasu* under the new Akkadian rulers. The chief goldsmith was known as *rab nappah hurasi* and the workshop *šakunu*. The hammering of gold sheet was *takaku*, the pressing of gold leaf was *labanu*, and gold leaf itself *pašallu*. The art of overlaying with *pašallu* was *ahazu*. As the technology at Ur improved and goldsmiths began simple refining and alloying of gold, so the terminology expanded; *hurasu* sarpu for refined gold, *hurasu samu* for red gold (with copper alloy), *hurasu ellu* for white gold and *hurasu damqu* designated gold of good quality. Electrum was, probably, *hurasu pisu*.[20]

This lexicon of gold terms indicates that, by 2000 BC, the technologies of ore preparation, preliminary smelting and cupillation in crucibles were understood. Cupillation was practised using little clay pots to remove base metals from silver and gold by oxidising or 'slagging them off' through repeated meltings as a current of air was blown over the surface. The more complicated parting of gold and silver by cementation, which involved the adding of salt, had probably not yet evolved, although it may have been developed later after Babylon took over the old Sumerian mantle. Definitions of the purity of fineness of gold already appear, however, in texts from the 3rd Dynasty of Ur. Three qualities were identified: a 'red' almost pure gold, 'mixed' gold and 'normal' gold. Expressed on a gold:silver ratio, 'red' gold with a touch of copper was between 1:21 to 1:15, 'mixed' gold was 1:14 to 1:11, and 'normal' gold was 1:10 to 1:6.5.[21] This is a rather loose range, implying that alluvial gold of differing qualities from a variety of sources was available. Moreover, purity was not yet an imperative. "The concept of 'pure' metals did not exist then," British Museum metallurgist Susan La Niece has pointed out. "The only classification was by colour and properties, such as hardness or resistance to corrosion."[22]

Five hundred years later in Babylon, after 1600 BC, the precision had improved radically; 'bright' or 'normal' gold was specified at 1:4 against silver, and 'red' gold at 1:8. A ratio between 1:8 or 1:9 remained fairly consistent over centuries, suggesting the ability to refine gold to precise standards and assay it accurately.

However, it is not clear when fire assaying was first used in Mesopotamia to determine fineness. Nor is there any hard evidence of the introduction of touchstones, the smooth, fine-grained, slightly abrasive black stone, usually quartz or jasper, used to test the purity of gold by the colour of the streak left when it is rubbed with metal. Gold-streaked stones have been found in a possible 'goldsmith's' tomb at Larsa, just across the Euphrates from Ur, and at Assur in the north, but are judged to have been used for burnishing jewellery, not testing its fineness. However, the technique, first confirmed by Greek authors around 550 BC, may have been applied in Mesopotamia much earlier (and it was still in use in local gold markets of the Middle East and India when I first visited them in the 1960s).

The tools at the goldsmith's disposal were simple and have changed little over time. The basics were a wooden block, a hammer, an anvil, chisels to cut, awls to pierce, punches for relief or *repoussé*, gouges, and stones for burnishing. He was aided by a charcoal fire stimulated by a blow-pipe or bellows, clay melting crucibles, moulds and dies to make ornaments by the 'lost wax' technique, solders and fine sand for polishing. The alluvial gold at his disposal was malleable and ductile and could be beaten into shape with relative ease. Gold could be hammered cold into sheets less than 0.0025mm thick.[23]

Thin gold sheet, probably beaten with a stone hammer on hard, flat stones, was produced soon after 4000 BC. The delicate sheet or leaf was used to overlay cores of wood, copper or bitumen to adorn, first, beads, then bracelets, harps and even ceremonial spear shafts. When great temples were built, it covered furniture, ivories, statues of deities or bulls or lions, colonnades and the inner walls themselves. The gold sheets were fixed by using egg white as an adhesive, or possibly lightly heated to fuse with the surfaces of copper or silver. The skin of gold created the illusion of a statue of solid gold, though it was only microns thick.

The technique of depletion gilding to create that same surface effect was developed remarkably early. Recent metallurgical research at the British Museum has revealed that three 'solid' gold chisels found in Queen Pu-abi's tomb at Ur were very early examples of depletion gilding. The chisels were analysed because their surface showed signs of flaking. The tests showed a surface skin, a millimetre thick, beneath which was a gold, silver, copper alloy. So the goldsmith had started with this alloy, in which copper was 30% and then removed most of the silver and copper from the surface. The copper was removed by heating to make it oxidise as a black or red film on the surface, which could be removed with extracts of citrus or other plants. The silver was removed, possibly by an early form of cementation with salt or a strong corrosive medium such as ferric sulphide, leaving a gold-rich surface layer. "These objects provide material evidence for the ability of the goldsmiths of Ur to remove both copper and silver from gold in the 3rd millennium BC well before the technique appears to have been applied to gold refining," concluded Susan La Niece.[24]

The understanding of how to work with the metal grew ever more sophisticated. The sheet-gold beakers and bowls from the Royal Cemetery at Ur were hammered out with patient skill. "This probably began as a thick cake of gold, which was hammered to a round flat sheet," the American metallurgist C. S. Smith has suggested, "from which the main cup shape was made by raising, that is by a sequence of local hammer blows from a slightly convex hammer against the sheet metal held at a slight inclination against the rounded edge of an anvil, so producing innumerable little bends in concentric circles or in a close spiral which eventually integrate into the formation of a progressively deepening cup."[25]

Goldsmiths were also adroit at making wires that could be used in a multitude of chain designs or for the delicate tracery like plaited grass on the sheath of Meskalam-dug's dagger. Lacking the modern steel draw-plate, the goldsmith may have hammered out an ingot into a thinner and thinner strip, or possibly have cut a strip of metal and pulled it through a succession of smaller and smaller holes in hard wood or bone.[26] The lost-wax casting technique, staple of the modern jewellery industry, was pioneered. The ornament was first modelled in wax (or possibly clay) around which moulds of three or four pieces were made and filled with molten metal. The moulds were then taken apart and the gold ornament extracted and polished up. An exquisite little gold monkey mounted on a bronze pin was an early triumph.

Cloisonné inlay of semi-precious stones in little cells of gold on rings or necklaces was also perfected; several *cloisonné* rings were found in the Royal Cemetery, and a fine lapis, carnelian and gold ring turned up at Lagash, just north of Ur (it is now in the Louvre). The prize, though, was the necklace of large onyx beads set in gold belonging to the priestess Abbabashti at the temple of Eanna at Uruk during the 3rd Dynasty of Ur. The stones were capped with heavy gold rims ornamented with filigree work. "The jeweller was … an obvious master of his craft," wrote Kathleen Maxwell-Hyslop. This unique necklace is also one of the few surviving ornaments from the period 2100–2000 BC.[27]

A more controversial question is the extent to which early goldsmiths used granulation – laying a pattern of small grains of gold on a metal surface and then joining them to it. A ring found in Queen Pu-abi's tomb at Ur was adorned with six such granules. They appear to have been fixed in place by 'sintering', that is, heating both grains and the surface to which they were to adhere to a point just below melting. Other early examples of granulation show evidence of soldering. Metallurgists are cautious, suggesting that several different techniques were employed, and warning that 'granulation' was sometimes simulated with tiny gold nails, whose heads create the same effect. In any event, the technique of granulation, spread east to Persia, north to the Caucasus, west to Byblos on the Mediterranean, and ultimately to Minoan Crete and Mycenæ during the 2nd millennium BC.[28]

The fruits of the goldsmiths' labour were dedicated to the temple or palace for which they worked. "Gold was pre-eminently used for ceremonial and prestige purposes," concluded P. R. S. Moorey. "It was amassed in temples and royal treasuries where it was largely reserved for the decoration of buildings and furniture, for the adornment of high-ranking people, or gifts and offerings in both religious and secular contexts."[29]

Gold contracts at Assur

Written records, however, reveal gold beginning to have a broader role during the long history of Mesopotamia. In the Akkadian period, when Sargon (2200–2145 BC) forged an empire of all the Sumerian cities, a more secular, technocratic government was installed. Local city governors reported to him as king, not god. A new standard language, written script and standard weights (very important for precious metals) were imposed. Sargon also strengthened trade routes into Syria and Anatolia.

Significantly, in this more secular society, merchants operated private businesses outside the aegis of the temples. Women were sometimes involved in investment. At Umma on the Tigris, records show a *dam-gar*, a professional business agent, called Eli, paying silver to various women who invested with him. Another woman, Ama-e, wife of Ur-Sara, invested in food, aromatics and wood with one *dam-gar* and silver with another. Silver and grain were the two basic commodities doubling as units of value and media of exchange. "When an official household … needed to buy commodities, silver could be used," reported Benjamin Foster, after extensive deciphering of Sargonic business records. "Silver could be bought and sold like any other commodity … (and was) widely used in personal loans and was often in the possession of both private citizens and officials. A businessman might have silver on deposit in various places."[30]

In international trade, gold and silver were used to underwrite long-distance operations. By 2300 BC merchants at Assur, built on a hill above the Tigris in northern Mesopotamia, were regularly trading with the town of Kültepe (also known as Kanes) seven hundred kilometres to the west in Anatolia. Eventually, they established their own colony there. Wealthy merchants sent their sons to live in Kültepe and, ultimately, perhaps two thousand people were involved in what is called the Old Assyrian Trade (Assyria takes its name from Assur). This commercial expansion marks the rise of Assyria as a power in the north of Mesopotamia that would eventually rival the ascendancy of Babylon in the south and finally subdue it.

Donkey caravans between Assur and Kültepe went back and forth, bearing tin and textiles and returning with gold, silver and, probably, copper. The gold arriving in Assur was always exchanged for silver which was used to purchase goods to be sent back to Kültepe. Two different qualities of gold were recognised: lesser quality gold was exchanged at a ratio between 1:6.66 to 1:7.33, the better quality at 1:8.25 to 1:8.66.

Much of the gold went to temples for ornaments, but a part was invested in unique gold contracts, known as *naruqqum*, which were at the heart of the Old Assyrian Trade between 2000 and 1600 BC. *Naruqqum* means, literally, the 'sack' or bag of a travelling trader. And a surviving tablet spells out a *naruqqum* set up by a merchant named Amur-Istar. Fourteen people invested a total of 30 minas of gold (13.5 kg/434 t.oz) in his *naruqqum*; some chipped in three minas, others two minas, and a couple one mina each. The contract read: "30 minas of gold, the *naruqqum* of Amur-Istar … he will conduct the trade for twelve years. Of the profit he will enjoy one-third. He will be responsible for one-third. He who receives his money back before the completion of his term must take the silver at the exchange-rate 4:1 silver for gold. He will not receive any of the profit".[31] Dividends and any profit were taken in silver. Proposed dividends did not always please investors. A letter to investors about another contract revealed "the investors of Ikunum (a trader) have realised on their gold each two minas of silver for every mina of gold". They responded tartly, "If you see that he can give you more than two minas – say three minas for each (mina of gold), then make a deal with him". Although all *naruqqum* were reckoned in gold, it appears that investors may sometimes have put in silver instead, at that rather artificial 4:1 ratio mentioned in the *naruqqum* above. So, instead of two minas of gold, eight minas of silver would have been contributed. However, what is unique about these contracts, which had a long life, is that gold was the bench-mark among the merchants of Assur four thousand years ago.

Prudently, the merchants often split the risk by investing in several *naruqqum*. The merchant Pusu-ken, who had a capital of 18 minas (8.1 kg/260 t.oz) of gold, divided it among eight contracts, putting the customary two minas (0.9 kg/29 t.oz) into seven, but risking four minas on one *naruqqum*. This is a significant stake and implies the amount of gold in circulation among Assur's merchants might have totalled several hundred kg. While this would not be enough to challenge the role of silver as a standard of value or regular unit for exchange for goods throughout Mesopotamia, it does show for the first time gold being regarded as a safe long-term investment.

The *naruqqum* of Assur do not appear in other Mesopotamian cities, but were tailored to the specific needs of the non-stop, round-trip trade with Kültepe, with family connections at both ends.

The rise of Babylon

In Babylon, the coming political and commercial centre of the south after 1900 BC, the merchants did things differently. They made *tapputu* contracts, which were joint-ventures for a single voyage down the Gulf to Dilmun (Bahrain) and beyond, and silver, preferred in the east, was more important. Babylon, however, would eventually become the first city-state to adopt gold as its standard of value and medium of exchange (albeit for a brief period after 1400 BC). The city, just south of modern Baghdad, has always cut an exotic image with its glittering temples and Hanging Gardens. Yet it was a late starter. While its powerful neighbours, Al'Ubaid, Uruk, Jemnat, Nasr and Ur, competed for over a thousand years, Babylon was but a village, quite unknown until 2000 BC.[32] Then the collapse of Ur's 3rd Dynasty to invaders from the east left a power vacuum in the land between the rivers. Two centuries of turmoil ensued. The local cities of Isin and Larsa enjoyed moments of glory, but the whole countryside was in chaos. Skilled craftsmen, including goldsmiths and jewellers from the temples of Ur, were dispersed. The temples where they had worked were looted. Ultimately, a succession of tribal leaders from Babylon seized the moment to fill the political and commercial void. Babylon on the banks of the Euphrates, but also only fifty kilometres from the Tigris, was strategically placed to take over. New canals improved irrigation of arable land and access to shipping.

Finally, King Hammurapi (1792–1750 BC) made alliances with local rivals and, most famously, devised the Code of Hammurapi, a written text of 282 laws setting out his ideal aspirations for Babylon society. "These are the laws of justice," Hammurapi declared, "that the strong may not oppress the weak, to give justice to the orphan and widow." An adversary's eye put out or bone broken incurred a fine of one mina (450 grams/14.5 t.oz) of silver. Silver was clearly defined as a standard of value. Nine different commodities were listed by weight and volume as being worth one *shekel* of silver (7.5 grams/0.23 t.oz). The interest rate on silver loans was set at 20%, with a concession that the debt could be paid in grain, at the fixed silver-grain exchange rate, if the debtor had no silver. Silver was not yet coined, but was clearly integrated into the monetary structure; ingots, small bars and rings of specific weight were used in some payments, though probably not among the populace at large.

Babylon thrived as the hub of international trading links between east and west, as Ur had done for generations. The merchants, in their own community known as the *karum*, set up warehouses by the thriving wharves, handled bills of exchange and gold and silver. They had their agents in Dilmun and in Ugarit and Byblos on the Mediterranean coast. Merchants from abroad settled in Babylon. A comparison with Dubai, as today's great trading centre lower down the Gulf, is not out of place; certainly Babylon fulfilled much the same role in precious metals.

The temple treasuries, too, almost sound like prototype central banks. "As prestigious and literate institutions and wealthy repositories of silver and gold, temples were also the centres where records of payments and loans were made and kept," the British Museum's *History of Money* put it.[33] Although silver was the main instrument, gold loans were made to merchants on occasion against deposits of other securities.

The temples, of course, had their own use for gold sheet to adorn their furnishings and statues and as jewellery for ruling families who saw the temple as a symbol of their power on earth. Temple goldsmiths and probably private goldsmiths also had a prosperous clientele among the elite. Although surviving jewellery from the 'Old Babylon' of Hammurapi is limited, we can admire it in frescoes from the palace at Mari, just up the Euphrates from Babylon, which Hammurapi captured. The frescoes reveal a taste for triple-fluted earrings and elaborate 'choker' necklaces. One such necklace, recovered from Dilbat, a small town near Babylon, has wonderful pendants decorated with delicate granulation (the Dilbat necklace may now be seen in the Metropolitan Museum of Art in New York).

The empire created by Hammurapi did not long survive. Babylon's prosperity aroused the jealousy not only of tribal leaders to the south, but of immigrant Kassites from Elam in the western region of Persia. Their names turn up first in lists of migrant agricultural workers, but they gradually built up land holdings in Babylon, winning influence. Then, unexpectedly, in 1595 BC the Hittite ruler Murshili I swept down the Euphrates on a quick raid from Anatolia, sacked Babylon and plundered its riches (more gold scrap). In the ensuing chaos, the Kassites took over.

They ruled Babylon for the next four hundred years, longer than any other Mesopotamian dynasty. "The emergence of Babylon as the political and cultural centre of the ancient world took place under their aegis," observed Joan Oates.[34] It was a period of great national wealth. The only real challenge was from Assyria in the north, a rivalry that continued for centuries. The Kassites' strength, however, was quiet diplomacy. They left a famous legacy of diplomatic correspondence. Kassite kings cultivated a wide network of foreign contacts, especially with Egypt. They made diplomatic marriages, direct alliances and established an international courier network. Babylonian became the diplomatic language of the entire region.

Babylon's gold standard

Kassite rule in Babylon came as Egypt was enjoying its most productive period of gold mining in Nubia (*see chapter 2*). Output between 1500 and 1300 BC was at record levels. In Egypt, Tutankhamun's burial in a coffin weighing 110 kg/3,536 t.oz reveals a totally new scale of gold fabrication. The Babylon-Egypt alliance was first forged in 1457 BC when Thutmosis III from Egypt reached the Euphrates and the first of many exchanges of gifts took place. Later, Kurigulzu I of Babylon (c. 1390–1370 BC) sought gold from Egypt for the decoration of his new capital at Dur-Kurigalzu, offering horses, chariots, lapis lazuli, bronze, silver and perfumed oil in exchange. The Egyptians obliged. The inflow of gold transformed the economy. Suddenly the prices quoted on the ubiquitous clay tablets were for gold, not silver. Babylon was on the world's first gold standard. The bench-mark was the gold *shekel* at 7.5 grams. No coins were made, but spiral rings of gold were exchanged, although such payments were probably only at the merchant level.[35] The gold flow to Babylon naturally aroused the envy of the Assyrians in the north. Their kings wrote regularly to Amenophis III (1390–1352 BC) in Egypt, pleading for a gift of 20 talents (about 540 kg/17,361 t.oz). As the *Cambridge Ancient History* put it, the refrain of the kings of West Asia was, "Lo, in my brother's land gold is as common as dust. Send me, therefore, very much gold in great quantity".[36]

Such lavishness lasted but a few decades. The Egyptians learned to play off the Babylonians against the Assyrians for diplomatic advantage. The gold flow petered out. A despairing final plea came from Burnaburiash II of Babylon to Tutankhamun around 1330 BC complaining, "Now my brother has sent me as a gift two minas (900 grams/28 t.oz) of gold. If now gold is abundant, send me as much as thy fathers but if it is scarce, send me half of it … As for thee, whatever thou desirest of my country, write to me and it shall be brought thee".[37] There was no known response and silver again became the standard in Babylon.

The Babylonians' flirtation with a gold standard provides, however, an important, if obvious, lesson. A gold standard is not possible without regular and significant supply of gold. Again and again, throughout history, a true gold standard with significant gold coinage in circulation has been achieved only for short periods after new gold discoveries took place. It would happen in Lydia in Anatolia a few centuries later, then in Greece, then with the Romans (with gold from Spain), later still in Venice after a Hungarian gold rush, in Britain from 1700 on the strength of a Brazilian gold rush, and ultimately on a world-wide scale after 1850 following the Californian and Australian gold discoveries. That does not challenge gold's unique role as a symbol of wealth and power, but the metal cannot become the standard of value or a serious medium of exchange when it is scarce. Gold is a rare metal, as well as a beautiful one; that is the foundation of its unique appeal, first realised in Mesopotamia and, almost contemporaneously, in Egypt.

Kassite Babylon ultimately succumbed to the endless power games between Mesopotamian city-states. The Assyrian Empire of the north defeated Babylon decisively in 1230 BC, imposing its own puppet rulers. Later invaders from Elam, across the border in Persia, sacked Babylon around 1157 BC reducing it to a shadow of its former self. For the next three hundred years and more it was quiet on the sidelines. "Babylon for the Babylonians," as one historian put it.[38]

The Nimrud Treasure

Assyria was now the driving force in Mesopotamia. Babylon was conquered and the collapse of the Hittite Empire in Anatolia after 1200 BC took pressure off its northern borders. The Assyrians, under King Tiglath-Pileser I (1115–1077 BC), ranged north to Lake Van and west to the Mediterranean. This was all familiar territory from over a thousand years of trading links.

The capital, Assur, continued to be the market for gold coming in from Anatolia. A thousand years earlier the merchants in Assur had pioneered their gold *naruqqum* contracts. This time round, the new Assyrian Empire made its mark on the history of gold with the Nimrud Treasure.

Nimrud took the stage as successive Assyrian rulers sought to build ever grander cities and temples. In 879 BC Assurnasirpal II (883–859 BC) moved his capital there from Assur. Nimrud is set on a small hill surrounded by a fertile plain on the eastern bank of the Tigris, near the modern city of Mosul. Assurnasirpal II set out to surpass his predecessors. Not content with renovating eight temples, he created a splendid new one dedicated to his god, Ninurta. At all the temples, he declared, in a surviving tablet known as the Banquet Stele, "I made their images of their great divinity resplendent with red gold and sparkling stones. I gave them great jewellery … I adorned the shrine of the god Ninurta, my lord, with gold and lapis lazuli … installed dragons of gold at his throne … I created my royal monument with the likeness of my countenance of red gold and sparkling stones and stationed it before the gold Ninurta, my lord".[39] Assurnasirpal regarded gold as proof of his devotions, but it was equally a signal of his power.

His successors, against the grain of historical custom, proved strong leaders. His son built the great ziggurrat at Nimrud and the arsenal of Fort Shalmaneser on the edge of town. Babylon was brought firmly into the fold, Damascus in Syria was captured. By 705 BC the Assyrian Empire stretched from the Gulf to the Mediterranean.

The wealth flowed in. We can even witness its arrival on the twenty panels of the Black Obelisk of Shalmaneser III (859–823 BC) in the British Museum, which depicts tributes being paid to the king by countries he had vanquished. The first from Gilzanu in western Persia offered gold, silver, tin, horses and two-humped camels. From southern Anatolia, Qarparunda the Patinean sent gold, silver, tin, and 'fast' bronze, while from ancient Israel Jehu, son of Amri, gave "silver, gold, a golden bowl, a gold vase with pointed bottom, gold tumblers, golden buckets".[40] All symbols of power presented to a great ruler. Golden bowls, such as Jehu offered, feature throughout Mesopotamian history, and were often inscribed. The bowl of Mes-Kalam-dug, "Hero of the Good Land", was found at Ur; now at Nimrud, almost two thousand years later, the inscribed golden bowl of Samsi-ilu, a famous provincial governor and commander, was buried with him, as were those of several Assyrian queens.

The Nimrud Treasure, of which they form part, was found in 1988/9 by Muzahim Mahmud Hussein of the Iraqi Office of Antiquities and Heritage in three cleverly concealed vaults beneath the North-West Palace at Nimrud.[41] Within the tombs were the remains of Assyrian queens spanning almost two hundred years (kings were always buried in the ancient capital of Assur). Remarkably, the oldest tomb (known as Tomb III) contained the bodies of three men, one of whom is thought to be Samsi-ilu, as the inscribed bowl was near him. The men could rest there, too, since leading Assyrian officials were usually eunuchs, and thus could be buried alongside women.

Near the coffin of Samsi-ilu was a sarcophagus with the inscription, "Belonging to Mullissu-mukaanisat-Ninua, queen of Assurnasirpal (II), king of Assyria, and (mother of) Shalmaneser (III), king of Assyria". Here lay the wife of the founder of Nimrud. She died around 850 BC. Other coffins in the same vault contained the remains, not just of Samsi-ilu, who probably died about one hundred years later, but of other individuals, including children from the intervening years. The treasures within this tomb thus represent a century of goldsmiths' work. Among them was an exquisite gold crown, found resting on the head of a child (although too big for him). The crown was topped with an interlaced framework of vine leaves and grapes supported by winged figures, with the base decorated by rows of rosettes and pomegranates. A magnificent gold ewer, with a broad spout and gracious handle, was adorned with flowing *repoussé* patterns. Gold plates, cups with bold bases, jewellery and cylinder seals with gold caps almost filled one coffin. This tomb alone yielded 449 items, the gold and silver weighing 23 kg/740 t.oz.

The legacy of Assyria's queens continued in Tomb II, spanning the period 730–700 BC. Here lay the bodies of two queens, and some of the jewellery of a third; Yaba, wife of Tiglath-Pileser III (744–727 BC), Banitu, wife of Shalmanser V (726–722 BC) and Atalia, wife of Sargon (721–705 BC). The missing body is thought to be that of Queen Banitu. As the Iraqi archaeologists penetrated this tomb in April 1989 they found a warning inscription, "Mortal destiny caught up with Queen Yaba in death, and she travelled the path of her ancestors. Whoever, in time to come, whether a queen who sits on the throne or a lady of the palace who is favourite of the king, removes me from my tomb … or lays hands on my jewellery with evil intent, or breaks open the seal to this tomb, let his spirit wander in thirst in the open countryside". Queen Yaba and her successors had quite a collection to protect.

Just for a start it contained an electrum cosmetics box with a mirror of polished electrum in the lid, a diadem of closely woven gold ribbon 4 cm/1.6 in wide and 40 cm/16 in long with a tasselled fringe at either end, a necklace of closely worked gold framed with 28 pear-shaped pendants, two exquisite gold armlets inlaid with semi-precious stones and four studded gold anklets (one of which weighed over 1 kg/32.15 t.oz). A gold bowl, inscribed "Yaba, wife of Tiglath-Pileser III", lay near two others, one engraved with a scorpion and the name Atalia, the other inscribed Banitu, wife of Shalmaneser V. A gold plate, also with Queen Yaba's name, was engraved with a hunting scene, reminiscent of Egypt, depicting boats in a papyrus thicket, a crocodile and other animals. The collection was rounded out with 79 gold earrings, six gold necklaces, 30 finger rings, another 12 armlets, several other gold vessels, 90 necklace sets with semi-precious stones and over 700 tiny gold rosettes, stars, circles and triangles that had once been sewn on long-decayed articles.[42]

The puzzle is which queen is missing, Yaba, Banitu or Atalia? Only two bodies lay, one on top of the other, in the sarcophagus. The presumption is that Yaba's is the lower body; after all, it was her, ignored, prohibition against being disturbed. The electrum cosmetics box offered the vital clue; it was inscribed "Banitu, queen of Shalmeser V". But she was queen before Atalia. The conclusion is that Atalia inherited the cosmetics case from Banitu, and she is buried on top of Yaba. Such mystery adds only to the fascination of this last great collection of Mesopotamian jewellery, the finest in existence anywhere from the 8th and 9th centuries BC.

A modern mystery, too, has surrounded this treasure. It was taken in 1989 to the Baghdad Museum for detailed study. Shortly afterwards Saddam Hussein invaded Kuwait and the Gulf War ensued. Museum officials, fearful for its safety, put the treasure in three strongboxes in the vaults of the Iraq Central Bank, which were then flooded with sewage, presumably to make it unreachable, even to Saddam. Thirteen years later, after his fall, Iraqi curators, aided by the *National Geographic*, pumped two million litres of water out of the vaults; the boxes were there, seals intact, jewellery unharmed. And, briefly, on 3rd July 2003, the treasure was put on display for the first time to an invited audience in the Assyrian galleries of the Iraq Museum.[43]

The Nimrud Treasure showed how cosmopolitan Mesopotamia had become. "Both the gold personal ornaments and the other gold objects are of varied origin," observed the Ashmolean Museum's P. R. S. Moorey. "Many were of local manufacture … but others may either have been imported or made locally by captive foreign craftsmen."[44] The craft of the goldsmith, born in the land between the rivers more than two thousand years earlier, had spread to a wider world, which had added its own refinements (witness the golden bowl with an Egyptian scene) which came back to enhance the Mesopotamian repertoire.

Babylon re-visited

A final word is due on Babylon. On the endless roundabout of Mesopotamian power, the Chaldaean tribes, who lived in the marshes where the Tigris and Euphrates approach the Gulf (predecessors of the modern Marsh Arabs), gradually asserted control over Babylon and took on the Assyrians. The Chaldaean wealth came from their control of the shipping lanes to and from the Gulf. Babylon's full resurgence came under Nabopolassar (625–605 BC) and his son Nebuchadrezzer II (604–562 BC). The Assyrians were defeated, Babylon's Empire stretched from the Gulf to the Mediterranean, the city itself was rebuilt with walls 18 km/11 miles long. Nebuchadrezzer's long reign has been proclaimed the greatest in Babylon's history. The archaeologist Joan Oates saw him as "a statesman and general of exceptional talents, he was also a builder of ambition and imagination whose surviving monuments are without rival in Mesopotamia".[45] Herodotus, the Greek historian, writing scarcely one hundred years after the event, was in no doubt of their magnificence. He noted that in a country remarkable for the number of great cities, Babylon was "the most powerful and renowned of them all … it surpasses in splendour any city of the known world".[46]

The most important temple was that of the city-god Marduk (also known as Bel) which, Herodotus reported, housed "a great sitting figure of Bel, all of gold on a golden throne, supported on a base of gold, with a golden table standing beside it. I was told by the Chaldaeans that, to make all this, more than 800 talents (21.7 m.t/683,550 t.oz) of gold were used. Outside the temple is a golden altar".[47] The proposal that twenty-two tonnes of gold was required must be inflated, to say the least. For over two thousand years Mesopotamian goldsmiths had been adept at covering hard wood, copper or even bitumen with thin gold sheet or leaf. The gold on Bel's image may well have been only skin-deep, but the desired amazement was created. Certainly, when Nebuchadrezzer rebuilt another temple at Nabu, the cedar beams were simply overlaid with gold. The king also issued gold and silver to specific craftsmen to make "rich garments and jewellery for the statues of the gods and the temple women".[48]   The implication is that these were independent goldsmiths not employed in a palace workshop but, as in all ancient civilisations, still dependent on gold handed out to them by rulers or wealthy patrons.

The Babylonian renaissance was short. The balance of power was shifting from the land between the rivers after more than three thousand years. To the east, Persia was the new force, and King Cyrus took over Babylon without much resistance in 539 BC. In the west, King Croesus was already getting rich on gold in Lydia and, across the Aegean Sea from him, Greece was on the rise. The gold business, too, had moved on; it had been born in Mesopotamia, but had long since reached out to Egypt, Troy, Minoan Crete, Mycenæ, the Phoenicians and even the Celtic fringes of Europe. Mesopotamia, however, had shown the way and taught them what could be wrought with gold.

CHAPTER 2

Egypt:
A gift from the Nile

The popular image of gold in ancient Egypt is of the sensuous death mask of Tutankhamun, of his solid gold coffin (the heaviest single item of worked gold ever found) and the other treasures of his tomb in the Valley of the Kings. Their splendour cannot be eclipsed, yet Tutankhamun was a minor pharaoh who ruled for perhaps nine years and died at the age of eighteen or nineteen. Apart from the man revealed by his tomb, almost nothing is known about him. This poses the question – what must the treasures of some of the great pharaohs, Amenemhat II or Senusret I or Senusret III of the Middle Kingdom era, and Thutmose III or Amenhotep III or Rameses III of the New Kingdom period, have been like? Their legacies in gold have long since been taken by tomb robbers and melted down, denying us a complete perspective of Egypt's contribution to the history of gold, both as the world's first major producer and of its transformation into 'wonderful things', to quote the archaeologist Howard Carter as he first glimpsed by candlelight in AD 1922 the interior of Tutankhamun's tomb, closed up since 1327 BC.

Fortunately, precious glimpses of the surviving adornments of assorted pharaohs, their queens and princesses down the long roll call of Egyptian dynasties spanning over two thousand years, are amplified by the panorama of Egyptian life unveiled in reliefs and wall paintings inside pyramids and tombs. These illustrations reveal how the Egyptians, men and women, revelled in the splash and, above all, the colour of jewellery. "Jewellery permeated every facet of Egyptian civilization at every level of society," observed the British Museum's Carol Andrews. "In life, it might be worn as a sign of rank or office, as a military or civilian award, to be amuletic and protective, or merely to be decorative. All such pieces could be taken to the tomb with their owner for use in the Afterlife."[1]

Amulets (charms) and little jewellery clasps were tremendously popular and often bore cheerful mottoes such as 'joy', 'contented life' or 'all protection is around thee', offering simple good wishes to the living and the dead.[2] Jewellery was created in a rainbow of colours as gold was contrasted with the dark blue of lapis lazuli, the pale blue of turquoise, the green and yellow hues of jasper, the blood red of carnelian and the deep violet of amethyst. These semi-precious stones cropped up in the deserts and hills along the river Nile, along with plenty of gold.

That gold made Egypt the world's first major producer. Rich alluvial deposits along the upper reaches of the Nile in Nubia and mines scattered like stardust in the desert between the river and the Red Sea yielded gold on a scale not previously seen. Egypt's output launched the African continent as the largest contributor to the world's stock of gold built up over the last five thousand years. Today Africa still provides over 20% of annual gold output and gold exploration or production is active in Egypt and its neighbours Eritrea, Ethiopia and Sudan, all sources for Egypt in ancient times as it pushed its frontiers up the Nile.

The Nile was the life-blood of Egypt. Just as the contemporary civilisation of Mesopotamia flourished on the banks of the Euphrates and the Tigris, so Egypt was nourished by the long ribbon of the main river coming out of the heart of Africa and the Blue Nile from the high plateau of Ethiopia. "Egypt was a gift from the Nile," declared the French historian Maurice Vierya.[3] "The river," as everyone called it, was the highway that bound together the towns and villages along its banks, its annual flood carried silt to fertilise the narrow strip of fertile land between the oppression of the desert sands, while the low-lying islands and swamps of the great delta teemed with fish and wild life.

The river's influence on people's lives and their religious beliefs was profound. The pharaoh was the master of the Nile and his people so accustomed to it for their livelihood and transport that they considered it natural to depict Ra, the sun god (also the symbol for gold), travelling through the sky and the netherworld on his barge. They had over eighty words to describe the different types of boat plying the river. Since the prevailing wind in Egypt was from the north, the hieroglyph for travelling south (whether on river, sea or land) was a boat with billowing sails, while the sign for travelling north was a boat with its sails down (boats going north down the Nile were carried by the current and aided by oars).

The river made Egypt more self-sufficient than Mesopotamia, creating an independent and, in many ways, isolated society that did not have to become a hub of international trade to thrive. The Egyptians were in no hurry to embrace new technology; the potter's wheel appeared long after its regular use in Mesopotamia and bronze made a very late appearance as a useful hard metal. As for money, the Egyptians managed quite well with barter until the Persian invasions of 525 BC. "Economists register astonishment and even frustration when confronted with life in Egypt," observed the French historian Fernand Braudel; "fantastically well-ordered and intelligent, yet obstinately archaic … money remained of marginal significance, barter being the rule".[4]

Gold was valued, not as money, but a divine metal that never tarnished and was indeed the flesh of Ra, whose cult was worshipped from the tie of the pharaoh Raneb (c. 2865 BC). As such, gold was a magic substance that protected the wearer in a hostile world. The pharaoh also handed out honours in gold to reward his generals and officials; the Order of the Golden Collar was first awarded during the Old Kingdom (2686–2181 BC), while the Order of the Golden Fly was a New Kingdom (1550–1069 BC) innovation for military achievement, notably for securing new sources of gold in Nubia. The success of those operations made Egypt so

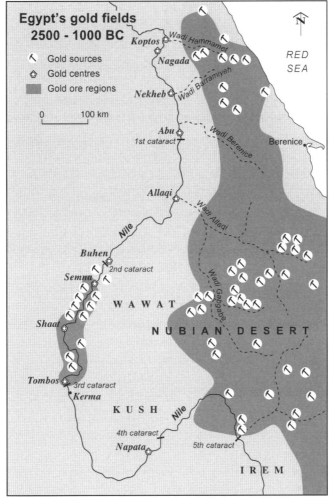

Egypt's gold fields 2500 - 1000 BC

Based on studies by J. Vercoutter, Journal of the Sudan Antiquities Service, Vol VII, 1959.

flush with gold for a while, that it became an important export item much sought by the rulers of Babylon, Assyria and elsewhere. Gold may not have been regarded as money, but pharaohs certainly valued what one historian felicitously dubbed 'diplomatically potent gold'.[5]

Gold also had a unique relationship with silver. Egypt had no silver mines as such, but much of the gold ore mined in the eastern desert had a relatively high silver content. "A large part of Egyptian silver was, in fact, natural aurian silver, or, put another way, a natural silver-rich gold ore," concluded the metallurgists N. W. Gale and Z. A. Stos-Gale, "Egyptians at first regarded gold and silver as two forms of the same metal, distinguished only by colour, so in a sense it was, initially, a rarer form of gold."[6] Indeed, during the Old Kingdom (2686–2181 BC) silver was valued more highly than gold, although this had much to do with the rarity of the metal. The gold:silver ratio may well have been reversed at 2:1, compared with a ratio around 1:13 or 1:14 in Mesopotamia, where silver was more plentiful. And it always remained in a narrow band. By the Middle Kingdom (2055–1650 BC) the gold-silver ratio was at 1:2 and that relationship did not change much for over one thousand years thereafter, until the Phoenicians began shipping large quantities of silver from mines in Spain. Until then, silver was always highly prized, and became a standard of value, as did copper. The price of major commodities was set in so many units of value of silver or copper, although that did not mean the purchase was actually paid for in the metal. Rather, settlement was made in several other commodities, such as oxen, fat, oil or even clothing, whose value was cross-referenced to units of silver and copper. But silver was the stable benchmark. The special relationship with silver keeps surfacing throughout Egypt's history. The pharaoh Psusennes I (1039–991 BC) was buried at Tanis on the Nile delta in a silver coffin filled with gold treasures.

The chronology of Egypt through several hundred pharaohs, thirty dynasties, three main kingdoms (Old, Middle and New) and 'intermediate periods' of chaos, is daunting.[7] The main outline, however, is relatively simple. Scattered towns and villages gradually developed along the Nile after 5500 BC and Egypt first became one nation during the Early Dynastic Period (3100–2686 BC). In the Egyptian mind the country was always divided into Lower Egypt, essentially the fan of the Nile delta, and Upper Egypt, which stretched from Memphis (near modern Cairo) one thousand kilometres up the Nile to the First Cataract at Elephantine (Aswan). The two parts were brought together by the pharaoh Narmer, c. 3100 BC, who came down from Upper Egypt to subdue the people of the delta. By then, Egyptian society was already well established, thriving on an abundance of game, wild fowl and fish. The profuse papyrus reeds that flourished in the Nile's waters were made into ropes, baskets, frail boats and, ultimately, sheets of 'paper' on which designs, hieroglyphs and writing were set down. Thus Egypt, like Mesopotamia, benefited at an early stage from a written language.

In this increasingly creative environment, personal adornment was important. Necklaces, girdles and bracelets were made of sea shells and beads carved from soft soapstone. Before long a stone drill, worked by a handle that could drill holes for beads, was invented. Thus beads became the staple item of jewellery. "The special contribution of Egypt to the jeweller's art was its bead jewellery," wrote the Egyptologist Cyril Aldred. "No other nation in antiquity produced such an enormous wealth of beads in so many shapes and substances."[8]

Sure enough, soon after 3500 BC gold disc-beads were being threaded on necklaces, mingled with roughly cut garnets, turquoise, carnelians and silver (perceived as a colour variant of gold). These were by no means the earliest workings in gold. A Neolithic gold wire bracelet, dated c. 4475 BC, has been found in a grave in the Wadi Elei, off the important gold mining area of Wadi Allaqi in the Nubian desert, and was on show at the British Museum in 2004. The bracelet was found on the arm bone of a skeleton; it was simple, but had one end fashioned into a hook, the other was flattened and pierced to enable fastening.[9]

From these humble beginnings, the goldsmiths' skills evolved. By the Early Dynastic Period their repertoire extended to amulets (charms), finger-rings, bracelets and diadems. The American archaeologist George Reisner came up with a bevy of ten gold amulets including representations of a beetle, an oryx and a bull at the ancient cemetery of Nag el-Deir five hundred kilometres up the Nile. They were made from two pieces of gold foil stamped out in *repoussé* and soldered along the edge. The same tomb revealed a small gold box within which was a gold cylinder-seal made from a strip of gold, rolled into a drum with caps at each end. Reisner's most elegant finds were a simple gold headband and a delicate necklace of twenty-four gold shells, each fashioned by hammering gold foil into a mould and then enhancing the shells' coils by *repoussé*.

While Reisner was digging, another pioneer of Egyptology, Flinders Petrie, was busy at the sacred site of Abydos just across the Nile. Abydos was the home of the ancient cult of the god Osiris, who presided over death, resurrection and fertility. Many early rulers of Upper Egypt were buried there, but their tombs had been ransacked. By chance, Petrie came upon the wrapped forearm of a woman, tucked into a crevice in the tomb of King Djer (c. 3000 BC). Unwrapping the bindings, he found four exquisite bracelets, each a different medley of gold, lapis lazuli, turquoise and amethyst. The finest bracelet was composed of thirteen gold and fourteen turquoise plaques each depicting the façade and ground plan of Djer's palace and surmounted by a falcon, one of Egypt's most sacred birds and protector of kings.

The craftsmanship in the jewellery points to the growing sophistication of the newly integrated Egypt. The foundations of a civilisation that would last three thousand years were in place. "These early people had achieved a written language of a very complex nature, they could fashion beautiful objects of the hardest stone, they had undertaken monumental architecture, their craftsmanship was … irreproachable," observed the writer Leonard Cottrell.[10]

The gold of Koptos

The location of these early gold relics in Upper Egypt is significant. Both Nag el-Deir and Abydos are less than one hundred kilometres downstream on the Nile from the twin towns of Koptos and Naqada. Koptos, on the eastern bank, was the collecting centre for gold from the eastern desert. Naqada, on the opposite bank, was one of the oldest towns in Upper Egypt, with a reputation for craftsmanship going back before 4000 BC. Indeed, two of the early 'civilisations' in Egypt prior to unification are known as Naqada I (4000–3500 BC) and Naqada II (3500–3100 BC). Naqada built a fine tradition for pottery, ivory combs and tiny figurines (one exquisite naked woman with two blue lapis lazuli eyes resembles a modern icon with sunglasses). The craftsmen strung almost any handy coloured article on necklaces. A necklace, dating pre-3600 BC in the British Museum, has beads of copper, carnelian, glazed steatite, shells and bird's leg bones. A slightly later necklace was strung with beads of alabaster, calcite, malachite, fluorspar, rock crystal, shell, feldspar and carnelian. Thus, gold arriving at Koptos from the eastern desert or down-river from Nubia was a natural addition to the inventory. Moreover, Naqada's original name was *Nubt* meaning 'gold town', which suggests this was the first home of Egypt's goldsmiths. *Nub* is the Egyptian word for gold and the debate had always been whether Nubia, a great source of gold, took its name from the metal or the metal from the country.

Access into the eastern desert was along the Wadi Hammamat, branching east off the Nile just above modern Luxor, and other dried-up watercourses. The wadis provided a link between the river and Quesor on the Red Sea coast and the gold mines and stone quarries that proved vital to the early dynasties. The town of Koptos, dating back before 3000 BC, serviced this traffic, as did Nekheb, a little further up-river. The gold was sprinkled in alluvial and shallow surface deposits only a few metres deep across a broad quartz plateau that sloped gently down to the Nile. The Egyptians called it the 'upland of Koptos'. And from an early date pharaohs made organised efforts to locate and mine it. "In principle, all mining operations were carried out for the sole benefit of the pharaoh," the German Egyptologist Professor Hans Müller noted. "He equipped the expeditions at royal expense and all gold as a result would be deposited in the royal treasury."[11] The 'brand' of the pharaoh Djet (c. 2980 BC) was carved in a niche in the rock close to the gold mines off the Wadi Barramiyeh, east of Nekheb, suggesting he had staked his claim. The energy that went into the search for gold was as great as that which built the pyramids.

The French archaeologist, J. Vercoutter, drew up a map of the three gold-bearing regions of ancient Egypt. First, the 'Gold of Koptos' found between the Wadi Hammamat and Berenice three hundred kilometres to the south-east; then came the 'Gold of Wawat' in the eastern desert beyond Aswan; and finally the 'Gold of Kush' in alluvial terraces on the Nile itself and at mines in the Nubian desert of modern Sudan. Vercoutter identified at least eleven ancient gold sites in the Koptos sector, over forty in Wawat and around thirty in Kush.[12] A later study by the Egyptian Geological Survey and Munich University in the 1990s covering only Egyptian terrain between the Nile and Red Sea located an astonishing 130 ancient mining sites, some dating before 3100 BC.

The research revealed how gold mining techniques had evolved over the centuries, from simple alluvial recovery to ever more ambitious mining of shallow surface deposits as recovery techniques improved. In practice, the initial surface mining did not have to be sophisticated. "The quartz veins are clear to see, so there is no difficulty tracking them," said Dr Tim Williams, a geologist with wide modern experience of the region. "The ore is oxidized and easy to get out. They crushed it to powder with circular granite stones that workers twisted." Over the centuries the miners went back again and again in Koptos, exploring for new and deeper deposits. The gold production continued, on and off, for over two thousand

Varna treasure, c.4250 BC; cut-outs of bulls from thin gold sheet.
Varna Museum of Archeology, Bulgaria

**Royal Cemetery at Ur, 2600-2400 BC;
gold cup from the queen's grave**
© *The Trustees of the British Museum.
All rights reserved*

**Royal Cemetery at Ur, c.2500 BC;
helmet of Prince Mes Kalam-Dug
hammered from a single sheet of
gold alloy**
Baghdad Museum

**Royal Cemetery at Ur, c.2600 BC;
headdress and necklace of gold,
lapis lazuli and cornelian**
© *The Trustees of the British
Museum. All rights reserved*

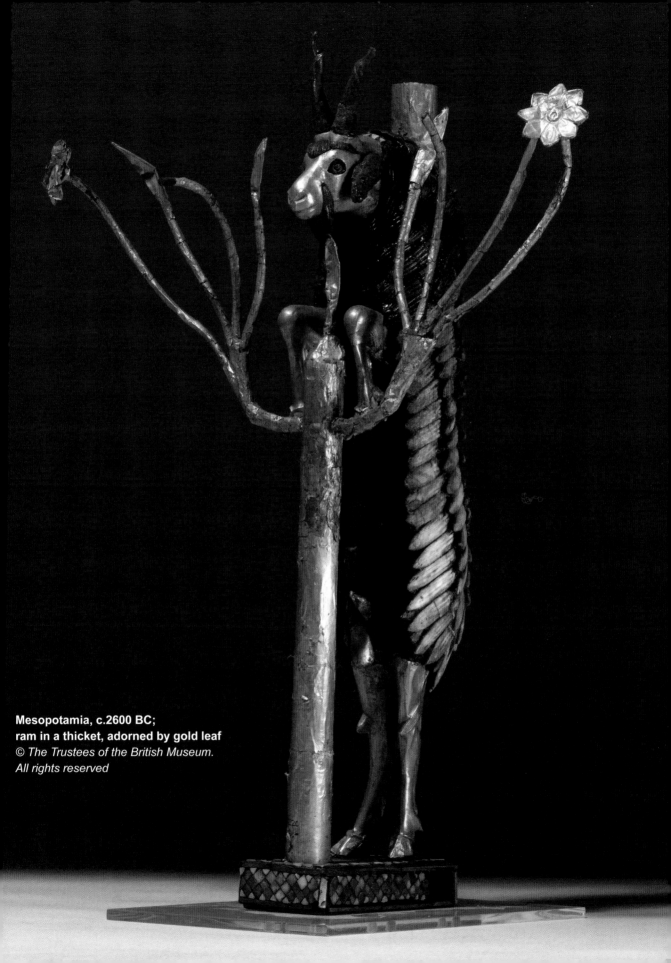

Mesopotamia, c.2600 BC;
ram in a thicket, adorned by gold leaf

© The Trustees of the British Museum.
All rights reserved

Egypt c.1327 BC;
death mask of Tutankhamun
Photo: Eberhard Thiem

**The throne of Tutankhamun, with the sun watching over the king
and his bride, Ankhes-en-pa-Amun**

Photo: Eberhard Thiem

Tutankhamun's tomb; collar ornament of thin chased gold foil with two guardian goddesses
Photo: Eberhard Thiem

Egypt; West Thebes tomb c.1550 BC; Nubians bring tributes of gold nuggets and rings
Photo: Eberhard Thiem

Tutankhamun's tomb;
scarab pectoral with
Isis and Nephthys
Photo: Eberhard Thiem

Tutankhamun's tomb;
gold and relief panel
of Tutankhamun and
Ankhes-en-pa-Amun
hunting in a papyrus
thicket
Photo: Eberhard Thiem

Troy treasure O;
hairpin with rectangular head,
surmounted by six miniature vessels,
weight 7.53g
Pushkin Museum, Moscow

Troy treasure F;
basket-shaped earring,
weight 6.6g
Pushkin Museum, Moscow

Troy treasure F;
'currency bars' with incisions,
weights 10.48g, 10.39g, 9.7g
Pushkin Museum, Moscow

years. The proof is the first known map of a gold mining region. On a fragile strip of papyrus 1.5 metres long, now housed in the Museo Egizio in Turin, the geological map, dating around 1150 BC in the reign of Rameses IV, covers the Wadi Hammamat between the Nile and the Red Sea. The best preserved section shows a network of roads intersecting in a pink coloured mountainous region with inscriptions indicating where the gold is located. An all-important reservoir is pinpointed, with four buildings nearby identified as "the houses where they wash the gold". The map is doubly interesting in that it was prepared in a period when gold output further south in Nubia was failing, and Rameses was seeking fresh sources. Hence the drive to go back over the ground along the Wadi Hammamat two thousand years after the first production.

Gold washers can be seen at work in a sculptured relief in the tomb of a provincial nobleman named Baqt III, dated c. 2050 BC. The relief shows four washers kneeling before two broad pans; the gold dust that settles is passed to a colleague who puts it through a gravity concentrating table; the concentrates are then put into an earthen jar with a lid ready for refining. At this early date the refining was limited to cupellation to remove any base metals from the ore by oxidising or 'slagging them off' with repeated meltings. The cementation process required for separating silver from gold by the addition of salt was not yet understood.

Output is hard to gauge. The sheer organisation, however, that went into the mining effort must have yielded several hundred kg annually, given that it was virgin territory with occasional rich outcrops. Modern geologists prospecting in these deserts have come across one or two 'high grade' deposits with gold 'caps' up to thirty metres thick. The upland between Koptos and Berenice was apparently the priority during the Old Kingdom. Wawat and Kush in Nubia were not then under Egyptian control, so any concerted mining programme had to be directed from Koptos. An unofficial traffic in high quality alluvial gold from the terraces between the Second and Third Cataracts in Nubia undoubtedly came down the river from the earliest times and found a ready market among the goldsmiths of Naqada, the gold town (the slim bracelet from Wadi Elei dating c. 4475 BC indicates how early gold was being recovered in that region). Arrivals would have been erratic; just a leather bag or two of dust on a passing boat bringing ivory, ebony or spices out of Africa.

The reliance on Koptos gold through much of the Old Kingdom period is confirmed by surviving ornaments which usually have a purity of 800–850 fine while, after 2000 BC, jewellery of 950–960 fine becomes more common, implying a switch in gold sources to higher quality alluvial from Wawat and Kush. While this could signal an improvement in refining techniques, it is more likely to reflect fresh supplies. The dependence on Koptos gold, with its relatively high silver content of 20% or more, also fits the Old Kingdom perception of the two metals as one, with a paler shade of yellow the higher the silver content.[13]

The curse of the tomb robbers

While the supplies of gold ebbed and flowed, the hidden bonus was scrap, especially from burial sites. Robbing from pyramids and tombs was almost as much a profession as building them (and often the same people practised both). Since the Egyptians believed that they should be buried with all their possessions, including food and seeds for next year's planting, ready for the Afterlife, most gold went into ornaments destined, ultimately, for the grave. Specific funerary jewellery was also prepared. Indeed, in the Book of the Dead, which laid down specific instructions for every phase of burial, section 157 required, "a vulture of gold placed at the throat of the deceased" and section 158 called for "a gold collar". The plundering of burial sites had much to offer. "It is the nature of a miracle that any ancient Egyptian jewellery should have survived reasonably intact to modern times," lamented Cyril Aldred. "The hunt for valuable grave goods has gone on relentlessly since a little after the time of the first burial in that land."[14]

Aldred chronicled the case of the stone mason Amun-pnufer, who was charged in 1116 BC with robbing the tomb of Sobkemsaf II (c. 1590 BC). After being beaten to encourage him to tell the truth, a surviving papyrus document reported, Amun-pnufer confessed, "We ... found the noble mummy of this king ... amulets and jewels of gold were upon his neck, and his headpiece of gold was upon him. The noble mummy of this King was completely bedecked with gold, and his coffins were adorned with gold .. we collected the gold we found". The gold, weighing 160 *deben* (14.5 kg/466 t.oz), was divided equally among seven other accomplices, the first of whom was a jeweller. Amun-pnufer sought to justify the robbery by saying everyone did it. Just a year later another team of eight robbers was rounded up after stealing 283 *deben* (25.5 kg/820 t.oz) from another tomb at Thebes.[15]   Tomb robbing was endemic and, although architects tried to thwart it with secret passages, sudden trap doors and dead ends inside pyramids, the thieves usually succeeded. Indeed, that is what makes the tomb of Tutankhamun unique, for although it had been partly disturbed, most of the treasures remained. "Sometimes the necropolis was well guarded," noted the French Egyptologist Christiane Desroches-Nobelcourt; "at others its workmen and inhabitants regarded old kings and their treasuries as their own rightful heritage".[16]

Thus much of the gold mined in Egypt was recycled, save exports which were not substantial until the New Kingdom era. The stock within the country was in constant play (even if it took Amun-pnufer four hundred years to get Sobkemsaf's gold). Scrap must have contributed significantly to market supply, especially as people would also have traded old ornaments for new while they were alive.

Goldsmiths at work

Thus sustained, goldsmiths were not just busy, but held in esteem. The position of Chief of Goldsmiths was occupied by a nobleman (a purely supervisory role) who sometimes rated his own splendid tomb. Apuia, the chief goldsmith to Amenhotep

III (1390–1352 BC) built a fine tomb for himself at Memphis, and his son, chief goldsmith and cup-bearer to the next pharaoh, was buried amid much splendour at Thebes.[17] Our benefit from these and earlier memorials is that they contained reliefs and wall paintings presenting a veritable pictorial guide to the goldsmiths' trade. They show the nubi (gold worker) and the more talented *hemu-nub* (gold craftsman) at their tasks. The earliest relief, dating c. 2500 BC, in a tomb at Giza, depicted a dwarf busy stringing together a collar, one of the most characteristic pieces of Egyptian jewellery, from an assortment of finished beads. Dwarfs feature in most early illustrations, leading to the somewhat bizarre suggestion that they were employed because they had short legs and so could not run away with precious metal.

The most comprehensive scene, from the tomb of the vizier Mererula at Saqqara, c. 2340 BC, illustrated every step in a workshop. First, the metal was carefully weighed out on scales, with a scribe noting details, then it was placed in a crucible in a furnace, whose temperature was raised by three workmen kneeling on each side puffing furiously through blowpipes. The molten gold was then poured onto shallow trays to be beaten into sheet with rounded stones. Craftsmen, some dwarfs, then fashioned a great collar surmounted by two falcons. There were even cartoon-like bubbles of speech, as one dwarf busy with a chisel is exhorted by his companion, "Make haste and get it done". Finally, they congratulated each other: "Good work, mate".[18] A similar relief at Giza showed gold being sent back with the caption, "Reheat this piece of metal, it has hardened".[19]

The wall paintings also reveal improvements in technology. By the New Kingdom the blowpipes had been replaced by a pair of leather foot bellows, operated by a workman constantly marking time, shifting his weight from one bellows to the other, so that as one filled, the other expelled air into the furnace. The crucibles of molten gold were now transferred from furnace to mould suspended between purpose-made rods, instead of flat stones used in earlier periods. As dynasty succeeded dynasty, scores of metal working operations were illustrated, sometimes with revealing technical captions. Thus, two beaters working with stone hammers comment that the metal is 'cooking' when it becomes hot as it diffuses into thinner sheet under their blows. Elsewhere, beads are bored with bow drills before being polished and strung, or a craftsman reheats an ornament in a little brazier before perfecting a detail. Semi-precious stones are ground up to provide the multi-coloured impact of collars or girdles. Gilding is demonstrated as a craftsman hands a strip of gold leaf to his colleague who is gilding a wooden shrine.[20]

All told, the pictures portray a highly professional trade, which steadily acquired the whole goldsmiths' repertoire over the centuries. Chasing with a blunt-edged chisel tapped by a mallet was practised before 3000 BC. Lost wax technology first revealed in a gorgeous solid gold cast amulet of a falcon, was perfected before 2500 BC, as was *cloisonné*, the inlay of semi-precious stones, to satisfy the Egyptian passion for rainbow jewellery. Granulation was mastered around

1900 BC, probably through learning by example from Mesopotamia. By then the goldsmiths were preparing a complex variety of solders combining copper, silver and gold, blended with natron, a natural sodium compound, as the flux. The only technique the Egyptians did not master was the drawing of wire. Instead, the wire for popular loop-in-loop chains was made by cutting gold sheet into thin strips with a chisel and then twisting it as one might a straw.[21]

Although goldsmiths usually worked for palaces and temples, there must have been an open market because every Egyptian wore jewellery of some kind, and even people of modest means were buried with a few gold beads or charms. In large cities, such as Memphis the first capital of united Egypt, there was a goldsmiths' quarter, where families passed on the trade from generation to generation. They were a privileged community, protected by pharaohs and the gods. The goddess of love and beauty, Hathor, watched over both jewellers and miners, among many other duties assigned to her.[22]

The goldsmith was as committed to making ornaments for deities as for his fellow citizens. "The gods, too, had their jewellery," explained Cyril Aldred. "Every shrine sheltered the statue or statues of gods, who had to have a change of raiment, including jewellery and especially collars, as part of the daily ritual of service."[23]

Royal beads, bangles and buckles

What remains physically from over two thousand years of jewellery production is, save for the Tutankhamun treasures, limited. Fortunately, to back up the wall-paintings and reliefs, a few prizes have survived from each Kingdom as proof of the goldsmiths' skills. The tomb of the Old Kingdom pharaoh Sekhemket (2648–2650 BC) at Saqqara yielded twenty-one gold hoop bangles made of sheet gold, with the edges carefully bent inwards, which confirmed the evidence of statues showing women with many bangles on each arm (as you still see in Egypt today). The fashion was to wear an uneven number of bangles on the left arm, and an even number of the right, as a way of warding off evil; the twenty-one bangles from Saqqara support this superstition. The hoard also contained a gold magic wand, a gold cosmetics box shaped like a scallop shell which opened on a hinge, and a broad bracelet of 388 hollow gold beads strung in ten parallel lines interspersed by spacer bars.[24] A bevy of silver bangles, inlaid with carnelian, lapis and turquoise, were found tucked into a box labelled 'box containing rings' in the tomb of Queen Hetepheres, mother of the pharaoh Khugu/Cheops (2589–2566 BC). They were badly corroded, silver not being so impervious to the elements as gold, but serve as a reminder that in the Old Kingdom silver was as highly, if not more highly, rated than gold and thus fit for a Queen.[25] The tomb at Giza of a princess of the same period contained a charming headband of gold foil backed by copper and adorned with golden marsh flowers; the style of this simple coronet was derived from Nile boatmen who often cooled their brow with a circlet of water weeds. The princess wore a unique necklace of fifty hollow gold beads shaped as beetles. The goldsmith had made each beetle by working a thin sheet of gold into a mould and soldering a ring to the head so that it could be strung on a chain.[26]   Tantalising glimpses of the innovative ideas of the early goldsmiths are occasionally unearthed. Two tiny limestone vases, dating c. 2700 BC, found at Abydos (now in the British Museum) were equipped with delicately made covers of gold sheet secured with gold wire, which look, at first glance, like golden panama hats. The expertise of the Old Kingdom craftsman is best demonstrated, however, in a belt with a solid gold buckle made for Prince Ptahshepses, which was inlaid with carnelian, obsidian and turquoise hieroglyphs giving his name and titles. The buckle, partly chased, partly inlaid, showed the seated figure of the prince on each side, watched over by two falcons with wings outstretched, creating a dashing image of a pharaoh's son around 2300 BC.[27]

The confidence that spurred such talent, whether channelled into ornaments or the architectural and engineering skills that built most of the greatest pyramids, did not endure indefinitely. The Old Kingdom petered out by 2181 BC, mired in rivalries within the royal family and the challenge of provincial governors competing for independence. Climate change and floods may also have caused disruption, as they did in Mesopotamia where the Sumer civilisation foundered. The united Egypt that had lasted almost one thousand years was in ruins. A wave of looting struck pyramids and tombs providing, no doubt, scrap gold to offset formal mining disrupted by the turmoil.

Middle Kingdom: In search of Nubia's gold

The interregnum was relatively short. Within fifty years, Thebes, five hundred kilometres up-river from Memphis, was the emerging power base from which Mentuhotep II (2055–2004 BC) finally stabilised and re-unified the whole country. The Middle Kingdom lasted four hundred years. In the story of gold the era was significant for the first successful attempt to control gold sources in Nubia and for some of the finest jewellery. "The court jewellers … brought this ancient craft to an unsurpassed height of excellence," reflected Leonard Cottrell.[28]

The challenge for Middle Kingdom rulers was not just political stability, but the economic resources to sustain it. Nubia held out the promise of gold and other minerals, with the added advantage of entry into the luxury trade with tropical Africa. The easily-mined gold of the eastern desert had largely been worked out during the Old Kingdom and declining output may have contributed to its demise. The immediate task now was to bring Nubia into the fold. Under Senusret I (1965–1920 BC), Amenemhat II (1922–1878 BC) and Senusret III (1874–1855 BC), the Egyptian frontier was pushed up the river beyond Aswan to the Third Cataract. A chain of fortresses was built to protect the frontier and the shipments of gold. Senusret III even had a short channel, 80 metres long, cut through granite rock around the First Cataract, so that his war galleys could proceed four hundred kilometres up to the Second Cataract at Buhen. This gave the Egyptians direct access to important new gold mining areas in the eastern desert of Wawat, along the Wadi Allaqi and the Wadi Gabgaba, and also to the rich alluvial gold terraces of Kush along the Nile itself between Buhen and Kerma at the Third Cataract. The fortress at Kuban at the junction with the Wadi Allaqi was the control centre for mining in the interior (which included copper in addition to gold) and for the smelting of gold dust into ingots or rings.

The waters of the Nile were crucial to many of the operations, and donkey caravans brought crushed ore from the interior for washing before smelting. At several points along the Nile sloping rock terraces have been found which served as gravity separation tables, from which channels led down into basins that acted as settling tanks for the slurry. The many shallow mines along the Wadis Allaqi and Gabgaba (Vercoutter, in his study of the Gold of Kush, had counted over forty) provided the Middle Kingdom pharaohs with much of their gold. The scales and weights for gold found at Quban, Kerma and other river forts indicate significant amounts of gold were recovered.[29]

The quantity is hard to estimate, but it could have reached well over 500 kg/16,075 t.oz in a few successful seasons. Crucially, the authorities' grip on the production was tight; they controlled (brutally) the mines of the desert interior and the output ended up in their strongholds on the river. Securing the open production from the alluvial deposits on the river itself may have been more difficult; throughout history they have always tempted unofficial gold diggers in remote regions. But for a few generations most of the output from the 'official' mining sector went into the royal treasury.

Enter princesses

A renaissance in jewellery was founded on Nubian gold. Some of the finest Egyptian ornaments were created in the century after 1900 BC when this gold flowed into royal coffers. Indeed, it is no coincidence that the most famous hoards of Middle Kingdom jewellery, found at Dahshur and el-Lahun, are those of wives and daughters of pharaohs closely involved in securing Nubian gold. They reveal the royal workshops in their prime. First came the discovery of three princesses, Ita, Ita-weret and Khnumet, who were buried within the walls of the pyramid of Amenemhat II, who died c. 1876 BC. Ita's remains had been disturbed and little remained beyond a bronze dagger with a golden hilt and a scattering of jewellery. Ita-weret was safe in her coffin, modestly adorned with a broad collar of beads and ornaments of gold, held in place by gold clasps, and bracelets of gold beads and semi-precious stones. Princess Khnumet's treasure was intact and spell-binding. The princess who is thought to have been the daughter of one pharaoh and perhaps wife of another, was buried, in a sense, in a goldsmith's showroom. She had a falcon collar of gold, inlaid with lapis, turquoise, carnelian, garnets and green felspar; seven rows of pendant beads were connected by horizontal strings of hundreds of gold beads, all connected to two soaring falcon head terminals.

Another gold collar, inlaid with a dazzle of red carnelian, dark blue lapis and pale blue turquoise, had strings of gold beads separated by little pendant hieroglyphs of vultures and cobras (symbols of Upper and Lower Egypt respectively) and abstract images of Life, Union, Strength and Stability.

The princess's necklace collection has fascinated archaeologists because wonderful butterflies and cockle shells suspended from perfect loop-in-loop chains, are decorated with gold granules – the first appearance of granulation in Egypt. They have led to speculation that this part of the treasure may have been made in Minoan Crete or at Ugarit or Byblos in the Levant or even by goldsmiths who had trained in those places. In short, clear evidence exists of the growing exchange of goldsmithing techniques, if not of an international trade.

The masterworks of Princess Khnumet's treasure were two diadems inspired by the Nile boatmen's circlet of cooling water weeds. The most informal, a circular tangle of gold wires set with flowers and berries in carnelian, lapis and turquoise, conjures up the impression of a young princess at court bedecked with a real garland of flowers. "No head-dress as fragile and delightful as this could be imagined from those illustrated in wall-paintings or sculpture," wrote Alix Wilkinson in her study of *Ancient Egyptian Jewellery*.[30]

Princess Khnumet's other diadem was more formal, with eight linked segments shaped like lilies or lotuses and inlaid with carnelian, lapis and turquoise. Over the forehead swept a gold vulture, wings curved downwards to create an arch. Alix Wilkinson concluded that the two crowns of princess Khnumet, along with another found at el-Lahun, were "the glory of Middle Kingdom jewellers".

The crown at el-Lahun belonged to Princess Sithathoriunet and was found by Flinders Petrie in the pyramid of Senusret II, who died c. 1874 BC. It was in a cache of jewellery which also contained ornaments bearing the names of Amenemhat III. The princess was Senusret's daughter, who lived on into Amenemhat's reign. Her regal crown was a simple band of burnished gold, set with fifteen rosettes, with a hooded cobra rising at the front, its head overlaid with brilliant blue lapis set with two red garnets as eyes. The triumph of her collection, however, were two pectorals worn on the breast that showed absolute mastery of the *cloisonné* technique of inlaying gold with semi-precious stones. In the most splendid of these set pieces, two falcons, their plumage of lapis and turquoise inlaid in cells of gold, their eyes tiny chips of garnet, rest their feet on palm branches of gold upheld by a deity, etched out in blue with a bright red carnelian kilt. On the plain gold reverse of this pectoral, the birds' feathers have been elegantly chased with lines of great delicacy.

Princess Sithathoriunet's pectoral had a rival, that of Princess Sithathor, also a daughter of Senusret II found near the pyramid of Senusret III at Dahshur. This pectoral was bordered by a multi-coloured shrine, within which two falcons perched on *nub* signs (meaning gold) representing the sky god Horus. It was dedicated to Senusret II, suggesting he gave both these famous designs to his daughters.

The twin pectorals represent the pinnacle of craftsmanship. "No more exquisitely fashioned example of goldsmith's and lapidary's work has survived from Egypt," wrote Herbert Winlock of the Metropolitan Museum of Art, "and no lighter and at the same time classically restrained design has come down to us to represent the Egyptian jeweller's art."[31]

The princesses were endowed with other jewellery of great simplicity yet sophistication. Sithathoriunet had one girdle of gold leopard-head beads interspersed with beads of dark blue amethysts and another of finely-chased gold cowry shells interspersed by blue and red beads. Sithathor also had a wonderful necklace of gold cowry shells; the cowry shell because of its resemblance to female genitalia, was believed to offer protection to young women from malevolent forces, especially when they were pregnant. The princesses' ornaments represent the pinnacle of Middle Kingdom jewellery, but the relative abundance of gold meant that it was worn by a large segment of the population. The fashion, above all, was for amulets (charms); they were available for every event from cradle to grave. Charms of the hippopotamus goddess Thoeris, with pendant breasts and swollen stomach, protected women in childbirth. Fish amulets prevented children from drowning in the river, frogs were a symbol of fertility, lizards of regeneration, coleoptera beetles offered general security and scarab beetles symbolised new life, while oyster shell amulets assured a sound, whole and healthy life (Princess Sithathor has 31 small gold oyster shells on a single necklace).[32] The rich kept their amulets in cylindrical gold cases, often decorated with the new fad – granulation. Such an array indicates, not just that amulets were all the rage in the 19th century BC, but that gold was plentiful. Nubia was delivering year after year.

The control over Nubia was demonstrated in a 'political' pectoral found at Dahshur amid the jewellery of Queen Mereret, daughter of Senusret III (who cut the canal round the First Cataract to get his galleys into Nubia's heartland). The pectoral cast Senusret III as a multi-coloured griffin trampling on his foes, including the Nubians shown with blue lapis bodies and red carnelian belts. A second pectoral, presented to the Queen by Amenemhat III (1855–1808 BC) also showed that pharaoh raising his mace to strike the enemy. The more warlike scenes hint that a century of great prosperity was ending. The enemy forces in contention were not just Nubians, but from Libya to the west and the Levant from the north. The pressure was such that, a few years later, in 1786 BC, Egypt withdrew from active occupations of Nubia and did not go back for 300 years. Gold output without the disciplined mining organisation imposed by Egypt was more haphazard. The interruption to the regular gold supply is mirrored by the fact that, after Queen Mereret's treasure, nothing of real significance has been found until that of Queen Ahhotep 250 years later. Obviously jewellery manufacture continued, but on a modest scale, with plenty of scrap supply from looted tombs during a period of unrest. However, it is not coincidence that the finest Middle Kingdom jewellery was created when Egypt was first controlling Nubian output and the next great collections to have been found, including Tutankhamun's, are from the New Kingdom era, when Nubia was back under the Egyptian yoke and gold in plentiful supply. Civil unrest over several centuries also inevitably took its toll of artistic talent. Those two pectorals of Queen Mereret signal the shift in public mood from harmony and creativity to war.

New Kingdom: Back to Nubia

The Middle Kingdom did not vanish overnight. Rather, political stability collapsed as rival dynasties squabbled and the unified nation broke in two. One dynasty stayed at Thebes in Upper Egypt, another set up at Avaris in the Delta. That was the fatal weakness. Waves of migrant nomads, known as Hyksos or 'rulers of foreign lands', pushed into the Delta from Palestine, Lebanon and Syria and settled there. This was not active conquest but, as one Egyptologist put it, "peaceful takeover". They arrived over many decades and were absorbed. They brought with them many new skills, especially in metalwork from Mesopotamia, along with horses, the wheel, and the war chariot. Such 'new technology' helped them gain power in Lower Egypt. Their influence on Upper Egypt was more limited, and it was from Thebes that the liberation struggle against the 'rulers of foreign lands' began. The last three kings of the 17th dynasty began the campaigns, but it was Ahmose I (1550–1525), founder of the 18th dynasty, who threw them out. The New Kingdom he created was to last almost five hundred years and see Egypt emerge as an imperial power, a conqueror and coloniser. The main economic resource of that empire was gold. Egypt became not just the major producer, but a substantial exporter of gold in the period after 1500 BC. The priority to achieve that was to reconquer Nubia.

Successive pharaohs now pushed the boundaries of Egyptian control up the Nile into Wawat and Kush and eastwards along the Wadis Allaqi and Gabgaba into the heart of the Nubian desert. Amenhotep I (1525–1504 BC) established a new fortress at Shaat between the Second and Third Cataracts, Thutmose I (1504–1492 BC) built the stronghold of Tombos at the Third Cataract, just above the ancient Nubian capital of Kerma. Finally, Thutmose III (1479–1425 BC) pressed Egyptian control through a region of rich grasslands up to the Fourth Cataract, where the fortified town of Napata was set up. This advanced Egypt's border up-river by almost one thousand kilometres. Her influence also extended several hundred kilometres beyond Napata through the Fifth and Sixth Cataracts to territory known as Irem, into which occasional Egyptian patrols ventured to demand 'tributes'. This 'colonialism' lasted almost four hundred years until the last of the New Kingdom pharaohs, Rameses XI (1099–1069 BC).

The location of prime mining areas and the 'tributes' they offered were carefully set out by a scribe for Rameses II when, much later, he was aiming to revive the industry. In each location hieroglyphics depict a man holding offerings on a tray, with the name of the mine inscribed over his head. One inscription read, "The Throne of the Two Lands (i.e. name of mine) … I bought to thee gold in many bags". The

Mountain of Amu provided "gold in enormous quantities" and the Mountain of Kush has "gold in heaps". The Desert of Ta Seti had "gold in millions", the Mountain of Djeb did even better with "gold by millions of millions". The Two Lands apparently designated mines near the Fourth Cataract, the Mountain of Amu embraced the mines near the Third Cataract, and the Mountain of Kush those around Buhen at the Second Cataract. The Desert of Ta-Seti was probably the harsh terrain of the Wadi Allaqi in Wawat and the Mountain of Djeb referred to mines along the Wadi Abbad in the original mining area of Koptos.[33]   In each area there was a scatter of gold deposits, just as we find today along the Carlin Trend in Nevada, or Kalgoorlie's Golden Mile in Western Australia.

The position of Viceroy of Kush was created to govern the two provinces of Wawat and Kush (each having a deputy governor), with responsibility for civil administration, collecting taxes and expanding gold mining. The Viceroy's authority was extended under Amenhotep III to include Upper Egypt's own gold mines in the desert east of Nekhen as part of a comprehensive plan to expand and improve the exploitation of gold mining areas. It was closely linked to Egypt's new foreign policy of active involvement in the affairs of the Levant and even Mesopotamia, which relied on regular Nubian gold. Gold had become an essential arm of diplomacy in the building of alliances with foreign rulers. Instead of trying to overthrow them by campaigning, they were bought off with gold.

In Nubia the major exploration thrust was into the desert, along the Wadi Allaqi system. The advance into the relentlessly hot barren and rocky terrain required careful planning. Water, both for survival and washing ore, was at a premium, food was scarce, wood or charcoal for smelting the ore was not to be found. The logistics were a nightmare. Donkey caravans hauled supplies into the interior, but they were often prey to nomads. Amenhotep III punished them for threatening the food supplies of the gold miners, and even sent an expedition down the Red Sea to march inland to subdue the tribes. Later pharaohs, Sety I (1294–1279 BC) and Rameses II (1278–1213 BC) made great efforts to improve water supplies. Rameses, a memorial to his Viceroy of Kush recorded, had "wells dug along the road (Wadi Allaqi) which is without water … when expeditions of gold washers went there, only half arrived. They would die of thirst on the way".

The Viceroys of Kush, of whom over thirty have been identified (many had their own fine tombs), had a tough assignment. By chance, the one about whom most is known from tomb paintings is Tutankhamun's Viceroy named Huy. Tutankhamun (1336–1327 BC) appointed Huy at a splendid ceremony in Thebes at which he gave Huy the gold ring of office. Huy then set off up-river in a fine barge, accompanied by his staff including 'an accountant scribe of gold'. Arriving in Nubia, he set about re-asserting authority, which had been neglected under the previous pharaoh Akhenaten, who had been preoccupied with a new religious cult. Taxes and tributes were exacted from local tribal leaders, often paid in bags of gold dust or gold rings, and expeditions were dispatched to the mines. Huy watched over as gold was weighed and registered by scribes. Ultimately he made a grand voyage back down the Nile laden with gold and other luxuries from the interior of Africa. Tutankhamun was delighted and rewarded Huy with a profusion of gold necklaces. The implication is that Nubian gold did not arrive regularly by courier, but rather in an occasional well-guarded convoy, much like the annual treasure fleet from the Americas to Spain centuries later. Its arrival was a grand event.

In the desert of Wawat, the gold minders of the New Kingdom faced a new challenge. The shallow surface deposits had largely been worked out in the Middle Kingdom era. Not only did they now have to explore further into the interior for new deposits, but also start working underground. Shafts were dug down over one hundred metres with radiating pillared galleries as they tracked the quartz veins.

The conditions were horrendous. The Greek geographer Agatharchides, who visited the mines c.125 BC, wrote of the pitiless treatment of slaves and criminals, bound by chains, who were forced to work day and night, without rest. The scene he witnessed must have been similar one thousand years earlier, and the mining techniques much the same. "The gold bearing earth which is hardest they burn with a hot fire," he reported, "and when they have crumbled it in this way they continue the working of it by hand; and the soft rock which can yield to moderate effort is crushed with a sledge by myriads of unfortunate wretches." He also told how they cut tunnels, "not in a straight line but wherever the seam of gleaming rock may lead". On the surface the ore was pounded with pestles in stone mortars and finally ground "until it has the consistency of the finest flour".[34] By Agatharchides' day, the gold was being refined by the cementation process using salt to separate gold and silver, but that technology was not understood yet by the New Kingdom miners. Their harsh endeavours, however, lifted Egyptian output to a record level.

Hard statistics are naturally sparse. The most direct evidence is from the Annals of Thutmose III, which record the 'tribute' brought into Egypt from Wawat and Kush in three years of his reign. They reveal:

	Wawat	Kush
Year 34 (1445 BC)	2555 *deben*/232.4kg	over 300 *deben*/27.5 kg +
Year 38 (1441 BC)	2884 *deben*/258.8 kg	over 100 *deben*/9.1 kg
Year 41 (1438 BC)	3144 *deben*/286.1 kg	195 *deben*/17.8 kg

These statistics indicate much higher production from the desert of Wawat along the Wadi Allaqi than from the alluvial terraces and open pit working along the Nile itself between the Second and Fourth Cataracts. This is no surprise. What is surprising is how little gold was being received. This is not enough gold output for it to be "diplomatically potent", not enough for it to be "as common as grains of sand", not enough to supply Babylon with enough to go on a gold standard, and not enough for Assyrian kings to be expecting 20 talents (over 500 kg) as gifts, let alone the gifts of golden rings being handed out to local courtiers in contemporary Egyptian wall paintings and reliefs. And we cannot talk of Kush as a major source if it delivered scarcely 20 kg/643 t.oz a year. The archaeologists T. Säve-Söderbergh and J. Vercoutter, who came up with this information, clearly recorded the right numbers.[35]   The catch, I believe, is the word 'tribute'. That may not equal production; merely what came into Thutmosis III's own treasury. There must have been parallel supply direct to temples (important sources of jewellery manufacture) and a 'black' market, even if the whole traffic was officially controlled. So much organisation, so much effort, so many workers were involved, that output cannot have been just two or three hundred kg.

My own view is that, for a few decades around 1450 BC, Egypt's output hit an exceptional level, but was falling off well before Tutankhamun's time a century later, and fell even more thereafter. I believe that by 1450 BC Egypt's gold production was over 1,000 kg/32,150 t.oz. annually and might have reached 2,000 kg/64,300 t.oz. in bonanza years.

In short, there was a genuine gold rush for a few years, even decades, such as we shall see throughout the later history of gold to Spain, Hungary, Brazil and, ultimately, to California and Australia. As recently as the 1980s, there was a huge, short-lived surge of output in Brazil, Indonesia and the Philippines from thousands of unofficial diggers lured to alluvial and shallow surface deposits by the high gold price. Brazil's unofficial output reached over 60,000 kg/1.9 million t.oz. for a couple of years. So, proposing Egypt at 1,000 to 2,000 kg may be grossly under-estimating; it could have been more under Thutmose III and his immediate successors.

Backed by gold, the pharaohs embarked on numerous campaigns along the eastern shores of the Mediterranean to the city of Byblos and confronted the Mittani, a rising power in Syria before reaching the banks of the Euphrates, gateway to Babylon. They were after tributes, trade and alliances sealed by diplomatic marriages sweetened with gold. The aim was not conquest, but securing a quiet life. Gold paved the way.

The dialogues thus established were revealed a few generations later in the Amarna letters, a cache of 382 cuneiform tablets recording communications around 1350 BC between Egypt's rulers and their counterparts in the cities of the Mittani, Babylonians and Assyrians. The letters discuss military needs, proposals for marriage, trade and gold. Thus Tushratta, ruler of the Mittani, pleaded, "May my brother send me much more gold than he did to my father. In my brother's country gold is as plentiful as dirt". Burnaburish II of Babylon complained to Tutankhamun that he had been sent only two minas (900 grams/28 t.oz) of gold, far less than his father received.[36]   The letters reveal just how much foreign rulers had come to rely on Egyptian gold a generation or two earlier, but were now disappointed to be receiving only token amounts, once output declined.

New Kingdom, new jewellery

Although the jewellery trade revived with the coming of the New Kingdom, standards had slipped. "The workmanship of the jewels is generally much cruder than that of Middle Kingdom craftsmanship," decided Cyril Aldred, reviewing the treasure of Queen Ahhotep (c. 1590–1530 BC), the mother of Ahmose I, founder of the new dynasty, which turned up in a coffin near the entrance to the Valley of the Kings. Her regalia included the usual amulets, bracelets, collars, chains and a fine pectoral. And Aldred did allow that a few of the latter pieces, bearing the insignia of her son Ahmose, showed "an improvement in quality".[37]

Not only did the goldsmiths get into their stride, but they acquired new techniques. Heavy bracelets for the upper arm were now made in two halves and hinged. Gold wire, instead of thread, was used to string beads on some bracelets, so that they stayed intact in the tomb, much to archaeologists' delight (thread always rotted). Earrings came into vogue for the first time, often with a grooved tube passed through the pierced ear with a 'button' of gold at each end to keep it in place (a style which may have come out of Africa through *Nubia*). And among Queen Ahhotep's regalia was a necklace of three flies suspended on a gold chain, each fly the perfect silhouette of a modern Stealth Bomber. The Order of the Golden Fly was primarily a military decoration, which featured frequently on New Kingdom honours lists. The most accomplished ornament in Queen Ahhotep's coffin was a six-ply loop-in-loop chain, a thin rope of gold over 200 cm long, with a goose-neck and head at each end and from which a scarab of two heavy gold plates was suspended. Its simplicity reassured Cyril Aldred that the goldsmith of the new Kingdom "was capable of work well able to hold its own with the best of the past".[38]

An outward-looking Egypt also widened goldsmiths' horizons, as they came into contact with the fashions of the Levant, notably the city of Byblos, with Babylon and Mycenæan Greece. The link with Mycenæ was close; Egyptian jewellery, including a gold scarab with the insignia of Nefertiti, was found in a 14th century BC cargo ship wrecked off the Turkish coast en route to Greece, while a Mycenæan merchant opened a shop selling fashionable pottery painted with octopuses in El-Amarna. The luxury trade was becoming internationalised.

Prosperity meant a wider market. Wall-paintings show royal concubines decked out with golden head-dresses and collars, and dancing girls clad in not much more than bracelets and girdles from their admirers. Such popular jewellery turned up in a hoard found after a flash flood in 1916 revealed a tomb near the Valley of the Kings, in which was found the treasure of three 'minor' wives of Thutmosis III, called Menhet, Menwi and Merti. Local villagers swiftly ransacked the tomb, but the ornaments later appeared on the black market and were acquired by the Metropolitan Museum of Art in New York. The three ladies, thought to have been 'diplomatic gift' brides from the Levant, did not possess the grandest of jewels, but the smart trinkets then in fashion; new-style earrings, rather flashy collars, gold shell pendants, a girdle of twenty-two gold fish amulets, finger rings, heart-scarabs, finger and toe stalls of gold, and dainty gold sandals. This delightful collection of the baubles of minor royals were but a curtain-raiser for the greatest show of the goldsmiths' art ever assembled – the treasure of Tutankhamun.

Face to face with Tutankhamun

The scene is one of domestic bliss. A rather frail young man sits at ease on a cushioned throne, one arm casually over the back. He is clad in a kilt-like robe of silver, an ornate collar adorns his neck, his headdress is turquoise topped by a crown of gold. Before him stands a young woman, also in a long robe of silver, ornate collar, turquoise head-dress and crown. In her left hand she holds a small jar of ointment or perfume with which she anoints his collar. The couple are surrounded by flower-garlanded pillars and the golden rays of the sun beat down.

Meet Tutankhamun and his queen, Ankhesenamun, depicted on a panel of sheet gold on the back of a throne. The throne was one of the first sights to greet the archaeologist Howard Carter in the antechamber to Tutankhamun's tomb when he first broached it in November 1922. "It was the panel … that was the chief glory of the throne," he recorded at the time, "and I have no hesitation in claiming for it that it is the most beautiful thing that has yet been found in Egypt."[39]

Carter could not envisage that this was but the beginning of the images of the young pharaoh that would be revealed on similar sheet gold panels, statuettes, coffin lids and masks as he spent the next six years clearing the thousands of articles in the four rooms of Tutankhamun's burial place deep inside a rocky cliff in the Valley of the Kings. For archaeologists, Tutankhamun's tomb is unique in that it is the only one of all Egypt's pharaohs spanning over three thousand years to be found virtually intact. And in the history of gold, it is the supreme example of this untarnishable metal providing a visual replay of someone's life. Tutankhamun is seen at court, hunting in the marshes of the Nile, or at war in his chariot, all captured on gold reliefs as if a photo album of snapshots had been prepared.

Beside such images were many of his possessions which, it was believed, were as essential to him in death as in life. Not just chests filled with clean shirts and underwear, but a royal robe on which over 3,000 gold rosettes had been sewn, three pairs of gold sandals and a small cap of fine linen set with beads of gold, lapis and carnelian, which he may have worn as a child. One chest was stuffed with a three-tiered gold corselet, which he had worn for his coronation; it comprised a collar, intermediary pectorals and a breast-plate of almost one thousand gold plaques. A royal bedstead, covered with burnished gold embossed with flowers and fruit, stood beside gilded chairs and footstools. Board games, embellished with gold, were there to keep Tutankhamun amused. His bow, covered with sheet gold, was to hand, along with a sceptre of thick sheet gold beaten onto a wooden core and an array of walking sticks mounted with gold and silver (so many, Howard Carter wondered if he collected them). Four chariots, two of them encased in gold reliefs, stood as reminders of pageants or hunts past. His dagger, set in a gold sheath embossed with wild animals, had a patterned hilt of finest granulated gold. All this baggage for the voyage to eternity filled three rooms around Tutankhamun's actual burial chamber.

The chamber itself was almost completely taken up with a massive wooden shrine, overlaid with gold the small gap between shrine and wall was occupied by a set of oars, neatly laid out, to aid the pharaoh on his voyage). Within the shrine was a nest of three smaller gold-covered shrines protecting a great sarcophagus of yellow quartzite with a matching lid of rose granite. And within the sarcophagus were three coffins, two of wood lined with gold foil, and the third of solid gold 2.5 to 3.5 mm thick, weighing over 110 kg/3,536 t.oz. The lid was shaped in the image of Osiris, the god who rose from the dead, but the face was that of Tutankhamun himself, who would hope to emulate his resurrection. In this gold coffin, the largest and heaviest gold object ever found in Egypt, lay the mummy of Tutankhamun. Over his head and shoulders was the death mask, beaten and burnished from heavy gold foil, showing the serene face of a young man with rather narrow eyes, thin nose and full lips. "The beaten gold mask, a beautiful and unique specimen of ancient portraiture," wrote Carter, "bears a sad but calm expression suggestive of youth overtaken prematurely by death."[40] The mask stands as a masterpiece of the Egyptian goldsmith's craft. Their skill was also evident in the 143 pieces of gold jewellery – amulets, bracelets, collars, daggers, earrings, sheaths on fingers and thumbs, necklaces, pectorals and rings – strategically placed at 101 different locations of the body, within the linen bindings of the mummy, exactly according to the instructions of the *Book of the Dead*. "The incorruptible metal endowed the protected creature with its own power," observed Christiane Desroches-Nobelcourt.[41]

The dilemma is that Tutankhamun's tomb revealed such an astonishing impression of the young man, but not a single inscription in it shed any light on his history. Who were his parents? What did he achieve for Egypt (probably not much in a nine-year reign as child and adolescent)? How did he die? The post-mortem on his mummy in 1926 shed no light on the cause of death, and a scan of it in 2005 showed only that he suffered a severe fracture of his left thigh bone shortly before. As Howard Carter himself admitted, "the outstanding feature of his life was the fact that he died and was buried".[42]

The received wisdom is that Tutankhamun was born at el-Amarna, the new capital for Egypt developed by the 'heretic' pharaoh Akhenaten (1352–1336 BC), who promoted the worship of the god Aten (the sun disc) instead of the 'official' god Amun. Akenhaten and his wife, the beautiful Nefertiti, made el-Amarna a thriving cultural and religious centre. Akhenaten was the son of the great pharaoh Amenhotep III and Tutankhamun *may* have been his younger brother. What is clear is that Akhenaten was so engrossed in his new city and religion that he neglected affairs of state. One conspiracy theory suggests that Nefertiti, anxious to save the dynasty, and encouraged by the grand vizier Ay (who ultimately succeeded

Tutankhamun as pharaoh), whisked the boy off to Thebes. There he was installed as ruler to reinstate the traditional supremacy of the god Amun and restore Egypt's fortunes. Tutankhamun married Ankesenamun, the third daughter of Akhenaten and Nefertiti. This young lady had, apparently, already been married to her father at the age of eleven, so that Tutankhamun, according to one Egyptologist, may have married his niece and his sister-in-law.

Despite such distractions, the gold business in Egypt had apparently prospered. A relief at el-Amarna showed Akhenaten and Nefertiti on a balcony lavishing gold collars on a crowd below. Under Tutankhamun, the voyage of his Viceroy of Kush, Huy, up the Nile to consolidate the hold on Nubian gold, had brought a handsome return. "The royal treasury was greatly enriched," concluded Christiane Desroches-Nobelcourt.[43] The goldsmiths of Thebes could once more cast statues of the reinstated god Amun, while occupying themselves with ornaments for Tutankhamun and his queen.

The splendour of their lives was captured in gold reliefs on the panels of a small shrine to the vulture goddess Nekhbet. The fourteen scenes depict, as Carter put it, "in delightfully naïve fashion, a number of episodes in the daily life of the king and queen. In all of these scenes the dominant note is that of a friendly relationship between the husband and the wife".[44] Sometimes they are just face to face, hand in hand, as the queen presents Tutankhamun with bunches of lotus and other flowers. In the two most famous scenes, Tutankhamun is hunting wildfowl in the marshes. First, he is standing in a boat made of papyrus stems throwing a boomerang with his right hand, while clutching four ducks, presumably already 'in the bag', with his left. Ankhesenamun, waving what looks like a fly-whisk, looks on admiringly. On the adjoining panel, Tutankhamun is seated on a stool on the river bank, bow at full stretch as he looses an arrow at wildfowl rising from the reeds. The queen on a cushion at his feet, holds another arrow ready, while pointing at a nest of fledglings in the reeds, seemingly cautioning him not to harm them. In four intimate moments the queen presents Tutankhamun with a heavy gold necklace and a musical instrument known as a sistrum; he proffers a vase full of flowers which she tops up with water; then, as she tenderly rests her left elbow on his knee, while he pours water or perfume into her cupped right hand; and finally she arranges his floral necklace, as he reclines in a chair covered with flowers. On the back panel of the shrine, Ankhesamun strokes her husband's arm as she wafts a cone-shaped ointment holder. More formally, the royal couple are depicted in court attire, Tutankhamun on his throne, wearing the crown of Lower Egypt, raising his hand to receive two notched palm ribs, the symbol of 'years' or a jubilee from Ankhesamun. All told, a gold collection worthy of any family album.

Considerable debate has surrounded the technique by which the goldsmiths made these panels. The initial notion was that they had made 'gesso' or plaster reliefs onto which sheets of gold were clamped hard to make the impression, with detail then chased on the raised surface of the metal. Later research has suggested the gesso was not robust enough, so the designs were embossed directly onto the gold sheet, and molten gesso then poured into the depressions on the back of the gold, so that each panel could be fixed to the wooden walls of the shrine.

A more athletic Tutankhamun, now on his own, is portrayed on a beautifully embossed and chased gold fan as he rides his chariot drawn by a pair of galloping horses in pursuit of ostriches. His bow is at full stretch, a hunting dog runs baying alongside. Tutankhamun triumphs; the reverse of the fan shows him returning home, ostrich feathers under his arm and two dead birds borne by his aides. Chariots themselves were ornate. The two state chariots found in the tomb were covered with gold, even on the axles, wheels and harnessing (the gold helped to protect the leather over the centuries). War-like gold panels within the chariots show conquered foes, their arms lashed behind them, kneeling before Tutankhamun. He probably never took part in battle, but the image of a ruler vanquishing his enemies was essential to his trappings.

The sheer spectacle provided by the gold reliefs, the gold coffin and the gold mask somewhat overshadows the collection of jewellery so precisely placed in the bindings of Tutankhamun's mummy. Moreover, Howard Carter found elsewhere in the tomb empty chests that probably held ever more ornaments, indicating that virtually all jewellery not within the funeral bindings had been looted. Thus, the full scope of the jewellery that was originally buried is not known. Yet what remained, literally on Tutankhamun, was impressive. It cannot all be catalogued here, but the neck ornaments alone were enough to bow any man down. Six layers of gold collars, both symbolic and amuletic, were draped around his neck and chest to protect him from the dangers of the underworld. The finest, a collar of Nekhebet (the Vulture), had a great rising sweep of flexible wings made up of 250 separate gold plaques; on the front they are patterned in pale blue turquoise and red and dark blue glass; on the back, each gold plaque was chased with a delicate feather pattern.

For all this brilliance and colour, the jewellery does not draw so many plaudits. Howard Carter himself felt that, while the personal jewellery of Tutankhamun – a diadem, pectorals, rings and bracelets – was of the highest order, the ornaments made specifically for burial were run-of-the-mill. "The actual technique … is perhaps not so fine as regards finish or simplicity as that of Middle Kingdom jewellers," he wrote, adding, "we are dealing with material from the very end of the 18th Dynasty. A certain ornateness and lack of high finish that may be visible here, are but steps in a decadence creeping in with iron and other foreign influences."[45]

Times were changing. But in the tomb of Tutankhamun lay the whole panorama of Egyptian life, still in its prime, 3,300 years ago. Its preservation owed much to gold. As the French Egyptologist, Christiane Desroches-Nobelcourt, summed it up in explaining the 'First Lesson of the Tomb', "Nearly everything was made of precious material, and gold, with its incorruptible surface, covered this whole assortment of articles so necessary to ensure eternity for the dead".[46]

Aftermath: last show at Tanis

While the New Kingdom endured for over two hundred and fifty years after Tutankhamun's death in 1327 BC, and enjoyed periods of prosperity, notably under Rameses II (1279–1213 BC) and Rameses III (1184–1153 BC), it was facing an increasingly perilous world. The final centuries of the 2nd millennium saw many migrations around the Mediterranean shores and in western Asia which threatened existing societies. Babylon declined, the Minoans on Crete had already been overwhelmed by Mycenæ on mainland Greece, which was itself now challenged by migration.

Egypt did not escape. The first rulers of the 19th dynasty, Rameses I and Seti I, who ousted Tutankhamun's immediate successors in 1295 BC, moved the Egyptian capital from Thebes to Qantir on the Delta. This shift in the centre of gravity of a united Egypt might have met invaders from the sea, but left the internal lines of communication and control, especially with Nubia, dangerously stretched.

On the gold front, that was a strategic error. A firm hold on Nubia was essential to high gold output. The mines there, however, were also past their peak, although every pharaoh sought to maintain production levels. Old mines in the eastern desert of Koptos were reopened, as the 'Turin map' of 1150 BC, already discussed, proved. Egyptian production probably fell below 1,000 kg/32,150 t.oz annually, not enough to offer the diplomatic clout it had provided in the days of Thutmosis III. The concerted effort by later pharaohs such as Rameses IX (1126–1108 BC) to round up tomb robbers and secure their looted gold for the royal treasury was also a sure sign of failing mine supply. Gold production did not cease. In the long decline of the 1st millennium BC from the heyday of its empire under the New Kingdom through periods of Persian and then Roman rule, Egypt rated as a gold producer. Agatharchides, the Greek geographer, visited the mines in the 2nd century BC, and reported on the misery there. But it ceased to be a major exporter after 1300 BC.

Goldsmiths worked on through this unsettled environment, but evidence of their ornaments is sparse, not least because of the plague of tomb-robbing. Two massive solid gold hinged bracelets bearing the insignia of Rameses II and richly patterned with impeccable granulation and bezels of a two-headed duck turned up by chance during railway excavations in 1906, but the pharaoh's tomb in the Valley of the Kings was plundered soon after his burial.

The pressure of events affected goldsmiths, indeed all craftsmen. "With the political and economic decline … came an artistic deterioration clearly visible in the wall paintings of the rock-cut tombs in the Valley of the Kings," noted Munich University's Hans Müller. "Nor are the surviving pieces of jewellery of a particularly high standard."[47] The exception, Professor Müller felt, was "a sumptuous pair of pendant earrings in the name of Rameses IX," but that only emphasised his disappointment with other pieces.

However, there was one great, late show of the Egyptian goldsmiths' talent, still to be unveiled. On 15th February 1940, the French archaeologist Pierre Montet, who had been excavating a site of several royal burials at Tanis in the north-east Delta for over a decade, opened the silver coffin of the 21st dynasty pharaoh Psusennes I (1039–991 BC). He beheld a gold mask beaten from extremely thin gold foil, finely chased, but not polished, so that it gave off a soft glow in the first light played on it for 3,000 years. This portrait in gold of Psusennes is more idealised than the intensely personal mask of Tutankhamun, but ranks as yet another masterpiece of Egyptian goldsmiths' skill. The silver coffin, incidentally, is an intriguing curtain-call for the metal which was the Egyptian's first love, valued more highly than gold, two thousand years earlier.

The treasure within the coffin was rich, with many of the ornaments showing the finest attention to detail; the fingernails carefully chased onto the finger-caps of gold, to say nothing of 36 rings on Psusennes' fingers. Around the neck of the mummy was a collar of over 5,000 gold discs, weighing 8 kg/257 t.oz and on his left wrist, a solid gold bracelet weighing 1.8 kg/58 t.oz (which rather gives the lie to any suggestion of gold shortages). Another pair of heavy bracelets (there were 26 in all) were inset with dark blue lapis lazuli and red carnelian, and decorated with a winged scarab.[48]

Alongside the ornaments were golden vessels; a carafe of beaten gold with a high neck that opened out into a papyrus umbel, a goblet like a half-open lotus flower chased all around with the leaves of the lotus, and a golden bowl with a long spout for pouring libations, and a long, thin handle like a graceful swan's neck and head. For all the tribulations of post-New Kingdom Egypt, the goldsmiths had not lost their touch. As Cyril Aldred wrote approvingly, "Some of these late examples of the goldsmith's craft are of excellent workmanship and novel design, showing that the best standards achieved in the New Kingdom could be maintained on occasion".[49]   Indeed, they were continuing a tradition begun over two thousand years earlier on the banks of the Nile, which in this treasure of Tanis showed great maturity.

CHAPTER 3

Troy:
The Jewellery Emporium

Sitting on a grassy knoll on the famous mound at Hissarlik that was once Troy, it is hard to imagine that three or four thousand years ago this was a vibrant citadel commanding a great plain below where, perhaps, the Greeks paraded their armies as Homer told in the *Iliad*. And that, on the sea, just visible on the western horizon, simple sailing or galley ships passed up and down the Dardenelles, the crucial link between the Mediterranean, the Aegean and the Black Sea and the bridge between Asia and Europe. Today, you do not feel at a crossroads of commerce. All you hear is the tinkle of bells on the goats chomping the grass of this hillock, still furrowed with the diggings of archaeologists. Out on the plain are a few sheep, a reminder that in ancient times large flocks provided wool for the textiles that became a notable export from this emporium, along with ceramics, copper, silver and gold in the 3rd millennium BC.

To see the best of the gold, however, you must travel to Moscow. In winter, dump your snowboots, fur hat and parka in the basement cloakroom of the Pushkin Museum of Fine Arts and climb a broad staircase leading to a cavernous, dimly-lit gallery filled with the soft gleam of gold. It is a calm room, usually with few visitors, so the ancient gold ornaments, simply displayed against black backgrounds, create a mood of mystery. Appropriate, actually, for the treasures were not only buried deep in the ruins of Troy for over 4,000 years, but were lost for another fifty years after the Russians looted them from Berlin in 1945. Only after a generation of speculation and rumour were they unveiled again at the Pushkin Museum in 1996.

Treasures is the correct designation. Gathered together at the Pushkin are thirteen collections, with an alphabet of codings from A to R. The Pushkin houses 259 items, of which 165 are of gold, weighing almost 3 kg/96.15 t.oz, along with silver, electrum, bronze, amber, carnelian and rock crystal.[1] Several collections are held elsewhere, notably the Archaeological Museum in Istanbul and the National Archaeological Museum in Athens. In all, 21 collections were unearthed by the German merchant-turned-archaeologist Heinrich Schliemann, who originally made his fortune in the California gold rush, in the mound at Hissarlik between 1872 and 1890. The prize collections, though, are in Moscow and, above all, what Schliemann thought was the treasure of King Priam. This hoard of ninety-six gold articles embraces diadems, bracelets, hair-rings, earrings, torques, strings of beads, beakers and a magnificent sauceboat. The most dramatic is the diadem or headdress, weighing 193.47 grams/6.03 t.oz, hung with a cascade of leaf-like gold plates. At the Pushkin it is fitted snugly, like a skull cap, over an anonymous black-stockinged head, the cloud of leaves falling to the shoulders. Confronted with it, you understand the excitement, the elation that Schliemann felt on the morning in late May of 1873 when, with a large knife, he dug out the treasure from the side of a trench, packed tightly together perhaps originally in a long decomposed wooden trunk. The enduring image of 'Priam's Treasure' is of his wife Sophia wearing the headdress in a photograph taken shortly afterwards in Athens. The only trouble (apart from that with the Turkish authorities after he smuggled most of the gold out to Greece) was that Schliemann was a millennium or more out in his dating. Despite his initial belief that he had proved Homer's stories of Troy (which he believed implicitly) and that the diadem could be that of the fair Helen over whom the Trojan war was fought, all the ornaments turned out to be much older.[2]

The ruins of Troy, later archaeologists have established, are a multi-layered cake containing nine cities, dating from 2920 to 500 BC. 'Priam's Treasure', Treasure A in the Pushkin catalogue, comes from Troy II level dated 2600 to 2450 BC according to the Pushkin timescale (but later by some others). The Trojan war (if, indeed, it took place) slots into Troy VII between 1250–1020 BC. Schliemann's dating error, however, must not detract from his dramatic find; he truly placed Troy, a city that had long captured the imagination, on the map. As the scholar Donald Easton, who has fought a number of battles in recent times on behalf of Schliemann's reputation, acknowledged it was "a perfectly genuine discovery … (although) he did promulgate a fairy-story about how it had been found".[3] Not least that his wife Sophia was with him at the time and hid the treasure in her shawl; in fact, she was far away in Athens. In short, while congratulating Schliemann on uncovering one of the finest gold treasures of the ancient world, one has to forget Homer and the heroes of the *Iliad*. Troy established its credentials as a player in the gold trade over a millennium before their campaigns.

Crossroads for 3rd millennium metals

Troy's trump card was its location. The citadel was first built around 3000 BC on the low hill of Hissarlik in north-west Anatolia (Turkey). The proximity to the Dardenelles placed it astride a unique cross-over of land and sea trading routes. Few places controlled such a strategic position in the outward spread of people, culture and trade from the city-states of Mesopotamia in the early years of the 3rd millennium. "The brilliant career of Troy … is the story of one such trading post," wrote Fernand Braudel, "which played an important role in the spread of metallurgy throughout the Aegean."[4] Troy thus became an important piece in the jigsaw puzzle of the evolution of gold. Before 3000 BC gold had been rare but, over the next one thousand years, jewellery manufacture became widespread, not just in Mesopotamia, as we have seen, but across Anatolia in such walled cities as Alaca Hüyük and Troy, on the Aegean island of Poliochini just offshore from Troy, at Euboea on the Greek mainland, on Mochlos off Crete, in Bulgaria (across the Dardenelles from Troy) and at Maikop and Tsarskaia in the Caucasus. The American archaeologist G. F. Bass called it an "Early Golden Age".[5] Gold was "reserved for ornament", Heinrich Schliemann noted, although silver was being used increasingly as weighted money among merchants in Asia. However, a selection of thin, notched gold bars found at Troy have raised debate about its monetary role.

The burgeoning regional metal trade between Anatolia, Mesopotamia, around the Black Sea and down to Egypt was not just in gold. Movements of tin and copper (the essential mix for high quality bronze), of silver and lead were all increasing. Merchants from Mesopotamia established a trading post at Kültepe, north of the Taurus mountains in Anatolia, during the 3rd millennium BC to win a better grip on the metal trade. The jewellery expert Kathleen Maxwell-Hyslop has pointed out, "The greater use of silver (at Ur) and the occurrence of many silver ingots at Troy suggest that Assyrian-Trojan contacts may have been one of the reasons for the decision of the Assyrian merchants to establish their colony at Kültepe and to trade their lead and other goods for Anatolian copper, with which they could buy silver. Silver was the common currency used in Babylonia and Assyria and it is possible that Troy was one of the main suppliers of the metal to the Anatolian traders and Assyrian merchants settled at Kültepe".[6] Another historian dubbed it the 'prestige network'.[7] There are even suggestions of caravans of 200–250 donkeys binding it together.

Silver-lead and silver-copper deposits abound in Anatolia and some were worked in ancient times. Alluvial gold deposits and perhaps some simple primary deposits were also exploited, but the precise sources of Troy's gold remain unclear. The geographer Strabo reported in the 1st century BC, "above the territory of the Abydenia in the Troad, lies Astyra. This city, which is now in ruins, belongs to the Abydenia; but in earlier times was independent and had gold mines".[8] Pliny, writing a trifle later, mentioned a gold mine at Lampsacus (the present-day Lapseki) about fifty-five kilometres north of Troy. These accounts were investigated by Frank Calvert, the local British consul, when Schliemann was digging at Troy. Calvert, an enthusiastic archaeologist and geologist, who had even probed the mound at Hissarlik, located ancient gold workings near Canakkala, but never published a report.

Modern geologists, however, have identified at least fifteen gold deposits in Turkey, of which thirteen are in the western provinces within two hundred kilometres of Troy, and two are close by at Canakkala. One, near the village of Kartal Tas, scarcely thirty kilometres north-east of Troy, has high grade ore and shows signs of ancient exploitation.[9] The most famous gold source in western Turkey was the rich alluvial deposit along the Pactolus river at Sardis, about 150 km south of Troy, which was to fund the empire of King Croesus around 600 BC (*see chapter*

8). It is possible that the Pactolus river or neighbouring streams also supplied Troy. However, the Pactolus gold had a relatively high silver content (in fact it was electrum) and, as the parting of gold and silver was not perfected until much later, Troy may not have taken much from there. Electrum articles have been found, but the finest pieces found at Troy are 950 fine; the implication is of other sources of purer alluvial gold. In short, Troy flourished in a gold environment, but the extent to which it was exploited is unknown. Equally, Troy's location could have given it access to gold coming across the Dardenelles from the Balkans or along the Black Sea coast from the Caucasus (modern Georgia), where the streams coming down from the high mountains were ancient sources for Mesopotamia.

An alphabet of treasures

What is not in doubt is that Troy had access to gold and became an important jewellery manufacturing and exporting centre before 2500 BC. The oldest 'treasure' from Troy (R2), consisting simply of a gold ring and some beads, is dated 2650 BC. The advantage of the many different treasures unearthed is that they offer a wide spectrum of gold ornaments, which enables us not only to admire the craftsmanship and technical know-how of the local goldsmiths, but to understand the extent of their trade.

The diversity of the ninety-eight gold pieces of Treasure A ('Priam's') alone are astonishing. The simplest are the forty-two spirals of hammered gold wire, known as hair-rings, which are thought to have been threaded over a long lock of hair. Between three and six spirals are soldered together and sometimes adorned with ridges of conical studs. They resemble a coiled snake with the gold wire perfectly tapered at the tail. The consistency of their weight suggests mass production; the smallest three spirals all weigh close to 2.8 grams/0.09 t.oz, the majority are between 4.3 and 4.4 grams, with two larger specimens over 11.6 grams/0.38 t.oz. Hair-rings turn up not just in Troy's treasures, but across Anatolia, on the island of Poliochini and in Mesopotamia. They were a favourite fashion item of the age, as were strings of gold beads of which Treasure A contains twenty-four. The beads were made in all shapes and sizes; as flat discs with smooth or toothed edges, as barrels, cylinders, mushrooms, spindles, butterfly or double-winged beads, and in two segments like the cracked shell of a nut. The archaeologist Carl Blegen, who assembled the most detailed analysis of Troy, counted at least seventeen types of gold beads on one layer of Troy alone. The sheer quality of beads on some strings, weighing up to 25 grams/0.8 t.oz, suggests a relative abundance of gold.[10] A single string may have up to 300 beads of all shapes and sizes, often strung quite haphazardly.

Intriguing evidence of bead manufacture is provided by two long, narrow strips of gold attached to one such string in which holes have been punched; twenty holes in one, twenty-one holes in another. A similar perforated strip also turns up in Treasure F, this time with nineteen punched holes The assumption is that the majority of beads were not made in moulds, but simply by punching holes in gold strip, and then fashioning the beads by hand. The perforated strips could be re-melted and combined into new ones.   The real skill of the goldsmiths, however, is revealed in larger articles. "Troy's gold repertoire consists of finely-worked basket earrings with elaborate chain and leaf pendants, diadems … and bracelets," wrote the metals expert Prentiss de Jesus. "Some pieces vividly show the advanced techniques of the Trojan craftsmen compared to that of their inner-Anatolian counterparts."[11]   The only possible rival was the output at Alaca Hüyük in north-central Anatolia.

Two pins (known as Treasure O) are among the most perfect articles of jewellery found at Troy. The larger has a sharpened shaft of round gold wire, surmounted by a rectangular plate framed by soldered rectangular wires. The front is decorated with four columns, each of seven miniature spectacle-shaped double spirals of filigree. A rectangular wire is soldered to the bottom of the plates, with each end rolled into six spirals. Six tiny two-handed vessels with disc-like rims on tall cylindrical necks are soldered along the top of the plate. The gold itself is a remarkable 958 fine (23 carat), and the pin weighs 7.5 grams/0.24 t.oz. The second pin has a more delicate air: the head is a flattened cylinder rolled from thin gold plate with a central pattern of a filigree rosette of eleven petals.[12]

Granulation, that other goldsmith's confection, adorns two basket-shaped earrings found at Troy (actually, their shape suggests stylish miniature gold handbags). The side of each 'basket' is striped with five rows of granulation, with a further pyramid of five rows of granulation at the base of the gold hook that goes through a pierced ear. Other slightly less ornate basket earrings are hung with five or six long gold chains, each often adorned with up to 24 leaf-like scales, with idol-shaped figures cut from gold sheet, attached to the end of the chains. The wearer must have swished by with earrings tumbling to the shoulders. Basket earrings originated at Ur, but Troy evolved its own style and the goldsmith probably cast the 'basket' itself in a mould. The two earrings with granulation are of almost identical weight (7 grams/0.23 t.oz) and perhaps came from the same mould. Basket earrings have turned up across Anatolia and at Poliochini, suggesting that they were regularly manufactured over a long period, becoming a standard fashion item. From Troy they were exported throughout the region.[13]

All these small, often exquisite, ornaments unearthed in the various layers of the Hissarlik mound, are almost eclipsed by a dozen or so spectacular finds which point to a society rich in gold. Among them are two bracelets, both from Schliemann's Treasure F, one in the Pushkin, the other in the Archaeological Museum in Istanbul, revealing remarkable artistic execution. The Pushkin bracelet, weighing a substantial 61.81 grams/1.99 t.oz in 958 fine/23 carat gold, is made of a wide gold plate decorated with spectacle-shaped double spirals of thin wire interspersed by four cross-wise rows, each of three rosettes. The rosettes are made of hollow studs surrounded by rings of narrow plate. The bracelet, after four thousand years underground, is somewhat damaged, but a confident reminder of Troy in its prime.

Yet it pales against two great vessels – the golden flask and the golden sauceboat. The flask, weighing in at almost 400 grams/12.84 t.oz in 833 fine/20 carat gold, is spherical with a short, cylindrical neck with very faint traces of an ornamental frieze. It is unique, no other has been found in metal. Its purpose is unknown, although similar Trojan ceramic flasks were used to store perfume and essences. The sauceboat, a colossus at 600 grams/19.26 t.oz in 958 fine/23 carat gold, is also unique. The vessel is indeed boat-shaped with the twin spouts rising like prow and stern at each end; one spout is more open than the other. The exterior is smooth, but the interior reveals marks made by the tools that shaped the vessel. The double handles sweeping up over each side are characteristic of Trojan pottery of the period.[14] Archaeologists have surmised that the sauceboat may have been used over a long period. Carl Blegen argued that it played a part in ritual ceremonies, unlike other gold, electrum or silver vessels, which were used regularly by rich Trojans. If that is correct, the Trojans did not stint themselves at dinner. One cylindrical gold beaker from Treasure A clocks up at 227 grams/7.3 t.oz of 958 fine/23 carat gold, while a more delicate tulip-shaped beaker, fashioned from a single sheet of gold, contains 70 grams/2.25 t.oz of 750 fine/18 carat gold.[15]

Headdresses for a queen

The splendour of the two diadems or headdresses that are the show-pieces of Treasure A confirms such luxury. When Schliemann first unearthed the treasure he overlooked them, for they were concealed in a large silver vase, along with sixty gold earrings, six gold bracelets, two small gold goblets, 8,750 gold rings and other assorted jewellery. A real measure of a wealthy ruler or family's collection that had been hastily hidden from attack. Archaeologists still argue over the date of the headdresses, but they could have been made before 2500 BC, while the whole collection of ornaments secreted in the vase could cover several generations. Once unravelled from this ancient cache, the two headdresses proved to be creations of immense technical and artistic complexity. From a narrow band of hammered sheet gold, which encircled the head, are suspended fifty short gold chains made of double links, framed by seven longer chain on each side. Schliemann counted 1,750 rings to the chains, while 354 gold plaques, each with a raised, perforated central rib, are hung on chains every four links. A gold idol, almost like a child's cut-out decorated with four dotted rosettes, was attached to the bottom of each chain. These pendants are similar to those on some basket earrings. They shimmer like falling leaves in the autumn sunlight. This small headdress weighs 85.52 grams/2.75 t.oz.

Was it a prototype for the more famous headdress in which Schliemann decked out his wife to be photographed? Dangling from a double horizontal chain round the head is a veritable hedge of 90 single, vertical chains decorated with gold leaves. Schliemann's scorecard showed 12,271 rings for the chains, and 4,066 leaves. The 74 central chains each have between 27 and 29 leaves, the frame of seven longer chains on each side has 106–111 leaves. A pawn-like idol, cut from sheet gold, hangs from the bottom of each chain. No wonder it weighs in at 193.47 grams/6.2 t.oz. The two headdresses, neatly placed over a cloth or leather skull-cap, have adorned cult figurines in a palace, or the ruler's wife. This is done to great effect at the Pushkin, with the larger headdress lit by a single spotlight from above that illuminates it as a tight-fitting crown around the brow, with golden plaits hanging down to the shoulders.[16]

The first 'currency' bars?

The insight that the treasures provide of the gold trade in the 3rd millennium BC is enhanced by assortments of jewellery scrap, notched rings and, above all, by five slender, hammered, round bars of gold, each with a series of incisions or notches (Treasure F). They are of almost identical length, 9.5–10.4 cm/3.7–4.1 ins, and weight, 9.87–10.48 grams/0.32–0.37 t.oz, and are divided into 53–59 parts by the notches. Similar bars from Troy are in the Archaeological Museum in Istanbul. The implications are intriguing. Are they a primitive version of today's London Good Delivery bars? Were the bars traded or even used as currency (some archaeologists have dubbed them 'currency bars')? Or were they simply preforms from which goldsmiths made beads? This notion is enhanced by several shorter bars with holes punched through them to be seen in both the Pushkin and Istanbul museums. One Pushkin bar has nineteen round holes from which globules for beads appear to have been created. The catch is that there is no exact ratio between the weight of the longer bars and the number of notches. Among the Pushkin's five bars, the snippets would weigh between 0.176 and 0.196 grams if they were chopped up. But this is a narrow variation in weight, especially if they were used for beads.

The answer may be that the bars had a dual function. They could be cut up or punched with holes for beads or other jewellery use, but each bar must have also had a clear 'market' value. That is to say, if a customer needed a specific weight of gold, it was roughly charted by the notches on each bar, just as a butcher may ask how many lamb chops (each of slightly differing weight) he should cut off. The exact weight could always be made up with filings or tiny bits of gold sheet. The bars probably had no actual currency function but a well understood value, certainly by professionals in the market. They are evidence of growing sophistication in the gold trade, with generally accepted standards.

Unquestionably, the bars reveal an organised regional gold trade in which Troy, because of its location, played a prime role by 2500 BC. Troy absorbed both the technology, such as filigree and granulation, and artistic concepts pioneered in Mesopotamia, adapted them and re-exported them to a wider world. "Troy was one of the leading centres of jewellery-making in western Asia Minor and the Aegean in the middle to the third quarter of the 3rd millennium BC," wrote Mikhail Treister, summing up for the Pushkin's catalogue.[17]

A high proportion of the gold artefacts found throughout the region around Troy came from its workshops or from nomadic goldsmiths who had learned their trade there. Jewellery unearthed at Poliochini on Lemnos, barely eighty kilometres offshore from Troy, bears all the hallmarks of Troy workshops.

Several of the alphabet of treasures (notably F, L and N) are thought to be from goldsmiths' shops rather than family hoards, because of the preform bars and half-finished or damaged jewellery which may have come in for re-working. This is entirely consistent with traditions throughout much of Asia even today, where old ornaments are constantly traded in for new. This scrap is an important source of gold supply; indeed, in countries such as Saudi Arabia, scrap gold from ornaments regularly traded in can provide a goldsmith with 50% or more of his supply annually. In ancient times, with erratic new mine supply, scrap must have been vital. Troy's workshops could have been kept busy re-making ornaments. The craftsmen were aided by small 'lenses' of polished rock crystal (Treasure L), used as magnifying glasses. Over forty of these lenses were found by Schliemann in one workshop, along with a jumble of gold, silver and bronze rings, beads, bits of chain, nails, gold foil, and small bars. Such lenses would be invaluable in the intricate assembly of headdresses or the careful positioning of gold grains in granulation.

Casting moulds, crucibles, blowpipes for furnaces, and ingots of gold, silver and bronze all build the impression of Troy as a metal-working centre with many workshops. The status of the metal-workers as independent artisans or part of a 'palace' system (as later at Knossos on Crete or in the Precolumbian cultures of Peru) is unknown. Their achievements, however, exceeded the other cultural achievements of Troy. The goldsmiths were real pace-setters, creating wealth for their small city and contributing to its role as an emporium for the region and a magnet for itinerant craftsmen. Troy was not an empire, never an empire builder, but a hot-spot of commerce, like Beirut before its tragic civil war and then Dubai today. Both have thrived as markets for through-trade, not least in gold, and evolved as jewellery-making centres.

The place of Troy as a landmark in gold's history is often overlooked because of the enduring stories told in Homer's *Iliad* and *Odyssey*. In legend, the city is so entwined with Greek heroes and the plight of Helen, that it escapes attention that Troy was in its prime almost a thousand years before Mycenæ, the first real civilisation on the Greek mainland, evolved. Certainly, the gold trade had moved on to Egypt and Minoan Crete long before the Trojan war. Yet, without the diligence of Heinrich Schliemann in pursuit of that war, we might never have known the real story of Troy. Moreover, our debt to Schliemann is greater because he also turned up the gold treasures of Mycenæ (*see chapter 5*). Never mind that his faith in Homer made him get that date wrong, too. No one else has unmasked two key stepping stones on the long trail to gold's origins.

CHAPTER 4

Minoan Crete:
To the 'Wine-Dark Sea'

The best way to capture the spirit of Minoan Crete is to get up early and arrive at the site of the ancient palace of Knossos as the gate swings open at 8 am. Walk up through tall stands of cypress and pine trees to a modest mound covered with a quiltwork of stone walls and, here and there, a row of pillars or a re-made roof over a fresco of a charging bull. The valley below is cloaked in olive groves. The wind sighs through the trees, doves and peacocks call. Pass into the great paved courtyard that was the heart of the palace, where the mythical King Minos held sway and dancers, male and female, leapt lightly over the horns of bulls before a crowd bedecked with golden ornaments. A lonely place now, but once the heart of a glittering civilisation.

Fifteen minutes down the road is the Herakleion Archaeological Museum. Buy an entrance ticket decorated with the image of a golden bee and go to Room VII. Before you, is the golden bee pendant itself, alongside it a showcase of 21 tiny gold double-headed axes (another famous symbol, along with bulls, of the Minoan culture) and, nearby, a gold finger-ring embossed with a scene of four tight-waisted, bare-breasted women (one of them a goddess) engaged in a sacred dance. These creations by Minoan goldsmiths express the vibrance of their unique society over 3,500 years ago.

By 2000 BC the world of gold was expanding around the shores of the eastern Mediterranean and the Aegean (Homer's 'wine-dark sea'). Economically, the region was becoming unified, criss-crossed by sea-borne trade, which brought with it architectural and artistic ideas and itinerant craftsmen, not least goldsmiths. The hub was the cities of Ugarit and Byblos in Phoenicia (Syria/Lebanon), with land links east to Mesopotamia and by land and sea to Egypt, thence westwards, now by sea, to Cyprus, Crete and mainland Greece. Troy, guarding the passage to the Dardenelles and the Black Sea, had already pioneered the way as a crucial commercial crossroads. This international interlocking of trade and culture stimulated the civilisations of the Minoans and the Mycenæans, as it already had at Troy. Today this is the itinerary of modern cruise ships setting out from Pireaus for a week's voyage around the ancient sites, with lectures on Greek mythology versus archaeological reality. Did King Minos really rule over the palace of Knossos where the Minotaur, part man, part bull, rampaged in the labyrinth? Did Agamemnon set forth through the Lion Gate at Mycenæ to rescue the fair Helen from Troy?

How much have archaeologists sought to fit legends and myths, re-told by Homer and others centuries later, to their own discoveries? Sir Arthur Evans, the discoverer of Knossos in 1900, christened it the Palace of Minos, seeing it as the hub of Minoan civilisation. "Did Arthur Evans simply discover the world of Minoan Crete?" ponders the British Museum's Lesley Fitton. "Or did he to some degree invent it?"[1] Similarly at Troy, Heinrich Schliemann had proclaimed he found King Priam's treasure, but later experts date the ornaments a thousand years or more before the siege of Troy may have taken place. Homer told that Mycenæ was 'rich in gold' and Schliemann duly turned up a gold death mask; but was it really that of Agamemnon? The reality is that these ancient city-states indeed flourished and the gold is proof of their prosperity. Whether Zeus, born on Crete, watched over them, or Hector slew Achilles at Troy or Theseus fell in love with Ariadne and won her by killing the Minotaur simply spurs the imagination as we wander the sites three thousand years later.

The initial stepping stone was Crete, strategically positioned for trade within a few hundred kilometres of the shores of Africa, Anatolia, mainland Greece and Sicily. Paradoxically, that immediate separation was also enough to secure Crete from casual invasion, unlike islands such as Cyprus, vulnerable from proximity to the Anatolian mainland. Thus, Crete was at the centre of growing Mediterranean trade, but able to evolve its own unique identity. "There are hundreds of islands in the eastern Mediterranean," the writer Leonard Cottrell observed. "Crete was the only one to achieve an indigenous civilisation as highly developed as the other great contemporary civilisations – those of Egypt, Mesopotamia and the Indus Valley."[2]

Sophisticated artistry and technology in gold contributed to that image. The achievement was greater because the island had no gold mines. Every ounce of gold had to be imported. Egypt was probably the prime and most consistent source, but metal also came, more erratically, from placer deposits in the Melas valley of Syria and from western Anatolia, near Troy. Thus the international gold trade began to spread westwards along the Mediterranean. Crete also imported silver, copper and probably tin, together with such luxury goods as semi-precious stones, ivory and ostrich eggs from African shores. It was well able to barter.

Mediterranean market garden

The Neolithic people who originally settled the island as early as 7000 BC had gradually built up a rich agricultural base, favoured by a slightly wetter climate than that prevailing today. "Agriculture was at the heart of the Minoan success story," notes Lesley Fitton.[3] Fine timber (notably cypress), famous wines and olive oil were cultivated along with grain, pulses, figs, almonds, pistachio nuts, pears, quinces, lettuce, celery, onions, garlic and herbs. Crete sounds a veritable Bronze Age market garden. Bees produced an abundance of honey, flax was woven into linen (used in the Minoan 'kilt' garment) and saffron was harvested for dyestuffs.

While many of these products went into the huge storage jars at Minoan palaces and country houses, they were widely exported. So, too, was the distinctive Minoan pottery fashioned from excellent clay beds found on the island. While high quality metalwork built a reputation for Minoan bronze swords and daggers, made from imported copper and tin, which were esteemed throughout the region; these weapons often had pommels and hilts adorned with gold foil. And gold ornaments, made by craftsmen who gradually adapted techniques learned from Mesopotamia, were widely exported, turning up not just on the Cyclades islands and Greek mainland, but even Egypt. There may have been a distinct class of wealthy merchants, with strong links to correspondents throughout the Aegean and in Phoenicia.

The first gold ornaments turn up in the 'prePalatial period' between 3200 and 1950 BC. The style began simply; just a cluster of olive leaves cut from gold sheet found on the offshore island of Mochlos that may date back to 2500 BC. Then came necklaces of gold daisies, roses and lilies (the Madonna lily became the Minoan emblem, just as it did for Italian art of the Renaissance three thousand years later), flower-shaped hairpins, pendants with chains and a tiny gold frog. One necklace in the Herakleion Archaeological Museum, which houses the best collection of Minoan gold, is made up of 70 delicate flower discs cut from gold sheet.

Crete, as Fernand Braudel put it, "was poised for take-off". Minoan culture reached its prime between 1950 and 1450 BC in two distinct 'palatial' phases. The first, beginning in 1950 BC, saw the initial building of great palaces at Knossos, Mallia and Phaestos, which were badly damaged by earthquakes around 1700 BC. They were rebuilt gradually during the second phase, lasting until 1450 BC, when the civilisation was at its height. Homer, much later, reminisced that Crete was then, "a rich and lovely island … boasting ninety cities". The plains were dotted with villas and country houses.

Palace powerhouse

Palaces were the powerhouses of Minoan Crete. "The palaces played a complex role," explains archaeologist Adonis Vasilakis; "they were centres of political authority and of religious life, and also large economic centres with warehouses, workshops and the residences of the 'royal family'."[4] The precise role of the ruler is a matter of debate, but he was probably both priest and king. And although Homer spoke of King Minos of Crete, no one knows whether there was actually a king called Minos, or whether the term 'Minos' symbolised all Cretan rulers in their function as priest-king.

Without doubt, their political authority was enforced by a complex bureaucracy. The palaces had archive rooms where records were kept on tablets, in two famous scripts, Linear A (still undeciphered) and, later, Linear B with Greek affiliations. Linear B was decoded in 1952 by the Cambridge historian Michael Ventris shortly before his untimely death in a car accident. The symbols or ideograms for gold, silver and bronze have been identified; the one for gold is somewhat akin to two crossed swords or palm trees. At Knossos the symbol for gold appears only on an incomplete tablet, with a special pictogram indicating a gold drinking cup shaped like a bull's head. However, other Linear B tablets, discovered at Pylos on the south-west coast of mainland Greece, revealed specific amounts of gold held in a local governor's palace. "The amounts of gold vary from 1kg to about 62 grams; the most common figure is 250 grams," noted John Chadwick, who continued the work of Michael Ventris. The tablets at Pylos listed 5 kg/160 t.oz in all.[5]

This information provides a unique insight into the modest quantities of gold available in both the Minoan and later Mycenæan world. The smallest amount at 62 grams/2 t.oz, and the most common at 250 grams/8 t.oz in a governor's treasure house provides a useful sense of perspective. A few kilograms went a long way in the 2nd millennium BC.

Yet gold was abundant enough to enhance the prosperous, almost cosmopolitan, society within the palaces of Minoan Crete. The enduring images of that culture are preserved, not just in its jewellery, but by the surviving frescoes. They reveal the excitement of the legendary sport of bull dancing, where young acrobats somersaulted up over the horns of a bull and then over the tail into the arms of a colleague, to the delight of an excited crowd. The fashion of their fans can be admired in the 'ladies in blue' fresco showing three Minoan belles in their finery. The ladies have gold filigree twined through their piled up hair and are adorned with gold necklaces and bracelets. Another famous fragment shows a young woman with large eyes, bright red lips and curly hair adorned with gold. An early French visitor to the site at Knossos dubbed her 'la Parisienne'.

The bull, so central to Minoan life, makes frequent appearances. A libation vase in the form of a bull's head is crowned with soaring gilded horns. A bull dancer sweeps around the golden hilt of a sword, and a delicate earring has a bull's head and muzzle simulated by gold granulation, surmounted with two touching horns of gold. The double-headed axe was another emblem of Minoan society, not as a weapon of war, but rather as a sacred votive offering and practical tool for ship-building in a sea-faring nation. A single showcase in the Herakleion Archaeological Museum houses 21 of these tiny votive axes, each like a child's toy, crafted in gold. Bronze swords and daggers, often decorated with elaborate gold pommels and hilts, show Cretan craftsmanship at its best and they were important export items.

The initial simple hammering of gold sheet into flowers or leaves in the prePalatial period soon matured into ornaments that were both artistic and technically correct, employing widespread application of filigree and granulation. The palaces nourished these skills. Palace wealth, too, provided the raw material. "The craftsmen creating precious works in … gold, ivory and semi-precious stones may well have been full-time craft specialists," argues Lesley Fitton, "totally dependent on the palaces and working constantly with them, their products in demand both for immediate use and possibly for exchange quite far afield."[6]

The golden bee

Among the most memorable creations was that golden bee pendant, reproduced today on museum tickets. Two golden bees, wings raised, hold with their legs a honeycomb dappled with granulated gold, above their heads is a cage containing a gold bead. "An exquisite pendant … filigree and granulation are used with great effect," the Greek jewellery expert, Reynold Higgins, wrote admiringly.[7] The bee pendant, uncovered in a tomb known as Chrysolakkos, the gold pit, because of the variety of gold ornaments found, at the palace of Mallia, dates from around 1600 BC. The bees are in keeping with many Minoan ornaments, which celebrate the animals, the birds, and insects and the flowers of the island. This is the goldsmith as naturalist, designing pendants or rings depicting lions with granulated manes, falcons, ducks and owls, monkeys and greyhounds, scorpions, spiders and snakes. Even a signet ring is embossed with two goats mating.

Presiding over them all is a famous gold pendant known as the Master of Animals from the Aigina Treasure, now in the British Museum. The pendant shows a Cretan god standing in a field of lotus flowers; in either hand he holds a goose by the neck, behind him are two curved tubes, thought to be sacred bulls' horns. The 'master' wears a tall feather headdress, large circular earrings, bracelets on his wrists and upper arms, a tightly fitting tunic and a tight belt with an embroidered tassel.[8] This little ornament, probably from a dress-pin, fashioned out of sheet gold, shows strong Egyptian influence, yet the god's dress marks it clearly as Cretan.

Mystery still surrounds the origin of the pendant and the other gold objects, including three diadems, earrings, beads, a bracelet and inlaid finger rings, that make up the Aigina Treasure. The British Museum paid £4,000 (over £300,000 today) for the treasure in 1892 to a firm of sponge-dealers on Aigina, the Aegean island that is first stop for ferries south of Athens. The sponge-dealers explained that one of their partners had come across the treasure while digging his vineyard or renovating his house (the story varied).

The treasure caused much excitement, coming on the heels of Heinrich Schliemann's discoveries at Mycenæ, just across the sea on mainland Greece. Dr Arthur Evans, then Keeper of the Ashmolean Museum in Oxford, initially suggested they were 'Mykenaean';[9] a pardonable error, given it was another decade before Dr Evans embarked on his own exploration of Knossos and 'discovered' the Minoan civilisation. Yet it was not until the late 1950s that a curious assistant keeper at the British Museum, Reynold Higgins, began to ponder the treasure's true origin. He determined the Aigina treasure had all the hallmarks of Minoan Crete (not least the clothing style of the Master of Animals).[10] He dated it 1700–1500 BC and proposed it came from the notorious Chrysolakkos (gold pit) at the ancient palace of Mallia, which had been subject to much modern grave-robbing in the 1880s. Since the Turks then ruled Crete, he felt the finders had decided to pretend it had been found on Aigina to avoid too much fuss. That was fine until new witnesses, descendants of people on Aigina in the 1890s, recalled the treasure really had turned up in an ancient Mycenæan (not Minoan) tomb uncovered when a windmill was being re-built. So what was a Minoan treasure doing in a long-forgotten Mycenæan tomb? The final (or rather, most up-to-date) theory is that the Aigina treasure was part of a much larger haul by tomb robbers on Crete some time before 1000 BC, when both the Minoan and Mycenæan states were in decline. It was an unstable period, and perhaps the tomb-robber could never come back for his loot. The best advice is not to worry whence it came to Aigina, but, if you are in the British Museum, pause to admire the Aigina Treasure as one of the finest examples of the Minoan goldsmiths' art.

The Minoans themselves, men and women, loved their jewellery; it was almost an addiction. Their hair was kept in place by gold pins surmounted with gold flowers, double and triple-decker earrings dripped from their ears, gold bands adorned arms, wrists and ankles, necklaces cascaded onto their breasts. Their zest for life is summed up by that gold finger ring in the Herakleion Museum, with a scene of four tight-waisted, bare-breasted women (one a goddess) in flowing skirts, surrounded by and garlanded with flowers, whirling in a sacred dance.

In creating such snapshots in gold, goldsmiths pushed their design and technical skills to the limit, especially in their use of granulation and filigree. These were not new techniques; they had a long history in western Asia, going back to the royal tombs at Ur. They had spread west, first to Troy and Alora Hüyüti in Anatolia, and now to Crete, both by example (a Babylonian cylinder seal with granulation was unearthed at Knossos) and through immigration by goldsmiths. The Cretan goldsmiths also win credit for developing looped gold 'cable' chain, something the ingenious Mesopotamian goldsmiths apparently did not come up with.

An intriguing question remains. How much gold was at their disposal, since Crete had no local sources? Supplies must have been erratic. Archaeologists report that most gold ornaments they find are from the second Palace period after 1700 BC. That coincides with rising gold production in Egypt, where output peaked around 1500 BC with the development of the Nubian goldfields up the Nile (see chapter 2). Since Crete enjoyed strong trading links with Egypt by then, more regular shipments may have been secured, at least of a few kg at a time. The surviving Linear B tablets from Pylos on the mainland showed that 250 grams/7.8 t.oz was the most common weight for ingots. They could be stretched a long way. The finest Minoan ornaments, the bee pendant and the Master of animals, are tiny, delicate creations, weighing but a few grams. Compare that with the opulence in Egypt at the time; Tutankhamun's coffin of sheet gold weighed 110 kg/3,536 t.oz. The implication is that the Minoan goldsmiths had to be thrifty because gold was indeed precious.

The lack of jewellery from the first Palace period could also be explained by constant recycling of old jewellery for new. The Greek jewellery expert Reynold Higgins pointed out that, in communal tombs, such as the 'gold pit' at Mallia, which were used over generations, the gold left with the dead by one family was removed by the next mourners burying their dead. "Once flesh had left their bones, the dead were evidently considered to be of no importance, to be robbed with impunity," he concluded.[11] Coupled with gold re-sold by contemporary tomb-robbers, scrap must have been an important factor. Families may also have traded in old ornaments for new, a common custom even today in the Middle East and India.

The Minoan diaspora

Constraints on gold supplies did not prevent the reputation of Minoan goldsmiths spreading around the Mediterranean. An ornament similar to the Master of Animals pendant, and dated 1780–1740 BC, was unearthed in excavations on the Nile in recent years; it may have been a Minoan export.[12] The greatest influence, naturally, was on neighbouring Greek islands in the Aegean and on mainland Greece. There, the rising power of Mycenæ challenged the Minoans' sway, especially after Knossos was severely damaged by fire or earthquake around 1450 BC. Incidentally, Crete seems to have escaped relatively lightly from the great Thera/Santorini volcanic explosion, now dated around 1628 BC, although the Minoan colony there at Akrotiri was wiped out. After 1450 BC, however, decline was relatively rapid. Mycenæ took increasing hold over Crete. Palace records in the final Palace period 1450–1375 BC, were kept in Mycenæan Greek, with Linear B taking over the Linear A. This is a crucial switch. No one is sure what dialect or language the Minoans originally spoke (hence the problem decoding Linear A), but now they were being absorbed into the nascent Helladic world of the mainland. Mycenæ became a power to be reckoned with, but they learned and adapted much from the Minoans.

The modern Athenian master goldsmith, Ilias Lalaounis, much of whose work has been inspired by the Minoans and Mycenæans, has no doubt of the debt. The Minoan impact on early Greek cultures was immense. "(They) were profoundly … influenced by Minoan art," he has written, "not only Mycenæ … but other local kingdoms … Pylos, Tiryns, Thebes were exposed to the pervasive influence of Minoan civilisation … Minoan art was grafted onto this new and vigorous tree … Out of this fertile union new treasures were born … Vases, weapons, objects of gold. Violent hunting scenes alternate with representations of peaceful rural life, while austere death-masks are found side by side with sumptuous gold chalices."[13]

Physically, Mycenæ eclipsed Minoan Crete; the island people emigrated (not least the goldsmiths) or retreated to the hills. Yet the myths of an elegant, almost magical civilisation lingered on. It fell to Sir Arthur Evans a century ago to restore the aura or weave his own spell around it. As his half-sister and biographer, Joan Evans, put it, "Time and Chance made him the discoverer of a new civilisation … fortunately it was exactly to his taste: set in beautiful Mediterranean country, aristocratic and humane in feeling; creating an art brilliant in colour … that drew inspiration from the flowers and birds and creatures that he loved."[14]

The reality was certainly rather harsher. Recent archaeological excavations on

Crete have suggested a bloodthirsty streak imposing on this idyll, with evidence of human sacrifice. And the rampages of the Minotaur in the Labyrinth killing all those sent to appease him hardly smacks of gentility. That does not deny Minoan Crete as a splendid and animated world of its own. In the evolution of gold's story, Crete was the essential springboard launching the metal around a widening Mediterranean world.

CHAPTER 5

Mycenæ:
Heroes Ancient and Modern

Tucked away on an inside page of The Times on Saturday 25th November 1876, beneath a discreet heading, 'Mycenæ', was this telegraphed report:

Argos, 24th November, from a correspondent:

"In the great circle of parallel slabs beneath the archaic sepulchral stones, considered by Pausanias[1] as the tombs of Atreus, Agamemnon, Cassandra, Eurymedon and their companions, Dr Schliemann has discovered immense tombs containing jewellery. He found yesterday in one portion of a tomb human bones, male and female, plate, jewellery of pure archaic gold weighing five kilograms … it is impossible to describe the rich variety of the treasure."

Five days later, The Times correspondent telegraphed:

"Dr Schliemann found yesterday. A helmet, two diadems, a woman's large comb, a large breastplate, three masks, six vases, two bracelets, two rings, three brooches, an immense mass of buttons, leaves and other articles, three large girdles etc."

All told, in five shaft graves just inside the famous Lion Gate at the citadel of Mycenæ, Heinrich Schliemann, just six years after finding 'Priam's Treasure' at Troy, turned up a treasure trove amounting to 15 kg/482 t .oz of gold relics, more than has ever been found in any other Greek graves. Mycenæ was revealed as the heart of the first great civilisation to evolve on mainland Europe over 3,500 years ago. Ultimately, Mycenæ became the dominant political and commercial power in the Aegean after about 1400 BC. Its influence spread not just to similar strongholds nearby at Tiryns and Pylos, but throughout the Greek mainland to Corinth, Thebes, Athens, Sparta and beyond to the islands of the Aegean. It became a commercial hub, with strong trading links to Anatolia, Syria and Egypt in the east and with Sicily in the west.

Initially, though, it was overshadowed by Minoan Crete, the first society to be caught up in the ripples of culture and trade pushing west along the Mediterranean after 2000 BC. The Mycenæans rode this trend about two or three hundred years later than the Minoans, but from first contact with those islanders realised they had much to learn. "All the refinements of civilisation on the mainland in arts and crafts seem to have been borrowed from Crete," wrote John Chadwick in his Mycenæan World.[2] The Mycenæans, however, were always of a different character. This encounter was pastoral Minoans meeting a clan of tough hunters and warriors.

The Mycenæ stature, moreover, was enhanced by myth and legend. Mycenæ was founded, so the story went, by Perseus son of Zeus and Danae, was the scene of some Labours of Hercules and long ruled over by the House of Atreus. From here, Homer's heroes of the *Iliad* and the *Odyssey*, led by Agamemnon, king of men, set forth through the Lion Gate to rescue fair Helen from Troy. Agamemnon sacrificed his daughter, Iphigenia, to obtain fair winds, but upon his final return with King Priam's daughter Cassandra, was slain by his wife Clytemnestra and her lover, Aegisthus.

Untangling such myths from reality has tested the skills of archaeologists and historians. Indeed, one could argue this is a story of heroes ancient and modern; of the kings and warriors who made Mycenæ great, of poets like Homer who retold their triumphs and, much later, Heinrich Schliemann, Cristos Tsountas, Alan Wace and Carl Blegen, who dug up the ruins. Above all, credit must go to the two Cambridge dons, Michael Ventris and John Chadwick, who cracked the code on the clay Linear B tablets found at Knossos on Crete and Pylos on the mainland which provided detailed tallies of the goods and chattels of palace life. Their achievement reminds one of the Enigma codebreakers (many of them also Cambridge dons) in World War II.

Initially, Schliemann believed he had found the graves of those very protagonists immortalised in Homer's *Iliad* and in Aeschylus' trilogy, the Oresteia. However, the story that he telegraphed the King of Greece, "I have gazed upon the face of Agamemnon," when he located the most stunning gold death mask, is not true. Rather, the graves were later proved to be much older, dating between 1600 and 1500 BC, almost four hundred years before the possible dating of the Trojan war. Thus, as at Troy six years earlier, when he found the treasure of 'King Priam', which turned out to be at least one thousand years older, Schliemann was over-eager to fit his finds to Homeric legend. Actually, most archaeologists have found it hard to ignore the myths. The American archaeologist Alan Wace, who dug at Mycenæ for many years in the early 20th century, wrote sternly at the beginning of his account of Mycenæ that he was omitting the family feuds of the House of Atreus. Then added, touchingly, "I should like to say, however, that I believe Agamemnon to have been an historical character who flourished at Mycenæ about 1200 BC".[3] Perhaps the ghosts got to him.

Mycenæ was a natural stronghold. It was built on a hill secured on three sides by mountains with few passes, yet with easy access to the sea in the Gulf of Nauplia just twenty-four kilometres away across the plain of Argos. The plain was well watered and rich in fruits, vegetables and cotton. The site was first occupied between 3000–2800 BC, but really began to thrive between 2200–1700 BC. The catalyst was several waves of war-like newcomers arriving from the north and north-east, who established themselves in central Greece and the northern Peloponnese around Mycenæ. Mixing with the indigenous people they created both a new social order and language – Greek. It is not true that the newcomers

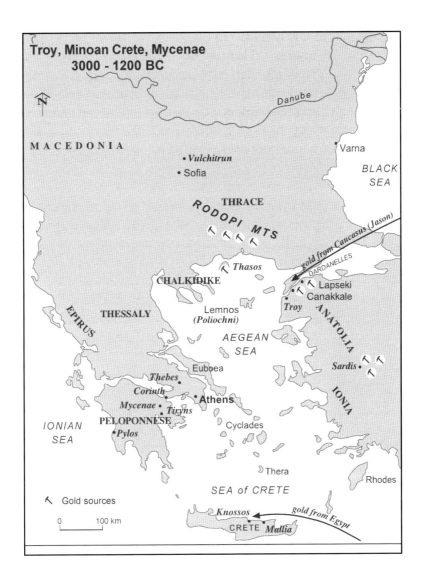

spoke Greek, nor did those they conquered. Greek emerged from this melting-pot. Thus, Mycenæans were the forefathers of what became Classical Greece in the 1st millennium BC. Incidentally, the Greek word for gold, khrusos, was 'imported' from the original Assyrian word, *hurasu*, used in Mesopotamia.

This growing community, much given to hunting (lions still roamed Greece) and fighting, soon became caught up in the cross-currents of Mediterranean trade.

It won control of the other cities on the plain of Argos and was eager to venture further afield. Mycenæ blossomed just as Crete was in its prime between 1700–1450 BC. The ultimate diversity of Mycenæ's overseas trade has been revealed by the sunken wreck of a Mycenæan cargo ship of around 1375 BC, which sank off the south-west coast of Anatolia. The ship was apparently on a voyage back to a Mycenæan port with a cargo of copper (from Cyprus), tin and glass ingots, elephant and hippopotamus ivory (from Egypt), figs, myrrh, olive oil, wine, pottery and gold and silver ornaments. They included a gold chalice, possibly of Cypriot origin, and a gold pectoral of a falcon with outstretched wings with a hooded cobra in each talon, probably from Ugarit in Phoenicia. A gold scarab of Queen Nefertiti, wife of the Pharaoh Akhenaten, implied the vessel might have been to Egypt, or, at least, carried exports of Egyptian gold ornaments. The cargo also included scrap gold and silver, suggesting either that an itinerant goldsmith had taken passage or that such scrap was a source of supply in Mycenæ.[4]

The link with Egypt matches the suggestion by the French historian Fernand Braudel, writing before the wreck was explored, of how the Mycenæans, and the Minoans before them, benefited from trade with Egypt. "The parallel rise of Cretan and Mycenæan trade in the 16th and 15th centuries is sufficient to explain the wealth of the tombs at Mycenæ," he argued. "The abundance of gold objects (the gold came from Egypt) and in particular the amazing gold masks covering the faces of the dead; this was a non-Cretan custom, probably imported, like the gold, from the banks of the Nile."[5] Braudel even ventured that Mycenæ may have sent mercenary warriors in 1580 BC to help the pharaoh Amosis fend off Asian invaders, receiving payment in gold.

This suggestion fits neatly with the warriors in the five shaft graves at Mycenæ, for the gold relics themselves point to a war-like society. As Basil Petrakis, curator of antiquities for Attica, put it, "War activities were very prominent with the Mycenæan civilisation, witness the frequent war scenes on vases, daggers and swords found in graves".[6] Four magnificent Mycenæan bronze swords with handles and hilts covered in gold sheet set the scene in the National Archaeological Museum in Athens, where most of the Mycenæan gold is housed.[7] A gold signet ring from the fourth shaft grave depicts robust fighting between four men. Two are contending with swords, with one already forced to his knees, while a third, half-hidden behind his shield, strikes out with a javelin, and the fourth lies on the ground naked and unarmed. Battles with wild animals are equally graphic. A 16th century BC bronze dagger is inlaid in gold, silver and black niello with a dramatic scene of four hunters with spears and long shields in combat with three lions, who have already knocked down one of their comrades.

The graves at Mycenæ contained a host of weaponry. The fourth grave, which included the above signet ring, contained no less than forty-six swords around the remains of just three warriors. Their bodies were covered with breastplates and their faces by masks of beaten gold. In the fifth grave lay another man with the most splendid of the gold masks and a breastplate of beaten gold with a thin strip of gold across it attached to his sword. The mask itself is by a master goldsmith, with impeccable *repoussé* representation of strong eyebrows, an aquiline nose, firm mouth, moustache and graceful beard. No matter that it is not Agamemnon, but of an unknown leader of about 1550 BC. It is a sublime portrait of a warrior at rest that is almost as moving to confront as the death mask of Egypt's Tutankhamun.

A classic example of how gold can capture an image and preserve it untarnished down the centuries.

Indeed, walking into the Mycenæan gallery of the museum, it is not just this mask, but the sheer array of gold that creates an astonishing impression of a rich, powerful society 3,500 years ago. You are surrounded by masks, breastplates, a whole showcase of 14 cups and bowls, another of belts and sword straps (one nearly 100 cm/39 ins long), a necklace of ten golden foils each shaped like an eagle (a symbol of power) and a wooden hexagonal box decorated with *repoussé* gold plates depicting lions chasing a deer and an antelope through palm trees. From the 'Grave of the Women' at Mycenæ there is a marvellous diadem formed by an elliptical band surmounted by seven tall golden leaves embossed with circles, and an elegant selection of cups and jugs. Standing before these displays you hear a multilingual repetition of the word 'gold' as visitors pass by.

"Schliemann's finds from Mycenæ remain one of the most impressive sights we have inherited from the ancient world," acknowledged Lesley Fitton of the British Museum. "The massed effect of them … in the National Museum in Athens is extraordinarily rich, the predominant impression is one of gold … all are interesting, many beautiful and some showing exquisite detail and fine workmanship."[8]

The debt to the Minoans was substantial. Many designs were executed by goldsmiths still living in or originally from Crete, particularly during the 16th century BC when the gold ornaments for the shaft graves were made. "Some of it was pure Cretan," argued the jewellery historian Reynold Higgins. "Some was made by Cretans for the Minoan market; some by Mycenæans from Cretan models."[9] Higgins also detected eastern influence in designs, particularly diadems worn by men and women which were enriched by leaves and rosettes of gold, which were reminiscent of styles in Mesopotamia before 2000 BC, as was jewellery made of a double spiral of gold wire, which long proved popular at Mycenæ.

However, as Mycenæ evolved into a serious power in the Aegean world, the balance changed, especially after the destruction of Knossos by earthquake and/or fire around 1450 BC. Shortly afterwards, Mycenæ conquered Crete and its civilisation reached its zenith between 1400–1200 BC. As the Minoan world shrunk, so goldsmiths and other craftsmen must have emigrated to the mainland. The clientele was there.

Excavations at several Mycenæan strongholds have provided clues to the spread of the goldsmiths' trade. In the ruins of two palaces at Thebes, north of Athens, the remains of three gold workshops have been found; one dates from 1400–1350 BC. At Pylos, the palace of King Nestor (another of Homer's heroes) in south-west Greece, the American archaeologist Carl Blegen turned up in 1939 stacks of the clay Linear B tablets, first found at Knossos on Crete (*see chapter 3*) but then undeciphered. When the writing on the tablets (an early form of Greek) was finally decoded by Michael Ventris and his collaborator John Chadwick at Cambridge University in 1952, an astonishing inventory of palace supplies was revealed. Tallies of deliveries and stocks of honey, wheat, olive oil, saffron, figs, wool, flax, and other goods were unveiled. Lists of gold vessels held at the palace turned up on two tablets. The sign for gold (akin to crossed swords or interlocked palm trees) was prefixed by a pictogram of the gold cup itself on one tablet. On another tablet, recording religious offerings, thirteen gold cups, some plain, some more ornate, were accounted for (of the cups themselves there was no trace). A list of tradesmen on another clay tablet included four goldsmiths among potters, bowyers and saddlers.[10]

The accountants kept close control on their Linear B tablets of the issuing of metal to palace craftsmen, particularly in bronze, matching it with the returned articles. No such tablet for gold has survived. However, one tablet has a curious listing of gold contributions from local governors, perhaps to meet some tax or urgent expense. Since the tablets date from around 1200 BC when the Mycenæan Empire was close to collapse, this may indicate a desperate call for gold. The contributions totalled a modest 5 kg/160.5 t.oz, in amounts varying from 1 kg/32.15 t.oz to 62 grams/2 t.oz, with 250 grams/7.8 t.oz the most common quantity (from Mycenæ there is also some evidence of rings or spirals of gold wire of 8.6 grams being used as units of value of one talent, but this was not widespread).

This is a fascinating insight into the small scale of gold transactions, giving us a rare sense of perspective on the amounts of gold available to the Mycenæans. John Chadwick decided, "This is a very large quantity of what must have been a scarce commodity".[11] So the two hard numbers we have for gold in the Mycenæan world are the five kg at Pylos and fifteen kg of ornaments in the Mycenæ shaft graves which date from four hundred years earlier. The implication is that, as on Minoan Crete, a little gold went a long way. Goldsmiths throughout the Mycenæan domain may not have had that much at their disposal in a year or even for several years. This is borne out even during the most ebullient period of jewellery-making after 1400 BC. Most gold ornamentation was of light, wafer-thin discs and wires.

Even so, in Mycenæ's prime there was a relative abundance of jewellery. Taste and style, though, were very different from the early days of the warriors in their shaft graves. Diadems, fancy long pins and earrings were out, gold beads, clothing ornaments and finger rings were in. The impression is of prosperous high society enjoying itself. "Jewellery belonged first and foremost to the world of women, especially ladies of the privileged classes," suggests the guide to gold jewellery in the Benaki Museum in Athens. "Elaborate coiffures were held in place by coil hair ornaments made of gold or bronze and ribbons garnished with beads."[12] The American archaeologist Alan Wace noted that women's clothes "were certainly as richly decorated as means allowed. The skirts of the rich had gold or silver discs of various patterns stitched on between the groups of flounces, and their hems and borders of the jackets were trimmed with bands of thin sheet gold with embossed ornament … jewellery was much in evidence. Beads of all kinds, gold, stone, faïence, glass, and amber were used for necklaces … in many cases beads of glass or terracotta covered with gold leaf were substituted for real gold beads".[13]

Beads were all the rage. "Globular beads, in gold and many other materials, are numerous," observed Reynold Higgins. "A large globular bead richly decorated with circles and lines in fine granulation … is typical of Mycenæan jewellery at its best."[14] Their shapes were myriad – melons, pomegranates, grains of wheat, crocuses, drums, wheels, lanterns, and wire cages with blue glass interiors. The most popular style was relief beads, stamped in shallow relief out of sheet gold. A backing of sheet gold was soldered on, with the space between the two sheets being filled with magnetite sand. Some were then decorated with granulation or touches of blue *repoussé* enamel. Output was so prolific between 1450–1400 BC that Reynold Higgins concluded, "Something like mass-production seems to have been introduced".[15] The designs created in this period were perpetuated for almost three hundred years, although as time went by less gold was used, the beads being made of glass and covered with gold foil. The beads evoked marine life, plants and religious symbols. In vogue were cockles, argonauts, roses, lilies, papyrus, ivy, bees, bulls' heads, and single axes.

The quality has astonished archaeologists and historians of jewellery. "The craft of the jeweller … was one in which the Mycenæans excelled," wrote Alan Wace. "Everything, even the smallest object of gold, is beautifully and most carefully finished. The granulated work of tiny beads of gold on rings, pendants, and other decorative work is unrivalled in fineness and accuracy, for each little grain is attached separately. The soldering together of the two halves of the hollow gold beads and the ring bezels is admirably executed. Some of the gold work is chased with designs in low relief produced by a combination of embossing and engraving."[16] The goldsmiths' finesse at setting precious stones in gold mounts, or inlaying gold in bronze daggers was so delicately done that Alan Wace admitted he found it difficult to believe it was achieved in the Bronze Age.

The scenes on the oval bezels of some finger rings offer an impression of Mycenæan life. A ring from the Tiryns 'treasure' depicts a leave-taking as passengers embark on a Mycenæan ship. Another shows a fertility procession with a goddess sitting on a folding chair, with a bird behind her, being presented with libation vessels by four lion-headed demons. A ring from Mycenæ itself shows a goddess, possibly Athena, seated beneath a sacred tree, holding three poppies. Before her are three full-breasted women, probably worshippers, carrying lilies; the sun, a half moon and a double axehead loom in the sky, from which a deity with spear and shield descends to earth. All this on an oval bezel scarcely four centimetres long. The drama of the hunt is caught on another bezel as a hunter in a chariot pulled by two horses draws his bow at a stag.

As time went by, elaborate rings became scarcer and gold beads gave way increasingly to glass, sometimes covered with thin gold foil. The trend was noticeable from 1300 BC. "After 1200," reported Reynold Higgins, "jewellery is rare in Mycenæan lands."[17] What had happened? The Mycenæan Empire itself was coming under threat from various invaders, sometimes vaguely described as 'the sea people'. The decline in gold use, however, pre-dates those incursions, probably because output from Egypt and Nubia was falling. The pharaoh Ramasses III even despatched expeditions down the east coast of Africa seeking new sources. Mycenæ, too, sought fresh supplies abroad.

Which brings us back to myths – specifically, Jason and the Argonauts setting sail in search of the Golden Fleece. According to legend, Jason was the heir to the throne of Ioclos (now Volos), a mercantile city of the Mycenæan Empire in north-east Greece. His birthright had been usurped by his step-uncle Pelias, who ultimately said he would relinquish the throne if Jason could prove his worth to the city by seeking out and bringing back the Golden Fleece. The cry was "Mycenæ needs gold, find it and you will be rewarded". As the Cambridge historian Janet Brown put it, "It was a real quest for real gold".[18]

So Jason undertook a perilous 1,500 mile (2,400 km) voyage, up through the Dardenelles and across the Black Sea to Colchis. This region, now part of Georgia, had been a source of alluvial gold for centuries (the city states of Mesopotamia probably got gold from Colchis before 2500 BC). The streams coming down from the Caucasus mountains there were rich in gold brought down from the high country in melt-water each spring. The mountain people, known today as the Svans, used sheepskins to trap the flecks of gold. Both Strabo, the geographer in the 1st century BC and, later, Pliny, recorded their technique. Strabo noted they used "perforated troughs and fleecy skins".

Nothing has changed three thousand years later. The explorer Tim Severin, who followed in Jason's wake in 1984 in a replica of the Argo, found Svan prospectors working ankle deep in the waters of the Enguri river. They pinned sheepskins to a board to catch the silt drifting downstream, then scraped it off the fleeces into a simple wooden trough and panned out the gold. They even presented Severin, just like Jason, with a gold-gathering fleece.[19] The high level of gold in the stream was confirmed in a report by the Georgian Academy of Sciences in 2001 which noted grades of 5.3 grams/ 0.17 t.oz had been recorded.[20]

Jason, it seems, was an ancient gold prospector, a forerunner of gold diggers rushing to Brazil in the 18th century (AD) and to California and Australia after 1849. He might have agreed with an Australian digger who wrote, "The mischief is that you hear so many wonderful stories that are false". Gold prospecting always was the stuff of myths.

At least Jason, as the legend suggests, struck gold. Yet, what he brought back was not much help to a Mycenæan Empire under increasing pressure. The strains of war were taking their toll. The Trojan war is thought to have been fought around 1275–1250 BC, not long before Jason set out. That war and other conflicts brought Mycenæ to the verge of collapse after three centuries of power. Tiryns, Pylos and Thebes were laid waste. The citadel of Mycenæ itself was burned and looted around 1200 BC. The civilisation it had spawned slipped away into the myths of history by 1100 BC.

The Dark Age of Greece, which was to last for over three hundred years, closed in. Historians and archaeologists argue over the cause. Was it climate change bringing famine or plague? Was it invaders, perhaps Dorians from the north-west or unknown raiders from across the sea? Certainly there were large migrations of people in this period, including refugees from mainland Greece settling on the islands of the Aegean and on the western shores of Turkey. No one knows what really took place.

There remain the ruins of the strongholds. They confirm a civilisation of great engineering skill that at Mycenæ built the Lion Gate, the Tomb of Atreus, and magnificent walls, and within them created frescos, pottery and ornaments of gold that provide tangible evidence of its artistic and technical sophistication. From those foundations the legends were spun, passing down by word of mouth until, about four hundred years later, Homer wove them into the *Iliad* and the *Odyssey*. John Chadwick, codebreaker with Michael Ventris of the Linear B tablets, deserves the last word. He wrote, "Some sort of continuity made possible the transmission … of some stories of the great days of Mycenæan Greece down to the time when a master poet could use them as background to two great narrative poems".[21]

CHAPTER 6

The Phoenicians:
World Travellers

You have to look hard to find Phoenicia on most maps of the ancient world. It was just a slip of a country reaching scarcely a hundred kilometres north and south of modern Beirut and hemmed into a coastal strip ten to fifty kilometres wide between the Mediterranean and mountains. Indeed, it was more a handful of neighbouring cities, Aradus, Byblos, Sidon and Tyre, strategically placed on coastal promontories or offshore islands, all with good harbours and possessing commercial, shipbuilding and navigational skills, along with fine craftsmanship, whether working gold, silver, bronze, ivory or marble. Together, this maritime league secured a remarkable hold on trade throughout the Mediterranean and beyond for seven or eight hundred years after 1200 BC.

The Phoenicians, above all, created the first truly international long distance trade in metals, not just in gold and silver, but copper, tin, lead and, before long, iron as the Bronze Age evolved into the Iron Age during the early 1st millennium BC. They ventured into the Atlantic beyond the Pillars of Hercules (Straits of Gibraltar) to the south-west of the Iberian peninsula for silver and gold, to the Celtic world of Britain for tin and down the west coast of Africa for gold.

Around 950 BC they embarked every three years on joint ventures with their neighbours in Israel down the Red Sea to the mysterious Ophir for gold, silver, ivory, sandalwood and precious stones. Starting again in the Red Sea, they even circumnavigated the entire African continent around 600 BC, at the behest of the Egyptian pharaoh Necho, seeking new sources of gold and luxuries. We know they succeeded because they reported back that, for a while, the sun was in the north at midday as indeed it would be passing southern Africa – a claim dismissed out of hand by early historians such as Herodotus, who could not conceive of such a thing.

This relentless search for metals was sustained by the colonies, trading posts really, that the Phoenicians established at Kition in Cyprus, Motya in Sicily, Thassos in Sardinia, Gadir (Cadiz) in south-west Spain, Lixus in Morocco and, most famously, at Carthage in North Africa near modern Tunis. Carthage took on a life of its own to become, by 550 BC, the most powerful city-state on the Mediterranean shores.

The Phoenicians' success in cornering the metals trade for centuries had a profound effect on the relationship between gold and silver. They secured such an abundance of silver from the mines of south-west Spain between 750 and 500

BC, that there was virtually a glut in Assyria affecting prices, because it was on a silver standard, while in Egypt, where silver had always been a rare metal, the gold:silver ratio widened from 1:4 to 1:13. The flow ultimately encouraged the shift from silver simply as a standard of value or money of exchange to silver coinage, although the Phoenicians themselves came late to coinage, well after several of their neighbours.

The curious thing is that despite such achievements, historians still find it difficult to agree on precisely who the Phoenicians were. For a start, they never called themselves Phoenicians. That name was given them by the Greeks, who saw them as traders of purple (phoinix) textiles dyed from the juices of murex sea shells. Homer, in whose writings the Phoenicians first turn up, also knew them as Sidones, from Sidon. The Spanish scholar Maria Eugenia Aubet remarked that the Phoenicians were "a people without a state, without territory and without political unity".[1] The mystery deepens because, although they bequeathed us an early version of our alphabet, no account by their own hand of their history has survived.

The best deduction is that Phoenicia emerged from the land of Canaan, which embraced the whole coastal region along the eastern Mediterranean between Turkey and Egypt during much of the second and third millennia BC. Canaan was always under the thumb of Mesopotamia or the Hittites or Egypt. Its early cities of Ugarit and Byblos were important trading centres before 2000 BC, offering the surrounding empires a gateway to the Mediterranean world. Ugarit was the centre of the metal trade for much of the 2nd millennium, switching copper from Cyprus, silver and tin from Anatolia, and gold from Egypt to Babylon and Assyria. Byblos was an artistic centre, learning the goldsmiths' skills from Mesopotamia, and passing them on to Egypt, the Minoans and Mycenæ.

This is the heritage the 'Phoenicians' acquired around 1200 BC when Canaan fragmented under the pressure of various migrations, including that of the 'sea peoples', which destabilised the entire region. Many communities were transformed as the controls previously exerted by the Hittites, the city-states of Mesopotamia and even Egypt disappeared. In this turmoil the Arameans took over in the north (modern Syria), the Israelites captured the mountains in the south around Jerusalem, and the 'Phoenicians' were left with the mid-Levant coastal strip (modern Lebanon). This gave the cities of Aradus, Byblos, Tyre and Sidon a new sense of independence, but also a need for new sources for raw materials, because trade routes with Anatolia to the north and Egypt to the south were often interrupted. Equally, the Phoenicians needed new export markets for their own luxury goods. The Mediterranean offered the obvious route for expansion, so the Phoenician diaspora grew not from a lust for conquest, but trade. And they had the commercial, financial, shipbuilding and navigational expertise 'in-house', thanks to their long history on the brink of that sea, doing the bidding of other powers. Moreover, although local kings and temples were sources of finance, there was

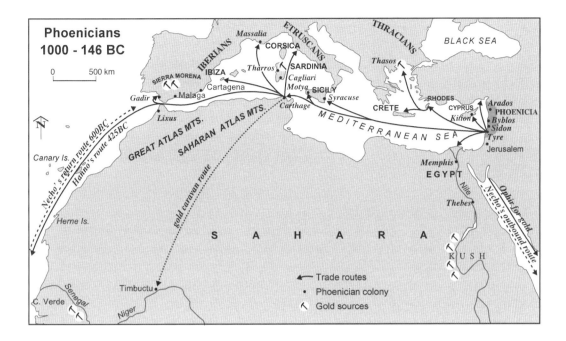

already an independent merchant aristocracy. The Phoenicians, indeed, sound very much like the Venetians who were to become commercial power brokers in the Mediterranean over two thousand years later. The only ancient city out of this loop was Ugarit in the north, but that had always been focused on metal trading from Anatolia or Cyprus, while the Phoenicians had their eyes on wider horizons (and the metal traders of Ugarit could easily have migrated a hundred kilometres to Byblos or Tyre).

Initially, Byblos staked out a leading role, given that it already had a substantial port, through which the cedarwood of the mountains had long been exported, along with the jewellery and ivory carving of its craftsmen. They had existing links with Mesopotamia, Egypt, Cyprus and Mycenæ, whose empire still held sway in mainland Greece. But as the New Kingdom foundered in Egypt and Mycenæ declined in the waning years of the 2nd millennium, these traditional links became less important. Gradually Tyre took command, looking further afield, east down the Red Sea and west along the Mediterranean.

The gold of Ophir

Tyre was well positioned on a tiny island off the coast that was protected from the open sea by reefs, but offered a snug harbour within. The Phoenicians' "golden age", as one historian put it, really began under Tyre's King Hiram I (969–936 BC), who allied with King Solomon in Israel to make a series of voyages down the Red Sea to Ophir in search of gold, silver, ivory, precious stones and other exotica. Solomon, eager to complete his lavish temple at Jerusalem, had the finance, Hiram contributed the Phoenicians' navigational skills. The location of Ophir remains elusive; it may have been Eritrea or Ethiopia or Yemen or even India, and probably the expeditions stopped at several places. They certainly were successful. The Book of Kings in the Bible related, "Once in three years came the navy … bringing gold, and silver, ivory and apes and peacocks. So King Solomon exceeded all the kings of the earth for riches and wisdom".[2] The Bible reported that Solomon gained 420 talents' weight of gold from a single expedition, which implied around 12,000 kg/385,800 t.oz. This quantity sounds extravagant, given our estimated levels of gold production in that period, when Egypt's high level of output as the major producer was probably back under 1,000 kg annually. (It is also three times what Spain ever received in a single year, in the first flush of supplies from the Americas in the 16th century AD.) It may be prudent to knock a zero off the supplies from Ophir, although Solomon and King Hiram had obviously tapped directly into a useful source of gold. This treasure was supplemented when, as the Bible reported in the same chapter, the Queen of Sheba travelled from Yemen to visit Solomon apparently bringing a gift of 120 talents of gold (3,000 kg/96,000 t.oz). Ancient gold workings of quartz veins have been discovered in the Jawf region of northern Yemen, but again Sheba's bounty is extravagant (quite apart from the fact that modern historians see her as a mythical figure).[3] One explanation of these quantities of gold offered both in the Bible and by early historians such as Herodotus, is that as silver was the standard of value at the time, the quantities of gold suggested in what are, after all, legends, were expressed in their value in silver talents; that is, 120 silver talents' worth of gold which, depending on the gold: silver ratio, would weigh much less. The Queen of Sheba's gold at a 1:10 ratio would amount to only 300 kg/9,600 t.oz – still a handsome present. By the same token the Ophir voyage would have yielded just over 1,000 kg, a handsome return by the standards of the day.

That said, Tyre benefited enormously from the gold-seeking voyages to the east, which broke the monopoly the Egyptians had long enjoyed as major producers of gold. The Phoenicians simply tapped directly into supplies coming out of Africa or Arabia, which had probably previously come down the Nile to Egypt. "Direct access to the metal producing countries … allowed the monarchs of Tyre not only to increase their profits, but gradually to widen their commercial sphere of influence," asserted Maria Eugenia Aubet. "This strategy would make Tyre the foremost naval and commercial power in Asia."[4]

To the 'far-west'

Tyre next turned its attention to capturing the metal sources around the shores of the Mediterranean, to meet the demand of the new Assyrian Empire arising in Mesopotamia after 900 BC (*see chapter 1*). The first step was a Phoenician colony at Kition (modern Larnaca) on Cyprus founded around 820 BC to secure copper supplies from the mines inland. In search of gold they colonised the island of Thasos in the northern Aegean just off the coasts of Thrace, according to Herodotus. He reported, "I have seen these mines myself; much the most remarkable are those discovered by the Phoenicians who came with Thasus the son of Phoenix to colonise the island … a whole mountain has been turned upside down in the search for gold". Herodotus was writing c. 450 BC, and does not indicate when the Phoenicians had arrived, but he implies they were the pioneers there.[5]

The Phoenicians' greatest legacy, of course, was Carthage (meaning 'new town'), which was established on the North African coast in 814 BC. The legend has it that the princess Elissa-Dido fled from Tyre to avoid persecution of her brother King Pygmalion and eventually settled there. Carthage offered the usual safe haven – a rocky promontory with sheltered lagoons on either side. Carthage thus secured direct access to the caravan trails coming north from West Africa through the Sahara bearing gold dust. Previously the caravans had turned east to Egypt when they reached the coast at Djerba, not far from Carthage. Now the Phoenicians, once again, cut behind Egyptian trade lines for gold, tapping this supply for over six hundred years. The city also intercepted other caravans arriving along the North African coast in what is now Algeria, and sent expeditions down the Atlantic coast of Africa seeking direct access to the goldfields. Meanwhile, its twin harbours provided shelter for Phoenician ships returning from south-west Spain laden with silver. Outward bound from Tyre these vessels followed a northerly track along the Mediterranean to take advantage of prevailing winds and currents, but the return voyage was easier along the North African coast. The Phoenicians were confident navigators, travelling by night guided by the Little Bear (North Star), which became known as the 'Phoenician star'.

The northerly route was secured by other carefully selected trading posts. Motya, a tiny islet off western Sicily with a causeway to the mainland, was strategically chosen as the shortest sea crossing to Carthage. On Sardinia outposts were established at Thassos, Sulcis, Nora and Caligari, all positioned on high promontories guarding sheltered bays. Besides these safe havens, Sardinia later offered silver from mines developed around 450 BC and probably a little alluvial gold. Approaching the Iberian cost, the Phoenicians set up on the island of Ibiza and established a series of small settlements along the Costa del Sol near Malaga, where vessels were secure and crews could rest. The outward voyage took most of a summer season, so they had the winter to recuperate. The Costa del Sol staging post placed them poised to venture through the dangerous waters of the Straits of Gibraltar into the Atlantic, where they could trade at Lixus in Morocco and Gadir (Cadiz) in south-west Spain before embarking on the homeward voyage to Tyre.

The Phoenicians made three trial voyages to south-west Spain before setting up their colony on the island of Gadir in the estuary of the river Guadalete directly across from the region of Tartessus with its gold and silver mines, according to the Roman geographer Strabo. Strabo and other early historians, repeating centuries-old legends, declared that the Phoenicians founded Gadir in 1100 BC (or, rather, 80 years after the supposed fall of Troy). Modern archaeologists disagree. They can find no trace of a Phoenician settlement there before 800 BC. That date matches the establishment of the other posts along the Mediterranean and a rising demand for silver. "It was a time when, in the east, especially in Assyria, silver was in great demand," the Italian archaeologist Sabatino Moscati has pointed out, "so the founding of Gadir is to be seen as the immediate response to a particular market situation, which could immensely enrich the kings and merchant princes of Tyre … (it) became the most important Phoenician colony in the farthest-west. Its economic and culture sphere of interest spread as far as the Atlantic towns of Morocco."[6] The mines of the Sierra Morena inland were to supply the East with most of its silver for over 250 years, along with a modest helping of gold from the mines and alluvial sources.

Whatever the quibble about starting dates, historians ancient and modern concur that cornering the silver trade was the Phoenicians' objective. The great sweep of the Sierra Morena north-west of modern Seville and the river Guadalquiver was peppered with mining prospects. At least ten specific silver mines, three gold deposits and over ten gold/silver deposits have been charted, while a dozen or more villages with old slag heaps and furnaces for smelting have been identified by archaeologists.

The Rio Tinto valley in western Andalucía contained the richest deposits of gold and silver ore. At the mining settlement of Cerro Salomon, near the source of the Rio Tinto, clay lamps, miners' tools, bellows and crucibles have been found. Moreover, the Phoenicians appear to have introduced more advanced technology that enabled more efficient refining of the gold and silver ores. "Analyses carried out on samples of ore indicate that … (they) knew a great deal about silica fluxes and how to treat the ore by adding lead to collect silver," reported Maria Eugenia Aubet, "so we are dealing with a well-organised mining enterprise using advanced technology previously unknown in Tartessos. It is not by chance that all this activity in Rio Tinto began at the same time as the first traces of a Phoenician presence appear in the region."[7] While initial smelting seems to have taken place close to the mines, more sophisticated metallurgical centres were established at Huelva, at the mouth of the Rio Tinto, and San Bartolome closer to Gadir. Oxidised ores with a high gold, silver and lead content was processed by fusion and cupellation. Initially, the crushed ore, together with a silica flux, was heated to separate out the slag from the other metals, with lead 'capturing' the gold and silver. The mixture was then subjected to cupellation, with the cupel absorbing the lead, leaving just the gold and silver to be separated (this technology was perfected in Lydia in Turkey by 600 BC or earlier and the Phoenicians would have known about it).[8] Although the Phoenicians provided the know-how and improved the management of the mining industry, the actual back-breaking work on the mines and in the refining centres was undertaken by the local people of Tartessus.

How much was produced? Contemporary accounts all speak primarily of silver and that was clearly the motive; gold was a welcome by-product. The best clue to silver production is a report of a vessel from the Greek island of Samos that loaded sixty talents, about 1,500 kg/48,225 t.oz. There is an anecdote that Phoenician captains took on so much silver that they sometimes disposed of their iron anchors to sail home with new anchors cast of silver. A sense of perspective can be gained from the shipments the Romans made several centuries later. In 200 BC they shipped almost 14,000 kg/450,000 t.oz from New Carthage in southern Spain and six years later shipped just over 8,000 kg/257,000 t.oz. The implication (and that is all it is) is that the Phoenicians could have secured a similar scale of output annually. As for gold, the output was modest; perhaps a few hundred kg annually. Gold was not the mainstay of the trade, but enough to help finance voyages and supply thriving local jewellery fabrication in southern Spain.

In exchange, the Phoenicians bartered the ubiquitous purple-dyed textiles, wine, olive oil, perfumes, glass beads, handsome bronze jugs, gold and silver jewellery and other trinkets. The Tartessian rulers were flattered with gifts of finely-wrought bowls of gold, silver and bronze and ornate sarcophagi for their burials. As Diadorus Siculus wrote disdainfully, "The Phoenicians, expert in commerce, would buy silver in exchange for some other small goods. Consequently, taking the silver to Greece, Asia and all other peoples, the Phoenicians made great earnings. Thus, practising this trade for a long time, they became rich, and founded other colonies".

Carthage: Mediterranean power-house

The rising star of those colonies was Carthage. Its great asset, apart from providing a pipeline into the resources of Africa, was its location far removed from the Phoenician cities of the Levant. While their commercial success depended on sales to the markets of Assyria and later a renascent Babylon, these neighbours frequently threatened their independence. Tyre fell to Nebuchadnezzar from Babylon in 574 BC. Thereafter the newly powerful Persians took on Sidon. Finally, Alexander the Great came calling in 333 BC, en route to destroying the Persian Empire. That attack virtually ended the concept of Phoenicia as a 'free' country.

Carthage, two thousand kilometres away in North Africa, was safe from such incursions, but was forced to take charge of its own destiny. The Phoenician world became the distinctive Punic world of Carthage seeking to dominate the Mediterranean. The Carthaginians occasionally put their naval power at the disposal of the Persians to thwart the Greeks, and in alliance with the Etruscans saw off the Greeks at the battle of Alalia on Corsica in 535 BC, winning firm control of much of Sicily and the western Mediterranean. Such success attracted merchants, mariners and mercenaries; the population exceeded 100,000 people. Carthage became, as the Tunisian archaeologist Mohammed Fantar put it, "the most prestigious city, the capital of a thriving empire and the hub of a brilliant civilisation". The people, he added, "enjoyed an open and liberal society which fostered a high degree of self-expression, encouraging self-confidence, a spirit of initiative, enthusiasm for action and even adventure".[9]

The adventures of Hanno

The appetite for adventure served the Carthaginians well. From the outset they established strong links across the Sahara desert, which had a slightly wetter climate in those days and was thus more accessible. They profited from the regular caravans (using horses, then, not camels) coming up to the coast with gold, ivory and slaves from West Africa. The trans-Sahara gold trade remained a source of supply almost to modern times. For the metal traders of the Phoenician network this African gold was more important than the gold from Spain which (until Roman times) merely supplemented the silver flows. Carthage built its own reserves of gold, while also becoming an important gold jewellery fabrication and export centre. No doubt goldsmiths from Byblos, Tyre and Sidon migrated there.

Along the caravans' routes, however, there were intermediary tribes taking their cut. The Carthaginians were determined to by-pass them to get to the origins of the gold, just as the sailors of Tyre had done on their voyages to Ophir. They had already made connections with small ports in Algeria and Morocco where trans-Sahara caravans turned up, but a bolder approach was needed to reach the actual goldfields.

Thus, a major expedition was reportedly mounted in 425 BC by an intrepid navigator named Hanno. The story is told in a Greek transcription of a stele at Carthage commemorating the voyage. The Greek document, which is of dubious origin, told how Hanno set out with sixty galleys bearing 30,000 men and women to set up colonies down the Atlantic coast of Africa. The landmarks they passed on their southerly voyage have enabled historians to hazard guesses at certain stopping places. First, in the bay at the mouth of the Rio de Oro in modern Spanish Sahara, they found a tiny island called Herné which fitted the Phoenician formula for a trading post. The bay was a destination for caravans out of Mauritania, Senegal and Mali, all important sources of alluvial gold to this day. The next stop was probably the river Senegal itself, down which gold dust could have come from the alluvial goldfields of Upper Senegal. The travelogue reported Hanno then pressed on, passing the Gold Coast of Ghana, as far as Douala in Cameroon. That final destination is implied by descriptions of fiery lava flows, which could match the high peak of Mount Cameroon. Lack of supplies then forced Hanno to turn back. Modern historians are sceptical that Hanno got to Douala, citing the difficulties of adverse winds and currents on the return voyage north. Yet in 600 BC, the Phoenicians had circumnavigated Africa in a clockwise direction, thus sailing back home up that very same coast; historians accept that account because of the crucial statement that the sun was to the north as they rounded the southern tip of Africa. The voyage of Hanno may well be a compound of tales of Carthaginian gold-seekers on the Atlantic coast. They had every reason to go. As Donald Harden remarked, "The riches of Africa were a powerful incentive".[10]

The classic account of how the Carthaginians bartered on such voyages was told by Herodotus, a contemporary of Hanno. First, he conjured up a wonderful anecdote about an island off the coast called Cyrauis, a pleasure dome of olive trees and vines. "In the island is a lake," wrote Herodotus, "and the native girls dip feathers smeared with pitch into the mud at the bottom of it, and bring up gold dust − … I merely record the current story, without guaranteeing the truth of it."[11] Herodotus went on to explain how the Carthaginians traded on Africa's shores. "On reaching this country," he reported, "they unload their goods, arrange them tidily along the beach, and then, returning to their boats, raise a smoke. Seeing the smoke, the natives come down to the beach, place on the ground a certain quantity of gold in exchange for the goods, and go off again to a distance. The Carthaginians then come ashore and take a look at the gold; and if they think it represents a fair price for their wares, they collect it and go away; if, on the other hand, it seems too little, they go back aboard and wait, and the natives come and add to the gold until they are satisfied. There is perfect honesty on both sides; the Carthaginians never touch the gold until it equals in value what they have offered for sale, and the natives never touch the goods until the gold has been taken away."[12] Such were the subtleties of gold trading in the 5th century BC.

Gold stocks, gold coins

Through such bargaining Carthage built up a substantial gold reserve, as another contemporary commentator observed. The Greek general Thucydides (c. 460–400 BC), in his authoritative History of the Peloponnesian War, recounted a debate at Syracuse on Sicily in 415 BC when that city was threatened by Greek invasion. Hermocrates, son of Hermon, argued that Syracuse send a delegation to ask the Carthaginians for help. "Certainly, if they are willing," he declared, "they could help us more than any power in existence, since they have the greatest quantities of gold and silver, which is what supports both war and everything else."[13] On this occasion help was apparently not forthcoming, but Syracuse defeated the Greek fleet a couple of years later anyway.

An indication of the size of Carthage's stock of gold is that when the Romans made their first conquest of Carthage two hundred years later they secured its treasury of 3,270 kg/105,000 t.oz, according to Livy, the Roman historian. Livy added that prior to that campaign, Rome's own treasury held a modest 1,300 kg/41,800 t.oz. These statistics, given by Livy in Roman pounds (one pound = 324 grams/10.4 t.oz), provide an important sense of perspective on stocks of gold towards the 1st millennium BC; they may not be exact, but they are the beginning of a long series of figures on Roman (and Greek) treasuries and gold imports over the next five or six hundred years that are consistent and therefore may be taken as relatively realistic. The 'ball-park' of precious metal statistics had been established much more precisely than was possible for ancient Mesopotamia or Egypt. For this reason the more extravagant stories of so many hundred talents from Ophir or the Queen of Sheba must be regarded with caution.

The French historian Fernand Braudel accused the Carthaginians of filling up their treasury with precious metals "without putting them to work".[14] Certainly, relatively little gold or silver was turned into coin. The Phoenicians, both in the Levant and Carthage, came late to coins, primarily because the peoples they bartered with in Africa or southern Spain had no use for them. The first silver and bronze coins were struck in Sidon, Tyre and Byblos between 450 and 400 BC, well over a century after the first coinage in Lydia and Greece, and long after the wealthy Persian Empire introduced its gold *daric*. The coastal cities never minted their own gold coins, preferring to let the Persian *daric* circulate, a prudent policy given that they were increasingly in the Persians' sphere of influence. The sole gold coins to turn up with Phoenician characters on them were minted at Kition on Cyprus between 361–312 BC. Carthage, however, began its own monetary system with silver coins, bearing Punic lettering from 410 BC and introduced gold coins before 350 BC. The prime motive for the coins was to pay soldiers and mercenaries in Carthage and Sicily, a custom that was becoming widespread around the Mediterranean world. The gold coins of Carthage, with the head of the goddess Tanit on the face, and a lion, horse or palm frond on the reverse, gained acceptance around the western Mediterranean in the 3rd and 4th centuries BC, but they never achieved the reputation of Persian or Greek coins, let alone that of the budding Roman Empire.[15]

The Phoenician jewellery 'brand'

Phoenician gold jewellery and metalwork was always more abundant than coin, being among the most important creations of craftsmen, initially in the Levant coastal cities, but later in Carthage, Thassos on Sardinia and in southern Spain. The Phoenician 'brand' became known throughout the Mediterranean. The prime Phoenician creation was decorated bowls of gold, silver and bronze that have turned up in ruined palaces and tombs from Persia, Assyria, Cyprus and Greece to Praenaste in Italy and southern Spain. Homer sang their praise in The *Iliad*, when one was presented as a prize at funeral games:

> The prizes of the runners, swift of foot
> Achilles next set forth; a silver bowl,
> Six measures its content, of Sidon's costliest art
> The product rare; thence o'er the misty sea
> Brought by Phoenicians, who, in port arriv'd.[16]

The manufacture of these bowls began in Ugarit well before 1400 BC and may be seen in a golden bowl with a hunting scene embossed on its base, at the Louvre in Paris. Later the metalworkers of Tyre and Sidon refined this technique through the centuries, revealing an exceptional artistic sense of composition in delicate, yet dramatic, scenes. Some of their finest work is to be seen in six bowls of the 7th century BC found at Praeneste (Palistrina) just south east of Rome and now in the Museo Archeologico di Villa Giula there. The 'day of the hunter' is in a bowl of gold and silver that is alive with three circles of action; hunters in their chariots taking aim at wildfowl, a grand procession of horses and warriors walking in front of prisoners and trampling others beneath their feet. Six golden serpents rise from the rim of another gold and silver bowl adorned with processions of birds, animals and warriors. Although the bowls are thought to have been made in Sidon, Egyptian themes are often strong. A pharaoh is shown slaying his enemies in the centre of a gold and silver bowl found on Cyprus, while hunters circle above. The bowls were prestige goods to be used as gifts in a deeply-rooted system of exchange on ceremonial, diplomatic or commercial occasions in the orbit of the social and political elite.[17]

Phoenician jewellery has survived as widely as the metal bowls, but archaeologists are often hard put to tell whether it was made in Byblos, Tyre or Sidon and exported, or made locally by a goldsmith who had migrated from there, or simply been influenced by the Phoenician brand. The Phoenicians, in turn, had learned their trade from Mesopotamia, and Egypt used much the same motifs. They loved lotus flowers, rosettes, palm fronds, scarabs, falcons, griffins and lions.

The ubiquitous amulets (charms) and the cases to carry them were universally popular. Often the cylindrical gold cases, shaped like a butterfly chrysalis or crowned with a falcon, lion, or ram's head, contained flimsy sheets of gold leaf bearing engraved designs of magic formulae. Style and taste changed subtly as the Phoenicians migrated west along the Mediterranean. A distinct Punic character, with strong Egyptian influence, was displayed by early Carthaginian scarab rings depicting the swivel-eye of Horus, the falcon-god, and Isis, the mother figure, and pendants with granulated solar discs or down-turned crescent moons.[18] Later, Greek jewellery often dictated Carthage fashions.

The most memorable jewellery, however, was made at Thassos on Sardinia. "Thassos has proved the richest source as regards quality and quantity for jewellery," asserts the Italian expert Giovanna Pisano. "Among the earrings there are some complex pieces … each unique in its delicate colouring, achieved through the skilful application of various techniques, such as embossing, granulation and filigree."[19] The finest Thassos ornaments date from around 650 BC, when the Phoenicians were closely involved with the Etruscans, whose central Italian state of Etruria was approaching the peak of its power. Phoenicians and Etruscans shared a remarkable affinity – the Etruscans even adopting the Phoenician alphabet. They allied their navies against the rising challenge of Greek expansion in the Mediterranean and worked closely in business. Their goldsmiths who achieved remarkable virtuosity with granulation (see next chapter) probably learned much from their eastern Mediterranean allies. The durability of this alliance is attested by three inscribed gold sheets, dating from the 5th century BC, found at Prygi, the Etruscan port north of Rome. Two of the golden pages bear inscriptions in Etruscan, the other in Phoenician, dedicating them to the Carthaginian goddess Astarte.[20]

Phoenician and Etruscan fingerprints can be detected on much of the gold jewellery from this era that has been found in southern Spain. The Phoenicians themselves set up workshops on Gadir, which created gold and silver jewellery and ornaments, as gifts for the Tartessian rulers. "A study of the Tartessian-orientalising … discloses one of the most significant aspects of Phoenician trading in the West," wrote Maria Eugenia Aubet. "In exchange for gifts of prestigious and luxurious objects – ivory, jewellery, metal bowls – the Phoenicians were granted a sort of right of transit to the territories that were richest in silver and agricultural produce."[21] The Gadir workshops nourished local goldsmiths so that, as time went by, it became hard for archaeologists finding such artefacts in Tartessian burials to determine whether they were truly from the hand of a Phoenician goldsmith or an 'orientalised' Tartessian craftsman.

Gold treasures in Spain

Three famous gold treasures, those of La Aliseda, El Carambolo and Ebora, have been found in Spain, all dating from the 7th century BC. The primary influence was Phoenician, but distinct Punic touches from Carthage are evident on some pieces, as are those of the Etruscans and even, on occasion, of Greek goldsmiths. Tartessian goldsmiths added their own ideas. "In local designs … the jewellery has a decorative exuberance, which is well supported by the precocious virtuosity of the workmanship," decided Giovanna Pisano.[22]

The first of these treasures was located at El Aliseda, near Caceres, just south of the river Tagus (a major source of alluvial gold) in central Spain. The collection comprised the whole repertoire of rings, bracelets, necklaces of gold beads, amulet cases, a diadem and a belt, all of diverse provenance. The most spectacular was a belt, 68.5cm long and 6.6cm wide, made up of 62 gold plaques, beautifully granulated and embossed with motifs of a man fighting a lion, a griffin and palm fronds. The basic design was Phoenician, but a Spanish archaeologist detected Etruscan influences 'creeping in'. A splendid pair of earrings with a circle of open-work lotus flowers flanked by hawks, alternating with palm fronds, were completely covered with delicate granulation, at which the Etruscans excelled.[23]

The El Carambolo treasure found near Seville, in the heart of the gold and silver mine area, embraced twenty-one pieces, all gold. What strikes you when you confront the treasure, spotlit against a black background in Madrid's Museo Arqueológico Nacional, is how robust and heavy most of the ornaments are, with a singular lack of figurative designs. Two studded bracelets that might have been worn by a warrior, and two hefty pectorals are set out alongside eight gold plaques.

The only delicate ornament is a necklace made of double chain ending with a loop catching eight small chains carrying seven rings or seals decorated in filigree. El Tresore de Ebora, found near Cadiz and now in Seville's Museo Arqueológico, is more modest, but its star attraction is a diadem of almost one hundred small gold plaques, each elegantly patterned with granulation exhibiting local themes.

These treasures demonstrate just how internationalised gold jewellery design had become around the Mediterranean by 600 BC. But that was the Phoenicians' legacy. They travelled to, traded with and commanded much of the Mediterranean world for most of the 1st millennium BC. They cramped the westward expansion of the Greeks and finally succumbed to the Romans in 146 BC, only after three bitter Punic wars (during one of which Hannibal from Carthage marched right to Rome). In so doing they formed a bridge between the very ancient world of Mesopotamia and Egypt and the sophisticated new societies of Greece and Rome.

CHAPTER 7

The Etruscans:
Virtuoso Goldsmiths

The testimonials are legion. "The masterpieces of Etruscan goldsmiths' work remain unmatched and unmatchable even today," declared the Sorbonne's Raymond Bloch.[1]   Guido Gregorietti, director of the Museo Poldi-Pezzoli in Milan, wrote, "Etruscan work maintained a happy equilibrium … producing ornaments whose significance as works of art was as great as their decorative value".[2]   The catalogue of the major Etruscan exhibition at the Palazzo Grassi in Venice in 2001 spoke of "an authentic explosion of jewellery production especially in the first half of the 7th century BC, one that reached unequalled levels of excellence".[3] Graham Hughes, in The Art of Jewellery, summed it up, "Etruscan jewels showed the most extraordinary virtuoso technique".[4]

These goldsmiths thrived in the brilliant, if short-lived, civilisation of Etruria, which was in its prime from around 700 to 500 BC. Etruria, whose heartland was modern Tuscany, was no more than a loose league of a dozen or so city-states, including Populonia, Vetulonia, Vulci, Tarquinii and Caere (Cerveteri) close to the Tyrrhenian Sea and Arretium (Arezzo), Curtun (Cortona) and Perusia (Perugia) inland. Its influence also spread north to Felsina (Bologna) and south for a while to Rome and Praeneste (Palestrina). The Etruscans were an artistic, energetic, pleasure-loving society. Yet they left no written history and a language which is not fully decipherable from the limited inscriptions that survive, most of which were short. Instead, they are remembered by the colourful frescoes, the terracotta sculptures and the gold jewellery buried in countless tombs (miraculously not all robbed) scattered among the orchards, vineyards and cypresses of the Tuscan landscape. "Their life," Raymond Bloch added, "is in the immense pictorial documentation of the tombs."

What a life it was. "Death, to the Etruscan, was a pleasant continuance of life, with jewels and wine and flutes playing for the dance," wrote D. H. Lawrence after a pilgrimage through candle-lit tombs.[5]   In the Tomb of the Feast at Tarquinii he gazed at a fresco in which "the band of dancing figures that go round the room still is bright in colour, fresh, the women in their spotted dresses of linen muslin and coloured mantles with fine borders … wildly and delightedly dances the next woman, every bit of her, in her soft boots, and her bordered mantle, with jewels on her arms". Throughout his tour he remarked on the equal place of women beside men. Viewing a banqueting scene in the Tomb of the Leopard, he reported, "They lie in pairs, man and woman, reclining equally on the couch, curiously friendly".[6] More sedately, Dennis George, an earlier chronicler of the tombs for more than four decades in the 19th century, put it, "The Etruscans were the great civilisers of Italy".

Despite such plaudits, the origins of these stimulating people remain a mystery. Herodotus, in his Histories, proposed that they came from Lydia in western Anatolia where, after a long famine, the population was divided into two, half sailing along the Mediterranean and ending up on the western coasts of Italy. The Etruscans certainly exhibited strong eastern influence in their customs and religion and much of their jewellery was 'orientalised'. Today, historians and archaeologists propose that they did not arrive from any single migration, but rather from the constant roaming of small groups of people by land and sea. Etruria was something of a melting pot of people from the north of Italy and beyond the Alps, from southern Italy, and from Greece. Above all, the Etruscans had a rare affinity with the Phoenicians and, particularly, those who colonised Carthage and Sardinia just across the Tyrrhenian Sea. The sudden surge of growth in Etruria came less than a hundred years after the foundation of Carthage by the Phoenicians, who then pressed on with their expansion of the international metal trade to southern Spain and Thassos in Sardinia.

In that orbit, the Etruscans had much to offer. While the interior of Tuscany had thriving agriculture, the shore region known as Campigliese Marittima, the island of Elba just offshore and Mount Tolfa, further south between Tarquinii and Caere, had rich deposits of copper, tin, lead, silver and, most important in the new Iron Age, iron ore.

Etruria's metals were just what the Phoenicians' network needed. "The extraction and exploitation of the country's metallurgical wealth was, to an overwhelming extent, the determining factor not only in its urbanisation, but the whole process of its development, and the cause of its rapid rise to prosperity," wrote the historian Michael Grant.[7] The link was confirmed by the establishment of a Phoenician trading post, Punicum (i.e. Carthage), strategically placed between the mining community of Caere, which was close to copper and lead mines at Mount Tolfa, and Vetulonia, which smelted the iron ore from mines on the mainland and offshore in Elba. The impression is almost of an industrial revolution on the coast of Tuscany in the 7th century BC. Forests were cut down to provide charcoal for the furnaces, whose glow lit the night sky. Small villages merged into well-laid-out towns with a growing industrial and merchant aristocracy. A network of roads built to carry heavy traffic was built, with cuts and tunnels dug out to ease the way – an excellent example for the Romans to follow later.

Plugging in to the Phoenicians' metals network, stretching from the Levant, Egypt and Mesopotamia to North Africa and Spain, turned a cottage industry into a prosperous urban society, and made Etruria a naval and trading power. Metals and metalware (especially in high quality bronze) were exported, luxuries, including gold which was the only metal the Etruscans lacked at home, were imported. The archaeological evidence suggests that gold jewellery was also imported from Phoenicia and Greece, and their style adapted to Etruscan tastes, either by local or migrant goldsmiths. The 'orientalising' of Etruscan jewellery, as archaeologists like to call it, produced more imaginative and delicate ornaments than had been made in the so-called Villanovan period prior to 700 BC. Artistically and technically, Etruscan jewellery was in a class of its own over the following century. The most characteristic ornament was the fibula, an ornate clasp or brooch worn by men and women, wonderfully powdered with granulated designs of which over thirty have survived.[8]

The gold had to be imported. The original sources of gold for both the Etruscans and earlier Villanovan goldsmiths were relatively close to home (the Phoenicians' gold supply came later). Alluvial gold could be panned in limited quantities in the river Po in northern Italy, but the main resources were just over the Alps in what are now Switzerland and Austria. The Celts, who then controlled a territory from Burgundy in France to Austria, recovered gold for their own distinctive ornaments and exchanged it with the Etruscans for wine, bronze drinking vessels and pottery. This gold connection has been investigated by the French metallurgist Christiane Eluère of the Musée des Antiquités Nationales, who compared analytical data of Celtic and Etruscan jewellery of the 7th century BC. The fine gold content of both bore remarkable similarity; gold content was around 690 fine, silver at 280 fine, with traces of copper at 30 fine. "The available information seems to indicate," she concluded, "that the gold used in the 7th century BC on both sides of the Alps was often rich in silver … the possibility remains that the distribution, or redistribution, centres for gold might have been the same for both sides of the Alps."[9] There is also later evidence of the Etruscan skills with granulation and filigree being adapted by the Celts, suggesting long-term interchange.

However, by the 6th century BC, Etruscan gold jewellery had a much higher gold content, up to 930 to 970 fine, with only traces of silver and no copper. This could be due to improved refining (the parting of gold and silver had been pioneered in Lydia), or because the Etruscans were receiving, through the Phoenicians, African gold, which contained little silver.

Their colony of Carthage, increasingly a powerful city-state in its own right (*see chapter 6*), controlled both the gold coming on caravan routes across the Sahara from West Africa, and was scouting direct supplies with expeditions down the Atlantic coast of Africa. The gold may have come direct from Carthage or, more likely, via the Phoenician trading post of Thassos on Sardinia, which was becoming an important jewellery-making centre in its own right. Indeed, the goldsmiths on Thassos were influenced by Etruscan styles, and Etruscan jewellery was exported through the Phoenicians' network around the Mediterranean. Some jewellery that has been found in Spain was either of Etruscan origin or made by local goldsmiths copying Etruscan techniques.

Tangible evidence of a close alliance between Etruscans and Phoenicians in the gold trade turned up in three inscribed gold plaques discovered in a sanctuary near the Etruscan port of Pyrgi in 1964. The short text on two of the plaques is in Etruscan, on the third in Phoenician. They commemorate the dedication by a local Etruscan ruler around 500 BC of a temple to the goddess Uni of Etruria or Astarte in Carthage. The bilingual inscriptions on the gold Pyrgi plaques "confirm the coexistence of Phoenicians and Etruscans on the Tyrrhenian Sea and Sardinia," argued the archaeologist Sabatino Moscati.[10]

The driving force for Etruscan jewellery was the swift accumulation of wealth on the back of metal trading, which led to a show of opulence and power. This was manifested not just in jewellery, but in the grandeur of carriages for parades, weapons, sceptres, fans, inlaid furnishings, sumptuous tableware, delicacies and fine wines. The prosperity lured craftsmen in metal, glass, ivory, wood, semi-precious stones, amber and gold from abroad, who brought the latest techniques, adapting them to Etruscan tastes. The high esteem in which women were held, whether wives with long black braids or the blonde courtesans often features in tomb paintings, assured that most of the ornaments were for them. They were laden with brooches, hair-rings, earrings, necklaces and bracelets. There was "an insistent search for decorative effects through the use of granulation, filigree, sequences of small buttons, terminals with plaques of human, leonine or serpentine heads … female figures with sceptres or fans, real or fantastic animals in heraldic patterns … crescent moons, palmettes, lotus flowers, loop-in-loop chains," noted the catalogue of the Etruscan exhibition at Palazzo Grassi, Venice, in 2001.[11] Men, by contrast, had to make do with fancy brooches and buckles, though these, too, had exquisite granulation.

The lavishness of the jewellery was revealed in 1836 when a priest, Alessandro Regoline, and a general, Vicenzo Galassi, opened a tomb near Caere and found within the skeleton of a woman named Larthia, either a princess or a priestess. She wore a robe heavily embroidered with gold, held together by an elaborate gold disc fibula (brooch). The disc showed five lions on a three-quarter moon-shaped field bordered by two fringes of palmettes and was hinged by two gold cross bars to a gold plate decorated with seven rows of upstanding tiny ducks – fifty in all. "Everywhere the wonderful *repoussé* work is enriched with long rows of finest granulation, the infinitesimal golden balls of which are barely recognisable to the naked eye," recorded the archaeologist Werner Keller. "They outline the animals and plants and are attached with such skill they seem barely to touch each other or the background."[12]

Etruscan goldsmiths loved creating processions of birds and animals. The Etruscan chronicler George Dennis, who was one of the first into the Bernadini tomb at Praeneste (Palestrina) forty kilometres south-east of Rome when it was discovered in 1876, was equally astonished. He beheld in "a mere pit, sunk two yards below the surface", the body of a chieftain "in all its panoply of rich vestments and gorgeous ornaments". The most remarkable was "an oblong plate of gold, eight inches by five, studded all over with minute figures of beasts and chimeras, not in relief, but standing up bodily from the plate, and numbering not less than 131 in that limited space. There are five rows of tiny lions, arranged longitudinally, some standing with their tails curved over their back, some couchant, others sitting on their haunches, two rows of chimeras, and two of sirens, flanked transversely at each end of a row of exquisitely formed little horses, full of life and spirit".[13] Nearby was a two-handled cup "of pure gold, bright as if newly polished". These treasures, along with others from the Barbarini tomb at Praeneste, which housed delicately granulated pins and fibulae, are now in the Museo di Villa Giulia in Rome. Praeneste was outside the main territory of Etruria and the tombs also contained ornate Phoenician gilt and silver bowls; the gold ornamentation is all thought to have been fabricated at Caere.

The Caere workshops were the earliest and most important in Etruria, but those at Vetulonia, the capital of the main mining area, evolved their own style to please the prosperous local clientele. They perfected very fine granulation, almost gold dust, set out in sinuous elongated patterns. The solid mass of tiny granules created an opaque effect, thus silhouetting the surrounding polished surfaces. This technique was used to wonderful effect in a pendant of Achelous, the river god, in which his shining gold helmet and face are set off by the granulation of his beard and his brow. Looking at the tiny pendant, little bigger than a postage stamp and bearing a remarkable resemblance to Ernest Hemingway, at the Louvre in Paris, the almost microscopic granules are a miracle. At Caere, the granulation had normally been applied as an outline around the edges of the ornaments. In both cities, however, the great achievement was to enhance the granulation with a delicacy hitherto unknown.

The question has long been – how did they do it? "The Etruscans had no temperature control, no high precision tools, no refined metals, no metallurgical science, no accurate drills, cutters or measuring equipment, and no accurate magnifying glasses with which to survey the details of their superlative work," wrote an admiring Graham Hughes.[14] Modern metallurgists have struggled, and argued, as they tried to work it out. Half the problem is that the technique of granulation died out well before AD 1000, and was not re-discovered until the 1930s, through work at the British Museum and in Munich and Cologne. The initial step in granulation is relatively easy, as Dr Nigel Meeks of the British Museum explained as we admired a magnificent fibula with a long 'catch plate' decorated with lions' heads, sphinxes and horses' heads. "The granules are made from little bits of wire snipped up and put on a matrix of charcoal and heated; when they melt they coalesce naturally into balls," Dr Meeks said. "You then paint on the design with animal sinew glue, and put the balls on like decorating a cake. Such fine, intricate work needed fantastic eyesight – it's stunning when you think of it." The hard technical part, however, was to solder or bond those microscopic granules to the surface of the plate. And that was where the argument came in.

A lively debate took place in the pages of the American Journal of Archaeology for a decade between Italian and American metallurgists over the merits of three techniques, each hailed as the ancient one.[15]   The first proposed that a wafer-thin foil of gold, silver and copper welding alloy was used to bind granules to the base gold sheet. The second, strongly favoured in Italian circles, was a finely powdered copper-salt with added carbon which was imposed between the two surfaces and heated to reduce the salt to metallic copper which bonded with the gold. The third magic formula, from Diane Lee Carroll of the California Academy of Sciences, was 'sintering' in which adjacent surfaces can be bonded without any intermediary solders, by heating them to a high temperature, but just below their actual melting temperature. She pointed out, "7th century BC Etruscan goldsmiths often selected grains so small as to resemble powder when seen with the unaided eye – seventy or more such grains to form a line one centimetre long". And she argued that with such tiny specks of gold dust, the application of a solder became virtually impossible without the surface to which they were being applied becoming flooded. The Italians countered by saying the Etruscans lacked the sensitive temperature control required by sintering. Diane Carroll replied, "Those experienced in modern sintering might despair at the prospect … but it nonetheless can be done with an experienced eye and the patience to go through an experimental period".

That 'experienced eye' may be the key. Both Caere and Vetulonia were metal-working communities schooled in handling the complete range of processes for a variety of metals from first smelting to finished products. Their bronze articles, combining copper and tin, had a high reputation in export markets. Inevitably, craftsmen there grew up judging temperatures and melting points with 'an experienced eye'. Their patience and perseverance also puts the modern jeweller to shame, Graham Hughes remarked.[16]   So 'sintering' to fix granules of gold in their intricate patterns could have been a practical proposition. The conclusion of this metallurgical debate was that all three techniques were employed in different Etruscan cities at different times, but that, probably, sintering proved the most practical for the tiniest granules. What no one challenges is that Etruscan granulation cannot be bettered. "Granulation … was carried to greater heights of technical excellence than by any other people at any other period," concluded the jewellery historian Reynold Higgins.[17]

Surprisingly, the granulation vogue was relatively short-lived, being almost over by 625 BC. This had led to speculation that perhaps a single workshop or family of goldsmiths in Vetulonia was responsible for the finest 'gold dust' granulation. After all, there have been 'virtuoso goldsmiths' throughout history and why not in Etruria in the 7th century BC? Thereafter, Etruscan jewellery, while retaining its own character, left fewer splendid pieces. Granulation gave way to the simpler, but still subtle, filigree, weaving a web of wires on new-style earrings known as bauletto, because they were shaped like a small bag. Similar gold wire, incidentally, was employed by the Etruscans for pioneering dental work. They used gold wires to hold in place substitute teeth, usually from a cow or calf, when their own fell or were knocked out.[18]

Meanwhile, Greek, rather than Phoenician, influence on jewellery fashion became strong. The Greeks already had their own colonies on the island of Pithecusae (Ischia) in the Bay of Naples and at Cumae across on the mainland. Both were centres of Greek crafts and culture, with their own jewellery workshops. They became a force to be reckoned with. The squeeze was harder because Greek outposts in southern France, notably Marseille, were expanding their presence in the Tyrrhenian sea. The Etruscans, in alliance with the Phoenicians, defeated the Greeks at Alalia off Corsica in 535 BC, but were slowly undermined. The Etruscans' ad hoc league of city-states, despite its excellent road network and well-planned cities, never became a real political and military union. That left them vulnerable. Before long, the individual cities were being picked off one by one. An alliance of Greeks with local Latin tribes forced the Etruscans out of Rome by 500 BC and, in 474 BC, Greek ships defeated them decisively off Cumae in the Bay of Naples. Celts from north of the Alps were also advancing. Before long, Raymond Bloch observed, "Etruscan power was only a memory".[19] The last Etruscan stronghold, Volsinii, was mopped up by an increasingly powerful Rome in 260 BC.

An obituary of the Etruscans might conclude that, in a dangerous age, their zest for life was a fatal flaw. While the Phoenicians, the Greeks and, shortly, the Romans displayed immense discipline and determination in creating empires, the Etruscans bartered their metals for luxuries and the good life. Their legacy was tomb paintings of banquets, dancing, music-making, hunting and fishing, along with terracotta sculptures of men and women at the banquet table, adorned with golden ornaments. Fernand Braudel saw the Etruscans as "the original creators of Italy".

Aftermath

There is a reminder of the Etruscans' supremacy in modern Arezzo which, as Arretium of the Etruscan league, specialised in bronze miniatures. Arezzo is the capital of the modern Italian jewellery industry, which enjoys a world-wide reputation, if for a slightly different gold product – machine-made chain. On the outskirts of the town at the factory of Uno a Erre, hundreds of chain machines unceasingly 'knit' gold wire into miles of chain, the little automatic pincer heads turning and twisting the gold that glistens under a coating of oil as the new chain spindles down into the plastic buckets beneath each machine. The chain machines, really a glorified version of the sewing machine, were the creation of Antonio Zucchi, a superb technician, working with Vittorio Gori, a wizard marketing man, to bring mass chain production to the Italian industry. A whole generation of Italian chain-makers started their careers in Gori and Zucchi's factory, observed how the machines worked, then set up on their own. Often they started with a couple of home-made chain machines chuntering away in their kitchen or garage before establishing their own emporiums.[20]   Watching the chain machines chattering away, gobbling up the gold wire, you realise that, once again, an initiative in Tuscany 2,500 years after the Etruscans, has brought a new dimension to the world of gold.

CHAPTER 8

Lydia/Persia:
The coins of Croesus;
The Persians' Challenge

The name Croesus is synonymous with wealth and with the launching of the first true gold and silver coins. Yet his short reign as king of the western Anatolian state of Lydia from 561–547 BC is even more of a landmark in the history of gold. Those coins were minted only as a result of one of the crucial technical breakthroughs for the metal – the 'parting' of gold and silver through refining the natural alluvial alloy with nothing more sophisticated than common salt. Thus both metals could be produced to a guaranteed high purity, the pre-requisite for widely accepted coinage.

Beyond the economic significance of the introduction of coinage, Croesus played an accidental, even foolish, role in initiating over two centuries of conflict between the nascent Persian Empire to his east, and expanding Greek domains to his west. The Persian armies of Cyrus the Great (550–530 BC) marched on his capital, Sardis, one of the great cities of the ancient world, not least because of the gold in the river Pactolus which flowed through its market-place. With their empire extended to the shores of the Aegean, they harried the Greek city-states for generations. The Persian wars ended only after Alexander the Great (336–323 BC) took Sardis en route to demolishing the empire of Darius III (336–331 BC) that ranged from the Aegean to Afghanistan. In all these campaigns, gold coins, often minted in Sardis, paid for mercenaries and diplomatic intrigue.

Initially, Lydia itself evolved through local power struggles across the whole of Anatolia (Turkey) between 900 and 700 BC, as three regional factions, Urartu, Phrygia and Lydia, fought each other and marauding bands of Cimmerian and Scythian nomadic horsemen sweeping down from the Black Sea shores. The Greeks, meanwhile, were consolidating city-states on the western shores of Anatolia at Phocaea, Smyrna (modern Izmir), Ephesus and Miletus. Immediately inland from them was the burgeoning kingdom of Lydia; Sardis was just eighty kilometres due east of Smyrna. And it was in Sardis, around 685 BC, that the king, Candaules, was deposed by a courtier, Gyges, who founded, according to Herodotus, a new dynasty of Lydian rulers. The Histories of Herodotus (c. 490–420 BC) are the guide to the fortunes of Lydia and of the 1st century or more of the ensuing Persian wars. Herodotus, being Greek, naturally presented the story from that point of view, so that the picture he recorded of Lydia was of a powerful, wealthy and menacing state.[1]

He enjoyed telling how Gyges won the throne, because Candalus was so proud of the beauty of his wife, that he invited Gyges, his bodyguard, to view her secretly naked as she prepared for the royal bed. The queen, however, spied Gyges and threatened to denounce him unless he killed the king and married her. Gyges obliged. The deed done, the queen wed, Gyges' next act was to dispatch to the temple of Apollo at Delphi an array of golden vessels, including six gold mixing bowls. The bowls alone, according to Herodotus, weighed over 1,000 kg/32,150 t.oz – a weight that is open to question.[2] Clearly the Lydian already possessed gold, although this may have come as much from plundering their neighbours, notably the Phrygians, whose king Midas also enjoyed the reputation of a golden touch, as from local alluvial sources. The contemporary Greek poet Archilochus referred to "the wealth of Gyges rich in gold". And the new king understood its diplomatic potency to win friends or favourable omens from the Delphic oracle.

Gyges and his successors were initially preoccupied with establishing Lydia as the foremost power in Anatolia by bringing the Greek cities along the Aegean coast under their domination and consolidating their eastern borders against the Medes, whose empire extended through northern Mesopotamia and western Persia. The most successful Lydian king, Alyattes (c. 610–561 BC), captured Smyrna, giving Lydia access to the Aegean sea, before waging a six-year war against the Medes. This conflict was brought to an abrupt halt in 585 BC after a famous battle during which a solar eclipse suddenly turned day into night. Both sides interpreted this as a bad omen and a peace line was established along the Halys river, which circles through eastern Anatolia to the Black Sea. Thereafter, Lydians and Medes each enjoyed their own sphere of influence on either side. Lydia prospered and Alyattes is credited with introducing the first electrum coins, from a gold-silver alloy, around 575 BC. The face of the coins bore the image of a lion, a symbol of royalty. In some later versions the name Alyattes was inscribed between two facing lions. Thus Croesus inherited, around 560 BC, both a secure and wealthy state. "It was Croesus, Alyattes' successor, who reaped the rewards of his predecessors' wars," wrote the historian Amelia Kuhrt.[3]

Sardis itself had become a thriving city, with tiled houses adorned with terracotta friezes, an Acropolis at its heart, and the gold-rich Pactolus river flowing through its midst. The city had become the crossroads of Anatolian commerce and a magnet for craftsmen and curious Greek businessmen and philosophers intrigued by its riches. To cap this, there was a genuine gold-rush between 560–550 BC, as substantial fresh deposits of alluvial gold were located in the easily worked sand and gravel of the Pactolus river and other local streams. For a few years they provided Lydia with exceptional wealth.

The Sardis expeditions

Our knowledge of the Pactolus gold and its refining and coining at Sardis has been broadened by the long-running series of Harvard-Cornell Sardis Expeditions, which began in 1958 and are still going strong. Their work on gold has been enhanced by collaboration with the Department of Scientific Research at the British Museum, notably after the discovery in 1968 of the first gold refinery from the ancient world. The resulting book, King Croesus' Gold by Cornell's Andrew Ramage and The British Museum's Dr Paul Craddock, provides an indispensable guide to the technical breakthrough of separating and purifying gold and silver, without which distinct gold and silver coinage could not have been introduced.[4]

The origin of the gold was in the towering massif of Mount Tmolus, just south of Sardis, which still hosts metamorphic rocks with intrusive gold-bearing quartz veins. From this range many small streams dropped precipitously to the flat floor of the valley below. They fed the Pactolus, today a lazy stream fringed by tall poplars, that flowed right through Sardis. Beyond Sardis the Pactolus joined the larger Hermus river, but most of the gold was deposited in the Pactolus between Mount Tmolus and Sardis. "All the gold scoured out of the oxidised ore in the mountains would have been precipitated into the river bed century after century, building up a huge alluvial deposit," explained the mining analyst Robert Weinberg after a visit to Sardis in 2004. "That was what Croesus 'mined' – it would have been an open-pit operation." The gold rush, like many throughout history, did not last long. The Harvard-Cornell team have suggested that "discovery and exploitation took place over a relatively short period".

Such exceptional riches gave Croesus' rule its lasting fame. Gold was recovered in quantities exceeding anything seen before. The parallel, already mentioned in earlier chapters, is the modern experience of local alluvial gold rushes in Brazil, Indonesia and the Philippines in the 1980s, which produced literally tonnes of gold for a few years. The best indication of output at Sardis, according to the Harvard-Cornell investigators, is that the one small gold refinery they found could have processed "several hundred kilograms of gold a year".[5] This was no grand industrial complex. The workshop was in a domestic area. "The fittings and equipment give the impression of domestic items pressed into service for special requirements," decided Andrew Ramage and Paul Craddock. "Thus the furnaces give the appearance of domestic ovens and the vessels for the parting process are derived from domestic jugs." Such a humble place could have been one of several in Sardis, each treating a few hundred kg annually. A total output of 1,000 to 2,000 kg/32,150–64,300 t.oz a year is entirely possible. That level of production might have been sustained for five to ten years.

The abundance was illustrated by a famous story in Herodotus about Alcmaeon, who had helped Croesus in his consultations with the oracle at Delphi. When Alcmaeon visited Sardis, Croesus offered him as a reward as much gold as he could carry on his person. "Alcmaeon thought of a fine way of taking advantage of this offer," Herodotus related. "He put on a large tunic, very loose and baggy in front, and a pair of the widest top-boots … and thus clad, entered the treasury. Here he attacked a heap of gold dust; he crammed into his boots, all up his legs, as much as they would hold, filled the baggy front of his tunic full, sprinkled the dust all over his hair, stuffed some more into his mouth, and then staggered out." Croesus, highly amused, not only allowed him to keep the gold, but gave him more. And Alcmaeon, once back in Athens, "was able to keep race-horses, with which he won the chariot race at Olympia".[6] Judging by the standards of modern gold smugglers, who used to board aircraft (before the days of high security) with up to thirty kg of gold in concealed jackets, Alcmaeon took quite a haul.

'Parting gold and silver'

The anecdote of Alcmaeon filling up with gold dust, not nuggets, is matched by the Harvard-Cornell team's conclusion that what was recovered from the river Pactolus was fine alluvial dust, which initially was stored in the King's treasury. Any refining necessary for coinage came later. The gold coming down from Mount Tmolus contained 17–30% silver, plus copper and traces of other metals. Traditionally, the base metals were removed by cupellation, leaving a gold-silver alloy. This sufficed for ornaments or the great bowls the Lydian kings sent to the oracle at Delphi, but not for consistent high purity gold and silver coins. As the Sardis investigators observed, "Without the requirement of gold of guaranteed purity for the specific needs of coinage, there was no incentive to refine gold."[7]

An intriguing question remains. Was the technique of parting gold and silver developed by accident or design? Did Croesus demand distinct gold and silver coins, instead of electrum, and his goldsmiths came up with the technology? Certainly Croesus was anxious to exploit the gold of the Pactolus to underpin his expansionist policies. "Croesus had a craving to extend his territories," Herodotus noted.[8] In that pursuit, coin was useful to pay mercenaries and the better the quality the more welcome it was. Local warlords in Anatolia were increasingly stamping their own personal electrum 'badges' to reward retainers and mercenaries.[9] Croesus may have wanted his coins to stand out as superior. In short, the incentive existed. Moreover, the basic technique of using sodium chloride (common salt) to enhance the surface colour of gold by removing the whitish tinge of silver had been used in Mesopotamia almost two thousand years earlier (*see chapter 1*). Experimenting with the reaction of gold-silver alloys to salt under heat and pressure undoubtedly led to the 'cementation' process that separated the two metals.

The refinery excavated at Sardis in 1968 unveiled the procedure frozen in time. The gold dust was placed in an earthenware container, usually a rather coarse cooking pot, and was surrounded by the 'cement' of salt. After the lid of the pot was sealed with clay, it was heated for many hours, even several days, at a temperature just below the melting point of unrefined gold. The vapours of the salt under heat and pressure attacked the gold-silver alloy. "Vapours of chloride ions and chlorine

**Minoan Crete, 1700-1500 BC;
golden bee pendant; two bees,
wings raised, hold a honeycomb
dappled with granulated gold**
Heraklion Museum, Crete

**Minoan Crete, 1700-1500 BC;
Aigina treasure, Master of Animals,
standing amid lotus flowers, holds a
goose in each hand**
© *The Trustees of the British Museum.
All rights reserved*

**Minoan Crete, 1700-1500 BC;
'ladies in blue' from the Palace
of Knossos have gold filigree
in their hair and wear gold
necklaces and bracelets**
Heraklion Museum, Crete

**Mycenæ 1600-1500 BC;
gold death mask found by
Schliemann, erroneously called
Mask of Agamemnon**
National Museum of Athens

**Mycenæ c.1200 BC;
gold kylix with hunting scene**
Benaki Museum, Athens

Etruscan c.525-500 BC; gold brooch with a bow in the form of a winged chimaera

© *The Trustees of the British Museum. All rights reserved*

Etruscan c.480 BC; pendant, with granulation, of the head of the river god Acheloos
Musée du Louvre, Photo RMN / © Gérard Blot / Christian Jean

 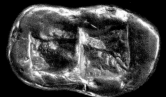

Lydia (Turkey) c.550 BC;
gold croesid coin issued by King
Croesus, weight 8.003g
© The Trustees of the British
Museum. All rights reserved

Oxus treasure; griffin-headed armlet which was a gift of honour at the Persian Court
© The Trustees of the British Museum. All rights reserved

Oxus treasure; Achaemenid Persian c.400 BC; embossed gold plaque of a Mede involved in religious ritual, weight 75.5g
© The Trustees of the British Museum. All rights reserved

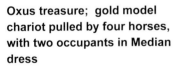

Oxus treasure; gold model chariot pulled by four horses, with two occupants in Median dress
© The Trustees of the British Museum. All rights reserved

Macedonia, Royal Tombs,
Vergina, 336 BC; gold burial
casket of Philip of Macedon,
discovered in AD 1977
*© Archaeological Receipts Fund,
Athens*

Macedonia, Royal Tombs, Vergina,
350-340 BC; gold quiver of Philip
of Macedon, probably made by
Scythian goldsmith
*© Archaeological Receipts Fund,
Athens*

Scythian, Issyk Kurgon, c.400 BC; the 'golden man', found near Alma-Ata in Kazakhstan, with coat of 2,400 tiny gold plates
Museum of Archaeology of Kazakhstan, Alma-Ata

Scythian, c.500 BC; recumbent stag with swept back antlers, a symbol of the wildlife of the Steppes
© State Hermitage Museum, St Petersburg

**Scythian, c.400 BC, Solokha Barrow, Ukraine; gold comb, cast and chased, of
Scythians in battle, weight 294g/9.5 t.oz**
© *State Hermitage Museum, St Petersburg*

at elevated temperatures attacked the surfaces of the impure metal, penetrating deeply into the interior of the metal along the grain boundaries," noted the British Museum's Dr Paul Craddock. "The silver was converted into silver chloride, which is also volatile, and was absorbed by the walls of the parting vessel and furnace." This left almost pure gold, while the silver could be recovered by smelting the pots and furnace lining with lead to absorb the silver salts, followed by cupellation to release the pure silver.[10] The gold itself was simply washed and melted. This method, pioneered at Sardis, remained the basic technique for separating gold and silver for the next two thousand years. "We believe the Sardis refinery is likely to be among the earliest, if not the very first, refinery in the world," Andrew Ramage and Paul Craddock concluded.[11]

Opening the way to a monetary economy through the progression from electrum to gold and silver coins made sense. As Herodotus remarked, "The Lydians were the first people we know of to use a gold and silver coinage and to introduce a retail trade".[12] While Aristotle, two centuries later, observed that the adoption of stamped coins was simply one of convenience to save weighing lumps of metal for every transaction.[13]

A bi-metallic coinage

The original electrum coins, issued by Alyattes around 575 BC, had been mere 'blobs' of metal on which the figure of a lion – a symbol of royalty – was stamped on the face. Another version had Alyattes' name inscribed between two lions.[14] The reverse of the 'blobs' had simple punch marks. Later, more sophisticated coin 'blanks' were cast in shallow circular pits. The early coins had a surprisingly high silver content. The Harvard-Cornell archaeologists have suggested that they were made from natural alluvial gold to which silver may have been added, since the normal silver content of gold dust from the river Pactolus varied between 170 and 300 fine. Analysis of nine early coins, now in the Ashmolean Museum at Oxford, showed a range of 500–600 fine gold, 380–480 fine silver with traces of copper. The basic unit was the stater of 13.93 grams/0.45 t.oz, with smaller coins of one-third stater at 4.44–4.74 grams, one-sixth stater at 2.36–2.38 grams and a tiny one-twelfth stater at 1.17 grams. A study of eight other electrum coins in the British Museum revealed similar gold and silver content, but a one stater coin weighed 14.24 grams/0.46 t.oz. Otherwise weights were remarkably consistent.[15]

Once the separation of metals had been achieved under Croesus, the high purity stood out. Analysis of gold coins in the British Museum collection shows uniform 990 fine gold, with under 10 fine silver, and traces of copper, lead and iron; this is higher purity than the modern *sovereign* or *krugerrand*. Among eight Lydian silver coins at the British Museum, six are 990 fine, one is 970 fine, and one virtually 1000 fine.[16] The cementation process for separating gold and silver produced consistent purity worked to perfection. However, with the introduction of the bi-metallic coinage the basic unit, the gold stater, was reduced, initially to 10.2

grams/0.33 t.oz and later to 8.2 grams/0.26 t.oz (almost the same weight as the *sovereign*).[17]

These early coins from Lydia are known as croeseids, because they are assumed to have been minted under Croesus around 550 BC. The gold coins are the only ones thought to have been produced anywhere during the 6th century BC, but it is possible that they continued to be made in Sardis after Croesus' death when the city was under the Persians. These coins did not bear Croesus' name or head, but several variations of the royal lion symbol, with a lion confronting a bull in one series. The idea of coinage spread to the neighbouring Greek city-states on the shores of the Aegean: Miletus, Ephesus and Phocaea all opened mints, but produced only electrum coinage. Lydian gold coins remained unique.

The concept of a 'mint' must be treated with caution. As Charles Seltman pointed out in his standard book on Greek coins, a mint "would normally be nothing better than a small hut of sun-dried brick or a wooden shanty, containing in one corner a little clay-built furnace fed with charcoal", an observation that foreshadowed the 'refinery' found by the Harvard-Cornell archaeologists a few years later. Seltman also spelled out that "the tools required were of the simplest; a balance for weighing the metal 'blanks' …. a graver and a little punch, both employed for engraving dies …. tongs …. for placing the 'blank' upon the anvil in which was sunk the lower or anvil die". A heated blank was then positioned on the anvil and a punch, with the upper die engraved on it. This punch was struck with a hammer, implanting a design on each side, thus 'minting' the coin.[18]

The Persians' challenge

The gold and silver coinage that underpinned Lydia's prosperity fuelled Croesus' imperial ambitions. The truce with the Medes that had been established along the Halys river after the solar eclipse battle in 585 BC collapsed. In 550 BC the Median king Astyages was deposed by his grandson Cyrus, head of the ruling house of Persia in south-western Iran. Thus Cyrus the Great founded the Achaemenid dynasty that ruled the Medes and Persians for over two hundred years. This regime change established the Persian Empire from the Halys river to the Oxus river in Afghanistan. "This gave Croesus food for thought," wrote Herodotus. "He wondered if he might be able to check Persian expansion before it had gone too far." Accordingly, he began sounding out oracles on whether to attack the new Persia. Above all, he sent the oracle at Delphi a magnificent gift. "He melted down an enormous quantity of gold," Herodotus continued, "into one hundred and seventeen ingots about eighteen inches long, nine inches wide and three inches thick; four of the ingots were of refined gold weighing approximately a hundred and forty-two pounds each; the rest were alloyed and weighed about a hundred and fourteen pounds. He also caused the image of a lion to be made of refined gold, in weight some five hundred and seventy pounds". For good measure, he sent along huge gold bowls, one apparently weighing nearly 250 kg/8,037 t.oz.[19]

These weights are open to debate, and some early translators of Herodotus in the 19th century were puzzled by them. If correct, the refined ingots would have weighed nearly 65 kg/2,090 t.oz each, and the unrefined just over 50 kg/1,600 t.oz. That difference poses no problem, as the unrefined bars would contained lighter silver and base metals. Together, the 117 ingots would have weighed over six tonnes/193,000 t.oz. This would have amounted to several years' production in the region. Moreover, judged by the refinery at Sardis, which relied on domestic cooking pots, there might be some difficulty casting such heavy bars. Or at least a great many small melts would have been required to make up a single bar. By comparison the largest 'good delivery' ingot for today's gold market weighs just 12.5 kg/400 t.oz, with a volume of just under 1,000 cubic centimetres.

However, there is a rough correlation between the bars ancient and modern. The volume of the ancient bars was just over 8,000 cubic centimetres, using Herodotus' measurements (incidentally, in the original Greek text, he gave them in palms, which is 3 in/2.54 cm per palm), or about eight times that of the modern bar. The weight of the ancient refined bar would have been about six and a half times that of the modern one. This is not an exact match, but the respective volumes and weights taken together are close enough to suggest that Croesus indeed sent big bricks of gold to woo the Delphic oracle, especially when the inevitable variations of weights and measures over the intervening 2,500 years are considered.

Certainly, the ingots made the right impression. The word came back to Sardis from Delphi that not only could Croesus attack, but he would destroy "a great kingdom". Thus encouraged, Croesus became the catalyst for centuries of conflict between the Persians and the Greeks. He formed up his army, paid mercenaries in gold coin, and crossed the Halys river. Cyrus was waiting for him with a large army. "After a sharp struggle in which both sides lost heavily," reported Herodotus, "night fell and the battle was broken off without decision."[20]   Croesus decided that, with winter coming on, he would retire back to Sardis and seek fresh allies for a spring offensive four months hence. Cyrus deduced correctly that, meanwhile, Croesus would disband his forces. So he marched immediately on Sardis, took Croesus by surprise and captured the city after a fourteen-day siege. As Herodotus put it tartly, "the oracle was fulfilled; Croesus had destroyed a mighty empire – his own".[21]

Croesus and his family were consigned to a funeral pyre. As the fire was lit, Croesus sighed deeply, apparently recalling the words of the Greek philosopher, Solon, who had visited him and was not impressed by the splendour of Sardis or by a king who equated wealth with happiness. Cyrus asked why he sighed, and when Croesus told him, granted him a reprieve. But the fire had taken hold and could not be put out. Croesus prayed to Apollo and, out of a cloudless sky, a sudden thunderstorm broke, dousing the flames. Then Croesus sat with Cyrus and watched his city plundered.[22]

When Cyrus withdrew, he left his general Harpagus as satrap (governor) with orders to consolidate and take the Greek city states along the Anatolian coast. The

Persian Empire now extended from the Aegean to Afghanistan; within a few years Cyrus had added Babylon, then the Phoenician cities of the Levant, and was at the threshold of Egypt. The expansion was financed not just by the gold initially looted from Sardis, but by the ongoing production. The Persian Empire was also receiving gold from Bactria (Afghanistan) and even won a yearly tribute of several hundred kg from India, but their new province of Lydia was the prime source for several decades. Archaeologists suspect there was a concerted effort to exploit more local ore deposits. Certainly, in the reign of Darius I (522–486 BC), who completed the full sweep of the Persian Empire to the borders of India and into Egypt, the gold from Sardis was crucial. Darius' own palace at his capital Susa was adorned with Lydian gold. The link was confirmed with a 'royal road' with posting stations 2,500 km long from Susa to Sardis along which relays of horsemen could carry a message in a week.

Enter the *daric*

Darius' legacy to the history of gold coin was the *daric*, the imperial coin that circulated throughout the Persian Empire and far beyond for nearly two hundred years. The *daric* was the first truly international gold coin, a forerunner of the Roman *aureus*, the Venetian *ducat* and the British guinea and *sovereign*. The precise dating of the first *darics* is unclear, although the assumption is that they were named after Darius, whose reign began in 522 BC. But what of Persian gold coinage under Cyrus the Great, who overthrew Croesus and his successor Cambyses? There is a twenty-five-year gap between Croesus and Darius. The Persians had no previous experience of their own coinage, having used only unstamped small ingots of varying purity in exchange. Now they adopted the Lydian practice of coinage. Numismatists argue that croeseids, as the early Lydian gold and silver coins are known, continued to be minted in Sardis for the first two Persian rulers. Indeed, they were the only gold coins that can definitely be dated before 500 BC.[23]

By that time, Darius had extended his empire to Sind on the Indus river, and into Egypt and Libya and the royal road from Susa to Sardis was complete. His empire embraced twenty provinces, each with a satrap (governor), and each paying him an annual tribute. The annual tribute from India, via Sind, was set at 360 talents of gold (c. 800 kg/25,680 t.oz).[24] Darius would also have been receiving some gold from Lydia (Herodotus mentions 700 talents, but seems to mean silver) and from Bactria (Afghanistan) and, beyond the Oxus river, from Sogida (Tajikistan). Moreover, Darius was organising assaults on the Greek mainland that were checked only by the Greek victory at the Battle of Marathon in 490 BC. The moment for imperial coinage had arrived. "The European campaigns of Darius and Xerxes (his successor) are the obvious occasions to look for large issues of Persian coinage," suggested the numismatist Ian Carradice, "not for the payment of Persian troops, but for logistical and diplomatic expenses and the hire of mercenaries."[25]

The 'regal' coinage of the Persian Empire consisted of gold *darics* and silver sigloi. Both coins bore the same image of a royal archer on the face; over time five different versions of the *daric* were minted and six of the sigloi. The *daric* always depicted a running crowned and bearded figure, with a quiver on his shoulder. On the early *darics* he was drawing a bow; in later types, he was holding a spear and bow or short sword and bow.[26] The contemporary nickname for the coins was 'royal archers'. Thus, when a Greek general claimed he had been driven back from Anatolia by a later Persian ruler's "thirty thousand archers", he did not mean bowmen, as on the field of Agincourt, but by Persian coins that had been used to raise revolt against Sparta to require his return home.[27]

The gold *daric* weighed 8.35 grams/0.27 t.oz, slightly more than the gold stater of Croesus, because the Persians had adopted the Babylonian system of weight which varied marginally from the Euboean scale used in Lydia and Greece. The first silver siglois were 5.4 grams, the later ones 5.6 grams. The evidence from coin hoards found in Asia and around the Mediterranean shores is that the majority of 'royal archers' minted between 500–400 BC were silver siglois. If anything, more croeseids than *darics* have been found, indicating that the original Lydian gold coins continued in circulation for well over a century, possibly until 430 BC. Gold croeseids and *darics* that have turned up also tend to be in much better condition than their silver counterparts, not just because the gold was resistant to corrosion, but because the turnover was less. Silver circulated from hand to hand, gold coins were tucked away, so they were less worn. A key reason why so few *darics* appear before 400 BC must be that gold output was less. The alluvial output from the Pactolus river at Sardis declined soon after the Croesus era, and the Indian 'tribute' mentioned by Herodotus may be more contemporary with his own writing c. 430 BC. Without doubt after that date and into the next century after 400 BC gold became more plentiful. More gold coins were minted, not just in Persian domains, but in Greece, Carthage and around the Mediterranean.

However, one anecdote in Herodotus was intriguing. He reported that when Darius' successor, Xerxes, was marching through Anatolia on his campaign against Greece in 480 BC, he encountered a wealthy Lydian named Pythius, who said he wished to contribute to the war, and offered him 2,000 talents of silver and 3,993,000 gold *darics*. The *darics* alone would have weighed 33 m.t./1.1 million t.oz). Xerxes was so overwhelmed by this gift, that he declined it and said instead he would give Pythius 7,000 more gold *darics* to make his treasure up to a round four million.[28] There is no evidence to suggest that *darics* were minted so early in anything like this quantity; if so, they would have turned up in hoards all over Asia and beyond. This sounds like Herodotus relaying a boast over dinner in the king's tent, but is the first written testimony of the daric's existence.

A more plausible tale was told by Xenophon (c. 430–55 BC), the Greek general and writer in The Persian Expedition recounting the famous march of 10,000 men he led in support of the revolt by the pretender Cyrus against Artaxerxes II (404–359

BC) of Persia in 401 BC. Rounding up support for his cause, Cyrus gave Clearchus, a Spartan exile, ten thousand gold *darics* (83 kg/2,668 t.oz) to raise an army. This is a realistic sum, given that, later, Cyrus paid the full expeditionary force one gold *daric* each per month at the outset, but had to increase this to one and a half *darics* when the going got tougher on the march from Anatolia into Mesopotamia to cross the Euphrates river. Cyrus later added a one-off bonus of five minae of silver (c. 2.24 kg/72 t.oz) each if his men pressed on to Babylon. The invasion ended in disaster, when Cyrus was killed in battle against Artaxerxes, but Xenophon led his Greek forces safely back by a tortuous route through mountains to the Black Sea and thence to the Bosporous. The Persian Expedition was a wonderful account of military adventure, and its credibility was enhanced by Xenophon's first-hand report of the minutiae of a campaign – including the going rate in gold for mercenaries.[29]

Without question, by 400 BC, Persian imperial coinage was strongly established and circulating widely beyond its own domains. As Charles Seltman put it, perhaps a trifle too emotionally, "These, the most celebrated of ancient coins, were minted by their millions by all the Achaemenid kings for two centuries and were destined to play a part in history of the widest significance, to promote the downfall of Athens, to corrupt the morals of Sparta, to ruin greedy satraps, to finance Sicilian wars, and to serve as the 'gold bait' which lured the famous 'Ten Thousand' into the midst of the Persian Empire".[30] During the next hundred years gold coinage was to assume an even greater dimension as the Greeks, the Egyptians and the Carthaginians launched their own coins.

The Oxus Treasure

Coin underwriting military operations was not the only aspect of gold on which Xenophon reported. Passing through Tarsus in southern Anatolia on the way to Persia, he watched the pretender Cyrus woo local rulers with 'gifts of honour'. The ruler of Tarsus was presented with "a horse with a golden bit, a gold collar and armlets, a golden scimitar and a Persian robe".[31] Just such golden armlets are in the British Museum amidst the splendours of the Oxus Treasure, the most important hoard of Achaemenid gold and silver objects, which turned up in Bactria (Afghanistan), the furthermost province of the Persian Empire, over two thousand years later.

The story goes that in May 1880 Captain F. C. Burton, a British political officer in Afghanistan, rescued some merchants from bandits on the road between Kabul and Peshawar. The grateful merchants showed him a collection of gold objects they said had been found on the banks of the Oxus river (now the Amu Dayra) which forms the border between Afghanistan, Uzbekistan and Tajikistan. Captain Burton himself bought a gold bracelet from them and, soon after, the rest of the hoard was somehow acquired by the director-general of archaeology in India who, in turn, sold it privately to Sir Augustus Franks, who was a curator at the British Museum in London. Mysteriously, all the papers about the transactions disappeared and there has been much dispute about its true origin.

Provenance aside, the treasure is there in the Museum for all to see. It is composed of 180 items, almost all gold with a few handsome silver pieces, mostly dating 500–300 BC. The majority are of the Archaemenid Court Style, which was familiar throughout the Persian Empire, although a few show Greek or Central Asian influence. Along with the treasure were 1,500 gold and silver coins, ranging from royal archer' *darics* to local gold Bactrian coins minted just before 200 BC. "To what extent this treasure is a single, discrete find must always remain a matter of speculation," admitted the British Museum's John Curtis. "We can never be sure that all the pieces were found together in a single spot ... but as far as we know all the pieces now in the British Museum are authentic."[32] The thesis is that the treasure, including the coins, was gathered together, perhaps in a temple on the banks of the Oxus, over a period of two or three hundred years and was buried in some sudden emergency around 200 BC. The site may be at Tahkt-i Kuwad, on the north bank of the Oxus. This does not mean the ornaments were made there, rather that they came to the temple as gifts over the centuries (much as some Indian temples today retain great wealth in gold).

This collection is very different from those buried with rulers in Mesopotamia, Egypt, Troy or Mycenæ. For a start, there were 51 gold plaques or sheets, thought to be votive offerings to the temple, each with an engraved or *repoussé* design. They show men dressed in plain or decorated, belted tunics with long trousers and men or women with long gowns. Usually they are holding bundles of sacred rods, spears, flowers or bowls. The workmanship is not always sophisticated; it is almost as if a pilgrim at the temple could have a sheet of gold, large or small according to his means, decorated by a local goldsmith. The most famous and largest plaque, however, measuring fifteen by three centimetres, has become something of a symbol of the Persian Empire. It depicts the bold figure of a man with a soft hood over his head and down to his shoulders, a belted tunic and trousers, a short sword in his belt and a bundle of rods in his hand. Some say he was a priest, but he has the air of a ruler. This golden plaque even commands the cover of the British Museum's own book on Ancient Persia.[33]

The oldest article in the Oxus Treasure, dated c. 500 BC, is a scabbard, almost thirty centimetres long, of thin gold sheet, decorated with a vivid royal lion hunt. Men on horseback gallop at full speed, bows drawn, spears thrusting towards lions. The whole scabbard is covered with lively snapshots of leaping animals. The scene closely matches those on stone reliefs at Persepolis, the great monument to the Achaemenid kings begun by Darius I and continued by his successors. An assortment of vessels, including a gold drinking cup and a jug with a ribbed body and a handle ending in a lion's head, are wonderfully crafted. So are a hollow gold fish with a finely engraved pattern of scales and a large hollow gold head, with an imposing face and delicately etched wavy hair. The most entertaining piece is a model gold chariot, 18.8 cm long, drawn by four small horses harnessed by golden wires leading to the hands of a charioteer, beside whom a grandee, turned to the left, might be reviewing a parade of troops. The chariot rolls along on two large golden wheels, each with eight spokes and the rim studded for a better grip. At the British Museum it entrances visitors, especially children.

This is not to ignore a handsome pair of massive golden bracelets, reminiscent of those reported by Xenophon. Each has impressive terminals in the form of winged griffins, that give them a slight air of handcuffs for royalty. The treasure also comprised gold finger rings with oval bezels engraved with everything from recumbent lions and stags to a crowned woman holding flowers and a wreath, and men kneeling to play a game with knuckle bones. A necklace of cylindrical gold beads, almost one metre long, was mingled among slender gold bracelets with terminals of animals and snakes, and a quizzical lion-griffin figure of Scythian origin. All told, a slightly eccentric collection of ornaments and artefacts assembled haphazardly over centuries.

The coins presumed to have been found with the Oxus Treasure demonstrated the widening circle of gold coin minting. The collection included two 'royal archer' *darics* minted in Lydia around 500 BC, and a double gold *daric*, still of a 'royal archer' imprint, minted in Babylon c. 320 BC (although these double *darics* continued to be produced until 300 BC). This was just after Alexander's conquest; henceforward Persian gold coinage switched to the standard of the Greek stater. The stater, originally launched by Philip of Macedon (*see next chapter*), weighed 8.64 grams, slightly more than the *daric*'s traditional 8.35 grams. The Oxus collection, embracing three centuries of coinage, also included a gold double stater of Seleucius I (312–281 BC) bearing his portrait and minted in Susa c. 300 BC and gold *staters* with a youthful image of his successor Antiochus I (281–261 BC) which were minted locally in Bactria. Mints proliferated, encouraging local rulers to issue their own coinage. Thus the final coins in the Oxus assortment were of the Bactrian ruler Euthydemus I (c. 235–200 BC).

The Oxus Treasure is an important historical find in its own right, the more so because it is the only major collection of Achaemenid gold work to survive. However, another glimpse of the immense skill of Persian goldsmiths and silversmiths was revealed in the British Museum's special exhibition "Forgotten Empire: the World of Ancient Persia in 2005".[34] Among the displays were gold treasures from the National Museum of Iran in Teheran. The most dramatic was a gold dagger, thirty-six centimetres long, with ibex heads adorning the hilt at the top of the blade and lions' heads astride the pommel – a handsome, savage weapon.

The splendour of the royal dining table was demonstrated by gold and silver vessels and cups. Notably, a horn-shaped gold rhyton or drinking cup in the form of a winged lion, with a frieze of lotus and bud decorations just beneath the rim, and a golden bowl, embossed with fluted and floral decorations, with a cuneiform inscription to 'Xerxes the king' (the successor of Darius). "The wealth of the Persian court is encapsulated in these vessels," John Curtis, the exhibition's curator, pointed out. "They travelled round with the king to his palaces at Persepolis, Hamadan and

Susa. As well as being used at banquets, the bowls were also valued as bullion." That was the tragedy; many of the finest creations of Achaemenid goldsmiths later went into the melting pot to make coins in Alexander the Great's image. As the jewellery historian Graham Hughes reflected sadly, "The finest display of gold jewels of the Persian court is carved in stone on the walls of Darius' ceremonial way at Persepolis".[35]

CHAPTER 9

Athens Goes for Silver; Alexander for Gold

The turning point in the fortunes of the Persian Empire built by Cyrus the Great and Darius I came with the battles of Salamis in 480 BC and Plataiai the following year in which a loose alliance of southern Greek city-states, including Athens, defeated the Persians and threw them off mainland Greece forever. The Persians remained a brooding presence across the Aegean for another 150 years but the Greeks could get on with their own affairs (often internecine warfare). Greece had emerged from its 'dark age' between 1000 and 700 BC into a quiltwork of self-governing cities on the mainland, the islands of the Aegean and the coast of western Anatolia. As Aubrey de Sélincourt, translator of Herodotus, put it, Greece was "all islands, whether actual islands of the sea or 'islands' of the mainland".[1]

Athens was in its prime as leader of the Athenian League, a defensive, anti-Persian alliance of several cities, and the heart of the intellectual and artistic debate that inspired Classical Greece. The 5th century BC was the age of Aeschylus, Euripodes, Socrates, Aristophanes and Plato, of Perikles, who dominated politics and inspired the Parthenon, and of Pheidias, the master sculptor, who built it. Herodotus and Thucydides chronicled the events of these turbulent times. Although the Persians presented a buffer to the east, the Greeks were successful in challenging the Phoenicians and the Etruscans to establish colonies in southern Italy, Sicily, southern France (where they founded Marseille) and across the Black Sea on the shores of Scythia (*see chapter 10*). A notable feature of these colonies was the artistic contribution of Greek goldsmiths, who migrated to avoid civil strife at home and benefit from wealthy patrons abroad, especially in Scythia.

Laurion silver, Siphnos gold

The prosperity of Athens was enhanced by the silver mines of Laurion, barely forty kilometres south-east of Athens towards Cape Sounion. The silver deposits, also containing significant amounts of lead, had been worked initially in Mycenæan times, but were not fully exploited until after 500 BC. They now provided Athens with abundant silver for coinage, plate and statues. Each citizen even received an annual dividend of ten drachms (c. 44 grams) of silver, until that bonus was switched to pay for warships. The mines extended in a narrow strip for almost twenty-five kilometres north from Cape Sounion towards the modern ferry port of Lavrio. Over 2,000 ancient shafts have been located from which an estimated

8,000 m.t./260 million t.oz. of silver and one to two million tonnes of lead were produced, in antiquity.[2] In peak years silver output reached 50 m.t/1.6 million t.oz.

The most widely circulated Athenian silver coin was the *tetradrachm* (c. 17.4 grams/0.56 t.oz), bearing the helmeted head of Athena, goddess of Athens on one side and an owl, symbol of Athena, on the other. The *tetradrachm* became the most widely-used trade coin of the Greek world. Silver coin was also minted by other Greek city-states, islands in the Aegean and in the 'East Greek' cities on the western shore of Anatolia. By comparison, gold coinage was limited throughout the 5th century BC, appearing only on occasional commemorative coins or in emergency issues in time of war, because of the shortage of gold. The Athenians had secured gold from the Persian army after its rout at Plataiai. "Treasure there was in plenty," Herodotus reported, "tents full of gold and silver furniture, bowls, goblets and cups, all of gold; and wagons loaded with sacks full of gold and silver basins … from the bodies of the dead they stripped anklets and chains and golden hilted scimitars".[3] This loot was not melted, but given as votive offerings to the temple at Delphi.

There was no significant gold production to underwrite coinage. Three small gold mines were worked on the island of Siphnos in the Cyclades. According to Herodotus, "the Siphnians … were at the height of prosperity; they were richer than any of the other island peoples, having gold and silver mines so productive that a tenth part of their output was enough to furnish a treasury at Delphi … the remainder of the yield was shared out each year among the islanders themselves"[4]. The neighbouring islanders sometimes raided, demanding a few talents of gold; when refused they ravaged the crops. Ultimately the greed of the Siphnians cost them dear. The legend had it that each year they sent a solid gold egg to Delphi, but one year the egg was found to be only gold coated. The oracle exacted its revenge; the mines were flooded around 510 BC and never reopened.[5]

Gold was also mined on Thasos, the most northerly of the Aegean islands, which was colonised by Greeks around 700 BC (and also by the Phoenicians, according to Herodotus). The island hosted good resources of gold, silver, lead, iron, copper and marble. Much of the gold was deposited in fractured cavities in the marble after being weathered out of veins in older iron and copper sulphides.[6] Herodotus himself visited Thasos to investigate. "I have seen these mines myself," he wrote. "A whole mountain has been turned upside down in the search for gold." He noted that gold mines yielded 80 talents annually towards total income for the island of 200 talents, which would amount at around 160 kg/5,144 t.oz of gold, a reasonable output from relatively small operations, but not enough to sustain coinage.[7]

Thus for all its intellectual and artistic brilliance, the Classical Age of Greece was not remembered for its achievements in gold. An international gold coinage and lavish ornaments had to wait for Alexander and the Hellenistic era. In Classical Athens the most notable features were limited to eight statues of Nike, the goddess

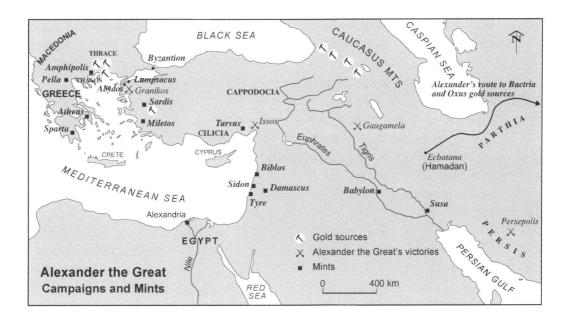

Alexander the Great
Campaigns and Mints

Map labels: BLACK SEA, CASPIAN SEA, MACEDONIA, THRACE, Byzantion, Amphipolis, Pella, THASOS, Lampsacus, Abydos, Granikos, GREECE, Sardis, Athens, Miletos, Sparta, CAPPODOCIA, Tarsus, Issos, CILICIA, X Gaugamela, CRETE, CYPRUS, Euphrates, Tigris, MEDITERRANEAN SEA, Biblos, Sidon, Damascus, Babylon, Tyre, Susa, Alexandria, EGYPT, Ecbatana (Hamadan), PARTHIA, Persepolis, PERSIS, PERSIAN GULF, RED SEA, Nile

Alexander's route to Bactria and Oxus gold sources

Gold sources
X Alexander the Great's victories
■ Mints
0   400 km

of Victory, which were covered with detachable gold sheet (very practical as it turned out), and the gold-covered statue of Athena herself on the Acropolis. The popular fashion was wreaths with golden leaves of laurel, myrtle, olive or oak, worn for processions and dedications or for burial of the dead. Each leaf had its place in Greek mythology; the oak was sacred to Zeus, the olive to Athena, the laurel to Apollo and Myrtle to Aphrodite. Boat-shaped earrings were in fashion and Aristophanes referred in Lysistrata to women adorned with necklaces of golden acorns. The relative absence of gold jewellery may also be because the metal was so rare that ornaments were constantly recycled within families. Moreover, Athens had restrictions on the burial of jewellery in graves (because of its shortage) and that is the way most ancient jewellery has come down to us. The result of the shortage of gold was that the talented goldsmiths migrated elsewhere.

Emergency gold coins

The scarcity of gold was reflected by the widening gold/silver ratio, which had long been at 1:13, but was 1:15.6 by 434 BC.[8] A crisis then brought gold into play. The strong leadership of Perikles had made Athens belligerent towards its neighbouring city-states ultimately triggering the Peloponnesian war from 431–404 BC as the cities set about destroying each other. The cost virtually bankrupted Athens. The city's treasury had originally had reserves of 9,700 talents in silver (254 m.t./8.2 million t.oz.), mostly in coin. Perikles' expenditure on the Parthenon and punitive expeditions had reduced the reserve to 6,000 talents when war broke out. The treasury also held 500 talents of uncoined silver and gold taken as spoils from the Persians years before, and a collection of sacred vessels.[9] This fighting fund was steadily eroded over the next three decades, not least because hostilities severely disrupted the output of the silver mines at Laurion. After 410 BC a scramble for any silver or gold for coinage began. The Athenian government and citizens were forced to liquidate their holdings. "Private individuals sold their silver and gold plate to pay for the *tetradrachms* with which to pay taxes and subsidise their military service," reported Thomas Figueira in his study of the Athenian economy.[10] So much gold was melted that, according to Figueira, the value of gold actually fell so that, briefly, the gold/silver ratio narrowed from the 1:15.6 on the eve of war to 1:11.

The gold came from some of Athens' finest statues, including seven of the goddess Nike, each stripped of two talents (4.4 kg/140 t.oz.) of gold sheet encasing their exteriors. The statue of Athena, the very symbol of Athens, provided 40 talents (88 kg/2,830 t.oz.) of gold according to Thucydides. Promises were made that when peace came the statues would be refurbished in gold, but it took until the days of Alexander the Great for that to be fulfilled. Meanwhile, the gold was coined at a special mint on the Acropolis into *staters* of 8.6 grams/0.28 t.oz and half *staters* of 4.3 grams. Over 100,000 coins were probably made, with Athena's head on the face and the Athenian owl on the reverse. The minting took place in 407/6 BC, but the limited gold stock swiftly ran out. The following year the mint was reduced to making a ghastly yellowish copper coinage covered with a thin veneer of silver. When Aristophanes produced his play The Frogs, in the spring of 405 BC, his Chorus lamented these 'worthless' new coins, compared with the previous year's "fine new-minted gold … all of perfect die and metal, all fairest of the fair, all of workmanship unequalled, proved and valued everywhere".[11]

An exhausted Athens surrendered to Sparta in 404 BC, but war rumbled on between Sparta and Thebes for nearly half a century, each becoming weaker by the decade. This endless inter-city strife paved the way for the rise of Macedonia. The age of Philip of Macedon and his son, Alexander the Great, was founded amidst turmoil in the rest of Greece and funded by new gold and silver mines.

The legacy of Philip of Macedon

On the 8th November 1977, Professor Manolis Andronicos of the University of Thessaloniki lowered himself down a wooden ladder into a tomb secreted beneath a great tumulus in the village of Vergina, recently identified as Aegae, the ancient capital of the Macedonians on the slopes of the Pieras mountains just north of Mount Olympus. The floor was cluttered with bronze and silver vessels, a pair of gilded greaves, a helmet, a sword, a great shield splashed with gold foil, an iron breastplate lined with leather and fringed with gold sheet, and a Scythian-style *gorytos* or quiver for a bow and 74 arrows clad in gold sheet embossed with battle scene. At one end of the tomb was a marble sarcophagus. When that was opened Professor Andronicos recalled, "We saw a sight which it was not possible for me to have imagined … an all-gold larnax with an impressive relief star on its lid". The casket was gingerly lifted out, the gold lid swung up easily on its hinge (after

2,300 years). "Our breathing stopped," he remembered. "There, unmistakeably, were charred bones placed in a carefully formed pile and still retaining the colour of the purple cloth in which they had once been wrapped. In one corner lay a very heavy gold wreath, now folded, which had covered them". The bones were those of Philip II of Macedon (356–336 BC), the father of Alexander the Great, who was assassinated at Aegae.[12]

The discovery rivalled that of Schliemann at Mycenæ 101 years earlier. Indeed, it was more significant in that it could be linked directly to Philip (examination of the bones revealed evidence of injuries to an eye and a leg that the king was known to have suffered), whereas Schliemann found the treasure of an unknown ruler of uncertain date (*see chapter 5*).

Today, it is a moving experience to stand before that gleaming gold casket, which rests on two lions' feet and weighs almost 8 kg/260 t.oz, with the wreath of gold oak apples and leaves suspended above it in the eerie light and silence of the carefully reconstructed subterranean tomb at Vergina. Alexander the Great, just twenty years old, supervised the placing of his father's bones in the casket, perhaps laying the gold wreath on them. He had attended to every detail of Philip's funeral after the assassination at a wedding ceremony in the amphitheatre near the royal palace a few hundred metres up the hill from the tomb. The scene is the more dramatic because just across from Philip's casket is another slightly smaller gold larnax found in an antechamber of the tomb. This contained the bones of a young woman, possibly Philip's last wife, Cleopatra, resting beneath a gold wreath of myrtle leaves and flowers.

The display of these treasures in the confines of their original resting place, rather than an impersonal museum gallery, makes the Royal Tombs at Vergina one of the most dramatic places in which to confront the history of gold.[13] They form a fitting tribute to the power and prosperity that Philip brought to northern Greece. He not only raised Macedonia to prominence, but imposed his mantle over the warring Greek city-states, including Athens and Thebes, whom he finally defeated in 338 BC at the battle of Chaironeia. Macedonia now became dominant on the Greek mainland. "Philip raised the Macedonian Kingdom to a high pitch of greatness because he had an abundance of money," wrote N. G. L. Hammond. "All the mineral deposits of the Kingdom …. were the personal possession of the king … and the gold and silver of his coins were of a pure quality."[14]

The wild, mountainous country north of the Aegean sea, which embraced Macedonia and Thrace (now north-east Greece, Turkey-in-Europe and Bulgaria up to the Danube) was rich in minerals. The best deposits lay within the Rhodope range and in the rivers coming down from that massif. The gold mines on Thasos, just offshore, pointed the way to larger deposits on the mainland. Soon after 400 BC miners from Thasos crossed to found a small settlement at Krenides to exploit fresh discoveries of gold and silver at Mt Pangaion just inland. The primary gold deposits were in quartz veins and associated iron and copper sulphides, while weathering had carried alluvial gold down the Strymon, Angitis and other local rivers.[15]   The young Philip of Macedon, eager to participate in the mining boom, captured Kenides in 356 BC, fortified the town and renamed it Philippi, after himself. He reorganised the mines on a grand scale They soon provided him with a serious income, of one thousand talents annually, for several decades. If all the output had been gold that would be over 2,000 kg/64,000 t.oz. a year; if it were all silver it would amount to 26,200 kg/842,000 t.oz. In practice, both metals were produced, but the gold contribution might have been 1,000 kg. A Greek geologist has estimated that over several centuries the mines of the Mount Pangaion region produced up to 300 m.t./9.6 million t.oz. of gold, with peak output during the reigns of Philip and his son Alexander the Great.[16]   No nation west of Asia had hitherto owned so much gold.

The gold production enabled Philip of Macedon to begin regular issues of gold coinage in 348 BC, just as Croesus had done almost two hundred years earlier on the back of a mining boom. Gold *staters*, half *staters* and one eighth *staters* were minted at his capital, Pella (near modern Thessaloniki) and named, not surprisingly, Philippeioi. Each stater weighed 8.64 grams/0.28 t.oz, with a portrait of a long-haired Apollo on the face and the goddess Nike (Victory) riding in a two-horse chariot on the reverse. The gold coins were on the Attic weight standard (that of most of mainland Greece); by contrast, silver *tetradrachms*, which Philip also issued extensively, were on the local Macedonian Thracian standard, with each at 14.52 grams/0.47 t.oz. This produced an awkward gold/silver ratio of 1:13.5, which Alexander the Great later rationalised. Initially, there was good reason for the different standards. The silver coin was widely accepted not just in Macedonia, but in Thrace and much of south-east Europe to the Danube. By contrast, the Attic standard of the gold coins was familiar to the Greek cities, which Philip had unified into his kingdom. The *staters* soon became acceptable throughout the Mediterranean world, particularly for payment of mercenary soldiers. Thus, Philip was satisfying his own region with silver coin, and a growing international demand with gold. The testimony is the coin hoards containing Philippeioi which have been found, not just around the Mediterranean, but across southern Europe and in Asia. "The economy of Macedonia became fully monetary," noted N. G. L. Hammond, "and Alexander inherited the strongest currency in Europe."[17]

Alexander's succession

Alexander came to the throne abruptly in 336 BC, after Philip's assassination at Aegae (Vergina). Thereafter, in the short space of thirteen years, he carved out an empire stretching to the borders of India and won himself a reputation equalled by few rulers in history. He was strong in body and mind (tutored by Aristotle), independent of judgement and always concerned for the well-being of his troops. A great athlete, he would practise mounting and dismounting a horse from a speeding chariot. For virtually all of his reign he was not in Macedonia or Greece, but on the road with his armies in Asia. He set foot across the Dardenelles in May 334 BC and never came home. He died, possibly of malaria, at Susa in south-eastern Persia on 10th June 323 BC at the age of thirty-two. In the meantime, he had defeated the Persian Empire of Darius III, built cities, and journeyed through Bactria (Afghanistan) to the Oxus river and beyond. His campaigns were funded initially by the gold and silver of Macedonia, and then by the Persian treasure he captured en route, which resulted in the first major transfer of gold stocks from one continent to another.

Initially, Alexander issued the gold Philippeioi and silver *tetradrachms* of his father to ensure immediate continuity. "It was wise to do so," his modern biographer N. G. L. Hammond decided, "because these coins were as acceptable everywhere as the Victorian gold *sovereign* proved to be."[18] They were essential for hiring mercenaries for the expedition against the Persians, that was in his mind from the outset of his reign. But he also began minting his own smaller silver coins on the same Attic standard as gold so that, for operations in Asia, the ratio between the two metals was clearly fixed at 1:10. This ratio, incidentally, acknowledged the fresh output of gold as it narrowed from the 1:13 around which it had hovered for at least two centuries, except in occasional emergencies. On this new standard Alexander also minted throughout his Asian campaigns a silver *tetradrachm* of 17.28 grams/0.56 t.oz, with the head of Heracles dressed in a lion's skin on the face, and Zeus seated on a throne holding an eagle on the reverse. Five of these *tetradrachms*, which became the main trade coin, were equal to one gold stater.[19]

In 335 BC Alexander also began issuing his own stater of 8.67 grams/0.28 t.oz which bore the head of Athena (an astute political tribute to Athens) in a triple-crested Corinthian helmet. The reverse of the gold coin showed a winged Nike (Victory), implying that he, Alexander, would be victorious in all he did. While the older Philippeioi coins continued to be minted at Pella, the Macedonian capital, Alexander's new ones were minted at Amphipolis at the foot of Mount Pangaion, close to the gold and silver mines. Each coin bore the symbol of a monetary magistrate to verify its authenticity. Perhaps over one million *staters* and thirteen million *tetradrachms* were struck at Amphipolis during Alexander's lifetime and for years after his death.[20]

First victories in Asia

On the road in Asia, Alexander established mints, like calling cards, wherever he went to coin treasure as it was captured to meet his operational expenses. He probably had a travelling mint in his baggage train to strike coin as necessary. The complexity of having cash in hand on an eleven-year journey was a nightmare. Indeed, gold and silver coins were the engine that kept his army going. The basic daily pay for his front-line infantrymen was one drachma (4.36 g of silver) and for cavalrymen, two or three drachma. When he first crossed into Asia in May 334 BC his army numbered around 90,000 men. Calculations suggest that he needed 20 talents of silver (524 kg/16,850 t.oz of silver) a day to keep on the march.[21]

With this in mind, Alexander had an eye out for new sources of precious metals. His staff included not just surveyors to improve the roads and bridges of Asia and long distance runners to pace them out, but prospectors to search for minerals, one of whom, Gorgos, was a mining expert. Alexander's route took him ultimately to the interior of Asia beyond the Oxus river and then southwards to the borders of India, a long-standing source of gold. His expedition was not just conceived to overthrow the Persian Empire, but to replace it with a Hellenistic model with good infrastructure and a sound economy. "It is hardly coincidence," observed the British Museum's Dyfri Williams, "that the route of Alexander's conquests after 331 BC passed through all the main gold-supplying regions of the former Persian Empire."[22]

Precious metals soon began to accrue. Within a month of crossing the Hellespont Alexander had defeated the local Persian satrap (viceroy) at the Battle of Granicus. This brought him not only the uncoined bullion and coin of the defeated satrap, but access to gold and silver from mines at Mount Ida, just inland from the Dardenelles, which were already minted in the city of Lampsacus. The Lampsacus mint promptly switched production to the gold *staters* and silver *tetradrachms* of Alexander. Before long he was in Sardis, whose mint had originated both the coins of Croesus two hundred years earlier and the gold *darics* of Darius the Great (*see chapter 8*). Although the Pactolus river was no longer the gold mine it had been then, Alexander picked up bullion and coin from the Persian satrap he ousted there.

The real test for Alexander, however, was yet to come – as was serious treasure. Through much of 333 BC he pressed east along the royal road built by Darius the Great before 500 BC to link the Persian Empire from Sardis to Susa. Simultaneously, the current Persian king, Darius III (336–331 BC) was moving west to intercept him as he came down out of the high mountains through the Cicilian Gates to the plain of Tarsus and the Mediterranean shores. Alexander was too fast for him. He took Tarsus, capital of Cicilia, which was a prosperous Persian province with its own mint. Seizing all the assets of the local viceroy, he immediately ordered the chief engraver at the mint to make dies for his own gold and silver coins. Over the next few years Tarsus became the third most important mint in Alexander's burgeoning empire, fed by treasure sent back from the campaign trail.

Darius, meanwhile, had caught up with Alexander. The confrontation came at the Battle of Issus on 1st November 333 BC. Alexander triumphed. His cavalry, the Companions, whom he had personally trained and mounted on specially-bred horses brought from Macedonia, won the day. Their swiftness simply bowled over Darius' forces, earning the Companions an enduring reputation as one of the finest cavalry squadrons ever assembled. Darius himself fled, escaping into the night before Alexander and the cavalry could catch him. Around midnight, according to Didolus Siculus, one of the first chroniclers of the campaigns, an exhausted

Alexander arrived at Darius' forsaken royal tent. Within he saw "bowls, pitchers, tubs and caskets, all of gold, most exquisitely worked and set in a chamber which breathed a marvellous scent of incense and spices."[23]

The real prize, however, was in the abandoned royal baggage train which contained uncoined silver reportedly to the value of 3,000 talents – enough to keep his army in the field for almost half a year. Another rich cache awaited at the Persians' main base in Damascus, where gold to the value of 2,600 talents (c. 500 kg/16,000 t.oz.) was recovered. Thus sustained, Alexander began a prolific coinage in the mints at Tarsus and Myriandrus (now Iskenderun), the wealthy seaport that was the terminus of the trade route from Babylon. As at Tarsus, the engraver at Myriandrus, who had previously made dies for the Persians, made fresh ones for Alexander's coins.

Financially secure, Alexander was in no hurry to follow Darius toward Babylon and Susa in the heart of the Persian Empire, but preferred to win over the allegiance of the Phoenician cities down the Mediterranean cost, picking up the tributes they had previously paid to Darius. Only Tyre resisted and was destroyed; Arudus, Byblus and Sidon accepted his rule and shortly their mints were issuing coinage under his emblem. He pressed on to Egypt in December 332 BC, to be received as a conquering Pharaoh, a welcome god. The Persian commander surrendered, making Alexander ruler by acclaim.

The legacy of his visit was the city of Alexandria which he founded, laying it out on a grid system facing the sea, surrounded on land by fifteen kilometres of walls. Two well-protected harbours made it ideal for communication with Greece and as a hub of Mediterranean commerce. The nascent city did not immediately need a mint, but one was established in 326 BC initially producing high quality silver *tetradrachms*, bearing a head of Heracles that bore remarkable resemblance to Alexander himself. Gold coinage was later initiated by Ptolemy I, the first viceroy and then king of Egypt in the division of Alexander's empire after his death.

Darius at bay

The challenge for Alexander, with the Persians eliminated from the Mediterranean shores, was to press on to Babylon, Susa and Persepolis, the heart of Darius' empire. After six months in Egypt, he set out, while reinforcements were dispatched from Macedonia, to join him at the Euphrates. In high summer he crossed the river with 47,000 men and cut through the cooler foothills of Armenia to reach the Tigris river just north of modern Mosul. Darius was waiting for him. On 20th September 331 BC an eclipse of the moon was taken as a good omen, and Alexander marched to meet Darius, exhorting his men to "fight for the rule of all Asia". The Battle of Gaugamela, fought on 1st and 2nd October 331 BC, spelled the end of the Achaemenid Empire that had ruled Persia and so long threatened Greece. Once again, the speed and flexibility of Alexander's cavalry, outmanoeuvring a huge Persian army on an open plain, won the victory. Darius, as at Issus two years earlier, escaped, but was in no position to challenge again. He was on the run for months before Alexander, having already taken Babylon, Susa and Persepolis, finally caught up with him, in the desert of Kavir south of the Caspian sea in July 330 BC. Alexander, acting on a tip-off and riding day and night with just sixty men, overhauled a small convoy of carts. While they searched it, a Macedonian officer saw a battered wagon off to one side; looking in, he saw Darius mortally wounded by his own disgruntled men. Alexander, in an instant act of reconciliation, wrapped the dead king in his own cloak and ordered that the body be sent to Persepolis for royal burial. In that moment in the desert, he took on himself to be heir to the empire which he had come to punish.

The ultimate treasure

Alexander could afford to be magnanimous. He had already secured the main treasure of the Persian Empire at Susa and Persepolis and exacted his revenge for the Persian sack of Athens over a century earlier by putting the palace at Persepolis to the torch. The quantity of gold and silver that he had seized was without precedent. For over two hundred years the Achaemenid rulers had squirreled away the precious metal paid them as tributes. Most of it lay as uncoined gold and silver in a small mud-brick treasury just behind the Hundred-Column-Hall of Xerxes at Persepolis. The Persian coinage had been limited to the gold *darics* and silver *sigloi* used for foreign expeditions; the domestic empire got by on barter. So the precious metal bars piled up in a treasury lit by two small skylights. This explained the scale of the treasure; it was not related to annual gold and silver output, but a stockpile amassed over generations. The overall treasure, according to assorted ancient sources, was worth over 180,000 talents. Of this, 50,000 talents, mainly in silver, were seized at Susa and 120,000 talents of uncoined gold and silver in the treasury at Persepolis, together with 8,000 talents worth of gold coin (1.6 m.t./51,000 t.oz.) in Darius' former bedchamber (presumably a nest-egg kept against sudden flight). A further 6,000 talents, probably in silver, were located at the small palace of Pasargadae, outside Persepolis, that had been built by Cyrus the Great.

The question is, how much of this was gold and how much silver? If it had all been silver, the 180,000 talents would have weighed over 4,700 m.t./151.1 million t.oz. Obviously it was a mix of the two metals, with the predominance in value and certainly by weight in silver. The coinage that Alexander commissioned over the next few years from up to twenty mints is the evidence. The silver *tetradrachm* of 17.28 grams/0.56 t.oz was most widely struck as the coin of daily trade throughout the empire. A buried coin hoard of the period found in Egypt early in the 20th century (AD) contained almost exclusively eight thousand *tetradrachms* from mints all over Alexander's empire. In other smaller hoards, silver coin usually outnumber gold. One exception was the stunning hoard of 51 gold *staters* of Philip of Macedon and Alexander the Great found at Corinth in 1930 and now in the Numismatic Museum in Athens; not only are they a dazzling sight, but the finish and quality of each coin was remarkable.

In practice, the make-up of the treasure must have borne some relationship to the gold/silver ratio, then 1:10, but at a wider 1:13 for most of the period over which it was assembled (which implies less gold by weight). My assessment is that by weight, the gold component of the 180,000 talents was between 36 m.t./1.15 million t.oz. and 47 m.t./1.51 million t.oz. and silver, broadly, around 4,200 m.t./135 million t.oz.[24] In making this split, the starting point is that the 180,000 talents reported refers to the value of the treasure. As the distinguished Danish numismatist Otto Mørkholm said, "One's general impression … is that silver not only provided the common means of exchange but was also regarded as the fundamental measure of value for all commodities including gold".[25]

This brings into question the calculation by some earlier numismatists and biographers of Alexander the Great that the value of the treasure was £44 million, based on the sterling price of gold in 1913 just prior to World War I. They can only have arrived at that figure by assuming the whole treasure was gold and then multiplied by £3.89 per troy ounce, the price of standard, 916 fine, gold for sovereigns at which the daily London gold price was then fixed.[26] More correctly, on the 1913 price, the gold proportion of the treasure was under £6 million. The error was repeated without challenge for almost one hundred years. Updating this to the gold price of 2007, at close to $650 an ounce, the value of the gold acquired by Alexander was between $750–$980 million (£375–£490 million). An immense treasure by any standard, which would have sustained Alexander for at least twenty-five years of campaigning.

Actually, the treasure galvanised the economy of Alexander's empire for almost that time-span, in terms of coin production, jewellery fabrication and the prosperity of communities far and wide. The treasure was won in 330 BC and the noticeable feature was the high levels of coins minted in the next fifteen years, then tailing off, especially in gold, before 300 BC. The jewellery-making boom lasted right through to 300 BC (see below). Putting into circulation precious metals which had lain dormant for generations was bound to affect economic life in almost every town and village as troops and mercenaries came home, not just with their pay and bonuses, but additional gold and silver coin or ornaments they had plundered privately. The dispersal of the treasure was remarkably rapid. A king was expected to live lavishly and to make gifts to loyal followers and strategic allies. Scarcely 50,000 talents was said to be left in Alexander's treasury when he died in Susa in 323 BC, shortly after returning from his great swing through Bactria and the fringes of India. By previous fortunes, that was still a handsome sum, but it, too, dissolved quickly in the turbulent succession squabbles.

Minting bonuses

The immediate payout by Alexander was bonuses to his troops. His cavalrymen, the Companions, were given one talent each (26.2 kg of silver or 2.6 kg of gold), equivalent to eight years' pay. Infantrymen received 1,000 drachma (4.37 kg silver or 437 grams gold) each, which was all paid in silver coin. The total cost was around 12,000 talents (c. 314 m.t. silver).

Such payments were the first of many settlements on veterans from Macedonia, and mercenaries from mainland Greece, Thrace and other Balkan countries. Ten thousand Macedonian veterans were paid off in 324 BC alone and the following year 31,000 mercenaries were on their way home to southern Greece. The Macedonians, in particular, were eager to show off their wealth acquired from years on the road, spending their gold and silver on fine residences and tombs. These men who, in the words of Arrian, another early chronicler of Alexander's exploits, became "great instead of small, and rich instead of poor", wanted to preserve some tangible evidence of their epic experience. One Macedonian veteran, Karanos, presented each guest at his wedding in Pella with golden trinkets. By contrast, mercenaries from Thrace who, in a sense, had just been doing a job, often buried their earnings, including a proportion of gold coin, to judge from the number of coin hoards of the era found in that province.[27]

The task of payment of the armies called for a succession of new mints on their roads home. Alexander had already commissioned a mint at Babylon in 331 BC, which issued gold *staters* and silver *tetradrachms* even before the main Persian treasure was in hand. Each coin, minted to the Attic standard, bore the letter M (for Metropolis), a sign that it had been issued at this great trading crossroads. Some of the *staters* carried a new symbol of a running lion-griffin or Athena's helmet adorned by a sphinx. Care was taken to monitor the exact weight and finish of the gold coins, compared with the mass production of silver *tetradrachms* of which Babylon made three to four million specimens in little over a decade, making it the most prolific mint in Asia. "Alexander used a gold and silver coinage of real value, which was valid through Asia," wrote N. G. L. Hammond. "Alexander was able to stabilise the relationship between gold and silver and to avoid inflation by his control of the output of coinage."[28] Where the Persians had made little use of coined money and relied heavily on barter, he effected a swift change from barter to capitalism. In all, twenty principal mints were operating within his empire during his lifetime, of which Babylon was the most easterly. He did not establish any mints on his way through Bactria and along the borders of India, which has suggested he was supplied from Babylon, or had his travelling mint. However, Bactria, with its own direct gold supplies from the interior of Asia, opened its own mint soon after Alexander's death.

Notably, minting at Sardis, the capital of Lydia, was revived in 330 BC with issues of gold *staters* over the next five years, fed by gold brought by Companions and mercenaries on the royal road back from Susa to their homes. Sardis provided a glimpse of the movement of precious metals from the Persian heartland towards Europe. The output in Sardis eased after 325 BC, with only small silver drachms being made, but there was another surge in gold minting between 321 and 318 BC, shortly after Alexander's death, suggesting the remaining spoils of his campaigns were being split up.

Sardis was not the only busy mint. For over a decade after 330 BC, mints at Alexandria in Egypt, on the island of Cyprus, and the 'East Greek' cities of Abydus, Lampsacus and Miletus in western Anatolia were occupied; so was Amphipolis in Macedonia itself. Their coins of that brief period, which have turned up in hoards in modern times, are the visible proof of the dispersal of a unique treasure. "All mints supplemented their silver by substantial issues in gold," reported Otto Mørkholm, "sometimes in the form of posthumous *staters* of Philip II's type. Gold issues were especially large at Lamsacus and Abydus."[29]   The latter cities were on the shores of the Hellespont where the veterans crossed over into Macedonia. They may have wished to legitimise their loot with coins acceptable at home before making the crossing.

Just as Philip of Macedon's coins were still being minted because everyone was familiar with them, so those of Alexander himself retained their popularity long after his death. Indeed, many mints completely ignored Alexander's immediate successors, Philip of Macedon's son Arrihidaeus (323–317 BC), who was mentally retarded, and Alexander's own posthumous son, Alexander IV (323–309 BC), who were theoretically joint kings. The real power rested with a triumvirate of the viceroys of Macedonia and Asia and a general named Craterus. In this political vacuum it was prudent to issue well-known coins of the conquering hero.

The Hellenistic Empire created by Alexander soon fragmented into a loose alliance of the kings of Macedonia presiding over the Greek mainland, the Seleucid dynasty controlling the main Asian provinces of the former Persian Empire, the Ptolemies ruling over Egypt and assorted local kings setting themselves up along the southern Black Sea coasts and in Bactria. And it was these newcomers, seeking to enhance their own authority, who began issuing new coins bearing their own portraits a generation after Alexander. Even then, they often trod carefully. Ptolemy I (305–283 BC) in Egypt tactfully had a life-like portrait of himself on one side of gold *staters* issued by the Alexandria mint and an idealised portrait of Alexander holding a thunderbolt and surrounded by elephants on the other. Ptolemy hoped a touch of greatness would rub off on him.[30]   By contrast, Seleucius I (312–281 BC) in Persia was confident enough to issue gold *staters* at a new mint in Ecbatana (whither much of the original Persepolis treasure had been taken) with his own portrait on the face and Apollo on the reverse. And at a new mint in Bactria his successor Antiochus I (281–261 BC) issued gold and silver coins bearing his portrait, with a bridled, horned horse on the reverse (very much a symbol of that wild Afghan terrain).

However, the strict gold/silver ratio of 1:10, under which Alexander had issued his coins, was slipping. Alexander's strength had been the gold from the mines of Macedonia and then the Persian treasure. Once that was dispersed, gold supply was again erratic; and, as was demonstrated time and again throughout history, a regular gold coinage demands regular gold supply. The Seleucid rulers in Persia, for instance, soon lost control of Bactria, cutting themselves off from the gold that had long come across the Oxus from the interior of Asia. Inevitably, the value of gold rose against silver, so that between 310 and 290 BC the ratio widened from 1:10 to 1:12 and later reverted to 1:13, where it had been before the gold mining boom of 360 BC.[31] New gold coin issues became increasingly rare after 300 BC, although the existing circulation of both gold and silver coin had expanded without precedent during the previous sixty years, particularly through the mobilisation of that long dormant Persian treasure. Conceivably, over ten million gold coins were struck in that period, giving a new dimension to the stock of Asia and the Mediterranean world.[32] As Otto Mørkholm summed it up, "The enormous output had made … gold and silver coins acceptable throughout the Greek world and beyond. By 280 they dominated the monetary circulation, enjoying an immense popularity in international exchanges".[33]

The goldsmiths' diaspora

The precious metal brought back from the Persian Empire stimulated a renaissance among Greek goldsmiths. After generations of shortage of gold and few wealthy patrons commissioning fine ornaments, both were, literally, in abundance. Earrings and rings from the 5th century BC usually weighed a modest four or five grams; now earrings were dazzling drapes three times that weight, while necklaces hung with golden beechnuts turned the scale at 35 grams/1.1 t.oz and gold wreaths called for 200–300 grams/6.22–9.33 t.oz of fine gold. Step into Gallery Six of the Benaki Museum in Athens, for instance, and you are confronted with an opulent spectacle. A bevy of gold wreaths of oak, myrtle, olive leaves and flowers are surrounded by earrings dangling with images of doves, heads of antelope, dolphins, bulls and lions. Nearby is a large gold medallion of Eros, son of Aphrodite the goddess of love, and a favourite icon on rings and other lavish ornaments of that time. The impact of the gold on Macedonia, Alexander's own region, was even greater. Today the entire first floor of the Archaeological Museum in Thessaloniki is dedicated to 'The Gold of Macedonia', almost all being ornaments from the tombs of rich Macedonians who came back from the campaigns determined to commemorate their immediate and their after-life in magnificent jewellery. A galaxy of over 500 bracelets, charms, chains, earrings, necklaces, pins, rings and wreaths are virtually all dated 350–300 BC. An array of lozenge-shaped gold sheets to cover the mouths of the dead mingles with thin ornaments of gold sheet that decorated textiles, furniture and armour, while gold thread was used in the garments of the wealthiest.

The sheer inventiveness of the goldsmiths was demonstrated in 1994 at a major exhibition, Greek Gold, at the British Museum spanning 500–250 BC; of the 157 prime pieces, 92 were made between 350 and 300 BC, and of those the majority were dated to the narrow band of 330–300 BC – in the immediate wake of the Persian treasure.[34] That exhibition also highlighted the dispersal of the Greek goldsmiths in the 4th century BC. They were at work, not so much in Athens, mainland Greece or the islands, but in Macedonia, the 'East Greek' cities along the Aegean coast of Anatolia, the 'North Pontic' cities of the Black Sea shores in the Crimea and the Sea of Azov (*see Scythia, chapter 10*), the Greek cities of southern Italy and Sicily, and in Cyprus and Egypt. This dissemination had evolved during the 5th century BC, when the long Peloponnesian War not only brought Athens to its knees, but prompted the flight of architects, sculptors, potters and goldsmiths. They had opened workshops abroad, wherever the necessary duo of gold and rich patrons existed, and never came back. That alliance was vital. The patron provided the metal and paid the goldsmith 'making charges' of between six and seven percent (a system that still prevails in much of the Middle East and India, where a part of any goldsmith's work is remaking family ornaments for a similar fee).

The jewellery revival was kick-started by Philip of Macedon's development of the mines around Mount Pangaion after 356 BC. "This was to release an explosion of gold working in northern Greece," wrote the British Museum's Dyfri Williams. "Many Greek jewellers were drawn to the Macedonian capital to work for Philip and his successors …. The Macedonian court now became the leader in jewellery fashion."[35] The momentum was maintained by the gold later brought back from Persia by Alexander's Companions and other veterans, many of whom commissioned ornaments and drinking vessels of exquisite workmanship in gold and silver.

The Macedonian goldsmiths introduced new motifs, drawn both from the local environment and the exposure to Asian cultures through Alexander's conquests. At home, they took inspiration from the acanthus leaf, which grew wild in their region, adding it to the repertoire of oak, myrtle, olive and laurel leaves on wreaths and other ornaments. Gold beechnuts as pendants became popular on necklaces, as a variation to acorns and seeds widely used elsewhere; again the beech tree was a native of Macedonia, not southern Greece. Some academics have argued the pendants were of spear heads, not beechnuts, but after analysis of the facets of spear heads and beechnuts, beechnuts have apparently won. These necklaces had straps made up of three or more doubled loop-in-loop chains with a fringe of sixty or more beechnuts, in all weighing up to 40 grams/1.24 t.oz. From Alexander's campaigns came back ideas for diadems and belts adorned with the Heracles knot (reef knot), long popular in Egypt, and for jewellery set with carnelians, quartzes, garnets and other semi-precious stones providing a rainbow of colours. The Heracles knot was both a symbol of marriage, and regarded as an amulet (charm), especially for healing wounds, and remained popular until Roman times. The profusion of jewellery was reflected in Macedonian tombs, where whole sets were buried with the dead (and thus have survived), compared with the ban in Athens on ornament burial because of scarcity of gold a century earlier.[36]

The bustle spread to Delphi, where the authorities, inspired by the fine workmanship of a new generation of goldsmiths, decided in 330 BC to melt down ancient votive offerings to make new ceremonial vessels. They set up a tendering system under which twelve craftsmen were invited to Delphi to bid for the contracts. The bidders included a goldsmith named Nikocrates, who also turned up in inventories of the temple of Athena on the Acropolis in Athens for whom he made twenty-six gold and silver vessels between 334 and 311 BC.[37] Temples throughout the Greek world benefited from the gold boom; ornaments, particularly wreaths, were stored by sanctuaries as the preferred way of keeping their wealth, rather than in gold coin. They made a better show for ceremonies and processions.

The stimulation of new-found wealth and ideas from Asia made special impact in the 'East Greek' cities of Madytos and Abydos, on either side of the Dardennelles, where the returning veterans crossed over, and of Phokaia, Kyme, Smyrna and Mylasa strung out southwards down the Aegean coast of Anatolia. They were not only the first communities to enjoy the troops' free spending, but had a fresh sense of independence after two centuries living on the doorstep of the Persian Empire. The magnificence of the jewellery the goldsmiths, particularly at Kyme, just north of Smyrna (Izmir), created was revealed in a collection of almost one hundred ornaments found in a local tomb in the 1870s and acquired by the British Museum. They included two pairs of elaborate earrings, each consisting of a disc intricately decorated in floral filigree patterns, from which was suspended the winged figure of the goddess Nike (Victory), who in turn held an inverted pyramid pendant adorned with flowers picked out in filigree and granulation; on either side, suspended by chain was the winged figure of Eros. Each earring weighed between 15 grams/0.47 t.oz, some even more.

The Kyme treasure also contained a splendid necklace of six-fold loop-in-loop chain, dripping with rosettes and beechnut pendants. The original necklace had places for seventy-five beechnuts, of which fifty-five remain. The two most sophisticated masterpieces were gold tie-necklets, with long two-fold loop-in-loop chains which fastened behind the neck and in front passed through a biconical bead, like a slip-knot, so that the chain could be adjusted; below, each chain flared out, on one necklet into myrtle flowers, the other into golden pomegranates. Each necklet weighed around 30 grams/0.96 t.oz. Technical similarities between all these ornaments from the Kyme treasure suggest they were produced in the same talented local workshop.[38]

Intriguingly, in an analysis of the fine gold content of 23 articles included in the British Museum's 1994 Greek Gold exhibition, those from Kyme proved to be of the purest gold; of four earrings tested two were 997 fine, one was 975 fine and the fourth rated 961 fine. Kyme, of course, was just down the road from Sardis, where gold refining was perfected under Croesus two hundred years earlier. Not too much should be read into such a small sampling. However, of the 23 ornaments tested, 17 rated 940 fine or above, three at 850–870 fine, two at 810 fine and one a mere 520 fine.[39] The more debased items came from Cyprus and the 'North Pontic' cities of the Black Sea coast. That implied different sources of gold for the latter. The purer items, especially from the 'East Greek' cities, may have been made from melted coin from one of Alexander's many mints in Asia. Coins were the most acceptable way to bring back the metal from the wars.

The concentration of jewellery production into the short span of years from 350–300 BC was remarkable. Although Raymond Higgins, doyen of the history of Greek jewellery, broadly classified Hellenistic jewellery from 330–27 BC, its heyday was over much earlier. "Most of the recorded material comes from tombs of the late fourth or early 3rd century BC," he conceded, "and it comes from every corner of the Hellenistic world, as a direct result of the sudden abundance of gold in Greece …. After about 250 (BC), except in certain favoured quarters, gold was evidently scarcer than before."[40] That brief age of gold, in jewellery and in coin, in the aftermath of Alexander the Great, was, of course, the third such era in what is modern Greece; the Minoans and the Mycenæans had made their contribution over one thousand years earlier, giving Greece a unique place in the story of gold.

CHAPTER 10

Black Sea Shores: Scythia: Nomad Warrior Meets Classical Goldsmith

The relationship was a curious one. Swift-riding nomad warriors from the steppes of Central Asia rubbing shoulders with migrant goldsmiths from classical Greece, on the northern coasts of the Black Sea. The nomads, the Scythians, swept in soon after 700 BC, and settled in the northern Caucasus, around the Sea of Azov and the Crimea and ultimately pressed across the Dneiper river into modern Ukraine, driving out the resident Cimmerian people. A century or two later Greek colonists, fleeing Persian incursions and then the Peloponnesian wars, established trading posts on the narrow Bosporus leading from the Black Sea into the Sea of Azov and at Olbia at the mouth of the Dneiper; they were known as the 'North Pontic' cities. Trade prospered. The Scythians offered furs and skins from the interior and, above all, controlled the grain business on the rich black soil of the forest steppes of the Ukraine; Greece needed grain and Scythia soon provided half her supplies. The Greeks, in turn, sold fine pottery, olive oil, wine and other luxuries to the wealthy Scythian elite. Migrant Greek craftsmen, especially goldsmiths, found them eager patrons.

The Scythians had long had a love of gold; their warriors, their women, their horses, their weapons were adorned with gold, both in life and in death. As nomads of the steppes with no settled homes, their gold travelled, literally, on them. Their warm leather or fur clothing was covered with small gold ornaments hammered out from alluvial gold plucked from the rivers of Central Asia. These plaques bore images of the wildlife of the steppes – the eagle, the leopard and the stag were favourites. A recumbent stag with swept-back antlers effectively became their emblem. The Greek goldsmiths, by contrast, were schooled to design images of gods, mythical heroes, or fantastic creatures and were trained in the technology of filigree and granulation. What emerged from this engagement between Scythian patron and Greek goldsmith over a period of over two hundred years from 500–300 BC was an astonishing cross-fertilisation of ideas and techniques that produced several of the most outstanding pieces of gold ornament of the ancient world. Academics argue tirelessly about whether the renowned set pieces were actually created by Greek goldsmiths to precise guidelines from their patrons, or whether Scythian goldsmiths learned from the Greeks, but always added their own ethnic touches. Terms like 'barbarian' patron and 'sophisticated' goldsmith are bandied about. Actually, what was created was unique: genuinely Scythian and differing in a subtle way from the Greek tradition, whoever was the master goldsmith.

The 'golden man'

The passion for gold that the Scythians brought with them out of deepest Asia was shared by many of the nomad tribes who ranged through the vast grasslands, deserts and mountains from southern Siberia and the borders of China to the Altai mountains and Kazakhstan and onwards to the Aral and Caspian seas, the Ural mountains, and the Volga, the Don and the Dneiper rivers. Other people and cultures – the Pazyryk, the Sakas, the Massagetae and the Sauromatians – adorned themselves with the gold they found in the rivers, especially those of the Altai and Tien Shan mountains. "The early nomads of the Eurasian steppe in the 1st millennium BC placed great value on gold for its ornamental and possibly symbolic qualities," wrote the American scholar Esther Jacobson, "and ... they routinely simulated solid gold by wrapping fine gold foil around superbly carved objects of wood, bone or leather."[1]

The lavishness of such ornamentation was revealed when the archaeologists K. Akishev and A. Akishev opened up a 5th century BC *kurgan* of the Saka people at Issyk fifty kilometres east of Alma-Ata in Kazakhstan in 1970. It contained the body of a young man in all the regalia and symbols of power of an ancient nomad. "It had not been touched," they reported. ".... The Issyk *kurgan* is a single monument of its kind." This chieftain was shrouded in over 4,000 plaques of gold and they nicknamed him

"the gold man". He wore a short coat (kamzol) covered with 2,400 tiny gold plates shaped like arrows in the form of trefoils and lions' heads, creating an armoured jacket. His belt was of gold plaques in the shape of stag and elk heads; around his neck was a gold torque with three loops, the terminals shaped as lions' heads. He had a sceptre with gold head and a whip wound with a gold band. His dagger was in a sheath with plaques of an elk and a horse. The gold ornaments, many of thin foil, had been made by hammering, stamping, engraving and soldering. "The Issyk *kurgan* illustrates a mature, highly original art, well worthy of the highest appreciation," the Akishevs concluded.[2]

This was the environment from which the Scythians began a long, slow migration westwards out of Central Asia around 900 BC. Their wanderings over several generations took them on a two-pronged front; some moving north of the Aral and Caspian seas, others swinging south of those inland waters, bumping up against the Assyrians in northern Mesopotamia and coming up over the Caucasus mountains to the river Kuban and the Sea of Azov. The Cimmerians, who had lived in the region for centuries, were subdued or fled.

The ubiquitous Herodotus, who wrote up the Scythian clashes with Assyrians and Persians, also visited the Greek outpost of Olbia in Scythia around 450 BC to

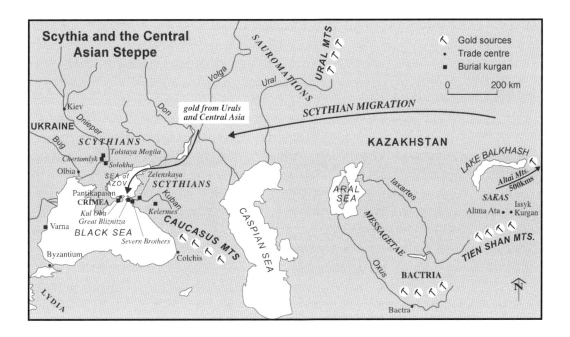

gain first-hand knowledge of the nomads. "A people without fortified towns, living… in wagons which they take with them wherever they go," he reported, "accustomed, one and all, to fight on horseback with bows and arrows, and dependent not upon agriculture but upon their cattle." In war, he noted, "the Scythian custom is for every man to drink the blood of the first man he kills". Normally they got drunk on fermented mare's milk. Herodotus admired their great *kurgans* where a ruler was laid to rest, "with one of his concubines, his butler, his cook, his groom, his steward, and his chamberlain, all of them strangled. Horses are buried too, and gold cups … and a selection of his other treasures".[3] Herodotus also remarked on Scythian "agricultural tribes" along the Dneiper river, where "no crops grow better anywhere than along its banks". It was their grain which the nomad Scythian overlords sold to the Greek merchants in Olbia and the other North Pontic towns to feed Greece. Little is known of their individual rulers. Apparently three kings ruled simultaneously, each with responsibility for a different region, of whom one was designated king-in-chief. Beneath them were 'nomarchs' who controlled large estates. The best known Scythian king was Ateas, who was killed in battle against Philip of Macedon in 339 BC at the age of ninety.[4]

The long haul gold trade

Although the forest steppes were a breadbasket, no gold was produced in the Scythians' new domain. They had migrated from the plentiful deposits of the Altai mountains (Altai meant 'mountain of gold') and eastern Kazakhstan to the Ukraine with none. However, trading links along caravan routes stretching from Olbia far into the interior of Asia were maintained. Herodotus noted that on this lengthy journey to trade for gold the Scythians employed seven interpreters speaking seven languages.

Archaeologists have determined that both open-cast and shallow underground mining took place in the Altai and Kazakhstan as early as 1500 BC. A Soviet survey in 1941 listed 70 ancient gold mines in Kazakhstan alone and some of their waste dumps have been processed in modern times. The ancient miners were not efficient, extracting only nuggets and larger veins, before breaking down the ore and washing it on the shores of lakes, using mortars, stone pestles and sledgehammers. Vertical shafts went down thirty metres, with the miners descending and ascending by wooden climbing posts. In the Altai the skeleton of a miner, who had been killed in an accident, was found with a leather bag filled with gold ore at his waist.[5] This region, incidentally, remains a major centre of gold exploration and development, showing that the miners 2,500 years ago barely scratched the surface.

The other main source of gold for the Scythians was in the rivers coming down from the Caucasus mountains into Colchis where the legend of Jason and the Golden Fleece originated (*see chapter 5*). These alluvial deposits (still tapped today by the sheepskin technique known to Jason) were scarcely three hundred kilometres south of the Kuban river, along which many of the early Scythian *kurgans* with their gold treasures were sited. Colchis was also easily reached from the Greek 'North Pontic' city of Pantikapaion at the entrance to the Sea of Azov where many of the gold workshops were located. Although the peak period of Scythian gold ornamentation was between 400 and 300 BC, the goldsmiths apparently did not benefit directly from the new mine production of Macedonia or from the huge transfer of gold reserves from Persia to Europe after Alexander the Great's victories, discussed in the previous chapter. An indication of the differing sources was provided by technical analysis of some of the items of the British Museum's Greek Gold exhibition in 1994, which showed that ornaments from the Greek/ Scythian workshops were of lower fineness than those from mainland Greece or the 'East Greek' cities of Anatolia. It was a limited study, but the North Pontic articles were under 850 fine, while most others were over 940 fine.[6] Scythian ornaments were often of a paler gold, implying more silver, and some rated as electrum (gold/silver).

Inside The Hermitage

The evolution of Scythian gold from the robust simplicity of wildlife images around 600 BC to the figurative subtleties of scenes played out in gold on ritual vessels, weapons' sheaths, pectorals and necklaces by 300 BC shows the transformation of a people. The story is best set out in the dedicated Jewellery Galleries of The Hermitage Museum in St Petersburg, which presides over the finest collection of Scythian gold. The credit for the foundation of this collection goes back to Peter the Great. In 1715 he arranged with Prince Mikhail Gagarin in Siberia to send to St Petersburg two hundred ancient gold articles, mostly of animals, purchased from grave robbers (who never recorded where they found them). This collection was later transferred to The Hermitage and, from that nucleus, other treasures were added as they turned up. Impetus came in 1830 with the excavation of the Kul-Oba *kurgan*, close to Pantikapaion, which contained the bodies of a high-born Scythian, his wife and an attendant surrounded by gold dress plaques, bracelets, a scabbard with gold overlay of mythical animals, a shield plate of a recumbent stag and an electrum ritual vessel with remarkable scenes of Scythian life. Since then, over one hundred *kurgans* have been excavated and no doubt more will be discovered. Two splendid items, a pectoral and a golden helmet, were found only in 1971 and 1988.[7]

Within The Hermitage a guide leads the way through subterranean passages until confronted by a vault-like door. She taps in a code, the door swings open revealing a long, narrow gallery. Gold gleams on either side. Here are gold-covered quivers for bow and arrows, gold scabbards, a battle-axe with a gold handle, golden bowls, gold harnesses and belt buckles, gold plaques that emblazoned shields, a golden comb, along with earrings, necklaces and bracelets all laid out in historical sequence. The first set pieces are the famous plaques of a stag and a panther that once marked out a chieftain's shield. They are heavy; both weigh in at 685 grams/22 t.oz and are 833 fine. The stag, a sacred animal symbolising the sun, is a compact silhouette, its antlers flowing gracefully streamlined along its back, its hooves in the form of predatory birds. The panther, dedicated by the nomads to the moon, is also a sleek silhouette with each of its paws in the shape of a curled panther, and six small panthers studding its tail. The stag shows up, too, on the sheet gold decoration of a *gorytos*, the Scythian quiver of wood and leather for both bow and arrows; this time twenty-four small stags are embossed on the gold, making it look like a sheet of commemorative postage stamps. A gold scabbard is similarly adorned with a panoply of fighting beasts armed with bows and arrows. The long, thin handle of a ceremonial battle-axe is covered with gold sheet emblazoned with stags, wild boars, panthers, hares, a horse with a bridle and a fantastic beast with its paws transformed into birds' heads. They are the epitome of Scythian animal style. "The ornamentation of weapons and horse harness with images of strong, swift animals had a special significance," wrote The Hermitage's Liudmila Galanina, "because the Scythians believed that such qualities as strength, speed, a keen eye and an acute sense of smell could be transferred from the images to the warrior, his weapon and his horse."[8]

The grandeur of this weaponry showed how Scythian rulers marked themselves out from their fellow nomads with the trappings of wealth and power. "The Scythian king in his war regalia was literally covered with gold and all the objects he wore were essentially works of art," observed Esther Jacobson. "Since (they) didn't have palaces, they carried their wealth on their own bodies … gold was not intended for royal treasuries or temples, but to be worn in this world and taken with them to the next."[9]

The original Scythian ornaments were animal orientated. After 500 BC, however, a subtle transition began as the nobility, growing wealthy from the grain trade, bought Greek pottery, fine painted vases, chased metal vessels and textiles, whose designs opened their eyes to more cosmopolitan visions. Locally, migrant Greek goldsmiths of the North Pontic cities sought to meet the tastes of what some scholars condescendingly call "the barbarian aristocracy". The compromise was evident in a fine, heavy, strap necklace of six strands of loop-in-loop chain, adorned with rosettes, with delicate filigree patterns on the connections to the clasps which were of horseheads. The necklace, found in 1990 in a *kurgan* on the east bank of the Dneiper, was pure Greek style – save the Scythian horses' heads.[10]

Animals on other articles became more fantastic or aggressive, with winged beasts attacking grazing animals. Gold plaques to be sewn on clothing or for harnesses began to feature sphinxes, helmeted heads, the Athenian owl, cockerels, and winged lions with their tails ending in a bird's head. The gold overlay for a drinking vessel found in the Seven Brothers *kurgan* near Pantikapaion depicted a winged lion killing a goat, while the same burial mound contained two superb gold rhyton (drinking horns), probably imported from Archaermenid Persia, one with a ram's head terminal of amazing grace.[11]

The interaction between the Scythian and Greek communities was increased by fresh migration of goldsmiths from mainland Greece fleeing the Peloponnesian wars, which rumbled on for decades after 431 BC, bankrupting Athens and other city states. The lure of rich Scythian patrons north of the Black Sea was too tempting. That mix fuelled the peak of Scythian goldwork over the century from 400–300 BC.

Prime time in Scythia

The impact of Philip of Macedon opening gold mines and minting gold coins in Macedonia and his son Alexander the Great conquering the Persian Empire brought prosperity to the Greek world from which Scythia inevitably benefited. Scythian society reached its zenith. The gold coins of Philip and Alexander achieved wide acceptance north of the Black Sea. Pantikapaion issued its own gold *staters* each of 9.2 grams/0.3 t.oz (marginally heavier than those minted in Greece). Significantly, these coins bore the image of an ear of corn as a reminder that Scythians' wealth was founded on grain shipments to Greece.

Pantikapaion now had numerous gold workshops producing everything from overlays for weaponry, to ritual vessels, necklaces, earrings, bracelets, and signet rings, along with the customary plaques for garments and harness. "Greek jewellery enjoyed great popularity, especially among women of distinction," noted The Hermitage's Liudmila Galanina. "Ceremonial attire and lavish head-gear were decorated with elegant ornaments."[12] The familiar animals, however, gave way to the gods, mythical heroes and epic scenes of the Hellenistic world. Pegasus, the winged horse, took to the air, hippocampi (sea horses) came out of the sea, satyrs danced. A shallow golden bowl was decorated with relief masks of the Gorgon Medusa and Silenus (a drunken friend of Dyonysus) amid a swarm of bees, dolphins and wild boars. A pendant in gold and enamel bore the resplendent relief head of Athena in a helmet with three crests, supported by a sphinx, two winged horses and little griffins. Floral earrings were draped with beads on chains.[13] Gold hairpieces, chased with fine wavy hair and adorned at each end with the figure of the goddess Nike, were all the fashion. The discriminating Scythian patron could even order a touchstone with a splendid gold cap to demonstrate the purity of his ornaments when showing them off to friends.

The jewellery prize went to a pair of heavy gold bracelets with sphinx terminals on which the feathers on the head-dresses were carefully chased and the horses' veins of their bellies were clearly defined. "These are the most magnificent of all Greek bracelets," declared the British Museum's Dyfri Williams.[14] Yet, in all depictions the sensibilities of the Scythians were honoured. They did not approve of nudity, so women were prudently draped and male genitalia were not exposed.

The output at Pantikapaion must have approached mass production for simpler items which could be hammered out in matrices by semi-skilled workers. Many of these were, no doubt, Scythians learning the trade, but there was no reason why they should not have become, in turn, master goldsmiths. They had long experience of hammering the metal of their animal images and, although they had not acquired the skills of casting, filigree and granulation out on the steppes, they could have learned them in a settled city. Esther Jacobson declared, "It is foolhardy to argue that a skilful Scythian craftsman could not have mastered the technique of granulation, just as before him the Greeks had learned that technique from their Near Eastern and Egyptian neighbours".[15] Moreover, the Scythians built their own fortified metalworking centre on the lower Dneiper at Kamens'ke Horodyshsche (Stone City). There, under direct supervision of Scythian rulers, weapons, armour and horse trappings were made; the city was close to a major iron ore deposit and had ample local timber for charcoal for smelting. Gold and silver workshops were also installed.[16]

The *gorytos* workshop

While jewellery was made on a grand scale, with even poorer Scythians sometimes being buried with gold earrings or rings, select workshops at Pantikapaion turned out truly astonishing pieces on which the high reputation of Scythian gold rests. The hand of at least three master goldsmiths has been detected. Among their finest pieces are four identical gold overlays for gorytoi, the Scythian quivers to hold both a bow and up to 200 arrows, the essential weapon of their attack (the sky was said to cloud over with flights of arrows discharged every few seconds). The metals expert Mikhail Treister believes that all four overlays were made in the same workshop. Two more overlays from the same shop, but with slightly different scenes, have turned up; one in the famous Kul Oba *kurgan* near Pantikapaion and the other in the tomb of Philip of Macedon at Vergina, who may have received the *gorytos* as a diplomatic gift or as a trophy from his victory over the Scythian ruler Ateas. Several fine scabbard overlays probably came from the same goldsmith's hand.[17]

The most admired overlay, from the Chertomlyk *kurgan* on the west bank of the Dneiper river, measuring 27.3 cm by 46.8 cm is an astonishing embossed panorama on gold sheet. Around the fringe, animals fight; a lion and spotted leopard attack a stag, a lion and boar confront each other, as do a lioness and a bull, a hound pursues a hare. Two figurative friezes command the centre of the *gorytos* cover depicting, it is thought, the life of Achilles. The story begins with scenes of Achilles being taught to use a bow, Achilles being found by Odysseus on the island of Scyros and relaxed with his sword and shield in front of King Lycomedes. On the second frieze, four women bid farewell to Achilles, who is then shown flanked by Odysseus and Diomedius as if being fitted with leg greaves before his fatal encounter and, finally, a greaving woman, possibly Achilles' mother, is shown holding either an urn with his ashes or a dead child. At first glance, it seems a perfect narrative of a Greek legend, but closer examination has revealed that the bow with which 'Achilles' practises is of Scythian style and the women are all draped and the otherwise naked Achilles has his genitals modestly covered. The goldsmith had made the necessary adjustments for his Scythian patron.[18]

Three other virtually identical *gorytos* covers have been dug up from *kurgans* at Melitopol, Illirtsi and Five Brothers, although there are subtle differences to each suggesting that the matrix or matrices in which they were hammered may have been slightly revised or repaired. Mikhail Treister who examined in detail the Melitopol overlay, housed since 1998 in the Museum of Historical Treasures of Ukraine in Kiev, concluded that each *gorytos* overlay was formed in multiple matrices. "The use of matrices to decorate different types of objects and the use of several separate matrices to create large narrative compositions were unprecedented innovations of a fourth century North Pontic workshop," he reported. "We have no earlier parallels for such complicated production methods."[19] He has also detected that some of the individual matrices used to build up panoramas were used in addition not just for sword scabbards but for the base of bowls, or diadems. In short, a workshop held a stock of matrices of lions and griffins or flying ducks or draped women and could take them off the shelf to hammer out a section of a larger article. "The workshop of the *gorytos* and scabbard overlays operated most probably in Pantikapaion from about 360 to 340 BC," Mikhail Treister reported. "It was one of about a dozen workshops in the capital of the Bosphoran kingdom … when Pantikapaion was one of the leading centres of gold work in the ancient world."[20]

The magnificent four

The workshops also came up with four strikingly original figures for special commissions. A golden helmet found just north of the Sea of Azov in 1988 has two dramatic scenes of Scythian warriors in a bleak steppe landscape. In each, two young men, one of whom had fallen wounded, attempt to keep at bay a fierce, bearded, older aggressor thrusting with a long sword. One young man, with an almost god-like head, challenges with his spear, "The heads of the Scythians are the work of an extremely skilled hand," decided Dr Ellen Reader, Curator of Ancient Art at the Walters Gallery in Baltimore. "The rest of the scene, including the rendering of the Scythian garments, was executed by less-skilled craftsmen who certainly could have been Scythian."[21]

Other 'snapshots' of Scythian life, clothing and customs appear on the famous electrum ritual bowl from Kul-Oba. Around the bowl are four scenes in high relief. Each shows two men, fully equipped with bow, arrows, *gorytos*, spear and shield. In one scene they simply chat, later one strings his bow, then one warrior helps to bandage his companion's left leg and, finally, one man appears to be probing a painful tooth in his friend's mouth. The impression is of an evening in camp attending to chores. "The Scythians' appearance, dress and weapons are reproduced … with amazing realism and ethnographic precision," wrote The Hermitage's Liudmila Galanina.[22] Although different in style, these 'snapshots' are reminiscent of scenes of Tutankhamun and his bride in gold overlays of shrines in his tomb (*see chapter 2*); both capture moments from life in the ancient world.

Among the most memorable of all Scythian artefacts in The Hermitage's subterranean Jewellery Galleries is a gold comb. The simple description is "comb crested with recumbent lions, fighting figures and horses". That hardly does justice to a unique article weighing a hefty 294 grams/9.5 t.oz that stands over 12 cm/7 ins high. The comb was unearthed in 1950 in the Soloka *kurgan* by the Dneiper and was recognised at once as without parallel in Scythian art. The comb has nineteen long teeth fixed into a bar supporting five recumbent lions sandwiched between another bar bearing sculptures of combat between three men with two horses (one already dead). They are cast in the round, so that the comb may be viewed from either side. It is a fascinating assembly, with the men, the lions, the horses and even the teeth all cast separately and soldered together. A bearded warrior in full armour on a rearing horse wielding his spear confronts another on foot with shield and short sword. From behind comes another warrior, *gorytos* on hip, a short sword in hand. The fallen horse, its neck pierced by a spear, is on its back beneath the *mêlée*. The tension is palpable, but who were these combatants? No one can agree. Their costumes and weapons are Scythian, although the helmet of the rider is judged to be Corinthian style from Greece. The confrontation on the comb may represent a Scythian myth, or even a contest between the triumvirate of Scythian kings for title of king-in-chief. But, as one critic remarked, it was "rendered with a Greek realism and Greek mannerisms".[23] Which brings us full circle to that basic question of the patron-goldsmith relationship in Scythian gold. Did the Greek goldsmiths work from close Scythian briefing, or did Scythian goldsmiths learn all the tricks from the Greeks? Or was it a mixed marriage?

The final test for this conundrum was a magnificent pectoral found by the Ukrainian archaeologist B. N. Mozolovsky at the Tolstaya Mogila *kurgan* by the Dneiper in 1971. This massive piece, a whole breastplate really, has a span of 31 cm/12 in and weighs 1,145 grams/36.76 t.oz. The novelty is that it illustrates, not hard-riding nomads at war, but pastoral Scythians caught in a domestic setting with their flocks (and in that setting may unintentionally have foreshadowed their fall as warriors became agriculturalists). The framework is four twisted ropes of gold, like the supports of a suspension bridge, within which are three curved friezes. The central one is a pattern of flowers, leaves and birds; with one bird actually pecking an insect from an acanthus leaf. Below, the sweeping panorama of the outer frieze is crowded with animals and even insect confrontations. Two griffins attack a horse, a boar confronts a lioness as his hind-quarters are savaged by a lion, a dog chases rabbit, grasshoppers face off. The top frieze presents the tranquillity of a Scythian farm. Two men, stripped to the waist, are sewing a fleece, a young man is milking a ewe with intense concentration to make sure the milk is caught in a tall jug, while another youngster is checking the content of an amphora after milking. Between them a mare suckles her foal, a cow her calf, a lamb, a foal and a goat lie about, birds with half-spread wings take off or land.

"The sense of reality and vitality of the elements in all three friezes is extraordinary," wrote Esther Jacobson. "One finely sculptured bird, for example, sits on the edge of a blossom … and seems about to peck at its centre."[24] Each person, animal, bird, insect or flower was cast individually and then soldered or pinned in place; a task of great complexity. "In the variety of its imagery, the pectoral is unequalled by any other artefact from Scythian times," declared Liudmila Galanina.[25] The pectoral, now in the Museum of Historical Treasures of Ukraine, is one of the finest works in gold of the ancient world. The patron who commissioned it and the goldsmiths, whether Scythian or Greek, who created it, are unknown. That is irrelevant. As Esther Jacobson summed up, "It is awkward at best, mistaken at worst, to force the gold objects of the Scythians into boxes labelled 'Greek', 'barbarian', and so forth. It would be more useful to think of the artistic arena represented by this material as representing its own tradition; one that was fragile and ephemeral, perhaps, and related to other Mediterranean gold-working traditions, but with its own distinctive expressive power".[26]

The pectoral's setting was, indeed, a premonition. Scythian life had changed, the nomads had settled down in the Ukraine. Within a few decades another band of warrior nomads, the Sarmatians, rode west out of the Central Asian steppes and swept them from the banks of the Dneiper. "The golden age of Scythia came to an end," said the Walters Art Gallery's Dr Ellen Reader sadly, "(and) the wondrous stream of gold objects abruptly ceased".[27]

Thrace: Treasure troves

Thrace was a maverick country of wild terrain, unruly tribes and uncertain borders, hemmed in by the Black Sea, Macedonia, the Danube river and the Carpathian mountains; broadly, it related to modern Bulgaria. Herodotus argued that "If the Thracians could be united under a single ruler, or combine that purpose, they would be the most powerful nation on earth, and no one could cope with them … but … such a thing is impossible – there is no way of it being realised, and the result is they are weak".[28]   They had no written language of their own and left no account of their history, so, apart from Herodotus and other Greek writers, the evidence was largely visual (as with the Etruscans) from tomb friezes and several collections of gold and silver vessels embossed with dramatic imagery of gods and warriors and hunting. Their lifestyle of combat and hunting was depicted, too, on hundreds of gold and silver ornaments made for the harness of their horses and chariots. Homer commented on their arrival as mercenaries at the siege of Troy, "Yonder are the Thracians … their king is Rhesos Eionides … his chariot is a masterwork in gold and silver".[29]   To cap this, an excavation in 1972 at an ancient necropolis at Varna on the Black Sea yielded gold axe-sceptres, bracelets, necklaces and hundreds of beads from the 5th millennium BC. Another hoard, mainly of gold rings dating from around 4200 BC, was unearthed in a tomb at Davene, just west of Sofia in 2005.

Thrace's story was episodic. The people of the Varna culture vanished and there was not much to report until 1500 BC, when the Vulchitrun treasure of thirteen exquisite gold vessels was created (contemporary with the best of Mycenæan gold). Thereafter it was almost another one thousand years until Thrace reached its peak between 500 and 300 BC, not least as major contributor of mercenaries to both the Peloponnesian war in Greece and later to Alexander the Great's Persian campaigns. The gold and silver the mercenaries then brought home created another surge in metalwork. The linking threads in Thrace's history were the fertile valley of the Danube which, as with the Euphrates in Mesopotamia and the Nile in Egypt, provided thriving agriculture, the high mountains of the Rhodope massif with their deposits of gold and silver, the Black Sea offering trading links, and the Bosphorus and the Hellespont, the bridge to Asia, whence invaders, including Darius the Great and Xerxes, came trekking through Thrace to attack Greece. The Greeks themselves also established colonies along these shores after 700 BC, paying tributes to the Thracians or hiring them as mercenaries.

Within their borders, the tribes fought each other, kings came and went. Thrace had no settled capital or cities where great monuments could be built. The kings were in constant royal passage around their domain, often seated, as early coins show, on carts drawn by oxen, their valuables in train. "Although the Thracians and the Greeks were neighbours, who fought and traded with each other for centuries, they did not live in the same historical age," wrote Professor Ivan Mazarov of the Bulgarian Academy of Sciences.[30]   And Thracian gold was not the sophisticated jewellery of the Greeks, but the cult vessels of hard drinking warlords who, unlike the Greeks, did not mix water with their wine. These vessels, jugs, shallow bowls, and *rhytons* (drinking horns), used for ritual ceremonies and feasting, became prestigious symbols. "Thracian kings actually used their magnificent insignia to express their power in the social hierarchy," Professor Mazarov argued. "As gold signified the order of the world, the attributes of high status in the Thracian cosmogony and in the social and religious hierarchy were made of gold."[31] The goldsmiths' task was to glorify the king's position. They worked at the royal court and, presumably, followed its peregrinations to cult centres or war lords' enclaves. This "power insignia" theme was even apparent in the ancient Varna treasure from the 5th millennium.

The Varna treasure: the earliest gold ornaments

The first impression of the Varna treasure is of its simplicity, when compared with the ornate vessels of later eras. The three axe-sceptres, each from a different grave in the necropolis at Varna just inland from the Black Sea, have a modern sophistication; just a haft of wood wrapped at intervals with tubes of sheet gold. On one the copper axe-head itself was elegantly shaped like a bow, on another it was sheathed in gold. The graves dated from the late Neolithic (or Chalcolithic) period between 4500 and 4000 BC, just before the transition to the early Bronze Age. In one grave lay a dead chieftain, who was originally wrapped in a tunic covered with several hundred gold beads and discs; a pectoral was on his breast, bracelets on his wrists, his sceptre in hand and, by his side, a copper spear with gold plate handles. The gold, in all, weighed 1.5 kg/48 t.oz. A single, beautifully fashioned concave bracelet alone weighed 194 grams/6 t.oz, while the rectangular pectoral, a sheet of 980 fine gold punched with holes so it could be fastened to a garment, was equally heavy. Other trinkets included two child-like cut-outs from thin gold sheet of bulls, their outline then enhanced with a pattern of punch marks. Besides an axe-sceptre in one grave, to confirm the dead ruler's status, was a gold phallus cover, with holes for sinews to tie it on, to emphasise his powers as chief procreator of his tribe. The ornaments in the graves at Varna were mostly related to men, a set of gold jewellery found tucked into a niche in the walls of a building being excavated in a nearby village, showed that women, or at least a priestess to whom it may have belonged, were not neglected. The parure included a necklace of 39 rings of gold wire, a snake-like bracelet of wire and four small amulets (charms) of thin gold sheet; together they weighed a substantial 312 grams/9.7 t.oz of gold at 980 fine.[32]

The technical achievement of the early goldsmiths at Varna, the quantity of gold available and its high purity at 980 fine are intriguing. In most other ancient civilisations gold ornaments were light, because they simply lacked gold. Here almost 200 grams/6.5 t.oz could be used for a bracelet or pectoral. Of course, the ornaments were for a chieftain, but the implication is that on the Black Sea shores before 4000 BC, gold was readily available. It must have been from alluvial sources. In that respect Varna was well placed. Streams coming down from the Rhodope massif in central Thrace carried placer gold eroded from the main quartz deposits. The alluvial beds in the stream must then have been almost virgin and gold abundant. Around the Black Sea were other alluvial sources, notably in Georgia, and downriver from the interior of Russia. This may have been traded around the coasts. But the Varna settlement probably relied on local gold sources. The high purity was also not uncommon for alluvial gold. The mystery was the fate of the Varna people. Their culture died out around 4000 BC. Their goldsmiths, however, left them a fine legacy.

The Vulchitrum treasure

Thrace emerged as a fledgling nation during the 2nd millennium BC through the same migrations from which Mycenæan Greece evolved. Little is known of its rulers, but the Thracians won a reputation as fierce warriors, which made them ideal recruits as mercenaries for Agamemnon's expedition against Troy c.1200 BC. And, just as the wealth of Mycenæ was marked by the gold found by Heinrich Schliemann, so the Vulchitrun treasure, ploughed up in 1924 in a vineyard near the Danube north-east of modern Sofia, revealed the riches of an unknown Thracian king c.1500 BC. The treasure of thirteen gold vessels, weighing 12.5 kg/402 t.oz, are thought to be from the sanctuary of a solar cult.

The most remarkable piece resembled three identical sauceboats, each ribbed with concentric grooves and shaped like the body of a duck. They were soldered together and connected to a silvery electrum handle. The ensemble weighed a hefty 1.2 kg/39 t.oz; no similar article in metalwork has been found elsewhere. The sauceboats, possibly used to mix a sacred drink, may have rested on a small cart representing the chariot of the Great Goddess of the sun. The potion-mixing notion was supported by the companion vessels. The grandest was a great bowl, almost a soup tureen, with two large handles, which weighed an amazing 4.4 kg/141 t.oz; it could have held an immense brew. With it were one large and three small gold ladles for dipping and serving. This highly original assortment of utensils was completed by seven golden lids that once fitted cauldrons (no cauldrons were apparent when the treasure was ploughed up, but suspicions remain that part of it went missing before the find was reported officially). The biggest lid, 37 cm/15 in in diameter and weighing 1.75 kg/56 t.oz, was inlaid with a swirling pattern in black niello (a fusible alloy of silver, sulphur and lead or copper); it had a domed knob for lifting. Six smaller lids, some damaged, lay about.[33] The impression is more of a richly equipped kitchen than a sanctuary, but three vessels had their place in the rites performed there, while also enhancing the prestige of the unknown chieftain.

The Vulchitrun treasure is an isolated relic of Thrace in the 2nd millennium BC, but more trophies of cults and chieftains may well turn up. The veil on Thracian remains has only been lifted since World War II, with dramatic new discoveries in each decade. The Bulgarian archaeologist Dr Georgi Kitov found a handsome two-handed gold cup in the tomb of King Seuthes III (c.330 BC) near Kazanluk in the summer of 2004, with the king's name engraved in Greek letters on the inside.[34] Given there are an estimated 1,500 tombs around the country, the majority not yet excavated officially, Dr Kitov anticipates revelations will continue.

The Panagyurishte treasure

That gold drinking cup of Seuthes III was fashioned during the most prolific period of gold and silver working in Thrace, following the expansion of the mines at Mount Pangaion, which Philip of Macedon took from Thrace, and the trickle-down prosperity from the metal transferred from Asia after Alexander the Great's conquests. The blip in surviving ornaments dating between 350 and 300 BC was just as marked in Thrace as in Macedonia and the Greek world. The money, the patronage was there to commission rings, bracelets, necklaces dripping with acorn-like pendants picked out with fine granulation, and the ubiquitous wreaths of laurel leaves. The jewellery was of distinctive Greek style and much of it may have been imported from Macedonia or the Greek colonies around the Aegean, Hellespont and Black Sea; but probably Thrace was prosperous enough to attract goldsmiths who had learned their trade in the Greek diaspora. The best of this jewellery was made at Seuthopolis, close to modern Kazanluk, which was Thrace's capital in the late 4th century BC, as kingship became less itinerant and, for the first time, rulers built permanent residences. These ornaments rest in the History Museum of Kazanluk, a town more famous today for producing the world's finest attar of roses for the perfume industry; by coincidence, when this writer visited Kazanluk, one kilo of finest rose oil fetched almost the same as one kilo of gold.

Even the horses were superbly decked out with the precious metals from Alexander's loot. Their harnesses were studded with gold, silver-gilt and silver ornaments, often of elaborate design. The Dolna Koznitsa, Kravelo, Lukovit and Letnitsa treasures yielded several hundred such pieces decorated with hunting and wildlife scenes. One can imagine competition among the elite for the most ornate trappings for their entourage in the field. A tomb at Kralevo, excavated in 1979, contained a complete set of forty-seven gold harness pieces, weighing 185 grams/5.75 t.oz. They included a figure-of-eight bridle frontispiece surmounted by an eagle's head, two rectangular plaques, each bearing the figure of a griffin in high relief with a delicate filigree pattern around the edge, and thirty-six little trinkets of thin gold sheet, each with a loop in the back for the bridle strap – shimmering regalia for the hunt.[35] The Letnitsa treasure, of twenty-two gold and silver-gilt harness plaques, offered a dramatic sequence of a mythical hero-warrior undergoing trials against lions, bears and a dragon, whom he overcame; he was rewarded with marriage to a princess, daughter of a goddess, with whom he enjoyed a graphic scene of copulation.[36]

The jewellery and harness trappings reflected a new Thracian elite, back from the wars, enjoying its prosperity. The more traditional status symbols of gold vessels for the king had to trump all that. The Panagyurishte treasure, unearthed in central Thrace in 1946, did so. The find embraced nine superb gold vessels, weighing in all 6.1 kg/196 t.oz, including seven *rhytons* (ceremonial libation horns), an amphora, and a phiale or shallow golden bowl. "The significance of the Panagyurishte treasure lies in the fact that the vessels were of a type more commonly found in the East, particularly Persia, than in Europe," observed Professor Mazarov. "However, many of the images with which they were decorated were Greek in origin. Thus the treasure embodies a conflation of the tastes of the Greek and Eastern world."[37]

The amphora is the most imposing piece, standing almost 30 cm/12 ins high and weighing 1.7 kg/55 t.oz. The smooth neck of sheet gold is framed by two handles of centaurs. The scenes embossed on the main body are in dramatic contrast. On one side two men are in quiet conversation, possibly looking for an omen in the entrails of an animal. Turn the amphora round and two armed men, naked save for flying cloaks, are beating down the door of a house as the terrified occupant peers out. The seven *rhytons*, however, are all models of peace and tranquillity. Three are in the form of a helmeted female head, with a serene face and curling locks, who may be the goddess Athena or, some archaeologists argue, an Amazon. They were probably the work of the same goldsmith, and two of them, of almost identical weight (c.460 grams/15 t.oz), may be from the same mould.

Three other *rhytons*, shaped almost like the curve of a foot and booted ankle, have a stag's head as the 'foot' and scenes of Athena, Hera, Apollo, Nike and other deities on the 'ankle'. A fourth has a wonderful he-goat as the foot. Each of these *rhytons* weighs nearly half a kilo. The outsider in this collection was a grand dish, also weighing nearly one kilo, which has five bands of remarkable ornamentation on its broad base. First, a ring of rosettes, then a ring of acorns, then, surprisingly, three rings of African heads. Interspersed between each ring was a quiltwork of palmettes and lotus flowers. The golden bowl, very different from the rest of this treasure, suggested a trophy of Asia or Egypt.

Articles of such splendour must have been commissioned by someone inspired by their experiences on Alexander's campaigns. The natural candidate was Lysimachus, one of Alexander's generals, who won the governorship of Thrace in the carve-up of Alexander's Empire after his death in 323 BC and later ruled as king in his own right from 308–281 BC. Lysimachus took over much of Macedonia and extended his empire across the Hellespont into several provinces of Asia Minor. He issued gold and silver coinage at the great mint at Amphipolis in Macedonia and at Lampsacus, Sardis and Smyrna in Asia Minor. His coins achieved wide acceptance after posthumous issues of Alexander's coins ceased.[38] So Lysimachus had all the credentials to have commissioned the Panagyurishte treasure. Archaeologists have not assigned it to him; after all, it was ploughed up in a vineyard in central Thrace and he died on a battlefield in Asia. But it is a fitting tribute to the warrior-king who briefly gave Thrace a mini-empire of its own.

The golden age was short-lived. Lysimachus was succeeded by a succession of less talented kings, and the Celts from central Europe were soon pushing at the frontiers of Thrace. The patronage that goldsmiths had enjoyed vanished. "The disappearance of Thracian art in periods of crisis is explained by its very limited patronage," admitted Professor Mazarov. "After the Celtic invasion (c.270 BC) … no metalwork was made for at least a century."[39] Indeed, Thrace never really re-established itself as a viable independent state. The Roman Empire was expanding eastwards; Macedonia became a Roman province in 148 BC. The Romanisation of Thrace took longer, although many Thracians served as mercenaries in the Roman armies. It was finally absorbed into the empire in AD 45. In the story of gold it will be remembered for a unique collection of treasures, beginning in Varna before 4000 BC.

CHAPTER 11

On the Fringe: Celtic Craftsmanship

The links between the burial of a prince decked out in gold at Hochdorf near Stuttgart, around 540 BC, a thirty-five-year-old princess with a torc of gold around her neck laid to rest by the river Seine in Burgundy c. 480 BC, an eighteen-oared boat of gold buried by an Irish lough c 100 BC, and nests of gold torcs hidden, c.75 BC, at Snettisham, England, are tenuous. Yet these four treasures, widely dispersed in time and place, are often cited as the masterworks of the elusive tradition of Celtic goldsmiths. "Our appreciation of the place of gold and silver in Celtic art and of the way in which their properties were adapted to the Celtic aesthetic is inevitably coloured by a small number of spectacular finds," observed the Oxford metals expert Peter Northover.[1]

The archaeological thread seems even thinner because historians often do not agree on who the Celts were, or even if they existed as a 'people'. "The Romans identified themselves – Civus Romanus sum (I am a Roman citizen)," wrote the archaeologist Miranda Green, "(but) we cannot tell whether a comparable Celtic consciousness ever existed … did these people think of themselves as being Celtic?"[2] The initial heartland of the Celtic tradition covered much of central Europe from the Danube through Austria, southern Germany, Switzerland, and eastern France after 600 BC, with its influence spreading gradually over succeeding centuries into northern Italy, northern Spain, the Atlantic coast of France (notably Brittany), Britain and Ireland. And it is on the latter peripheries in Brittany, Wales, Ireland and Scotland that it persists to this day, as an estimated two million people speak local languages descended from the original Celtic. No mean achievement for a nation that did not exist. As Christiane Eluère of France's Musée des Antiquités Nationales said, "The Celts never achieved a truly centralised power or an empire in the political sense of the word".[3] Their legacy, however, is unquestioned. "Among the great works of art in the ancient world, many stand out as being uniquely Celtic," wrote the French scholar, Paul-Marie Duval. "This art was developed in a temperate climate that fostered a sense of the mysterious allure of the forest and powerful animals."[4]

The Celts were real enough, too, to the Greeks, who called them Keltoi and the Romans who knew them as Celtae or Galli. "The whole nation … is war mad and both high spirited and quick for battle," reported the Roman geographer Strabo (c. 63 BC). Ferociousness aside, the Celts astonished the Mediterraneans with their white skins and fair hair. "Their hair was of gold, the clothing was of gold … their milk white necks had gold collars around them," noted Virgil.[5] The Greek historian Polybius (204–122 BC), who visited Celtic Gaul, observed, "Each man's wealth took the form of cattle and gold, since these things could be taken with them anywhere they moved".[6] He added that they went into battle naked save for gold collars and bracelets (which may explain why, when the Romans defeated the Celtic Boii tribe in northern Italy, they looted 1,471 gold torcs). Their marauding expeditions took them to Rome, which they sacked in 386 BC, securing a ransom in gold, and to the great oracle at Delphi in 279 BC, about which there are conflicting accounts of how much gold (if any) they got away with, as the gods intervened with thunder and lightning. In sum, the Celts were a vital force in Europe from 600 BC to around 50 BC, building hilltop forts at strategic river crossings and later laying out well-planned oppida (towns).

The Celtic love of gold as a symbol of wealth and power was remarked on by every ancient commentator. Their advantage over contemporary Etruscans and Greeks was that they had indigenous supplies of gold. As the Roman historian Didolus Siculus wrote, with a touch of envy, "In Gaul, there is plenty of native gold that the inhabitants collect without difficulty or mining". Actually, he was in error, for open-cast mines were developed in the Massif Central of France from the 5th century BC, and expanded by the Romans once they conquered Gaul. And, throughout the Celtic sphere, alluvial gold was recovered from Transylvania (Romania) and Austria, from the central Alps in Switzerland, and rivers of the Rhineland, France, Wales, Scotland and Ireland. Moreover, the recovery and fabrication of gold in those regions pre-dates the Celtic era by over a thousand years. Celtic gold is not the beginning of the story.

Ireland: the case of the crescent moons

By the Early Bronze Age, c. 2000 BC, simple sheets of gold were being beaten into ornamental shapes to adorn clothing or into long ribbons for simple necklaces or bracelets that were often buried with the dead across much of continental Europe and the British Isles. Thousands of these trinkets have turned up in graves or in wooden boxes concealed in the ground, jute sacks and bronze or ceramic pots. Surprisingly, Ireland hosted the greatest number of these treasures, with over 1,000 pieces being found, compared with a few hundred in mainland Britain or France. In one detailed analysis of 1,425 European gold objects of the Bronze Age, the Stuttgart metallurgist Dr Axel Hartmann studied 507 of Irish provenance.[7]

The reputation of Ireland as a production centre during the early 2nd millennium BC rests, however, not on the scale of output, but on the originality of around eighty *lunulae*, large crescent moons of gold perfectly engraved with geometric patterns. The finest of them, known as Classical *lunulae*, have virtually all been found in the north and west of Ireland, with only a scattering of exports, three turning up in Cornwall, England, and two in Scotland, although more dubbed 'unaccomplished' or 'provincial' have been found elsewhere in the British Isles and northern Europe. They are sweeping thin curves of gold often over 70mm/28in across, with diamond and triangular patterns as regular engraved motifs; the classical lunula usually weigh just over 50 grams/1.6 t.oz. "Each classical lunula appears to be the work of a master from its initial beating out to its decoration," decided the archaeologist Joan Taylor. "Symmetry seemed desired, understood, and aptly carried into the decoration, which was executed so well that the motif fits its allocated space with seldom a line overrun or an obvious slip of the hand."[8] Several are thought to be the creation of a single master goldsmith, while the whole collection (of which, of course, countless are missing) were the work of a coterie of specialists of successive generations, living in the heart of Ireland between 2000–1600 BC. The *lunulae* had deep religious significance; indeed, several have been found beneath large standing stones indicating the ritual burial as a votive offering.

The origin of the gold for the *lunulae* is uncertain. The best source in Ireland for alluvial and mined gold has been along the rivers of County Wicklow, south of Dublin; analysis of some *lunulae* matches modern nuggets from that region. Ancient alluvial deposits were also worked further north in Tyrone (where active modern exploration is going on), Derry, Donegal and Antrim. Suggestions that this early goldwork was made from imported gold are doubted, for the creative initiative behind the *lunulae* must have come from a craftsman or craftsmen working with local gold always to hand. Indeed, their work shows the same innocent originality that was displayed by the earliest Precolumbian goldsmiths of South America working totally isolated from any outside influence.[9]

Re-creating the Mold Cape

Beside the crescent moons, one of the finest examples of Early Bronze Age sheet-gold working is the Mold Cape. In AD 1833 the skeleton of a prehistoric chieftain was found in a grave at Mold in north Wales, surrounded by flattened pieces of beautifully patterned gold sheet, weighing just over one kilogram (32.15 t.oz). Archaeologists were not certain whether the crushed object, dating 1800–1500 BC, was fancy trimming for a horse or a warrior's cape. The puzzle was solved in 1965 by Ian McIntyre of the British Museum's conservation department who assembled and re-shaped the pieces. It was, indeed, a short shoulder cape. Ian McIntyre made further adjustments to his original restoration in 2003. Standing by the cape in his laboratory at the museum he explained how the ancient goldsmith created it. "He knocked it up out of a single sheet of gold weighing over a kilo, beating the living daylights out of it until it was one-third of a millimetre thick," he explained. "Then he probably shaped it into a bowl and cut out an opening in the base for the warrior's head to go through."

The cape fits snugly on the shoulders of a small man or woman and is decorated with neat patterns punched in the gold. "The goldsmith didn't make a mistake, he had very precise control," McIntyre went on. "I'm sure he used a press tool." To prove it, he had made up a simple wood press of two slanting arms, with small wooden press tools, male above, female below, and a wooden lever on top so that he had only to press down lightly for a consistent indent to be made. He demonstrated it on a sheet of copper; the indent was perfect. The Welsh goldsmith four thousand years ago, likewise could insert gold sheet and press out exquisite patterns.

This insight into a goldsmith's tools aside, Ian McIntyre's real achievement was to shape the flattened sheets of gold back into the original curves of the cape. This proved an object lesson in the ductility and malleability of gold that made it so appealing to ancient craftsmen. McIntyre explained that he started pushing gently at some of the flattened corners of the gold sheet and found the metal almost willed itself back into its original shape. "Gold is a forgiving metal ... it talks to you," he said. "It is so easy to work."[10] The friendly gold may have come from the Clywydian hills above Mold, which have gold-bearing quartz veins, or from the Dolgellau gold belt in the Cambrian mountains, whose rivers lead down to the sea. Dolgellau was the most prolific gold-producing area in Wales with scores of ancient shafts.

Late Bronze Age gold boom

Gold was an exclusive metal in the Early Bronze Age before 1500 BC, reserved primarily for tribal rulers to wear in life and death or, like the *lunulae*, to appease the gods. Local tribes produced their own styles. The 'Wessex' culture in southern England made pendants of amber set in gold leaf; in Brittany the encrustation of sword and dagger hilts with thousands of minute studs made from threads of gold was fashionable among noble warriors; in eastern France and northern Germany long gold pins to fasten clothing were preferred. These local favourites were swept aside in the Later Bronze Age by the widespread introduction of twisted bars or bands of gold used for belts, bracelets and necklaces. These torcs, as they are known, were made either by simply twisting the metal under tension or, in central Europe, by casting. Quite massive pieces were often produced, implying ready gold supplies. Gold leaf and foils were popular, and carefully controlled alloys, using more copper, were introduced. The art of filigree was perfected, especially in Ireland, where a flourishing jewellery industry developed, making buckles from slender gold threads, twisted and soldered.[11] The Irish gold trade was now being supplied partly by imported gold, particularly from alluvial deposits in southern Scotland (the connection has been detected by traces of platinum in the jewellery which match the make-up of the Scottish ores). In this growing international trade the emphasis was not on grand pieces, like the Mold Cape, but on ornaments, often quite heavy, for a wider clientele. France was at the crossroads of this Bronze Age gold boom, with bracelets and spirals being found in several hoards. French designs were widely copied. Many gold ornaments recovered in the British Isles show French influence, although local goldsmiths produced their own interpretations of continental styles.[12]

This spirited trade, which foreshadowed the Celts in style and technology, petered out in Europe soon after 1000 BC, just as it did in Greece, Italy and elsewhere in the Mediterranean world. Shortage of gold was the problem; some of the rare pieces found have a high copper content, revealing a need to conserve gold. As Christiane Eluère explained, "The great flourishing in the art and practice of making precious metal jewellery and ornaments … died away. During the Iron Age which followed, gold apparently was much less available and it became an exclusive attribute of 'princes' and their funerary wealth".[13] The initial reputation of Celtic goldwork was founded on that princely wealth.

Hallstatt: salt paved the way

The supply of gold, or rather lack of it, was critical in the evolution of Celtic gold between 600 and 400 BC. Scarcity meant that gold leaf and foil were extensively used. The strong new swords of the Iron Age had their hilts covered with gold leaf or were carved of ivory inlaid with amber. The very shortage of gold meant that a gold collar or torc on a warrior or chieftain was the supreme symbol of power. Another mineral, salt, became the source of wealth for rulers who controlled its growing international trade. Salt helped to preserve food and improve livestock. One of the earliest communities of the 'Celtic' tradition was around the salt mines of Hallstatt, by an isolated lake locked in the Salzkammergut mountains fifty kilometres south-east of Salzburg in Austria.

Between 700 and 500 BC the salt miners of Hallstatt dug passageways and galleries deep into the mountains. The excavation of over 2,000 graves in the Hallstatt cemetery has revealed how an original and dynamic culture evolved there – giving its name to the first period of Celtic history. Hallstatt's customs spread along the salt routes. The Celts favoured strategically secure citadels, each controlled by strong local dynasties, which commanded wide stretches of good arable land or river crossings. The pattern spread west through southern Germany to Switzerland and eastern France; Heuneburg overlooked the Danube, Hohenasperg was founded near Stuttgart, Uëtliberg near Zurich, and Mont Lassois by the upper Seine in Burgundy. The ruler of each territory was independent, but he formed alliances and was buried in splendour on great four-wheeled wooden wagons, surrounded by every comfort for the after-life.[14]

This veneration was demonstrated in the Eberdingen-Hochdorf tomb, excavated near Stuttgart in 1978, which revealed the body of a wealthy prince, aged about forty, lying on a couch of sheet bronze. He had been buried around 540 BC. A heavy torc of hammered sheet gold was around his neck, a gold bracelet circled his right wrist, his garments were fastened with gold pins, sheets of gold were fixed to the hilt and sheath of his dagger, his belt and his leather shoes were trimmed with exquisitely patterned gold foil. Nine drinking horns adorned with gold foil lay around, while a gold drinking cup was thoughtfully placed on the rim of a Greek bronze cauldron that once held mead or honey (to judge from the residue left). An iron razor and nail scissors were in the prince's toilet kit, and three fish hooks were in his breast pocket; a quiver filled with arrows was at his side.[15]   The Hochdorf tomb offered the finest collection of early Celtic gold, confirming its role as a mark of high prestige. Other tombs in southern Germany at Bad Cannstatt, Heuneburg and Ditzingen-Schöckingen have also provided an array of torcs, bracelets and pendants worn by the elite between 600 and 500 BC.[16]   Women, however, were usually buried with less ornaments than men, often with a few hair trinkets. Christiane Eluère has suggested this "confirms the idea that the precious metal was first and foremost a symbol of power".[17]

That custom changed, however, after 500 BC; women were increasingly endowed with ornaments. Indeed, one of the most notable treasures of the later Hallstatt period was that buried with a thirty-five-year-old Burgundian princess on the banks of the river Seine at Mont Lassois around 480 BC. The lady, known as the Vix princess (after the neighbouring village), was undoubtedly a great ruler in her own right. She lay on a small wagon with a magnificent gold torc, weighing 480 grams/15 t.oz, around her neck. Where the round terminals joined the main circle of the torc, two little winged horses trod over a perfect patterned field of tiny gold granules and filigree threads. "One of the finest and most controlled applications of filigree is in the terminals of the Vix collar," wrote Peter Northover. "This collar, with a thick, smooth sheet body and complex multicomponent terminals with cast, chased, punched and filigree ornaments, is unique."[18]   The collar indicated that the goldsmiths at the princess's court at Mont Lassois had learned much from the contemporary virtuoso Etruscan goldsmiths (*see chapter 7*) in the detail of their work, yet the massive circle of the torc itself remained true to Celtic tastes. The improvements were striking compared with bracelets and earrings in an earlier 6th century barrow at Sainte-Colombe nearby. "Goldsmiths were now seeking originality at all costs, using many different techniques," noted Christiane Eluère. "The high quality of the precious metal objects found in the grave at Vix could only have been achieved in workshops where master goldsmiths were working … nevertheless a Celtic vein pervades their work."[19]

That search for originality led to the Celts not only adopting Mediterranean technology, but motifs, thus ushering in the La Tène style to replace the Hallstatt. La Tène was named after the site by Lake Neuchâtel in Switzerland where graves revealed four-wheeled burial wagons giving way to light two-wheeled chariots, long swords to spears and much wider use of animals, birds and plants in design. Lotus flowers and palmettes sprouted on drinking vessels and vases. A princely tomb at Schwarzenbach in the Rhineland yielded a handsome cup trimmed with an open network of gold leaf embossed with plant designs. La Tène was also characterised by high quality metalwork. Gold and silversmiths now worked on the metal with compasses to map out exact patterns (tell-tale pin-pricks on the metal show where the compass point rested).[20]

Gallic gold mines

Although gold leaf still predominated, except on special pieces like the Vix collar, the availability of gold was set to increase. Between 500 and 400 BC small open-cast mines were dug in France, mainly in the Limousin, Haute Vienne and north Dordogne regions around modern Limoges. The current Michelin road atlas of that area is studded with little crossed pick-axes marking ancient mines near such villages as Beaune les Mines, Crôs Gallet, La Forge de Tindeix, Les Lanvers à Ambazac, and Sirejes. A survey by the archaeologist Beatrice Cauuet during the 1980s and 90s identified two hundred and fifty mines, many of them dating back to the La Tène era beginning in the 5th century BC. The mines continued to be worked for several centuries and were actively developed by the Romans after they conquered Gaul in the 1st century BC. The gold was in quartz veins, typically grading 80% gold, 20% silver, and the open pits were up to 100 metres long, 20–30 metres wide. The output was hard to judge, but Beatrice Cauuet put it at "several tonnes during the Iron Age".[21]

The miners learned as they went along. "The ancient miners had developed a rule of thumb in understanding their geological environment enabling them to identify the mineralised areas," Beatrice Cauuet reported. "You can even see in areas of poor mineralisation traces of prospecting which were never followed up … preliminary soundings and little trenches have been found at several mines". During the La Tène era the mines were opencast, going down to a maximum of 20 metres after which drainage became a problem. Underground mining started later, probably in Roman times. The early miners apparently understood the difference between easily worked oxide ores near the surface and complex sulphide ores at depth. Beatrice Cauuet has suggested they tackled the sulphide ores by roasting them in little pits, with the broken ore mixed with fragments of wood or charcoal to oxidise it, thus unlocking the grains of gold in the network of sulphides. After crushing with mortars and rotating granite millstones, the resulting powder was washed through pits leading to little trenches down an incline into a terminal tank, where the gold was deposited in troughs filled with woven material or sheep skins (as in Jason and the Golden Fleece). The gold was then heated in crucibles to remove most trace metals.

While output was modest, it provided goldsmiths in south-west France with a reliable supply over the centuries – and it is notable that some of the best La Tène period gold ornaments have been found in that region. The most original find was a magnificent helmet of gold, coral, iron and bronze discovered in a cave at Agris, near Angoulême in 1981. The inner core of the helmet, dated c. 350 BC, was of iron and bronze overlaid with gold leaf embossed with patterns of plants that were so popular with the Celts in the La Tène period. The gold leaf was consistently 990 fine. "Gold of this purity has so far only been found in ornaments from south-west Gaul, whose sources were the mines of the Massif Central," reported the analyst José Gomez de Soto.[22] The same high purity has also been noted in torcs and bracelets of the 3rd and 4th century BC from this region. Elsewhere in the Celtic world other sources of gold were being generated.

The wages of war

Celtic migration after 400 BC probably accounted for most fresh supplies of gold. As they pressed eastwards along the river Danube and down into northern Italy as far as Bologna and Ancona, marauding yielded more than mining. Their foray against Rome in 386 BC was particularly profitable. The Celtic leader demanded a ransom of 1000 Roman pounds (324kg/10,400 t.oz), then 'loaded' the weights against which it was measured out. When the Romans protested, he added his sword to the weights, warning, "Woe to the defeated". The Celts' ferociousness in war also secured them contracts as mercenaries around the Mediterranean, for which they were paid in the gold coins that circulated widely after 350 BC – a circulation enhanced by the transfer of huge gold stocks from Persia after Alexander the Great's victories (*see chapter 9*). The *staters* of Philip of Macedon and Alexander were welcome throughout central and western Europe. Celtic tribes along the Danube are thought to have encountered Alexander before he set out for Persia in 335 BC and exchanged gifts. "Enormous quantities of Mediterranean gold passed into Celtic Europe in the hands of returning warriors during the 4th and 3rd centuries BC," wrote the numismatist Daphne Nash Briggs of Oxford's Ashmolean Museum. "The Celts were the most popular barbarian soldiers of the day … (and) preferred their salaries in gold at a time when silver was the normal currency medium in the Mediterranean."[23]

A 'going-rate' for mercenaries was established. Livy recorded in his History of Rome that when Perseus of Macedon (179–168 BC) hired Celts from the Danube region for "a season's campaign", he paid five gold *staters* (42.5 grams/1.32 t.oz) for each foot soldier, ten *staters* (85 grams/2.64 t.oz) per cavalryman, and 1,000 *staters* (8.5 kg/264 t.oz) to the Celts' leader Cloadicus.[24] Assuming perhaps 1,000 infantry, 300 cavalry and Cloadicus himself, this called for 76.5kg/2,486 t.oz) of gold. Such estimates provide a sense of perspective to the amounts of gold changing hands in this period. The Celts had settled on a ransom of 324 kg/10,400 t.oz from Rome and now, for a summer's campaigning, a battalion of mercenaries could be hired for well under 100 kg/3,250 t.oz. As for mercenaries, the more fearsome their reputation, the higher the fee; it was a bit like signing up international footballers today. The fee was enough to melt into ostentatious gold torcs and bracelets to be worn in battle. Celts hired themselves out, not only to the Greeks and the Carthaginians (for their Punic Wars against Rome), but to fellow tribes in need of a hand. Polybius reported that the Insubres and the Boii in northern Italy signed on the Gaesatae from across the Alps in 225 BC "to make war on Rome, offering them an immediate large sum in gold".[25] Actually, this may not have been gold well spent, for just three years later the Romans drove the Celts out of Mediolanum (Milan), a sign of the growing Roman might that defeated the Celts in Gaul itself, within a few generations.

Celtic coinage

Meanwhile, it was the flow of gold coin from the Mediterranean that was the main source of Celtic gold, especially for their growing oppida (towns) in central Europe and Gaul. The coin served three purposes: to underwrite trade between the major oppida, such as Manching on the Danube which was a crossroads of traffic for central Europe; for melting into local coinage (often debased as time went by); and for melting into ingots from which ornaments could be made. While the coins brought back by mercenaries were usually full *staters*, local gold issues at Manching and Stradonice in Bohemia included ⅓, ¼, and even 1/24th of a stater (0.4g). These coins were sometimes shaped like shallow dishes and adorned with the heads of birds, dragons or stags, as well as the image of a local chieftain. "The range of denomination of gold coins is indicative of a developed and differentiated money economy, further proved by the great quantities of silver coins, which largely served as local currency," noted the numismatist Hans-Jörg Kellner.[26]   However, there was no universal Celtic coinage, unlike Greece or Rome, and minting was sporadic to meet sudden political or economic needs. The philosopher Poseidonis reported that around 150 BC the ruler of the Averni tribe in central Gaul issued coins in an attempt to win popular favour and rode around the countryside distributing gold and silver coins to the populace.

Gold coin was used normally for official payments, taxes, tributes, fines or as religious offerings and dowries. In moments of danger it was buried, especially as the Celtic world came under increasing pressure from the Romans. Such hoards have provided a unique insight into the coinage. The one thousand *staters* of the Irsching hoard from the 1st and 2nd centuries BC, which turned up in Bavaria in the 1850s, weighed an average 7.5g/0.23 t.oz and were 692 fine gold with 228 fine silver, showing considerable debasement from the *staters* of Philip or Alexander. Remarkably, although 85 of the coins were preserved in the Royal Numismatic Cabinet in Munich, 300 were sold and over 500 were melted down by the Royal Bavarian Mint to make new *ducats* (a classic example of ancient gold being recycled after two thousand years).[27]

Renaissance in jewellery

The imported mercenaries' gold coin was the main supply for jewellery fabrication in several Celtic regions, such as Britain. Jewellery, in turn, became less exclusive. And a notable shift took place after 400 BC from grand tombs filled with ornaments to votive offerings of ornaments and coin to the natural cults the Celts worshipped. The sky, the stars, mountains, lakes and plants (especially mistletoe) had great religious significance in their lives. A hoard of seven gold torcs and bracelets concealed under a huge rock at Erstfeld high in the Swiss Alps on the trail to the St Gotthard Pass is thought, for example, to have been an offering to the supreme powers who ruled the mountains.[28]   Such ornaments were the staples for both daily wear and offerings, along with gold fibulae for pinning garments together. While

Celtic goldsmiths constantly picked up ideas from their Mediterranean colleagues, whether Greek, Etruscan or Iberian, relatively little jewellery was imported. The Celts always preferred their own enduring La Tène designs.

Technology, however, improved significantly, particularly in deeply textured torcs comprising patterns of twisted wires. The technique was initially perfected in Gaul between 200 and 100 BC. The goldsmiths' speciality was lost wax (*cire perdue*) casting of collars, terminals and torc bodies in moulded, three dimensional abstract plant forms. Each item was hollow with thin gold walls. It was "a triumph of contemporary casting technology," decided the metallurgist Peter Northover.[29]

Such expertise spread to Britain and Ireland where jewellery fabrication had been virtually absent for several centuries. In both countries the new era came, not from significant migration of Celts from mainland Europe, but through the flow of samples across the English Channel from the Champagne/Marne region of northern France and the Belgae people (in what is now Belgium). Champagne, in particular, had long been an important centre of jewellery-making in gold and bronze. After 300 BC metalworking achieved a high status in southern England; swords with ornate scabbards, parade shields and ornate horse trappings were made in iron or bronze for an aristocratic ruling class. Women admired themselves in decorated mirrors of polished metal, and gold torcs began to be made in East Anglia, usually from melted coin. "Metalworkers were significant figures in the community," noted the Celtic historian Barry Raferty.[30]

Gold for a sea-god

A similar revival took place in Ireland, where the great jewellery tradition of one thousand years earlier had been lost. A buried hoard at Broighter on the shores of Lough Foyle in County Derry in the north of Ireland, dating c. 100 BC, has revealed that the skills had been revived. The treasure, a votive offering to the local sea-god (an Irish Poseidon or Neptune), comprised seven pieces. The most impressive was a highly decorated tubular gold torc, which Barry Raferty declared "a spectacular example of native craftsmanship". The provenance of four bracelets is not certain, but two are judged to be from the eastern Mediterranean and two were local copies of Roman designs. Evidence, at least, of limited international flow of jewellery, but only enough for local goldsmiths to adapt Mediterranean designs from the occasional example that turned up. The most original item was a golden boat, the earliest known model of a Celtic sea-going vessel. Fashioned from sheet gold and wire, it was equipped with a mast and yard-arm, benches for eighteen rowers, wispy oars of wire, a steering oar at the stern and a grappling hook. It is a simple, enchanting creation sustaining the proposition that the Broighter hoard was an offering to the local sea-god Manannan mac Lyr. Archaeologists believe the workshop in which the boat, the torc and a small gold cauldron (which completed the treasure) were made was in a community close by.[31]

Snettisham: the grand finale

Back in Britain the final display of La Tène style Celtic gold was spectacular. In 1948 deep ploughing of a field at Ken Hill, Snettisham in Norfolk, turned up the first of at least a dozen distinct hoards of gold torcs. Over the next forty years no less than 75 complete torcs and pieces of 100 more, along with bracelets and coins, were recovered. The combined treasures yielded 15 kg/482 t.oz of gold and 20 kg/643 t.oz of silver – the largest deposit of gold from Celtic Europe.[32] They were buried in a series of carefully excavated pits, where the torcs rested like worms in a nest. Scrap metal, rough alloy bars and even crucible waste were tucked into some pits, the implication being that these caches were associated with a nearby workshop, and may, in part, have been used for secure hiding of the stock-in-trade. Other nests of perfect torcs were votive offerings, or hiding places for torcs recovered for religious rites from time to time.

The finest are classic examples of twisted torc bodies. "The most elaborate show great inventiveness in creating different, regularly patterned surface textures from twisting and bundling the wires in different ways," observed Peter Northover.[33] The gold content of the torcs, however, varied widely, from purity over 900 fine, down to 250 fine, with high silver and/or copper content. The goldsmiths understood alloys, and on occasion debased the gold deliberately (perhaps for a torc for a less important occasion or client). Moreover, they were working mainly with imported Celtic coin from Belgium and northern France which, in itself, was already adulterated. The local tribe, the Iceni, also made their own coins from such imports, which would have led to inevitable debasement. The confirmation that coin was melted for jewellery is that some of the small rings found at Snettisham match the weight of contemporary coins. The goldsmiths lacked a regular supply of new gold, and worked with whatever came their way. The Snettisham workshop operated over several years or even decades around 75 BC.

The reliance on imported coins, rather than local gold recovery, meant that a workshop, such as Snettisham, was vulnerable to the changing Celtic scene in Europe as the Romans pressed their advantage northwards. Indeed, this treasure was the last example of gold being used for large ornaments in the La Tène tradition which had endured for four hundred years.

After Snettisham the curtain came down. Julius Caesar defeated Vercingetorix, leader of the Celtic Gauls at Alesia on the Cote d'Or (scarcely forty kilometres from the Vix princess burial), in 52 BC. Gradually, all of Gaul came under Roman control. The indigenous coinage was replaced by Roman coin, and the customs were slowly Romanised. Caesar plundered Gaul for gold, dispatching so much back to Rome that the local price there momentarily fell. Britain retained its independence for another century, despite Julius Caesar's brief invasion. A meagre local Celtic currency was maintained until after AD 60 when Britain also came under the Romans, whose gold coinage ruled for three centuries. Elsewhere Germanic tribes swept aside Celtic oppida in Bohemia and along the Danube. "Celtic culture per se is generally considered to have come to an end," wrote Miranda Green.[34]

Despite this eclipse, the Celtic presence is still felt around the Atlantic fringes of Europe today, most directly in language, but also in an inherent awareness of ancient traditions. In gold, the legacy is the diversity of objects to be seen in museums large and small right across Europe. The main collections are in The National Museum of Ireland, The British Museum, Musée des Antiquités Nationales just outside Paris, and small regional museums in Angoulême and Châtillon sur Seine, Museo Provincial, Lugo in Spain, Schweizerriches Landesmuseum in Zurich, Museo Civico Archeologico in Bologna, and Museu Archeologico in Padua, Rheinissches Landesmuseum in Bonn, Württembergisches Landesmuseum in Stuttgart, Musées Royaux d'Art et d'Histoire in Brussels, and the Magyar Nemzeti Muzeum in Budapest. That pan-European roll-call qualifies the Celts as 'the first Europeans'.

Part Two
Empires (AD 1 - 1200)

CHAPTER 12

China:
A serious player:
Ancient and Modern

The Chinese have long adored gold. Catchphrases and proverbs, ancient and modern, laud gold, *chin* in Mandarin and *kam* in Cantonese, as a symbol of happiness and prosperity. The child of a wealthy family is said to be born, not with a silver spoon, but with golden chopsticks in his mouth. Yet China is an enigma in gold's history. At the beginning of the Christian era its emperor, Wang Mang (AD 9–23) held the world's largest reserve of gold, around 155 m.t/5 million t.oz, in his treasury, but that was the higher-water mark, not exceeded until modern times. China was also the cradle of alchemy, the search for the elusive agent to transmute other metals into gold, which was pursued diligently by its scientists for centuries. The implication, to some historians, was that China lacked regular gold supplies and so tried to create it, although the most recent research suggests that gold has been mined in every province of China, although not in abundance.

For all that auspicious gold reserve two thousand years ago, China never had a true gold coinage and was the only major nation not on the gold standard at the beginning of the 20th century, remaining firmly wedded to a silver standard until 1935. Today, however, China has an active gold industry, ranking third in the world as a gold producer in 2006 and potentially second before 2010, and already second in jewellery fabrication (after India).[1] (a good deal being unofficial), while its central bank has around 600 m.t/19.3 million t.oz in reserves – just four times the amount the emperor held in AD 23. In short, China was a serious player in gold two thousand years ago, just as it is becoming once again in the early 21st century.

Remarkably, the measure of gold's weight in both eras has the same name – *liang* in Mandarin and *tael* in Cantonese – indicating one Chinese ounce, although the actual weight of the ounce has changed. At the beginning of the Han dynasty in 206 BC, one *liang/tael* weighed 15.25 grams/0.49 t.oz, compared to 37.43 grams/1.2 t.oz today.[2] The Han dynasty, surviving from 206 BC until AD 220, was nourished by gold. "By the Han period, for the only time in China's history, gold bullion was extensively used in commercial transactions," observed Peter J. Golas in his study of mining in China. "Even the early Han government seems to have had remarkably large amounts of gold available to it."[3]

Thus China came relatively late to the gold scene. While there is sound archaeological evidence for the use of copper and the making of bronze (copper/tin alloy) in northern China around 2000 BC or a little later, there is scant trace of gold until after 1500 BC and not much before 1000 BC. The first signs are scraps of gold foil 0.2mm thick or gold leaf hammered into a thin flake 0.01mm thick. They were used for decoration on metal or wooden vessels and ornaments by the Shang dynasty (1500–1050 BC). One early tomb contained the remains of a local ruler encased in this gold sheet attached to the body by red lacquer. Several bronze heads found in Szechuan province were covered with gold foil. Overall, however, gold was scarce; jade and bronze were the early symbols of prestige and incorruptibility. The perception began to change with the steady infiltration of gold ornaments from the nomads of the steppes, the vast grasslands rolling across Central Asia from Mongolia to the Ukraine.

The Central Asian connection

From the earliest times China was known as the creator of luxurious silks, traded with her nomadic neighbours of the northern steppes and later welcomed around the Mediterranean world as the height of fashion. What is less appreciated is that, in turn, her neighbours were largely responsible for introducing gold into ancient China. Not just the metal itself, but every important metalworking technique, from cupellation to mercury gilding, along with casting, filigree, granulation, loop-in-loop chain and lost-wax casting, was transmitted by way of the steppe people of Central Asia, who had themselves learned them from the West.[4] The early gold ornaments of northern China are cast plaques of stags with swept-back antlers, grazing horses or wild asses or ibex and crouching leopards. They match the ornaments of the Scythian nomads who rode west out of Central Asia soon after 700 BC to settle by the Black Sea (*see chapter 10*). The golden animals of the steppes were symbols of rank and wealth to Eurasian nomads living between Bulgaria in the west and the Great Wall of China from the 7th to the 6th centuries BC to the 1st century AD, according to Emma Bunker, the pre-eminent scholar on the art and culture of these nomadic people.[5] The source of this tradition lay in the gold of the Altai mountains of south-eastern Siberia and western Kazakhstan. The open-cast and shallow underground mines there, some dating back to 1500 BC, were a prime source of gold for the nomads and for northern China.

Contact between the settled nomads and agricultural people of the feudal states of north China was close. The Chinese bartered silk for horses, furs and gold ornaments. The furs moved on the 'Fur Route', forerunner of the Silk Road, which stretched from north of the Caspian Sea along the fiftieth parallel to Lake Baikal and thence down the Amur river, which today forms the border between China and Russia. The Amur was, and still is, an important source of alluvial gold, which also took the Fur Route. The likelihood is that gold from the Altai and the Amur reached northern China, not as dust, but as ornaments which could easily be melted as the Chinese acquitted their own metalworking skills.

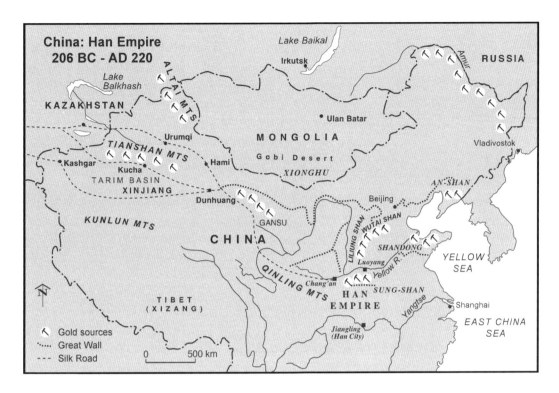

By the 6th century BC gold earrings, necklaces, cast belts and bridle ornaments for horses were common in a wide arc from north-east to north-western China, especially in the Ordos region skirted by the upper reaches of the Yellow River. In these competing feudal states, butting up against nomad territory (the line on which the Great Wall of China would soon be built), small gold pectorals of horses, wild asses (*kulan*) or leopards worn on the chest, became status symbols for local chiefs. The vogue gradually spread south into the Central Plains around modern Beijing, where these talismen were a mark of rank by 500 BC. Weaponry was also highlighted with gold. The British Museum's China Gallery displays a bronze sword of the Warring States period with a gold inscription on its blade, a crossbow inlaid with gold and silver, and a fine open-work dagger handle with gold wires plaited like intertwined ivy.

Gold had joined jade and bronze in the triumvirate respected as signs of wealth. "Gold became the major metal for luxury items," noted Emma Bunker, describing gold vessels from the tomb of the Marquis of Zeng in Hubei province, "which reflect the secular, not the ritual aspects of society. Ornate garment hooks cast or enhanced by gold proclaimed their owner's wealth, not his beliefs. Power, politics and prestige were the chief concerns."[6]

The technology of working gold was increasingly understood. The tomb of Prince Jing (577–537 BC) in Shaanxi province revealed a fine cast gold tiger, a golden bird and a gold buckle with a duck-headed hook.[7] The Chinese goldsmiths later evolved their own variation of lost-wax casting by using a coarse textile to reinforce the wax. This 'lost wax and lost textile' trick was revealed in gold plaques which showed a woven pattern on their backs. "This casting technique developed somewhere in the ancient Chinese world to allow craftsmen to produce a very thin wax model … reducing the amount of metal required to cast the final product," Emma Bunker decided.[8]   Later the goldsmiths used 'mother-molds', in which a whole series of identical plaque designs could be made, an early step towards mass production.[9]   Another significant advance, after 400 BC, was the adoption of mercury gilding to put a thick sheen of gold over bronze, replacing gold foil which had enhanced the appearance of bronze for many centuries. This proved a strategic technique in trying to pass off bronze as gold, whether by forgers or alchemists.

The full maturity of goldsmiths' skills was reached under the brief Qin dynasty that unified China and the long-running Han dynasty that followed from 206 BC. Their repertoire was completed with the mastering of granulation, which became fashionable, especially in the Imperial Workshops. The fabrication was not only for the emperor and the court, but splendid gifts for rulers of vassal states and provincial governors. The style by now had become distinctly Chinese, shrugging off the nomadic images of steppe wildlife in favour of splendid dragons. Belt buckles became ornate with inlaid quartz for eyes and moving tongues to fasten them. The *repoussé* design on one sophisticated buckle showed a dragon entwined with a fantastic creature. "The plaque is a superbly crafted example of Han goldsmith work," declared Emma Bunker, "produced by hammering sheet gold over a matrix and then chasing the front surface to enhance the details … microscopic examination reveals the use of granulation, producing a border of granules around each eye."[10] The buckle was as subtle and sinuous as anything created by Greek goldsmiths for the Scythians in the same era. The lavishness of the workmanship was also unveiled in the royal tombs at Mancheng in Hebei province, with everything from gold seals to acupuncture needles. The emperor Liv Sheng and his wife Dou Wan were buried in suits of articulated jade plaques sewn together with gold thread, merging two incorruptible materials to preserve the human body.[11]

The goldsmiths did not forget the traditional ornaments of their northern neighbours on the steppes. They had, meanwhile, been partly unified by the Xionghu tribe into a nomadic empire, always on the move with no fixed cities. The Chinese goldsmiths cast gold plaques of their favourite animals for export, carefully marking their weight and origin on the back. Such trade goods were important. The Han's military power depended on the horses they bought from the Xionghu. Gold ornaments along with exotic Chinese lacquers and, of course, silk were popular with the roving stock breeders. Gold was portable wealth, just as it was for Scythian nomads around the Black Sea for whom Greek goldsmiths made luxury articles.[12]

This two-way traffic in gold has continued for two thousand years. Placer deposits are no respecters of borders. Alluvial mining has flourished along the

Amur River, between north-east China and Russia. The Russian writer Anton Chekhov, travelling down the Amur by steamship in June 1890, wrote, "To our left the Russian shore, to our right the Chinese … China is as wild and deserted as Russia; you sometimes see villages and guard huts, but not very often. The people living along the Amur are most unusual … all they talk about is gold. Gold, gold – nothing else".[13] A century on again, I reported from Beijing in 1993, "Cross-border smuggling had developed since the collapse of the Soviet Union. Russian gold is bartered for consumer goods that are increasingly plentiful in China".[14]

Gold 'stamps' by the sheet

The first recognition of gold as a symbol of wealth was in ornaments. As money, it made a slower start and then only in the Central Plains along the Yellow River after 700 BC. Previously, during the Western Zhou period (1050–771 BC), when China was still a quiltwork of independent states, bronze and copper 'money' circulated. In the north, bronze 'knife' or 'spade' money shaped like those utensils, was widespread. Elsewhere, copper coins with square holes in their centre were used for small transactions, their weight being based on *shu* in multiples of 100 grains of millet. Silk and textiles made from vegetable fibres also became acceptable, the latter because they could be used for clothing as well as exchange. Silk was exchanged by the 'bundle', which was made up of five rolls, each about one metre in length. Silk was regarded as an 'investment item' at home as well as the major export item.

Gold was first used as money in the southern state of Zhou on the Central Plains. The 'coins' were small, flat squares, 2.3cm across and 5mm thick, produced in sheets of up to twenty from which each square was cut off, like a postage stamp. The earliest 'stamps' were punch-marked *Ying-yuan*, meaning 'treasure of Ying', the Zhou capital on the Yangtze river. Ying was founded about 700 BC, but the gold 'stamps' probably date from 500 BC. Sheets of the stamps, some with the mark of other cities, have turned up at archaeological sites in seven provinces of modern China.[15] These samples have been up to 990 fine. A variation on the 'stamps' were small ingots of *huang-chin*, meaning actual gold or yellow gold. They were square with rounded corners, not of uniform thickness, but rising in the middle and thinning out at the edges, like Chinese pastry cakes. Indeed, they were known as *ping-chin* after the cakes.

Reviewing these early forms of money (or 'method of round', as it was known), an early Zhou minister, quoted in Han Schu 24, the earliest economic history of China, observed, "The most precious medium of exchange was gold. The convenient one was the knife money. The one which flowed (i.e. like water) was coins". The 'round' of textiles from vegetable fibres, he added, was 'the widespread one', while silk was stored up (as investment) by the 'bundle'.[16] The precise weights of these monies are uncertain in the early period, for there was little standardisation in the states (or the Warring States as they become between 480–221 BC).

Those wars, however, led to the unification of China under the Qin dynasty by 221 BC. The first Qin ruler set about regularising the monetary system. "When the Qin united all under Heaven currency was issued in two denominations," the Han Schu 24 history recorded. "Actual gold which weighed an *i* or one *catty* (twenty *taels*) was given the name of *shang-pi* (currency of the first class), and … copper coins".[17] The actual gold ingot at twenty *taels* thus weighed 305 grams/9.8 t.oz, which cannot be called a coin. It was decreed that other items such as pearls, jade, tortoise shell, cowries, silver and tin were not to be used as money, but only for vessels, ornaments, or treasures. The new Imperial China wanted clearly defined currency – gold and copper. The Qin dynasty was short-lived, lasting only until 207 BC. The take-over was by the Han, who survived for four hundred years, sustained, like its contemporary, the Roman Empire, by substantial quantities of gold.

The sources of gold

The sources of gold that enabled the Han to acquire the world's largest stock of gold by AD 23 have caused much debate. The original suggestion, advanced in the 1940s by Homer H. Dubs of Duke University, was that, "China did not then mine any large quantities of gold". He proposed that the gold came primarily from Siberia (the Amur River) paid for by Chinese silk, and along the Silk Road itself from the Mediterranean world, whither much Roman gold and silver was transported after 110 BC (he was helped in that by Pliny the Elder commenting on this drain of precious metals).[18] However, a broader picture of the sources has emerged in recent years revealing that placer gold deposits were extensively tapped in China well before the Han period.

Placer deposits were already being worked in Kansu province of north-west China by 1000 BC, but the real thrust came around 500 BC, as the Warring States period leading to unification was beginning. Chinese miners and prospectors started coming to grips with the realities of the geology of gold and other metal and mineral deposits. The early notion was that gold and other minerals grew in the ground, like vegetables, but one needed to understand where the 'vegetable' patches might be. A mineral inventory, the *Wu Tshang Shan Ching* or The Five Storehouse Mountain Classic, written in the 5th century BC, identified nearly one hundred metallic and non-metallic minerals, together with jades, rocks and clays. "These chapters … testify to a keen awareness … of the variety of useful minerals and materials available from the surface of the earth as well as from underground," noted Peter Golas. "They also give us some idea of how the Chinese were trying to make sense of the variety in the mineral world, including efforts to generalise about where minerals were to be found, which minerals tended to be found together, the properties of minerals and rocks (hardness, colour, lustre, etc.)."[19]

The focus on mining evidently paid off. Terms such as sha chin, strictly meaning sand gold but indicating placer, and shan chin meaning mountain gold or veins, turn up in texts. Wooden washing pans, some shaped like boats, finely woven bamboo baskets and triangular wooden boxes for separating slurry have been found by archaeologists who date them around 500 BC. Thick cloth and felt were also employed to trap particles of gold in running waters, in the 'Golden Fleece' manner, although it is not certain how early this technique was adopted. "The Chinese became very skilful panners," declared Peter Golas, who had watched modern ones at work, "matching the patience and manual dexterity that have marked so much of Chinese handicraft production."[20]

The richest deposits were in pre-Cambrian granite in the Wu-thai and Lu-liang mountains of Shanxi up on the northern border with Inner Mongolia, the An-shan mountains of Lianoning on the north-east frontier, the Thai-shan range of Shantung, and the Sung-shan mountains of Honan. The placer deposits were often shallow, and usually relatively easy to work. Over fifty mining sites have been identified in north and north-east China, dating before 200 BC, mostly from the Warring States period.[21] Peasant miners discovered two such open-cast trenching operations in Hopeh province in 1984, each with trenches up to three metres deep and thirty metres long.

Their discovery was a reminder that little changed in gold mining in China into modern times. Until the early 1990s it remained, for the most part, a primitive, village-orientated business. Talking with Chinese mining officials in Beijing in 1993, I was shown, unofficially, a booklet on mining in Hebei province, which listed 175 village gold mining collectives in the county of Qinglong alone. The officials had no firm idea how much gold was produced for it vanished into the black market. The total unofficial output in China at that time was estimated at around 25 m.t/800,000 t.oz annually.[22] That is not to suggest it was as much in ancient times, but merely to demonstrate what can be achieved in hundreds of villages with local people scouring out gold.

The foundation of the gold stock that sustained the Han dynasty came about in just that way over two thousand years ago, mostly from skilful gold panners. "Given that simple panning of gold has remained the overwhelmingly dominant method of working gold placers right down to the present," Peter Golas concluded, "the likelihood would seem to be that any significant increases in placer gold production during the Warring States and Han periods owed more to discoveries of new deposits and increases in the number of people engaged in gold washing rather than to technological breakthrough."[23]

The precise date of the arrival (from the west) of cupellation to refine the gold by separating out the base metals is uncertain; probably it was practised in the Han period. A later manual, from around AD 300, included precise instructions:

"Method of refining crude gold taken from streams. Use clean earthy clay to make a crucible, and dry it by taking over fire. Use pinewood charcoal and place the crucible in the furnace, and when the metal had melted put powdered salt in with it, stirring well. Watch until full fusion has taken place and then use a thornwood stick to remove the slag. Continue to add powdered salt, and then go on stirring and removing slag. When the process is complete, pour the metal into a mould making sure no cracks or fissures appear."

If they did, further refining was recommended with a mixture of powdered iron filings, ash of burnt cow-dung and powdered salt added to the gold, which was beaten into thin sheets. A mixture of yellow alum, poplar balsam and mud was to be smeared on the gold sheets, which were then heated several times over a charcoal fire to get "the best quality of red gold".[24] This confident recipe suggests a process already long established for the refining of domestic gold production.

Gold along the Silk Road

The local output was always supplemented by the gold, mostly as ornaments, from Central Asia. This was enhanced during the Han period by the growing importance of the Silk Road, the five thousand kilometres long overland route linking China with the Mediterranean world. In 148 BC the Chinese emperor sent an emissary, Zhang Qian, to investigate the 'Western Regions' beyond Ganzhou to the north of Tibet towards the Tarim Basin and, ultimately, Samarkand. After an odyssey lasting ten years, much of it in captivity, Zhang Qian returned with tales of thirty-six walled cities, their riches and their trade.

On the basis of his information, China not only pressed its trade along the burgeoning Silk Road, and established diplomatic links, but began military campaigns beyond the Tarim Basin and the Pamirs, reaching almost to Samarkand, emporium of the Silk Road, by 121 BC.[25] The hazards of sustaining such long supply lines prevented further expansion, but China's links along the Silk Road remained for a thousand years. Fine gold ornaments, especially heavy belts, came through on the caravans from the workshops of Samarkand, while gold from the Tien Shan mountains was picked up in Kucha, the city-state bordering the Tarim Basin and the Gobi desert.

The Silk Road was the direct link (albeit a journey of many months, even years) between the newly unified China and the expanding Roman Empire. The drain on Rome's coffers as gold and silver were dispatched to the east to pay for Chinese luxuries, above all silk, has been much debated; notably because of contemporary remarks by Pliny. Even in the 1st century BC wealthy Romans became so enamoured of Chinese silk that they sewed small pieces on their cloth or woollen togas as badges of prestige. By AD 14 the custom was so popular that the Senate in Rome voted to forbid men wearing silk, because of the cost in precious metals.[26] The silk trade did not diminish. Doubt exists, however, as to how much gold from Rome really ended up in China. Few Roman coins have been found there, unlike India, where significant hoards have turned up, although the coins would presumably have been melted down as China had no internal market for foreign coin (unlike Europe and the shores of the Mediterranean where the *aureus* was accepted everywhere). The Roman coins were certainly carried as far as Samarkand and then perhaps went into goldsmiths' workshops to be made into the fashionable belts beloved in Central Asia. So the gold may have arrived in China already fabricated. Even so, Rome was not a regular, or reliable, source of supply. Domestic production and Central Asian deposits were the foundations of the Han dynasty's stockpile.

Golden Age of the Han

The Han dynasty, coming to power in 206 BC, after the brief interregnum of the Qin, the unifiers of China, inherited a substantial stock of gold built up during the Warring States era from the blossoming of placer gold mining in several provinces. The gold did not circulate in the nation at large, where copper coin, known as *gian, guan, or wen*, and later christianed cash in pidgin English, was the standard common currency throughout most of China's history for everyday payments. Gold was the province of feudal landlords, the nobility, military chiefs and, of course, the emperor. The Founder of the Han, as he was billed in official documents, decided on monetary reform. "When the Han arose the money of the Chinn (Qin) was heavy, and difficult for practical purposes," the Han Schu 24 history noted.[27] The *catty*, the basic (but uncoined) monetary unit was reduced from 305 grams to 244 grams/7.8 t.oz, with its fineness determined by 'colour' (which implies the use of touchstones). Free copper coinage by the people was permitted for what were called "elm-pod-coins". One *catty* of gold was worth 10,000 elm-pods. "It does seem clear that money of the Han period in China was on the gold standard, the gold unit remaining constant," concluded Nancy Lee Swann, translator and commentator of the Han Schu 24 documents.[28] On this twin gold and copper track, the Chinese economy proceeded for the next four hundred years. The range of copper coins varied, with up to six denominations at times, but the underlying relationship of a gold *catty* for 10,000 copper 'cash' was maintained.

The Han emperor benefited from the custom of nobles and princes presenting him with gifts of gold, *huang-chin*, each year on the occasion of sacrifices offered in the eighth month of the lunar calendar. The expected gift was four *taels* (61 grams/1.96 t.oz) for every one thousand fiefs on a noble's domain. Each gift was carefully scrutinised, according to the commentator Ju-Shun in AD 40, to make sure the weight and colour were acceptable; if not, the errant patrician was punished.[29] Since alchemy was becoming all the rage in China (even with emperors) and metal was often passed off as gold (see below), such caution was prudent.

Controls were presided over by the Superintendent of Metals and Minerals, known as *Chih Chin*, at the Imperial Palace. His duties covered regulations on gold, jade, tin, precious stones and rare pigments, according to contemporary records. His role was defined thus:

"He receives the consignments which come in from taxation and distinguishes the quality of the materials, whether refined or crude as well as recording their quantities and weights. He then marks them with the imperial seal. He deposits the gold and the tin in the Armoury, and the jade, stones and pigments in the Treasury ... he is also charged with receiving fines paid in metals and money."[30]

The gold and tin (for bronze) were placed in the Armoury because they were 'sinews of war', needed not just for military expenses, but to reward generals and their men after major campaigns. The salaries of the Superintendent of Metals and of senior ministers were frequently designated in gold, although in practice they were paid partly in copper coin and grain. The first minister and the minister of military affairs were paid 60,000 copper coins each month, equivalent to six *catties* of gold or 1.464 kg/46.8 t.oz. In a full year, 12 moons, that amounted to 17.568 kg/564.48 t.oz which, at a 21st century gold price of $650 per ounce, would be worth $366,000, which is not entirely out of line with a modern cabinet minister. A good horse for the minister could be had for 4,500 'cash' copper which, by the same calculation, would be $2,290.

The gold stock of the Han dynasty circulated constantly into the imperial coffers as tributes, taxes or fines and out again as salaries and rewards; one moment they were full, the next almost barren. The Han Schu 24 documents recount that during 124–123 BC, the general Wei Ch'ing successfully attacked Hsiung-nu in north China, earning himself and his officers 200,000 *catties of huang-chin*, actual gold, amounting to 48.8 m.t/1.6 million t.oz in prize money. That sum drained the gold reserves, so officials begged for an imperial order that would permit people to purchase official titles or government posts. Top jobs cost the equivalent of 30 *catties* (7.3 kg/267 t.oz of gold), payable in gold or copper coin. Sales were brisk. A handsome sum, equal to 300,000 *catties* or 73.2 m.t/2.25 million t.oz was raised.[31] The job-seekers, however, must have been paid largely in copper, because four years later another campaign by Wei Ch'ing brought rewards equal to 500,000 catties, which were all paid in copper coins.[32] The shortage of gold may be deduced from the fact that a short-lived attempt was made between 120–115 BC to introduce a new coin of silver-tin alloy in three denominations, but it on little acceptance.[33]

Wang Mang builds the ultimate hoard

The imperial gold reserve was, however, gradually re-built during the 1st century BC, so that, by the new millennium, the stock was again substantial. The sinologist Homer H. Dubs, in his famous paper on the Chinese stock of gold, pointed out that for two centuries under the Han nobles had been required to pay the emperor four *taels* of gold annually per thousand fiefs. This steady accumulation had always concentrated gold in the treasuries of nobles and the emperor. In AD 6, the first minister of the Han dynasty, Wang Mang, ordered not only nobles but all the people, to bring their gold to the national treasury and receive in return lightweight bronze coins of high denomination which had been 'washed with gold' (i.e. gilded). Three years later Wang Mang staged a coup, dismissed the Han nobility, declared himself emperor and demonetised the gilded coins. "In this way he mulcted his people of their gold," Homer Dubs commented sternly.[34]   The usurping emperor then issued five types of new currency in gold, copper, silver, carapaces of tortoises, and cowrie shells. Criticism of these tokens drew dire punishment, but few accepted them and before long they were withdrawn.[35]

Wang Mang himself, flush with China's entire gold stock, presented the family of his second wife with 30,000 *catties* (7.3 m.t/235,000 t.oz) of gold, along with horses, chariots, slaves, silks and jewels to the same value. Vengeance was swift. In AD 23 Wang Mang was killed by his own troops. The inventory that his generals then made of his gold holdings amounted to 155.5 m.t/5 million t.oz, quoted by the Chinese historian Pan Gu in his *History of the former Han Dynasty* written about AD 80. According to Pan Gu, "In the inner apartments of the Wei-Yang Palace, ten thousand *catties* of actual gold were put into one chest and there still remained sixty chests. In each office of the Yellow Gate and of the Intendent of Palace Parks and in the workshops of the Master of Recipes (court alchemist?) there were also several chests".[36]   This implies 2.44 m.t./78,446 t.oz in the specific chest mentioned, equal to 196 of today's 'London Good Delivery' bars of 400 t.oz, a pile just over one metre high. This might fit into a single chest – although moving it would be another matter. But was the same amount of gold in all the other chests? The total hoard of over 150 metric tonnes is questionable. Homer Dubs admitted as much, but argued Pan Gu probably got his figure from a contemporary account made to the new emperor, which must have been tolerably accurate. Dubs concluded, "I think it is rather likely that Wang Mang actually possessed at least a large proportion of the gold with which Pan Gu credited him".[37]

Indeed, it is not an unreasonable statistic. Half a century later in Rome, the great recoinage of the *aureus* by Nero, between AD 64–68, used perhaps 240 m.t/7.6 t.oz of gold recalled from general circulation (*see following chapter*).[38]   So a Chinese emperor who had corralled most of the nation's stock in his own palace could have held half that amount. It is also on the same scale as the rewards being paid out to Han generals over one hundred years earlier. The 'ball-park' amount has credence.

The Wang Mang interlude cut the Han period neatly in two: the original dynasty, often known as the Western Han, was now replaced by the Eastern Han. Yet they never achieved the power or security of their forbears, being beset by internal rivalries and, increasingly, by nomadic tribes from the north migrating into China as the Xionghu confederation on the steppes fell apart. Military expenses were heavy and the gold reserve inherited from Wang Mang was dissipated and not replaced by domestic production. Modern Chinese historians have suggested that gold became increasingly scarce under the Eastern Han due to the exhaustion of easily worked placer deposits and the diverting of gold into jewellery and large vessels.[39] What did not diminish (or perhaps was even encouraged) was alchemy.

Alchemy: first make your gold

A parallel world of gold existed in China for centuries; alongside the normal gold business was the relentless search for the magic formula that would turn base metals into gold. The belief was that, not only was alchemical gold superior to the real stuff, but that the conjuring up of the imperishable metal would secure earthly imperishability for the conjuror and for anyone who would buy his 'gold'. Thus, China became the pioneer of alchemy. "This concept of the elixir of immortality became firmly crystallised by 300 BC," wrote Joseph Needham.[40] All manner of alchemists – some of serious scientific bent and many charlatans, set themselves up everywhere from the imperial court to the humblest back street. It is a measure of how firmly alchemy gripped China and its influence on scientific evolution in chemistry, metallurgy and pharmacology over the centuries, that Joseph Needham's ongoing series on Science and Civilisation in China has devoted a good part of two whole volumes to its role.

Emperors were, in turn, captivated and irritated by it; intrigued at the prospect of its creation, angered when nobles paid their annual levies in fake gold. Imperial workshops were set up with enthusiasm and closed when the genuine article did not materialise. The Superintendent of Metals and Minerals was kept busy passing annual gifts to goldsmiths for assay. The Han emperor Wên Ti (179–156 BC) banned alchemists because, "in the end they did not succeed in fabricating gold, in spite of heavy expenses, mutual deceptions and magniloquent claims". A century later, however, the Imperial Workshops were again busy making 'superior gold'.[41] The temptation persisted because of the belief that it was the elixir of life. The incentive for the alchemist was not to create a gold reserve for the emperor (though no doubt that would have been welcome), but to get the right prescription for him to live for ever.

The actual challenge to create 'gold' was not so difficult. "The range of possible gold-like and silver-like alloys is very impressive," Joseph Needham pointed out.[42] The catch was that if the Superintendent of Metals turned the 'gold' over to a goldsmith for assay by cupellation, the bluff would be called. The easiest thing was to debase the gold by making an alloy with silver, nickel, tin or zinc, and pass it off as pure gold. The trick was possible because gold keeps much of its colour when it is diluted (witness modern jewellery of 8, 9 or 10 carats, instead of 24 carats, that retains the aura of gold). Another easy option was mercury gilding of bronze or brass to add a thin sheen of gold.

The subterfuge most favoured by Chinese alchemists was to make alloys entirely of metals other than gold, but which combined to match its appearance. The best alloy was brass composed of a blend of 60% copper and up to 40% zinc, with an occasional dash of tin, lead and even iron. This mix made a passable imitation for gold, always provided it was not assayed. Over the centuries many other combinations of non-precious metals were tried, but brass was most likely to pass.[43] "No later than the beginning of the 2nd century and perhaps some time before, brasses of various compositions are the explanation of what was done," Needham concluded.[44]

Brass continued to be used widely in China in coin and ornamental vessels throughout the 1st century AD, much more than in Europe. Indeed, the initial use of alchemical gold was in plate and vessels, from which people ate and drank in the belief they possessed a magical property conferring longevity or immortality. The next step was to ingest elixirs, often seemingly lethal potions. An extensive literature recommended a multitude of remedies. Pao Phu Tzu's elixir book, composed c. AD 320, had much on offer. He advised a subtle blend of 'gold, hog-fat and strong vinegar' to ensure longevity of 2000 years. The Grand Purity elixir contained vinegar, red salt, calomel (a chloride of mercury), lead and gold for certain immortality. A tasty cocktail of wild raspberry juice into which was stirred gold leaf, saltpetre, salt, vinegar and magnetite sounded promising.[45] The simplest remedy was gold leaf in wine, which secured insensibility to heat or cold, together with levitation and immortality (at least a potable drink similar to Japanese saki with gold leaf offered to this writer in Tokyo).

Pao Phu Tzu was a forerunner for what is billed as The Golden Age of Alchemy between AD 400 and 800, during the Northern, Sui and Tang dynasties. The most celebrated alchemist was Thao-Hung Ching (AD 456–536), renowned as a physician and pharmaceutical naturalist and very much into herbal medicines. The Emperor Wu Ti was so taken with his skills that he provided him with gold, cinnabar (crystals of mercury sulphide) and copper sulphate for his elixirs. They were a tempting vision of crystals like "frost and snow" and, so the word went, "really did make the body feel lighter".[46] A more fearsome recipe of this era mixed eight ounces of gold with mercury, realgar (a disulphate of arsenic), orpiment (also known as yellow arsenic) and vinegar. The lethal nature of such elixirs was brushed aside by the alchemist Chang Yin-Chu in his *Discourse on Metals*, AD 713, who said that, while a single substance might be poisonous, if compounded with others, the poisonous effects could be overcome. He added, "Gold is the seminal essence of the sun … after taking gold the skin will not wrinkle, the hair will not go white, and no one will either be affected by lapse of time nor disturbed by ghosts and spirits".[47] Such universal aspirations nourished Chinese alchemy through the centuries.

Gold for the Buddha

Returning to real gold, the puzzle is why China peaked so early. After the fall of the Han, Imperial China continued for almost seventeen centuries, through many dynasties, some great like the Tang, Ming and Qing, and others that were swiftly dethroned. All this time gold fulfilled essentially a niche role. A tradition of minting gold and silver coins never developed; the every-day currency was copper, with silk and other textiles serving in settlement of many transactions. Even paper money was issued between the 11th and early 15th centuries as promissory notes against copper coin, but faded out when notes depreciated against coins. China was also a significant importer of silver, offering a tempting 1:5 gold/silver ratio when Marco Polo visited in the 13th century. Venice dispatched silver to China in the 15th century via Black Sea ports and the Silk Road (*see chapter 16*), and after the Spanish discoveries of silver in Mexico in the 16th century even more went by sea through the Philippines and, later, with the Dutch and English East India Companies. Most of it, however, went into the fabrication of silverware, not coin.

Chinese economic historians today have suggested that because gold and silver were in relatively short supply in ancient China and again after the Han period, the custom of using precious metals as money never took off. The British Museum's Helen Wang has suggested "gold and silver coins were 'special purpose' money, often for use within the court".[48]   Gold continued to be used among the nobility during the Six Dynasties era from AD 265–589, when China was divided into rival north and south factions, for payments among themselves or for hoarding. The reality is that the vast population of China was always tied to the land on the Central Plains. In their villages they had little use for money, save a few copper coins.

Gold production certainly continued with placer deposits being worked in many provinces, but not at the level of the Warring States and early Han era. An account of alluvial recovery in Yunnan province during the Tang dynasty (AD 618–906) described how, "between spring and winter they first dig pits a *chang* (3 metres) deep … in the summer months when the rain comes down in torrents, it carries mud into the pits. The natives then spread out this alluvium and pick over the sand or rock (for gold). They may get flakes or nuggets".[49]   Underground mining for vein gold may have evolved during the later Han period, and certainly before AD 600. The most productive area was on the Shandong peninsula, north-east of modern Shanghai, where the Jao-Yuan mine has been worked for over one thousand years. This area is just touched by epithermal deposits of gold, which circle the Pacific Rim – but they can only be unravelled by modern technology. That is the catch; China has much to offer the modern gold miner, but had less for his forbears. The output was never sufficient to sustain a gold coinage.

Whatever gold there was, was taken up by fabrication.   The Tang era, beginning in AD 618, was a period of high quality craftsmanship. The standards of granulation, filigree and *cloisonné* were exceptional, in ornaments, small boxes and long hairpins. Tang figure painting depicted women with elaborate hair combs and hairpins crowned with birds or lotus flowers. Examples in gold, however, are few, perhaps because they have been melted down, but more likely because output was limited. Walking through the Chinese galleries of museums, it is striking how many ornaments and vessels are of gilded bronze, not gold, while wonderful silver bowls, cups and vases are abundant. "Silversmithing, more than any other craft, embodies the quintessence of … Tang taste," observed Bo Gyllensvärd in his book on the Carle Kempe Collection of Chinese gold and silver in Stockholm.[50]

The soaring new demand for gold, however, was to satisfy the requirements for ornate pagodas and statues as the religion of Buddhism swept China. During the Six Dynasties era (AD 222–589) the influence of Buddhism spread from India and Tibet to grip much of China. The aura of gold abounded in Buddhist texts that encouraged the faithful to make offerings of gold, silver and precious stones, and endow statues of precious metal in the Buddha's image. "The texts conjure up paradise in which the ground is made of gold, steps leading to terraces are made of gold and silver and lapis lazuli," John Kieschnick pointed out in his study of Buddhism and Chinese materialism.[51] While Buddhist monks themselves took vows of austerity and restraint, Buddhist art and architecture assumed a whole vocabulary of opulence. A 4th century monk, Zhi Daolin, praised the "colour and loveliness of purple and gold", while *stupas* (pagodas) were "ornamented with gold to make them splendid and dazzling".[52] Since gifts to the Buddha enhanced social prestige, offerings flowed in. A cautionary tale also warned of the penalty of reneging on offerings; one patron, Hou Qing, had a bronze image of the Buddha made, promising to cover it with gold leaf, but he ran out of money. The Buddha then appeared to his wife in a dream saying that, as punishment for not gilding him, he would take her only son. The child was taken ill and died.[53]

Emperors were soon in despair; Buddhist devotion was draining their gold stocks. As gold went into the *stupas* and even books of Buddhist texts were adorned with gold leaf, the emperor was already trying to curb the custom by AD 490. The Emperor Wuzong in AD 845 went further; he issued an edict forbidding the use, not just of gold, but silver, copper, iron and gems in Buddhist images. Buddhists must make images of clay or wood which are sufficient to express respect," he declared.[54] The order was withdrawn on his death, but over the centuries emperors repeatedly tried to forbid the application of gold and gold leaf to Buddhist shrines, with little success. As John Kieschnick concluded, "The metal taken up by Buddhist images was so great that it was persistently coveted by the state. From medieval times up to the 1960s, the Chinese government repeatedly called for the melting down of Buddhist images to fill state coffers or provide metal for construction or the military".[55] Which may help to explain why gold never achieved a foothold in coinage in China after the Han era that ended in AD 220.

CHAPTER 13

Rome:
An Empire Built on Gold

By tradition Rome was founded on 21st April 753 BC, a humble town at a strategic crossing point of the river Tiber. Nine hundred years later, in AD 150, Rome was a city of one million people commanding an empire of perhaps fifty million, embracing not just the whole Mediterranean world, but much of Europe. The Roman Empire reached from the Atlantic Ocean to the Black Sea, from Hadrian's Wall in the north of England to the deserts of North Africa and Egypt. *Pax Romana* was maintained by up to thirty legions guarding the far-flung frontiers. Their presence provided not just stability but, unwittingly, established the first really international economy, broader even than that encompassed by today's Euro. For the legionnaires were paid in hard cash, gold and silver coin, bearing the portrait of their emperor. Their wages became the major component of the empire's budget, and pumped cash to every corner.

"In the Roman world the availability of money permitted the creation of a professional standing army and of a system of salaried officials," wrote Christopher Howgego of the Ashmolean Museum. "The normal use of coin as a means of exchange was ubiquitous … that is to say that coin was used both in towns and in areas of settled agriculture, and in the 'less developed' as well as the 'more sophisticated' provinces … money was embedded in the structure of the economy."[1] Gold coin predominated; of the 13,000 coins recovered from the volcanic ash of Pompeii, destroyed by the Vesuvius eruption in AD 79, the gold coins were worth twice as much as silver and base metal coins put together.[2]

The quantity of gold in circulation was on a scale not previously seen, even after Alexander the Great captured the Persian treasure. Indeed, it was not equalled again until modern times, after the gold rushes of California and Australia in the mid-19th century. One calculation has put the weight of gold coin in circulation throughout the empire in AD 160 at 880 m.t/28.3 million t.oz made up of 120 million *aurei*; this is a dimension otherwise unknown in the ancient world. Silver coin then in circulation was also assessed at 5,766 m.t/185.4 t.oz).[3]

These amounts are realistic when the stepping stones by which the Roman Empire was pieced together are analysed. The accumulation of gold and silver took the best part of four hundred years, starting shortly before 200 BC. Rome was initially at a disadvantage. The Roman Republic, founded in 509 BC, had virtually no domestic gold or silver production (unlike Egypt which had mines in the eastern deserts and Nubia, or Greece with silver at Laurion and gold and silver in Macedonia). The precious metals were acquired only after Rome had won internal wars between 350 and 270 BC to control all Italy. In those wars, as Fernand Braudel put it, "The Roman legion was forged as an instrument of victory".[4]

Thus prepared, the republic was ready to take on its greatest rival, Carthage, for control of the Mediterranean, picking off lesser powers on the way. "Rome laid its hands by stages on the stored up wealth of the whole of the Mediterranean," Christopher Howgego observed. "First Carthage and Spain, then Macedon, Greece, Asia, Numidia, the East, Gaul, and finally Egypt fed the Roman coffers. The sums involved were massive and the immediate impact of these accretions of wealth would be dramatic."

The historian Livy (59 BC–AD 17) catalogued the booty. Rome's first foray against Carthage itself in the Second Punic War (218–202 BC) netted it 3,270 kg/ 105,000 t.oz in gold, which enhanced the *aerarium* (treasury) stock which previously was a mere 1,300 kg/41,800 t.oz.[5] The capture of New Carthage (Cartagena) in south-east Spain in 209 BC also won Rome control of the region's silver mines, then the major source of supply. The conquest of Macedonia in 167 BC also brought a mixed treasure of gold and silver. In all, Livy reckoned Rome secured 12,315 kg/ 396,000 t.oz of gold between the second Punic War and 157 BC, when the *aerarium* held 5,640 kg/181,326 t.oz, plus 11,291 kg/363,000 t.oz of silver. Temple treasuries also held stocks of precious metals, given as votive offerings, but liable to be called back in time of war (as had happened in Athens). The dictator Sulla 'borrowed' 2,916 kg/93,750 t.oz of temple gold in 88 BC to finance expeditions in Greece and Asia against Mithradates, ruler of the Black Sea shores. Fortuitously he returned victorious in 81 BC with 4,860 kg/156,250 t.oz in gold and a huge bonus of 37,260 kg/1.2 million t.oz of silver. Julius Caesar took almost 1,000 kg (32,150 t.oz) for 'expenses' when he set out to conquer Gaul in 59 BC, but also returned with much more loot. So he felt justified in tapping the *aerarium* for a further 1,340 kg/ 43,000 t.oz in bar form after his crossing of the Rubicon in 49 BC to seize control of Rome. He promptly struck large quantities of gold *aurei* in his own image, a direct challenge to the authority of the state.

In fact, these were the first significant gold coins of the Roman republic. A limited issue of gold *staters* of 6.82 grams/0.22 t.oz and half *staters* and smaller coins had been made between 216 and 209 BC with some of the first booty from the Second Punic War, but Rome still lacked regular gold supply. By contrast, the war assured the control of the Spanish silver mines. Thus, through the next 160 years, the silver *denarius* provided the main circulation, along with bronze coins, and became the standard form of payment to the army. A scattering of commemorative gold coins was struck in the 80s BC to mark Sulla's victories, but it was Julius Caesar who initiated the era of gold coin. In 46 BC the regular issues of Rome's moneyers became his issues. After his murder on the Ides of March 44 BC, the ruling triumvirate of Mark Antony, Lepidus and Octavian each

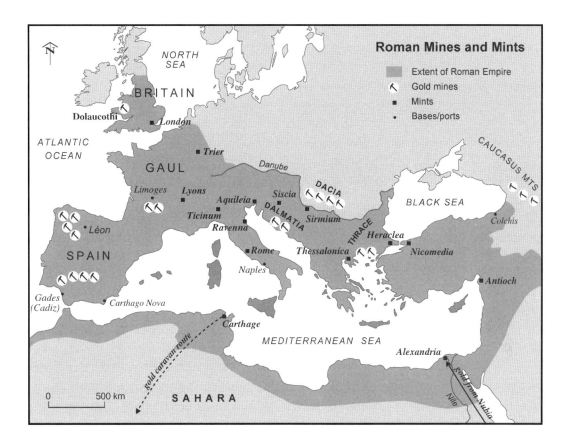

issued their own gold coin until 38 BC when Octavian, already assuming supreme power, determined that only his name should be on coinage. With the creation of the empire, under Octavian, taking the name Augustus, in 27 BC, a new monetary system for Rome emerged with gold as a major element.[6] The coinage was part of Augustus' strategy to bring Rome peace and stability after a century of civil strife.

Coins became a symbol of the new imperial authority, bearing a portrait of the emperor or of his immediate family. At the heart of the system was the gold *aureus* of 8.1 grams/0.26 t.oz, normally 993 fine. One *aureus* was worth 25 silver *denarii*, each of 3.86 grams, giving a gold:silver ratio of 1:11.9. The prime initial use was army wages. The pay of the normal legionary was equal to nine *aurei* or 225 *denarii* annually, which was issued as *stipendia* three times a year on the first of January, May and September. The *stipendia* were usually paid in a mix of gold and silver coin for convenience, although the proportions are not clear. The advantage in making payment in gold was that it was much easier to transport to distant forts; each *stipendia* for a legion of 3,000 men would require scarcely 75 kg/2,400 t.oz of gold coin, compared with nearly one tonne of silver. The vast network of military bases also gave coin wide circulation. "The monetary economy of Roman Italy was spread throughout the empire, primarily by the Roman legions, paid in coin and with enormous spending power in relation to the areas where they were stationed," Michael Crawford noted. "They bought from and 'married' into these areas, bringing with them the monetary usages to which they were accustomed … the empire for the next two and a half centuries possessed a monetary unit which covered almost the entire Mediterranean world".[7]

Yet paying the army put Rome under constant pressure to find fresh gold and silver supplies. Booty from conquests was finite; after the submission of Egypt in 30 BC little more was forthcoming. The imperative, the Emperor Augustus (27 BC–AD 14) realised, was new gold mines.

Gold mining – the Empire's lifeline

The strong Roman economy was founded originally on gold and silver hoovered up as booty, but was sustained through the succeeding centuries by mine production. When that faltered in the 3rd century AD, the empire was fatally weakened. The Romans had already secured the silver mines of southern Spain in 209 BC when they took New Carthage (Cartagena) and added the silver sources of Macedonia some years later. The priority was gold and the prize mining prospects were in the harsh mountains of north-west Spain. Their conquest was one of Augustus' first goals. In 26 BC he went to Spain himself, backed by three legions. Resistance was tenacious and the terrain almost impenetrable (as any visitor there today will testify). The territory was finally subdued by Augustus' son-in-law Agrippa in 19 BC, but legions had to remain on duty, mainly in the ancient town of León, for almost two hundred years.

The gold resources were worth it. The Romans brought in their best engineers and miners who worked with ingenuity and technical skill to recover gold from alluvial beds in rivers, alluvial terraces like cliffs high above, and from hard-rock quartz deposits in the depths of the mountains. They created the world's first long-term gold mining industry with projects on a grand scale. Close to 250 Roman mine sites have been identified. Indeed, until the gold discoveries in South Africa in the 19th century AD there was no other precedent for major operations being maintained decade after decade. Most gold rushes were boom and bust. "The gold mines were the most important in the empire, serving as the essential source of the raw material necessary for guaranteeing the monetary system that Augustus based on gold and silver," the Spanish historians Almudena Orejas and F. Javier Sánchez-Palencia pointed out. "These mines were worked for approximately two hundred years as *ager publicus* (imperial domains) under the direct management of the state."[8] Technically, the emperor owned gold and silver mines, but usually leased the right of exploration to contractors, while his provincial procurator kept track of output, and legions provided military security. Legion VII Gemina, for instance, long made its base at León, the gateway to the gold mining region.

The Romans did exploit other mines in Gaul, in Britain (at Dolaucothi in Wales), in Dacia north of the river Danube, and the Balkans, but none was so prolific for so long. Spain's gold production fluctuated between five and ten m.t/160,000–320,000 t.oz annually during much of the 1st and 2nd centuries AD. By comparison, Spain also provided 60–100 m.t of silver a year, and even over 100 m.t occasionally in the 1st century BC from mines in southern Spain and the Pyrenees.

The major gold output was in the brooding mountains of the present provinces of Galicia, Orense and León, and the rivers Sil, Duerna, Mino, Narcea and Navia that flow down from the divide of the Cantabrica Cordillera to the Bay of Biscay and the Atlantic. "The mountains, with the vein gold they contain, are also the original source for the alluvial and placer gold deposits found in the rivers that flow from them," reported P. R. Lewis and G. D. B. Jones in a detailed survey.[9]

As the Elder Pliny explained in his *Natural History*, "Gold prospectors begin by collecting *segullum*, that is, placer-deposits indicating the presence of vein gold. After the auriferous material is washed, the sediment allows an estimate of the actual vein to be made … Gold found by this method is called *talutium*, a term that covers placer-deposits in general. It is … the wealth of placer-deposits that brings prosperity to the dry, barren mountains of the Spanish provinces".[10]

The easily accessible deposits in the rivers were the initial attraction for the Romans (and were certainly worked before they arrived), but over time they tracked the gold back to high level alluvial terraces and ultimately to the parent ore-bodies themselves. That was where they brought a new dimension to mining with massive hydrological operations channelling millions of litres of water for kilometres through aqueducts to flush out the gold. "The Romans were great miners, they really knew how to take advantage of water," remarked the modern mining consultant Dr Tim Williams. However, Pliny complained:

"It was laborious and expensive running aqueducts along mountain ridges to wash away mining debris. The aqueduct channels are called *corrugi* … The problems are innumerable; the incline must be steep to produce a surge rather than a trickle of water; consequently high level sources are required. Gorges and crevasses are bridged by viaducts. Elsewhere protruding rocks are cut away to allow the placing of flumes. Workmen cutting the rock face are suspended on ropes; man thus brings water through places he cannot himself pass. The washing process is ruined if the water is full of silt … to avoid this the water is made to flow over gravel or pebbles. On the ridge above the minehead, reservoirs are built measuring 60 metres each way and three metres deep. Five sluices about a metre across occur in the walls. When the reservoir is full, the sluices are knocked open so that the violent downrush is sufficient to sweep away rock debris".[11]

The longest aqueducts, to the Las Medulas site on the Rio Sil, spanned up to twenty kilometres and were capable of delivering up to 34 million litres of water per day. The Romans worked all along the Rio Sio, even tunnelling through an escarpment at Montefurado (which means 'pierced mountain') to create a canal to their diggings. "Every major meander of the Sil exhibits the tell-tale rock piles of placer workings," reported Lewis and Jones. Las Medulas itself was not only a high level alluvial operation at a thousand metres above sea level, but one of the best preserved of the Roman period, because apparently there has been no later working. Bright red alluvial deposits still stand out below eroded cliffs that remind visiting geologists of the weathered pinnacles of the 'badlands' of the American west.[12] Seven aqueducts, drawing on streams coming off Mount Guiana (1,848 metres), channelled water to Las Medulas benefiting from a drop of up to 800 metres to build up pressure. Tanks were then ranged along the brim of the alluvial terraces from which a powerful cascade of water could be dumped continuously to break them down – a process known today as hydraulicking. Once the terraces began to crumble, water from smaller tanks was released to wash away waste overburden, a process known as hushing. The final task, Pliny noted, was at ground level. "Water conduits ... are cut in steps and floored with gorse, that collects gold particles [ed: as did the Golden Fleece]. The conduits are boarded with planks and carried over steep pitches. Thus the tailings flow down to the sea and the mountain is washed away ... the gorse is dried and burnt and its ash is washed on a bed of turf sods, so that the gold is collected."[13]

The main rival to the vast Las Medulas complex was scarcely fifty kilometres to the south-east in the valley of the Rio Duerna, in the shadow of the Sierra de Teleno which rises over two thousand metres. This task was easier; there were no high cliffs to be eroded by water pressure, but a series of orange-brown alluvial deposits like sand bars along the banks of the upper fiver. The Duerna and its tributaries tumbling off the heights of the Sierra provided ample water for 'hushing'. The Roman miners tackled at least twenty-one deposits along a thirty kilometre stretch of the river; almost all of them were on the right bank indicating the gold had originally been eroded from the Sierra de Teleno. A series of short aqueducts was built to each site, feeding into a crescent-shaped dam above the workings. Sluices then funnelled the waters into gullies on a gentle downhill slope to the ridge of alluvial material. The top soil was washed away to reveal the auriferous deposit from which the gold could be sluiced out. The ridge was steadily cut back in a series of steps up the hill.[14]

The Duerna valley was a significant source of gold through much of the 1st and 2nd centuries AD. The French geologist C. Domergue estimated it produced up to 3,000 kg/96,450 t.oz annually for a period of 130 years.[15] While such long-term consistency may be challenged, modern experience with alluvial deposits that can be worked relatively easily indicates that such an amount could be obtained annually. Moreover, Roman inscriptions indicate a continued military presence close to the Duerna well into the 2nd century.

The ultimate engineering achievement was in the high country on the northern watershed of the Cantabrica Cordillera. The challenge was two-fold. Roman geologists had tracked back to a primary quartz gold deposit at Puerto del Palo, a ridge at 1,170 metres dividing the two river systems of Rio Navia and Rio Narcea which descend to the Bay of Biscay. This was a hard-rock open-cast mine for which abundant water-supply was essential. The nearest source was ten kilometres away in the headwaters of the Rio Del Oro at just over 1,200 metres in another valley. So the intrepid engineers built an aqueduct along the western flank of the Puerto del Palo, with just enough decline to build up a good head of water, especially when winter snows melted. They even cut a tunnel, another Montefurado, through an intervening ridge. "The Montefurado tunnel serves the lower of two aqueduct systems that can fairly be claimed to represent one of the most outstanding examples of hydrological engineering known in the Roman world," decided Lewis and Jones.[16] The resulting open-cast pit, now known as Cueva de Juan Rata, scoured out by the water, is so immense that visiting geologists have been tempted to regard it as a natural formation. It is over 500 metres long, with vertical sides of 200 metres ranging up a wall of highly weathered quartz to the summit of the mountain. Another smaller open-cut nestles nearby.

This project alone justifies describing Roman mining as an 'industry'; it took years in the making and then excavation of the hard-rock. And the Romans had no hesitation at going underground where necessary. Indeed, they tackled all the basic problems of ventilation, lighting and drainage (for which they developed water wheels and Archimedean screws to lift out water).

Pliny outlined some of the operations:

"Vein gold may be obtained by underground or open-cast working. It can be found in a crystalline matrix … traces of the veins appear here and there along the walls of the underground galleries and the overburden is supported by wooden props …. By the light of lamps long galleries are excavated into the mountain. The lamps measure the shifts, and the men may not see daylight for months on end. This class of mine is termed *arrugiae* (deep mining). In them sudden collapse can crush the miners …. As a protection the overburden is supported by rock arches at frequent intervals. Whatever the underground mining methods employed, hard quartzite masses will be encountered. These can be split with the help of fire-setting involving the use of acid. More often fire-setting in adits makes them too hot and smoky; instead, the rock is split by crushing machines incorporating 150 pound (c. 50 kg) iron weights. The miners then carry the ore out on their shoulders, each man forming a human chain working in the dark, only those at the end seeing the daylight …. If the quartzite seems too large a mass, the miners divert the drive to go round it. Yet rock of this kind is considered relatively easy in comparison with *gangadia*, a form of conglomerate, that is almost insuperable. The method … is to attack it with iron wedges and the crushing machine …. When the work is completed the miners cut away the roof props, beginning with the last. A crack, seen only by a watchman perched on the slope above, is the prelude to the collapse. With a shout or wave he orders the miners away … the overburden falls apart as it collapses with an incredible crash and blast of air".[17]

193

Mining was a perilous business in dreadful conditions with high loss of life, only urged on, as Pliny put it, by "the greed for gold". The workers were mostly criminals or captives, but above them was an elite of geologists and mine managers, whom the Romans moved from mine to mine, not just in Spain, but in Gaul, Wales and Dacia. Pliny himself was a procurator for the imperial treasury in Spain and Germany and thus wrote from first-hand knowledge of the industry. His assessment that Spain had long been the main gold-producing area yielding 20,000 pounds (6,480 kg/208,332 t.oz) annually carries credence. The modern estimate by Domergue that the Duerna valley alone produced 3,000 kg a year at its peak fits this pattern. However, well before the end of the 2nd century, Spain's output of gold (and silver) was in sharp decline. Grand projects gave way to small operations, probably run by locals, as Rome's control weakened. Good deposits, however, were left untouched. The Canadian mining company Rio Narcea Gold developed, in our own time, successful open-pit and underground operations in the high country of the Cantabrica Cordillera close to the original Roman workings that yielded around five m.t/160,750 t.oz annually for over a decade after 1994.

Elsewhere in the empire production was fitful and modest compared to Spain. The mines in Gaul, which had been developed by the Celts from the 5th century BC (*see chapter 11*) were expanded by the Romans, but detailed studies by French archaeologists during the 1990s have suggested they contributed at best a few hundred kg annually.[18] The Dolaucothi mine in South Wales, where significant hydrological works were carried out to facilitate open-cast and underground mining, was also a limited contributor. There was a flurry in Dalmatia (Croatia) and northern Albania under Nero in AD 54 where one new discovery was widely reported to be yielding 50 pounds (16 kg/514 t.oz) a day. While this would amount to almost 6,000 kg in a year, it was a short-lived boom.

The solid supply to the empire's gold stocks, as Spanish output faded in the 2nd century, came from Dacia (Hungary/Romania) north of the river Danube, which the Romans under Trajan conquered in AD 107 and held for over 160 years. Placer deposits in Dacia along many small rivers coming down from the mountains of Transylvania were already being worked. The Romans developed them extensively, even bringing in experienced miners from Albania. They also probed local sulphide ores, which they had experience of roasting to unlock the gold. Dacian gold was credited with financing many public works in Rome during the Trajan period, not least the forum with its column to his memory.

The miners themselves were mostly free men whose families had already scoured the rivers for generations, so they offered an experienced workforce. They had to pay an annual tax in gold and sell their main output to the provincial Roman procurator for the imperial treasury at "competent prices" and were paid in silver *denarii*.[19] The production never achieved the same levels as Spain, as the declining gold coin minting and reduction of the weight of the *aureus* by the late 2nd century testify. However, the mines of Dacia provided some output well into the

4th century, by which time many miners had forsaken their profession in favour of agriculture – a sure sign that the accessible gold was petering out. Long before that the Romans had lost control of the province as the empire faced increasingly hostile challenges from the north.

Looking back, however, the great achievement of the Roman mining industry, underpinned by Spain in the first two centuries of the Christian era, had enabled primitive economies throughout the empire to be truly monetised with gold, silver and base metal coinages.

The golden era of coin

While coinage had become indispensable in the running of the Roman state by the 2nd century BC, it was limited to silver and bronze. The crucial introduction initiated by Julius Caesar and confirmed by Augustus as first emperor from 27 BC was gold as the benchmark of a new monetary system. The relationship of one gold *aureus* to 25 silver *denarii* endured long after much of the silver coin had been debased by the 2nd century AD. Indeed, a situation developed in which *denarii* of differing silver content were circulating, all with the same official value. Gold, by contrast, was not significantly debased, although the weight of the *aureus* was marginally reduced from time to time. Caesar gave the Roman mint a target of 8.1 grams/0.26 t.oz for the *aureus*, Augustus allowed it to slip to 7.87 grams by 11 BC, and his successor Tiberius (AD 14–37) shaved it to 7.78 grams.[20]

For all three emperors, however, the priority was to get gold coin minted, not only to carry their public image, but because they needed a cash reserve to meet the ceaseless pressure of paying the army and servicing the empire. "The Roman government did without credit," the historian Richard Duncan-Jones remarked wryly. "There was no resort to large banks at times of crisis, and from what we can see, no large banks to resort to."[21] Unlike, one might add, Renaissance princes in Italy fifteen hundred years later, who bankrupted many a banker.

The enhanced role for gold was demonstrated in the ashes of Pompeii in AD 79 where, as already mentioned, the value of gold coins was found to be twice the value of silver and base metal coins. Estimates of mint production into the 2nd century AD suggest that, by value, gold normally accounted for 70% of mint production. Pompeii's ruins also revealed that gold was hoarded as a means of savings; a stock of 1,000 *aurei* weighing 7.3 kg/235 t.oz was found in one villa. Such hoards have been found throughout the empire from Britain and Gaul to the Danube province, Egypt and Syria. The coins from hoards are the clues from which the frequency and quantity of mint outputs can be roughly estimated.

Nero (AD 54–68) was the most prolific producer of gold coin. To begin his reign he reduced the weight of the *aureus* to 7.69 grams/0.247 t.oz, but after the disastrous fire of AD 64 destroyed much of Rome, he embarked upon a massive recoinage of even lighter *aurei* and *denarii* partly to meet costs of rebuilding the city.

The new *aureus* weighed 7.34 grams/0.236 t.oz and the *denarius* 3.36 grams (compared to 3.80 grams under Augustus). The fine silver content of the *denarius* was also reduced from 980 fine to 935. The minting of new *aurei* between AD 64–68 has been estimated at 32.26 million coins, an average of 8.07 million per year; this astonishing total would call for 236.79 m.t/7.6 million t.oz of gold at a rate of over 69 m.t per year. At the same time, an estimated 31.9 million *denarii* were struck, requiring 107.2 m.t/3.4 million t.oz of silver, according to Richard Duncan-Jones.[22]

Clearly, these quantities were not met by new supply, although at this moment the new gold deposit in Dalmatia was said to be producing over five m.t/160,750 t.oz a year which, added to Spain's output, might have provided Nero with over 10 m.t annually. Additional supply came from taxes paid in gold coin, but there must also have been a massive general recall of old, and heavier, coin. The only historical recoinage that bears some comparison was the major recoinage of guineas in Britain between 1774–7, when the mint struck 155 m.t/4.98 million t.oz, of which 85% was estimated to have come from old guineas. Curiously, if new mine output provided Nero with 40 m.t/1.28 million t.oz during the four years of recoinage, the ratio would be about the same. Nero's achievement, however, was not exceeded until the gold rushes to California and Australia, which spawned 908 m.t/29.21 million t.oz of coin in Britain, France and the United States between 1850–4.[23]

Nero also transferred most precious metal coinage to the Rome mint. Previously, from the time of Julius Caesar and Augustus, gold coins had usually been struck at the mint at Lugdunum (Lyon) in Gaul. Logistically, this made sense; Caesar captured ample bullion in his Gallic campaigns and this could be struck at once in his image and used to pay his troops in the field. Augustus also took advantage of the Lugdunum mint, which was not only closer to his main sources of gold and silver mining in Spain (and to the smaller Gallic mines near Limoges), but offered swift dispatch of new coin to his legions guarding the empire's frontiers on the Rhine and Danube. The upgrading of Rome's mint by Nero for the recoinage of AD 64–68 was logical because most of the old coins called in for melting must have been in Rome and Italy. Thereafter, Rome's mint remained the centre for gold coinage, although gold coins were struck sporadically throughout the empire by the 3rd century AD, as it became less cohesive and local heroes produced their own issues.

Nero's troubled rule saw the high point of Roman gold coin output. Domitian (81–96) initially sought to restore the weight of the *aureus* to the pre-Nero level of 7.78/0.25 t.oz grams, but soon let it slip back to 7.64 grams, while his successor, Trajan (98–117), settled for 7.34 grams. The increasing scarcity of gold, as Spain's output declined, encouraged Trajan to conquer the province of Dacia, north of the Danube, to secure its gold mines, which supplied Rome through much of the 2nd century AD. Even so, annual minting of *aurei* was a shadow of the Nero era. During the first 80 years of the century, under Trajan, Hadrian, Antonius Pius and

Marcus Aurelius, the annual issue of *aurei* was just over one million, requiring scarcely 8 m.t/257,200 t.oz of gold, which could probably have been met largely by the depleted mine supply. Silver *denarii*, by comparison, were struck at between 15 and 19 million a year, calling for 50–60 m.t/1.6–2.1 million t.oz. This quantity would have been met by new mine supply, especially as the fine silver content was sliding.

Although the annual gold mintings were low, the gradual build-up of gold coin through the 2nd century has led to the calculation, mentioned earlier, that by the 160s the total gold circulation for the empire might have reached 880 m.t/28.3 million t.oz.[24] This is realistic as many coins from Nero's great recoinage of 64–67, which had pumped almost 240 m.t/7.7 million t.oz into the economy, were still around after 200. His coins had great staying power for well over 100 years, and even after 200 often accounted for over 15% of hoards. Thus, an average of only six to seven m.t annually over the following century would suffice to get 800–900 m.t in circulation. However, the word circulation might be a slight misnomer, given that gold coin was now primarily hoarded as security against inflation and the debasement of silver. Under Marcus Aurelius (161–180) the fineness of the *denarius* fell to 800 fine, compared with the traditional 900 fine, and under his successor, Commodius (181–192), it slipped to 750 fine. Silver was becoming token money. That encouraged people to sit on gold coin and pay with silver when possible. In effect, gold coin almost disappeared from daily circulation.

Previously, in what one might call the golden era of Rome coinage from 27 BC until AD 117, gold coins had become widely accepted. They were used not just to pay the army (and navy) or senior government officials, but for taxes or paying large fines, for buying slaves and luxury goods. Pliny complained that the empire was being drained of precious metals to pay for exotica from the East and, although he may have exaggerated, hoards of Roman gold coin of Augustus, Claudius and Nero have been found on the south-west coast of India.[25] "We can document the role of gold in the good life," wrote Christopher Howgego, "as prizes in the games, a stake for gambling or a reward for sexual favours."[26] Special events, such as the succession of an emperor, the betrothal of his children, the naming of heirs or military victories, were honoured with *congiaria* (cash hand-outs) to privileged officials and citizens, almost always paid in gold coin. The normal dispensation was 3, 4 or 6 *aurei* to each recipient. *Congiaria* were usually made between three and six times by each emperor (Augustus granted five, Nero one, Trajan three and Hadrian seven) and were eagerly sought. When Marcus Aurelius returned to Rome from a triumph in 177, hopeful citizens held up eight fingers urging a *congiaria* of eight *aurei* each. They probably did not get it; gold was scarcer by then and a *congiaria* required up to 90,000 *aurei* or 675 kg/21,667 t.oz.[27]

The era of abundant gold coinage was over. In the years ahead, as the empire was increasingly beset by wars of succession, it was more sporadic and the weight of the *aureus* was to tumble. While gold coinage has rightly made the historical headlines during the first two centuries of the Roman Empire, a significant amount of metal was also fabricated into lavish, even ostentatious, jewellery.

Jewellery: international fashion

The scope of the Roman Empire inevitably meant that the jewellery worn by its people far from the hub of Rome in northern Britain, the coasts of North Africa or on the desert fringes of Syria, reflected local styles. In Britain or Gaul, Celtic traditions were strong, in the eastern Mediterranean Hellenistic fashions persisted, while in Rome itself many goldsmiths were immigrants from Greece or the east (throughout ancient history goldsmiths had always followed the trail to new prosperity). Yet from these varied strands evolved what Catherine Johns of the British Museum dubbed "Roman international fashion".[28]

The ornaments, like the *aureus* gold coin, were disseminated by soldiers and their families posted to the farthest frontiers where local goldsmiths copied them. Thus the necklaces, bracelets and finger rings that have turned up in hoards in Algeria, Belgium, Germany, Hungary, or Syria often match those recovered from the ashes of Pompeii. A charming colour portrait from Egypt of the 2nd century depicts a Roman-Egyptian lady who could equally pass as a pillar of fashion in Rome itself. "Roman jewels are of sensible design, suitable for everyone, everywhere," decided the jewellery historian Graham Hughes. "Rome brought order and solidarity to jewellery, just as it did to politics."[29] The jewellery was also for the living, not for burial with the dead. Certainly it was shown off as a sign of rank and wealth, but also was cheap and cheerful. A mass market for popular ornaments welcome throughout the empire was born.

Originally Roman jewellery had been of Etruscan design when the nascent city was under Etruria's wing before 250 BC (*see chapter 7*). Thereafter, during the Republic, Hellenistic fashions from the Greek city-states of southern Italy predominated and consisted primarily of rings for the elite, given Rome's lack of gold. Jewellery became abundant only with the blossoming of the empire under Augustus after 27 BC when it became flush with gold from the new mines in Spain. Goldsmiths now migrated to Rome. Their signs '*aurifex brattiarius*' sprouted and strictly controlled guilds were formed. They soon forsook many Hellenistic styles, although the Heracles knot on bracelets endured. Grand wreaths and diadems disappeared, as did seals and rings engraved with gods and epic heroes. In came images of seahorses, dolphins, woodpeckers, Cupids or bezels set with coloured semi-precious stones and, before long, betrothal rings with touching inscriptions. Lightweight earrings of little gold hemispheres hung by a simple wire hook through a pierced ear were all the rage, especially if a shake of the head made them jingle.

The eruption of Vesuvius on 24th August AD 79, which shrouded Pompeii and neighbouring villages in a cocoon of ash and mud within hours, preserved unique collections of gold jewellery, coin and silver plate. Gold plate was rare, although a splendid twin-nozzled lamp embossed with lotus leaves was excavated in

1863.[30]   Jewellery was scattered far and wide, but hoards were found at a villa at Boscoreale and in the house of the poet Menander in Pompeii. At Boscoreale a vat in the cellar wine press contained gold jewellery, over 1,000 gold coins and a complete set of 109 pieces of silver plate; beside the vat lay the skeleton of a woman, evidently overcome as she tried to recover her ornaments before fleeing. They included heavy gold pendant chains, and a rather flashy gold bracelet of interlocking double hemispheres – evidently a popular item as seven others have been found elsewhere beneath the blanket of volcanic ash. Over eighty pairs of fashionable lightweight earrings of gold beads or hemispheres were recovered, not only at Boscoreale, but all over the area, as were snakes coiled into rings and bracelets. In the finest snake pieces the texture of their scales, incised into the gold creates a ripple effect. These snake ornaments, originating in the earlier Hellenistic period as a symbol, not of fear, but of healing and regeneration, remained popular throughout the Roman era and were made by goldsmiths across the empire.

At the house of Menander in Pompeii two wooden chests in the basement contained family jewellery, gold and silver coins and 118 pieces of silver plate, each wrapped individually in cloth. Among the jewellery was a handsome pouch-shaped gold amulet or *bulla*, weighing over 14 grams/0.45 t.oz, that was reminiscent of Etruscan designs, along with earrings set with emeralds or clusters of pearls. Emeralds and mother-of-pearl were also set in an elaborate necklace of gold mesh. They revealed a growing Roman passion for coloured precious and semi-precious stones and pearls. Indeed, in the house of a gem cutter, Pinarius Cerealis, at Pompeii, engraving tools and a box containing 114 cut carnelians, sardonyx, amethysts and agates were found.

Pompeii was a snapshot of Roman jewellery in transition. The gold *bulla* was a hangover from Etruscan times, but the abundance of light earrings and bracelets and the use of coloured stones to dazzle pointed towards an emerging mass market. A light-hearted fresco in the House of the Vettii at Pompeii even illustrated a goldsmith's workshop with seven Cupids busy weighing, melting and hammering gold.

Post Pompeii came new trends. Gold coins or medallions were favoured on the bezel of rings or as pendants on necklaces (making them much easier to date) while goldsmiths developed a new technique, *opus interassile*, rather like fretwork. A pattern was sketched out on gold sheet and then chipped out with a chisel, creating a delicate tracery. Among the finest examples is a bracelet of the 4th century, from Tarsus in Syria, fashioned as a broad band, the outer edge of which forms a curving hexagon decorated so minutely that it has the appearance of gold lace.[31] *Opus interassile* was used on bracelets, rings, necklaces and around the borders of medallions across the empire. Later, a vogue for massive chunky bracelets flourished in the 3rd century, possibly as a prudent response to the long-running instability of the empire after the assassination of the emperor Severus Alexander by the Imperial Army in 235. Heavy gold ornaments were a walking insurance policy (much gold coin was also hoarded then).

The delight of Romans at an ostentatious display of wealth, however, was nothing new. Writers had always enjoyed making fun of such extravagance. Gaius Petronius, director of pleasures at Nero's court, earlier wrote a satirical romance in which the key episode was a dinner party at which the host's wife, Fortunata, arrived with golden anklets and gold embroidered slippers, her 'great fat arms' laden with bracelets and her hair encased in a gold net. "She must have six and a half pounds (Roman) on her," boasted her husband, Trimalchio. "Still, I have a bracelet myself … and it weighs not less than ten pounds." So Fortunata weighed in with 2.1 kg/67.5 t.oz and her husband with 3.2 kg/102 t.oz of trinkets.[32]

Modern critics are not always complimentary about the ornaments. "Technically, Roman jewellery sees some falling off in the standards of workmanship, " wrote Reynold Higgins, the expert on both Roman and Greek jewellery, before conceding, "although good work could still be produced." In making ornaments for an empire, not just a fastidious elite, quality did not always come first. Yet, looking at the jewellery that has been found at Amiens, Eauze and Lyon in France (Gaul), at Beaurains in Belgium, at Thetford or Hoxne in Britain, at Ténès in Algeria or Tarsus and Palmyra in Syria, an acceptable international standard was maintained from the earliest days until after AD 400. Reviewing the Hoxne treasure, dating c. 407 and found in Britain in 1992, which included six necklaces, a magnificent foxtail body chain and nineteen bracelets, Catherine Johns noted, "The very finest class of jewellery available was thus found in Britain in the late Roman period just as it was in the 1st century when the province had recently become part of the empire".[33] Romans abroad demanded the best.

They were also sentimental. Finger rings and bracelets were inscribed in Latin and sometimes Greek, with pledges of love and passion. "Polemios's love-token" and "May you live, Aemilia" declared the messages on two rings found in northern Britain, and "I love you too little" was engraved on a ring from Amiens in France. The tracery of an *opus interassile* bracelet from the Hoxne treasure bore the words "VTERE FELIX DOMINA IULIANE" – "Use happily Lady Juliana". Rings were also engraved with symbolic hand clasps or facing portraits of bride and groom encircled by such pledges as "The future groom to his amorous love". By the 4th century Christian thoughts such as "VIVAS IN DEO" – "May you live in God" – were being inscribed.

Such messages stimulate curiosity. Who were Valerianus and Paterna, whose names were carefully inlaid in black niello (a late Roman vogue) around the edges of a wedding ring that was part of the Beaurains treasure in Belgium, where this couple were stationed around 300? What were their lives like at this outpost of the empire? How happily did Lady Juliana live at Hoxne by the River Waveney on the borders of Norfolk and Suffolk a century later, as the Romans' grip on Britain faltered? Her wealthy family probably buried in haste their jewellery along with over 15,000 coins, many of them gold, when threatened by some marauding force.

In complete contrast, a fashion for gold crossbow brooches (*fibulae*) spread

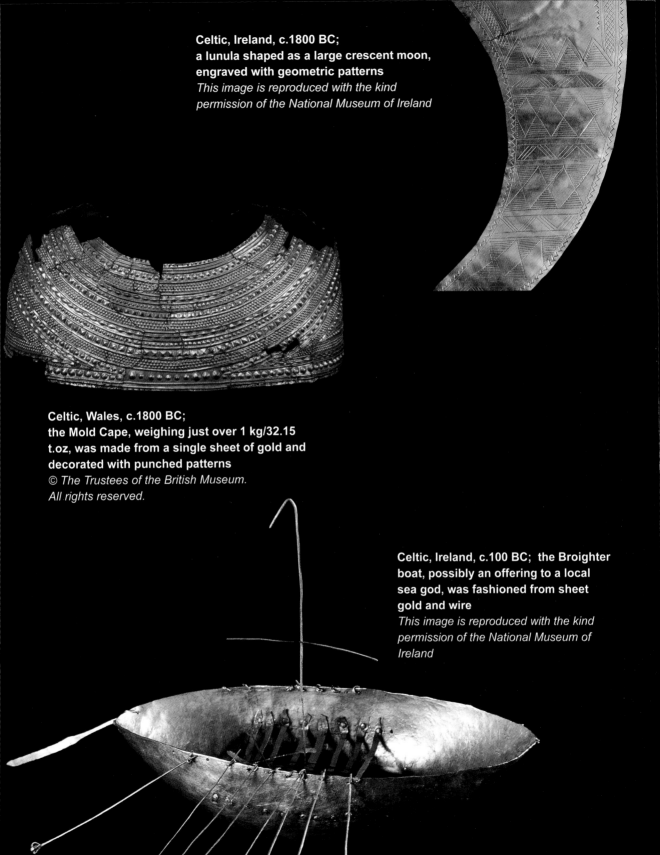

**Celtic, Ireland, c.1800 BC;
a lunula shaped as a large crescent moon,
engraved with geometric patterns**
*This image is reproduced with the kind
permission of the National Museum of Ireland*

**Celtic, Wales, c.1800 BC;
the Mold Cape, weighing just over 1 kg/32.15
t.oz, was made from a single sheet of gold and
decorated with punched patterns**
*© The Trustees of the British Museum.
All rights reserved.*

**Celtic, Ireland, c.100 BC; the Broighter
boat, possibly an offering to a local
sea god, was fashioned from sheet
gold and wire**
*This image is reproduced with the kind
permission of the National Museum of
Ireland*

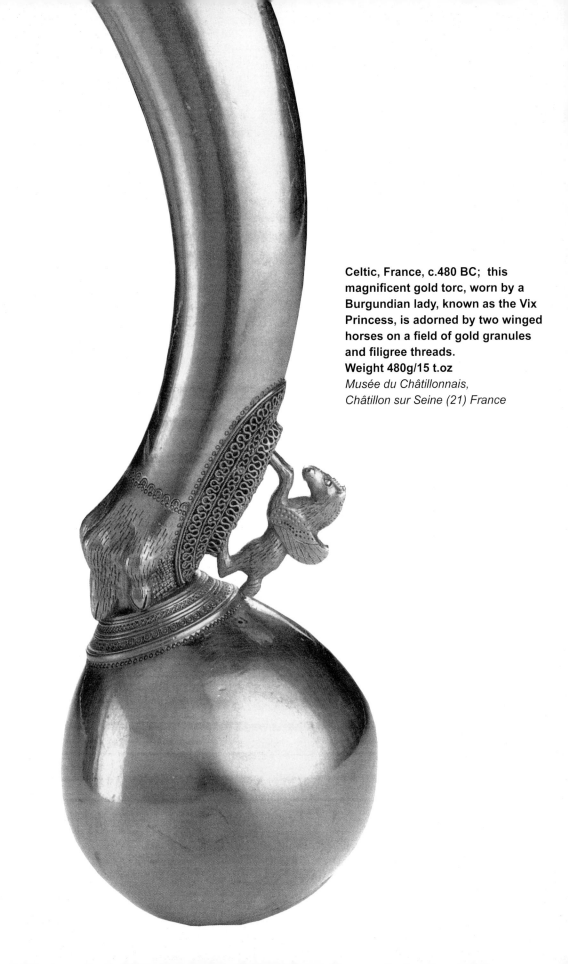

Celtic, France, c.480 BC; this
magnificent gold torc, worn by a
Burgundian lady, known as the Vix
Princess, is adorned by two winged
horses on a field of gold granules
and filigree threads.
Weight 480g/15 t.oz
*Musée du Châtillonnais,
Châtillon sur Seine (21) France*

Roman; gold aureus of Nero, minted AD 64-68 as part of his great recoinage
© *The Trustees of the British Museum.*
All rights reserved.

Roman; gold medallion showing Constantine the Great at prayer, minted AD 306-337 in Siscia (Croatia)
© *The Trustees of the British Museum.*
All rights reserved.

Roman Britain; the Didcot hoard of 126 gold coins was equivalent to 10.5 years of a soldier's pay; it was buried c. AD 160-169
© *The Trustees of the British Museum. All rights reserved*

Roman, c. AD 375-40; gold bars with assayers' stamps, all c.980 fine.
Weights: 343.03g, 345.00g, 133.67g, 476.20g
© *The Trustees of the British Museum.*
All rights reserved.

Roman, c. AD 54-68; mummy portrait of a woman wearing gold ball earrings and a gold necklace with a pendant crescent and circular terminals

© The Trustees of the British Museum. All rights reserved

Roman Britain, Thetford treasure, c. AD 390; gold belt buckle with a dancing satyr

© The Trustees of the British Museum. All rights reserved

Roman, c. AD 250; brooch with a coin of Emperor Philip I. Coins were then often included in jewellery items as their purity was more assured

© The Trustees of the British Museum. All rights reserved

Roman, Turkey, c. AD 350-400; gold plaque of a hunt, with rider on a rearing horse over a lion or panther

© The Trustees of the British Museum. All rights reserved

Ravenna AD 548; the Byzantine Empress Theodora, draped in jewellery, surrounded by a halo of gold tesserae, in the mosaics at San Vitale

Basilica di S. Vitale, Ravenna

Ravenna AD 548; the Byzantine Emperor Justinian (AD 527-65), surrounded by his court, against a background of gold tesserae, in San Vitale

Basilica di S. Vitale, Ravenna

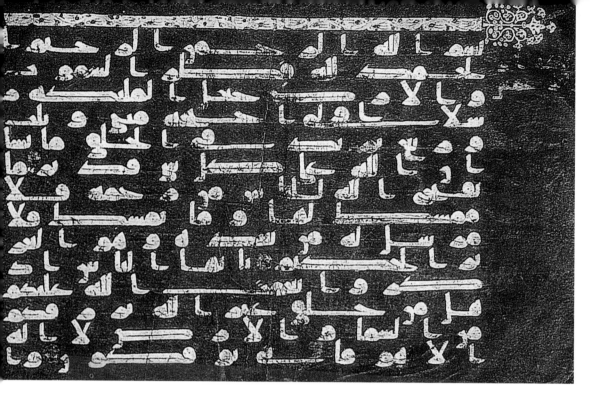

Gold script on a blue-dyed parchment of the Qur'an
Musée des Arts Islamiques,
Qayrawan, Tunisia

Gold dinar of Caliph Abd al-Malik, AD 696-7, probably minted in Syria as part of his reform of Islamic coinage
© The Trustees of the British Museum.
All rights reserved

The gold coin boom, 1250 - 1350

Venice, ducat of Doge Giovanni Dandolo (1280-89), weight 3.49g
Fitzwilliam Museum, Cambridge

Florence; florin, first issued in 1252, weight 3.52g
Fitzwilliam Museum, Cambridge

Genoa; Genovino, first issued 1252, weight 3.5g
Fitzwilliam Museum, Cambridge

Hungary; ducat (or gulden), of ruler Charles Robert (1303-42), minted from local gold rush. Weight 3.53g
Fitzwilliam Museum, Cambridge

Benvenuto Cellini's Salt Cellar, created in
Paris for Francis I of France between 1540-41,
showing Sea and Earth with their legs entwined.
Made from melting 1,000 gold crowns,
weighing 3.5 kg/112 t.oz
Kunsthistorisches Museum, Wien oder KHM, Wien

throughout the empire during the 3rd century AD. "Crossbows were an international late Roman type ... worn by men, including, or perhaps especially, men in positions of authority," noted Catherine Johns. "There is evidence that some of the finest and most valuable specimens were worn by individuals in the highest echelons of society."[34]   Many of the brooches were carefully decorated with inlaid black niello. The crossbows were imposing pieces, like formal wear, and served as clasps to fasten cloaks high on the right shoulder. Some were inscribed "HERCULI AUGUSTE SEMPER VINCAS" – "Hercules Augustus, may you always conquer" – read the dedication on a crossbow made c. AD 307, possibly referring to Constantine the Great. The brooches often had complex safety-catch mechanisms to lock the pin into the catchplate. These distinctive insignia have been found across Europe from the Moray Firth in Scotland (beyond Hadrian's Wall) to southern Germany and Hungary, in Ravenna (a leading city of the late empire) and across the Mediterranean at Ténès in Algeria.

Such austere ornaments for the elite were against the mainstream of late Roman fashions, which boasted a flamboyant rainbow of coloured stones in gold settings, even for rings. Of the 22 finger rings in the Thetford treasure, dated c. 390, virtually all were set with amethysts, garnets, emeralds, quartzes or glass, and several bracelets, necklaces and pendants were gem-set.[35] These styles persisted into the Byzantine era, when cheap coloured stones became ever more prominent as gold supplies declined and jewellery was often of non-precious metals (*see chapter 14*). Shortage of gold was already a challenge even before the 4th century, with gold coinage dramatically reduced and a smaller coin introduced. For goldsmiths the lifeline was scrap, with family collections of ornaments built up over the centuries constantly being re-worked. Since the Romans did not normally bury gold jewellery with the dead, that circulating pool of metal must have been substantial. However, secreting family treasures in the face of danger in an insecure empire also took considerable amounts of gold out of circulation. Our benefit is that, as they have been turned up by archaeologists or ploughmen, they have provided a showcase of Roman jewels from across the empire, while Pompeii's ruins preserved the early ornaments of Roman goldsmiths. Moreover, much more surely lies waiting to be ploughed up by chance or excavated, particularly at Pompeii, if ambitious international proposals come to fruition.

The fractured empire

The fault lines that would ultimately split the Roman Empire were already apparent before AD 200. Gold and silver supplies had dwindled. The Spanish gold mines were long past their peak and those secured by Trajan in Dacia were abandoned after a barbarian invasion in AD 167. The Spanish silver mines at Rio Tinto were disrupted in the same decade. Treasury stocks were sapped maintaining an army, itself demoralised on restless frontiers, and by bribes to the tribes beyond. Army pay, always the government's biggest running cost, had required the equivalent of 10,000 kg/321,000 t.oz in gold in 84; by 202 that had risen to 18,000 kg and 26,000 kg by 212.[36]   The legionnaire, who had received 225 *denarii* a year from Julius Caesar in 46 BC, was due 1,800 *denarii* by AD 235.

In practice, the troops had long been paid largely in silver; now only privileged officers got gold. Worse still, silver coin was rapidly being debased. Although army pay was met, in part, by recycling local taxes in the provinces, there was a limit to raising them to cover rampant inflation. "It was not possible for the treasury to make up the difference *in the long run* by increased exactions of whatever kind," observed Christopher Howgego.[37]

Consequently, there was a steady decline in the weight of the gold *aureus* and its minting, and in both weight and fineness of the silver *denarius*, which became a mere token. Originally, under Augustus in 27 BC the *aureus* weighed 7.87 grams/0.25 t.oz, before being reduced to 7.34 grams/0.236 t.oz by Nero's recoinage in AD 64; that weight lasted over one hundred years until AD 180, when it fell to 7.25 grams/0.23 t.oz (still respectable). Under Caracalla (215–17) it slid to 6.46 grams/0.21 t.oz and, by 235, when Severus Alexander was assassinated, the *aureus* was a slim 5.51 grams/0.18 t.oz. The few *aurei* surviving from the ensuing political turmoil, as emperors or usurpers came and went in rapid succession, varied between 3.60 grams/0.16 t.oz and 1.10 grams/0.35 t.oz. Stabilisation came only in 274 when Aurelian (born, apparently, in the gold region of Dacia) restored the *aureus* to 5.45 grams/0.18 t.oz. Through these gyrations, however, its gold content was not greatly debased.

Silver fared worse. The *denarius* of Augustus had been 3.80 grams at 980 fine; by 180 it fell to 3.36 grams at 734 fine, sliding on to 3.10 grams at 450 fine by 235. Then the rot set in. The *denarius* was replaced by the antoninianus in 238, with a notional weight of 5.11 grams, but a silver content of 50 fine (5%) and finally 25 fine (2.5%).[38]

This could no longer be regarded as a silver coin, rather it had become *billon* – base metals with a dash of silver. Moreover, low denomination bronze coinage became uneconomic to produce in some provinces. Genuine silver coinage was restored only in 294 by Diocletian. Meanwhile, the clear relationship between gold and silver, which had endured for over two hundred years, was broken. Gold was now priced purely by weight, with a common price for coin, plate and jewellery, which fluctuated from day to day. New gold coinage was rare. This explains the vogue for heavy gold bracelets for they were valued equally with coin.

The virtual breakdown of the monetary system weakened the fabric of the Roman Empire, faced not just with inadequate resources but constant warfare on all sides. In the east it was challenged by the new Sasanian dynasty pushing west out of Persia, which took over Syria and Egypt. In the west, local emperors set themselves up in Britain, Gaul and Spain. The fight back began with Aurelian (270–5) who quickly secured Egypt and Syria and, in AD 274, won the submission of Gaul at the battle of Châlons. He restored the *aureus*, initially at 5.45 grams/0.18

t.oz and then at 6.54 grams/0.21 t.oz, produced mainly at the Rome mint (where, not surprisingly, there had been a revolt by the moneyers at coinage chaos). The problem of silver coinage was not addressed. Sticking plaster had been applied to the monetary system and the fabric of the empire, but stability remained elusive.

The re-invention of the empire came under Diocletian (284–304) who proposed co-emperors, one for the east, one for the west, with each having a designated deputy to succeed him. This strategy was put aside by Constantine the Great (306–337), who favoured a principal ruler, but the concept that the empire was too vast for a single ruler had taken root and would ultimately lead to formal division in 395.

Initially, Diocletian tried to put the monetary system back together. He set the scene in a famous price edict in AD 294 which officially confirmed that the price for gold should be the same for coin or bullion (ingots) and could 'float', although with a maximum. The *aureus* was stabilised at 5.45 grams/0.18 t.oz, while a new silver coin, the *argenteus*, at 900 fine and theoretically weighing 3.41 grams/0.11 t.oz, was introduced (in practice the coins varied between 3.00 and 3.30 grams). This set the gold:silver ratio at 1:12 as in the time of Augustus three hundred years earlier. The mint in Rome remained the most important, but Diocletian established other mints across the empire. Gold coin was struck from Trier in Gaul to Aquileia in northern Italy and Thessaloniki in Greece to Antioch in Syria. Politically, the image of the Emperor was thus being re-established in many places. "The reform effected by Diocletian in 294 was the most thorough in the history of Roman coinage," decided Robert Carson of the British Museum.[39]

To spur things on, Diocletian made forced purchases of gold from private holders and, perhaps, money changers, offering a maximum price of 60,000 *denarii* (value) paid in base metal coins. This gave him gold to mint, while putting small value bronze coins into circulation – one essential of getting a widespread monetary system up and running again.

Constantine launches the *solidus*

If Diocletian set the framework for a viable coinage, it was Constantine who really made it work during the first four decades of the next century. His initial step was the launching of a new gold coin, the *solidus* of 4.50 grams/0.14 t.oz at 990 fine, in mints of the western Empire c. 309. The *solidus* was to become the most widely accepted gold coin throughout the late Roman Empire and the Byzantine Empire that followed, surviving for one thousand years (though later debased on occasions and variously known later as the *nomisma* or *hyperpyron*). Ultimately, its role, in an early form of gold standard, was matched by the Muslim *dinar* and later taken on by the Venetian *ducat*.

A lighter coin than the *aureus* made sense, being more convenient for accounting and calculating than its predecessor. Later, a half *solidus* at 2.25 grams/0.07 t.oz and an even smaller coin at 1.70 grams/0.05 t.oz were introduced. Together the three gold coins were practical for a wider range of payments, although gold always remained the province of the wealthy and merchants with international business.

The priority was gold for the new coins, in the absence of substantial mine supply. Constantine secured the metal by seizing the reserves of defeated rivals, through a new tax payable in precious metals levied on the wealthy senatorial class and, after his conversion to Christianity (which he declared the state religion in AD 323), by confiscating the stock of gold and silver held by pagan temples in Rome and elsewhere. No estimate had been made of the temple reserves but, given they had been acquired over centuries, a significant amount of gold must have been available for the mint. Constantine profited, too, from the overthrow in AD 312 of his rival Maxentius, who had proclaimed himself Emperor of Rome in 306, when his own power base was only Britain and Gaul. Maxentius had hidden precious metals in the basement of his palace, which fell into Constantine's hands. Similarly, when he defeated Licinius, 'emperor' of the eastern Empire, in AD 324 he gained its gold stocks, while uniting the whole empire under his mantle. Thereafter, the *solidus* was struck in Antioch in Syria and at a new mint opened in the budding city of Constantinople in AD 326.[40]

Progressively, therefore, more gold which had been frozen in private hoards or usurpers' stocks was mobilised. Constantine also insisted that all gold *solidi* or other old coin collected as taxes must be melted immediately into ingots and handed over to official channels for assaying and then re-striking into coin. The ingots were a practical option because it was easier to assay a smaller number of large bars than millions of individual coins. The ingots varied in weight. Four ingots of the period in the British Museum's HSBC Money Gallery, all with assay stamps, weigh in at 134 grams, 343 grams, 345 grams and 476 grams. This suggests that, unlike coins, precise standard weights did not always apply to bars, although two of the BM's bars are just over one Roman pound (324 grams/10.4 t.oz). Private coining of gold at mints was forbidden. The Emperor's coin was inviolate. "All *solidi* on which Our face and venerability is to be found are to be valued and sold at one price," said an edict in AD 317. Clipping or forgery was "to be capitally punished either by being handed over to the flames or some other death-carrying punishment".[41]

The *solidus* prospered. One calculation has suggested that a mere 60 m.t/1.93 million t.oz of gold coin was circulating in the empire in AD 310, rising to 200 m.t/6.43 million t.oz by AD 370.[42] This has been challenged as too low by some historians, but clearly coin could not be minted abundantly in the absence of significant mine supply; the amount available from confiscated stocks, temples or even taxes was finite. Nor was it minted year in, year out as in the early empire. After Constantine, coins were usually struck only on the accession of a new emperor to enhance his image or to mark the anniversary of his rule every five years, when large gold medallions were also given out. Over time, the portraits on coins became less individual, making the image more of an icon of authority. In moments of instability, emperors were prone to debase the *solidus*; those minted between 346–368 were only 945 fine, although the gold standard was restored in 369 to 990 fine by Valentinian I, emperor of the western Empire. His successor, Valentinian II, launched a small new gold coin, the *tremissis*, in AD 383, which was one-third of a *solidus* at 1.51 grams/0.05 t.oz; the coin circulated widely through the later years of the empire – a sign perhaps that people welcomed such a tiny coin in turbulent times as a practical means of saving or payment.[43]

The division of the empire became ever more likely. Indeed, Constantine himself probably made it inevitable by building his 'new Rome', at Byzantium on the Bosphorus, naming it Constantinople and declaring it his seat of power in AD 330. After his death in AD 337 his less talented successors indulged in turf wars over who should be *de facto* ruler of Rome or Constantinople. The status of Constantinople was enhanced by its mint, opened in AD 326, which became the most important of all imperial mints, with its stamped signature CONS being recognised throughout the eastern Mediterranean (the mint mark was changed to CONOB in AD 378). "Constantinople was the most regular and prolific producer of gold coinage," noted Robert Carson, "and ultimately the only mint for gold."[44]

The balance of power had shifted from Rome to Constantinople. The western Empire in Rome, its frontiers repeatedly breached by hostile tribes, was further weakened by a formal division in AD 395 after the death of Theodosius I. His sons, Honorius and Arcadius, took the western and eastern Empires respectively. Just fifteen years later the Visigoths invaded Italy and sacked Rome in AD 410. The western Empire was on its knees, being progressively dismembered as Britain, Gaul and Spain shook off four hundred years of Roman control. The emperor Honorius, writing from Ravenna, whither he had moved as a safe haven in AD 402, told the *civitates* of Britain to "look for their own defence". They had no alternative; there was no Roman army to protect them, nor Roman officials to administer them.[45]

CHAPTER 14

Byzantium:
The Thousand Year Gold Standard

The link between the late Roman and early Byzantine Empires may be compared to a gardener taking a cutting from his favourite plant, which then outgrows it, while the original withers. The gardener, of course, was Constantine the Great, who declared the former city of Byzantium his capital in AD 330 and renamed it Constantinople. It was a step of immense historical portent. As Philip Grierson pointed out, "Under Constantine it (the Roman Empire) acquired a new ideology with Christianity, a new political centre with Constantinople, and a new monetary system, with the *solidus* … replacing the *aureus*".[1]

The maturing of this 'new Rome' was protracted. Not until 395 did the sons of the Roman emperor Theodosius I, Honorius and Arcadius, divide Rome and Constantinople between them, each as emperor in his own right. Honorius later moved his capital from Rome to Ravenna in 402, prudently as it turned out, for Rome was sacked by Alaric the Goth eight years later. The last truly Roman western emperor, Romulus, died in 476, while in Constantinople the accession of *Anastasius* in 491 is sometimes taken as the 'official' start of the Byzantine Empire – at least for coinage. Although, as Philip Grierson added, "Byzantine coinage can no more be dated from a fixed point in time than can be the Byzantine Empire itself".[2]

During these two centuries of transition, from c.300–500, the two cities ran in parallel, particularly with their common gold coinage, which might be called an early gold standard. Ultimately, their fortunes diverged economically and militarily. The western Empire of Rome crumbled under a rapid succession of emperors whose military power had been eclipsed and whose resources were constantly drained trying to bribe the Germanic tribes to stay away. These annual 'subsidies' in gold rose from 113 kg/3,633 t.oz in 422 to a hefty 680 kg/5,208 t.oz.[3] The mint at Ravenna maintained sporadic output of the gold *solidus*, the staple coin of both empires launched by Constantine but, in the absence of gold from efficient tax collection or newly mined sources, had little metal to restrike.

By contrast, the eastern Empire enjoyed political and social stability. Only four emperors (plus one brief usurper) ruled in Constantinople between 408 and 491, enabling steady administration and the all-important gold tax collection. Since the law required all coin collected as tax to be melted immediately into ingots, there was always metal for the mints in Constantinople and Thessaloniki. The emperor

Theodosius II (408–450) enjoyed gold reserves of 32.4 m.t/1.1 million t.oz, made up of 7.2 million *solidi* or *nomismata*, as the coin came to be called in the Greek-speaking eastern Empire.[4]   The other favourable card for the budding Byzantium Empire was its compactness at this early stage. Constantinople, with a population of 400,000 by 500, was the crossroads of sea routes from the Black Sea to the Mediterranean and of the land routes between Europe and Asia. Its territory was essentially Greece, the Balkans and Anatolia (Turkey); there were, as yet, no far-flung frontiers to be protected. Admittedly, the emperor *Anastasius* paid a ransom of 648 kg/20,833 t.oz to procure peace with the Huns along the Danube, but he had substantial reserves to draw on. Incidentally, the details of such transactions become more frequent during the Byzantine period; while they are not completely accurate, they usually fall within a realistic range. Bribes/subsidies were often agreed at one thousand or two thousand Byzantine pounds (324 kg or 648 kg), with the pound weighing at this early period 324 grams/10.42 t.oz, the same as in Rome.

Anastasius' monetary revolution

Byzantium's strength from the outset was its monetary system, rooted originally in the reforms of Diocletian and Constantine around 300. The *solidus*, 4.5 grams/0.14 t.oz at 980 fine, had become the principal trade coin of the Mediterranean and was welcome far beyond. Even the Burgundian kings in France accepted this empire coin by the 6th century, adding their own monograms struck at the mint in Lyon. The seal of economic success came, however, with *Anastasius* (491–518), who initiated as drastic a reform of base-metal currencies as Diocletian and Constantine had done for gold and silver two hundred years earlier. He launched, in 498, a new copper coin, the *follis*, which was issued initially in denominations of 40, 20 and 10 *nummi*, weighing 9, 4.5 and 2.25 grams respectively. The *nummus* was the basic unit of account initially at 1/6000th of a *solidus*. A few years later *Anastasius* doubled the weights of each copper coin and introduced also a 5 *nummi* piece. The *follis* provided a stable and flexible subsidiary coinage which could be used by everyone for everyday transactions in town or village.[5] As contemporary commentator, John Chrysostom, wrote, "The use of coin welds together our whole life, and is the basis of all our transactions. Whenever anything is to be bought or sold, we do it through coins".[6] The absentee in Anastasius' reforms was silver, which had virtually vanished from daily coinage, its reputation tarnished by centuries of debasement; only ceremonial silver coins were struck occasionally during the early Byzantine Empire. The low esteem in which silver was held was reflected in the wide gold:silver ratio of 1:18.

This revolution in copper coinage marked the decisive change from Roman to Byzantine currency, setting a structure which was flexible enough to endure the triumphs and many crises of the next eight hundred years. It offered, too, an added advantage to the imperial coffers, for although many expenses, whether for public works, military expenses or the salary of officials and provincial prefects were paid in gold coin, minor payments could be made in copper. *Anastasius* had a reputation for financial prudence. The proof was that he left the imperial reserves holding 104 m.t/3.34 million t.oz of gold, a record level for known official gold stocks and the highest for any Byzantine emperor. It was just as well, for after a brief interregnum of Justin I (518–27), he was succeeded by Justinian I (527–65), who was bursting with ideas and projects to restore the ancient glories of the Roman Empire by reconquering provinces abroad and building churches, public baths, roads, bridges and aqueducts at home.

The golden age of Justinian

"The Emperor never sleeps," a courtier said, reflecting Justinian's passion for work during his thirty-eight-year reign. He was at once politician, administrator, war-maker (if not a warrior), and learned theologian. His 150,000 line Codex Justinianus of 534 was a compilation of imperial constitutions going back centuries, which clarified and preserved Roman law for posterity.[7] He stimulated Christian art and architecture in monasteries and churches from Haghia Sophia in Constantinople to Sant'Apollinaire Nuovo and San Vitale in Ravenna, where mosaics with magnificent gold grounds may still be admired (see below). He even set up a thriving silk-making industry in Constantinople, with silk worms initially bred (so the legend went) from eggs smuggled along the Silk Road from China by two patriotic missionaries, who concealed them in hollow staves. This imperial monopoly continued for centuries, with silk becoming a secondary currency for special payments and diplomatic gifts. Through it all, Justinian was encouraged and harassed by his wife Theodora. She was the daughter of a bear-keeper at the Hippodrome in Constantinople, whose early life had been as an actress and courtesan (to quote the politer descriptions) in Egypt and Syria. Back in Constantinople she charmed the emperor and became a powerful influence over him. She may be seen today in the mosaics in the basilica of San Vitale in Ravenna; a rather slight figure crowned by a halo of gold *tesserae*, draped in jewellery, her robe edged with gold, her feet in slippers of gold, blue and white.

This energetic, if eccentric, pair presided over a huge expansion of the empire, pressing up against the borders of Persia, retaking Egypt, sweeping the Vandals out of Carthage and North Africa, pushing the Visigoths from southern Spain and the Goths from much of Italy (Ravenna became the strong western enclave of Byzantium) and taking Sicily. The empire now stretched from the Danube in the north to the First Cataract of the Nile in the south, and east-west from Syria to Spain. Ever the administrator, Justinian established praetorian prefectures in the new provinces to run them and collect taxes.

New mines, new mints

These conquests brought gold from Armenia, Egypt and West Africa into the empire's treasury. Previously, newly-mined supplies had been scant, with small mines or alluvial pickings in the mountains of Macedonia, the Taurus mountains of Anatolia and, probably, erratic shipments coming via Trebizond and on the Black Sea from Georgia and Central Asia. The imperial authorities always tried to ensure they got their hands on gold, making levies on miners or prospectors and controlling operations if they could. Up in the mountains of Armenia some sites were jointly licensed to Byzantine and Persian miners at an annual rent of 100 pounds (32.4 kg), although in 530 one operator did an exclusive deal with the Byzantine prefect for his mines at Pharangim on the Anatolia/Armenia border. The fees involved, however, suggest production was small.[8] Mining on a more organised basis was carried on at Bir Umm Farakir in the Wadi Hammamat of Egypt's eastern desert (an ancient source before 2000 BC) between AD 400–600 and provided Constantinople with gold at least under Justinian and his immediate successors.[9] Gold was also being bartered for in a region known as Sasou on the Blue Nile south of Khartoum. According to Cosmos Indicopleustes, the 6th century merchant-writer, the local people exchanged their alluvial gold from the river for oxen, salt and iron. In a system reminiscent of Herodotus' description of Phoenicians trading for gold on the coasts of Africa, the traders made a fenced enclosure with thorny bushes, and inside displayed the carcasses of oxen, alongside salt and iron. The local people then came and placed little piles of gold on the goods they wanted and drew back. If the trader was satisfied, he took the gold; if not, he waited until enough gold was added to make the exchange.[10]

The recapture of Carthage also gave the empire direct access to the gold coming across the traditional Sahara routes from West Africa. The Carthage mint, which had previously coined it for the Vandal kings, now made new dies with the emperor's image. Justinian ordered his praetorian prefect "that gold marked there shall exactly resemble that in this Great City (Constantinople), they shall place their seals on it according to the weight preserved in the coined money".[11]

These new sources, however, only provided the empire with marginal amounts of gold. "New metal appears to have made but a very limited contribution to renewing the money supply," wrote the French Byzantine scholar Cécile Morrisson. "Our period never witnessed an influx … comparable to the one that made possible the monetary enrichment of the (Roman) Empire."[12] The coinage depended, therefore, on the profits of trade and constantly recycling the gold already within the system through tax collection, which could work effectively in times of stability, but not during turmoil.

The extended domains of the 530s and 540s, however, enabled Justinian to open new mints for gold coin, not just at Carthage, but Alexandria, Antioch, Thessaloniki, Ravenna, Rome and Syracuse in Sicily (which had already been an entrepôt for African gold via Carthage for centuries). The *solidus* remained the pivotal coin, although the smaller *semissis* of 2.5 grams/0.08 t.oz and the *tremissis* of 1.5 grams/0.05 t.oz were also struck regularly to bridge the gap between the gold and copper currencies. Lightweight *solidi* with varying gold contents of 958, 896 and 833 fine were also struck occasionally, although the reason is not clear; it may have been a momentary shortage of gold for the mints or, as some argue, the coins were made for payments to the Germanic people of central Europe. Justinian also struck at least one heavy medallion, equal to 36 *solidi*, of 162 grams/5.2 t.oz, which ended up in the Bibliothèque Nationale in Paris from where it was stolen and melted down in 1831.[13] The significant change on all coins was the striking of Christian symbols, an angel and, later, the cross on the reverse, replacing the traditional Winged Victory of Roman coins.

The actual production by the mints can only be estimated roughly, based on surviving coins, for records (which certainly existed) have not survived. Constantinople's output was possibly five to ten times that of the provincial mints and could have exceeded one million *solidi* in some years, calling for 4.5 m.t/144,675 t.oz of metal, which would have been met primarily by recycling gold collected as taxes. This helped ensure consistent weight and fineness. "The relatively high rate at which Byzantine coinage was extracted from circulation and cycled, by way of the fiscal system, through the mint will have acted towards maintaining its general level of weight," concluded Michael Hendy.[14]

The weight of coins was usually expressed in terms of carats, the ubiquitous measure in the markets of the eastern Mediterranean based on the carob seed (*Caratonia siliqua*). One carat weighed 1/1728 of a Byzantine pound or 0.189 grams. The *solidus* weighed 24 carats and that remained the standard bench mark for much of the Byzantine period (the secondary meaning of carat, more readily used today, relates to the fineness of gold, with 24 carats being the equivalent of a fineness of 1000).[15]

The integrity of the coinage was guaranteed by the regulations of the Codex Justinianus of 534, which spelt out the strict supervision by the state over weights and measures, clipping, and forgeries. Dire penalties were threatened for forgers, although they flourished. The gossip was that the best counterfeiters were mint workers. The Codex also required that weights of gold, silver and copper coins be posted in churches, "so that both the collection of revenues and military and other expenses may take place according to them". The stipulation indicated that churches had become an integral part of everyday life; in Roman times such regulations were put up in post houses on major routes. The publication in church even bore the design of a hand holding a balance.[16]

Transactions in gold, particularly through the money-changers, were meticulous procedures which took time. Each coin had to be examined and weighed. Large transactions were often accomplished by the use of sealed purses bearing the number and weight of coins within. The purses, originally known to the Romans as *sacculum signatum* and in Greek-speaking Constantinople as *balantion*, contained anything from 20 to 2,000 *solidi*, with a 500 *solidi* purse of 2.25 kg/72.3 t.oz being common in the merchant community.[17]   Such security, despite the inevitable forgeries, made Byzantine coins unrivalled. Contemporary merchant, Cosmos Indicopleustes, wrote that the *solidus* "is accepted everywhere from the ends of the earth. It is admired by all men and in all kingdoms, because no kingdom has a currency that can be compared to it".

The Great Church

The coin was proof of the vitality and wealth of the empire under Justinian in the mid-6th century. The gold coins, struck at the imperial mint within the shadow of his palace, went into its vaults and then out to pay not just for the army and administrators of the empire, but for an array of public works. They encompassed churches, hospitals, city walls, roads, bridges, aqueducts, reservoirs, theatres and public baths (and from those who grew wealthy building them, gold was recycled back in taxes). The enduring monument to this age was Justinian's 'Great Church', Haghia Sophia, rising high on a bluff above the Bosphorus in Constantinople.

The original church, built in 360, had burned down during riots forty years later; its replacement was likewise destroyed in the Nika revolt of 532, a mini-civil war within the city. Justinian and his architect Isidorus of Miletus then set out not just to create an imposing building, but to furnish it within with ornate decoration in gold and silver. The total budget has been estimated at over 1.1 million *solidi*, almost 5 m.t/160,750 t.oz of gold.[18]   The new Haghia Sophia was inaugurated in Justinian's presence on 26th December 537. It has suffered damage from earthquakes and neglect on occasions since and, after 1453, became a mosque. Yet the view today from the waters below or what emerges on a walk up from the Galata Bridge, through the modern gold market, is essentially Justinian's church. His court poet, Paulus Silentiarus, lauded the grand scale of the gold and silver work within. Its columns were sheathed in gold leaf, the marble screen between the main nave and sanctuary had 12 columns sheathed in silver, the main altar was covered in gold and silver studded with precious stones. One modern calculation is that over 11 m.t/323,650 t.oz of silver went into this decoration. Gold mosaics covered the interior of the great dome, the semi-dome, many walls, vestibules and galleries, giving the church an interior radiance. Unlike the famous mosaics in Ravenna (see below), they were not figurative, but consisted of large grounds of plain gold *tesserae* adorned around the edges with bands of geometric or floral designs. The scholar Marlia Mango has calculated that the original mosaics covered 9,925 square metres and, assuming the gold foil on the tiny tiles was 2 microns thick, required 353 kg/11,350 t.oz of gold.[19]

The commitment to Haghia Sophia demonstrated the transformation in the uses for gold and silver for fabrication in the early Christian period. Rulers, provincial aristocracy and wealthy families put their money, not in the gaudy ornaments of Roman times, but into the endowment of churches. Gold and silver were fashioned into altarpieces, chalices, crosses, reliquaries or sceptres and other symbols of office for bishops, along with rich gold brocade for their vestments. The creation of the mosaics became a specialised art in its own right. The Church thus built up its own stocks of precious metal to rival those of the emperor, which became reserves of last resort (as had those of temples in pagan times), when the imperial treasury ran out. Goldsmiths in the imperial workshops close by Haghia Sophia worked largely in the service of the emperor and his Church. Emperors and empresses always required diadems and crowns and sometimes made extravagant demands. Justinian's successor, Justin II (565–578), had his throne room lined with gold mosaics, set golden lions beside his throne, with jewelled birds sitting on gold and silver trees around the chamber. Save for Church and State, goldsmiths had few calls on their talent. The French critic André Grabar lamented the "narrowing of the repertory … with no important developments in the decorative art of the goldsmiths and silversmiths".[20] The single new creative application was in mosaics, in which Christian art of the Byzantine Empire made a unique contribution to the history of gold with a fresh demonstration of the metal's versatility.

Ravenna: mosaic masterpieces

The last rays of the afternoon sun streaming through the west window of the basilica of Sant'Apollinaire Nuovo in Ravenna fall on the mosaic pattern of a 6th century royal palace creating a warm glow on the tiny gold *tesserae* that outline its loggias and colonnades. The light also catches a dynamic portrayal of the Magi, the three wise men, their robes edged in gold, their leader bearing a dish of gold, and filters along a procession of twenty-two virgins in embroidered gold tunics, framed against a background of gold. The mosaics, marching above graceful arches down either side of the nave, look as bright as the day they were created almost fifteen hundred years ago around 550. The freshness of their magnificent golds, blues and greens owes much to the dampness of the area, which prevented them flaking or crumbling, for Ravenna was first built as a safe harbour on islands in lagoons (like Venice, just to the north). Almost one thousand years on, the Renaissance artist Ghirlandaio called them "Paintings for Eternity". While André Grabar acknowledged, "These mosaics owe their compelling power to the brilliancy of the gold grounds".[21]

The mosaics of Ravenna are to be found not just at Sant'Apollinaire in Classe (the ancient port of Ravenna) and San Vitale, but other ancient baptistries and mausoleums around the city. They combine to offer a unique record of the great period of early Christian art, which peaked with Justinian, when the Byzantium Empire was in its prime and Ravenna became its Italian stronghold. Originally, Ravenna had become a Roman city in the 2nd century BC and, in the 1st century AD, was selected by Caesar Augustus as the port for his eastern Mediterranean fleet, because of it protected harbour. After the Roman Empire split, it became the capital of the western Empire in 402, until it was taken by the advancing Goths in 476. Fortuitously, the Goth Theodoric, who became king in 493 and ruled for several decades, was a cultivated man, and an advocate of religious tolerance. He built Sant'Apollinaire Nuovo and the palace depicted in its mosaics. The city was retaken for the Byzantine Empire in 540 and flourished throughout the reign of Justinian.

The incentive for mosaics to develop in Ravenna had stemmed originally from an imperial decree by Constantine the Great two hundred years earlier, granting tax exemptions to this art form. It was further stimulated by close contact with the eastern Empire flourishing in Constantinople. A "great school" of mosaic artists grew up in Ravenna, according to Gianfranco Bustacchini of the Mosaics Group at the Academy of Fine Arts in Ravenna.[22]

Mosaics, of course, were nothing new. They had been the vogue on the floors of many earlier Roman villas and public buildings. But floor mosaics had to be of stone cubes to withstand wear and tear. What the Ravenna mosaicists perfected was wall mosaics in which the *tesserae*, from the Greek word 'four' or 'square', could be of tinted or gilt glass positioned on a bed of mortar. That was how gold made its entry. Very fine gold leaf, usually 2 microns thick, was applied to a sheet of plain or lightly tinted glass about 8mm thick. The gold was then covered with a layer of powdered glass and the whole cube fired. The resulting tessera, Gianfranco Bustacchini noted, "was ideal for producing colour effects because the unevenness of the powdered glass and consequently of the overall thickness, created variations in tone that enabled gold to be used on very large areas".[23] A single halo might be made up of almost one thousand gold cubes.

The wall mosaics had two benefits. They not only gave extra stability to the walls, but could flow with them. "The use of small juxtaposed *tesserae* made it possible to clothe the curves of arches and vaulted ceilings with a wealth of scintillating colours," wrote André Grabar. "Once the mosaic workers realised the possibilities this opened up … some of the finest mosaics that the world has seen came into production."[24]

The mosaicists' first triumph was the Mausoleum of Augusta Galla Placida, empress of the western Roman Empire in Ravenna, who died c.450. The dome of her mausoleum has a wonderful midnight blue sky peppered with golden stars. The style was still Roman. The apostles Peter and Paul, clad in togas, look like Roman senators as they stand on a carpet of pale gold beneath a canopy of deeper gold hues.

Over the next century the mosaic artists, confidently marshalling myriads of tiny glazed cubes of all sizes, created infinite chromatic variations, often employing between 250 and 400 shades in a single mosaic, but giving it a remarkable unity of composition when viewed from a distance. They used gold on a grand scale as the backcloth on which figures and objects stood out.[25] Their style also drew increasing inspiration from Constantinople, where dramatic mosaics were being created in Haghia Sophia and other churches, although they were not figurative and many were later damaged or destroyed.

The Byzantine influence reached its peak during the reign of Justinian and his wife Theodora, who are each depicted with their clergy and courtiers in the apse of the basilica of San Vitale in Ravenna. Justinian, surmounted by a golden halo, wears a jewelled crown, holds a golden bowl and his cloak is fastened with a fibula of gold. The Bishop Maxminian, who originally consecrated San Vitale in 548, wears a golden cassock, while a guard of soldiers bears an oval shield in gold, blue and emerald. The entire court is framed by a golden backdrop of thousands of *tesserae*. Across the aisle, the empress Theodora is draped in jewellery, her robe edged in gold, her feet encased in slippers of gold, blue and white. Her ladies are decked out in robes and shawls of multicoloured patterns. A sumptuous lady has an entire robe with stripes of subtly differing shades of gold, another wears a jazzy mix of gold, red and green. One almost senses a mosaicist turned fashion designer. Seen close up, the designs reveal the irregular shapes and sizes of the *tesserae*, fitted together like pieces of an immense jigsaw puzzle to form a coherent whole.

The imperial mosaics are surrounded by a wealth of biblical scenes, alive not just with figures, but animals, birds, flowers and trees. A brilliant blue peacock with brown and orange tail feathers struts across a lawn of the palest gold dotted with white flowers. A basket of fruit is set off against a quiltwork of golden cubes. The head of a young, clean-shaven Christ is surrounded by a gold halo made up of over two thousand individual *tesserae*. The impression given visitors is that they are seeing something of enormous antiquity, yet so bright it might have been created yesterday, a feeling that is echoed at Sant'Apollinaire Nuovo with its vivid scenes of the life of Christ. "The Sant'Apollinaire Nuovo mosaics, enriched with a wealth of colours, gold, white, emerald-green, and spangled with broken gleams, rank justly as one of the masterworks of Byzantine art," decided André Grabar.[26]

As dramatic is the huge panorama that sweeps across the apse of Sant-Apollinaire in Classe on the outskirts of Ravenna. The top half of the mosaic, depicting the transfiguration of Christ, has a great cross in gold, with His face as a medallion at its centre, set against a blue sky filled with golden stars. On either side, Moses and Elijah appear amid the clouds of a gilded sky. Below, Sant'Apollinaire, the archbishop of Ravenna who founded the church, presides over a pastoral landscape of sheep, flying birds, trees and flowers, with a background of grass that is a remarkable blend of shifting shades of pale golds merging into greens.

The gold brings a special advantage to this mix. "Gold *tesserae* in particular have a property of exploiting the dynamism of light refraction," Gianfranco Bustacchini pointed out. "Anyone who has seen the Ravenna mosaics at different times of day has remarked that the gilded background 'relives' at each instant." Actually, the virtual generation of light by gold mosaics was already appreciated by the artists' own contemporaries in 6th century Ravenna. An unknown poet wrote, in the corner of a mosaic at Archbishop's Chapel there, "*Aut lux hic nata est aut capta hic libera regnat*", "Light, either born or imprisoned here, rules freely".[27]

The Empire at bay

The Empire of Justinian was prosperous, powerful throughout the Mediterranean world and a worthy successor to the Roman Empire in its own prime. A century later all that had been swept away by crisis after crisis that left it with scarcely one-third of the territory it commanded in 565 when Justinian died. The seeds of the disaster were already planted in his own overblown style. He had over-spent on vast projects and over-taxed trying to pay for them; the army had been neglected so that the frontiers were porous; and corruption, which he had eradicated early in his long reign, had crept back. Bubonic plague ravaged the population in 558 and earthquakes damaged buildings (including Haghia Sophia). "He left the State bled white, the frontiers pillaged, the government weak before the great proprietors, the people riotous and seditious," wrote C. Previté-Orton in a harsh obituary, although praising his achievements in stimulating Byzantine art and codifying Roman law.[28] The stability of the empire was undermined. Justinian's successors were at once preoccupied by incursions from the Slavs pressing down from the Danube and the Sasanians moving west from Persia. In Italy the Lombards threatened to overrun Rome. In 579 the emperor Tiberius II in Constantinople received a tribute of 972 kg/31,250 t.oz in gold from Rome with a plea for help. Tiberius, busy with eastern wars, sent the gold back, telling the Romans to use it either to hire the Lombards as mercenaries to aid his own eastern campaigns (and so distract them from Rome) or bribe the Franks to attack the Lombards from the north.[29]

A short reprieve came under Heraclius (610–41), potentially a great emperor, but running an exhausted empire surrounded by enemies. With little reserve in his treasury, he persuaded the churches of Constantinople to 'loan' him their gold and silver plate and votive treasure for a crusade against the infidel Sasanians in Persia. The Church's treasures were melted for coinage to finance the campaign. Heraclius left Constantinople in 622 for a six-year struggle which was won finally at Ninevah in 628. Heraclius, fortuitously, more than recouped his initial investment with the capture of the Persians' treasure. It was a bitter reward; in his absence the Slavs, aided by the Persians, had besieged Constantinople behind his back. The city held out, but much of the Balkans was lost to the Slavs. Meanwhile, the Visigoths had retaken Spain. As for the Church, they never recovered their gold and silver, since the Persian treasure was coined.

The gold coin output at the Constantinople mint during those years matched Heraclius' activities. Between 610 and 632 the estimated annual gold use striking *solidi* rose from under four m.t/128,600 t.oz to over six m.t, as he coined first the Church treasure and later that of the Persians. After 632, however, coin output fell to around three m.t annually, and before long to even lower levels. For Heraclius' efforts had been in vain.[30] In 632 the Prophet Mohammed died in Medina and the next year militant Islam rode out of the deserts of Arabia into Palestine and Syria. The Byzantine army was powerless to stop the invaders, suffering two major defeats in 634. The cities of Aleppo, Damascus and Antioch surrendered. The Arabs were checked by the Taurus mountains in Anatolia, but swung east into Mesopotamia and south to Egypt, taking Alexandria in 642. In less than a decade the Byzantine Empire had lost all its south-eastern provinces and was driven out of Carthage and North Africa within a few decades. What was left of the empire was western Anatolia behind the barrier of the Taurus mountains, Constantinople itself, Cyprus, Crete and Sicily, along with several Aegean islands. This rump at least served as a buffer between Islam and Western Europe, but its administration was in tatters and its economy ruined. Tax revenues withered, trade (for which Constantinople had been an international hub) was curtailed. The best source of newly-mined gold, Egypt, was in the hands of Islam. Constantinople itself became a smaller city; the population fell from 500,000 to under 100,000 people. Everywhere towns were depopulated and became defensive 'islands', while agricultural output in the countryside slumped. Gold coin striking dwindled, as did silver (which was always minimal) and copper coin. In town and country many went back to barter. The army often had to live off the land and in 743 the emperor Constantine V paid his troops in 'coin' made of leather. For at least 150 years, from 650–800, the Byzantine Empire was a shadow of its former self.

'Image smashers'

This dark era also provoked a religious upheaval. In the eastern, Greek-speaking part of the empire, there had always been vocal groups against all religious images (as, of course, in the new Islamic faith). In the turmoil of the early 8th century, they gained the upper hand. Under Leo III (717–40) an edict was promulgated banning all images in churches. The iconoclasts, 'image smashers' E. H. Gombrich called them, set about destroying mosaics, icons and wall paintings which depicted not just the image of Christ, but saints, bishops and all figurative Christian art. Given that the previous three hundred years had witnessed the great evolution of religious art in churches, there was much damage to be done. Church treasure was also appropriated by the state. New art and literature, including illuminated books often illustrated in gold, were stifled. The mosaics at Ravenna in Italy, being in the old Roman Empire, escaped this desecration, but this Byzantine foothold in northern Italy fell to the Lombards. Its mint ceased striking Byzantine gold coin in 752. Recovery from this 'Dark Age' was slow.

Buying peace with gold

Surprisingly, throughout this bleak period the minting of *solidi* was maintained without loss of weight or debasement of its gold content at 980 fine. The coin stood as a durable symbol of imperial finance, upholding the image of the emperor. To keep that in the public mind the *solidus* was often struck bearing two faces, that of the current emperor and his chosen successor to provide a sense of continuity. When the successor took over, his first act was a new coin also bearing his successor's face. The actual output of the Constantinople mint, the only one remaining in the

Empire save that of Syracuse in Sicily, was limited to perhaps 250,000–300,000 *solidi* at a time, not always annually; that would call for around one m.t/32,150 t.oz of gold.[31] It was enough to maintain Constantinople as the capital of gold coin, for Western Europe, also in its Dark Ages, survived only with silver coinage for four hundred years after 700. However, the new Islamic Empire had launched its own *dinar* in 697 and increasingly it rivalled the *solidus* (*see following chapter*).

The Byzantine and Islamic Empires had no doubt what gold was for – bribing each other to keep the peace, although it was something of a one-way business. Constantinople, under constant threat from the newly-established Caliphate in Damascus, found gold paved the way to uneasy truces. Their tributes, the emperor hoped, would also impress the Caliph with their importance. The emperor Justinian II sent the Caliph al-Walid a gift of 100,000 *dinars*, weighing 423 kg/13,600 t.oz in 705. Not that it stopped a siege of Constantinople by the Arabs in 717, which was ultimately repulsed.

Thereafter, gold flows during the 8th and early 9th century were mainly subsidies for peace or outright hijacking of Byzantium's gold shipments to its armies in the field. The Empress Irene (797–802) sent the Caliph in Baghdad, the new capital of Islam, an annual gift of 140,000 *solidi* (630 kg/20,255 t.oz). Her successor Nicephorus I (802–11) knocked this down to an annual 135 kg. Even this modest amount so drained his treasury that Nicephorus took to making compulsory loans of 3.9 kg to Constantinople's goldsmiths at 16.6% interest – payable in gold. Nor were his stocks helped when the Bulgarians captured a Byzantine army payroll of almost 80,000 *solidi* (360 kg/11,574 t.oz) and an Arab raid snatched another payroll of 95,600 coins (421 kg) in eastern Anatolia.[32]

These varied examples offer a unique perspective on the quantities of gold in transit for bribes or military purposes around the year 800. They are much smaller than in the heyday of the Roman Empire, when Nero recoined 237 m.t/7.6 million t.oz between AD 64 and 68, but are hard evidence of gold flows around Constantinople while Western Europe was operating entirely on silver. Constantinople was the market for gold, just as Venice and London would become in later periods. If gold was momentarily short, silk from the imperial workshops was sent as an alternative gift to foreign rulers.

Re-birth of the Empire

The Byzantine Empire that began to revive soon after 800 was a different creature from its predecessor. It had thrown off Roman trappings, was Greek-speaking (the *solidus* by now was always referred to as the *nomisma* and was eastward-looking to stay on terms with Islam on its borders). Ambassadors from Constantinople and Baghdad went back and forth with 'gifts' to keep the peace. The seeds of recovery lay in growing populations (the last serious onset of plague was in 747), which initially helped bring more land back under cultivation and then to a revival in towns as more crops came to their markets. The towns, and trade between them, also benefited from a greater feeling of security. As the Byzantine economic historian, Angeliki Lailou, aptly put it, "Glimmers of a turnaround, though not yet a takeoff, can be seen in virtually every major economic activity".[33]

Monetary development was aided by reforms of the Emperor Theophilus (829–42), who launched a new range of four copper *follis*, ranging from 3 grams to 14 grams. These coins put hard cash back into the hands of people in town and country who had virtually gone back to barter. "The copper coinage," Philip Grierson noted, "was abundant, well designed and carefully produced."[34] Theophilus also issued silver *miliaresion* of around 3 grams at 980 fine with the aim of getting silver back as an accepted monetary coin, rather than the ceremonial medal it had become. The gold *nomisma* were also struck in quantity on his accession, and on two later occasions. Gold minting was not an annual event and, before 900, rare. The smaller gold *semissis* and *tremissis* were occasionally struck. The imperial gold stocks, however, grew steadily and when Theophilus died in 840 he left 6,984,000 *nomismata* (31.43 m.t/1.10 million t.oz) in the treasury. His widow Theodora, who then ruled jointly as regent with Michael III (842–67) until 856, improved the holding to around 35 m.t. That gold was soon squandered after her death by Michael who, according to reports, left barely 21,600 *nomismata* (97 kg/3,118 t.oz) in the treasury when he was murdered.[35] His successor, Basil I, who had started out as a groom in the imperial stables before becoming a court favourite, had to melt palace jewellery to pay salaries. Basil (867–86) assumed the throne on a spurious claim that he was descended from Alexander the Great, but his Macedonian dynasty provided the empire the stability and military confidence it required for a full comeback. The lack of an inheritance in gold, however, was dire. His successor, Leo VI (886–912) did not issue any gold coins for the first twenty years of his reign, and minting by his successors was irregular.

Goldsmiths' and money-changers' charter

Leo VI himself is remembered for his *Book of the Eparch* of 911–12, a collection of legal provisions governing key trades in Constantinople in which the state has a close interest, including goldsmiths, money-changers and silk makers. The goldsmiths, with their workshops close to the imperial court, were a well-organised guild. They worked under the direction of the prefecture and ranked above money-changers in the social hierarchy. The goldsmiths, *argyropratai*, worked in gold, silver, pearls and gemstones, as buyers and sellers. They paid out primarily in silver coin when they bought back and were limited to buying one pound (320 grams/10.3 t.oz) of gold or silver at a time.[36] Informally, at least, they acted as goldsmith-bankers, lending out the metal at interest. Their prime clients were the imperial court and the Church. The court required not just crowns for the emperor or empress, but gold pieces as votive offerings to churches. Michael III, for example, commissioned a gold chalice set with precious stones and pearls, which was carried up to the altar of Haghia Sophia by the goldsmith who designed it.

Gold vessels were also commissioned by wealthy citizens as gifts to the patriarch of the Church or his bishops and clergy. Extravagant diplomatic gifts were ordered; a single girdle for the governor of Armenia took 8.6 kg/276 t.oz of gold inlaid with enamel.[37] Ordinary gold jewellery for the people at large was rare.

The money-changers, in their turn, sitting in their little booths, a scale at their side, were central to the daily functions of the urban economy. Across their tables gold, silver and copper coins were exchanged, quite profitably given the wide margins between them. The money-changers alone could give out gold *nomismata* to shopkeepers trading in copper coins from their customers. The changers also took in old gold coin, passing it on for reminting. Regulation was strict. A money-changer was admitted to the guild only after unassailable witnesses had confirmed his moral character. He was forbidden to hoard coin, could not clip or counterfeit, and was supposed to inform on forgers. How far these rules were honoured is debatable.

The money-changers were offered a new chance to deploy their skills as arbitragers with the launch of a new, lighter gold coin, the *tetarteron*, in 963 by the emperor Nicephorus II (963–9). This was supposed to replace the traditional *nomisma*. The *tetarteron* weighed 4.10 grams/0.13 t.oz (against 4.5 grams/0.14 t.oz for the *nomisma*) thus matching the Arab *dinar*, suggesting to some numismatists that it was conceived to aid exchange in trade. Sceptical contemporary commentators saw it as a ruse for the government to collect taxes in full weight *nomismata*, while making payments in the lighter *tetarteron*. To complicate matters, both coins looked almost identical, although later the *nomisma* was struck from larger, thinner blanks. The *tetarteron* never achieved wide circulation and was discontinued by the 1030s. The launch, however, indicated the Byzantine economy was picking up in the final decades of the 1st millennium.

The credit for this resurgence went to the Macedonian dynasty, founded by Basil I in 867, that had brought stability and won new territory. Although Sicily was lost to Islam, Crete and the northern Balkans had been regained. The real lift-off came during the forty-nine-year reign of Basil II (976–1025). Basil, otherwise known as the 'Bulgar-slayer', was a man of great energy and foresight, who ran an austere regime at home and hard-hitting campaigns abroad. Bulgaria was subdued (hence his nickname) pushing the empire's frontier back to the Danube. He then secured Syria, including Antioch, and the upper valley of the Euphrates, gathering booty along the way, probably recouping much of the gold that had been lost in army payroll ambushes or given as 'gifts' in preceding generations. When Basil died, the imperial reserves held 65 m.t/2.1 million t.oz of gold – the highest level since *Anastasius* five hundred years earlier.

'Take-off' in the new millennium

By the year 1000 under Basil II, Constantinople was again a great city, the bridge between Europe and Asia, between Christianity and Islam, and entrepôt of trade between the two civilisations. Western Europe's economy was waking up, Venice was emerging from her lagoons as a trading force, Egypt under the Muslim Fatimid dynasty was rich in African gold and eager for luxuries. Through the warehouses and wharves of Constantinople passed brocades, carpets, furs, metalwork, pearls, precious stones, slaves and spices. Silk, officially still an imperial monopoly not to be exported, was widely produced and sold to all comers. Delegations of merchants arrived from Russia (they were permitted to enter at a specific gate and lodged nearby) and Venetian ships could tie up on the Golden Horn. Local merchants were encouraged to visit Islamic countries, not least to gain intelligence. International trade fairs were organised in Constantinople, Thessaloniki and Trebizond, the Black Sea gateway to the Caucasus and Central Asia.

This traffic brought gold into Constantinople, sustaining the currency and continuing the situation that had prevailed since 700 that the Byzantine monetary system (and that of its Islamic neighbours) was on gold, while Western Europe had silver coinage. The local gold:silver ratios explain the flows. In the year 1000 the gold:silver ratio in Constantinople was as wide as 1:18 and 1:14 in Baghdad, compared to 1:10.7 in Venice and 1:9 in London. Constantinople was the magnet for gold, because it was more highly valued there.

The Byzantine Empire, though, was delicately balanced. Merchants and bankers were becoming prosperous and powerful, confident enough to challenge imperial rules (as in unofficial silk exports). By contrast, after Basil's death in 1025, a succession of profligate and militarily inept emperors undermined his legacy. While Basil lived, the empire was secure, but his territorial gains had left it dangerously over-stretched. Basil's immediate successor was Constantine VIII, who lasted barely three years. The real power, however, lay with his two daughters Zoe and Theodora. Zoe, a scheming lady, married three emperors or, rather, they married her to get the title. She also ruled for a sickly nephew, and for a while in her own right with her sister Theodora. Zoe prevailed from 1028–1050 and Theodora kept going until 1056. Not much was left by then. "Neither, unhappily, possessed any capacity to rule," wrote a stern critic, "and on their passions and caprice hung the fate of the declining empire."[38]

The great debasement

Zoe's second husband was a former money-changer, if not counterfeiter, who, at her whim, became Michael IV (1034–41). Michael knew all about manipulating currency. He promptly debased the *nomisma* to 900 fine and then to 870 fine. Overnight he broke the seven hundred-year tradition on the purity of the *solidus/nomisma* that had been maintained at 980 fine (with only momentary lapses) since the days of Constantine the Great.[39] Militarily the empire's frontiers were constantly challenged and reserves drained by attempts to buy peace, Constantine IX, another of Zoe's husbands, sent 216,000 *nomismata* and 300,000 Islamic *dinars*, weighing in all 2,341 kg/74,400 t.oz in gold, to the Caliph in Baghdad in 1046 to smooth treaty negotiations.   This "affluent gift", noted in the *Book of Treasures*, which recorded such profligacy, was the largest ever sent by a Byzantine emperor.[40]

The Byzantine system was spiralling to disaster as each emperor further debased the *nomisma* in the face of rising aggression on all fronts. The greatest danger was from eastern Islam united under a new banner of the Seljŭks Turks, migrants from the steppes of Central Asia. They defeated the emperor Romanus IV at the battle of Manzikert, near Lake Van in eastern Anatolia in 1071, capturing the emperor himself. It was a major setback. Gold coins plumbed new lows; debased at once to 580 fine, the *nomisma* slipped to a minimal 106 fine by the accession of Alexius I in 1081. His long reign of 37 years until 1118 managed to halt the monetary, political and military rot. However, even Alexius did not act for a decade. He inherited a badly-debased gold coinage and let it deteriorate further. "Gold was a greyish alloy in which there can have been little, if any, gold, but some silver and much copper," noted Michael Hendy.[41]

Salvation in the *hyperpyron*

Reform came only in 1092 with a complete reconstruction of the monetary system. A new gold coin, the *hyperpyron*, weighed 4.3 grams/0.14 t.oz at 870 fine; no attempt was made to return to the traditional 980 fine of the *solidus*/*nomisma*. The *hyperpyron's* companions were an electrum coin of 4.3 grams, with average 230 fine gold and the balance in silver, a *billon* coin, also at 4.3 grams, with 2% to 6% silver on base metals, plus two copper coins of 4.0 and 2.0 grams. The *hyperpyron* was "passably good gold" wrote Philip Grierson, a trifle condescendingly, but the whole package "conferred upon the empire a high degree of financial stability for at least another century".[42]   The *hyperpyron* won street credibility throughout the Mediterranean world, where the Venetians called them *perpero* and elsewhere in Europe they were *bezants*. Alexius may have minted ten million of these coins at the Constantinople mint over the rest of his reign, which would have called for 37.5 m.t/1.2 t.oz of fine gold.[43]   This gold came from reminting old coins that circled back into Constantinople from international trade and a tough tax regime imposed by Alexius, which could have tapped hoards of high purity coins from earlier days. New gold output was still scarce; indeed, between 1000 and 1100, mine supply was at an exceptionally low level, and most African gold went to the Muslim rulers of Egypt, North Africa and Spain.

The financial stability that Alexius brought to the empire was aided not just by his own long reign, but those of his successors, John II (1118–43) and Manuel I (1143–80), both powerful and influential men. So the Byzantine Empire had just three emperors in a span of ninety-nine years, in contrast to the comings and goings of the previous century. Yet the world around it was changing rapidly. Venice was becoming a formidable maritime and trading power; her famous Arsenal, the shipyard that built warships and trading vessels, was established in 1104. Western

Europe was stirring economically and militarily as its populations and cities threw off the Dark Ages. The First Crusade, which established the kingdom of Jerusalem in 1099, and two further crusades during the following century, changed the dynamics of the eastern Mediterranean, not least in precious metals.

The Crusaders, coming from Europe, paid their way in silver and took home gold, thus re-establishing the interchange of the metals between east and west. They also had to pay local demands in gold. The Knights Templar paid 100,000 *hyperpyrons* (374 kg/12,000 t.oz) in fine gold to secure a base on Cyprus in 1192 and 622 kg/20,000 t.oz as ransom for a leading Crusader.

Although Constantinople stood out as a bastion of Christianity, the crusades ultimately spelt disaster for the empire. Moreover, after the death of Manual I in 1180, it swiftly descended into rivalry for his title; there were seven 'emperors' and several usurpers between 1180 and 1204, some of whom met ghastly deaths. As the French and Venetians began to plan the Fourth Crusade in 1201, Constantinople was in turmoil. The French advanced over 20 m.t./645,000 t.oz of silver to the Venetian Doge, Dandelo, for ships to be built and supplied at the Arsenal. Crusades were now the pursuit of power, wealth and fame or, as one historian said, "criminal brigandage". The mayhem in Constantinople provided the crusaders with the opportunity to side with one feuding usurper or another in the hope of installing a sympathetic 'Latin' emperor. The Crusaders' fleet sailed up the Bosphorus in the summer of 1203, got a foothold in the Galata harbour and spent months intriguing. One 'emperor', Isaac II, died of fright; another, Alexius IV, was murdered. Finally, the exasperated Crusaders took matters into their own hands, breaking the defences of the city on 12th April 1204 and indulging in a three-day rampage. A Latin 'emperor' was put on the throne, and the empire divided between the Venetians and the Crusaders. Doge Dandelo secured three-eighths of the city for Venice, plus several islands in the Aegean and useful trading ports around the Balkan peninsula, confirming his city as the new maritime power in the Mediterranean.

The Byzantine Empire was fragmented into a handful of individual cities and its administration shattered. Although the Greeks won back Constantinople in 1261 and the ghost of the empire carried on until the Ottoman Turks took the city in 1453, the capture in 1204 was a disaster from which it never recovered. As for its gold coinage, the *hyperpyron* was minted erratically, but increasingly debased, first to 750 fine, then to 500 fine by 1300. The coin petered out completely by the reign of the emperor John V, beginning in 1341, leaving the empire with only a silver coinage. It was a sad last gasp for a coin that had a pedigree going back one thousand years to the Roman Empire.

CHAPTER 15

The Rise of Islam: Cornering African Gold

The sheer speed with which a small army of Muslims riding out of the deserts of Arabia in 632 effectively demolished the eastern Byzantine Empire and the Sasanid dynasty in Persia within a couple of decades has always astonished historians. By 700 they had also taken North Africa and were poised to move into Spain, spreading the word of the Prophet Muhammad from Central Asia to the Atlantic. "Within little more than a century after the Prophet's death, the whole area had been transformed," wrote Bernard Lewis, "in what was surely one of the swiftest and most dramatic changes in the whole of human history."[1]

This new empire, bound together by a mission to bring the Prophet's message of one God and his Divine Law to the rest of the world, was at the same time a military, political and economic force. "It was, first and foremost, a vast economic territory … more extensive, more varied, and more powerful than anything which had preceded it," observed the French historian Maurice Lombard.[2] It stitched together a new monetary system, combining the gold standard of its conquered Byzantine territories with the silver standard of Persia, to create a bimetallic currency bloc that served as a dual carriageway between two major economies – India, which liked silver, and the Mediterranean, which operated on gold. The coins, both gold and silver, won acceptance far beyond the immediate empire in southern Russia, India, China, Africa and parts of Western Europe to become the most widespread and uniform system in existence. "Its uniformity," Philip Grierson has pointed out, "resulted from the fact that almost the whole of it is epigraphic and employs Arabic script, contrasting with the pictorial coin types that have dominated the Western tradition."[3] The simple Arabic inscriptions from the Qur'an remained the same for generations, unlike coins in the west whose pictorial images came and went with successive rulers. What the coins did inherit was their names: the gold *dinar* derived its name from the Latin *denarius aureus* (gold coin), and the silver *dirhem* from the Greek *drachma*.

The Muslims' original advance had met little resistance. Byzantium, under the Emperor Heraclius, was already exhausted from a decade of wars against the Persians (*see previous chapter*), who, in turn, were riven with internal disputes among their Sasanid rulers. Heraclius had also overtaxed his eastern Empire and neglected, or could not afford to subsidise, Christian Arabs on the borders of Syria. They had turned for help to their fellow Arabs in Arabia, who had just embraced the religion of Islam as revealed to the Prophet Muhammad. The message of that new faith was the passport to empire, for although war was engaged in to displace rulers, and plunder was sought, fraternisation with the people at large was the key. Islam had something to offer them, a religion, a political system, a fresh way of life. Thus it was embraced and the new believers often helped the empire to spread.

Muhammad had first received his revelation from God in 609 in Mecca, an ancient sanctuary and trading oasis on the trans-Arabia caravan route. The heart of the belief was in one God and the Prophet Muhammad as his messenger. Muhammad fled with his followers from Mecca to Medina in 622 (the year from which the Islamic calendar begins), when his nascent sect ran foul of the authorities. In Medina the first mosque was built for Muhammad's community or *Umma*. Just eight years later, in 630, Muhammad went back to conquer Mecca; his *Umma* was already a mini-state, poised to become an empire. Muhammad, however, died suddenly on 8th June 632, and was succeeded by the eldest of his companions, Abu Bakr. Since Islam declared there could be no other God and no other prophet but Muhammad, Abu Bakr became the Caliph – the sovereign title in the Islamic world. And it was his general Khalid, the 'Sword of God', who swept out of the desert to take Damascus in 634.

This initial campaign against Byzantine territory revealed the Arabs' unique advantage. The desert was their natural environment, to the people they were conquering it was a hostile one. They emerged out of the sands and could vanish back into them. The garrison towns they built, such as Fustat in Egypt (now Cairo), were located at the meeting of desert and fertile land. They became the urban centres in which the Arabs were most comfortable, where they could build mosques and an ordered administration. Some, like Cordoba in Spain, became centres of culture and learning. One historian called them urban 'islands' on strategic trade routes, rather like the oases of Mecca and Medina from whence they came, which were astride the caravan routes of Arabia. The Arab migration from the desert may have been stimulated by over-population in those barren lands, but it was not a mass movement. Rather, the Arabs became an army of occupation with a dominant class of the military, senior administrators and landowners. The general population got on with their lives and were encouraged, rather than required, to embrace Islam, often with the carrot of paying lower taxes.[4] Gradually, Arabic became the official language through much of the Muslim Empire, replacing Greek and Persian.

The Caliph, the supreme leader, was located first in Damascus and, after 762, at a new capital in Baghdad. Two dynasties, the Umayyads from 661–750, and then the Abbasids, took the empire to the peak of its powers. The Abbasids were the titular heads of much of the Muslim world until 1250, but after 850 lost the real power, which was taken over by sub-dynasties in Egypt, North Africa and Spain. The Caliph was, as was once said of a British prime minister, "in office, but not in power". They just gave their blessing to *de facto* rulers. The sense of

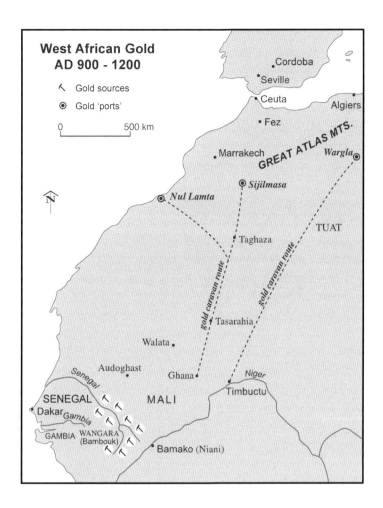

mission, however, was not lost. Many down-trodden peoples found Islam brought new meaning and structure to their lives. The Persians were not just converted, but helped spread the message into Central Asia; the Berbers in North Africa, after initial resistance, aided the conquest of Spain and took the Islamic faith south across the Sahara to the gold-bearing regions of West Africa.

That was a step of great significance, for the strengthening ties along the caravan routes enhanced the gold flows out of Africa, producing the largest quantities since the era of Roman mining in Spain eight hundred years earlier. Africa provided the Muslim Empire, particularly Spain, North Africa and Egypt, with enough gold to keep the mints busy.

A new Islamic coinage

The newcomers out of Arabia had approached the issue of their own coinage gingerly. For the first few decades the gold *nomisma* of Byzantium and the silver *drachm* of the Sasanians continued to circulate. A suggestion that a coinage of camel skins might be tried brought the explanation to an early Caliph that there would be no camels left alive. The first expedient was to copy the Byzantine *nomisma*, with a Caliph's head, but omitting the cross and other Christian symbols. Islam's growing reluctance to permit any images, however, mitigated in favour of an epigrammatic coinage, simply bearing inscriptions from the Qur'an. The decision was hastened by the Byzantine Emperor, Justinian II, objecting to official papyri from the Caliph bearing phrases on the 'Oneness of God'. His response was to propose *nomisma* bearing Christ's image. The matter was settled by the Caliph Abdul al-Malik (685–705), with the issue in 696/7 at the former Byzantine mint in Damascus of a gold *dinar* or *mithqal* of 4.25 grams/0.14 t.oz at 970 fine without any pictorial design. The face was inscribed "There is no God, but God alone; he has no associate, Muhammad is the Prophet of God". The message on the reverse read "God is one, God is eternal, he begets not nor is he begotten". A silver *dirham* of 2.8–2.9 grams was issued two years later, but it was the *dinar* that was to become the symbolic coin of the Islamic world, minted in many cities from Central Asia to Spain over the next five centuries. Indeed, the diversity of mints was astonishing. A display of *dinars*, with subtly differing Arabic scripts for their inscriptions, in the Islamic Gallery of the British Museum in London, shows coins from over twenty mints, dating 696–1244. They were struck as far apart as Ghanzi in Afghanistan to Aden in Yemen and Isfahan in Persia to Ceuta in North Africa and Cordoba and Seville in Spain. The *dinar* was truly an international coin.

The first Arab mint was established at Wasit, on the Tigris south of modern Baghdad in 703, by the governor of the region, al-Hajjaj bin Yousuf. According to the 9th century writer Baladhuri, al-Hajjaj "inquired into the matter of coining *dirhams* of the Persians, and then erected a mint and assembled men to do the stamping. He marked by tattooing or branding the hands of the coiners". Mint workers and money changers, who dealt in coin, were closely supervised to ensure there was no forging. The penalty was the chopping off of hands.[5] The mint was transferred to Baghdad after 762 when the Caliph declared it as his new capital.

The sources of gold

The Caliphs had diverse sources of gold. The initial conquests brought them the gold and silver stocks of the eastern Byzantine Empire – including its churches and monasteries – and of Persia, where much gold coin had been hoarded in Sasanian palaces, although silver formed the main coin circulation. In Egypt, tomb robbers, known as *ashab al-matalib*, scoured the tombs of the ancient Pharaohs for gold, giving 20% of their finds to the government and working closely with the Fustat (Cairo) mint. Contemporary sources suggest they may have come up with at least 4 m.t/128,600 t.oz. Thus dormant gold was brought back into circulation, while, through the money-changers, Byzantine *nomisma* were called in, melted and recoined as *dinars*.

This metal was supplemented by "gifts" of gold from Byzantine and other rulers in an effort to keep the Muslims at bay. Justinian II sent Abd-al-Malik's successor a welcoming present of 100,000 *dinars* (423 kg/13,750 t.oz) in 705, although this did not stop an abortive Muslim assault on Constantinople in 717. Gifts flowed constantly; the Empress Irene (797–802) sent coins weighing 630 kg/20,250 t.oz annually to Harun al-Rashid (786–809) in Baghdad. Her successor offered a more modest 135 kg/4,340 t.oz during his reign, but lost 93,600 gold coins (421 kg/13,535 t.oz) in an army payroll ambushed by Arabs in Armenia. The Emperor Theophilus was said to have offered 1,440,000 coins (6.48 m.t/208,330 t.oz) as ransom in 838 for the release of prisoners after a Muslim rout of Byzantine forces at Amoriun in central Anatolia, which was rejected as being insufficient (the amount, anyway, was probably vastly exaggerated). The largest confirmed tribute from Constantinople was sent in 1046 by Constantine IX who dispatched 216,000 *nomisma* and 300,000 *dinars* (2,250 kg/72,340 t.oz) to mark the signing of a peace treaty with the Caliph in Baghdad.

The gifts were something of a ritual, with frequent counter-gifts from the Caliphs to maintain their own prestige. The reaction of al-Mamum (813–33) to a gift from Theophilus was, according to an Arabic source, "Send him a gift a hundred times as much as his, so he recognises the glory of Islam". He then enquired what the emperor valued most and was told "musk and sable". Gold, it seems, always went to Baghdad.[6] The Caliph received gifts in gold, too, from the regional dynasties who were increasingly ruling his empire. The Tulunids in Egypt paid an annual tribute of 300,000 *dinars* (1,275 kg/40,500 t.oz) to Baghdad in this period. The Fatimids, who ruled Egypt from 969, were equally lavish with gold *dinars* minted from their growing supplies from West Africa.

Cornering the gold of Africa

The broad sweep of Islamic lands enabled them either to control the mines for precious metals or command the trade routes along which they flowed. Gold came from Armenia and the Caucasus, possibly from the Altai mountains of Central Asia, and from the upper reaches of the Nile in Egypt and Nubia. It was even mined in Arabia at Hijaz, south-east of Medina around 723, from which *dinars* were minted locally bearing the inscription "the mine of the Commander of the Faithful in Hijaz".[7] The serious gold, though, came from West Africa, between the Senegal and Niger rivers, a region often referred to as 'Sudan' in early accounts and not to be confused with modern Sudan.

The key to this gold was mastery of the Magreb region, Berber territory, stretching through the Atlas mountains of Algeria and Morocco in whose foothills the caravan termini from the south were located. "The entire political and dynastic history of North Africa was governed by the desire to control the arrival points of the gold caravans," Maurice Lombard noted.[8] The Arabs first advanced into the Magreb after their capture of Carthage in 697 taking the inland route along the northern foot of the Atlas mountains. They were resisted – a natural reflex action – but by 700 the Berbers had embraced both Islam and its empire. They became cohorts in the conquest and colonisation of Spain between 711–14 and many Berbers later migrated there. The advance was halted only at Poitiers in France in 732 by the Franks under Charles Martel. To the south, beyond the Sahara, they not only colonised, but converted, many of the tribes to Islam. These ties of blood and religion consolidated the gold trade in their hands.

The strategic staging posts, 'gold ports', were often in places where the desert butted up against the Atlas ranges. The two most easterly were Djerid and Wurgla (now Ouargla), which had good access to the city of Kairouan built by the Arabs, south of modern Tunis, on the main route to Carthage and Egypt. To the west the 'gold ports' in Morocco were Sijilmasa, at the foot of the Atlas, and Nul Lamta on the coast near modern Agadir.[9] Initially, most of the gold from all four termini was directed onwards to Egypt and beyond to Baghdad, then the centres of gold coinage. But by 900 under new alliances to control the gold trade, Nul Lamta and Sijilmasa supplied Spain, where the independent Umayyad dynasty began striking *dinars* at the Cordoba mint.

Sijilmasa, an oasis renowned for pure water between Fez and Marrakech, came under the wing of the Zanata, a powerful merchant family, in 757. They established it as a centre for fitting out caravans embarking on the two months' march to the goldfields. "The way to them is dangerous and troublesome," reported the chronicler Ibn Haukal, who ventured there c. 950, "but the mines are of the most pure and excellent gold." The destination was a frontier town called Ghana (not the present state). En route, they paused to load their camels with salt at the mines of Taghaza twenty days' march into the desert. Salt was the currency for buying gold. "They travel in the desert as it were upon the sea, having guides to pilot them by the stars or rocks," wrote another anonymous traveller. "When they reach Ghana they weigh their salt and sell it against a certain unit weight of gold, and sometimes against double or more of the gold unit, according to the market supply."[10]

On the gold fields

The precise location of Ghana is unknown, but it was a market town north of the Senegal river to the west of Timbukto, another historic trading post. The gold was recovered from alluvial deposits in an area known as Wangera, a wedge between the Senegal and its tributaries and the Upper Niger river (which flows east at that point making early travellers suspect it was the Nile). Wangera matches a region now called Bambouk, between the towns of Kayes and Bamako in Mali, where alluvial gold is recovered to this day. The deposits were then so rich that, according to one report, all nuggets were reserved for the local king and only gold dust went to traders. The king was also said to tether his horse to a gold nugget large enough to secure it.

The digging was seasonal. The rainy season each August brought the rivers into flood. Once the waters retreated, the local people began the search in deposits laid bare or in sediment newly brought down from the hills. Traders from Ghana and another market at Audoghast, fifteen days' march to the west, then came to barter for the gold. The procedure followed the 'silent system' described almost fifteen hundred years earlier by Herodotus and by Cosmos Indicopleustes in Nubia in the 6th century AD.[11] The Arabic author Yaqut, who compiled a geographical dictionary, wrote that when the foreign traders reached the Senegal river they beat on drums to signal their arrival and set out their trade goods, including salt, and retired. The gold diggers approached and put gold on each pile and, in turn, retired. If the quantity was sufficient, the merchants again beat their drums, took the gold and departed. If not, they waited for more gold to be added until the deal was done.

These accounts do not explain the extent to which the traders from the north purchased gold in Ghana or Audoghast from local brokers, or bought directly at the gold fields. Judging by modern experience on the ground in Africa and South America, it was probably a bit of both. The gold fields were scattered and it would have been impossible to visit them all. Outsiders going into remote areas today have to rely largely on a host of small brokers living on the fields to round up much of the metal. What is fascinating is how much gold still comes to market every year from such West African round-ups. In the 1980s and 90s, I monitored the gold dust being dispatched from Bamako in Mali from precisely the same areas on tributaries of the Senegal river. It no longer came by camel, but on the weekly Swiss Air flight from Bamako to Geneva, where it went to a local refinery. It was high purity gold, well over 900 fine; between 1 and 2 m.t/32,150–64,300 t.oz turned up each year – a latter-day example of a trade that has gone on for over one thousand years. Moreover, those original alluvial diggings were the clues to huge low-grade deposits, which have been unlocked since 1995 with the benefit of new technology, making modern Mali a significant producer of close to 50 m.t/1.6 million t.oz a year.

The output a thousand years ago can only be guessed, but it is recorded that, around 950, the mint established by then at Sijilmasa in Morocco was producing up to 400,000 *dinars* annually, which required 1,700 kg/54,655 t.oz.[12] Given Sijilmasa was only one of four main 'gold ports', it is likely that the 'Sudan' of West Africa was producing at least 6,000 kg/192,900 t.oz a year.[13] This would have amounted to the largest regular supply of newly-mined gold since Roman times.

This steady flow of gold over the centuries underwrote prosperous Muslim societies in Spain, North Africa, Sicily and Egypt, as the original empire built around Baghdad fragmented into increasingly independent segments, each with its own ruling dynasty owing token allegiance to the Caliph in Baghdad.

Cordoba's golden age

Spain was a particular beneficiary under its own Umayyad dynasty, established in Cordoba in 756 by Abd ar-Rahman I (756–88), who sought to emulate the grandeur of the eastern caliphate from which he had been exiled. He made Cordoba into a prosperous centre of culture and learning and began the first stage of its great mosque, the Mesquita, still the pride of the city. A new mint in Cordoba struck silver coinage in abundance after 768, using the metal from Spain's own mines. Gold coinage, however, was reserved for the eastern mints in Damascus and Baghdad. Only after 850 did gold coinage become more widespread at mints throughout the Muslim world. The Umayyads of Cordoba only got their hands directly on the growing African output after 900, through an alliance with the Zanata merchant dynasty in Morocco, who controlled the crucial Sijilmasa and Nul Lamta caravan termini.

The switch to gold was dramatic, underwriting the long reigns of Abd ar-Rahman III (912–961) and his successor al-Hakim II (961–976), who brought Muslim rule in Spain to its apogee. "In Cordoba it maintained the supply from which *dinars* were coined, it kept the court in luxury, paid for the huge mosque, and contributed to the patronage of the arts," wrote Maurice Lombard.[14] The treasury of Abd ar-Rahman contained close to five million *dinars* when he died, amounting to over 21 m.t/675,000 t.oz of gold. Al-Hakim paid forty million *dinars* into his treasury during his reign, according to contemporary reports. If they did not exaggerate (a common occurrence) that would have amounted to 170 m.t/5.47 million t.oz, or an average of 11.33 m.t/365,000 t.oz annually. These receipts would not all have been newly-mined gold, but tax receipts or tributes of gold already in circulation. Even so, Cordoba mint was producing serious gold coinage that circulated not only in Muslim Spain, but north into Western Europe to pay for imports – which included slaves for whom Spain served as a transit point to the east. "Muslim coins provided an internationally recognised standard of payment," noted Philip Grierson.[15]

The coins were also imitated by the Christian kings of Castile and north-west Spain, just outside the Muslim domain. The wide distribution of the *dinars* has been confirmed by hoards turned up in Europe in modern times, which include *dinars* from Spanish and North African mints. Such coins were highly desirable in a Europe still on limited silver coinage. *Dinars*, or even imitations of them, were welcome for re-export in payment for luxuries from the east. Indeed, at this moment just before the year 1000, the fortunes of the Byzantine Empire were reviving, with Constantinople again a major trading entrepôt. The *dinars* circulated there to pay for silks and spices, thus aiding the replenishment of the Byzantine treasury of the Emperor Basil II (976–1025). The Umayyads of Cordoba prospered until 1031, when their dynasty imploded in internal strife. Although *dinars* continued to be struck by other Muslim family dynasties at Cordoba, Seville and Granada until the 15th century, the heyday of the *dinar* had passed.

Fatimid riches

Meanwhile, the Fatimids of North Africa profited from their control of the two eastern 'gold ports' of Djerid and Wargla, where the surging West African output injected new life into the economy after 900. The Fatimids were minting *dinars* at

Kairouan by 912 and shortly thereafter founded a new capital nearby at Mahdiyya, where *dinars* were also struck. They secured control of Sicily, where *dinars* were minted at Palermo, along with a profusion of quarter *dinars* known as *kharruba*. Finally, under al-Mu'izz (953–75) they conquered Egypt in 969, where the dynasty remained in power until 1171.

In Egypt they benefited from the gold of the Upper Nile and Nubia, as well as West Africa, which enabled them to keep up high quality gold coinage at the mints of Cairo and Alexandria for two centuries. Before long, Syria was also in their control, with *dinars* being struck in Damascus, Tripoli and Tyre until well after 1100. In Cairo itself, the Fatimids maintained a magnificent court, built palaces, mosques and *souks* (markets), while expanding their commercial ties down the Red Sea towards India. One leading Fatimid minister was said to have six million *dinars* (25.5 m.t/820,000 t.oz) in his treasury – not an impossible amount given that the Emperor Basil II in Constantinople had a similar stock in his treasury in the same period.

Thus the Muslim gold standard survived almost intact for the first two centuries of the new millennium, despite Islamic domains being chipped away on many fronts. Persia had already become an independent Muslim state in 946. The Byzantine Empire won back some territory in Syria, Christian Europe was stirring, first pushing back the frontiers of Muslim Spain, and then embarking on the four Crusades that re-shaped the eastern Mediterranean world. As a forerunner, the Normans took Sicily in 1091. "Henceforward the Muslim World was not a united whole," remarked Maurice Lombard. "There was a Turkish Islam, a Persian Islam, a Syrian Islam, an Egyptian Islam, and a Magreb Islam."[16] Muslim mints, notably those of the Fatimids, maintained the fineness and uniformity of weight of gold coins ensuring their acceptability as international currency. The *dinar*'s status was enhanced when the Byzantine *nomisma* went into free-fall debasement after 1050 (*see preceding chapter*). Control of African gold sources and caravan routes was also maintained, with output rising in the 11th and 12th centuries.

The silver famine

The gold *dinar* became more exclusive after 1000 because of the virtual absence of silver coinage throughout the Muslim world. The Islamic currency, as launched in 697 by Abd al-Malik, was bimetallic; both gold and silver were minted, depending on the availability of the metals; Spain had minted silver *dirhems* alone until after 900, importing *dinars* from Damascus or Baghdad. In the new millennium, however, silver coin vanished. Baghdad struck no silver after 1010, in Syria and Anatolia where *dirhems* had been minted in a dozen towns, they disappeared before 1030. In Egypt *dirhems* were minted, but the fineness fell from 860 to 340 fine between 1000 and 1100. The disappearing act continued across North Africa and Spain. "From the Atlantic coast to the borders of India no Islamic ruler was striking silver coins," wrote Andrew Watson in a seminal research paper: *Back to Gold – and*

Silver.[17]   The absence of silver was explained partly by the capture or closure of several silver mines in Persia, Afghanistan and Sardinia, but also by the very fact that the Muslim diaspora controlled the gold routes from Africa and that, for the time being, gold was more highly valued in their territories. The gold:silver ratio was between 1:14 or 1:15 in the Muslim Near East, and as wide as 1:18 in Constantinople. By comparison, the ratio in much of Europe was 1:10 or narrower, valuing silver higher. Market forces attracted gold to underpin the Muslim and Byzantine gold standards, while silver went to Europe or India and China where it was also sought after. Even the fabrication of silverware collapsed.

Yet that balance was on the cusp of change. Over the next two centuries, the precious metal flows reversed completely. By 1250 the gold:silver ratio in Baghdad, Damascus and Cairo was hovering between 1:5 and 1:7. The Damascus mint started striking silver coin in 1174 for the first time in 200 years; gradually Baghdad, Cairo, Cordoba and the North African towns followed suit. The silver trail spread along the trade routes to Samarkand and Tashkent in Central Asia before 1300.[18] Silver simply replaced gold as the basis of currency throughout the Muslim world. The other side of the equation was that Europe forsook silver, the foundation of its coinage since 700, and went over to gold. The catalyst for this reversal of fortunes was the Crusades.

The Crusaders' challenge

Crusaders from all over Europe, making common causes to win back Jerusalem and the Holy Land from Islam, set out on the First Crusade in 1096. Within three years they had set up the kingdom of Jerusalem, and over the next century struggled to maintain their foothold in the eastern Mediterranean, with three more Crusades. They paid their way largely in silver (although taking counterfeit Arabic gold coins when possible), thus inaugurating an eastward flow of the metal through the force of war and not the market. The tide increased with the pilgrims and merchants who came in their wake. The Second Crusade, beginning in 1147, and the Third in 1189, kept up the momentum. Each wave of Crusaders brought more silver to a region starved for generations. Silver coin became more commonplace in the markets of Antioch, Aleppo, Damascus and Jerusalem. The Crusaders even started striking silver *dirhems* at the local mints they had captured. The silver at their disposal was increased by the opening up of fresh silver deposits in the Vosges and Jura regions of France and in the Black Forest, Harz mountains and Freiburg region of Germany. Silver output in Europe probably doubled between 1100–1200.

In the Near East this brought daily market-making between gold and silver to the money-changers' tables. The Crusaders found it essential to have gold in hand for securing strategic locations or paying ransoms for kidnapped comrades. The Knights Templar paid almost 450 kg/15,500 t.oz in 1191 to lease a base on Cyprus. Arab potentates were also encouraged to pay 'tributes' to the Crusaders to be left in peace. Two tributes, each of one million *dinars* (4.25 m.t/136,600 t.oz), were rumoured to have been offered by one supplicant, although they may not have been fully paid up.[19]   Taxes were also exacted in gold.

Indeed, the Crusades were increasingly seen as a licence to plunder. Twenty gold lamps were even taken from the temple in Jerusalem. Gold was not just for expenses on the ground, but to take back home, initiating a two-way flow of gold and silver that ultimately reversed the gold:silver ratio. The Crusaders also began minting imitations of Muslim *dinars*, particularly those of the Fatimids in Egypt, at mints in Tyre, Acre, Tripoli and Antioch. Therein lay the real threat to the international acceptability of the coin, for they were often light and of doubtful fineness. The Fatimids themselves were still meticulous on such standards. The Crusaders' counterfeits, however, undermined the *dinars'* reputation in the markets of the east.

Meanwhile, the Fatimids were overthrown in 1171 by the Ayyubid dynasty, whose inspiring leader Saladin challenged the resident Crusaders. Saladin took Damascus in 1174 and Jerusalem in 1187. In Damascus he promptly minted silver *dirhems*, the first struck there for 200 years, and in Egypt coined them on a large scale. A few gold *dinars* bearing Saladin's name were made, but essentially Egypt went over to silver as the official coinage. Gold became simply a commodity sold in the market by weight after the year 1200. The *dinar*, the backbone of Muslim currency since its launch in 797 by Abdul al-Malik, was finished. The contemporary historian, al-Makrizi, sighed that to find a pure gold coin any more was "Like crossing the gates of paradise".[20]

The gold trade was moving on. The eclipse of the Islamic *dinar* after five hundred years coincided with the last gasp of the Byzantine *nomisma* after a life of one thousand years. Those two gold currencies had bridged the gap between the ancient and modern worlds. "From now on, the nerve centres and centres of influence of an expanding economy were no longer in the East, in the cities of the Muslim world," concluded Maurice Lombard. "They moved westwards and became established in the mercantile cities of Italy and Flanders."[21]   The responsibility for striking a gold coin of international acceptance was shortly to be shouldered by Venice.

The artistic legacy

The Arab ascendancy in military, political and monetary power endured from 650–1250, but their faith, their language and their law remain to this day. So, too, does the visual legacy in art and architecture which the prescriptions of the Islamic faith made unique. The doctrine that artists must not usurp the creative role of God by depicting human images pervaded everything, sometimes to advantage. "Art as such cannot be so easily suppressed," observed the art historian E. H. Gombrich. "The craftsmen of the East, who were not permitted to represent human beings, let their imagination play with patterns and forms. They created the most subtle lacework ornamentation known as arabesques … Muhammad directed the mind of the artist away from the objects of the real world to this dream world of lines and colours."[22]

The goldsmiths' art was hedged by themes imposed by Muslim patrons on jewellery and mosaics. Gold earrings framed verses from the Qu'ran in elegant script of gold filigree, bracelets bore benedictory inscriptions in niello. Although the Qu'ran permitted adornment, it urged moderation and strict Muslims often shunned vessels of gold or silver, preferring brass in which wonderful ewers were created for washing before prayers. The mosaicists, working on great new mosques in Damascus, Jerusalem and Cordoba, left out the human form, often covering the gold background with graceful trees beside rivers, replicating the Islamic vision of Paradise as a garden with running waters.

The common factor in many works of art was the calligraphy, regarded as the supreme art of the Islamic world and the means by which the word of God in the Qu'ran was conveyed to the people. This powerful angular Arabic or rather *Kufic* script (named after Dufah in Iraq where it was perfected in the first century of Islam) became ubiquitous. The message was on every medium – coins, jewellery, vessels for eating and drinking, and framing around mosaics. The calligraphy was at its most splendid in early versions of the Qu'ran, bound in wood and leather, with the script written in gold on parchment dyed deep blue, as if the message was etched against a night sky.[23]

For the goldsmith the tracery of the arabesque, or the geometric and zodiac styles approved by Islam, were best served by filigree with its delicate creations in thin gold wire. An early fashion was set by Zubaida, wife of the Abbasid Caliph Harun al-Rashid (786–809), who wore a famous serpent collar of interwoven gold wires. The collar, like much Islamic jewellery and plate, has not survived; most ended in the melting pot. But we know there were occasional flights of fancy; the Caliph al-Muqtadir (908–32) commissioned a tree of gold and silver with fruit of precious stones and birds twittering in its branches. The best of what may be seen today was created by the Buyid dynasty in Persia between 960 and 1055, and by the Fatimids in Egypt at their court in Cairo in the same era. The Buyids, living on either side of the Tigris river, are remembered by a handsome gold ewer resplendent with animal and plant designs and a delicate gold wine bowl with a *Kufic* inscription in praise of wine around the rim, above a decoration of birds. The golden bowl was part of the Nihavand treasure found near the ancient city of Hamadan, which also comprised silver gilt belt ornaments and an amulet (charm) case.[24] The high standard of Persian metalwork revealed in such rare articles in gold is backed up by silver and brass artefacts from the province of Tabaristan on the southern shore of the Caspian sea and from the city of Herat, then in Khurashan. Persia, after all, had an ancient tradition in working gold and silver, going back to the days of Darius the Great, and all the goldsmiths had to do was adapt to the new parameters.

As usual, they were also mobile, moving during the centuries of Islamic supremacy to Isfahan, Baghdad, Damascus, Mosul, Cordoba or Cairo, depending on which city was in the ascendancy. Cairo was definitely the place to be under the Fatimids between 969 and 1171. The goldsmiths there excelled in filigree and granulation of the highest quality, created in both palace and souk workshops. Palace inventories suggest that gold ornaments were constantly being ordered, with old often being melted down for new. An exquisite gold necklace of biconical and spherical beads totally fabricated from gold wire and then decorated with granulation is an outstanding survivor.[25] After the Fatimid collapse, some goldsmiths migrated back to Syria and Iran, but others moved along the North African coast, now controlled by the Almohad Berber dynasty of Marrakech, where they produced filigree earrings in which verses from the Qu'ran were spelt out within a square frame.[26]

Such sparse examples are hardly a fair way to judge Islamic jewellery, except that they prove the high standard achieved; but that was inevitable because ornaments were always melted to make new ones. The first thing I had to understand in visiting gold *souks* from Casablanca and Fez to Cairo in the late 1960s was the extent to which gold was recycled. Morocco and Egypt, like all Middle East countries, had scores of little workshops busy making ornaments in cubbyholes in the depths of the *souks*, without any apparent new supply of gold. As I sat in the goldsmiths' shops in the evening until 10 pm, sipping glasses of tea, the reason became apparent. Each shop was a social centre, where veiled women gathered with old ornaments wrapped in paper bags to be traded in for the latest designs. No doubt it was much the same a thousand years earlier.

Mosaics of Paradise

The history of Islamic mosaics has an intriguing twist. The great schools of mosaicists were in Ravenna and Constantinople (*see preceding chapter*) and Islamic artists relied considerably on their technical ability in making the tiny gold tiles or *tesserae*, while adhering to their own constraints of not depicting human imagery, but the cool gardens and waters of Paradise. The Emperor Justinian II even sent forty mule loads of gold *tesserae* from Constantinople to the Caliph al-Walid I in Damascus in 705 to provide the golden background to the mosaics in the Great Mosque that he was building. They gleam still in the *Barada* mosaic at this mosque, which shows a palace hung with jewels surrounded by tiny houses and framed by tall trees before the river *Barada* which flows through Damascus.[27]

Help was also sought 250 years later by al-Hakim II (961–976) in Cordoba when he embarked upon a ten-year expansion programme for the great mosque there (now the Mesquita). He wrote to the Emperor Nicephorus II asking him to send a mosaicist who could create mosaics similar to those in the Great Mosque in Damascus. Whether anyone was sent is not known, for the style is as much Andalusian as Byzantine. The *mihrab* in Cordoba, acclaimed as one of the most beautiful of Islamic prayer rooms, is approached through endless elegant columns, capitals and arches that create a tranquil impression of peace and space. The arch opening into the *mihrab* prayer recess is flanked by marble columns and adorned with foliage motifs on gold grounds, which themselves are rimmed with *Kufic* inscriptions from the Qu'ran in gold on a blue background. Above the inscriptions is a row of blind niches with gold grounds on which flourish the 'trees of life'. Within the *mihrab* itself (not normally open to the public) a shell-like dome is sheathed with gold mosaics.[28] The Mesquita today is both an Islamic and a Christian shrine, for in the 16th century, after the Muslims were driven from Spain, a small cathedral was built within this immense Muslim mosque. So it is appropriate that the mosaic technique of Christian Byzantium, a real breakthrough in the technical application of gold, should have inspired one of Islam's most famous shrines.

Part Three
New Horizons (1200 - 1700)

CHAPTER 16

Italy:
Venice: first gold 'fixing'

The Roman *aureus*, Byzantine *nomisma*, Islamic *dinar* and then the Venetian *ducat* make up the roll call of gold coins that served as internationally accepted currency for centuries at a time during the last two millennia. It was like a family title, with each assuming the role when the preceding monetary standard waned. Add in the British sovereign, launched in 1817, and the chain from ancient to modern is complete. National gold coins abounded, but these were the famous international five.

Venice, of course, was thoroughly familiar with gold long before its own *ducat* of 3.56 grams/0.11 t.oz at over 995 fine was first struck in 1285. Her merchants had been trading to and through Constantinople for three hundred years and so used, first, the ailing *nomisma*, and then its reincarnation as the *hyperpyron*, which they called '*perpero*'. "Many of them may have thought of gold as 'real money', the true standard of value, and reckoned their fortunes in *perperi*," wrote Frederic Lane and Reinhold Mueller in their great study of the evolution of money and banking on the Rialto. "After 1285 the 'good old *perperi*' … were disappearing or had disappeared. But those who thought of gold as the 'true' standard of value could find their standard resurrected materially in the *ducat*."[1] It endured until the fall of the Republic in 1797, weight and fineness unchanged, as Venice became the first international bullion market (a role much later taken over by Amsterdam and then London).

The early financial expertise was enhanced by the establishment in 1104 of the Arsenal, the great shipyard that built galleys and warships for the trading and protection of the growing maritime power. The Arsenal's ultimate assignment was the fitting out of the Fourth Crusade, for which French Crusaders paid the Doge, Enrico Dandelo, with over 20 m.t/645,000 t.oz of silver. They went on to sack Constantinople in 1204, awarding the Doge for his help with three-eighths of the city, plus islands and trading posts in the Aegean and Mediterranean from which it could watch over its new trading routes to the Black Sea, Cyprus, the Levant and Egypt.

That was the breakthrough for Venice. Her influence now stretched far and wide. "Venice was something unique," wrote James Morris, "half eastern, half western, half land, half sea, poised between Christianity and Islam, one foot in Europe, the other paddling in the Pearls of Asia."[2] The Venetian Republic's *raison d'être* was trade; profit was sought as an intermediary, whether in precious metals or luxury goods. Supply and demand ruled, not the need to build up a king's treasury. Venice was a self-governing city-state. The Doge was the titular head, but his responsibility was to execute the decisions of councils of merchant-nobles, of which he was but a member. Monetary policy and the operation of the mints were run by officials chosen by the Commune's councils headed by the Doge. The members of those Councils benefited from the financial health of the state.[3]

From the earliest days, Venetian merchants dealt in two monetary systems: silver, which was the basic currency and standard in Western Europe from 700 until well after 1200, and gold, which circulated in Byzantine and Islamic lands. "That experience," Lane and Mueller observed, "prepared them for their future role as middlemen able to profit in the bullion trade from handling both markets."[4]

Playing the silver card

At home the initial strong card was the Venetian silver *grosso* of 2.19 grams/0.07 t.oz at 965 fine that Doge Dandolo pioneered. The French silver paid for the Crusaders' ships was minted into four million *grossi*, establishing it as an international trade coin, especially in the east, where the Crusades had provoked the reversal of bullion flows between Muslim lands and Western Europe (*see preceding chapter*). The *grosso* was sustained by rising output from silver mines near Freiberg in Germany, in Bohemia and Hungary, which came across the Alps or the Adriatic in the hands of German entrepreneurs. They established themselves beside the Grand Canal near the Rialto Bridge in the Fondaco dei Tedeschi, which served as custom house, storage and lodging for German merchants for centuries. One merchant, known as Bernard the German, was soon said to be the richest man in Venice through marketing silver; he even made loans to the Commune. With a strong silver market established, Venice became a magnet for fresh silver from new mines in Serbia inland from Ragusa (now Dubrovnik), just across the Adriatic, in the 1250s and mines in the Tyrol of northern Italy opened up after 1270. The appeal of Venice was competitive prices and mint charges in a well-regulated, but relatively free, market. The steady supplies ensured that the *grosso* became a symbol of Venice's financial standing. Not only *grossi* but silver ingots of 25kg/800 ounces and, later, of just 200 grams/6.22 t.oz at 965 and 925 fine bearing the 'chop' of the San Marco mint were exported to North Africa, the Black Sea ports and the Levant.

Gold fixing on the Rialto

The approach to gold was more circuitous, perhaps because merchants were proud of their silver *grosso* and comfortable with the old Byzantine *perperi*. Moreover, as the status of the *perperi* and the Islamic *dinar* declined, they could often be bought cheaply against *grossi*. Once Venice opened its gold mint in 1285 many of the first *ducats* were made from melted *perperi* acquired at a discount.

Meanwhile, the pace-setters in gold were Venice's trade rivals, Florence and Genoa. Both struck gold coins in 1252; the *florin* and the *genovino d'oro* each weighed 3.55 grams/0.11 t.oz and were close to 995 fine. Contemporary merchants' tables logged them as 24 *carati* or 'pure' gold.

The main source of the gold, particularly for Genoa, was from West Africa, which came across the Sahara to Tunis or by way of Seville in Spain, often as local gold coins, sometimes as dust. This was the main orbit of Genoa's trade throughout the western Mediterranean, while Venice's eye was to the east. Florence blossomed into a centre of early banking houses such as the Bardi and Peruzzi, which established a branch network that stretched to Bruges (the money market of the north) and London. Both banks kept their accounts in gold from 1296. Florence's gold came from African production by way of Sicily and recycling of old Byzantine and Islamic coins. The *florin* acquired its own status as an international coin for over a century, especially at the great trade fairs of Champagne, in Bruges and at Lübeck, centre of the Hanseatic trade along the Baltic, as well as in the Levant.

Venice did not follow Florence and Genoa with its own gold coin for over thirty years, but the city had already made its mark as a distinctive bullion market through its silver trading, and they never equalled it as a turntable of precious metals.[5] Market regulations were clearly set out by the Great Council in 1266.

All importers, Venetian or foreign, had to register incoming bullion, gold or silver, with the official Assay Office on the Rialto for weighing and assaying. Salaried officials for gold and silver were appointed, with two weighers for gold and two for silver, plus three assayers who were elected for life. Gold that arrived as dust (*paglola*) had to be cast before assay and it was forbidden to sell more than two marks (477 grams/15.3 t.oz) of *paglola*. Assays were recorded, and the decision of two of the three assayers was final. The assayers worked with needles (*toche or virgule*) graded from 1 to 24 carats (42–999 fine) which they rubbed on a black touchstone to judge the subtle grades. Initially, assayers worked a battery of 96 needles, measuring a single grain of difference in fineness (4 grains per carat). But in 1345 the Great Council ruled that a set distinguishing half-grains must be made, which implied the ability to differentiate between, for example, 990 and 993 fine gold just by rubbing a *toche* on a touchstone. Such meticulous attention to detail enhanced Venice's credentials. A resolution by two senators in 1414 declared that the Assay Office was "the foundation and base on which depends our honour and profit".[6]

The Rialto, where the Assay Office was located, was the heart of the market; crowded with money-changers' tables, bustling with brokers taking importers of coin or precious metals from one to another. Everyone soaked up the latest intelligence from Alexandria, Bruges, Constantinople, Damascus, Florence, Genoa, London or Lübeck. Such gossip on the Rialto served as the *Financial Times* of the day. The German merchants, coming across the Grand Canal from their headquarters at the Fondaco dei Tedeschi, on the St Mark's side of the canal and today the main post office, were the most conspicuous traders. They had first made their presence felt selling the silver from soon after 1200 Central Europe; by 1300 they had metal not only from their traditional sources, but from the huge new silver mines at Kutna Hora in Bohemia, yielding over 20 m.t/643,000 t.oz annually, and the first consignments from new gold mines in Hungary that were producing perhaps 1,000 kg/32,150 t.oz and would soon provide much more. The Germans and others with precious metals to sell responded twice a day to the ringing of a bell in mid-morning and at Vespers to summon them to the Rialto, where auctions through local brokers (charging 0.25%) were held. In effect, these were daily price 'fixings', forerunners of the London silver 'fix' that started in 1897 and the gold 'fix' in 1921. If they did not like the bids on the Rialto, the gold or silver could be sold directly to the respective mints, who wooed them with low charges or faster payment.

Introducing the *ducat*

The mints, like the Assay Office, operated under the auspices of the Great Council, which, on 1st October 1284, approved the establishment of the mint for coining gold. The coin was to be of the same weight and fineness as the *florin*. The proposed *ducat* was to weigh 3.559 grams (usually shown as 5.36 grams/0.11 t.oz) at 24 *carati*, implying pure gold; in practice, the *ducat* was between 995 and 997 fine, no mean technical achievement and matching today's 'gold delivery' standard on the London market. The first *ducats* were issued in March 1285, with the face showing Giovanni Dandolo, the current Doge, kneeling to receive a banner from St Mark, and the reverse depicting Christ in the act of blessing. During the early years much of the gold came from recycling old coins, particularly the old *perperi*. They were only 20 *carati* or 833 fine, but could be melted and refined up to title. The mint led a somewhat hand-to-mouth existence, picking up gold as it came along. There were only four small furnaces and ten craftsmen employed in the processes of beating gold into sheets, cutting it into squares, and shaping the blanks (*flaoni*), ready for them to be 'struck' by the moneyers after careful weighing. They were busy in December 1286, when a consignment of 24,000 *perperi* suddenly turned up from Constantinople and the Great Council ordered they be rushed through, yielding around 26,000 *ducats* (the *perperi* being heavier, but of lower fineness).[7] This was an exception, not the normal monthly throughput. No records of annual production have survived, but it may not have topped 100,000 *ducats* often before the 1320s.

The mint was strict in the gold it would accept and worked in close liaison with the Assay Office, who sent them written reports on the amounts of gold at the auction on the Rialto, with the names of the buyers. Initially, the mint would accept only gold of 23 *carati*/979 fine, later giving preference to 23.75 *carati*/990 fine. They then refined it themselves aiming for 24 *carati*/999 fine. "The technical skill attained in such medieval mints as Venice and Florence was high enough to deserve our admiration," wrote Lane and Mueller, pointing to a detailed process reported by

Francesco Balducci Pegolotti, a Florentine manager in the Bardi banking house between 1310 and 1340, who compiled a comprehensive book of market data from across Europe and the Levant.[8]

Pegolotti devoted three pages to a '*Ricetta d'affinare oro*', complete with little sketches, which read like a pasta cookbook. He explained that a crucible was filled with alternate layers of gold sheet and a flux (*cimento*) of sea-salt and crushed red tile (essentially silicon). The *cimento* was then spread over the gold "*comme gittassi formaggio grattugiato sopra lasagne*" – "like sprinkling grated cheese over lasagne". The crucible was then placed in the furnace "*uno giorno e una notte*" – "a day and a night". The accompanying sketch looks precisely like a neatly layered pasta dish. This refining process did not yield 999 fine gold, but modern tests on *ducats* have shown them up to 997 fine.

The Great Council's original specification was that 67 *ducats* should be made from one mark (238.5 grams) of gold, which was 3.559 grams each, a shade more than the *florin* from the Florence mint at 3.536 grams. Most merchants, however, rated them both of equal value at 3.55 grams on their books. At first the Venice mint charged 3% on coining gold, meaning they made 67 *ducats* and paid the supplier with 65 *ducats*, but later, in the bid to secure more gold, the charge was dropped to 0.8%, giving back the equivalent of 66.46 *ducats* per mark. That 0.8% was shared equally between the mint for its expenses and the government as seigniorage. A tolerance of one grain (0.0517 grams) was originally permitted on the weight of a *ducat*, but this was reduced to half a grain in 1317 and a mere quarter grain in 1330. Venice took the credentials of its gold *ducat* seriously, and the authorities made frequent spot checks at the mint. By comparison, the mint in Florence permitted a one and a half grain tolerance. Legally, all Venetian *ducats* were of equal weight and treated equally regardless of the date of issue. "One reason, " suggested Lane and Mueller, "why the *ducat* proved a more widely accepted international standard of value in the long run."[9] Large payments were often made with sealed bags of 100 or more *ducats* that bore an assayer's seal '*ducati bullati*', which circulated widely as the mint's output increased in the 1320s.

The gold boom: from Mansa Musa to Hungary

Within a couple of decades in the first half of the 14th century the new gold supply available to Europe reached its highest level since Roman times. Gold coinage, which had been rare for centuries, became almost the norm, eclipsing silver, not just in Venice, Florence and Genoa, but in France, Germany (sixteen mints struck gold coins during the century), Flanders and England. In Venice, minting of the *ducat* exceeded that of silver *grossi* by 1328. "The Victory of Gold," declared Peter Spufford, one of the great experts on medieval mints and markets.[10] Most of them were national coinages, but both the *florin* and the *ducat* were confirmed on the international stage, the *florin* particularly in north-west Europe, the *ducat* in the Eastern Mediterranean.

The first injection of gold came in a somewhat eccentric manner. The ruler of Mali in West Africa, long a prime source of gold (*see preceding chapter*), set off across the desert to Egypt in 1324 on the first stage of a pilgrimage to Mecca. To meet his expenses en route he was accompanied by between 80 and 100 camels each laden with three kantar (110 kg/3,40 t.oz) of gold. That amounted to 8–10 m.t/257,200–321,500 t.oz of gold which had accumulated in his treasury over the previous twenty years. The contemporary writer El Omari, who worked for the Sultan in Cairo, recorded that Mansa Musa and his entourage spent much of the gold on fine clothes and female slaves, often offering five *dinars* where one would have sufficed.[11] The Egyptian market was awash with gold, narrowing the local gold:silver ratio from 1:11.7 to 1:8.1. The effect spread like a ripple over the next two or three years to Genoa (normally the main channel for African gold) and Venice, where the gold price also weakened. Mint production figures are not available in either city for those years, but output probably rose as some of Mansa Musa's gold arrived on galleys from Alexandria.

That one-off event came just as the Hungarian gold rush was gathering pace. Itinerant German miners had been there for over a century looking for silver and both Hungary and its neighbour Bohemia had produced upwards of 30 m.t/964,500 t.oz between them in the early years of the 14th century, along with perhaps 1,000 kg of gold annually, often a by-product of the silver. Around 1325 new gold deposits were discovered around Kremnica, north of Budapest, in what is now Slovakia. The gold was in surface deposits which could be mined as open cast or by shallow underground mines. Mining villages mushroomed, the region around Kremnica was pock-marked with little operations. By the 1330s they were yielding upwards of 3,000 kg/96,450 t.oz annually under the watchful eye of Demetrius Nekcsei, Hungary's chief treasurer, who controlled the mining on behalf of the King. Nekcsei contracted out the mining to local landlords, who paid the miners fixed prices for their ore according to grade. Private buying and selling of gold was forbidden (that is not to say it did not happen), as was export of gold bullion. The ore was refined and sent to the royal mint. A new coin, the *gulden*, was launched, at 3.52 grams/0.11 t.oz at 989 fine (23.75 *carati* on Venetian money-changers' books). The margin between what the miners were paid for their gold and the *gulden* sold for was apparently 40%.

The spate of silver from Bohemia and the gold from Hungary provoked a monetary crisis between the two countries, which was settled in 1327 by a meeting of their two Kings who agreed to co-ordinate the relationship between Hungary's *gulden* and Bohemia's silver *groschen* at an exchange rate of 1:14.5. The *groschen* became the trading currency of central Europe. The *gulden* was traded west to Bruges, Paris and London (an exchange table for incoming gold coin at Dover featured the coin), but its main destination was south to Venice and Florence, where many were melted and restruck as *ducats* and *florins*.

A spate of European gold coins

The Hungarian mines provided Europe with its first regular supplies of new gold for centuries. The precise output is uncertain. The historian Oszkar Paulinyi, who researched the gold rush, put it at 3,000 to 4,000 kg/96,450 to 128,600 t.oz on average annually between 1330 and 1380.[12]   This sounds a generous allocation, given that mint output of gold coin was tailing off well before 1380, but Hungary could have added 150 to 200 m.t/4.8 to 6.4 million t.oz to gold stocks in the 14th century. Paulinyi conceded that, by 1380, "The upper layers were mined, which were more concentrated due to oxydation". This was always the problem confronting early gold miners, who found it difficult to tackle deeper sulphide ores. Europe was also in depression by the late 14th century, after the ravages of the Black Death had killed perhaps a quarter of the population and slowed all economic activity. However, even with recovery in the next century, Paulinyi found there was no major new development of the mines, because of lack of capital to construct deep galleries and the installations necessary to protect the mines from flooding.

The clearest evidence of the Hungarian output from 1330 was the soaring production of mints across Europe. A bar chart of their combined output between 1300 and 1500 resembles a mountain range arising rapidly in the 1330s, peaking between 1350 and 1360, and then fading away, never to recover. "The money supply was … at a high point, not reached again for several centuries," Peter Spufford noted.[13]   In France, Philip VI issued a new *ecu* gold coin for which the mints used almost 11 m.t/350,000 t.oz in 1338/9, while in England in 1344 over 1.1 m.t/36,500 t.oz was used for the new *noble*.

Much of this coin was minted, not from the proceeds of, or for, trade, but for war. As England and France entered the early stages of the Hundred Years War, both sides sought financial aid from Italy. Edward III of England borrowed over 1.5 million *florins* (5.3 m.t/170,000 t.oz) from the Bardi and Peruzzi in Florence, from which he offered 360,000 *florins* to the Duke of Brabant, and 300,000 *florins* to Lewis IV of Bavaria to support him. Philip VI in France benefited from 3,517,000 *florins* (12.5 m.t/400,000 t.oz) over a decade, some directly from the Pope, Clement VI, and the rest from papal levies raised in France that were diverted to his cause.[14]   That kept the northern European mints fully occupied (at least two of them, incidentally, recruited mint masters from Italy).

Overtime at the Venice mint

Meanwhile, in Italy itself, Florence and Venice were geared up to handle the main flow of Hungarian gold, coming overland via Zagreb to the Adriatic and then by sea, watched over by the German merchants who controlled the trade. The Venice mint was on overtime work at night by 1341 because, beside the Hungarian gold, the galley fleets from the Black Sea were bringing in gold from Armenia and Central Asia that was exchanged for silver at the ports of Trebizond and Tana, at the mouth of the river Don. The mint staff demanded a pay rise – and got it. More artisans were recruited to strike *ducats*, while the number of mint masters was increased from three to four and supervisory weighers from two to four. The mint masters were paid 120 *ducats* a year, and a bonus, depending on throughput of gold, which could amount to 60 further *ducats* (in all, 640 grams/20.5 t.oz a year, worth just over $13,000 at a modern gold price of $650 per t.oz). The mint now had up to 600 marks (142.8 kg/4,591 t.oz) of gold 'in house' at a time, enough to produce 40,200 *ducats*.[15] The new capacity was tested when young Louis I of Hungary sent into Italy in 1343 over 1.4 million *gulden* (almost 5 m.t/160,750 t.oz), accumulated by his father over the previous decade, to meet expenses in pursuing a dynastic claim to the kingdom of Naples (Louis also dispatched 6.4 m.t/205,760 t.oz of silver).[16] The *gulden* were largely melted and restruck into *ducats* or *florins* in Venice and Florence, partly accounting for exceptionally high output at the mints in 1344–5. Thereafter, production at both mints remained high for the remainder of the decade.

Bullion fleet to the East

The flow of precious metal through Venice grew during the 1340s as her fleet of merchant galleys, specially designed to take large amounts of silver to the east, was expanded. Two convoys set out each year, one bound for Cyprus, a transit point for Egypt, the other to Constantinople and the Black Sea. In 1343 nine galleys went to the Black Sea alone, guarded by Venetian war galleys. Individual merchants sent consignments of silver on the vessels, often in small ingots of 200 grams/6.22 t.oz, which were the most acceptable bars around the Black Sea and across the steppes of Central Asia. One Venetian trader dispatched 55 kg (that is 275 small bars), with orders that they be invested in gold for return to Venice, provided the net profit was 8% – if not, the silver was to buy cotton or spices.[17] The anticipated margin on gold showed that old Byzantine coin could still be had at a discount. Another Venetian merchant on Cyprus collected 7,000 *ducats* worth of old coin, including copies of Byzantine coins made in Alexandria, which were sent to Venice for sale in 1344.

Francesco Pegolotti's table of *monete d'oro* listed *Bisanti vecchi d'oro d'Allessandria* at 23 *carati* (958 fine) and 23.5 *carati* (979 fine), along with *Pezzi di bisanti d'oro a carati* 12 (500 fine). He noted no less than 12 other varieties of *perperi* between 18 and 11 *carati*. All told, Pegolloti recorded 39 different types of gold coin from Italian, Black Sea, Levantine, Egyptian and North African mints.[18] Among them were *Tanghi d'oro* that could be picked up at Trebizond or Tana on the Black Sea. The *tanghi* came from the city of Sarai on the Volga river, which was ruled by the exotically named Khan of the Golden Horde, and was a market for Central Asian gold. Much of the silver that was exchanged for this spectrum of gold coin was destined for China, which was in the process of phasing out paper money, and India, where Hindu princes had been overthrown by Muslim rulers who wanted silver coinage.[19]

The final market place for the gold was the Rialto in Venice, where the Assay Office and the mint were fully occupied. The traffic increased in 1345, after the Pope lifted a ban on direct trade with the Mamluks in Egypt, enabling Venice to send an annual convoy to Alexandria. This gave fresh access to West African gold, much of which still came to Cairo, as it did with Mansa Musa's famous expedition. The gold was paid for primarily with silver at first, but when an acute silver shortage occurred in the late 14th century, *ducats* were exported to trade against the unrefined gold and other imports.

"The great bullion famine"

The growing status of the *ducat* as the principal trade coin in the eastern Mediterranean was enhanced by a banking crisis in Florence, as the houses of Bardi and Perruzzi collapsed due to their unpaid gold loans to Edward III of England. The image of the *florin* was tarnished and output fell. In Venice, meanwhile, output rose to around 600,000 *ducats* annually in the late 1360s, against scarcely 30,000 *florins* from the Florence mint. In Genoa, with its close connections to African gold, the mint managed around 200,000 *genovinos* in good years, but was still no match for Venice.

The Rialto was now the premier bullion market, secure in that role as long as northern Europe sent precious metal there to pay for the luxuries she imported from the east. Those luxuries were paid for increasingly by the *ducat*, as it overtook the *florin* as the international standard of value and medium of exchange. Moreover, Venice was such a flexible market that, during the years between 1380 and 1420, when Europe suffered from a silver 'famine' due to declining output in Germany, Bohemia and Hungary (all greatly affected by the Black Death), Venice had its hands on output from new silver mines in the Balkans which it re-routed to Bruges and other northern European cities, meanwhile sending gold to the east. "Venice's position as the central bullion market was so strong at the end of the 14th century," wrote an admiring Frederic Lane and Reinhold Mueller, "that she could maintain that position during the reversal in the direction of bullion flows."[20] In fact, this was the second time the Rialto's money changers and bankers had adapted to such a switch; gold had been replaced by silver in the Levant in the wake of the Crusades (*see preceding chapter*). Now gold was going back again. "To the end of the Middle Ages, annual exports of gold to the East normally exceeded annual exports of silver by a wide margin," concluded John Day in The Great Bullion Famine.[21]

While the 'famine' was primarily of silver, less gold was available as Hungarian output declined sharply. Gold coin output shrank across Europe. An analysis of production by Peter Spufford revealed that, in the decade 1401–10, coin minting in eight European nations was less than one-tenth of what it was between 1361–70. There was a revival between 1411–30 to one-third of the peak level, but European minting of gold between 1400 and 1500 as a shadow of the previous century.[22] The simple lesson was, as in earlier eras, that substantial, sustained gold coin production could be achieved only on the back of a significant gold discovery, such as in Hungary. The next would not come until after 1700 with the gold rush to Brazil.

The striking of coins in the 15th century was essentially limited to Venice and, to a lesser degree, Florence and Genoa, which secured most of the African production. After the collapse of the Mali Empire in West Africa soon after 1350, the caravan routes switched west to the old gold port of Sijilmasa south of Fez in Morocco, from whence it passed, often as locally minted *dinars*, to Seville in Spain and then to Genoa. Saharan routes were also sustained towards Tunis, so that, by 1436, Venice was sending an annual escorted convoy to the North African port to pick up gold. The gold mint in Venice, after two or three quiet decades, experienced a sharp revival in 1422, achieving a record output of 1.2 million *ducats* (4.3 m.t/137,000 t.oz), according to Doge Tommaso Mocenigo, praising his city's achievements.[23] The gold came partially from re-coinage, but the vintage minting confirmed an improvement in gold flows. Genoa also bounced back with its mint striking 244,528 *genovini* in 1428/9, the best since the 1360s, and some years around 200,000 coins during the next few decades. Florence, by comparison, minted 45,166 *florins* in 1423/4, and there is no record of her mint reaching 100,000 coins for the rest of the century.[24] Venice and Genoa were the cities with the galley fleets to seek out African gold in their trade with North Africa and Spain.

Ducats for spices

The operations of Venice's commercial shipping lines were impressive. "The striking feature of the galley service was its regularity and this was undoubtedly one of the reasons for Venice's great success," wrote Professor Eliyahu Ashtor, diligent historian of the Levantine trade.[25] Ashtor tracked the schedules of the galley fleets from Venice to Beirut and Alexandria every year from 1380–1496; usually there were three or four convoys to each destination, with up to six convoys to Alexandria for several years between 1485 and 1492. The service was suspended only in six years in over 100 years due to wars or disputes with the Sultan in Egypt. The volume of trade grew steadily, to reach its peak between 1450 and 1500.

The Venetians had several advantages. Merchant vessels built by the Arsenal now carried cargoes of between 1,000 and 1,500 tonnes, compared to 600–700 tonnes in the 14th century. They were equipped with maritime compasses and portolan charts of shipping routes and harbours. Colonies of Venetian merchants settled in Egypt and Syria, complete with consular officials. They marshalled the spices, cotton, dyes, silks, sugar and pearls to be dispatched to Venice. The spice trade was the most important, embracing over twenty-five different varieties. Pepper was paramount, but there was a selection of at least six kinds of ginger (green ginger, ginger in lemon, or Colombo ginger for a start), cloves and clove stalks, cinnamon and cinnamon stalks, cubeb (a pungent, pepper-like grain), cardamom and roots of turpeth and zedoary that were used as medicinal drugs.[26]

This medley of eastern flavours to titillate the palate or mask the odour of stale food cost upwards of 400,000 *ducats* annually, 80% of Venice's imports from the Levant. The other major item was cotton from Syria, costing around 50,000 *ducats* a year. The imports were set against exports of olive oil, cloth and base metals, but the major share was paid in *ducats*. Doge Tommaso Mocenigo, besides mentioning the mint's peak output of *ducats* in 1422 in his famous speech, claimed that Venetians invested 300,000 *ducats* in the Levant annually. His remark was confirmed by an agent of the merchant Lorenzo Dolfin in 1423, who cited just two Venetian galleys leaving for Beirut with 200,000 *ducats* aboard.[27] Even the Ottoman Turks' capture of Constantinople in 1453, which was an immense set-back for Venice in its Black Sea trade, disrupting its gold sources in Trebizond and Tana, did not halt the spice flows from the Levant. Professor Ashtor found that even in the late 15th century, "merchants travelling on board the spice galleys carried more than 300,000 *ducats* with them, and at least 50,000 *ducats* was sent to Syria for the cotton fair in the spring".[28]

However, shipments now included silver, of which there was an abundance by the 1470s following the opening of new mines at Schneeberg in Saxony and the Tyrol region close to Innsbruck. Venice, still the premier precious metals market, took most of this silver – even launching a new coin, the *mocenighi*, of 6.52 grams, in 1472. The coins were initially sent on the Tunis convoy to buy West African gold, but were dispatched in huge quantities to Alexandria in the 1490s. Two convoys alone took up to 12 m.t/385,800 t.oz of *mocenighi* in 1497.[29] There has been some confusion about the balance of *ducats* and *mocenighi* sent in this era, because the value was often expressed only in *ducats*, making it difficult to assess accurately the proportion of each metal in the cargo.

The differing gold/silver ratios between Venice and Egypt from the 1470s onwards certainly made it more profitable to send silver, if it was available, without diminishing the image of the *ducat*. Venice was a practical, flexible market; if it made sense to dispatch silver, they did so. "Venetian supremacy in the economic life of the Near East was so great," concluded Professor Ashtor, "that the *ducat* became the currency in which most transactions were made, even when the partners were not Venetian."[30] In short, merchants thought in *ducats*, deals were priced in them, even if payment was part (or even all) in silver. An unforeseen challenge, however, was about to sink Venice's virtual monopoly of the spice trade. In 1498 Portuguese navigator Vasco De Gama landed in India, having successfully sailed round the Cape of Good Hope. The sea route from India direct to Europe was open. Moreover, the Portuguese had already been pressing down the west coast of Africa for fifty years, establishing trading posts that picked up gold directly from Senegal and the Gambia, siphoning off metal from the traditional caravan routes to the Mediterranean. A new gold coin, the *cruzado*, was first struck in Lisbon in 1457. Venice was about to be by-passed in spices and gold. "The discovery of the route by the Cape of Good Hope was a harsh blow to the great transit traffic in the eastern Mediterranean," sighed Professor Ashtor in an essay dedicated to the doyen of Mediterranean trade studies, Fernand Braudel.[31] Braudel himself spelled out the impact, "The spice-market shifted from Venice and its Fondaco dei Tedeschi to Antwerp (with a short sojourn in Lisbon) and then to Amsterdam".[32]

The eclipse of Venice as the great trading emporium for Europe was also heralded by the discovery of the Americas by Christopher Columbus in 1492, which was to change even more the patterns of international trade, not least in precious metals. The first shipments of gold landed in Spain in 1503 and by the 1530s were significant enough for the Seville mint to begin striking *escudos* (*see chapter 18*). Those gold coins and silver ones, which followed the huge inflow of silver from the Americas later in the 16th century, largely migrated to Antwerp and the Netherlands to pay for Spain's military adventures there, although Venice and, particularly, Genoa benefited from some of this metal. The mint in Venice was striking up to 200,000 *ducats* a year for a while in the late 1520s, and the coins remained widely accepted in Europe and around the Mediterranean. Indeed, among the new national gold coins minted in the 16th century, none achieved such international status. Once the gold supply from the Americas peaked by 1560, gold coinage was on the wane. Silver, from the huge deposits at Potosi in Bolivia and Zacatas province in Mexico, was coined, instead, in abundance across Europe.

In Venice itself, the *ducat* continued to be minted in modest measure and unchanged in weight and fineness for another three hundred years until, in 1797, Napoleon marched in. The coin had survived for 512 years, the longest production run in history of a gold coin from a single mint. The Rialto, too, was the premier precious metals market for three hundred years from 1200 to 1500 and only began to be replaced, first by Amsterdam and then London in the 17th century.

Florence:
Renaissance goldsmiths

In the middle of the Ponte Vecchio over the river Arno in Florence, with its phalanx of little jewellery shops on either side, is a small statue of Benvenuto Cellini (1500–1571); a tribute to one of the city's finest and most flamboyant craftsmen. "The greatest goldsmith of whom the world has ever heard," an admiring Michelangelo, his Florentine contemporary, once said. Cellini worked wonders with his chisel; a master sculptor whether in gold, silver, bronze or marble. And he did not mind telling people how good he was. He was a boaster, a brawler, almost a bandit at times. For him, an artist was a virtuoso for whose favours cardinals, princes and kings had to compete. "Picking quarrels and earning laurels, Cellini is a real product of his time," declared the art historian E. H. Gombrich.[33]

Cellini was the most celebrated of a unique school of goldsmiths working in Florence between 1400 and 1600, borne along by the intellectual and artistic energy that was unleashed in that cosmopolitan city and then through all Italy in the early 15th century as the Renaissance took hold. Florence spawned Lorenzo Ghiberti, Donatello, Verocchio, Botticelli, Michelangelo and Leonardo da Vinci, several of whom served their initial apprenticeships as goldsmiths and later drew many designs for them. Donatello first worked with Lorenzo Ghiberti on bronze doors for the Baptistry in Florence in 1401, which marked the beginnings of the Renaissance stepping away from the flat, stylised designs of medieval art in pursuit of reality. The journey to rediscover the ancient technical skills of Greece and Rome in creating a harmony based on the reality of anatomy and perspective had begun. Metalwork in gold, silver and bronze played a core role in that search into the past, in which the 'goldsmith' was often a sculptor in all three metals.

The original stimulus owed much to the prosperity brought to Florence, Venice and Genoa by their international trading in the 13th and 14th centuries, which created a wealthy merchant nobility eager to patronise art. Florence, in particular, had its great banking families of the Bardi and the Peruzzi and later the Medici. In Venice, elaborate gold and silverware of plates, bowls and cups were fashionable because they enhanced status, while creating a reserve of wealth that could be melted and minted into coin in emergencies. In the 'War of Chioggia' between Venice and Genoa from 1378–81, the citizens of Venice brought their precious metal utensils and ornaments to the mint to meet the war's expenses.[34] A depiction of the scene may still be seen on the ceiling of the Sala del Maggiore Consiglio in the Palazzo Ducale, an ominous forecast of the fate of most of the later work of Renaissance goldsmiths, very little of which survives. "Every goldsmith must have known, as he worked on his latest creations, that the preciousness of its material condemned it to destruction as soon as it became unfashionable or its owner needed ready money," observed J. F. Hayward in *Virtuoso Goldsmiths*. "While the painter or sculptor was producing works of art which would continue to please future generations … the goldsmith could not look forward to more than a life of thirty years or so for his best creations, however splendid or costly they might be." Hayward called it "the curse of the goldsmith".[35]

Hence, what is known of Renaissance goldsmiths comes less from admiring the few surviving creations, but from contemporary books or archives. Cellini had much to say in his egotistical *Vita*, the rare autobiography of a Renaissance artist, and in his *Trattati* on goldsmithing techniques, while Giorgia Vasari's *Vite* on the lives of Renaissance artists, published in 1550, was a unique contemporary account (not least about Cellini). Visually, the elaborate sketches and designs prepared by goldsmiths (or sometimes for them by artists such as Michelangelo) for their own guidance or to tempt potential patrons, are in themselves mini-works of art. The invaluable invention of printing also meant that designs and patterns were disseminated widely among goldsmiths, not only in Italy, but across Europe (where many looked to Italy for the latest ideas, just as they have in the modern jewellery industry). And inventories of the *Guardaroba* of great families, such as the Medici, list golden bowls and *tazzas* (shallow ornamental bowls), flasks, lamps, and salt cellars of gold or silver. Renaissance goldsmithing was less about jewellery than a cornucopia of vessels as a sign of wealth.

Goldsmiths – a rigorous training

In Florence, the goldsmiths' workshops were gathered together along the Via Vacchereccio which leads into the Piazza della Signoria. The master of each workshop usually had two or three qualified journeymen and a couple of *discepolo* or apprentices. "Florentine goldsmiths' shops had a reputation for offering vigorous training in draughtsmanship and design, skills that provided the springboard for all sort of careers," noted Patricia Lee Rubin and Alison Wright in their study of *The Art of the 1470s* in Florence. "Painters who started their training as goldsmiths, such as Botticelli and Ghirlandaio, as well as Verrocchio … were a distinctive feature of the Florentine milieu, almost unknown in other cities with strong traditions of art production."[36] Verrocchio first trained in the workshop of the well-known goldsmith family of Antonio de Giovanni Dei. Sandro Botticelli not only began as a *discepolo* goldsmith, but his brother, Antonio, became *battiloro* or goldbeater and supplied gold leaf for Sandro's paintings and their frames. "The passage from goldsmith to painter that in all likelihood occurred in Botticelli's career was not uncommon in Florence," added Rubin and Wright. "The ties between a goldsmith's training and painting probably nourished the fascination with evoking the precious and luxurious in the depiction of sumptuous cloth and jewellery that is characteristic of Florentine painting of the 1470s."[37]

Goldsmiths of all the talents

This alliance was fostered by the goldsmiths being part of the *Arte della Seta*, the silk workers' guild. The manufacture and sale of fine silk was a mainstay of the Florentine economy, with a particular speciality in cloth of gold, which was made by wrapping silk thread in ribbons of beaten gold from the *battilori*. The goldsmith often had an integral role in the designs. Antonio del Pollaiuolo (1431–98), perhaps the most versatile of all Florence's goldsmiths on the Via Vacchereccia, oversaw the designs and manufacture of embroidered vestments for the Baptistry, while painting portraits and frescoes, etching engravings, serving as architect for the façade of the Duomo in Florence and working in gold, silver and bronze. He was, indeed, the goldsmith as multi-faceted Renaissance Man. "The principal master of the city … in the opinion of all intelligent people perhaps there was never a better," declared his patron Lorenzo de Medici.[38]

This overlapping of talents was apparent from the birth of Renaissance art, often cited as the competition, announced in 1401, for the second bronze door of the Baptistry in Florence which was open to "skilled masters from all the lands of Italy". The very idea of a contest signalled innovation was welcome. Seven sculptors took part. The winner was Lorenzo Ghiberti (1378–1455), who went on to become one of the most successful sculptors in bronze of the early Renaissance, while also working in precious metals. In the competition, Ghiberti just beat Filippo Brunelleschi (1377–1446), who had trained as a goldsmith, but became the architect of two of Florence's great basilicas, S. Lorenzo and S. Spirito. The disciplines of design and draughtsmanship that had been instilled during their training in goldsmiths' workshops served them well. Lorenzo Ghiberti, in particular, attached great importance to drawing, which he regarded as the 'foundation and theory' of sculpture and painting while raising the status of professions that had previously been considered merely a craft.[39] The goldsmiths' workshops were the seed-bed from which much of the sculpture, painting and even architecture of the Renaissance grew.

Strictly speaking, the word 'goldsmith' is something of a misnomer during the 15th century, for gold and silver were in short supply during the precious metal 'famine' already described in the section of this chapter on Venice. Bronze or, at best, gilt bronze, was the primary metal used for great reliefs on church doors or for busts and statues. Once silver became more readily available from the opening of new mines in Germany after 1460, silver candlesticks, incense burners and incense boats for ecclesiastical purposes or silverware for the rich man's table were commissioned. Gold itself was principally for the *battiloro* making gold leaf for picture frames or thin strips for embroidery.

The most splendid examples are twenty-seven surviving panels from the set of liturgical vestments for feast days commissioned from Antonio del Pollaiuolo by the Merchants' Guild for the Florentine Baptistry. The embroideries employed a technique known as or *nué* (naked gold). The base canvas of each embroidery had a horizontal foundation of silk thread wrapped in thin ribbons of beaten gold. It was then worked vertically with coloured silks, allowing more gold to show through in lighter areas, creating the subtlety of a painting. In one dramatic panel of St John the Baptist at the court of Herod, the whole scene appears set on a rich gold ground, like those of the great 6th century mosaics in Ravenna, but with gold threads in place of *tesserae*. The entire project took Pollaiuolo and his embroidery team over twenty years to complete at a cost of thousands of gold *florins*, paid in instalments of 90 at a time, the first in 1466, the last in 1487.[40] The panels are the legacy of the grand conceptions and enduring patience of one of Florence's most versatile goldsmiths.

The genius of Cellini

The 16th century brought precious metals in greater quantity from the Americas, first to Spain but then dispersed throughout Europe. Vessels that had previously been made of bronze or even brass were now fashioned in silver and, increasingly, in gold.[41] It can be no coincidence that Benvenuto Cellini's most productive period working in gold, between 1530 and 1560, coincided with the largest arrivals of gold from the Americas.

Cellini was born in Florence in 1500, son of a maker of musical instruments, who hoped he would be a great performer on the flute. Young Benvenuto had other ambitions. When his father challenged him, "You take no pleasure in playing?" he replied curtly, "No". So his father placed him, at thirteen, as an apprentice with the goldsmith Michel Agnolo. The engagement was short-lived; he transferred, against his father's wishes, to another goldsmith, Antonio Marcone.[42] Marcone permitted him to indulge his passion for drawing, which proved an advantage, enabling him to catch up quickly with "the best young craftsmen in our business". The lesson of his predecessors, Ghiberti and Pollaiuolo, on the importance of drawing, was well-taken.

Cellini's precocious talent was soon recognised. "When he applied himself to goldsmiths' work in his youth he was unequalled," wrote his Florentine contemporary, Giorgio Vasari. "The medals that he made in his youth in gold and silver were executed with such incredible skill that it is impossible to praise him enough."[43] Ever restless, he moved to Rome when he was nineteen to join the master goldsmith Giovanbattista Sogliane, and then a young goldsmith Lucagnolo, who specialised in large silver plate but was happy for Cellini to take more glamorous commissions. Flitting about to the fine houses of potential patrons, he encountered the wife of one, Madonna Porzia, who was "as courteous as could be, and of surpassing beauty". She admired his drawings, supposing him to be a sculptor or painter. When he confessed he was a goldsmith, she said he drew too well for a goldsmith, but got her maid to bring a brooch of diamonds set in gold. Could he re-set the diamonds really well in a new gold design, she enquired? "I ... began before her eyes to make a little sketch for it, working all the better because of the pleasure

I took in conversing with so lovely and agreeable a gentle-woman," he recorded in his autobiography. His design for a *fleur-de-lys* set with diamonds met instant approval. She handed him the diamonds in their old setting, plus twenty gold *crowns*, saying, "Set me the jewel after the fashion you have sketched, and keep for me the old gold in which it is now set". He completed the *fleur-de-lys* in twelve days, "ornamenting it with little masks, children and animals, exquisitely enamelled, whereby the diamonds which formed the lily were more than doubled in effect".[44] Madonna Porzia became his patroness and shortly advised him to open his own shop. "This I did," he wrote, "and I never stopped working for that excellent and gentle lady, who paid me exceedingly well, and by whose means perhaps it was that I came to make a figure in the world."[45]

Getting paid was not always so easy. He made a large gold medal engraved with Leda and her swan for another patron, Gabbriello Ceserino, to show off on his hat, but when it came to payment, assessed by a professional valuer, the price appalled Ceserino, so Cellini kept the medal. He could afford it. He was making silver candelabra for the Bishop of Salamanca, while "Cardinals and others of the Holy College all kept me well employed, so I earned plenty of money". Before long he was being commissioned by the Pope. Among the handful of surviving examples of his work are medals he struck for Pope Clement VII, for whom he also designed new coinage. His most famous piece for Pope Clement was an ornate gold morse, or clasp, to fasten his cope. The morse has vanished (though three drawings survive in the British Museum), but Cellini boastfully declared, "It was held to be the finest masterpiece which had ever been seen in Rome".[46] Cellini, always ready for a brawl, also fought for the Pope in internal Italian campaigns. He grasped his sword as readily as his chisel.

One thousand gold *crowns* become a salt cellar

His brawling eventually landed him in prison from which he was fortuitously released at the request of Francis I of France, who had heard of his skills and appealed to the Pope. Cellini spent five years in Paris at the court of Francis I, from 1540–45, and there created the gold salt cellar for which he is renowned. Initially, he set up his workshop at the court, surrounding himself with many journeymen goldsmiths as assistants. His first assignment was three silver statues of Jupiter, Vulcan and Mars, for which the king gave him over 100 kg/3,250 t.oz. The king became intrigued, however, by a proposal Cellini had made to the Cardinal of Ferrara for a gold salt cellar, which the latter found too lavish. François called him in and asked how much gold he would need. "A thousand *crowns*, I answered," Cellini wrote. "He called his treasurer to come at once … and ordered him that very day to disburse me a thousand *crowns* of good weight and old gold."[47] The *crowns* weighed around 3.5 kg/112 t.oz. The treasurer took Cellini to his office, counted out the coins, amid much delay and muttering to his servants. Cellini tucked the gold into a small basket and set off into the night – alert for an ambush. "I was well armed with shirt and sleeves of mail, and having my sword and dagger at my side," he wrote. His suspicions were well founded; four men with swords came at him out of the dark. He drew his sword and saw them off. "Next morning, I made the first step in my work upon the great salt-cellar," he concluded.[48]

The salt cellar represented Sea and Earth, seated, with their legs interlaced. Cellini described it thus:

It was oval in form, standing about two-thirds of a cubit (30cm/12in.), wrought of solid gold and worked entirely with the chisel. The Sea carried a trident in his right hand, and in his left I put a ship of delicate workmanship to hold the salt. Below him were four sea-horses … the water was represented with its waves, and enamelled in the appropriate colour. I had portrayed Earth under the form of a very handsome woman, holding her horn of plenty, entirely nude like the male figure; in her left hand I placed a little temple of Ionic architecture, most delicately wrought, which was meant to contain the pepper. Beneath her were the handsomest living creatures which the earth produces; and the rocks were partly enamelled, partly left in gold.[49]

Cellini added that when he showed it to the king, "his Majesty … uttered a loud outcry of astonishment, and could not satiate his eyes with gazing at it". But he allowed Cellini to take it home that evening, where he dined "gaily" with his friends around the salt cellar.[50] From a modern professional standpoint, it is still admired for its superb modelling in gold, finished with chasing and engraving of rare precision.[51]

This exotic work by an extrovert goldsmith launched a new trend in gold and silverware throughout Europe. Known as Mannerism, it dictated the tastes of customers and fashion in goldsmiths' workshops for a hundred years. "More than competent exercise of his craft was expected of the goldsmith," explained J. F. Hayward. "The more complex the design and original the invention, the more admiration it attracted. As a result, profuse and fantastic embellishments were imposed upon familiar utensils of every-day life."[52]

As for the salt cellar that paved the way, it came close to being consigned to the melting pot in France in 1562 in a royal budget crisis, but was reprieved and presented as a gift to the Archduke Ferdinand of the Tyrol in 1570 by Charles IX. And it came to rest finally in Vienna's Kunsthistorisches Museum, from where it was stolen in 2003, almost on a whim by an expert in alarm systems. He kept it in a suitcase under his bed for a while, but later buried it, carefully wrapped in linen and plastic in a metal box in woods outside Vienna. After trying unsuccessfully to blackmail the insurance company, the police tracked him down in January 2006 and dug up the box.

Admiring the salt cellar afterwards in its new secure and well-alarmed showcase standing alone in the centre of a gallery, so that you can circle it, the first impression is what a sumptuous sculpture it is. It is larger than photographs imply, being almost 26 cm/10.2 in. high and 34 cm/13.4 in. long; a worthy centrepiece for any table. The proportions are perfect, with both figures, Sea and Earth, leaning back, relaxed, as if in conversation. Looking over the Sea's shoulder their eyes seem to meet. Cellini's mastery of the gold in these figures is astonishing. Earth's left hand, resting gently on her breast, is delicately formed, her back is slender, while the golden muscles of the Sea's torso and legs ripple. The only apparent sign of damage after the robbery is a slight graze on Earth's left shoulder. But it enhances the fascination of the salt cellar being an escapade reminiscent of Cellini's own adventures and it has, no doubt, burnished his image.

Not that he needed much promotion, for he was his own publicist, puffing himself up in his autobiography, written between 1558 and 1562, though not published in Italy until 1728. His legacy was enhanced by the German poet Goethe, who translated the memoir into German and dubbed him a true Renaissance man. "Typical of his age and perhaps typical of all humanity," declared Goethe, "such personalities can be considered spiritual pivots." On a more practical level, Cellini is remembered for the goldsmiths' technical manual that he wrote in 1568, shortly before his death. The English goldsmith and historian Graham Hughes observed it was "a technical manual … upon which any modern workshop could base its activity".[53]   A real compliment offered by one professional to another over four hundred years later.

CHAPTER 17

Precolumbian Gold: A Unique Legacy

Charles Darwin's theory of evolution stemmed from his observations on the Galapagos islands, far out in the Pacific from South America, on the way plants, birds and reptiles adapted to that isolated environment. Gold-working on the mainland, in what are now Colombia, Ecuador and Peru, also evolved in complete isolation from and ignorance of the tradition around the Mediterranean that successively produced the treasures of Ur, Egypt and Minoan Crete, although the goldsmiths' techniques were largely identical. As the metallurgists Susan La Niece and Nigel Meeks of the British Museum observed, "Goldsmiths in Central and South America, independent of outside metallurgical influences … (chose) designs that incorporate universal features … filigree, granulation, relief decoration and surface colouring".[1]

Yet, as Darwin realised on the Galapagos, there were subtle divergences. The lost-wax process for casting ornaments was not developed in Peru, because bees providing the right kind of wax did not survive there, but thrived in the forests of Colombia. More significantly, the Precolumbians had a more focused perception of gold's role, with its symbolic relationship to the sun (as in Egypt) and to many other gods and spirits of the air, earth and water. Goldsmithing was about making votive offerings for the gods or a symbol of power for rulers and nobility who represented them on earth. No one regarded gold as money; that concept, the Spanish invaders of the 16th century found, was incomprehensible.

The Precolumbians' inventiveness and energy, therefore, always went into enhancing gold's brilliance and colour. The purity of the gold was irrelevant; they always aimed at achieving the maximum effect with colour, by making a rainbow of alloys. Sicán goldsmiths, for instance, working on the north coast of Peru after AD 700, made breastplates, bangles, earspools and grand ceremonial headdresses in gold surmounted by brilliant feathers to adorn their rulers. "The Sicán lord wearing this full headdress was probably carried on a litter to magnify the visual effects," one archaeologist wrote. "With each step of the litter-bearers, the bangles, gold and bird feathers … would have been set in motion to create a dazzling visual and auditory effect that would have captivated and impressed onlookers."[2] The ruler, shimmering by, symbolised the sun's power.

Thus gold was just one of the triad of metals, along with silver and copper, upon which the complex and sophisticated Andean metallurgy developed. The varied colours and textures that could be created by the mix of these metals in alloys was at the heart of the technology. The tinge of red from copper could be subtly alloyed with gold to enhance the rich burnish of the surface of a mask or breastplate. Gold-copper alloys, known as *tumbaga*, were widely used, but a touch of silver was also in many ornaments for its cooling colour effect. Appropriately, silver was regarded as tears of the moon, while gold was the sweat of the sun. It was the ready availability of these three metals, with alluvial deposits often providing a natural *mélange*, that distinguished New World metallurgy from the Old. Moreover, because gold was not used as money, there was no need to purify it to a constant standard, as there would be for acceptable coin.

Luck helped. "The Andes are a veritable mine, and the Andean peoples were sitting right on that mine," wrote Heather Lechtman of the Center for Archaeological Materials at M.I.T. "The Andes … contain some of the richest ore deposits in the world …. The placer golds of Colombia and Ecuador … the rich and complex copper ores of Peru and Chile, the silver deposits from Peru to Bolivia … were liberally exploited in Precolumbian times."[3] And because gold was most readily found in alluvial deposits in many of the rivers coming down from the Andes throughout South America, it was almost certainly the first metal people used, unlike the Old World where copper came first.

The first evidence of fabrication in South America came from a burial site in the village of Waywaka, high in the central Andes of Peru. Just a handful of tiny sheets of gold foil were found by the archaeologist Joel Grossman, along with a metal worker's kit of a mushroom-shaped anvil of polished porphyry and three stone hammers of differing weights and hardness that had fashioned more scraps of foil. They date from around 1500 BC and so were contemporary with the finest Minoan ornaments on Crete (*see chapter 4*). From this dawn in the Andes, the use of gold spread slowly from one mountain valley to another and then down the short rivers flowing to the Pacific, as people became adept at working it. Over the millennia a succession of cultures in Peru, Colombia, Central America and the Caribbean created a unique legacy in gold, which the Spanish *conquistadores* unveiled three thousand years later.

Peru: the Chavín – mastering the technology

Gold first came to real prominence around 800 BC, in the earliest known Peruvian civilisation of the Chavín people. They lived in the high country of northern Peru in cohesive villages, grazing llamas (the ubiquitous beast of burden and source of wool for weaving) and trading with people on the coastal plains down the valley of the Lambayeque river. This river proved a useful source of gold, silver and copper from the first. A rich gold-silver deposit at Cerro Morro de Etén may have been worked before 1000 BC. The most consistent supply to successive Peruvian cultures, however, came from the eastern slopes of the Andes, where rivers such as the Maranón drain into the Amazon basin of Brazil (the forty-odd short rivers coming

down to the Pacific from the western Andes have little alluvial gold). Knowledge of this trans-Andean gold trade is scant, but it fits with discoveries in Brazil centuries later (*see chapter 19*), where alluvial gold still enriches the river beds and streams. This pattern is the same today. When I visited South America regularly during the gold mining boom of the 1980s, Brazil, along with Colombia and Venezuela, was yielding an abundance of alluvial gold, but I could track little in Peru. The geology was just totally different. Peru's real gold reserves were not unlocked until the immense Yancocha mine opened in 1993 taking advantage of modern heap leach technology to recover gold from ultra low-grade ores. Today, Yancocha is Latin America's largest mine, yielding nearly 100 m.t./3.2 million t.oz. annually.

Even without that modern benefit, gold was prominent in Chavín culture during its prime from 800–200 BC. "Gold seems to have dominated the Andean scene until around 200 BC," reported M.I.T.'s Heather Lechtman. She added that the Chavín showed "superb mastery in the handling of the metal" and their artefacts were "exquisitely fashioned".[4] They hammered gold into sheets, from which they put together three-dimensional forms by soldering and welding. The welders were skilled enough to heat the pre-shaped sheets along the edges until they melted and fused. *Crowns* and breastplates of gold were decorated by punching or stamping from the back (*repoussé*) into high relief with motifs such as plumed jaguar heads.

Their achievements reveal confidence and wit. A tomb in the Lambayeque valley contained three tall gold *crowns*, a gold head-band, earspools and gold tweezers for removing body hair (a popular implement in successive cultures). Another tomb, at Chavín de Huántar in the high country north-west of modern Lima, revealed a head-band, 66 hollow beads, 29 gold snail shells, finger rings and pins, all of gold.

Chavín technology extended to making alloys. Although some ornaments contain 80% gold, 15% silver and 5% copper and could be from natural alluvial sources, one alloy excavated had 53% gold, 40% silver and 7% copper, which is unlikely to have occurred naturally. The Chavín were setting the stage for a long-running love affair with these three metals, which turn up in all manner of exotic combinations throughout the Americas for the next two thousand years, as goldsmiths sought to enhance brilliance and colour.

The commitment to religious or ceremonial functions was always apparent. "Chavín art creates a tremendous impression," wrote historian Richard Burger, "and may have been created by full-time specialists dedicated to developing an artistic style capable of communicating the power of Chavín religious ideology."[5] This was the foundation from which successive Peruvian cultures grew.

The origins were in the highlands, because that was where alluvial gold was most accessible. However, as coastal communities became more established, irrigating the desert, creating stable agricultural, fishing and shell collecting industries, so exchange of goods between coastal and highland peoples grew. From the interior came not just gold, but brightly coloured birds' feathers from the rain forest of the eastern Andes, charcoal, and soft alpaca wool for weaving, all bartered for salt, fish, shells or cotton textiles from the coast. Everything was carried by the alpaca's cousin, the llama. Craftsmanship matured not just in metals, but ceramics, where sound technology was equally essential to provide refractory furnaces, crucibles and moulds capable of holding molten metals. In ceramics and metals, the coastal people set the pace for the next 1,500 years. Only the Incas, in their mountain fastness of Cuzco, ultimately took goldsmithing back into the central Andes, but even they did so only by transplanting the goldsmiths from coastal towns they had conquered.

Peru: the Moche – the finest metal workers

Learning from the Chavín, a scattering of cultures along the Pacific coastal plain began working with gold by 200 BC. The Paracas, Siguas and Nasca peoples in the south were soon hammering out sheets of gold to be fashioned into soaring birds with outstretched wings, snakes and human faces. The Vicus, to the north, developed simple granulation for ornaments soon after 100 BC. The legacy of the Chavín, however, was really picked up by the Moche (or Mochica) living near the modern city of Trujillo, along the Lambayeque valley. This became the heartland of goldsmithing from around AD 100 until 1475, sustained first by the Moche, then the Sicán and finally by the Chimú cultures.

The achievements of the Moche have become fully recognised in recent years through the excavations of their 'royal tombs', dating from AD 200–400, at Sipán on the lower Lambayeque river. "These are the richest unlooted tombs to be excavated in the hemisphere," noted archaeologist Michael Moseley. "Each individual was accompanied by much precious metal, a presentation goblet, and uniforms."[6] Actually, some looting did take place, not least of a splendid headdress depicting a sea god with eight waving 'tentacles'. It vanished in 1988 and was not recovered for almost two decades. Then in 2006, through diligent detective work by Scotland Yard's arts and antiques squad in London working with the Peruvian government and a Dutch art dealer, it was located. The dealer, Michel Van Rijn, had labelled the headdress 'the Mona Lisa of Peru' and posted its picture on his web site, 'outing' the alleged trafficker who turned it in through a London lawyer and fled. The headdress reveals, not just the strong religious iconography in Moche craftsmanship, but its artistry and supremacy in metallurgy.

"The Mochica put metallurgy on its feet," argued Heather Lechtman.[7] Their understanding of complex *tumbaga* gold-copper alloys set the pattern that was to be copied throughout the Americas. The Moche mixed endless cocktails of gold and copper which were melted together to form an entire range of alloys providing the colour and the hardness required. Their subtle use of copper could give *tumbaga* of quite modest gold content the burnished look of real gold. Not content, they learned to gild copper with a thin, seamless layer of gold, a process now known as electrochemical replacement gilding. Moche metallurgists, lacking electric current, made up a potion of common salt, saltpetre and potash alum, which was heated gently for two to five days (according to modern experiments) until it dissolved. This acidic solution was neutralised with sodium bicarbonate and boiled. Copper ornaments were immersed in this solution which plated them with gold.[8] This chemical breakthrough shows the desire in Moche culture to create the colour and appearance of solid gold even if it was in short supply.

Equal admiration has been earned for their technical skill in joining sheets of gold. Listen to M.I.T.'s Heather Lechtman, "The sweating-welding joins used in the manufacture of a set of hollow jaguars made of sheet gold are as elegant as any goldsmithing techniques in the ancient or for that matter the modern world. The Mochica metalsmiths were probably the finest metal craftsmen who worked in the Central Andean area in the prehistoric period".[9] One of their bravura pieces was a nose ornament of tiny gold spiders on a rectangular gold web; each spider was meticulously soldered to a silver plate to make it stand out, and the silver plates in turn were soldered to the gold web.

Moche metalworkers in action are shown in a surviving ceramic bowl within which the sculpted figures of three men blow into tubes inserted in a dome-shaped kiln to sustain the high temperature needed for smelting, while a fourth colleague arranges ingots[10]. Their work was well organised in specific compounds at the two great sun-dried brick complexes of Huaca del Sol (Pyramid of the Sun) and Huaca de la Lune (Pyramid of the Moon) on the Moche river. These huge pyramids (Huaca del Sol is the largest architectural structure ever build in the Andes) served as administrative centres housing the aristocracy, workshops for hundreds of craftsmen, mausoleums and tombs.[11] Archaeologists call this 'Urban Craft Production'. Areas were set aside for metals, ceramics, cotton processing and weaving, and Spondylus shell decoration (these red or purple shells were harvested by divers in warm waters off the coast and strung into necklaces and other ornaments).[12]

This seemingly well-ordered society, trading its craft goods along the coast and into the highlands, was abruptly cut short just before AD 600 by a series of devastating El Niño-type floods which swept banks of sand inland, covering the whole area, save the tips of the two pyramids. Although some Moche nobility did relocate further north to Pampa Grande in the Lambayeque valley, where similar craft complexes were established, further flooding caused more setbacks. Pampa Grande, too, was abandoned. For a century or more, life was disrupted; the order and style of the Moche era disintegrated.

Peru: the Sicán – scintillating symbols

Centralised rule and a fresh sense of direction emerged after AD 700 as a new regional culture Sicán (also known as Lambayeque) evolved. "Sicán crystallised as a sharply defined corporate style," argued Michael Moseley. "The central design element is a male figure called the Sicán Lord. The richly-attired image is often depicted with small wings on each shoulder, a beak-like nose, and occasionally with talons instead of feet."[13] The goldsmiths faced a fresh challenge to create scintillating symbols. The Sicán capital of Batan Grande was on a fertile plain of the river Leche at the foothills of the Andes, which offered silver and copper deposits, along with algarroba, a local hardwood good for making charcoal. Gold came from alluvial sources on the Chinchipe and other tributaries of the river Marañon about two hundred kilometres away in the eastern Andes. The huge low-grade deposit of today's Yancocha mine was but a short distance away, unknown to those early metallurgists. By AD 1000 Batan Grande was the main metalworking centre in Peru, turning out a range of *tumbaga* alloys mostly containing 60–65% gold, 30–40% silver and 10–20% copper, and quantities of silver ornaments. Both sun and moon were emphasised. This production underpinned Sicán society. "Metals became the prestigious media of political, social and religious expression," reported an archaeology team.[14]

Output was prodigious. One tomb in the Huaco Loro pyramid at Batan Grande, where successive Sicán lords were buried, contained 67 kg/2,558 t.oz. of gold ornaments and 147 kg/4,726 t.oz. of silver. A 'principal man' had his face covered with a gold mask, four bangles in his nose, a pair of large earspools and beside him a pair of gold gauntlets made of two layers of thin gold sheet. The left glove held a gold beaker with a skilled *repoussé* representation of a Sicán lord, with a staff in each hand. Each earspool weighed almost 75 grams/2.4 t.oz.[15]

"The gold mask and earspools can be justifiably described as a *tour de force* of prehispanic goldsmithing in terms of innovative designs, careful planning and flawless execution," wrote the archaeologists who excavated the site.[16] The mask itself was made from a single large sheet of gold-silver-copper alloy measuring 46 by 26 cm. To anneal such a sheet would have required a large brazier and several workers just to charge it with charcoal. Moreover, it was hammered to a subtle thickness that gave some flexibility, but still rigidity. The technical and creative flair of the Sicán goldsmiths suggested to the archaeologists that they "may have vied with each other, showcasing their talent for personal gain and social prestige. The gold objects they created were the standard-bearers and pace-setters of Sicán crafts".[17] Their purpose, too, was clear – to emphasise through gold and silver the great symbolic importance of the sun and the moon in Sicán ideology.

Peru: the Chimor – brilliant gold for the nobility

In its prime, between AD 900–1100, the Sicán culture influenced several hundred kilometres of coastline north and south of the Lambayeque valley, until further El Niño flooding destroyed Batan Grande. This disaster cleared the way for an emerging rival, the budding Chimor Empire (AD 1000–1470) in the former Moche heartland to the south. Ultimately, the Chimor controlled one thousand kilometres of the Pacific coast. Their capital, Chan Chan, became a vast metropolis, with the civic centre alone covering six square kilometres. At its peak, after 1350, up to 26,000 craftsmen were engaged in wood, stone, ceramics, weaving and, above all, metalwork. A complex social order existed among these workers, who lived in rooms built of cane around small patios. Metalworkers apparently took weavers as wives, enjoyed the privilege of wearing earspools and were buried in their own cemeteries. They evolved a distinctive new culture, Chimú, drawing on the sea for many of their motifs, depicting fish, sea birds, mythical monsters and waves.[18]

The Chimor Empire secured most of its gold from the long-tapped alluvial sources of tributaries of the river Marañon on the eastern slopes of the Andes; copper for *tumbaga* alloys was closer to hand in the Lambayeque valley. The trans-Andean trade routes also supplied Chimú craftsmen with colourful feathers of the blue-and-yellow macaw and other tropical birds of the rain forest, already employed by the Moche and Sicán cultures, to top off golden *crowns*. The Chimú metalworkers inherited, too, their metallurgical knowledge. Indeed, it is likely that goldsmiths, much sought after for their skills, could be tempted (or simply transported) from one community to another, just as they were around the Mediterranean world where there was constant migration. The art historian Karen O'Day suggested "retained artists in the barrio may have been regarded as 'items' to acquire, like gold or feathers".[19]   Their role was clear: to provide brilliant goldwork for the nobles at the apex of Chimor's social order. "The privilege of wearing gold ornaments was largely restricted to the highest social echelons," O'Day reported. "There was a direct connection between gold and the nobility, for the technology and iconography of metalworking served to display their unique position and status and to assert their divine authority to rule."[20]   The Chimú outdid the Moche and Sicán goldsmiths in creating complex ornaments. A single earspool might contain more than one hundred pieces of sheet gold soldered or stapled together in an architectural pyramid. Two groups of specialists contributed, the first hammering the gold or *tumbaga* into sheets, the second assembling them into a work of art. "They were superlative engineers," observed Karen O'Day.[21]   Their dazzling multi-component pieces swayed as the wearer moved, out-shimmering anything that had gone before, evoking luxury and sanctity.

The Chimú style shows the Precolumbian goldsmith at his best.   What the Chimor Empire created between 1000 and 1470, when they were conquered by the Incas from the Andean highlands and blended into their vast empire, was the apogee of almost three thousand years' work.   That first simple metalworker's kit with a few scraps of foil found at Waywaka led to the Chavin, the Nasca, the Moche, the Sicán and the Chimú building a legacy which was snatched by the Inca and shortly thereafter astounded Francisco Pizarro and his *conquistadores*.

Peru: the Incas' inheritance

Historically, the Incas grabbed the world's attention because of the sheer size and wealth of their empire that confronted Pizarro in 1532. "Their sprawling realm Tahuantinsuyu, or Land of the Four Quarters … probably surpassed Ming China and the Ottoman Empire as the largest nation on earth," Michael Moseley observed.[22] Stretching along the Andes from southern Colombia to Chile and upland Argentina, it embraced Peru and Ecuador on the Pacific coast and penetrated east into Bolivia and the Brazilian rain forest in the upper Amazon basin. The empire was bound together by a network of over 30,000 km of all-weather roads that aided military control and trade. The true Inca numbered perhaps 40,000 individuals, yet they ruled ten million people. Their conquest of the Chimú in 1470 knitted in the last crucial slice of territory, giving them the fertile, irrigated plains of the northern coast, the copper and silver mines of the Lambayeque valley, and the technical know-how of the craftsmen and metallurgists of Chan Chan. Many of these metalworkers were forced to move to the Inca's provincial capital of Cajamarca and to Cuzco itself.

Cuzco, in the very heart of the Andes, was regarded as the home of the Sun, the god Inti. Gold was his essence. The Inca emperor and empress considered themselves the children of the Sun and the Moon. Gold was "sweat of the sun", silver was "tears of the moon". These metals were embodied in the human forms of emperor and empress and their control was central to Inca rulers. "Both metals were mined ... throughout the four quarters of Tahuantinsuyu on a grand scale," noted M.I.T.'s Heather Lechtman. "Gold was collected from placer deposits, but was also mined from auriferous quartz veins. The gold-silver focus was ... transformed into a state-monopolised industry and one to which the state committed substantial resources of labour and energy."[23]

The goldsmiths, hammering away at their sheets of gold, followed the 'architectural' style of the Chimú, assembling them into more and more complex designs. No wonder the Spanish invaders were awe-struck when they reached the city of the sun god to behold palaces, temples and shrines glowing with gold. The best description comes from the *conquistador* Cieza de León in his *Chronicle of Peru*. He visited the great temple, the House of the Sun, at Cuzco and reported it was more than 400 paces in circuit: "Round the wall, half way up, there was a band of gold, two palms wide and four dedos (fingers) in thickness. The doorways and doors were covered with plates of the same metal ... within were four houses ... with walls ... covered with plates of gold, within and without. In one of these houses, which was the richest, there was the figure of the sun, very large and made of gold, very ingeniously worked".[24]

Close by the temple was a garden all in gold and silver, which was recalled somewhat later by Garcilaso de la Vega, El Inca, a Spanish-Inca traveller. He wrote, "It contained many herbs and flowers of various kinds, small plants, large trees, animals great and small, tame and wild, and creeping things such as snakes, lizards and snails, butterflies and birds ... there was also a great maize field ... fruit trees with their fruit all made of gold and silver ... men, women and children cast in gold and silver ... to the great majesty and ornamentation of the house of their god, the Sun".[25] Beside such symbolic exhibitions, Inca rulers distributed gold trinkets as tokens of royal esteem to the nobility and military commanders. Status among the elite was indicated by the length of the long loops of their gold earspools or by conical flat-topped hats. Gold depilatory tweezers, too, remained in fashion.

Goldsmiths' work was held in high regard. Gold was both a physical and psychological support to an emperor's prestige, its brilliance enhancing his unique place in society. Yet not for a moment was gold thought of as money by the Incas nor any of their Peruvian predecessors. That distinction, when Inca came face to face with Spaniard (*see chapter 18*), was to highlight that although Old World and New World had evolved largely in parallel with the technology of working gold, they had diverged on its role in society.

Colombia: the gift of the stingless bee

The real treasure at the Banca de la Republica in Bogotá is not a modest stock of ingots in its vaults, but the unique hoard of over 33,600 gold ornaments in its Museo Del Oro[26] revealing the people and cultures of Colombia over the last three thousand years. The spectacle is almost overwhelming. Diadems, helmets, breastplates, trumpets, masks, earrings, earspools, ear danglers, nose ornaments, necklaces, rings, bracelets, bells, beads, shells, penis covers, lime-flasks and lime-dippers, depilatory tweezers, even fish hooks, all crafted in hammered and cast gold or *tumbaga* surround you. A single necklace comprises 260 plaques of cast gold. Animals, amphibians (especially alligators), bats (very spooky), birds, fish, frogs and insects have been fashioned in gold, along with men, women and children, and half-human and half-animal figures. It is a world in gold.

If you cannot venture as far as Bogotá, then view the Treasure of the Quimbayas in Madrid's Museo de América.[27] The treasure, dating AD 200–1000, is regarded as the most important collection of Precolumbian gold in terms of aesthetics and technique. In confronting the history of gold, these exhibitions in Bogotá and Madrid rank with the Tutankhamun treasures in the Cairo Museum, or the Scythian gold in the Hermitage in St Petersburg, as testaments to early goldsmiths' skills. They also help us understand why the Spanish later sought the legendary El Dorado, source of all this gold.

What is also intriguing is the contrast with Peru. While there are naturally similarities, the barrier of the Andes meant that different metallurgy, symbolism and designs evolved. Above all, while Peru was the land of hammered sheet gold, Colombia became the home of lost-wax casting, thanks to the wax available there from the stingless bee, which the environment of Peru apparently did not suit. The Quimbaya treasure, for example, has sublime creations of human figures, animals, and great lime gourds cast in gold, quite unlike anything found in Peru.

From the beginning, the *cordilleras* of the northern Andes offered easily-worked deposits of placer gold. Imagine the central and western *cordillera* as two prongs of a fork probing north towards the Caribbean across much of Colombia. The streams coming down from these ranges into the river Magdalena to the east, to the river Cauca in the centre of the fork (both flowing to the Caribbean) and the river Calima off the western flank into the Pacific, were rich in alluvial gold. Copper was also available in the hills. Silver was less abundant, however, than in Peru (just as today, Peru is the largest silver producer in Latin America, but Colombia contributes virtually none). Colombian metallurgy, therefore, developed principally as a gold or gold-copper *tumbaga* province.

Colombia: 'very handsome nuggets'

The gold came primarily from alluvial deposits in river beds and along the banks. Fire-hardened sticks were used to break up the ground; gold dust and nuggets were then washed out in shallow wooden trays and transported in animal skin pouches down to the valleys. The Spanish invaders found large teams at work, often diverting streams to get at fresh gravel in their beds. The Spanish chronicler Vasco Nuñez de Balboa reported in 1513 "They wait until the rivers rise … and after the floods have passed, and they become dry again, the gold is exposed, having been washing from the banks and carried from the mountains in very large nuggets". Another Spanish observer, Martin Fernández Enciso, noted: "When it rains they stretch nets across the streams and when the water rises it brings nuggets as big as eggs which are caught in the nets". This strategy was akin to the legend of Jason's golden fleece, with sheepskins used to trap gold particles in streams. In the dry season the alluvial miners burned off vegetation in the high country revealing, according to Nuñez de Balboa, "great quantities of gold in very handsome nuggets".

Gold-bearing quartz veins were also tapped around the main mining centre of Buritica in the north-west of Antioquia province. Stone tools were used to dig narrow shafts, scarcely a metre wide, down to depths of 20–30 metres; but underground galleries were apparently not attempted. The quartz was crushed between stones and smelted in furnaces of fired refractory clay, with the temperature kept up by ceramic blowpipes. This process produced a small button of gold, but its fineness varied widely, implying limited quality control. Gold dust may also have been refined by heating it with a mixture of common salt and clay, with the chlorine in the salt combining with impurities to form chlorides (the magic ingredient that provided the refining breakthrough in Lydia to provide a constant standard for coins).[28]

Buritica was strategically placed at the crossroads of many Colombian trade routes, so that gold could be distributed throughout the country, being bartered for salt, cotton cloth, maize or even manufactured gold ornaments. Usually, gold was fabricated in distinct communities, often inhabited largely by goldsmiths.

Colombia: the regional styles

Initially the gold came down from Buritica or other mining sources on the Saldana and Nechi rivers to the villages of the Calima, Cauca and Magdalena valleys, but was then traded along rivers flowing to the Caribbean plains. Thus, over time, a dozen or more regional styles of goldsmithing evolved; Narino and Tumaco-La Tolita down on the border with Ecuador, Calima on the Pacific coast, Malagana and Quimbaya along the river Cauca, San Agustin, Tolima and Muisca along the Magdalene, the Zenú and Tairona living mainly on the Caribbean plains. Ultimately, the tradition spread into Central America.

The provenance of gold ornaments from some of these regions is not always clear, because most have been recovered, even today, through tomb-robbing, not organised archaeological excavation. A whole new 'culture' can even turn up. A tractor driver working his sugar cane patch on the flood plain of the Cauca in 1992 literally fell into an unknown tomb. He spied gold and the resulting rush brought over 5,000 robbers to the scene. They made off with at least 150 kg/4,822 t.oz. of gold ornaments (some say much more), and initially drove off archaeologists from the Museo del Oro in Bogotá, who hastened there. The archaeologists did get their hands on 150 pieces of this 'Malagana Treasure', but more remains in private hands. Later excavation around the settlement of Malagana suggested it thrived from 300 BC–AD 300, with the goldwork itself pinpointed between 180 BC–AD 90. Analysis of the individual iconography on the gold won Malagana the accolade of its own regional 'brand', thus rating it as one of the earliest gold 'cultures' in Colombia.[29]

The Malagana style fits into the jigsaw of south west Columbia along with their neighbours, the Calima and Tumaca, across the western cordillera on the Pacific coast. The Calima are credited as the first substantial goldworkers in Columbia, with a tradition dating back before 500 BC. They began with a trump card. The local alluvial sources provided remarkably high grade gold which was easy to hammer into gleaming objects. Working with small, oval hammers of meteoric iron the Calima goldsmiths beat out plates of wafer-thin gold on cylindrical stone anvils. Ana María Falchetti of the Museo del Oro described how they proceeded. "A design was then drawn on the sheet and working over a soft surface – thick leather or a sack of fine sand – the goldsmith traced it with varying degrees of relief using chisels, engraving tools, and punches of metal, stone and bone. They joined sheets with gold nails."[30] They created nose ornaments shaped like twin birds or embossed with monkeys, and pendants with stylised human faces. A diadem with *repoussé* decorations came complete with ear discs and nose ornaments stapled on. Such workmanship was akin to that of Peruvian goldsmiths to the south on the Pacific coast.

Colombia: the art of lost-wax

What sets the Calima, and ultimately all Colombia, apart is that, in parallel with this hammered sheet gold, they were already experimenting with lost-wax casting. This involves the goldsmith fashioning the ornament in wax, encasing it in a clay mould, with a channel to the exterior. When the mould is heated the wax drains out and is replaced with molten gold which sets into a copy of the wax design. The earliest cast designs include lime-dippers, the long thin spatulas for access to the ubiquitous lime-flasks, which were surmounted by tiny but intricate human figures, birds or animals. Lime-flasks, often made from gourds, were essential accessories for Colombian Indians, alive or dead, along with a little bag of coca leaves. The flask contained, not lime juice as might be imagined, but lime powder from crushed shells. With each flask came a long, thin stick or dipper, often with an ornate top. When the dipper was poked into the flask after being moistened on the tongue, some lime powder adhered. This could then be licked off, while chewing a wad of coca leaves. Apparently this gave an agreeable taste, even a kick. The élite had their lime-flasks cast in gold, the fashionable cigarette cases of the day, which were later buried with them.

The reason the Calima first devised the lost-wax technique some time before AD 1 (compared with Egypt where the process goes back to 1500 BC) is that their local stingless bee provided ample supplies of beeswax. The significance of this humble bee, a member of the *meliponidae* family, was first observed by Junius Bird of the Department of Anthropology at the American Museum of Natural History. He was puzzled that, while the lost-wax technique was employed by goldsmiths from Colombia northwards through Central America into Mexico, in Peru its application was extremely rare.[31]   The answer was simple – no stingless bees. "They are found," he observed, "in Mexico, Central America and much of South America … they are absent, however, from the highlands and west coast valleys of Peru – the regions of gold working". By contrast, Colombia had an abundance of the bees and plenty of wax, which was esteemed by goldsmiths. They made full use of it in creating their remarkable legacy. Junius Bird concluded, "although the Peruvians achieved considerable artistry by hammering … I believe they were disadvantaged by a scarcity of the beeswax that was available in other goldworking areas".

Along with the Calima, the Tumaco culture further south on the coast on the border of present-day Ecuador/Colombia, pioneered casting and the technology spread ultimately to other cultures in the south-west, such as San Agustin, Tolima and Malagana. "The South-western jewellers were masters of lost-wax casting, producing huge quantities of miniature human and animal figures, beads and pendants," notes Warwick Bray, the Precolumbian metalwork specialist.[32]   The flora and fauna around them fascinated these early metalworkers. Their symbolic ornaments are an encyclopaedia of the birds, insects, animals, reptiles and fish of their region. An early Tumaco mask from 325 BC portrays the threatening jaws of a jaguar, the Tolima conjured up pendants of hovering bats, at San Agustin flying fish were featured, and the Narino, up in the high country, had leaping monkeys on their nose ornaments and ear pendants. The prize goes to Malagana, whose goldsmiths produced a profusion of beads in gold and *tumbaga* portraying armadillos, birds, crabs, flowers, lizards, even mosquitoes, along with semi-abstract creatures.

The Malagana goldsmiths were equally confident making large cut-out sheet metal human figures and flexible masks with simple eyes, nose and mouth like a modern cartoon character, with the added touch of hanging discs covering the eye sockets. The Malagana finds included an imaginative sheet metal creature that was combination bird, crocodile and human. "The goldsmiths of Malagana also had a liking for boldly embossed, curvilinear designs … depicting … animals (real or supernatural), human beings and stylised faces," observed Warwick Bray. "The imagery is charged with symbolic, and often religious, meaning, reflecting a system of beliefs about the nature of the universe, mankind's place within it, and the proper structure of society."[33]

The catalogue of Malagana ornaments outstrips other south-west cultures. It spans trumpets, gold-covered sea shells (they were adept at gilding), lime-flasks and lime-dippers with their tops hammered and chiselled into palm trees, breastplates, earspools, 'dropper' ornaments like Christmas tree decorations, diadems, delicate depilatory tweezers and large tweezers whose function is uncertain.

The Malagana settlement was the strategic centre of the south-west Colombia 'gold cultures'. Its location on the upper reaches of the river Cauca, which originated close to alluvial gold sources in the Andes and flowed on down through other settlements towards the Caribbean, was an advantage. The river was the artery for gold, both rough and worked, for trade and for ideas. Malagana's influence spread downstream to the Quimbaya living in what one archaeologist has described as "a primitive province of bamboo in green valleys" about 350 km to the north.[34]

Colombia: the Quimbaya – cool sophistication

The Quimbaya were actually a small tribe living on the middle reaches of the Cauca. Their name, however, has come to embrace all the people living there over many centuries, about whom relatively little is known, save their goldwork. The exact date of the best work is obscure; it was created some time between AD 200 and 1000, several centuries after the best of Malagana.

The Quimbaya's metallurgical skills were exceptional. First, because they had no immediate access to high quality alluvial gold sources, they relied mainly on *tumbaga* alloy. They learned, however, to enhance the surface colour by depletion gilding in which some of the copper on the surface was removed by heating the *tumbaga* in an open hearth until it oxidised. The black copper oxide scale was then dissolved in an acid of plant solutions, and the ornament burnished to create a surface sheen of purer gold.[35] Secondly, the Quimbaya excelled at lost-wax casting. Ana Maria Falchetti of the Museo del Oro has said their work was "the zenith of lost-wax casting, with its anthropomorphic vessels of striking realism, its lime-flasks in plant form and its embossed gold helmets".[36] Their heavy, naturalistic, three-dimensional pieces are distinct from the work of all other goldsmiths in the Precolumbian cultures of both Colombia and Peru.

The heart of the matter is the Quimbaya Treasure, found at La Solidad on the river Cauca in 1891 and given by the Colombian government to Spain the following year. It now has pride of place in the Museo de América in Madrid. The museum dates it broadly AD 200–1000, as the precise dating remains uncertain. The treasure is set out against a black background along a whole gallery wall. It stuns most visitors to momentary silence. The collection has 122 pieces, thought to make up the funeral dowry of six prominent people. They are represented by six lime-flasks cast as human figures, three seated, three standing; there are three men, two women (one apparently pregnant) and a boy. All are naked, except for jewellery, their plump bodies superbly modelled and finished. Their eyes are half-closed, creating a sublime, almost sensual expression. Around them are six embossed helmets, a trumpet, an incense burner, musical instruments, bells and a great assortment of necklaces, pins, pendants, nose and ear rings, and a diadem. The lime-flask figures are provisioned with other lime-flasks for their journey to another world. The largest lime-flasks stand up to 40 cm high and one is embellished, front and back, with a naked woman.

The abiding impression from the Quimbaya Treasure is of sophisticated goldsmiths of great technical ability. Their human faces reveal them as sculptors of immense confidence. The immediate comparison is with the death mask of King Tutankhamun of Egypt, that serene portrait in gold of a young man. The Quimbaya goldsmiths matched that expression.

The chance findings of the Malagana and Quimbaya treasures enhanced the lasting reputation of their respective cultures. Pity, therefore, the Tolima just across the central *cordillera*, who have won technical credit for their lost-wax casting, but are less well-known because few grand showpieces have been unearthed. Yet they were well positioned at the junction of the river Saldana, which was rich in alluvial gold, and the river Magdalena, which was as key an artery for exchange of goods and ideas as the Cauca. Moreover, Tolima ornaments were mainly of high grade gold, not *tumbaga*. They cast mythical animals in solid gold and hammered out pure gold pectorals that look like a child's cut-outs from coloured paper. They lack, however, the cool sophistication of the Quimbaya.

Colombia: El Dorado, the gilded man

The real sparkle came after AD 600 from the Muisca, living 500 km further down the Magdalena, beyond the modern city of Bogotá. The energy and inventiveness of their goldsmiths knew no bounds. They were the sole Colombian gold 'culture' to cast in stone moulds which could be used repeatedly, unlike those in clay. The Muisca created an astonishingly comprehensive picture of their society and the world about them. Yet their style comes full circle from the Quimbaya. They made no attempt to be naturalistic; instead, they produced flat, semi-abstract figures of gold or *tumbaga* sheet overlaid with gold wire cast from threads of wax. A tall, thin figure of a warrior, his bow and arrows in one hand, a trophy head in the other, the outline of his face, nose, mouth and eyes outlined in gold wire, resembles an early Cubist sculpture from Picasso or Braque.

The religious symbolism was pervasive. Over half of all Muisca gold artefacts were votive offerings, or *tunjos*, to a bevy of deities. Foremost were Chibchacum and his wife as creators of the world, Bachue and his son, creators of humanity, and Bochica who once saved the Muisca from floods and taught them cultivation and weaving. They also revered the sun and the moon, lakes and mountain tops. Their devotions were presided over by priests or shamans, who feature prominently in metallic figurines.

Tunjos depict everything from domestic chores and love life to household goods and weapons of war. Muisca goldsmiths cast cradles with and without babies, women with a child, or a bowl and tray, men with tools and weapons, perhaps with a staff in hand and birds on each shoulder. Couples make love, chiefs are borne on litters, an alligator swallows a human (a real-life fear) and sacrificial posts are raised. The range of wild life *tunjos* would do credit to a guidebook; eagles, hawks, condors, pheasants, doves, parrots, deer, lizards, turtles, snails, snakes (by the score, often with a human or jaguar face) and insects abound. "The figures reproduce … the real world of the Indian communities," argues Roberto Lleras-Pérez, deputy director of the Museo del Oro. "They evince an intention to represent and obtain control over nature and society."[37]

The most dramatic of Muisca gold *tunjos* in the Museo del Oro is a raft, which illustrates the legend of the gilded man, El Dorado. The raft is sketched out in cast gold wires. In the centre the ruler is seated on a high-backed stool; he is adorned with ornaments. Around him are other smaller figures, two with lime-flasks, two with rattles, two are masked. They are destined for a great ceremony on Lake Guatavita, a small, circular lake hemmed in by hills, just north of Bogotá, and home of the demon they worshipped. The raft *tunjo* commemorates the inauguration of Muisca rulers. The new ruler was covered with powdered gold (hence 'gilded man') and set sail on the lake on a raft of rushes laden with gold ornaments, accompanied by his chiefs, each with their own offerings of gold. Music and singing onshore wished them well, until a banner was run up on the raft for silence. Then the new ruler threw the gold into the lake; his companions did likewise. Over the centuries the gold accumulated at the bottom of the lake and the legend of El Dorado was born.

To the Spanish, who first heard the tale around 1535, El Dorado promised treasure beyond belief. They (and others) have sought it, without success, ever since (*see chapter 18*).[38] The personification of the Muisca ruler setting out on his raft is one of the most enduring images in Precolumbian gold. The raft, with its passengers and their golden offerings, encapsulates the search for El Dorado, that has spawned expeditions, books, films and television documentaries.

The ripple of gold expertise that spread north over the centuries down the Magdalena and Cauca rivers ended up on the Caribbean plains with the Zenú (or Sinú). The name embraces several local styles along the Sinú, San Jorge, Cauca and Nechi rivers, where a gold working tradition began almost two thousand years ago and peaked between AD 500–1000. This remains the heartland of today's gold mining in Colombia, especially on the Nechi. My own introduction to Colombian gold in the 1960s came from the manager at Pato Consolidated, which had dredges on the Nechi and fought an unending duel with local bandits out to steal their gold.[39] Pato was one of the earliest settlements for Zenú gold work. Further west in the Serranía de Abibe was the Zenú mining community of Buritica, while Finzenú on the Sinú river and Dabeida on the Sucio river in Antioquia province, still a key mining area with the modern Frontino mine, became important centres for goldsmiths. Their output was destined mainly for the fertile plains by the Caribbean, extensively irrigated by a network of canals. The picture is of a prosperous society, with its mining and jewellery manufacturing in the hills, and its clientele spread out towards the sea.

Colombia: the Zenú, masters of filigree

The religious symbolism of ornaments was, as ever, paramount. The Zenú conceived a three-tier universe, the upper and lower levels of which were inhabited by different spirits, the terrestrial one by humans. The most noted spirit of the underworld was a golden alligator, which supported the world and humanity. Water birds moved at will between these three worlds. Amphibians such as turtles and water snakes, which could move on earth and in water, also enjoyed special status.[40]

Homage was paid accordingly, particularly through ornate, heavy cast gold or *tumbaga* heads on staffs, carried like sceptres as a symbol of office by local chiefs or *caciques*. Alligators with ferocious teeth and water birds, such as egrets and ibis, with crests and long beaks, were popular. Staff heads also featured monkeys, dogs, a jaguar attacking an alligator, and humans (one playing a flute). The technique of casting from the first centuries AD was impeccable. The Zenú goldsmiths learned their metallurgy from their neighbours, the Quimbaya, to the south along the Cauca river. They evolved, however, special skills in casting thick wire, known as filigree or 'false' filigree, from long threads of wax (a technique the Muisca also perfected). Large, lacy, fan-shaped filigree ear ornaments became the vogue, as did bold, moustache-like, filigree nose ornaments. "The skill required to cast such complex shapes as Zenú earrings with all their intricate detail is extremely impressive," argued British Museum metallurgists Susan La Niece and Nigel Meeks, "not least for the ability to produce and manipulate the minute beeswax components and to add the appropriate runners and risers to control the flow of molten metal, so that it filled every part of the mould."[41] Such dexterity meant the Zenú goldsmiths hardly needed to bother with many other goldworking techniques. Yet they were equally skilled at hammering out crescent-shaped or circular breastplates and embossing them in immaculate *repoussé* technique with jaguars, snakes and earth-supporting alligators.

A bonus came with the plentiful supply of gold from the mines around Buritica or Zenufana, land of gold, as it was known. The gold miners themselves were accorded supernatural talents to use their hands as reels to get gold out of veins.[42] The goldsmiths congregated in Finzenú, which became an important ceremonial centre, also inhabited by *caciques* and priests. Here, as in other Zenú communities, the *caciques* owned gold as one symbol of their sacred powers and, when they died, their ornaments were buried with them (making Finzenú a target for Spanish tomb-robbers centuries later).

Within this society goldsmiths had status. "The role of the goldsmiths (contributed) to maintain the stability of Greater Zenú," Ana Maria Falchetti has noted. "Goldsmiths transformed a sacred metal which came from the rich deposits of Zenufana into objects with cosmological and social meaning."[43] Their output, especially of filigree ear ornaments, was traded for centuries throughout the Zenú lands and beyond. The Zenú 'brand', as it were, circulated not just to the Tairona people on the north coast of Colombia, but up the isthmus into Central America and out to the islands of the Caribbean. Payment came in fish, salt and cotton cloth.

The Tairona lived in the Sierra Nevada de Santa Marta and on the coastal plains where the rivers, Magdalena and Cauca, now merged, enter the Caribbean at the modern city of Baranquilla. They were thus last stop on the twin river lifeline of the gold trade stretching back over 1,500 km into the high Andes; between them the Magdalena and Cauca passed through all the major gold 'cultures' of Colombia, except the Calima. The Tairona must have received both raw gold and ornaments for centuries. Indeed, their early metalwork dates back to the first centuries AD.

Their prime, however, did not come until after AD 1000. They were an industrious people, digging irrigation canals, hewing out terraces to cultivate, building roads and bridges. The Spanish found a populous and prosperous community. Their work, in gold and *tumbaga* not surprisingly incorporated several styles, including the heavy ornate style of Zenú, with more than a touch of Quimbaya naturalistic roundness. They were adept, too, at cast filigree, which they must have learned from the Zenú or Muisca. Yet their own ornaments lack the inventiveness and flair of the other cultures. The Tairona, one suspects, were not the initiators of new technology or design, but copied what had gone before up-river. Being on the Caribbean shore, however, they participated in the dissemination of both ornaments and metallurgical expertise into Central America along the Caribbean trade network which existed as far back as 500 BC.

Central America: 'rich coast'

The gold trade itself reached Panama by AD 200, before moving on into Costa Rica. "Colombia, Panama and Costa Rica are really a single metallurgical province," argued Warwick Bray, "characterised by a preference for gold-copper alloys, lost-wax casting, depletion gilding and false filigree."[44]

Looking at the ornaments in gold and *tumbaga* of such Central American 'cultures' as the Tonosí/Cubitá (AD 200–700), Diquis/Chiriquí (AD 700–1500), and Coclé (AD 900–1500), the familiar pattern emerges. The ubiquitous alligator as a god-figure is ever-present, with similar homage paid to eagles and parrots. A spider spins his web as a pendant, butterflies and bats flutter. Frogs are everywhere and one anthropomorphic figure looks like a scuba diver with mask and webbed feet.

Gold and goldsmiths played a crucial role in these societies. "Gold objects, perhaps above all other artistic expressions, came to express transformative capacities and powers," suggested Jeffrey Quilter, Curator of the Precolumbian collection at Dumbarton Oaks in Washington DC. "High ranking shamans who wore and were buried in gold jewellery ... must have claimed command of cosmic forces as part of their rights to power."[45]

Our appreciation of their work is often somewhat sketchy because the Spanish *conquistadores* and later tomb-robbers took their pick. However, diligent archaeology at the Sitio Conte, Las Huacas and, most recently, the Cerro Juan

Diaz sites in Panama, has turned up Tonosí goldwork from AD 300 and cast gold birds and animals from the Cubitá culture AD 500/600. In Costa Rica the search has been more haphazard (someone wrote an article called "Bootleg Archaeology in Costa Rica") but the best finds come from the Rivas-Panteon de la Reina sites, nicknamed 'The General and the Queen', located along a wild river called El General.[46] This heritage has been preserved by the National Museum of Costa Rica and by Banco Central de Costa Rica with its own Museo del Oro, which houses many of the 'El General' finds.[47]

However, it is down to a railroad surveyor named Minor Keith, who worked for the United Fruit Company in San José, Costa Rica in the late 19th century, that one of the best collections of Chiriquí artefacts was assembled. While scouting routes for banana trains, Keith bought up over 3,000 Precolumbian relics in stone, ceramics and metal, including 881 objects in gold and jade. For years he was the bane of archaeologists and museum directors, because he always got the pieces first. A buyer for Berlin's Royal Ethnological Museum, however, had luck; he arrived in San José when Keith was out of town, securing the museum several of the best objects in Europe.[48]

While Costa Rica and Panama confirmed to the Spanish invaders the potential wealth from gold in the Americas, their first experience was with the Taino people living on Cuba, Haiti (Hispaniola) and Puerto Rico. The Taino culture, dating from AD 1200, was less sophisticated than other contemporary Precolumbian styles. They scoured dust and nuggets of placer gold from streams on the island, and hammered it between two stones into flat sheet, on which they made simply *repoussé* patterns. Smelting and casting was unknown. Pure gold was known as caona, but the Taino preferred a low-grade *tumbaga* alloy they called *guanin*. *Guanin* was up to 55% copper, 40% gold and 5% silver, reddish-purple in colour, with a pungent smell. The smell apparently was much appreciated and *guanin* was valued more highly than gold. The origin of this alloy is not clear, but it probably came from *tumbaga* workshops in Zenú or elsewhere in Colombia.[49]

The first Spanish encounters with the people of the New World out on the islands, therefore, gave them but a glimpse of its heritage in gold. The list of treasure Columbus brought back in 1495 from his second voyage, did include over one hundred items in gold, such as a frog pendant, masks and gold sheet, but that was like lifting the first of seven veils. The full picture did not emerge for almost forty years until the 1530s when Pedro de Heredia, governor of Cartagena, and Gonzalo Jimenez de Quesada revealed what the Zenú and Muisca had achieved in Colombia and Francisco Pizarro removed the seventh veil in Cuzco, Peru. Sadly, they did not perceive the golden ornaments as a unique cultural legacy built up over 3,000 years, but as potential money. So they hastened to melt it.

CHAPTER 18

Spain:
Squandered Treasure

Waterfront to the New World

Beside the river Guadalquivir in Seville a fortified tower, appropriately known as *Torre del Oro*, presides over a paved broadwalk fringed with jacaranda and palm trees, oleanders and bougainvillaea. In the quiet of early morning, before the first tourist buses arrive, you can imagine the bustle on this quay 500 years ago, in 1503, as the first shipments of gold from the New World arrived in Spain. Across this waterfront, over the next 160 years, came 180 m.t/5.8 million t.oz of gold, along with 16,810 m.t./540 million t.oz. of silver. Ox carts hauled it the few hundred metres to the House of Trade (*Casa de la Contratación*) where officials supervised weighing, refining and assaying, made sure the royal 'quint' (a fifth of all treasure) was assigned and secured the bullion in triple-locked wooden chests in the treasure chamber, guarded round the clock by three shifts each of 12 men. The House of Trade later arranged public auctions of the treasure and watched over minting of gold coins (into which most gold went) at the nearby *Casa de la Moneda*. Seville and its House of Trade were granted the monopoly of all incoming precious metals thus stimulating its own golden age and setting Spain on course for aggressive, if ultimately disastrous, empire-building.

The House of Trade has long gone and only a neat ceramic plaque in a quiet courtyard of the Calle Habana commemorates the mint, so the *Torre del Oro* tends to be taken as the symbol of that rich trade. Intriguingly, however, the records of how much gold and silver came in, ship by ship, remain close by in the *Archivo General de Indias*. This great four-square building (extensively renovated in 2003/04) first opened as a merchants' exchange in 1584, but later came to house all the documents relating to Spain's colonisation of the 'Indies' – that is to say, the Americas. A solid green treasure chest has rested for centuries at the top of the main staircase of the *Archivo*, a tangible reminder of the wealth that came through Seville.

Up that staircase, passing the strong-box, one day in 1926 came a young American scholar, Earl J. Hamilton. He had just crossed the Atlantic with his wife, Gladys, and six-week-old daughter, Sita, "To ramble over Spain", as he put it, "on the trail of old paper". Initially, the trail led to the *Archivo*, where he spent two years among letters, bills of lading and ledgers such as the *Cuenta y Razón* (receipts and disbursements) and *Carga y Data* (freight and articles), weaving together the first real assessment of the quantities of gold and silver imported into Spain from the Americas. Later, he scoured Spain for other dusty records to see what impact that tidal wave of metal had upon prices. Ultimately, Hamilton published *American Treasure* and the *Price Revolution in Spain 1501–1650*.[1]   The French historian, Fernand Braudel, greeted it as "a monumental work".

In the story of gold it stands out as a scoop; ferreting out those statistics was academic detective work of the highest order. For Hamilton gives us not just the gold imports, but an insight into the gold trade from diggings in the Americas, to the initial assaying and shipping of gold, from how many parcels came on what ship, to auction bids at the House of Trade. He tracked 154 separate parcels of gold on a single caravel in 1544, noting that the first six parcels together contained almost 8.5 kg/275 t.oz. of gold. From this mosaic of numbers emerges the pattern of gold flows starting in 1503, soaring quickly in the 1530s as Pizarro conquered Peru, and peaking in the 1550s from new sources in Colombia, Mexico and Chile. Thereafter, silver imports surged thanks to new extraction technology and the expansion of the Potosi mine in Bolivia.

Subsequently, rival historians have sometimes challenged Hamilton's statistics, arguing he ignored unofficial imports. Actually, Hamilton always admitted there was smuggling, conceding it could add anything from 10 to 50% to the official flows, though he inclined to the lower figure. Crucially, however, his pattern of flows meshes with both new gold and silver discoveries and major sequestrations, such as the ransom for the Inca Emperor Atahualpa. In short, Hamilton got the perspective right on the core New World flows.[2]

The promise of gold had been there from the first expedition by Christopher Columbus to the 'Indies' in 1492/3. He brought back samples of gold ornaments from the Bahamas, Cuba and Haiti (Hispaniola). The hunt was on. The pursuit of gold was relentless throughout the next sixty or seventy years, sustaining the newly united Spain created when King Ferdinand and Queen Isobella took over in 1492 the keys to Granada, the last remaining Muslim citadel. "Gold was the first great lure offered," noted Professor Henry Kamen, "Columbus, Cortés, Pizarro and every subsequent adventurer placed the search for gold at the head of his priorities."[3]

Pizarro's plunder

Yet patience was required. The first serious gold arrivals noted by Sancho de Matienzo, treasurer at the House of Trade, did not turn up until 25th February 1503.[4] Quantities were modest for the remainder of the decade; only 4.97 m.t/159,625 t.oz was imported in eight years. Set in perspective, that equalled a single year's output elsewhere in Europe and Africa at the time. Although the inflow doubled between 1511 and 1520, as new supplies came from Puerto Rico, it was not yet a gold rush. The gold was coming from both melted trinkets and modest alluvial deposits in the mountains of the Caribbean islands (bullion imports were all of

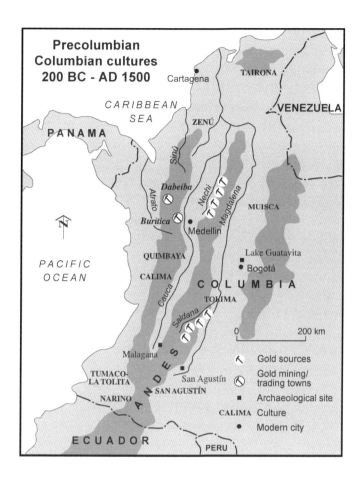

Precolumbian Columbian cultures 200 BC - AD 1500

gold until 1521, and then only a trickle of silver until Mexico was opened up in the 1530s. But it was that push in Mexico by Hernan Cortés, after the discovery of the Aztec Empire in 1519, that widened the horizons of Spain's ambitions on the mainland of the Americas, leading to firm footholds also in Panama, Colombia (New Grenada) and ultimately Peru.

Peru was to provide serious treasure, but at immense human cost and with the irreparable loss of cultures stretching back almost 3000 years. The metal-working skills of the Precolumbian civilisations of Central and South America, as they learnt how to fashion gold with much the same techniques as the Mediterranean world have already been described in the previous chapter. When Francisco Pizarro and his tiny band of 198 foot soldiers and 62 horsemen fought their way into Peru in 1532, the Inca Empire, ruled by Atahualpa, was at its height, having conquered the Chimu people sixty years earlier. The Chimu had brought Precolumbian craftsmanship to its peak; the Incas not only captured their treasures in gold, but moved many of their goldsmiths to their capital, Cuzco, in the central Andes.

What confronted Pizarro and his men, first at the Inca provincial capital of Cajamarca and then at Cuzco itself, was the fruit of well over 500 years' labour by goldsmiths. Life size figures of men and women, great jars and pitchers half of pottery and half gold, vases sculpted in relief with birds, animals and insects, a golden crayfish, and gold shoes like fashionable half boots. By the Temple of the Sun at Cuzco, its walls encased in sheets of gold, was a garden of golden plants and maize with silver stems and golden ears. To the Incas and all Precolumbian cultures before them, gold was an object of religious veneration; the concept of money did not occur to them. To their Spanish conquerors, the gold spelt money and went into the melting pot. As a young priest, Cristobal de Molina, travelling with Pizarro, sadly observed, "Their only concern was to collect gold and silver to make themselves all rich … without thinking that they were doing wrong and wrecking and destroying. For what was being destroyed was more perfect than anything they enjoyed and possessed".[5]

The collection and melting at Cajamarca of the ransom in gold for the emperor Atahualpa lasted from March to July 1533 and ended, not with his release, but his execution. The ransom yielded 5 m.t/160,000 t.oz of gold at 22.5 carats (935.5 fine). A second melt at Cuzco later in 1533 provided a further two m.t/66,500 t.oz of gold.

The first Peruvian gold came up in the Guadalquivir river to Seville on 5th December 1533 and was unloaded by the *Torre del Oro* (which probably won its nickname at that time), and transferred to the House of Trade. Three more treasure ships arrived early in January 1534. The city was agog. The treasurer at the House of Trade said, "The quantity of gold that arrives every day from the Indies, especially from Peru, is quite incredible; I think that if this torrent of gold lasts even ten years, this city will become the richest in the world".[6] And a thankful Emperor Charles V murmured, "I am extremely pleased at the timely arrival of gold from Peru – a great help for our present needs". A coded way of acknowledging the gold as a vital asset in securing and expanding his disparate Hapsburg Empire embracing not just Spain, but the Netherlands and parts of Austria, Hungary and Italy.

Hysteria gripped the populace. "Driven mad by greed, many priests and Spaniards and ladies and merchants took ship for Peru," wrote the early Spanish historian, Felipe Guaman Poma de Ayala. They were interested, he added, neither in the country nor the people of the Americas, but only in their gold.[7]

The result was the first intercontinental gold rush, foreshadowing what was to happen three centuries later when gold was discovered in California and Australia. But the surge in gold output was relatively short-lived. Half of all the gold imported into Seville in the entire 16th century, arrived in just three decades, 1530–60.[8] Moreover, much of this came from further looting, rather than mining; "mining" often meant the opening up of ancient tombs in search of gold among the burial goods. In New Granada (Colombia) alone, three expeditions in the 1530s picked up over 1.5 m.t/48,225 t.oz, including 836 kg/26,900 t.oz of ornaments from Zenu tombs ransacked by Pedro de Heredia, governor of Cartagena. Added to the melted Peruvian gold from Cajamarca and Cuzco, this alone accounts for 8.5 m.t/273,275 t.oz, or 60% of all official gold imports to Seville during the decade. Given that later widespread looting in Peru, where the Spanish installed a smelter in the Moche valley to melt down ornaments from the Pyramid of the Sun and other tombs, and similar pillaging in Colombia and Central America, such treasure probably made up over three-quarters of all incoming gold in the mid-16th century. Thus the gold from the New World largely supplemented mine output elsewhere, rather than expanding world production. The real transformation took place in silver production which rose ninefold between 1500 and 1600, while annual world gold output was up less than 50% by 1600.

Even so, the administration of the goldfields in the Americas, mostly still alluvial along the banks of rivers, became more organised. In Peru, private individuals could stake claims, but were bound by oath to bring gold to the royal assay offices in Lima, where it was assayed (not always accurately), cast in marked bars and 'quinted' (the royal one-fifth). Officials there also made sure they took their own salaries in gold. As a result, the King's quint was sometimes remitted solely in silver. Miners themselves often delivered the gold initially to financiers who had 'grub-staked' them or sold it (no doubt at knock-down prices) to itinerant dealers touring the mining areas. Transport in and out of the mining areas was by the llama, that ubiquitous Andean pack animal. Ultimately, the gold was shipped from the port of Callao near Lima, up to Panama and across the isthmus to Portobelo or Nombre de Dios, where treasure fleets assembled for the Atlantic crossing. Colombian gold, coming from such long-established Precolumbian mining centres of alluvial and quartz vein gold as Buritica on the river Cauca and Ibaque on the river Magdalena which the Spanish sought to exploit, was dispatched from Cartagena.

Treasure fleets to Seville

The treasure fleets themselves were well organised, especially as the volume of silver picked up dramatically after 1560, with the opening up of mines at Zacatecas in Mexico and at the great Potosi deposit in Bolivia. The amalgamation process of silver with mercury for more efficient recovery was also introduced in Mexico in 1557, and adopted at Potosi in 1571 after the discovery of the Huancevalica quicksilver deposit nearby in Peru provided ample local supplies of mercury.

The rapid expansion of silver output, tripling in the 1560s alone, and tripling again by the end of the century, had important consequences for gold. The abundance of silver widened the gold/silver ratio from 1:10.7 to 1:12 by the 1570s, making gold the more desirable metal to hold.

The destination of both gold and silver remained exclusively the House of Trade in Seville. Even if ships were blown off course and ended up in other Spanish harbours, the bullion had to be forwarded to Seville. Elaborate precautions were taken to prevent bullion being smuggled ashore as the fleet approached mainland Spain. Fishermen were forbidden to take their boats out to meet the incoming treasure fleet on pain of two hundred lashes and ten years as a galley slave. When the fleet arrived at San Lucar de Barrameda, the fishing port at the mouth of the river Guadalquivir, officials from the House of Trade and the Council of the Indies were first aboard. All travellers had to swear an oath that they had no unquinted gold or silver (or pearls).[9] As an additional control, once the quantities of silver increased, each fleet had a Silver Master, to whom both colonial officials and private passengers were supposed to deliver all bullion for the voyage. The Silver Master took a fee of 1% of all transactions.

Did these precautions contain smuggling? The sheer weight of silver, usually in large bars, made it harder to conceal, but gold was easily hidden in clothing and no doubt slipped through with officers, crew and passengers. Losses also occurred when vessels foundered (thus keeping modern treasure-seekers in the underwater recovery business), but a copy of the register of what was aboard each ship was dispatched on another, so that a record existed even if it vanished. The treasure fleet was natural prey for Dutch, English and French privateers, but apparently they were often thwarted. Documents at the House of Trade note many abortive attacks, but only in 1628 and 1658 were significant amounts captured.

On arrival at the House of Trade, the gold and silver was weighed by the *balanzario*, recorded, and placed in the treasure vault in triple-locked chests, a key held respectively by the *contador*, factor and *tesorero*. The control of parcels was now transferred from the Silver Master to the private owners. The House supervised the refining and assaying of the metal. The refining was done by local merchants, "usually," Earl Hamilton observed wryly, "with their wives, children and servants doing all the work". Sale by contract or public auction then took place to professional bullion merchants, *compradores de oro y plata*. At a sale on 14th August 1531, seven *compradores* made 24 bids for a shipment of gold, usually then contracting to deliver it to the Seville mint next door for coinage.

As the flow of bullion increased, so the auctions became more elaborate. A House of Trade document on gold brought in by Rodríguez Marcos, captain of a caravel, recorded, "We offered the said gold for sale at public auction in the presence of many merchants of gold and silver and sold it to Luis Hernández, the highest bidder, at 25½ maravedis per carat, plus one *ducat* over the amount offered for sale. The value of the gold is to be delivered to the treasurer of the mint of this city in gold of the fineness for coining *escudos*, within six days".

The *escudo* (*crown*), launched by Charles V in 1537, weighed 3.38 grams/0.109 t.oz with a gold content of 916 fine. Those specifications lasted for a hundred years, making the Spanish *crown* as well known in Europe as the Venetian *ducat*. Initially, its value was 350 maravedis, but was raised to 400 maravedis in 1566 by Philip II in recognition of gold's appreciation against the surge of silver coming from the Americas. The revaluation demonstrates the price revolution in Spain, and beyond, caused by bullion from the New World. While the bulk of *escudos* were minted in Seville, Charles V occasionally showed impatience at delays, sending gold instead to be minted at the Barcelona mint.

Gold as the sinews of war

Through the growing trail of Spanish *escudos*, we can track Spain's new-found wealth across Europe, and see how it was squandered on endless military expeditions. As Earl Hamilton put it, "Historians have generally agreed that American gold and silver fanned the flames of Hapsburg imperialism, added to the zeal with which Spanish rulers defended the Catholic faith against Protestant and Mohammedan, furnished sinews of war and, in short, constituted an important factor in Spain's aggressive foreign policy".[10]

Despite consistent Spanish attempts to limit the re-export of gold, it filtered swiftly into the monetary network of Europe and the Mediterranean world, including North Africa. Charles V (1516–56) himself used gold to set up credits with the banking families of Antwerp, Augsberg and Genoa who, in turn, opened representative offices in Seville. Precious metals were a monarch's best credentials. In England, Elizabeth I realised this when she came to the throne in 1558 and at once set about restoring the gold content of the *angels* and *crowns*, which had been debased by her father, Henry VIII. A Venetian writer in the early 17th century even ventured that precious metal was "the sinews of all government, it gives it its pulse, its movement, its mind, soul and it is its essence and its very life … it overcomes all impossibilities, for it is the master, the patron of all".[11] Such sentiment was a trifle over the top, but a widely held view at the time. Fernand Braudel, that acute French observer of Mediterranean economies, noted, "The role of precious metals had never seemed more important than in the 16th century".[12] Certainly, Charles V and his son, Philip II (1556–98) would have agreed.

Charles V, who succeeded unexpectedly to the Spanish throne in 1516 after a swift series of family fatalities, then became Emperor of the entire Hapsburg realm in 1519. This "vast disjointed empire", as one historian put it, stretched along the Mediterranean to Sardinia, Sicily and Naples, east to Bohemia, Austria and Hungary, and north to parts of Germany and the Netherlands, not forgetting the new lands of Mexico and South America. The peoples were different in tradition, and tension was heightened by a growing schism between Catholic and Protestant in northern Europe. Charles V (himself born in Flanders and speaking only French when he first visited Spain) had somehow to consolidate and hopefully expand this inheritance. In Spain he was accepted because he did not challenge Spanish tradition, harnessed the power of the church, and made an astute marriage to Isabella of Portugal. But his energies were constantly taxed in trying to master his immense domain and, in particular, by his determination to uphold the supremacy of the Catholic Church against the new Protestant order. In that pursuit the gold from the Americas (most of which arrived in his reign, while silver really followed under his son, Philip II) was life-blood. Indeed, it is debatable what both rulers could have achieved without the metals. All Europe saw Spain as a convenient reservoir of precious metals which were soaked up as by a sponge. The French ambassador in Paris wrote to Philip II in 1577, "In all the kingdom I see almost no money besides Spanish *reals, escudos* and *doubloons*, not to mention large quantities smelted every day in order to coin other money [i.e. French]".[13]

The gold couriers

The preference for gold was marked under both rulers, because of the devaluation of silver as supplies soared and the difficulty of transporting it in quantity except by sea. Shipment became increasingly hazardous during Philip II's long stand-off with Elizabeth I, as English warships patrolled the English Channel picking off ships from the annual treasure fleet from Cadiz to Antwerp, bearing silver to pay for Spain's military campaigns in the Netherlands and Germany. Re-routing silver along the Mediterranean to Genoa and thence overland to the Netherlands was tedious. So gold, so easily concealed, was spirited instead all over Europe. Over 400,000 Spanish *escudos* weighing 1,350 kg/43,400 t.oz were smuggled across France to Lyons in 1567, hidden in bales of leather.[14]

Officially, Philip II resorted to sending couriers to the Netherlands, each with 5,000 gold *escudos* sewn into their garments. This burden of almost 17 kg/550 t.oz, presumably worn for days on horseback, compares favourably with modern gold smugglers on aircraft who regularly carried up to 30 kg in special jackets before the days of airport security. By such subterfuge, Philip II was able to slip the Duke of Alva a quick 40,000 *escudos* in 1572 to meet urgent military expenses. Alternatively, he sent the gold by sea in fast galleys to Genoa, whence it was transferred onward overland to the Netherlands. During the 1580s and 90s the galleys sometimes carried 200,000 *escudos* at a time to Genoa, while the Fugger banking house on occasion lent Philip up to 1,500,000 *escudos* (5 m.t./160,000 t.oz.) payable in Italy and Germany.

The size of these gold shipments has an important implication – more gold was coming into Spain unofficially from the Americas. The official imports, as listed by Hamilton, drop sharply between 1560 and 1590. This is partly explained by the shift in silver mining, but if couriers in Europe could carry 5,000 *escudos* in hidden pockets, so could passengers from the New World. Thus, more gold probably arrived in this period than official statistics indicate. Moreover, besides the King's transfers, foreign merchants resident in Spain regularly sent gold coin home; coin they could have acquired in a parallel market. Unfortunately, regular annual mint production statistics have not survived before 1590; they would have provided a good comparison against imports. Fernand Braudel's explanation is that Europe's gold supply was only "meagrely replenished from the New World, so existing gold reserves were drawn down".[15] Certainly, taking the whole 16th century, the average annual official supply from the New World was only 1.6 m.t./50,000 t.oz. Even with unofficial imports providing another few hundred kilograms each year, this was no great augmentation to annual world supplies, which were around 4.7 m.t./ 150,000 t.oz. in 1500 and perhaps 6.5–7 m.t./210,000–225,000 t.oz. in 1600. By comparison, silver output, up almost ninefold in the same period, had entered an entirely new dimension.

The relative scarcity of gold is confirmed by limited gold coin minting in Europe (outside Spain) in the 16th century. Whereas two hundred years earlier the gold mining boom in Hungary had spurred minting not just in Venice, but in France, Flanders and England. This time the only significant move to upgrade gold coinage in England was Elizabeth I's launch of new *angels* and *crowns* in 1558, which happened to coincide with the peak decade of Spanish imports, implying more gold around for a bolder coinage venture. After 1560, however, the English gold coinage was usually under 300 kg/10,000 t.oz annually, reflecting the fading supply from the Americas.

Given that perspective, a preference for gold in face of rising silver flows is understandable. "In a period of silver inflation," Fernand Braudel summed it up, "gold became the safe investment, the metal that was hoarded and the one used for international payments. Unless specifying the contrary, Bills of Exchange were payable in gold. It was gold coin, too, that Flanders' army demanded to be paid, if not in full, at least in part. And finally, gold was the only metal that could be carried by courier".[16]

The message was also that silver was not much use to Spanish kings trying to hold together a fragmented, unstable empire across Europe. The historian Carlos Pereyra dubbed the Netherlands "Spain's folly", swallowing her American treasure in hopeless campaigns, when it might have been better employed at home building up new enterprises. Ultimately, Dutch protestant determination triumphed. In the wake of Spain's withdrawal, the Netherlands came into its own, with Amsterdam establishing itself as the emporium of northern Europe, setting the stage for both the Dutch and English East India companies to take over the silver trade from Venice and Genoa in the 17th century. Their success in forging the new silver route round Africa to India and beyond to pay for the luxuries of the east set the pattern for precious metals for the next three centuries. Europe might favour gold; the east had an endless appetite for silver.

The narrowing girdle of the gold/silver ratio around the globe pointed the way: 1:15 in Mexico or Bolivia, 1:12 in Europe, 1:10 in India, 1:4 in China. No wonder the Spanish sent an annual silver fleet direct from Acapulco on Mexico's Pacific shore to the Philippines for onward shipment to China.

Gold, on the other hand, became less and less of a lifeline for Spain. Although official imports were strong in the 1590s, and modest for the first two decades of the 17th century, they tailed off sharply from 1630 and were almost non-existent between 1651–60, the last decade monitored by Earl Hamilton. Indeed, in the 160 years he accounted for, a mere 15% of the gold arrived between 1601 and 1660; while almost 25% came in the single decade 1551–60, and 45% in 1531–60. In that perspective, Spain's 'golden age' was remarkably transient and accounted for in significant quantity by looted gold, not new production. Indeed, throughout the 16th century as much energy went into trying to find more tombs to ransack, if not the mythical El Dorado, as actually opening up new mining areas. The greatest efforts went into trying to drain Lake Guatavita, a small, circular lake just north of the present Bogotá, into which offerings in gold had been poured for generations from a raft on the lake at the inauguration of each new Muisca ruler (*see previous chapter*). Exhaustive attempts were made to drain the lake in 1545 and 1586, when a notch was cut in the surrounding rim. This lowered the level by 20 metres before the outflowing water eroded the cut, causing it to collapse. A mere 50kg/1,600 t.oz. of ornaments were recovered. Yet that only seemed to provide more incentive; for almost 400 years successive expeditions sought to recover the treasure of Lake Guatavita until, in 1965, the Colombian government finally brought the lake under protection, as part of the country's heritage.[17]

The sharp drop in official imports after 1600 probably reflected more smuggling, and less ancient treasures located. By the 17th century treasure fleets were often fitted out by Spanish merchants themselves, making it easier to avoid official declaration and the royal 'quint'. Yet even if smuggling channelled half of all supplies, overall output was limited. The reality was that no important gold discoveries were made. Output was on hold for a century. Not until the late 1690s did Minas Gerais province in Brazil turn up trumps, but that was to the benefit of the Portuguese and British empires, since most of the gold swiftly ended up in London. Marking time in the 17th century might be labelled 'waiting for the gold standard'.

Part Four
Gold Standard: Whence it Came, Where it Went (1700 - 2000)

CHAPTER 19

Britain and Brazil: The 'Accidental' Gold Standard

In the closing years of the 17th century a recoinage in England, the appointment of Sir Isaac Newton to the Mint in London, the founding of the Bank of England, and a gold rush in Brazil combined, each in their own way, to foster a new era in gold. The fragile, and accidental, child was the gold standard that, for the next two hundred years and more, was to provide the basic monetary system, initially uniquely for Britain, but ultimately for most nations, save China. The essence of the standard being a fixed price for gold, gold coin either forming the major circulation of currency within a country or with notes redeemable in gold, coupled with free import and export and all balance of payments deficits settled in the metal.

The word 'accidental' is apt because neither the institutions nor persons involved had the slightest intention of creating a new monetary standard based on gold. Indeed, the main purpose, even of Sir Isaac, great mathematician and physicist though he was, was to sustain silver as the prime coinage of the land. What was misjudged consistently over the next twenty years was that old rogue 'market forces' because many people in Britain realised it was more profitable to hold gold coin, while silver went into the melting pot and was shipped off by the East India Company to India and China where it commanded a better price.

That was nothing new. Ever since the price of silver in Europe had been devalued after 1560 by the tidal wave of silver being mined by Spain first in Mexico and then at Potosi in Bolivia (*see chapter 18*), it had normally been more profitable to dispatch it to the east, where it was more highly valued, to pay for silks and other luxury goods. This trend continued throughout the 17th century as the Dutch and English East India Companies expanded their trading links with India, Java (Indonesia), China and Japan. Silver also remained the prime coinage circulating in Britain and Europe, partly because the new gold supplies from the New World had been relatively limited (except between 1530–60), and because it was more practical in paying for day-to-day purchases. Gold's function was primarily for settling transactions between banking houses or merchants, or hoarded by wealthy men against dangerous days. Samuel Pepys recorded in his diary on 12th June 1667 that, after the Dutch fleet sailed up the Medway and London seemed threatened, he sent his wife and father into the country with £1,300 in gold coin, and had a special money belt made in which he could carry another £300 in gold, presumably the newly issued *guineas*, in case he had to flee the city.

Annual gold production through much of the 17th century was a modest eight or nine m.t/275,000 t.oz. The output was chiefly in West Africa and Colombia, with the Nambu mine in Japan also contributing nearly one m.t./32,000 t.oz. by 1640.[1] This was not enough to sustain widely circulating gold currencies. Although the *guinea* (8.7 grams/0.27 t.oz at 916.6 fine), named after Guinea on Africa's 'gold coast', was launched in England in 1663, only modest amounts were minted; scarcely eight m.t/255,000 t.oz of gold went into *guineas* in the first ten years. Moreover, they circulated little at home, the majority being exported. The Royal Africa Company, which was importing gold dust from Guinea, re-exported *guineas* to meet its overseas expenses, as did the East India Company, especially between 1671 and 1685, when a shift in the gold/silver ratio in India made it briefly more profitable to send gold. These shipments (the East India Company sent almost seven m.t/225,000 t.oz of gold between 1681–85) reflected, too, a rise in gold output, with the new Espiritu Santo mine in Colombia briefly producing over three m.t/100,000 t.oz by 1680.

Such exports kept gold coin circulation in England low, compared with silver. Sir Isaac Newton once calculated that, in 1688, total gold coin circulating was worth just over £5 million, compared with nearly £14 million in silver.[2] Later historians have suggested the domestic gold coin circulation was as low as £3 million. Even so, there had been an inexorable rise in the minting of gold coin since the mid-1670s; 45% of all gold coin struck in the entire 17th century was made after 1675, while little silver had gone to the mint. In short, there was already a subtle swing to gold.

The great recoinage 1696–9

The concern, however, was with silver, not gold. Silver had been the basic money standard metal for centuries. "In all men's minds the only true money of the country was the silver coin – crowns, half-crowns, shillings and sixpences," remarked Sir John Craig, the Mint's great historian.[3] But by the 1690s the silver coin in circulation was worn thin, often half its original weight and had been extensively clipped. Coins dating back to the Plantagenet kings of the 14th century were still used. Forgeries abounded. Thus, in 1694, a committee of the House of Commons recommended, "the best way to prevent clipping the Silver Coin of the Kingdom for the future is to new coin (*sic*) the same into milled money". The technique of 'milling' the rim of coins to prevent clipping had been perfected by a French engineer, Pierre Blondeau, for the Paris Mint in 1639 and adopted by the Mint in London in 1663. The recoinage was to be paid for by the public through a tax on the windows of their homes (to this day, windows of some 17th century houses are still bricked up).

The tax was necessary because the worn and clipped silver coin was being called in at face value and the government had to make up the silver deficiency; a detail that illustrates the different status of gold and silver. Both metals were accepted at the Mint for coinage and both were accepted in payment of debts and were legal tender to any amount, but there was no fixed rate value for gold coins. The price of the *guinea* floated. That paved the way to the 'accidental' gold standard.

Even before the Great Recoinage was announced by Parliament, the price of the *guinea* had been edging up because the poor condition and shortage of silver coin had encouraged people to prefer gold for many transactions.[4] The actual legislation prompted fears that silver would be written down, causing a rush for *guineas* that pushed the coin's nominal value of £1 up to 30 shillings (£1.50). The soaring price attracted foreign gold coin from all over Europe that was melted down and sent to the Mint for coinage. The Mint struck over half a million *guineas* in 1695, the year before the recoinage officially started, compared with scarcely 45,000 the previous year. The Treasury, alarmed that all the silver in the country would be melted down and exported against gold, persuaded Parliament to order the price of *guineas* down to 22 shillings (£1.10) each by mid-1696 Even then, the *guinea* was still over-valued.

The recoinage itself began with the first new silver coin struck on 23rd January 1696, and available in the market on 8th February. Five local mints were set up to expedite the task.[5] As worn silver coins came in, the need for recoinage was swiftly proved. In the first six months the coins traded in were found to have lost 47% of their weight; the Exchequer took in over £4.6 million at face value, but the silver was worth a mere £2.5 million. One-sixth of the returned coins were judged counterfeit. In all, £10 million worth of silver (at face value) was returned during 1696 alone. By the end of 1697, the Mint had used nearly 466 m.t/15 million t.oz of silver (equal to one year's world production), and 90% of the work was done. Relatively little silver was recoined in the next two years.[6] Yet Mint output lagged behind demand and many people had difficulty in exchanging old coins for new within the deadline set. Bullion dealers in London continued to receive silver coin for melt, which they bought by weight, not face value, for several years. People who could lay their hands on new coins found them handsome – and ideal for export, often after melting. While the tired old coins had previously had little acceptance abroad, the bright new ones were welcome. More significantly, while the Mint paid five shillings and two pence (£0.26) per ounce, the market price was invariably two or three pence higher, stimulated by Indian demand. The East India Company was regularly shipping over 31 m.t./one million t.oz. annually.[7]

After the initial new issue of silver coin, therefore, no incentive existed to take silver to the Mint for coining; it was more profitable to dispose of it directly in the market. Gold, by contrast, was over-valued at the Mint, at 22 shillings (£1.10), so the profitable thing was to have it coined. The proportion of gold coin in circulation in relation to silver, which had started to rise even before the recoinage, thus became more pronounced year by year. Sir Isaac Newton, who had become Warden of the Mint just as the recoinage started in 1696, and Master three years later, calculated that even by 1698 more gold than silver was circulating within the country; a complete reversal of the situation just ten years earlier.[8] England was on the way to being on a gold, rather than a silver, standard. Significantly, a further attempt was made to fix the price of gold by writing down the value of the *guinea* again in 1699 to twenty-one shillings and six pence (£1.075), but that still left it slightly more highly priced than its equivalent in rival European gold coins. Consequently, as one economic historian put it, "Had (the Mint) valued silver slightly higher than the market, England would have had a flourishing silver coinage. England went over gradually to the gold standard by default".[9]

The fascinating thing is that this swing to gold, while naturally debated, was seen as a temporary phenomenon, not a permanent structural change in the English monetary system. Silver was still regarded as the standard of value and the monetary metal by most observers. The issue was how to restore its domestic appeal without a formal devaluation. Any numbers of alternative suggestions were ignored in the hope that the gold/silver balance might somehow right itself. But in South America a new contributor to the equation, Brazil, was emerging. One requirement of a gold standard is the gold itself. The Romans had been able to pay their legions in gold coin because they tapped new supplies in Spain and elsewhere. The gold mining boom in Hungary in the 1420s had helped underwrite the power of Venice (*see chapter 16*). And the ultimate triumph of the gold standard in the late 19th century was on the back of Californian, Australian and then South African discoveries providing a new dimension to gold supplies. Now, the Portuguese colony of Brazil stepped on stage with a gold mining boom that lasted more than sixty years. Much of that gold turned up in London to nourish the gold standard.

Gold rush in Brazil

The first word filtered down to Rio de Janeiro from the high, thickly-wooded country beyond the Serre da Mantiqueira two hundred miles inland some time in 1694. Alluvial gold had been found in Minas Gerais province at Itavevera near the headwaters of the Rio Das Velhas, a tributary of Rio São Francisco. Then came news of more finds at Tabuate, and of 'steel coloured' gold at Ouro Preto, off the Rio Carmo. By 1697 the governor of Rio de Janeiro was writing to the King in Lisbon that new diggings at Caete, "extend in such fashion along the mountain ranges that the miners are led to believe that the gold in that region will last a great length of time".[10]

For once, gold diggers, ever optimistic, were right. The gold brought a new dimension to world output, which more than doubled within a few decades; by 1750 Brazil was contributing 65% of all production. During the 18th century Brazil's total output was between 900–1,000 m.t./28.9–32.1 million t.oz., four times what Spain got from its American colonies in the entire 16th and 17th centuries.

Not only was world output higher than at any time in history, but the level was sustained for much of the 18th century, unlike some earlier gold rushes which had soon exhausted deposits. In Brazil, decade after decade, new alluvial deposits kept turning up, first in Minas Gerais, then ever westwards into Goiás and the Matto Grosso. Every river, stream and brook coming down the flanks of the Sierra do Espinhaca, the oldest geological formation in Brazil, had payable gold. It gleamed in the stream beds. The diggers called the deposits *faisgueiras* because the larger particles glittered in the sun; the diggers themselves were christened *faisqueiros*.[11] (The nickname *garimpeiros* applied today originally referred only to diamond miners, after diamonds were found in Minas Gerais in 1723.) Once the stream beds were cleaned out, the *faisqueiros* ferreted out deposits in the banks and in clefts in the hills.

The first discoveries were by the roving bands of adventurers known as *Paulistas*, many of whom were deserters or fugitives, often of mixed Portuguese-Amerindian blood. They were soon joined by swarms of gold-seekers trekking up wilderness trails or along rivers from Rio de Janeiro, São Paulo and Bahia. The Jesuit priest Antonil, who spent forty years living in Bahia, wrote, "Each year a crowd of Portuguese and of foreigners come out in the fleets in order to go to the Mines. From the cities, towns, plantations, and backlands of Brazil come White, Coloured, and Blacks, together with Amerindians employed by the *Paulistas*. The mixture is of all sorts and conditions of persons: men and women; young and old; poor and rich; nobles and commoners; laymen, clergy, and religious of different orders".[12] The governor of Rio was less generous, accusing the miners of depopulating farms and ranches and "leading a licentious and unchristian life". Many brought with them African slaves who were either already working Brazil's sugar and tobacco plantations or newly shipped across the Atlantic. The slaves toiled, while their masters, as the Jesuit Antonil put it, led "louche lives". The slaves, often from West Africa where alluvial gold was common, were familiar with processes for washing and panning. They used a *bateia*, a shallow, cone-shaped basin of wood or metal in which the gravelly subsoil mixed with quartz that contained the gold was just covered with water. The *bateia* was gently rotated, with the water and quartz gradually tipped out, while the gold sank to the bottom. It was remarkably pure; usually 896–937 fine.[13]

An English traveller, John Mawe, who visited the diggings a century later, described a scene that can have changed little. "Suppose a loose, gravel-like stratum of rounded quartzose pebbles … covered by earthy matter. Where water of sufficiently high level can be commanded, the ground is cut in steps … Near the bottom a trench is cut to the depth of two or three feet. On each step stand six or eight Negroes who, as the water flows gently from above, keep the earth continually in motion with shovels, until the whole is reduced to liquid mud and washed below. The particles of gold contained in this earth descend to the trench where, by reason of their specific gravity, they quickly precipitate."[14]

Gold output rose swiftly, as up to 50,000 people worked the mining areas by 1705. Statistics are hard to confirm because much gold went undeclared to avoid the official levy of one-fifth for the king – the royal *quinto*. Smuggling back to Portugal was also relatively easy. Official shipments to Lisbon have been traced as 725 kg/23,300 t.oz. in 1699, 1,785 kg/57,400 t.oz. by 1701, and 4,350 kg/140,000 t.oz. in 1703.[15] Such amounts are realistic, but may be understated; caution is needed because over the years quantities were both exaggerated by some and under-estimated by others. Ultimately, the onward shipments to Britain, which became the main destination over the next seventy years, are a useful guide, because of the complete annual coinage figures at the Mint, which essentially used Brazilian gold.

Back in Brazil, confirmation of the blossoming mining industry was the establishment of the *Casa de Moeda* (mint) in Rio de Janeiro in 1702 (it struck 77,760 coins using 900 kg/30,000 t.oz. in its first two years) and a new Mining Code issued the same year. The Code stipulated that the first person to discover a new deposit had the right to stake two *datas* (claims), while a third was assigned to the Crown and a fourth to the Crown's representative. Each *data* was thirty square *bracas* (a *braca* being a fathom or six feet/1.84 metres). The Crown's *data* was auctioned to the highest bidder. All other *datas* were assigned by drawing lots, with the area depending on the number of slaves each master employed, with two square *bracas* per slave.[16] Such regulation was partly aimed at securing the Crown's *quinto*; the miners were supposed to bring dust or nuggets to designated smelting houses, or the Rio Mint, where the royal slice could be taken. Everyone tried to avoid it. Alternatives, such as capitation tax per *data* or per slave, did not work, because one claim might yield much more than another. Smuggling of unrefined gold dust down to the coast was rife. Itinerant friars were even suborned to carry gold dust out of the mining region concealed in the hollow images of saints, which became known as *santos de pau ouro*. To halt the traffic, a decree was issued forbidding the establishment of any religious orders in Minas Gerais. Even so, the local governor conceded that 60% of the *quintos reais* was never collected by the Crown's agents. Another official pragmatically observed, "Is it to be expected that anyone would voluntarily deprive himself of a fifth part of his capital, when he can conceal it with little risk and trouble?"[17]

One fact is not in doubt. Substantial amounts of gold were arriving in Lisbon on the annual fleets bearing gold, sugar, tobacco and other products from Brazil. The English consul in Lisbon reported to London in 1710, "I am assured that by the most modest computation the Fleet brings in gold the value of fifteen millions of cruzados".[18] This implies about 13.4 m.t./430,000 t.oz. of gold; a significant amount for a single season. Gossip on the Lisbon exchange may have exaggerated but, clearly, it was a huge consignment –virtually what was landed in Seville in the entire decade 1531–40, when the first major shipments came from in the New World (*see chapter 18*). In Lisbon, most of the gold was coined into *moedas de ouro*, or *moydores*, as they became known in Britain, whither most were destined.[19]

Portugal, like Spain before it, really became just a conduit for gold – but with one key difference. Spain had squandered gold on war and empire-building; Portugal was an importer of everything from cereals, beef and fish, to English woollen goods, manufactured articles and luxuries. This imbalance of trade was largely settled in gold (and later, diamonds). The English consul noted some years later that Portugal imported five times as much from Britain as it exported to it, with the balance paid in gold. The evidence in Britain itself was swiftly apparent. Since most of the coin taken aboard Royal Navy ships, returning East Indiamen, and the regular Lisbon-Falmouth packet boat, landed in Falmouth or Plymouth, *moydores* soon circulated widely in the West of England. An Exeter man wrote in 1713, "We have hardly any money current among us but Portugal gold".[20] In London, the Mint was busy melting *moydores* and making *guineas*. In the four years beginning 1713 the Mint transformed over 37 m.t/1.2 million t.oz of gold into *guineas*; in 1715 alone they used over 13.5 m.t/434,000 t.oz. which matches the amount in the Lisbon consul's report a few years earlier. Given that not all the Brazilian gold ended up in Britain, and some circulated as *moydores*, this is hard evidence of the amounts now available from the gold rush. In Britain, so much gold coin had never been minted before, naturally raising questions. Sir Isaac Newton was called upon by Parliament to investigate both the state of gold and silver coins in the country and their proportionate values in different currencies.

Sir Isaac Newton pronounces

By this time, Sir Isaac Newton had been at the Mint for twenty-one years, first as Warden, then as Master. He had thus been a close observer since the Great Recoinage when gold had first become over-valued. In his initial report to the Treasury in September 1717, he stressed the continued profit in sending silver out of Europe, where gold/silver ratio was 1:15. "In China and Japan, one pound weight of fine gold is worth but nine or ten pounds of fine silver," he pointed out, "and in East India it may be worth twelve. And this low price of gold in proportion to silver carries away the silver from all Europe."[21] This flow could be stemmed, Newton argued, only if the gold/silver ratio in Britain and Europe could be narrowed, effectively reducing the value of gold. One way to do this was to lower officially the price of the gold *guinea*, but initially Newton did not urge this course. He believed that silver was already in short supply and that market forces would shortly correct the imbalance. "If this be let alone till silver money be a little scarcer," he advised, "the Gold will fall of itself. For people are already backward to give silver for Gold, and will in a little time refuse to make payments in silver without a premium … and this premium will be an abatement in the value of Gold." Newton had a point. The market price for silver had crept slightly to five shillings and four pence (£0.28) per troy ounce, although the Mint price was still only five shillings and two pence (£0.26). Merchants in the City of London were building positions, anticipating a further rise. Abraham Mocatta, soon to become precious metals broker to the Bank of England, built up a position at the Bank of over 31.1 m.t/one million t.oz during this period on behalf of an unknown client. Curiously, the fact that silver production in Mexico had been increasing almost as rapidly as gold output in Brazil was not mentioned. Output in Zacatecas province had already doubled and continued to rise fast throughout the 18th century. Both precious metals were plentiful.

Newton did not address this issue; nowhere do the high flows of gold from Brazil or silver from Mexico enter the debate. However, in a fresh report to parliament in December 1717, Newton noted that, in the previous fifteen years, the value of gold coinage at the Mint was thirty times that of silver. Most members of Parliament were of the opinion that it was the over-valuation of gold that was leading to an excessive drain of silver from the country. During the parliamentary debate it came out that not only was there smuggling of silver coin out of the country, but unofficially imported gold was minted into *guineas* at a profit of fifteen pence (£0.06) on each coin. Parliament resolved that action was required to write down gold. On 22nd December 1717 George I issued a proclamation forbidding anyone to take a *guinea* at a price higher than 21 shillings (£1.05), thus reducing its value by six pence. The new maximum price was to be observed "upon pain of our highest displeasure and upon pain of the greatest punishment that by law may be inflicted on them for their default". The key phrase is 'maximum price'. The King was not setting a *fixed* price, merely the maximum. But it was this price of £3.17s.10½d (£3.89) per standard ounce of 916 gold in which the *guinea* was minted, equivalent to a fine gold price of £4.4s.11½d (£4.25), that was to be the benchmark for gold for over two hundred years. This gold standard might be unofficial, even accidental, but it was here to stay. Yet still no one thought in those terms. John Conduitt, Newton's successor at the Mint, observed a few years later, "Gold is only looked on as a commodity, and so should rise or fall as occasion requires. An ounce of fine silver is, and always has been and ought to be, the standing and invariable measure between nation and nation".[22]

The writing down of the *guinea* indeed strengthened the market price of silver to five shillings and seven pence (£0.28) per ounce, but since the Mint price for buying silver for coinage remained unchanged at five shillings and two pence (£0.26), there was no incentive to send silver there. The East India Company dispatched it to India as before – over 62 m.t/2 million t.oz in 1718. The Mint carried on with gold *guineas*, striking over 650,000 in 1719 and 840,000 in 1720. "With every decade the *guinea* becomes more surely the typical English coin for important transactions," wrote Sir John Clapham, in his *History of the Bank of England*, "although well into the 19th century England was not technically on a gold standard."[23] The Bank itself, the fourth protagonist in the rise of the 'accidental' gold standard, now came centre-stage as its manager.

The Bank of England as manager

Within a year of its foundation in 1694, the Bank of England had first instructed its Committee-in-Waiting to "buy gold and silver on the best terms it can for the service of the Bank".[24]   It was not involved, however, in the Great Recoinage then taking place, but by 1700 was eager to establish itself as the central depot for treasure. A committee was set up to consider the best method of buying gold for coinage. It was an auspicious moment. The following year the Mint bought almost 9.5 m.t/305,000 t.oz of gold to strike *guineas*, part of it supplied by the Bank. Thereafter the Bank became increasingly the turntable for Brazilian and other gold (chiefly from West Africa) arriving in London. In 1711, as the Duke of Marlborough's campaigns in the War of the Spanish Succession were ending, the Bank's Committee was buying "any quantities … to be coyned as it comes in".[25] Couriers were even sent to Chatham and other naval dockyards to meet incoming men-of-war that might have picked up gold in Lisbon. During the war, the Royal Navy had sometimes escorted the annual treasure fleet from Brazil to Lisbon, an indication how important the gold was in underwriting the war effort. The Bank also bought its gold from a variety of merchants and brokers, both as coin (usually the ubiquitous *moydores*) and bar, sent it to the Mint, and took it back into it "Accompt of Gold", as "cash coyned from the Mint". By 1715 this Accompt had a balance of almost 800 kg/25,700 t.oz. in gold; a nascent central bank reserve. After 1720 the traffic to and from the Mint accelerated. Clapham noted, "Great blocks of *guineas* – 63,000, 80,000, 109,000 coming from the Mint". He added, "The Bank becomes the chief furnisher of the Mint with gold and of the public … with *guineas* … the *guinea* has won … in London men of importance are all thinking in terms of gold".[26]   Moreover, London had taken over from Amsterdam as the foremost precious metals market, an integral part of becoming Europe's financial capital. While the Bank needed gold, the East India Company needed silver. Increasingly, the middle-man supplying both was Abraham Mocatta, the broker. The Mocatta name runs as a thread throughout the history of the London market. The original Moses Mocatta had set up in London in 1671 and first sent gold to India with the East India Company in 1676 (a modest 2.3 kg/75 t.oz).[27]   His son, Abraham, became official broker to both the Bank of England and the East India Company by the 1730s, an exclusive post the family firm held until the 1840s. Ultimately, nine generations of Mocatta worked in precious metals. The name is preserved in ScotiaMocatta, a fixing member of the London gold market.

The year after appointing Abraham Mocatta as its broker, the Bank of England opened its own Bullion Warehouse (later the Bullion Office). The Warehouse was open to all comers and most gold coming into the country was lodged and weighed there, before being collected by its owners. The Warehouse remained the heart of the London gold market until after 1850. Besides presiding over this private business, the Warehouse handled all bullion for the Bank's own account. The Warehouse initiated an account for "Foreign Gold Coin", which became one of its most active during the 1730s, and an "Account for Bullion for the Mint". A separate account was also maintained of precious metal (almost all gold) in the "Treasury or Vault".[28]   The latter was the Bank's reserve against its note issue. The reserve stood at 15.55 m.t/500,000 t.oz in 1730, rising to 28 m.t/900,000 t.oz a decade later. The Bank's notes were mostly £10 and £20, with a few of larger denomination, but no small ones. They were not legal tender; the confidence in them came from the promise on them to pay the bearer "on demand" in legal tender gold coin. The size of the Bank's reserve meant few were presented for redemption (although a run on gold in 1763, at the end of the Seven Years' War did reduce the Bank's stock briefly to under 3 m.t/96,000 t.oz).[29]

The maintenance of this "working standard" in gold, as Clapham dubbed it, by the Bank was underpinned by the continuity of production in Brazil. Indeed, the vintage years were between 1725 and 1760 as prospectors opened up new areas.

New frontiers in Brazil

The heartland of gold production was always Minas Gerais province (it still is). Year after year, the *Paulista* adventurers made fresh finds at Villa do Principe, Itabira and Sabara in the vicinity of the present city of Belo Horizonte. Villa Rica de Ouro Preto (Rich Town of Black Gold) was transformed from a rough mining camp into a flourishing city with its own royal mint, smelting houses, palaces, grandiose churches and public buildings. "In this town live the chief merchants, whose trade and importance incomparably exceed the most thriving of the leading merchants in Portugal," wrote a Portuguese traveller in 1734. "Hither … are directed and collected in the Royal Mint the grandiose amounts of gold from all the Mines."[30] Another contemporary visitor simply called it *Potosi de Ouro* in comparison with the great Bolivian silver mine.[31] Output in Minas Gerais was, conservatively, 11 m.t/350,000 t.oz annually between 1735 and 1744, then averaging 8 to 9 m.t/257,000 to 290,000 t.oz until 1759.[32]

The search along the rivers of the interior spread wider. In Bahia province to the north, gold turned up in many small rivers such as Rio des Contas, with rich strikes at Aracuahi and Fanado in 1727. The mint in the capital, Salvador, received up to two m.t/65,000 t.oz annually by 1729. The ladies of Bahia became famous for the massive pieces of gold jewellery they wore, while the churches were adorned with a profusion of gold artefacts.

The *Paulistas*, meanwhile, constantly pushed west, deep into Goias and the Matto Grosso towards the border between Brazil and Bolivia, in spite of great hazards. The journey to Cuiabá, where gold was first discovered in 1718, took up to seven months, along a network of small rivers linked by tough portages. Prospectors drowned, died of starvation or disease, were killed by wild animals, piranha fish, or local Amerindians. One season, no one made it safely through. Cuibabá did not become a real mining town for a decade. Yet, for the lucky few, the gold pickings were occasionally astonishing. A *Paulista* named Miguel Sutil scooped up 7 kg/225 t.oz in a single day near Cuiabá; his partner had to make do with 2 kg/64 t.oz. When news spread, other miners and their slaves rushed in, reportedly harvesting almost 6,000 kg/192,900 t.oz within a matter of weeks without having to dig deeper than one metre (this sounds far-fetched, but the swift returns from Serra Pelada and other alluvial deposits in the 1980s Brazilian gold rush showed what can happen there).

The Cuiabá workings were uniformly shallower than in Minas Gerais and quickly worked out. Moreover, their remoteness made it impossible to take in serious mining equipment, so that digging was often done with, at best, a shovel and even musket butts.[33] So the diggers scooped a shallow pit, but soon moved on. Consequently, output was erratic. Annual output is hard to gauge – not least because the gold had to be brought back to the smelting houses in São Paolo for refining, a seven-month return journey. The travelling was often undertaken by a fleet of canoes in the 'monsoon' season when rivers were highest. One year, 305 canoes bearing over 3,000 people set out. Ultimately the prospectors pushed on up the rivers Guaporé and Sarare right on the Bolivian border, leaving Cuiabá almost a ghost town. They were penetrating right up to the eastern slopes of the Andes, where the rivers had been a prime source of alluvial gold for the Precolumbian people of Peru for over two thousand years. The richness of the deposits now encountered by the Brazilian prospectors helps to confirm how much gold must have long been available for working in Precolumbian cultures (*see chapter 17*).

The story was similar in Goiás province, west of Brazil's modern capital Brasília, where gold was first found in 1725. Here, too, over the next thirty years, diggers shuttled from one find to the next. Mining camps mushroomed on the harsh, red-earth landscape but soon were deserted. Mining is hardly the word, because skills were few. A traveller some years later observed that the most ignorant miner in Minas Gerais was more skilled than the most expert in Goiás, and that the most ignorant in Goiás knew more about mining than the most intelligent in Matto Grosso.[34] Even so, after 1730, the two regions contributed upwards of 5 m.t/160,000 t.oz annually from shallow alluvial sources until the 1760s. Taken with the output of the more sophisticated operations in Minas Gerais, where large-scale hydraulic operations were put in place along river banks and hillsides, Brazil's total output in those years was in the range of 15.5 m.t/500,000 t.oz to 18.7 m.t/600,000 t.oz In certain years, it probably exceeded 20 m.t/643,000 t.oz. This compares with 6–8 m.t/190,000–260,000 t.oz from the rest of the world, where the main suppliers were other South American countries, notably Chile, Colombia and Peru, and Africa. Brazil was thus contributing upwards of two-thirds of the world's gold.

Once Brazil's production faltered after 1765, slipping to around 11 m.t/350,000 t.oz by 1770 and barely 7 m.t/225,000 t.oz by 1790, strains on the gold standard soon appeared. Britain had relied on Brazilian gold both to finance its growing international trade and as a treasure chest in time of war. The pipeline from Brazil through Lisbon had been an indispensable infusion.

The Lisbon connection

The gold from the mints and smelting houses of Brazil left for Lisbon, usually in March or April, in three fleets, each of twenty to thirty merchant ships with Portuguese naval escort supplemented by the Royal Navy in wartime. They sailed from Rio de Janeiro, Bahia (Salvador) and Pernambuco, laden with sugar, coffee, cacao, timber and hides, reaching the Tagus estuary by June or July. The gold consignments included coin from the Rio, Bahia and Ouro Preto mints, bars (of 1 kg/32.15 t.oz) and dust. The Rio fleet in the spring of 1749 brought 12.25 m.t/394,000 t.oz, of which 5 m.t/ 162,000 t.oz was in gold dust, 770 kg/24,700 t.oz in bars and the rest in coin (mostly held on private account). This declared gold was divided evenly between the two escorting warships to split the risk.[35] No doubt there was also smuggled gold on the twenty merchant ships in the fleet.

The mints in Lisbon and Oporto then transformed most of it into the *Moedas de Ouro*, in denominations of one, a half, and a quarter. The Treasury in England valued each *moydore* at 28 shillings (£1.40), the coin being slightly heavier than the *guinea*. The Portuguese took great pride in the design and quality of this coinage. The Portuguese painter, Vieira Lusitano, was commissioned to prepare a portrait bust of King Dom Joáo V for a new *moeda* in 1722, for which the dies were prepared by the French technician Antoine Mangin, at the *Casa de Moeda* in Lisbon. The resulting coin is considered one of the finest ever put in circulation. Such quality made the *moedas* welcome in financial markets throughout Europe, not just in London, but Amsterdam, Hamburg and Genoa. The 'foreign gold accounts' of merchants everywhere comprised mainly *moedas* and *guineas* because of their wide acceptability, like the Venetian ducat in earlier times, and the English *sovereign* in the 19th century. England was always the main destination, importing at least half and probably two-thirds of all Brazilian gold. Throughout the 18th century the Portuguese *moydores* circulated in the west of England, more so than the home-made *guinea*. "Very little specie of any other kind is to be met with," reported the Receiver-General of Cornwall in 1737.[36]

In Lisbon itself, the English community grew. The English consul noted 2,000 English living there in 1721 and often "one hundred sail" of English ships on the Tagus. In peace and war for over sixty years every Royal Navy ship or East Indiaman returning home found some excuse to call, even if it meant a long deviation. The Falmouth-Lisbon-Falmouth packet boat service, operated by the Post Office since 1703, offered regular courier service. The packet, like the naval ships, had the benefit of diplomatic immunity from searches by Portuguese customs – a great advantage since the export of gold coin was officially forbidden. Not that anyone paid much attention. Ships' boats slipped away from the waterfront to waiting vessels with gold, their crews armed with cutlasses, swords and pistols.

A colourful Irishman, James O'Hara, second Baron Tyrawly, who served as British Ambassador in Lisbon for a generation, took delight in telling the Foreign Office that the English merchants "will talk publicly upon the Exchange of what

Peru, Mochica culture, AD 1-800;
gold sheet diadem of a warrior
priest with a jaguar's head
Museo Larco, Lima

Chimor empire, 1300-1532, Imperial
Epoch; gold ear spools, shoulder
straps and pectoral of a chief
Museo Larco, Lima

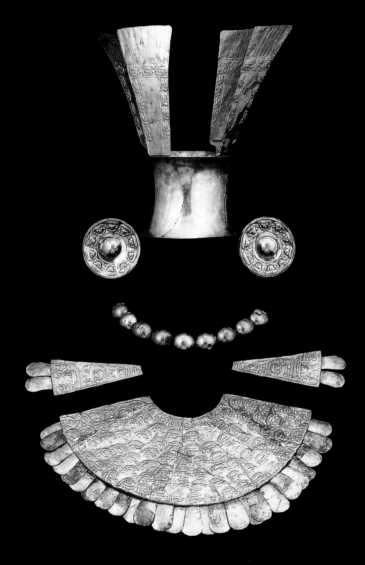

**Colombia, Quimbaya culture,
200-800; 'lime' flask of a man**
Museo de America, Madrid

Colombia, San Agustin culture, 0-AD 900; graceful flying fish, a rare item in Precolumbian metalwork.
Colección del Museo del Oro del Banco de la República en Bogotá, Colombia

Colombia, Zenu culture, 200 BC-AD 1600; staff head of a needle alligator
Colección del Museo del Oro del Banco de la República en Bogotá, Colombia

Colombia, Muisca culture, 600-1600; wonderful filigree raft showing a new chief assuming power with an offering to the gods in a lake
Colección del Museo del Oro del Banco de la República en Bogotá, Colombia

Brazil, c.1800; washing gold at Italcoloni, when Brazil was the major producer
Museo do Ouro, Sabara, Brazil.

Gold sovereign of George III, dated 1817, the first year of minting. Weight 7.7g at 916 fine

© The Trustees of the British Museum. All rights reserved.

THE MINT.

The Royal Mint in London making gold coins for the Bank of England in the early 19th century
City of London (Guildhall Library & Guildhall Art Gallery)

California gold rush, c.1851; placer mining at Foster's Bar on the North Fork of the Yuba river by the French artist, Ernest Narjot

Robert B. Honeyman Collection, Courtesy of The Bancroft Library, University of California, Berkeley

Today's fashion: 24K hand-hammered pure gold 'Square Matrix' collection by Gurhan, www.gurhan.com
© 2004 Gregor Halenda / courtesy of World Gold Council

India's tradition: bride adorned with the customary 22 carat gold ornaments
Courtesy of World Gold Council

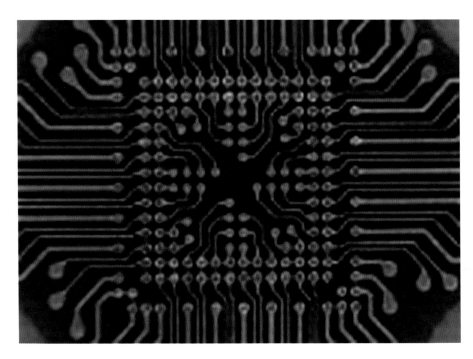

Spider's web of gold bonding wire on a high density board
Tanaka Kikinzoku Kogyo K.K.

**NASA's artist impression
of a Pioneer space craft**
NASA

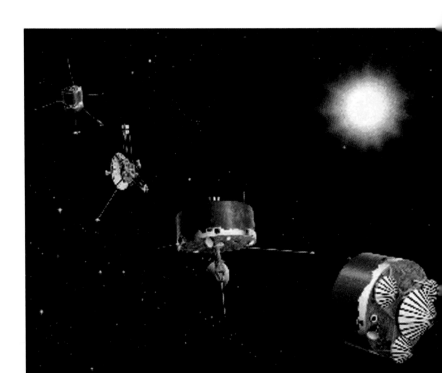

money they have shipped for England, and with as little secrecy send it on board, as they do a chest of oranges". He took note of consignments. The purser of HMS Winchester personally carried several thousand *moydores* daily on board over a three-week period; often carrying 61 kg/1,990 t.oz at a time. Captain Augustus Hervey RN sailed away in 1748 with 80,000 *moydores*, weighing 822 kg/26,400 t.oz [37] Lord Tyrawly summed it up, "There is not an English Man of War homeward bound from almost any Point of the Compass that does not take Lisbon in their way home ... everybody knows that (they) have no other business in life here but to get money". Tyrawly, an indefatigable correspondent, also reported that much gold in dust and bar, smuggled from Brazil by organised syndicates, "Has been bought chiefly by our English Factors, from whence our own Mint in the Tower has been ... so well supplied";[38] confirmation that official and unofficial supplies merged in Lisbon and that the gold going to England was a measure of the true Brazilian output.

The most reliable courier, after the Royal Navy, was the Falmouth packet. These fast, armed ships usually sailing once or twice a month, carried a good share of the gold for seventy years. Records of their consignments are sparse in the early years. Later, between 25th March 1740 and 8th June 1741, they carried 3.3 m.t/105,000 t.oz and, in 1746, the packet Hanover took 622 kg/20,000 t.oz in a single trip. Full records exist, however, from 1759–1769. In those eleven years, the packets took 67.4 m.t/2,167,675 t.oz – an annual average of 6.13 m.t/197,061 t.oz[39] Since the packets accounted only for part of the traffic, these statistics confirm how substantial and regular Brazil remained as the gold standard's supplier at least until 1770.

A landmark gold re-coinage

"The gold inflow was crucial to the increasing gold circulation in the country and to the gold standard," concluded H.E.S. Fisher, chronicler of Anglo-Portuguese trade.[40] That coinage, however, was badly in need of fresh minting by the 1770s. As Charles Jenkinson, 1st Earl of Liverpool, whose hobby was metallic currencies, put it, "Gold coin of this realm has been greatly diminished by clipping, filing and other evil practices". Gold coin was in as bad shape as silver before the 1696 recoinage. The recoinage occupied the Mint for four years, 1773–76, and its sheer scale confirmed how firmly planted gold coins had become as Britain's principal currency. In all, the mint coined almost £20 million pounds worth of gold, equivalent to over 155 m.t/5 million t.oz of metal, providing 18.5 million new *guineas* at 916.6 fine. 85% of the gold came from melting of old *guineas*, with the balance made up from foreign gold coin or bars. Newly-mined gold from Brazil, where production had now fallen sharply, made a relatively small contribution – but the majority of old coin melted would have been originally Brazilian gold.

The quantity of gold involved in this recoinage is virtually without precedent, not just in Britain, but anywhere. It was thirty times greater than the amount coined in tandem with silver at the recoinage of 1696–9. The volume was far greater than anything achieved in Spain from South American supplies in the 16th century, or at Venice in its prime in the 14th century. Indeed, I can track only one possible precedent. In Rome between AD 64 and 68, Nero initiated a recoinage of the *aureus* (making it slightly lighter to help meet his expenses after Rome was destroyed by fire). The Cambridge historian, Richard Duncan-Jones, has estimated this may have involved over 230 metric tonnes/7.6 million ounces of gold, which would be even more than the British recoinage of 1773–76.[41] This is a credible figure, given the amount of gold Rome had been getting from Spanish mines for almost a century. The British recoinage one thousand seven hundred years later was thus a landmark in the history of gold coin, and it, too, was not to be exceeded until after the gold rushes to California and Australia in the mid-19th century, which added a whole new dimension to the world of gold.

The recoinage was a formal admission that the country was on a gold standard. The basis of gold as the accepted measure was underlined by the fact that no attempt was made to recoin silver, despite the fact that the silver coin in circulation was in worse shape than gold, and was in such short supply that banks even gave a premium for it. Indeed, one of the biggest problems facing the pioneers of the Industrial Revolution, who were starting to build their canals, steel works, cotton mills and potteries in the Midlands and the North, was how to pay their workers. There were bank notes, both from the Bank of England and country banks, but they were not legal tender and by law could not be issued for denominations of less than £5 (the Bank issued none less than £10). The daily circulation, therefore, was really based upon the *guinea* and its small offspring, the half-*guinea*, which was worth ten shillings and sixpence. Five and two-*guinea* pieces were also minted in limited quantities. Yet these coins were really the prerogative of the rich; they were little use to ordinary working people, when wages were a few shillings a week, and most staple items of food cost but a few pence. Early industrialists sometimes wasted days scouring neighbouring towns for silver shillings, others resorted to issuing their own notes or tokens, which were accepted by local shopkeepers. The Recoinage Act not only ignored their needs, but actually down-graded silver, designating it henceforth as legal tender only up to £25. The concept that gold was a commodity while silver was the standard of value that had prevailed in Sir Isaac Newton's day half a century earlier had been abandoned. As Charles Jenkinson, the architect of the recoinage, wrote, "Silver coins are no longer the principal measure of property … gold coins are now become, in the practice and opinion of the people, the principal measure of property".[42] The 'accidental' gold standard had become the reality and it would last until 1931.

CHAPTER 20

London:
The 1810 Bullion Committee

On 29th August 1809 an article in the London *Morning Chronicle* by the young economist and stockbroker David Ricardo headed 'The Price of Gold' launched a debate on the relationship between the metal and paper money. The nub of Ricardo's argument was that since the Bank of England had suspended redemption of its bank notes in gold in 1797, due to the pressures of war, the discipline controlling note issue had gone. The Bank was guilty of over-issuing notes, leading to their depreciation. "The mint price of gold is £3.17.10½ (£3.89)," wrote Ricardo, "and the market price has been gradually increasing and was within these two or three weeks as high as £4.13.0 (£4.65) per ounce, not much less than 20% advance." There was a case to answer.

Within six months the House of Commons had set up a Select Committee to "enquire into the Cause of the High Price of Gold Bullion". The Committee was chaired by Francis Horner MP, a close friend of David Ricardo, with the Chancellor of the Exchequer, Spencer Perceval, by his side; other members included the banker Henry Thornton (author of an early book on banking theory) and William Huskisson, a rising star in the Commons on financial matters. They called twenty-nine witnesses, including participants in the gold market, the Governor and Deputy governor of the Bank of England, along with other bankers and merchants. A veritable Who's Who of the City of London attended. The 1810 Bullion Committee was the first wide-ranging investigation into gold, with every word transcribed and published. The Committee's evidence, report and statistical appendices remain a unique document in the history of gold. The enquiry ranged widely over trade, the exchanges, the financial responsibilities of the Bank of England and the pressures on the economy of the Napoleonic wars. The debate it provoked in Parliament and the City over the next decade was, declared J. K. Galbraith, "the most famous in all history on money and its management".[1] David Ricardo himself was not a witness, but remained a shrewd commentator on the sidelines as the arguments rumbled on until paper notes were again redeemable in gold from 1821.

The drama had three acts. Act One spanned the rise of Napoleon in France in the 1790s that precipitated the suspension of gold payments and the subsequent rise in its price. Act Two was the Bullion Committee itself. Act Three saw the fall of Napoleon, the launch of the *sovereign* and, at the final curtain, a blessing on an official, not an accidental, gold standard. This was all played out against a backdrop of the Napoleonic wars, without which the gold price rise and fall would not have happened.

The gold of French *émigrés*

The story begins with the French Revolution in 1789. As the mob took over the streets of Paris, the nobility pocketed any gold and silver coin they possessed and fled across the Channel to England. Just four days before the storming of the Bastille in Paris in July 1789, the Bank of England opened a special account in its ledgers for French silver crowns and, shortly afterwards, another for *Louis d'Or*, the French gold coin. Throughout the next four years, as the old order crumbled in France and the guillotine claimed its victims, the *émigrés* who escaped to London filled the Bank's coffers. The Bank took in twice as much bar gold in the second half of 1789 as in the first, of which close to 2 m.t/64,000 t.oz came from France. The flow accelerated as the franc of the *ancient regime* was replaced by *assignats*, notes theoretically redeemable in five years with the re-distributed lands of Church and State. The Bank's brokers, Mocatta and Goldsmid, picked up over 12.4 m.t/400,000 t.oz in bar gold from melted French coin in 1791.[2] It was welcome, because output in Brazil, the regular source for almost a century, had declined (*see previous chapter*). The Bank of England warned the Prime Minister, William Pitt, that the flow of Brazilian gold "had ceased for some time"[3]. The French dishoarding, however, helped to lift the Bank's reserves to over 56 m.t/1.8 million t.oz, a new record.

The breathing space was short-lived. The French gold supply dried up after 1793, as the new Directorate in France shelved their paper *assignats* in favour of a new gold and silver currency and the young Napoleon began to carve out a victorious path through Europe. French confidence revived, pushing the gold price in Paris back above London, promptly reversing the gold flow. Although Britain itself was shortly at war with France, making it illegal to dispatch any gold to France, no one paid much attention. There was a profit of seven shillings (£0.35) per ounce between London and Paris, which was too tempting to be ignored. As for the French, they were quite content to see smugglers slipping up their beaches by night with the enemy's gold.

The suspension of cash payments

War put multiple demands on the gold reserves. British armies had to be sustained in the field with gold and silver coins. Allies demanded 'loans' in gold. The Emperor of Austria negotiated with Pitt's government for a loan paid partly in silver, plus over 1.2 m.t/38,580 t.oz in French *Louis d'Or* from the Bank's special account. The Bank's reserves, recently so healthy, were down to 16.8 m.t/540,000 t.oz by August 1796, drained further by two poor harvests necessitating grain imports. There was no gold to be had in the market. Purchases by the Bank through Mocatta and Goldsmid were scarcely 2 m.t/64,000 t.oz in 1795 and a minuscule

144 kg/4,600 t.oz the following year.[4]   Starved of fresh gold, the reserves were a meagre 8.8 m.t/280,000 t.oz, worth £1.1 million by January 1797, against note issue and other liabilities of £15.5 million.

Rumours flew round the coffee houses that the French or the Dutch would invade at any moment. The navy had mutinies on its hands. A run started on the Bank for gold coin. The Committee of Treasury noted they faced "constant calls of the Bankers from all parts of town for cash".[5]   Gold was vanishing from the reserve at £100,000 a day. A desperate attempt was made to send a Royal Navy frigate to Hamburg for gold being rounded by the exchange house Goldsmid and Eliason, whose senior partner was the brother of Asher Goldsmid at the Bank's brokers. It was already too late. On Friday 24th February, the Bank lost another £130,000 in gold (just over 1 m.t/32,150 t.oz). A report reached the City that the French had invaded (a few men had come ashore from a French ship on the coast of Wales). There was no time to be lost. King George III was hastily summoned from Windsor early on Sunday morning, 26th February and, at an emergency meeting of the Privy Council, ordered the Bank of England to "forbear issuing any Cash in Payment until the Sense of Parliament can be taken on that subject". No one dreamed on that Sunday in the winter of 1797 that it would be twenty-four years before bank notes could again be redeemed for gold coin at face value.

Rather, everyone heaved a sigh of relief that a crisis was over. The Lord Mayor convened a large gathering of bankers and merchants at the Mansion House on the Monday morning, which passed a resolution declaring, "We will not refuse to receive Bank Notes in payment of any Sum of Money paid to us, and we will use our utmost Endeavours to make all our Payments in the same Manner". Such confidence caused *The Times* to comment wryly, "Yesterday was a phenomenon in the political history of the country. The Bank of England refused paying its notes in specie, and the credit of the Country immediately revived". The newspaper also reported a Bank of England director has ventured at the next Court of Directors meeting that "he trusted that a Bank-note would soon appear like a bar of gold".[6]

In reality it was less easy. As word spread through the country, many tried to get their hands on gold. "Our counting house, and indeed the offices of all the banks, were instantly crowded to the door with people clamorously demanding payment in gold of their interest-receipt, and vociferating for silver in change of our circulating paper," wrote Sir William Forbes, an Edinburgh banker.[7]   The practical question was, what could replace the *guinea*, worth £1.05, which had circulated widely? Over 50 million had been minted during the reign of George III. The Bank of England had issued only £10 notes until 1793, when it also began to print £5 notes. By law, neither the Bank nor the country banks could issue notes of less than £5. Parliament promptly authorised the Bank of England and country banks to issue notes of £1 and £2, but they were not declared legal tender. Domestic circulation of silver coin had been minimal for a century, and was in sorry condition. The stop-gap was Spanish silver dollars. The Bank told its brokers to buy up

500,000 Spanish dollars to be delivered within a week. The plan was to have them overstamped at the Mint with a small head of George III punched on the cheek of the Spanish king. This was greeted with derision. A contemporary wit sneered,

"The Bank, to make their Spanish dollars pass,
Stamped the head of a fool on the neck of an ass".

The Times was quite put out. "We must confess," lamented an editorial, "that we do not like this introduction of foreign specie to pass as current in this country; it does not look respectable."[8] Nevertheless, a motley collection of silver coins and home-made silver tokens (many of which have become collectors' items) circulated for the next quarter-century.

On the gold front, the *guinea* largely went to ground; the basic instinct was to hoard it or, if the price rose, to sell it for illegal melting and possible export. Immediately after suspension the market price in London remained at the Mint parity of £3.89 per ounce as the threat of invasion melted away. The British navy obliterated the Dutch navy, and Nelson destroyed the French fleet that had taken Napoleon to conquer Egypt at the Battle of the Nile, giving Britain naval supremacy throughout the Mediterranean. The (paper) pound strengthened and foreign gold flowed back into London. The Mint was busy melting it and making *guineas*. They took in almost 20 m.t/643,000 t.oz of foreign gold in 1797 and 22 m.t/700,000 t.oz the following year, enough to strike almost five million *guineas*.[9] By February 1799 the Bank of England's gold reserve was back to a healthy 61 m.t/1.96 million t.oz. Yet, not a word on the resumption of cash payments was uttered. Paper money was the vogue, while Napoleon, if momentarily tamed, remained a real threat. The cost of war had already been learned; prudence dictated strong gold reserves. So paper was printed – and the gold price began to edge up late in 1799, getting to £4.30 by January 1801. The City of London took that in its stride for it entered the new century in a buoyant mood.

Trading metropolis of the world

A guide book to London around 1800 enthusiastically declared, "London is the centre of the trade of the whole world, and more ships sail from it in a year than from all other places in the world united. It has fifty times more trade than ancient Carthage, than Venice in its glory; than all the Hans Towns, or Amsterdam could ever boast".[10] A trifle over the top, perhaps, but London was the growing trading and financial capital of the world. British trade had risen five-fold during the previous century and would continue to expand. Henry Thornton, banker, economist and Member of Parliament, who sat on the 1810 Bullion Committee, was just as proud. "London is become, especially of late," he declared, "the trading metropolis of Europe and, indeed, of the whole world."[11]

That position strengthened during the Napoleonic wars. As David Kynaston observed in his splendid history of the City, "The catalyst was the state of almost continuous European warfare between 1792 and 1815 which severely blunted the activities of Britain's main trading rivals and greatly increased the proportion of world trade conducted by merchants based in Britain. Amsterdam declined as the leading financial centre and was replaced by the City of London".[12]

In the realms of gold and silver, London was confirmed as the premier market. In gold it already held that position, but Amsterdam had received direct shipments of Spanish silver from the Americas; now London secured that too. In 1800 annual world gold production was around 19 m.t/610,850 t.oz, of which two-thirds came from the Americas (still mainly Brazil) and around one-tenth from Russia. The London market handled at least one-third of this entire output. In silver, London also saw one-third of the 870 m.t/28 million t.oz produced (over two-thirds from Mexico).[13]   The silver, of course, went primarily to India on East India Company ships; the traffic was hardly interrupted by the wars, with East India ships carrying upwards of 200 m.t/6.4 million t.oz (almost a quarter of world output) each year. Silver did not stay in London to be minted as an alternative to gold; the Indian silver price was always more tempting.

The Bullion Committee convened

Meanwhile, the gold price hovered at just over £4 an ounce between 1802 and 1808, marginally over the Mint price but not enough to cause concern. The Bank of England bought small amounts from time to time at £4, but was reluctant to send it to the Mint for coinage. The Mint made a handful of *guineas* each year but that business had ground to a halt. The Bank's own gold reserve fluctuated on either side of 50 m.t/1.6 million t.oz. The Bank's broker, Aaron Asher Goldsmid later told the Bullion Committee that gold prices were quoted relatively rarely between 1806 and 1808 as little went on in the market. The situation changed, however, in 1809 as the price rose from £4 in January to £4.65 by August when David Ricardo drew attention to the surge in his article. Within months the market was under the microscope.

The Bullion Committee first met on 22nd February 1810, hearing evidence over the next four weeks. The testimony from a cast of bankers, brokers, exchange dealers, merchants and refiners provided a unique portrait of the gold business in London at the beginning of the 19th century, while also probing the relationship (if any, in some opinions) between gold and paper circulation and the Bank of England's responsibility (again, if any) to manage the currency. The framework of the gold market that was initially set forth showed that all precious metal passed essentially through two parties: The Bullion Office at the Bank and their exclusive broker, Mocatta and Goldsmid.

The Bullion Office

The Bullion Office was almost as old as the Bank itself, though it began life as the Bullion Warehouse. John Humble, a venerable figure who worked in the Office from the 1770s until the 1830s, told the Committee, "It has been established upwards of 100 years. I understand it to have been instituted merely for the purpose of accommodation and safety between merchant and merchant as a place of deposit".[14] The name had been changed from Warehouse to Bullion Office around 1770. It was minder of the Bank's own gold reserves and crossroads of most gold and silver entering or leaving the country.

"The business of the office is divided into two branches," John Humble explained. "The first is for the purpose of weighing and ascertaining the value of the bullion in which the Bank is concerned; the other, in which individuals only are concerned."

The Committee wanted more explanation.

"What do you mean by ascertaining the value?" – "By weighing, calculating the fineness according to the Assayer's reports, and casting up the value according to the prices."

"Where do you get the prices?" – "From the Broker's reports made to the office, either on account of the Bank or of individuals."

"Does the Broker give you a general price, or the price of every transaction?" – "The price of every transaction."

"Is there more than one broker?" – "Only one house, there are several partners in the firm, the house of Mocatta and Goldsmid."

So both Bank and broker were privy to virtually every deal in the market. Physically, the metal crossed the Bank's doorstep as John Humble went on to set out. "The bullion is deposited generally by ship-masters, and lies in the office for the owners to whom it is consigned; we keep separate books for entering those deposits, one of which we call the packet-book, and the other the man-of-war book and in those books we enter what may be called a manifest of deposit, the name of the ship-master and the consignee, the name of the vessel by which the importation has been made, the number of packages, and what those packages are said to contain, for we receive them only as packages. When a sale takes place, that is transacted by the Broker between the seller and buyer, he giving a contract to each; the parties come to the office, and in their presence the package is opened, the bullion weighed, we deliver the quantity sold to the buyer and receive from him the price, which we deliver over to the seller … the whole of this is done by the Bank gratuitously."[15]

The Committee had a final key question. If there was only one recognised broker, Mocatta and Goldsmid, "have they, in your opinion, any power of control over the price?" – "None in the world, I believe."

John Humble later forwarded to the Bullion Committee the quantities of gold and silver moving through the Bullion Office in the fifteen months prior to their hearing. His statistics revealed that between 1st January 1809 and 30th March 1810, gold to the value of £176,958 had been deposited by the captains of men-of-war, and £343,267 by the masters of Post Office packets. Together these were equivalent to 4.16 m.t/133,734 t.oz in gold if Humble used the Mint price of £3.89, or 3.48 m.t/111,876 t.oz at the current higher prices up to £4.65.[16] Sales of gold by private dealers through the Bullion Office in the same period amounted to £683,067 in gold coin and £60,867 in bar gold.[17]   This amount exceeds the deposits from men-of-war and packets, because there were also deliveries by 'private persons'. Meanwhile, the Bank of England's own gold stock had declined from 36 m.t/1.15 million t.oz to 28 m.t/900,000 t.oz; not surprising given the low level of imports of the men-of-war and the packets. The Bank's directors were at least fully informed of what was going on. John Humble noted that, "Every transaction which is done for the Bank is daily reported to the Cashiers, passes through the Bank's books and into the Bank balances".[18]

The Broker's role

The team of Bullion Office and broker at the heart of the gold market was underlined by the first witness called before the Committee – "Aaron Asher Goldsmid Esq., Partner in the House of Mocatta and Goldsmid; Bullion Brokers; called in, and Examined".

"Are there any other Brokers in the same line besides your house?" he was asked. "Our house has been solely employed since the year 1694, at the establishment of the Bank," he responded.

"Are there any other dealers in Gold but yours?" – "I apprehend none of considerable amount."

"Are there others recorded in the Bullion Office in the Bank like yours?" – "None."[19]

Mocatta and Goldsmid's special relationship with the Bank was clear.   The Goldsmid family, moreover, with whom Mocatta had made a partnership in 1779, were well known in the City. Asher Goldsmid, the senior partner at the brokerage firm (who chose not to appear before the Committee) had over twenty years' experience in precious metals and his eldest son, Isaac Lyon Goldsmid, was also a partner and future entrepreneur in his own right. Asher Goldsmid's brothers, Abraham and Benjamin Goldsmid, were underwriters of government loans (though with somewhat disastrous results), while his other brother, George, was the senior partner at Goldsmid and Eliason, the exchange house involved in the last-minute attempt to bring gold from Hamburg to London in 1797. In turn, George's son, Abraham, also a partner, appeared before the Bullion Committee to explain the intricacies of exchange rates and the costs of shipping gold to the continent.[20] Between them, the Goldsmid family knew where all the skeletons were buried. This could explain why Aaron Asher Goldsmid, a young man of twenty-five with only a few years' experience of the market, was fielded before the enquiry. He was only twelve when cash payments were suspended, so he could, and did, plead ignorance on occasion.

That said, he outlined the daily practicalities of the market, above all on how the price was set.

"What is the present price of Gold?" – £4.10 (£4.50) standard Gold bars; foreign

Gold is comparatively higher."

"Can you state what tables (of prices) are the most perfect in your judgement?" – "Those published by Wettenhall are likely to be correct; they are made from our reports to the person who furnishes him with the prices."

"Is that price derived by Wettenhall from the information of others, or only from your reports to him?" – "From ours alone."[21]

Wettenhall published his price lists on Tuesdays and Thursdays, Aaron Asher Goldsmid went on, and if there had been no transactions in the meantime, no price was quoted. The prices quoted were always real ones, based on transactions and were never nominal. The members of Parliament were not easily reassured how genuine the price was. They wanted to know exactly how Mocatta and Goldsmid arrived at a price.

"Do you consider your house as having a considerable control over the Bullion market, so as to fix the price?" He replied, "Not so as to raise or depress it above or below its natural level."[22]   However, at a later examination (he was called on three occasions), the questions focused keenly on how the price was determined.

"In what manner do you fix the price of Gold as between buyer and seller? By ascertaining the general disposition of the buyer and seller?" – "By ascertaining the general disposition of the buyer and seller and stating the medium."

"Have you any reference in fixing the price, to the prices in the foreign market?" – "Certainly."

"How do you ascertain that?" – "By enquiring the last price of various merchants; and generally the disposition of the market concurs with the prices abroad, because persons are willing to buy up to that price."

"Are they governed by the antecedent price of Gold?" – "Guided by the general disposition of the buyers and sellers here and the prices abroad; there is seldom any great fluctuation unless some great influx or rise; for some considerable demand or large arrival will tend to fall the price; and any considerable repression of the exchange would tend to raise the price, which might arise from many causes."

"Enumerate those causes or give some instances." – "In fact there recently arise causes of which we are not aware of the original source, such as a particular demand for Gold on the Continent, as I believe is the case in the present instance; of money going out of the country for the payment of troops abroad to any considerable extent would naturally have that effect."[23]

This touched the heart of the matter. Armies on the march during the Napoleonic wars, whether British, French, Dutch or Austrian needed gold and silver coin to meet their expenses, creating an exceptional demand for precious metal.

Aaron Goldsmid suggested the rise in the price of gold during the preceding eighteen months had been due to the French armies moving into Spain. "As a proof of the probability of this circumstance," he said, "since the war in Spain, doubloons (the Spanish gold coin) have borne a greater premium on the Continent in proportion to other Gold."[24]   Gold was also flowing out of Britain because that was the cheapest way of paying for imports, mostly of grain, since the exchange rate for the paper sterling pound was weak. His firm's business was mainly with twenty Dutch or French merchants who bought up to £80,000 in gold (0.5 m.t/17,000 t.oz) a month. Amsterdam was the main destination being "the greatest mart for Gold on the Continent". He professed not to know where it went from there, displaying the discretion of a gold trader to this day.[25]

What worried the Bullion Committee was where this gold originated? They began a consistent challenge to Aaron Goldsmid, and later witnesses, to explain the source. Was it foreign gold, which could be re-exported legally? For instance, another witness, the refiner William Merle, stated, "I have had a great deal of African Gold this last year … within the last four or five months I bought about four thousand ounces". He refined this gold dust into bars for export. Despite Merle calling that "a great deal", it was a trifle. Aaron Goldsmid agreed with a question that over £500,000 in gold (3.5 m.t/112,000 t.oz) had been exported in the previous twelve months. The implication, therefore, was that *guineas* melted and passed off as 'foreign gold' were exported. William Merle honestly conceded, "If a bar is brought to me it is impossible for me to know where it is from; it is assayed and we buy it according to the assay".[26] Aaron Goldsmid was more circumspect, claiming, "We never sell any gold for exportation, unless melted in the presence of two witnesses, and sworn off before the Court of Aldermen". It became a mantra he repeated several times. A Committee member finally put it to him bluntly that it might be highly profitable for dealers to lie, accepting gold bars of melted coin.

"What profit would they obtain upon that transaction?" – "They would in the first instance obtain the profit which arises from the difference between the market and the Mint price of Gold (i.e. the price at which the Mint bought the gold to make *guineas*), and in the next place if they were to export it, they would derive the profit of the export merchant." He agreed the profit to be made on one hundred *guineas* (£105) would be £15.11.6d (£15.57).

The next exchange was terse.

"Then for one hundred *guineas* melted into bar, he could have obtained £121.11.6d in Bank of England paper?" – "Yes."

"If he could for £105 have £121.11.6d and contrive to procure more *guineas*, would he not have made a profit of £15.11.6d and be in a condition to repeat the operation?" – "Certainly."

"Is there not a positive temptation to melt all our English Gold coin that is not degraded for sixteen per cent?" – "Yes."[27]

The Committee had made its point; it was lucrative to melt *guineas*, pass the bars off as foreign coin and get an export licence. The implication, following Ricardo's thinking, was that if paper notes were repayable in gold, such an outflow would check note issue as the Bank of England stock fell. But with the present divorce between gold and notes, the metal still went abroad, while the printing presses rolled unchecked. Aaron Asher Goldsmid bluntly denied any connection, telling the Committee, "not perceiving that the increase or decrease of bank notes has any connection with, or influence upon, the price of Gold, we have paid no attention to that subject".[28]   A sentiment echoed by his cousin, Abraham Goldsmid of Goldsmid and Eliason, who repeatedly told the Bullion Committee he did not "profess himself competent to give my opinion on that".[29]   But both may have felt it prudent to voice no opinion, given Mocatta and Goldsmid's role at the Bank.

The Bank of England at bay

As for the Bank, it was in total denial. The Bank's case, presented jointly by the Governor, John Whitmore, and his deputy, John Pearse, was that they were not guilty of over-issuing bank notes, nor of indiscriminately dispensing notes through their discounting of commercial bills. The fact remained, however, that note issue before the suspension of payments in gold in 1797 had never topped £11 million, but was close to £21 million as the Bullion Committee sat. The value of bills under discount was up from £5.3 million to £15.5 million. Governor Whitmore argued the increase was in response to demand. "The Bank," he stated, "had never forced a note into circulation." His deputy added they discounted only "bills of real value, representing real transactions". So if trade was booming, he went on, they merely responded to a demand for more discounts with more notes. The Bank could not over-issue through discounting 'good bills' from people of unquestioned credit. This was the weak link. The Bank of England was acting like a commercial bank in search of profit from discounting, and not as the guardian of the currency.

The Governor and his deputy dismissed the suggestion that the depreciation of sterling on the exchanges and the resulting rise in the gold price had anything to do with bank notes. The Deputy Governor declared, "I cannot see how the amount of Bank notes issue can operate on the price of Bullion, or the state of the exchanges, and therefore I am individually of the opinion that the price of Bullion, or the state of the exchanges, can never be a reason for lessening the amount of Bank notes to be issued". Governor Whitmore agreed, "I never think it necessary to advert to the price of Gold or the state of the exchange, on the days on which we make our advances".[30]

The Bank was not yet thinking like a central bank. "The Bank of England was essentially a profit-making bank run by merchants on behalf of the mercantile rather than the banking community," David Kynaston observed. "There was no continuous sense in which it was a central bank regulating a national financial system."[31]   The Bullion Committee's Report would underline that obligation.

Diverse voices, including 'a Continental Merchant'

In the City itself opinion was divided, but two leading figures were forthright on the link between gold and paper. Sir Francis Baring, founder of the merchant banking house, saw the trouble as, "the increased circulation in the Country of paper". He pointed out that, during the Seven years War and the American War of Independence, the country had managed well without suspension of cash payments in gold. "Before the restrictions (of 1797), the experience of above a century proves that the administration of the affairs of the Bank had been wise and correct; the Public have been satisfied, the Country has flourished." He went on, "This experience points out the only principle on which the Public can rely with confidence, namely, to return again to payments in specie whenever it shall be in the power of the Bank to do so".[32]

The strongest advocate of the return to gold was the only anonymous witness before the Committee, described as "Mr ————, a Continental Merchant". His identity has been the subject of speculation, with the young Nathan Mayer Rothschild, relatively newly arrived in London, sometimes tipped as the mystery guest. The Bullion Committee Report singled him out as "a very eminent Continental Merchant" and as "being intimately acquainted with the trade between this Country and the Continent of Europe".

The real 'Continental Merchant' was almost certainly John Parish, a partner in Parish & Co., one of the largest merchant houses in Hamburg. Parish organised several discreet operations for the British government during the Napoleonic Wars, arranging the transfer of gold and silver to Austria and other allies. He is thought to have slipped into London from Hamburg (then under French occupation) on another clandestine assignment just two weeks before the anonymous witness stood before the Bullion Committee. It was imperative, therefore, that he appear incognito. A clue to his identity, however, was in the very first question directed to him. "Are you acquainted with the subject of the exchange between this Country and Hamburgh?" No one was better qualified to speak on that or the whole topic of undercover gold flows during the war. This explains why the Bullion Committee examined him at length no less than four times, and gave much credence to his opinions in their report.[33]

The 'Continental Merchant' set out his stall clearly. "I value everything by Bullion," he declared several times. Thus, on the issue of the exchanges, he added, "I first wish to state my general idea of a par of exchange; it is the expression in the coins of denominations of the two currencies which are to be compared ... I have no idea how a par can be ascertained without the precious metals being the foundation". He had little time for paper money. "To the best of my recollection," he went on, "a depreciation in the exchanges has always taken place whenever a paper currency has been put into circulation, that is not convertible into cash. The strongest instance is that of *assignats* in France. At the present moment we have a very strong instance in the paper currency of Austria and Denmark, where a forced paper circulation exists."

That reply prompted a Committee member to ask, "Do you then consider our paper as depreciated 10 to 13% in consequence of its non-convertibility into cash?"

John Parish the "Continental Merchant" replied, "As I value everything by Bullion,

I conceive the paper currency of this Country to be depreciated to the full extent of 15 to 20% or rather the difference in this Country between the price of Bullion and the rate at which the coin is issued from the Mint".

"Do you ascribe what you call a depreciation of the paper of Great Britain, in any degree to an opinion of any insufficiency of the Bank of England to fulfil all its engagements?" – "No, by no means; but to the circumstance of their not allowing Bullion to perform those functions for which it seems to have been intended by nature."[34]

Just in case the point was not taken, the 'Continental Merchant' later added, "In my opinion, there is no single cause that would tend so materially to have the effect of depreciating the exchange, and keeping it low, as an increased paper currency not convertible into cash". His evidence was the longest of any witness, save the Governor and Deputy Governor of the Bank of England, and it carried great weight. In the verbal sparring match between Bank and 'Continental Merchant', the latter prevailed.

His analysis was at odds with most merchants appearing before the Committee, who regarded the adverse balance of payments and heavy foreign expenditure by the government in the prosecution of the war as the cause of the falling sterling exchange rate. In their report the Bullion Committee singled out the merchant John Greffulhe as "most wedded to the opinion that the state of the balance of payments alone was sufficient to account for any depression".[35] They came down firmly, however, on the side of the 'Continental Merchant'.

The Bullion Report

The Select Committee's report, drafted by Francis Horner MP, the ally of Ricardo, was published on 8th June 1810. The central recommendation was unequivocal. "Your Committee," it said, "have formed an Opinion, which they submit to the House; that there is at present an excess in the paper circulation of this Country, of which the most unequivocal symptom is the very high price of Bullion, and next to that the low state of the Continental Exchanges; that this excess is to be ascribed to the want of a sufficient check and control in the issues of paper from the Bank of England; and originally, to the suspension of cash payments, which removed the natural and true control … No safe, certain, and constantly adequate provision against an excess of paper currency, either occasional or permanent, can be found, except in the convertibility of all such paper into specie."[36] The report went on to plead for "the Repeal of the Law which suspends the Cash Payments of the Bank of England". There need be no rush. "The period ought to be ample, in order that the Bank Directors may feel their way." They proposed a period of two years or, if there were a Peace Treaty with France, a return within six months.[37] In fact, it was to be eleven years.

Initially, as is still the fate of many Parliamentary enquiries, the Report was shelved for almost a year, not being debated in the House of Commons until May

1811. Elsewhere, argument raged, not least from the pen of Ricardo, who applauded its thesis. Indeed, the issues were given a thorough airing. The Bullion Committee marked not the end, but the beginning of a decade of debate in newspapers, pamphlets and Parliament on a gold-backed, as opposed to pure paper, currency. David Ricardo led the way; his articles, pamphlets and correspondence on 'the Bullion controversy' filled the best part of two volumes.[38] The crux, he argued, was that "for a currency, to be perfect, should be absolutely invariable in value". Precious metals provided the best base; they were not ideal because their prices fluctuated too. "They are, however, the best with which we are acquainted," he wrote. Without such a standard, currency "would be exposed to all the fluctuations to which the ignorance or the interests of the issuers might be subject". Bank notes, Ricardo allowed, were acceptable – and practical – but they should always be fully convertible on demand.[39]

The arguments unleashed show the real achievement of the Bullion Committee, for besides offering a unique insight into the gold business, it made people focus on the management of a national currency and the responsibility in that task of the Bank of England as a central bank. The outcome in 1821 was a fully fledged gold standard, monitored by the Bank.

Gold for Wellington

In the immediate aftermath of the Bullion Report the government was anyway in no mood to agree to a resumption of cash payments. The demands of war made that impossible. As George Canning, a future Prime Minister, said in the eventual House of Commons debate on the Report, while he sympathised with much of its theory, he could not vote for it until Napoleon was defeated. The government was having enough trouble rounding up gold at exorbitant prices to dispatch to the Duke of Wellington's armies in Spain. The Bank of England and its brokers, Mocatta and Goldsmid, were under constant pressure from the Treasury to lay their hands on any brand of gold coin. The contention of several witnesses to the Bullion Committee that the military needs for gold were bolstering the price were entirely justified, for the price topped £5 an ounce in 1812.

The new governor of the Bank of England, William Manning, wrote to the Chancellor of the Exchequer, "Since we supplied you a few days ago, for the use of the Marquis of Wellington's army, with the foreign gold you then desired, the price has risen very rapidly and the demand for individuals has much increased. The Bank broker states to me today that he had been offered five *guineas* (£5.25) an ounce for Portugal gold … There are also some Venetian *sequins* but the price would be equal to £6 per oz".[40]

Anything on offer was snapped up. The brokers also bought old *Louis d'Or*, *new Napoléons d'Or*, Imperial *ducats*, Dutch *guilders* and Indian *star pagodas*.[41] Indeed, what saved the day was gold from India. The consistently high price in London made it worth shipping gold back, despite the long voyage. An initial consignment of 500,000 *star pagodas* (2 m.t/64,300 t.oz), together with an assortment of *mohurs* and other coins arrived in England in February 1813 on the East India Company's *Modeste* after a five-month voyage. Mocatta and Goldsmid were instructed to acquire the gold from the East India Company for the Bank, eventually making the deal at £4.85 an ounce for *pagodas*, slightly less for other coins. The size of the consignment and perhaps doubts about the true fineness of the coins probably helped Mocatta negotiate a lower price. A second shipment a few months later brought 2.9 m.t/93,366 t.oz of Indian coins, which were similarly snapped up. In all, the Bank paid out £772,000 for Indian gold in 1813.[42]

The coins were dispatched to the Mint, which was geared up for an 'accelerated' programme of melting, refining up to title and striking *guineas* in days. The task of spiriting them through France (enemy territory) to Wellington's headquarters beyond the Pyrenees in Spain was entrusted to Nathan Mayer Rothschild, with the active co-operation of his brother James, fortuitously working in Paris. Thus Rothschild took on the role fulfilled earlier in the war by John Parish, the 'Continental Merchant' from Hamburg. Rothschild employed relays of couriers. Given that up to 5,000 kg of gold coin was smuggled through, this would have required many teams, assuming each courier carried up to 20 kg on horseback.

The successful operations throughout 1813 earned Rothschild the deep gratitude of the government and won him future confidential assignments. After the war Rothschild dined out on anecdotes about hoodwinking the French in getting almost £800,000 worth of gold to Wellington. The ability to pay his men and meet his campaign expenses aided Wellington's victory, leading to Napoleon's exile to Elba. With peace at hand and international trade freed from the constraints of war, the paper pound strengthened on the exchanges. No more Indian gold came in after the spring of 1814 and the price slipped down to £4.32.

The breathing space was short-lived. In March 1815, word reached London that Napoleon had escaped from Elba. The gold price jumped to £5.35 an ounce; the classic example of it reacting to 'bad news'. "There was an extraordinary demand," Isaac Lyon Goldsmid of the Bank's brokers later recalled before a House of Commons Committee. "At that moment we gave considerably more than the value of bar and Portugal gold, than anything would warrant, according to the rate of exchange, in the consequence of the return of Bonaparte from Elba. The current report was that the government were purchasers, through some medium of which we had no personal knowledge, for particular objects."[43]

The 'medium' was Nathan Mayer Rothschild buying directly for the Treasury at the request of John Herries, its Chief of Commissary. Rothschild's earlier success secured him the contract to mobilise gold needed quickly to get Wellington's army back in action. In his Memoirs, John Herries referred to "an arrangement entirely new which consisted principally in providing Specie required for these services through a single confidential agency". The agency was the Rothschild network. Herries dispatched Nathan Mayer Rothschild to Amsterdam and Hamburg to supervise the rounding up of French gold and silver coin (even getting it sent to Amsterdam from Paris) as little could be procured in the London market. The gold was then dispatched to Wellington direct from The Netherlands on British men-of-war. "By this means genuine French gold and silver currency was made to flow steadily into the military chest," Herries recalled. Thus financed, Wellington moved to his victory over Napoleon at Waterloo in August 1815.[44]

The price jump at the beginning of this crisis is an illustration that, despite what Ricardo and others might say, priority buying for an immediate campaign had real impact in wartime; over-issue of paper notes may well have influenced the gold price over time, but both in 1813 with the purchase of the Indian gold and in 1815 after Napoleon's escape, the urgent need for a significant amount of gold lifted the price. And it is a reminder that throughout the Napoleonic wars the normal international flows of gold were disrupted, putting a strain on markets to meet sudden demand. There was also the natural hoarding instinct of people to secure themselves from devaluations and the hazards of war by keeping a nest-egg in gold coins. The French émigrés fleeing the original revolution in 1789 had demonstrated that. Markets were not normal because much gold coin was frozen in the hands of hoarders.

Now, in the aftermath of Napoleon's defeat at Waterloo and his final exile to St Helena, people breathed easier and the gold price eased in turn. By Christmas, it was down to £4.00 an ounce, the lowest for a decade and, during 1816, slipped back almost to the Mint price of £3.89. This gave ammunition to critics of the Bullion Report, who argued the gold price had risen in response to the special circumstances of war. Note issue, they said, had nothing to do with it; armies no longer had to be paid, trade was unhindered, so the gold price was down. The truth lies somewhere in between. David Ricardo and his friend Francis Horner MP had, it can be argued, over-dramatised note issue as the sole concern. In reality, the gold price had been injected with a cocktail blending unrestrained issue of paper by the Bank of England, with the inevitable inflationary pressures of two decades of war.

Launching the *sovereign*

Gold might be back at Mint price, but there was no rush to resume cash payments for notes. Aside from the intellectual debate, two practical hurdles had to be overcome. First, the Bank of England's gold reserves were low, while the stock of *guineas*, not just at the Bank, but in the country at large, was depleted. Scarcely five million *guineas* had been minted since 1799 and none in recent years except those rushed through for Wellington in 1813. Pre-war *guineas* had either been hoarded or melted illegally for export abroad.

At the Bank the position improved as the country enjoyed good harvests, trade flourished, the exchange rate strengthened and gold flowed back in. The Bank's reserves rose from 21 m.t/675,150 t.oz in February 1815 to 61 m.t/1.96 million t.oz by August 1816 and to 94 m.t/3 million t.oz the following summer. In one brief period in the autumn of 1816 Mocatta and Goldsmid bought 28 m.t/900,000 t.oz for the Banks' account.[45]

The priority then became a major recoinage. But of what coin? The traditional *guinea* was worth £1.05, but in two decades of cash suspension people had become accustomed to the £1 note. The answer, a Privy Council Committee on the State of the Coins decided in May 1816, was a new coin, the *sovereign*, worth precisely £1. The *sovereign* would be 7.7 grams/0.25 t.oz of standard (916 fine) gold. Its champion was the Prime Minister, Lord Liverpool, himself a former Master of the Mint and the son of Charles Jenkinson, the instigator of the recoinage of the *guinea* between 1773–6. The *sovereign* was legalised by the Coinage Act of 1816, which declared it the sole standard of value and of unlimited legal tender. A new silver coinage was also authorised, but was to be legal tender only up to £2. The sole role of gold was finally confirmed. "Thus a century almost to the very day after the publication of Newton's famous report, which resulted by accident rather than design, in the establishment of the *guinea* at 21 shillings, as the standard coin, that coin was superseded," wrote Sir Alfred Feaveryear in *The Pound Sterling*. "The *guinea*, upon which had been founded the great economic expansion and prosperity of the 18th century, gave way to the *sovereign*, of which the 19th century became so proud."[46] The first *sovereigns* were issued in July 1817, and the half *sovereign*, worth ten shillings (£0.5), followed three months later. The Mint used 34 m.t/1.1 million t.oz of gold for the coins that year.

The resumption of cash payments

The road to a full resumption of cash payments was still bumpy, with opinion divided both among politicians and, even more, in the City on the merits. Initially the Bank of England edged into a return just before the first *sovereigns* were issued in the summer of 1817 by offering gold coin for all notes of £1 and £2 issued before 1812. Since few rushed to redeem the paper, they offered gold against small notes dated prior to 1816, and then, with their own gold reserve at a record high, honoured in gold all notes of every denomination issued prior to 1817. That was a step too far. The Bank still did not realise they must watch the relationship between the exchanges and the price of gold. They neglected to react as a bad harvest, a series of foreign loans and a rush of tourists to the continent, eager to enjoy its temptations after a generation of war, combined to put the balance of payments in deficit. "Byron went … and threw English money about," Sir John Clapham, the Bank's historian, wrote wryly, "so did Shelley and his mixed set. Lady Hester Stanhope queened it among the Arabs on English money."[47]

As the exchange rate dropped, the gold price climbed back to £4.15. Suddenly it became profitable to trade in notes for gold; £1 in paper secured a gold coin now worth £1.025. The freshly minted *sovereigns* flowed abroad. The banker Alexander Baring estimated up to 28 m.t/900,000 t.oz in gold ended up at the Mint in Paris alone.[48]   The Bank of England's gold reserves were under 30 m.t/964,500 t.oz by the summer of 1819, one-third of their level two years earlier. Both Houses of Parliament convened Secret Committees to investigate, quickly issuing interim criticism of the Bank for moving too hastily on cash payments when the exchange was deteriorating. They urged the whole process to be put on hold.

That relieved the governor of the Bank of England, George Durrien who, in his evidence to the Commons Committee, said, "It is difficult to say when the Bank could with propriety resume its cash payments, it must always be judged of by experience".[49]   The mood in the City was not to hurry. The state of the exchange did not warrant immediate resumption, so it was prudent not to set any date. The merchants had learned to manage quite well with paper for over twenty years. Their case was put most strongly by Nathan Mayer Rothschild who told the Committee that he was "in the foreign banking line" and that since he came to live in London (in 1805) he had known only a paper currency and "everything had gone smoothly".

So what would happen if cash payments were resumed? "I do not think it can be done without very great distress to this country," he cautioned. "It would do a great deal of mischief; we may not actually know ourselves what mischief it may cause."

"Have the goodness to explain the nature of the mischief, and in what way it would be produced." – "Money will be so very scarce, every article in this country will fall to such an enormous extent, that many persons will be ruined."[50]

Neither the Lords or Commons Committees were convinced. They recommended a return to gold within four years (by 1823). The House of Lords report argued the exchange would be steadied by restoring "to the country by the speediest and safest means, a metallic standard, as the regulator of its paper currency".[51]   A new Act proposed a gradual return to cash payments within four years, during which the Bank would reduce its note issue. Shortly before Parliament debated the upcoming Act, four or five hundred City merchants signed a petition to the government suggesting resumption would lead to a 'highly injurious contraction of the circulating medium of the country'.

The politicians did not listen. They were more concerned with the mood in the country at large, beset by high unemployment, created by demobilisation of the army, which led to social unrest. A return to gold payments in the wake of victory seemed a way of signalling a new beginning. "Somehow it was assumed that bringing the paper money era to an end would cleanse the body politic of unpatriotic speculators and generally repair the social fabric, damaged by war and its aftermath," David Kynaston observed.[52]

The tone was set in the House of Commons debate on the necessary legislation by Robert Peel, who had chaired their Secret Committee on Resumption. Peel admitted that he had originally not agreed with the 1810 Bullion Committee on the relationship between note issue, gold and the exchange, but his chairmanship of the Committee had changed his mind. "No one," he said, "not even Sir Isaac

Newton, had been able to find an alternative. Every sound writer came to the same conclusion, that a certain weight of gold bullion, with an impression on it, denoting it to be of a certain weight, and of a certain fineness, constituted the only true, intelligible, and adequate standard of value; and to that standard the country must return, or the difficulties of our situation would be aggravated."[53]

The initial strategy was for a partial resumption of gold payments in February 1820, with notes being redeemed for gold ingots of 60 ounces (1.87 kg) at a price of £4.50 (a minimum transaction of £270). This was prompted by a suggestion from David Ricardo, now a Member of Parliament, that notes should be interchangeable only for ingots, and that small notes of £1 and £2 should be legal tender. Thereafter the target was to get the price down to the Mint level of £3.89 by 1823. "The object, scientifically conceived," noted Sir John Clapham, "was to operate on the price of gold and the exchange without prematurely dissipating the Bank's limited stock of coin into the pockets of the public."[54]

This Act of 1819, often called Peel's Act, also legalised the export of gold, including gold coin of the realm or bars from melted coin. The findings of both the 1810 Bullion Committee and the 1819 Secret Committees was that illegal export could not be curtailed, so it was best to permit it. Freedom of export meant that the gold standard in its classic form came into full operation with the metal flowing into or out of the country according to the balance on the exchanges. The timetable for resumption was soon speeded up, as the winding up of several foreign loans, a good harvest in 1820 and deflation through reduced government expenditure brought prices down in general.

The exchanges turned and the Bank's gold reserves rose. From a modest 39 m.t/1.25 million t.oz in February 1820 they reached a new record of 96 m.t/3 million t.oz a year later. Meanwhile, the Bank had reduced its note issue from £29 million to £20 million which was now backed by over £11 million in gold, more than 50% cover. There was no reason for further delay. From 8th May 1821 anyone could walk into the Bank of England with a paper pound note and exchange it for a gold *sovereign*. The *sovereign* swiftly replaced small notes entirely as they were withdrawn from circulation. The Mint struck 9.8 million *sovereigns* that year (a level not reached again until 1853 in the gold rush era) and ample to meet the renewed demand. The first era of the paper pound had lasted twenty-four years and sixty-two days. The new gold standard would last almost a century.

CHAPTER 21

1848-1914:
Gold Standard Triumphant

As James Marshall later told it, he was walking by the millrace at a sawmill he was building for John Sutter on the morning of 24th January 1848 when "my eye was caught by something shining in the bottom of the ditch … I reached my hand down and picked it up; it made my heart thump, for I was certain it was gold. The piece was about half the size and shape of a pea. Then I saw another …". He ran back towards the sawmill, on the banks of the south fork of the American river coming down the western slopes of the Sierra Nevada in California, shouting, "Boys, I believe I have found a gold mine".

He had started a gold rush that captivated the world and brought thousands of diggers from across America, Australia, Europe, Mexico and China to California's shores. The news of men picking up more gold in a day than they could earn in a year unleashed "a contagion of optimism and ambition," wrote J. S. Holliday in *The World Rushed In*. "Responsible family men found their jobs and prospects unrewarding when set against all that California could provide."[1] Riding that wave of excitement, prospectors also found gold across the Pacific in Australia within three years. Annual world production rose from a modest 43 m.t/1.4 million t.oz before Marshall spied his gold to 203 m.t/6.5 million t.oz by 1855. Ultimately, ten times as much gold was mined in the second half of the 19th century as in the first.

In truth, there are really two histories of gold; one prior to 1848, the other thereafter. The scale of the gold business, whether on the mines or the markets, changed out of all proportion, as the metal now available dwarfed the size of the treasure of Alexander the Great, the output of Spanish mines for Rome, of African deposits to early Islam, of Hungarian mines for Venice, or even the Brazilian gold that first underpinned Britain's fledgling gold standard after 1700. Even a sharp rise in Russian production to 25 m.t/800,000 t.oz a year during the 1840s was quite overshadowed. Bankers and economists, especially in France, feared the gold price must tumble. On the contrary, it remained stable. Just as the gold rushes ushered in the era of the common man out to make his fortune as a gold digger, they also put gold coins into the pockets of millions of people world-wide, replacing silver coins that had predominated before.

The Mint in Paris made over 150 million *Napoléons d'Or* in just eight years, 1850–57, compared with 65 million in the preceding fifty years. The United States

Mint's output of gold *eagles* rose five-fold 1850–54, compared with the previous five years. In 1850 only Britain was on the gold standard, but by 1900 every major nation, save China, had gone over to gold, as opposed to silver, as their standard of value. And it was the price of silver, not gold, that collapsed as its main usage was abruptly terminated. In 1850 the gold/silver ratio was 1:15.5, with the silver price in London at £0.27 per ounce and New York at $1.42; fifty years on, the ratio was 1:33.33, with the London price at £0.13 and New York quoting $0.67. The gold price was unchanged. Yet, these years were the most dramatic in the entire history of gold.

California bound

The day James Marshall found gold, California was still legally part of Mexico. Just nine days later, on 2nd February 1848, after two years of war, Mexico signed a treaty with the United States ceding to it the land west of Texas and north to Oregon. At the moment of transfer a mere handful of men knew of the gold Mexico was bequeathing. Four days after his discovery Marshall rode over to Sutter's Fort to tell his boss of the find. John Sutter, who had set up his ranch and a store at the junction of the American and Sacramento rivers in 1839, hastened back with him. "I have made a discovery of a gold mine," he soon wrote to a friend, "which, according to the experiments we have made, is extremely rich." Through February word spread to the few homesteads along the rivers. Everyone turned prospector. Sutter could not hold his own workers. Sam Brannan, leader of a nearby Mormon settlement, came up and started digging through the rainy winter months. And it was Brannan who turned up in San Francisco on 12th May, with a bottle full of gold dust shouting "Gold! Gold! Gold from the American River". The flame had been lit. "The whole country from San Francisco to Los Angeles and from the seashore to the base of the Sierra Nevada resounds to the sordid cry of "Gold! Gold! GOLD!" reported the Californian on 29th May, "while the field is left half-planted, the house half-built and everything neglected but the manufacture of shovels and pick-axes".[2]

Yet California was still a little world of its own, cut off from the rest of the United States, with journeys overland or by sea taking many months. The military governor of California in Monterey, Colonel Richard Mason, wrote to his superiors in Washington DC on 1st June, "On the American fork of the Sacramento and Feather rivers … there has been within the present year discovered a placer, a vast tract of land containing gold in small particles". He set out to investigate the diggings. On the North Fork of the American river, he found one site where two men "had a short time before obtained in seven days $17,000 worth of gold". Mason reckoned there were 4,000 miners on the rivers, half of them Indians. He estimated production at $30,000 to $50,000 a day (up to 100kg/3,250 t.oz). Mason added, "No capital is required to obtain this gold, and the laboring man wants nothing but his pick and shovel and tin pan with which to dig and wash".[3]

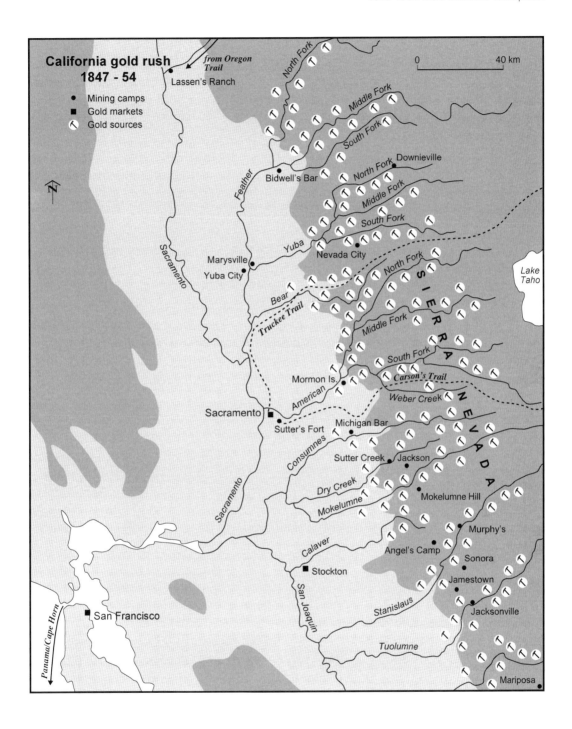

Scores of letters from diggers were soon arriving with their families in the East. The *New York Journal* ran a letter speaking of a prospector getting "eight to ten ounces a day". The Philadelphia North American quoted a note, "Your streams have minnows, and ours are paved with gold". Throughout the eastern United States everyone was agog. But was it really true? The seal of approval came on 5th December 1848, when President James Polk told Congress, "The accounts of the abundance of gold in that territory are of such extra-ordinary character as would scarcely command belief were they not corroborated by authentic reports of officers in the public service". The race to California was on.

"The spirit of emigration which is carrying off thousands to California … expands every day," reported the *New York Herald*. "All classes of our citizens seem to be under the influence of this extraordinary mania. Poets, philosophers, lawyers, brokers, bankers, merchants, farmers, clergymen – all are feeling the impulse and are preparing to go and dig for gold."[4] They were dubbed the '49ers', as upwards of 90,000 would-be diggers (almost all men) set out by land and sea. Newspapers were full of sailing dates and advertisements for money-belts, tents, India-rubber wading boots, patent medicines and machines, such as the hydro-centrifugal Californian Gold Finder or the Archimedes Gold Washing Machine. One bold shyster promoted an "aerial locomotive" capable of taking 100 passengers from New York to California in three days for $200 each.[5]

The reality was harsh. A long sea voyage around Cape Horn on overcrowded ships, a short cut across the fever-ridden Isthmus of Panama to the Pacific or the overland route across the Great Plains from St Louis, Independence, or St Joseph through the high mountains on the Oregon Trail, swinging down into California, a trek of over 2,500 miles. Over 40,000 emigrants went overland, often forming themselves into joint-stock companies both to buy wagons and provisions and for security against perceived attacks from Indians. Actually, the threat was cholera, which carried off far more men; the rutted trail was marked by graves. Indeed, the fear of cholera, apparently, kept the Indians at bay.

Their diaries and letters reveal the sheer determination of these men, who should have been tending their farms, or their customers, or their patients (plenty of doctors went) at home through the summer of 1849, but were battling mud, hailstorms, poor food, contaminated water and enforced companionship on a six-month slog. Letters for home tried to reassure families all was well; diaries were blunt. William Swain's entry for 28th May read, "This morning Mr Lyon, who was taken sick with the cholera last night, is dead. His mess and the doctor who attended him seemed to take but little care of him; otherwise he might in all probability have been saved. A gloom appears on the company. We started late, leaving … Mr Lyon's mess behind to bury him".[6] They tramped on, sustained by great expectations of the gold fields. "Neither the Crusades nor Alexander's expedition to India … can equal the emigration to California," wrote a Michigan doctor, far out on the plains in July 1849.[7]

On the diggings

In California, meanwhile, the diggings were becoming crowded. Upwards of 40,000 men were working along a 600 kilometre front on ten rivers coming down from the Sierra Nevada by late autumn in 1849. Life was gruelling. "Digging was the constant and endless task that faced every miner," observed J. S. Holliday. "Digging on a river bar in sand, gravel and rocks, between massive boulders, some of which had to be pushed aside … Always digging, down and down … through rock and gravel that dulled pickaxes and bent shovels."[8] The easy pickings of 1848, creaming gold off virgin sand bars or stream beds, were gone. The task was soon aided by the development of wooden rockers, 'long toms', worked by four men, with the upper end in the stream to provide a constant flow to wash gold out of gravels. Mercury, to which gold adheres naturally, was spread along the bottom riffles of the 'long tom'. In the evening the men scraped off the mercury, heated it until it vaporised and recovered the gold. It was a thankless task, often working many hours a day up to their waists in water, their boots rotting, their clothes always damp. "This mining … is a dog's life," William Swain wrote home. "A man has to make a jackass of himself packing loads over mountains that God never designed man to climb, a barbarian by foregoing all the comforts of civilised life."[9] Yet, for the lucky, rewards were handsome.

"On the North Fork of the American River, a company of men, thirty in number, turned the course of the river and took out $75,000. Their greatest yield for any one day was $6,040," another miner told his family.[10]

Supplies were sparse and over-priced (many made more money through supplying the diggers than by digging themselves). In the absence of authority, summary justice was often handed out. A man who stole $300 had both ears cut off and a T branded on his cheek. Heavy drinking was endemic, not least to offset the rain and cold in the winter months. Social life was spartan, though one trading post organised a ball for New Year's Eve 1850 – entry one ounce of gold. "Gold dust is the principal currency in this country," Edwin Hall told his family.[11] "When a man is asked the price of anything here, he does not tell the price in dollars, but will say an ounce, half ounce, or two ounces. Every person has a small leather bag to hold his dust." The maximum gold price on the diggings was $16 an ounce, compared to the New York price of $19.25 for 900 fine gold. The quality of the gold dust ranged from 760 to 960 fine, with the balance in silver and traces of iron.

Gold output in the early years is hard to quantify. No real records were kept and gold went by sea from San Francisco, principally to New York and London, but was taken home by diggers to Mexico, South America, Australia and, no doubt, to China, given the numbers of Chinese at work in California. The hard evidence through official imports or coin minting does not really emerge until 1851. The yields probably exceeded 10 m.t/320,150 t.oz in 1848, over 30 m.t/1 million t.oz in 1849, rising above 80 m.t/2.5 million t.oz in 1850, but the margin of error on an individual year is wide.[12]

'River mining'

The steady increase in production was maintained only by radical improvements in recovery techniques. Even by late 1849 the diggers realised co-operative efforts were needed to dam and divert rivers, so that they could trawl through tonnes of gravel and rocks of the river beds where gold was hidden in potholes and crevices in the bedrock. They called it 'river mining'. Each year operations were conceived on a larger, capital-intensive, scale. The California stamp mill was developed to crush rock to powder, as miners also tried to track gold back into quartz veins in the hills. Mills cost upwards of $50,000, requiring the formation of mining companies. The true day of the digger with pick, shovel and pan, picking up a few dollars' worth of gold each day was short-lived.[13]

The most significant technical advance was made on the Yuba river in 1853 by Edward Matteson, who conceived hydraulic mining, by directing a powerful jet of water on river banks to break them down and flush out the gold into a series of sluices. The *Sacramento Weekly Union* explained, "Thus banks of earth that would have kept a hundred men employed for weeks in its removal will now be removed by three or four men in two weeks". The concept caught on fast, for relatively low-grade deposits could be harvested. Construction companies were formed to build canals, tunnels, and aqueducts to channel water downhill for miles, stepping up the head for high pressure monitors with cast iron nozzles that were directed at the hillsides (the environmental damage was horrendous). Over 4,400 miles (7,000 km) of waterways were built by 1857, an achievement comparable with the Romans' aqueducts to their Spanish mines (*see chapter 13*). These projects pushed California's output towards 90 m.t/2.9 million ounces in 1851 and thereafter to just over 100 m.t/3.2 million t.oz annually until 1859 (with 1853, by general consent, the record at around 110 m.t/3.5 million t.oz). By 1860 the best years were over; output slipped back to between 60 m.t/1.9 million t.oz and 70 m.t/2.25 million t.oz for the next decade.

Marshalling the gold for market

The gold fields had to be sustained almost entirely by sea through San Francisco, whose population grew from a few hundred in 1848 to around 30,000 by 1850. Almost 700 ships entered her harbour in 1849 bringing not just would-be prospectors, but the supplies to feed them, the tools they worked with and the luxuries they indulged in. Many crews deserted their ships for the diggings; entrepreneurs took them over as warehouses, hotels, saloons and shops. A colourful array of merchants, bankers, speculators, shipping agents, gamblers, pick-pockets and prostitutes assembled to service the diggers coming into town with their money belt filled with gold dust. It cost one ounce just for a girl to sit at your table, more like ten or fifteen ounces to spend the night with her.

The initial priority was to get steamboat services going up the rivers to Sacramento, originally Sutter's Fort, and Stockton, the front-line towns, from which wagons and mules left loaded for the diggings. The *Pacific News* reported by early 1851, "Forty-four steamers [are] employed in river trade with Sacramento and Stockton and lesser towns; twelve ocean-going steamers connecting with Panama".[14]

The gold buying in Sacramento seemed casual to one miner. "I was struck all aback when I saw the merchants receiving and handling gold," Dr Isaac Lord wrote in his diary. "To examine the quality, they go through much the same manoeuvres as the wheat buyers of Chicago when inspecting a sample of wheat. If the gold dust looks clean and fair, it is poured onto the scales and weighed. If it looks dirty and has rock and sand in it, they take some in the palm, and stir it ceaselessly around with a forefinger and determined its value."[15]

A more organised service was eventually established throughout the diggings by the courier company, Adams & Co., which was set up in San Francisco in December 1849. They opened a network of small buying and assaying offices, backed up with armed expressmen, who ventured to the most remote camps to buy gold at $14 to $16 an ounce. They hauled it back down the river canyons in leather bags slung across mules. Adams & Co. accepted deposits of gold or bought it for their own account, issuing drafts payable in the eastern states so that miners could remit money to their families. They were the forerunners of the more famous Wells Fargo from New York, which opened in San Francisco in 1852.[16] Official regulation came in 1851 with the establishment of a US Assay Office in San Francisco, with a US Mint branch set up the following year, so that gold coins could be struck on the spot. Until then there had been shortages of gold coin in California (no one wanted paper notes) and some private mints had issued their own coins or tokens.[17]

Meanwhile, a young man named Heinrich Schliemann, who would later become famous as the discoverer of the gold of Troy and Mycenæ (*see chapters 3 and 5*), had turned up in San Francisco, scenting a profit. He had worked already as a successful commodity trader in St Petersburg for the London house of Schroder & Co. He was lured partly by gold, but was also anxious to find out what had happened to his younger brother, Louis, an early arrival at the gold rush, who had died in Sacramento. Schliemann arrived in San Francisco in April 1851, armed with an introduction from Rothschilds in London to their agent, Davidson, who was already buying up gold. He took a steamer to Sacramento, traced his brother's grave and erected a tombstone. Ever the opportunist, he decided Sacramento was the perfect buying location close to the gold fields. He placed an advertisement in the local paper:

H. Schliemann & Co., Bankers
in the Brick Building Cor. J. & Front Street.
We are now ready to purchase any quantity of
Gold Dust at the highest prices, for which we pay

principally in American coin, and drafts drawn on
San Francisco. We will sell Messrs Rothschilds' Bills
of Exchange on the United States & Europe.[18]

Schliemann was soon buying between 1,000 and 2,000 ounces a day, which he sent downriver to Davidson for dispatch to London. The connection was fortuitous, because Rothschilds banking house was about to take over the Royal Mint's refinery in London and this gave them a direct link into the California diggings. Between 19th October 1851 and 5th April 1852 Schliemann purchased $1,350,000 worth of gold (close to 2 m.t/64,000 t.oz), which was shipped through Panama to the London market.[19]

The impact of the Californian gold rush was not just in the physical delivery of gold to the markets, calling for more refining and coin-making capacity, but in creating a whole generation of gold prospectors for whom it was a way of life to rush anywhere at the hint of a new discovery. Their experience of battling for gold in the river beds of California gave them unique advantage. During the 1850s and 60s, they dashed to Oregon, to the Columbia river in Canada, to Virginia City on the eastern flank of the Sierra Nevada to tap the Comstoke Lode of gold and silver, and to Cripple Creek, Colorado. In the mid-1860s there were over a thousand mining camps scattered throughout the American West, five hundred of them in California and two hundred in Nevada. Prospectors were also scouting the Black Hills of South Dakota, where Homestake, America's oldest working mine, opened in 1877 – a direct legacy of the spirit of discovery that fuelled the Californian rush in 1849. The diverse sources helped to maintain American production close to 70 m.t/2.3 million t.oz annually. The new prize, though, was already across the Pacific in Australia.

Gold 'down under'

The spell cast by California soon caught Australians in its web. Early in 1849 a ship put into Sydney, not just with news of the gold rush, but 1,200 ounces of the metal. It captured the imagination of Edward Hammond Hargraves, who had wandered around the interior of New South Wales, then a British colony, for a couple of decades. "Fortune had not smiled so favourably on me," he acknowledged in his memoirs, "as to make me proof against the contagion."[20] He took the next ship to San Francisco, sharing a cabin with a sheep farmer and would-be geologist, Simpson Davison, who had come to Sydney to sell his wool, but decided to go for gold instead. On the voyage their discussion centred on how the geology of the river systems coming down from the Blue Mountains of New South Wales might match those of California.

The moment he set foot there Hargraves was almost more eager to get back home than dig for gold. He and Davison did get lucky on the Yuba river in the summer of 1850, but he was restless. "The greater our success was, the more anxious did I become to put my own persuasion to the test, of the existence of gold in New South Wales," he wrote.[21]   He took a ship back to Sydney, arriving in January 1851.   On 12th February he was on Lewis Pond Creek, a tributary of the Macquarie River, north-west of Sydney.   "I took the pick," he recounted, "and scratched the gravel off a schistose dyke … and with a trowel, I dug a panful of earth, which I washed in the waterhole.   The first trial produced a little piece of gold."[22]   Hargraves got the recognition he had long sought; he was appointed a Gold Commissioner to organise the field (he was never one for hard digging) and a reward of £500.   New South Wales produced 4.5 m.t/150,000 t.oz that year and, in 1852, an astonishing 25.5 m.t/820,000 t.oz.   Hargraves' hunch was right, as he never ceased to tell people, although the real bonanza was to the south in the rival colony of Victoria.

News of the finds in New South Wales sent prospectors hastening from Melbourne to the streams coming down from the coastal mountains towards the Murray river. On 25th August 1851 a prospector named Connor washed out thirty ounces in a day from a stream at Ballarat, north of the settlement of Geelong.   Within weeks discoveries were made near Bendigo, in creeks below Mount Alexander.[23]   Virtually the entire population of Melbourne decamped.   Twenty thousand men were digging at Bendigo by mid-December, reportedly recovering 2 m.t/64,300 t.oz per week. Licensing of claims was introduced and the government of Victoria provided armed escorts for the gold back to Melbourne.   The colony produced, officially, almost 7 m.t/225,000 t.oz in 1851 and over 71 m.t/2.3 million t.oz the following year.   Thus, within the space of less than two years, Australia was contributing close to 100 m.t/3.2 million t.oz, on a par with California.

Regulating the gold fields

While both gold rushes led to the growth of cities and the opening up of wilderness areas, the Australian approach was more regulatory than California's *laissez-faire* stance, where miners largely ran their own affairs.   Gold was on Crown Land in Australia, so claims had to be registered at a charge of £1.50 per month.   The Commissioner of Crown Lands set the size of claims.   Initially in New South Wales up to eight metres frontage was allowed along a river for two or three men, and 13 metres for a gang.   In Victoria, where much of the digging was on open ground, claims were six square metres for a couple of diggers, or 12 square metres for a party.

In both colonies armed escorts took the gold each week to Sydney and Melbourne, where banks eagerly bought, although often handicapped by having little gold coin to pay for it until shipments from London could be arranged – a lengthy process.   The banks usually paid cash at around £3.20 per ounce (compared to the London price of £3.89 for standard gold), or with a draft on London.   However, the avalanche of gold coming into Melbourne from Ballarat and Bendigo early in 1852 meant prices slipped briefly to £2.75 an ounce.   They revived to over £3.50 as the process of shipping gold to London became more organised. Some banks simply sat on the gold, watching their balance sheets bloom, but eventually began regular dispatches to London, at first not committing too much on any one ship. The Bank of New South Wales branch in Melbourne was ordered to send 5,000 ounces (155 kg) "by every first class vessel". They managed to get away 300,000 ounces (9.3 m.t) between August 1852 and March 1853 only by heavier shipments.[24] The *Illustrated London News* for 22nd January 1853 depicted 20,000 ounces (622 kg) being unloaded from the steamship *The Australian* on arrival in London. The delay between mine and market was many months, probably up to one year, until the local Australian banks got organised. In return, the Bank of New South Wales, for instance, ordered 40,000 *sovereigns* a month to be shipped out to Australia. Total British exports of *sovereigns* to all Australian banks amounted to 4.6 million in 1852 and close to 3 million the following year. Ultimately, the shortage of gold coins in the colonies was solved by the establishment of the Sydney Mint in 1855, as a branch of the Royal Mint in London.

A cosmopolitan cast

Meanwhile the population of New South Wales and Victoria exploded. Every Australia-bound ship from Britain, Europe and California was packed. Twenty thousand prospective diggers were arriving monthly by late 1852. The colonies, which had originally been peopled largely by convicts and their families, now took on a cosmopolitan look. At Mount Alexander, over 30,000 diggers were hard at work; Bendigo was probably home to 40,000 prospectors and hangers-on. They were a democratic medley, just as in California. One visitor, Colonel Mundy, observed, "Merchants, cabmen, magistrates and convicts, amateur gentlemen rocking their cradle merely to say they have done so, fashionable hairdressers and tailors, cooks, coachmen, lawyers' clerks and their masters, colliers, cobblers, quarrymen, doctors of physic and music, aldermen, scavengers, sailors, short-hand writers, a real live lord on his travels – all levelled by community of pursuit and of costume".[25]

For all Hargraves' original trumpeting, it was Victoria, not New South Wales, that was the easy champion. During the 1850s Victoria yielded, in all, over 650 m.t/20 million t.oz of gold, against a modest 90 m.t/2.9 million t.oz from its rival. Extracting the gold, however, was a different technical proposition than in California. Even in the early days around Ballarat, Bendigo and Mount Alexander, the miners had to dig down twenty feet for a bluish-grey 'pipe-clay' studded with pockets of gold, often including good sized nuggets. The largest nugget, turned up in a gully at Ballarat in January 1853, weighed 51.7 kg/1,664 t.oz. Dealing with the tenacious clay was the real problem, for which a new technique, the puddling tub, was developed. A barrel was cut in half and filled with clay. "Water is baled in from the creek, and the whole worked about with the spade," explained a contemporary account, "the miner cutting up and turning over the clay till it gradually dissolved in the water;

and as the water becomes charged with earth it is poured from the tub, and a fresh supply added." Eventually nothing remained but clean gravel and gold.[26]

The task became harder with the years. Gullies had to be cut down into the clay to depths of fifty metres to tap deep gutters in ancient watercourses where the gold lay trapped. Six months often elapsed while a new gully was channelled out. Once its underground gutters had been located, miners on neighbouring large claims tried to second-guess how they ran under their own property and started digging too. Ever larger puddling machines were devised, along with quartz crushing mills and steam engines for pumping. These called for capital and the establishment of co-operatives employing miners for wages.

Yet independent diggers persisted with their own small-scale operations, sometimes clashing with the miners seeking deep alluvial and quartz veins.[27] Coming up behind both parties were the Chinese, probably 33,000 by 1858, who specialised in 'paddocking'. They stripped out completely the topsoil of terrain that had already been worked, washing the dirt to get out the last traces of gold, then restoring the ground and moving on to the next section. They created their own environment with teahouses, educated letter-writers, even a theatre and circus.

Next stop – New Zealand

Rumours of new finds were always rife and the individual diggers responded with alacrity. "At the first whisper … of a new field, they shoulder their picks and shovels, and their swags and stalk away with all the speed they can put forth," wrote one *habitué*.[28] Usually they were disappointed, but a hot tip in 1861 was worth following up. In May that year, Gabriel Read, a veteran of the Californian and Australia gold fields, was on the sand bar of a stream below the Dunstan mountains of the south island of New Zealand. "I shovelled away two and a half feet of gravel, (and) arrived at a beautiful soft slate and saw gold shining like the stars in Orion on a dark frosty night," he later recalled.[29] He panned seven ounces in 10 hours. A Gold Commissioner was on the field by mid-August and 2,000 prospectors a week were arriving at the little port of Dunedin, most of whose population had already hastened to the interior. Rich pickings were found along the Molyneux and Arrow rivers. Instinctively the diggers organised themselves along Californian lines, assigning twenty metres of river frontage to each team. That first year, 1861, around 6 m.t/193,000 t.oz of gold was recovered, rising towards 13 m.t/420,000 t.oz the next year and close to 20 m.t/643,000 t.oz by 1863, as more elaborate river mining was developed.

Fresh discoveries in 1864 on the west coast of the south island along the Greenstone and Taramaku rivers, coming down from the Southern Alps, brought a new flood of prospectors to create the community of Hokitaka. Output surged to a record 23 m.t/740,000 t.oz by 1866, and was maintained just below that until 1871, helped by modest finds on the Coromandel peninsular of the north island. Despite New Zealand's remoteness, the usual international crowd assembled. "German,

French, Italian, Greek and several other tongues were to be heard," noted the New Zealand historian W. P. Morrell.[30]   The Chinese were soon on the scene trawling over the initial workings for second helpings.

With New Zealand's contribution, Australasian output stayed neck and neck with America into the early 1870s. The market was thus required to digest a combined total of over 200 m.t/6.4 million t.oz annually through the 1850s and not much less through the next decade. Supplies were boosted by Russian output which rose to 40 m.t/1.3 million t.oz annually in the 1860s. This flood of gold posed two questions. How could it be absorbed and what was to be the fate of silver, the primary metal for coinage in most countries? Economists and politicians became engrossed in a great debate on the merits or otherwise of bimetallism for the next half century. Congressional and parliamentary commissions pored over columns of figures outlining this new world of gold. The American presidential election of 1896 even turned on the whole issue; when the bimetallists' candidate, William Jennings Bryan, lost, the gold standard had won.

Strike up the gold

While much of the Californian gold initially went to New York, whence it was sent to the Mint in Philadelphia, the London market was also a recipient. "As creditor of the whole earth," Sir John Clapham observed, "London got the first of this gold."[31] The immediate fear was that the gold price was vulnerable. *The Economist* reported "excitement, especially on the Continent, that the price must fall".[32]   The City Editor of *The Times* was more sanguine. "There will be considerable surplus," he wrote. "In fact, on the Continent, which is on a bimetallic system, more and more payments are likely to be made in gold."

The real pessimist was Michel Chevalier of L'Institut Français, who wrote a book *On the Probable Fall in the Value of Gold*. Bowled over by the quantities involved, he worked out that jewellery fabrication was "very far from being sufficient for the purpose". As for gold use in gilding and gold leaf, beloved by the French, that could only take a tiny bite of the golden apple. He calculated that one tonne (32,150 t.oz) of gold would be enough to gild 144,000 salons and apartments in Paris, while whole hectares of French countryside could be spread with gold leaf before a similar amount was consumed. His solution was simple. "There is but one way of disposing of these masses of gold," he wrote. "It is by coining them." He still feared the value of the coins would depreciate, but at least the metal would be taken up. However, he misjudged the balance; silver, not gold, was the casualty.[33] As the Harvard Professor of Political Economy, J. Laurence Laughlin, later pointed out, "France began the march away from silver to gold … (that) willingness to take gold and give up silver sustained the value of the former."[34]

The switch to gold coin inevitably began in the United States. The US was then on a bimetallic standard, with a gold/silver ratio of 1:16, but relatively little gold was coined. The mood changed abruptly. Scarcely had President Polk confirmed the scale of the California discoveries in December 1848 than Congressman James McKay of North Carolina (scene of earlier small gold finds) introduced a bill for coinage of a gold one dollar coin and a $20 double eagle, in addition to the existing $10 eagle. The bill was swiftly enacted on 3rd March 1849. The one dollar was a tiny coin of 1.67 grams/0.054 t.oz (often known as the 'toy' dollar), while the handsome double eagle weighed 33.44 grams/1.08 t.oz; both were 900 fine. Newspapers were enthusiastic. "We go for gold, for gold coin, for the gold dollar," declared Washington's *Weekly Globe*. "The gold interests ... conquered virtually every horizon," wrote Don Taxay, historian of the US Mint. "Gold coinage emerged from literal obscurity to become the predominant specie."[35] The Mint, which had struck little over $4 million worth of gold annually before the California discoveries, minted over $62 million (91 m.t/2.9 million t.oz) in 1851 and a trifle less in 1852, the two record years.

In practical terms, the US was now on a gold standard. A formal relationship with silver was maintained, but it was a subservient coinage. "Gold is the only standard of value by which all is now measured," said a Congressman in a debate proposing a new three dollar gold coin in 1853. "It is virtually the only currency of the country."[36] Keeping up with this conversion, the US Mint established branches in San Francisco in 1852, in Denver in 1862 and Carson City in 1863, close to the main gold fields.

Like a surging wave the flow of metal then crossed the Atlantic to London, whose busiest years were 1852–4 (as Australia also came on stream), and finally engulfed Paris from 1854–7. Often it was the same gold, minted into *eagles* in Philadelphia and exported to London, melted there for *sovereigns* and, in turn, dispatched to France for melting before being struck as *Napoléons*. The Royal Mint in London once reckoned at least 25% of *sovereigns* were from re-melted American coin, with the proportion at least as high in Europe. A great deal of gold was on the move. British imports of gold soared from a mere 13 m.t/432,000 t.oz in 1848 (mostly from Russia) to 102 m.t/3.3 million t.oz in 1853 and 163 m.t/5.24 million t.oz the next year as Australia was in full spate. The Bank of England bought over 100 m.t/3.2 million t.oz of bar gold, plus almost 20 m.t/643,000 t.oz of foreign gold coin (including US *eagles*) in 1852, taking its reserves over 160 m.t/5.1 million t.oz, a new record. The Mint promptly turned much of this into *sovereigns*, delivering to the Bank nearly eight million coins in 1852 and almost 12 million the following year.[37] The Bank's Governor, Thomas Weguelin, told a secret Parliamentary Committee in 1857, "there has been ... an increase of nearly 30% in the gold circulation in the country". He put this down to "the increased wealth in the country, and the increased trade of the country".[38]

Britain, of course, had a head start. Gold coin had provided the main circulation for almost 150 years, so that had only to be added to, without a dramatic change from silver. Governor Weguelin pointed out that the real growth in gold circulation had been on the Continent, notably France. He estimated the total European stock of gold had risen by close to 700 m.t/22.5 million t.oz. Asked by the Committee if he had any 'observations' on the Bank of France, he could not resist a wry comment on the rival central bank. "The Bank of France has, no doubt, paid a premium upon gold," he responded. "The mode which they have pursued is not very intelligible; but we conclude that it has been paying a premium upon bar gold, which induced merchants to bring bar gold to them in exchange for their notes."[39]

Actually, this sudden appetite for gold in France was a matter of that usual suspect, 'market forces'. The Mint in Paris had long adhered to a fixed gold/silver ratio of 1:15.5, but gold had traded at a premium on the Paris market so that it had not paid to take gold to the Mint. Silver went to the Mint, most payments were in silver coin and even the Bank of France redeemed its own notes in silver. The abundance of gold from California and Australia knocked out the gold premium. Moreover, the Netherlands chose this moment to switch from a gold to a silver coinage (wrongly anticipating a fall in the value of gold), with gold no longer legal tender. Almost one hundred tonnes (3.2 million t.oz) of melted Dutch gold coin was dumped on the Paris market. Meanwhile, a strong demand in London for silver for India and China pushed up the silver premium, making it attractive to export silver from Paris to London, taking gold in return.[40] The contemporary observers Tooke and Newmarch noted, "The French mint had been over-burdened with accumulations of Gold Bullion presented for coinage … the relative proportions of the two metals in the French Coinage … have been reversed".[41]

The Paris Mint was in a league of its own, easily exceeding the combined output of American and British mints. Once it got into its stride by 1853, it struck regularly close to 160 m.t/5 million t.oz of *Napoléons* annually; in the eight years to 1859 almost 1,250 m.t/40 million t.oz of gold went into 214 million *Napoléons*. This was equivalent to 70% of all gold mined in those years (though some of the gold was the Dutch disposals). The shift from silver to gold in France was reminiscent of Britain's switch to the 'accidental' gold standard after 1700, with the catalyst again being India as a sponge for silver upsetting the subtle ratio between gold and silver, making it more attractive to hold gold at home.

The London market comes of age

Long before the California gold rush, London was the heart of the world's gold trade. It handled the gold of Brazil in the early 18th century and later from Russia, the largest producer immediately prior to 1848. In that decade it began to modernise, notably by ending the long-standing arrangement by which the Bank of England's Bullion Office was the sole crossroads of gold and silver, with all transactions handled by their exclusive broker, Mocatta and Goldsmid. The Bank ruled in January 1840 "that in the purchase or sale of gold in bars, the employment of a Broker on the part of the Bank be discontinued. That the Bank be open to purchase or sale of Foreign Gold Coin, Silver Ingots, Dollars (silver), or other Bullion, on the tender of any sworn Broker".[42] Mocatta were disappointed to lose their monopoly, but the market was more broadly based. Sharps & Wilkins, already brokers outside the Bank's orbit since 1811, were now on equal terms, as were Rothschilds (though Nathan Mayer Rothschild had often skirted the previous restrictions). The way was also opened for new brokers. The market was braced for what lay ahead.

Mocatta moved into larger premises immediately across the road from the Bank of England, installing their own bullion weighing and packing room, which became vital as the Bank's own Bullion Office would shortly become overloaded. A payment of £1.19.6d (£1.97) was also made in December 1850 for an "Electric Telegraph", heralding an age of swift international price quotes. As business grew, brokerage earnings took off; Mocatta's doubled from 1847 to 1849, while at Sharps & Wilkins, net profits tripled by 1853.[43] The Australian arrivals put the market under real pressure. "The Australian workings … commenced a new era in the bullion business," recalled the refiner Edward Matthey. "As the sailing vessels arrived … the Bullion Office … was sometimes flooded with gold. To meet the difficulty, the Bank of England sent to Hatton Garden and Johnson & Matthey were at once made 'Assayers to the Bank of England'." Working fifteen hours a day, they were often unable to cope, locking up bundles of assays overnight until they could build a new assay office with the latest instruments.[44] Johnson & Matthey, who had been refining since 1835, also later gained Bank of England 'good delivery' status for their bars. Yet more refining capacity was required, as Brown and Wingrove, long the Bank's official refiners, were swamped. The gap was quickly filled through the disposal by the Royal Mint of its small refinery to Sir Anthony de Rothschild, one of Nathan Mayer Rothschild's four sons. A Royal Commission had decided the Mint's priority must now be coinage, and Sir Anthony judged the Royal Mint stamp on his bars was a fine brand, especially as it enjoyed 'good delivery' status.

In its first full year for Rothschilds, the refinery processed 14 m.t/450,000 t.oz of Californian gold (thanks to the diligence of its agent, Davidson, in San Francisco, though no longer aided by Heinrich Schliemann), together with over 9 m.t/300,000 t.oz from Australia.[45] Another competitor, the banker Henry Lewis Raphael, started a refinery on the river at Limehouse, which secured Bank accreditation in 1856. The 'good delivery' list of approved refiners, still a hallmark of the London market, was growing. The Bank's definition of a 'good delivery' bar was a maximum of 200 troy ounces (the 400 ounce bar came after 1871) of 'standard' gold at 916 fine or 22 carats. The Bank bought on what it called the 'Trade Report' of a bar in carats, grains and eighths of a grain, with the symbol B indicating if it was 'better' than standard or W for 'worse' than standard. A bar reported B.1.2 meant it was 23 carats 2 grains or 980 fine; W.0.2 meant it was 21 carats 2 grains, or 896 fine.[46]

Alongside the assayers and refiners came new brokers. Stewart Pixley, a senior clerk in the Cashier's Office at the Bank, joined up in June 1852 with William Haggard, whose father ran the Bank's Bullion Office, to open a brokerage office across the street. Samuel Montagu, son of a Liverpool silversmith, set up a bullion and exchange business the following year in nearby Leadenhall Street. Montagu became a significant banking house, but always prided itself on its precious metal operations and produced the best annual bullion review until 1989.

The entire cast of the London gold market for the next one hundred years was now assembled: Mocatta, Sharps, Pixley and Montagu essentially as brokers, Rothschild as bankers and refiners, and Johnson Matthey as refiners and, later, bankers.[47] They were a tightly-knit club. The continuity was such that when this writer first reported on the market in 1966, Stewart Pixley, the fourth generation of his family in the firm, and Edward 'Jock' Mocatta, the ninth generation of Mocattas (since 1671), briefed me on their forefathers. 'Jock' Mocatta even opened up an ancient tin trunk to show me a fading page in neat small handwriting listing the firm's brokerage earnings annually since 1780 (they were £4,458 in 1847 and £9,784 in 1849 as California got into its stride). This market was the operations centre of the gold standard, taking the metal from the gold fields, and channelling it to a bevy of nations that would forsake silver for gold before 1900.

Raising the gold standard

A monetary earthquake took place in the second half of the 19th century. In 1850 only Britain and a handful of small nations, notably Portugal and Brazil, were on the gold standard; fifty years later China was the only major nation not to have raised it. The price of silver had halved as country after country forsook either bimetallism or a pure silver standard. Silver was the deserted metal, gold ruled in the international monetary system, with London as its financial heart. "It was a change without parallel in the known history of the world," Sir John Clapham remarked in his history of the Bank of England.[48] John Kenneth Galbraith observed, "Silver, from ancient times, the hardest of hard money, now became soft money".[49] The stock of monetary gold, that is the gold in central banks or official treasuries and the coin in people's pockets, rose eight-fold from under 1,500 m.t/48 million t.oz to over 10,600 m.t/341 million t.oz.

The trend was set by the United States and France, both of whom were on a de facto gold standard by the mid-1850s, though still legally wedded to silver on a bimetallic system, with both metals legal tender. They had been overtaken by events beyond their control; the United States by California's riches and France by a subtle shift in silver premiums due to India's appetite for the metal, that made it prudent to sell silver and buy gold. The shift was not the result of political or economic debate, but of market forces. Moreover, the price of gold for which doom had been forecast, especially in France, held stable, not least because France coined so much. Overall, the expansion of world trade during the second half of the 19th century enabled the huge influx of gold to be digested. Even India, long the sponge for silver, began taking gold, especially during the prosperity generated in her cotton industry in the early 1860s as she benefited from the disruption to American cotton supplies due to the Civil War. India took over 400 m.t/over 13 million t.oz of gold in the 1860s, most of it in ten-ounce bars (0.31 kg) bearing the 'chop' of London's refineries and brokers. The bars were hoarded or turned into ornaments as Indians began the love affair with gold that persists to this day. By the 1880s India was estimated to be taking up to 25% of annual world production (while still retaining a silver coinage for every-day purchases).[50]

The monetary switch from silver to gold gathered pace in Europe after 1870, when it was clear that the high levels of production initiated in the 1850s were being maintained. An international monetary conference in Paris in 1867 had paved the way, with most European nations, except the Netherlands which had perversely changed from gold to silver, coming out firmly for gold. Four years later, Germany, grown prosperous on an indemnity (paid partly in gold) it had secured from France after the Franco-Prussian war, started buying gold in the London market as the basis for a new currency, the Mark. The Imperial Mint used 364 m.t/11.7 million t.oz of gold (equivalent to two years' new mine output) in 1872–3 to launch the new coin. Simultaneously, the coinage of silver ceased, old coins were called in and melted for sale through Deutsche Bank on the London market. The initial sales pushed the silver price into the doldrums, while the threat of more sales hung over the market like a black cloud for several years. The German initiative was followed swiftly by Denmark, Sweden, Norway and even a contrite the Netherlands, not least because they all saw their own silver coinage and reserves depreciating. That put France, Belgium, Switzerland and Italy in an embarrassing position, for they had signed up to a Latin Monetary Union in 1865 on a bimetallic standard under which they had uniform and interchangeable coinage of gold and silver, with all gold coins and five-franc silver pieces being legal tender. The tumbling silver price undermined this early version of a European currency, and silver coinage was largely suspended from 1874, putting the bimetallic pact into suspension. All silver coinage for the Latin Union ceased by 1878, ending this trial Eurozone. Europe, effectively, was signed up to gold, with around 3,500 m.t/11.2 million t.oz of coin circulation and 850 m.t/27.4 million t.oz in central bank reserves.

Silver 'crusaders' rally, but gold wins

The United States, meanwhile, was in an ambivalent position. No silver dollar had been issued since 1853 (although they still circulated) and a new Mint Act in 1873 formally discontinued small silver coins and the silver dollar. But a trade silver dollar was authorised and made legal tender up to five dollars. In effect, the United States had gold coinage with full legal tender and, for convenience, a subsidiary coinage of silver, with very limited legal tender. This created outrage among silver miners and congressmen from mining states. "The friends of silver referred to 'the deep-laid plot' that had been engineered by a foreign conspiracy in order to increase our national debt, which would thus have to be paid in gold," noted Don Taxay, historian of the US Mint.[51] The rearguard action, a 'Silver Crusade', lasted over twenty years, with the silver lobby chalking up some transient victories. They secured the Bland Allison Act of 1878, which required the US government to buy 622 m.t/20 million t.oz of silver annually for coin and approved the resumption of the silver dollar with unlimited legal tender. Over 360 million silver dollars were struck by the 1890s, but few stayed in circulation because of the constant depreciation of silver; no one wanted to get stuck with the metal. The bimetallists also had great hopes for an International Monetary Conference in Paris in 1881 that was to set a new fixed gold/silver ratio. Neither the US Treasury nor the Bank of England bothered to turn up and the debate petered out.

The topic did get a thorough airing at the Royal Commission on Gold and Silver in Britain, which convened in 1886 and finally published a pro-gold majority report and pro-bimetallism minority report two years later. The Commissioners included Samuel Montagu MP, founder of the bullion house in 1853, and evidence came from all leading players in the London market. For historians, the Commission is a treasure-chest of statistics, but the conclusion was largely foregone. The bimetallists had tried to argue that the traditional link between gold and silver had been broken once the United States stopped the free coinage of silver and the Latin Union restricted its silver coinage. "For the first time, the system of rating the two metals ceased to form a subject of legislation in any country in the world," their minority report complained. "The law of supply and demand was left to operate independently upon the value of each metal; and simultaneously the ratio which has been maintained, with scarcely any perceptible variation, for 200 years, gave place to a marked and rapid divergence in the relative value of gold and silver, which has culminated in a change from 1 to 15 to 1 to 22."[52] They added a hostage to fortune that gold output was stagnant and might not long be able to sustain new gold coinage, ignoring the discoveries in South Africa while the Commission sat, although the scale of the find was not yet apparent.

All that cut little ice with the pro-gold majority on the Royal Commission. Britain was at the height of her imperial powers and had been on a gold standard for almost two centuries. The notion that she should change from a gold-backed sterling currency, with the *sovereign* as the most universally accepted medium of exchange, to an alliance of gold and silver was a non-starter. "This country is largely a creditor country of debts payable in gold," the majority report argued. For good measure, it pointed out that the British Empire included such gold-producing colonies as Australia, Canada and, most recently, South Africa. "Their deposits of gold are one of the principal sources of wealth," the report declared, "and any measure which tends to check gold mining or to depreciate that metal will … injuriously affect the prosperity of the Colonies, and re-act upon the trade of the mother country with them."[53] This was the death knell for bimetallism, especially as South Africa was shortly to reveal its true potential.

The silver 'crusaders' in the United States fought on regardless. They had a case. After the gold bonanza in California in the 1850s, silver output in Nevada and Colorado has surged since 1870 (while gold output was down). The United States and its ally in bimetallism, Mexico, were now producing over 80% of world output. Yet in the virtual absence of coinage there was no real market (photography, the ultimate saver of the silver price, was only just beginning). A lifeline was offered by the Sherman Silver Purchase Act 1890, which declared that it was 'the established policy of the US to maintain the two metals on a parity with each other upon the present legal ratio or such ratio as may be provided by law'. The Act obliged the government to buy 1,680 m.t/54 million t.oz of silver (more than US output) at market prices up to $1.29 (the price then being under $1.00). This lifted the price briefly to $1.18, at which point speculators, who had shrewdly built positions, sold out. The government also unwisely paid for the silver with Treasury notes which could be redeemed in gold or silver. Virtually everyone redeemed them in gold, causing a huge run on US gold stocks. In effect, silver was being sold for gold, via Treasury notes. Not surprisingly, the Sherman Act was repealed in 1893.

The final outing for the bimetallists was the presidential election of 1896 at which it was the central plank in the campaign of William Jennings Bryan, the Democratic candidate from Nebraska, against the Republican William McKinley. In his acceptance speech at the Democratic National Convention, Bryan declared, "We will answer their demand for a gold standard by saying to them, 'You shall not press down upon the brow of labor this crown of thorns, you shall not crucify mankind upon a cross of gold'". He lost.

Four years later The Gold Standard Act of 1900 confirmed that the dollar of twenty-five and four-fifths grains (1.67 grams/0.054 t.oz) of gold at 900 fine was 'the standard of value'. The roll call was complete, for Austria had joined in 1892, Russia a year later and Japan in 1897, while India went on a gold-exchange standard against sterling in 1898. The United States demonstrated its faith in gold by striking 1,416 m.t/45.5 million t.oz into coin between 1895 and 1904.

The world-wide standard was underpinned by 7,265 m.t/233.6 million t.oz of gold, with just over half circulating as coin or with commercial banks and the balance in central banks or treasuries (see Table 1). This was the gold standard at its peak, with coin in the pockets of millions. Central banks still regarded gold stocks primarily as backing for note issue, rather than as a war chest. The Bank of England, the pulsating heart of the system, held scarcely 200 m.t/6.4 million t.oz in 1900, although the Bank of France was more serious with 544 m.t/17.5 million t.oz and the US Treasury had 602 m.t/19.4 million t.oz. The leader was the Imperial Bank of Russia, which was sitting on 661 m.t/21.5 million t.oz, most of it from local production. Several smaller nations, while having domestic gold coin circulation, did not really bother with a reserve, holding sterling balances instead, which they regarded as being as good as gold (a perception that caused much woe a few decades on). The central banks' attitude would change rapidly as war clouds appeared after 1910, but for the moment the 'people's standard' flourished. Obligingly, too, fresh gold discoveries in South Africa, Western Australia and the Yukon territory of Canada were strengthening its foundations.

Table 1 - Monetary Gold Stocks[54]

	a Central bank stocks		b Gold coin in circulation or with commercial banks		a + b Total monetary	
	m.t	million t.oz	m.t	million t.oz	m.t	million t.oz
1850	110	3.5	1,350	43.4	1,460	46.9
1860	185	6.0	2,300	73.9	2,485	79.9
1870	715	23.0	2,835	91.1	3,548	114.1
1880	1,150	37.0	3,414	109.8	4,565	146.7
1890	1,970	63.3	3,368	108.3	5,337	171.6
1900	3,175	102.0	4,090	131.5	7,265	233.6
1910	5,820	187.1	4,699	151.1	10,608	341.0
1913	8,100	260.4	3,383	108.8	11,481	369.1

Gold discoveries: round two – the South African factor

Few forget their first journey to the centre of the earth in a South African gold mine. A steel cage plunges down over 2,000 metres in a couple of minutes to an intensely humid world lit by the dancing lights of miners' head lamps and filled with a cacophony of sound from rumbling ore trucks and chattering drills. In a honeycomb of low passageways, *stopes*, branching off the main gallery, narrow reefs, bright with rounded white pebbles and the occasional fleeting gleam of gold, are etched out in red paint waiting to be extracted like thin slices from an uncut cheese. The reefs usually contain 10-20 grams per tonne (g/t) of gold. Freeing the tiny particles from reefs a few centimetres thick that slope down from the surface at an angle of 25 degrees or more and that 'bottom out' beyond 5,000 metres calls for deep mining, skilled engineering and capital. Watching machines bite slices out of the wall of the stope the unique scale and nature of South African gold mining becomes apparent.[55]

An understanding of those reefs, best gained by going underground, took time. Prospectors, infected by news from California and Australia, were seeking gold in South Africa by 1853, but they were mistakenly looking for conventional placer deposits that might lead back to quartz lodes in the hills. Here, gold was hidden far below the flat *veld*. "The prospectors were slow, agonisingly slow, in their progress towards their unknown goal," wrote A. P. Cartwright in *The Gold Miners*. "They stumbled about as men do who are blindfolded, groping their way towards what they believed would be the 'mother lode' from which had sprung the traces of gold they had found so far."[56] All the time it was far beneath their feet.

Instead, they struck lucky with diamonds along the Vaal river, just within the borders of the two independent Boer republics, Transvaal and the Orange Free State, with a major discovery at Jagersfontein in August 1870. The plum pickings were on the farm of Johannes and Diedrich de Beer, a name to become synonymous with diamonds, and in a shallow depression a mile or so away, which became the Kimberley mine. During the next forty years the burrowings of diggers at Kimberley created the awesome Big Hole, one of the deepest open-pit mines ever dug. They were tapping into diamond pipes, each no more than a few hundred metres square, thrust up from the bowels of the earth by volcanic activity. While the pipes are geologically entirely different from the gold reefs, once the surface diamonds had been sifted out, they, too, called for organised deep mining, which in turn required capital.[57]

The discovery and development of the diamond mines around Kimberley brought together an assorted bunch of prospectors and entrepreneurs, among them Cecil Rhodes, Alfred Beit, Barney Barnato, Hermann Eckstein, J. B. Robinson, and Leopold Albu, who were quickly on the scene when serious gold deposits were ultimately located. "They brought together the necessary financial and technical resources to transform the mining industry … from a 'diggers' democracy' of small, independent producers into a highly capitalised, technically advancing organism," observed Sir Theodore Gregory in his study on the economic development of Southern Africa.[58]

Various champions have been proposed as the original discoverers of gold on the Witwatersrand, most notably George Harrison and George Walker, a couple of itinerant prospectors with some Australian experience. They certainly found an outcrop of what later proved to be the Main Reef Leader on Langlaagte farm, thirty-five miles south-east of Pretoria and just west of modern Johannesburg, early in 1886. Official records even show that Harrison registered Langlaagte Discoverer's Claim No.19 and George Walker lodged Claim No.21 (but not as a Discovery). Harrison soon sold his claim for £20 and vanished, never to be heard of again. Walker later got a pension from the Transvaal Chamber of Mines, and his tombstone at Klerksdorp declares, "The man who discovered the Main Reef series of the Witwatersrand at Langlaagte, in February 1886".[59]

The Kimberley diamond magnates were not far behind. They took mail coaches north towards Pretoria, jumping off at obscure camps to confuse their rivals. J. B. Robinson, with financial backing from Alfred Beit, promptly bought Langlaagte for £7,000, and soon bought more surrounding land for £13,100, defying rivals who scoffed "a fool and his money were soon parted". It was a close call. Extracting the gold sprinkled so finely through the reefs was a formidable challenge. "A large percentage of the gold was lost in working the ores," recalled the diamond mine manager Gardner Williams, an early visitor to the scene, "for the precious metal was so extremely minute that it floated away with the water, and, at no considerable depth, a portion of gold was held in the pyrites, and could not be recovered by means of the ordinary process of amalgamation".[60]

Salvation came through the MacArthur-Forrest process, developed in 1887 by two Glasgow doctors, Robert and William Forrest, with the chemist John S. MacArthur, which used cyanide to attract the gold. The ore had first to be crushed to a fine powder and circulated through tanks containing a weak solution of cyanide, which has an affinity for gold. The solution dissolved the gold (and any silver) but had no effect on the rock particles (in the same way that if sugar and sand were stirred together in tea the sugar would dissolve and the sand would remain as grains). The rock pulp could be filtered off. Zinc dust was then added to the cyanide solution to replace the gold, causing specks of gold to be precipitated out for refining. The MacArthur-Forrest Process extracted 96% of the gold from the ore. The South African gold mining industry was viable. J. B. Robinson got his reward. Langlaagte farm yielded 7.6 m.t/250,000 t.oz of gold in the first five years.[61]

His rivals from Kimberley swiftly circled. "The gold rush to the Rand was from the first dominated, not by a crowd of men who wished to make their fortune," wrote W. P. Morrell, "but by a few who had already made it."[62] Within two years, four of the great mining finance houses that were to dominate the industry had been founded. The first was launched by Hermann Eckstein in 1887; it was nicknamed 'the Corner House' and matured as Rand Mines. Immediately afterwards came Cecil Rhodes and Charles Rudd with Gold Fields of South Africa, the Barnato brothers with Johannesburg Consolidated Investment Company (JCI) and George and Leopold Albu with General Mining and Finance Corporation. A fifth group, later Union Corporation, was started in 1893 by Adolf Goerz, who first went to look over the gold fields for a group of Berlin businessmen. Thereafter, the only newcomer was Ernest Oppenheimer's Anglo American Corporation founded in 1917. The concept of each house was centralisation at a high level of the provision of financial, technical, geological and administrative services for mines within its stable. A new mine thus enjoyed first class supervision from the outset.

Between them, the mining houses began tapping into an almost infinite resource as the reefs encircling the rising city of Johannesburg were unveiled. The outcrop of Langlaagte farm was but one of a crescent of reefs around the whole Witwatersrand Basin. This gold-bearing conglomerate, usually grading 10–20 g/t, stretches from 60 km east of Johannesburg to 145 km west and then swings down south-west to the Orange Free State, over 300 km away. Another field, Evander, was found much later 120 km south-east of Johannesburg, outside the main Witwatersrand system. The reefs were laid down between 3,000 and 2,700 million years ago and include the Main, Ventersdorp Contact, Kimberley, Carbon Leader and Basals reefs.   Their average thickness is only 20–30 cm, requiring exceptional geological detective work to track them far underground.

Once the MacArthur-Forrest equipment was installed to treat the ore brought to the surface, output surged. By 1892 it was over 32 m.t/1 million t.oz and in 1898, on the eve of the Boer War, which disrupted mining for three years, it was almost

120 m.t/3.8 million t.oz, one-third of world output. As World War I loomed in 1913, South Africa was producing 280 m.t/9 million t.oz annually, 40% of world output.

The great beneficiary was the London market, which refined and distributed all the gold. The refiners took rough South African bars at 875 fine and turned it into 400 ounce 'good delivery' bars at 995 fine or ten-ounce bars for India. The refiners were under pressure; the South African gold arrived every Monday morning by Union Castle liner, and the ten-ounce bars for India had to be ready before 8 am on Friday to catch the noon P & O boat from Tilbury to Bombay. By agreement, Rothschilds' Royal Mint refinery took 60% of the material, and Johnson Matthey refined 40% with both contracting work out on a toll basis to Raphael's refinery.[63] The link between the South African mines and the London gold market endured exclusively until 1968, although once the Rand Refinery opened in 1921, most refining was done in South Africa. London still handled distribution, working closely with the South African Reserve Bank and the Bank of England. While that relationship lasted, London was unchallenged as the premier gold market, for South Africa would soon produce over half the world's gold.

Bonuses from Kalgoorlie and the Klondike

The spirit of the 19th century gold rushes lives on in Kalgoorlie, where Paddy Hannan and two fellow prospectors sifted out 100 ounces of good alluvial gold in June 1893. Visiting this remote town in the desert of Western Australia for its centenary celebrations in 1993, the excitement of a community that still thrives on new discoveries was tangible. The latest hot tip, confided stockbroker David Reed in the bar of the Palace Hotel (founded in 1897), was Bronze Wing. His family had been on the gold fields since 1896. The Yellow Pages telephone directory spelled out the action: A for Assay Offices (eight of them), D for drilling contractors, G for geologists (eleven set out their stalls), M was for Metal Detectors, and sixty-three Mining and Exploration companies, N for Nugget Shop ('Natural Nuggets from the Australian Gold Fields') and, most essential, T for twenty-nine Taverns. Out in the street the headframe of the Mount Charlotte mine was visible and machinery was rumbling along Kalgoorlie's Golden Mile, a great open pit which had then produced 1,400 m.t/45 million t.oz since the summer of 1893.[64] Over two-thirds of Australia's gold production since that time has come from Western Australia.

The early years were hard, plagued by water shortages in the desert, but output grew from a mere 8 m.t/250,000 t.oz in 1896 to 45 m.t/1.45 million t.oz in 1899. A branch of the Royal Mint opened in Perth that year to refine the Western Australian gold and to strike *sovereigns* (690,992 dated 1899). Overall, Australian output reached 119 m.t/3.8 million t.oz in 1903, with Western Australia contributing over half. This record was not exceeded until 1988. In that sense, the first Kalgoorlie gold rush was brief, with output slipping under 40 m.t/1.3 million t.oz by 1912 and below 20 m.t/650,000 t.oz by 1920, as easily accessible oxide ores close to the surface were worked out.[65] The revival came only with new technology enabling deep, low grade sulphide ores to be tapped in the late 1980s – hence the exuberance in Kalgoorlie for the centenary. Their gold rush had got its second wind.

The persistent prospectors who had ranged the mountains and streams of the American and Canadian west since the 1850s had their final fling in the brief Klondike gold rush from 1896. The story goes that in August 1896 an Indian hunter, Jim Skookum, and his brother, fishing for salmon in the Thron-diuck (hence, Klondike) tributary of the Yukon river, caught a gleam of gold in the stream bed. They panned out eighty ounces in eight days, and paddled back to register their claim. Word spread fast. The next spring every steamer on the west coast was overloaded with diggers, heading for Dawson City on the Yukon River. Perhaps 40,000 actually arrived in 1897, to find an icy wilderness and few supplies. A few were lucky, most were disappointed. The Canadian writer Pierre Berton reckoned that perhaps 5,000 men got out on the rivers in search of gold and a few hundred got rich.[66]   The 'Klondike' yielded around 75 m.t/2.4 million t.oz over three years, before the best pockets were worked out.

Thus the curtain came down on the last great migration of diggers in the 19th century, just as the United States went onto the gold standard in 1900. The rush to California fifty years earlier had been the stimulant for the world-wide switch from silver to gold coin, which might not have happened without that irresistible urge to get rich quick that set hundreds of thousands of men on the gold trail, triggering a chain reaction of gold finds. Their endurance paved the way.

A brief honeymoon

The gold standard that their labours underwrote worked because of strong commitment by its leading participants, Britain, France and Germany, through their central banks. The United States, although on board the system fully from 1900, was slightly sidelined because it still lacked a central bank (the Federal Reserve System was not authorised until 1913). "For more than a quarter of a century before World War I the gold standard provided the framework for domestic and international monetary relations," observed Barry Eichengreen in his analysis of its strengths and weaknesses. "Currencies were convertible into gold on demand and linked by fixed exchange rates. Gold shipments were the ultimate means of balance-of-payments settlement. The gold standard had been a remarkably efficient mechanism for organising financial affairs."[67]

The lever of control to maintain equilibrium and curb large gold flows from one nation to another was the Bank rate, that is to say the central bank's trend-setting interest rate. As the Governor of the Bank of England, William Campbell, explained to a visiting US Monetary Commission in 1909, "The Bank rate is raised with the object either of preventing gold from leaving the country, or of attracting gold to the country, and lowered when it is completely out of touch with market rates and circumstances do not render if necessary to induce the import of gold". The Governor also hastened to tell his American visitors that London was 'the only free gold market in Europe' and that the Bank liked to see gold coin, rather than paper notes in circulation. "If there were £1 notes in circulation they would take the place of gold in the pockets of the people," he added, "and thus tended indirectly to drive gold from the country."[68]

The Bank rate was crucial to the daily life of the gold standard. If sterling weakened, funds from Europe flowed into London anticipating a rise in the rate, providing self-correction in the exchange rate. The central banks, too, were ready to help each other out. "The Bank of England stood ready to let gold go when it was needed in the United States," Barry Eichengreen noted. "The Bank of France stood ready to lend gold to the Bank of England or to purchase sterling bills when the British gold parity was endangered. The Reichenbank and the Russian government came to the aid of the Bank of England in periods of exceptional stringency. On other occasions, the favour was returned."[69] Such international co-operation gave the standard credibility and secured the gold parities, for if one was under stress, the combined resources of several central banks came into play. But those strong links binding the gold standard network together could last only so long as the main players were friends. World War I quickly demonstrated what happened when they became enemies.

CHAPTER 22

1914-1933:
Goodbye Gold Standard

John Maynard Keynes tucked his lanky figure into the sidecar of his brother-in-law's motorcycle outside King's College, Cambridge on Sunday afternoon, 2nd August 1914, and set out for London, a city in financial turmoil. For a week ultimatums of war had been flying round Europe. That very day Germany declared war on Russia and Britain would be at war with Germany by midnight the next. In London financial markets had been turbulent all week, not least from a rush by people across Europe to get their hands on gold coin. Three million *sovereigns* had been dispatched to France and other continental capitals. Outside the Bank of England, five thousand people had queued patiently on the Friday to change £5 notes (the smallest denomination) into *sovereigns*. "Everyone got his notes promptly exchanged," *The Times* reported. The clearing banks, however, were in a panic. They had not only stopped paying out *sovereigns*, but were urging the government to suspend gold payments for notes completely. The gold standard was at stake.

Settling into the Treasury in Whitehall, Keynes, whose advice as an economist, though he was scarcely thirty, was often sought, saw no need for alarm. He penned a memorandum to the Chancellor of the Exchequer, Lloyd George, saying, "It is difficult to see how such an extreme and disastrous measure as the suspension of cash payments can be justified. The future position of the City of London as a free gold market will be seriously injured if at the first sign of emergency specie payment is suspended". He added that a number of countries kept part of their gold reserves in London and it was essential that their confidence in the City as a unique financial centre be maintained. "The existence of this confidence in the past," Keynes noted, "has been one of the most important *differentiations* between London and Paris or Berlin."[1] The chancellor agreed with him, telling a meeting of bankers the country was "not ready for the suspension of specie".

Indeed, much of the furore came from the bankers, who were trying to dun the Bank of England for up to £15 million in gold (120 m.t/3.85 million t.oz) for their own emergency reserve. Keynes later accused the clearing banks of 'a fit of hoarding', remarking that the internal drain on gold was not for the public, "but by the banks running on the Bank of England".[2] Cash payments in gold were never suspended during the war – they just became much more difficult to get. The pressure was defused that same week by a rush printing of £1 and ten shilling (£0.50) notes with unlimited legal tender, putting paper 'cash' in people's pockets. Minting of silver as subsidiary coinage was stepped up.

Such confidence did not exist elsewhere in Europe; France, Germany and Russia all stopped convertibility of paper into gold within days. The freeze was such that the US Congress authorised $35 million in gold coin to be shipped on a naval cruiser to beleaguered American tourists in Europe. The collapse of the cross-border teamwork that had made the gold standard work for a generation was put into limbo overnight, never to return in its classical international form. Actually, central banks had quietly been building war chests for some years. The reserves of France, Germany and Russia had doubled since 1900, US Treasury holdings had quadrupled. The balance of the monetary gold equation had also swung in their favour. In 1900 private holdings of gold coin exceeded central bank stocks but, at the end of 1913, central banks held over 8,000 m.t/257 million t.oz, compared to under 3,400 m.t/109 million t.oz in private hands or with commercial banks.[3] They were going to need it. "There was magic in gold," Sir John Clapham reflected, "ignorance of the costs of 20th century war, a great and only half-mistaken faith in gold reserves".[4]

The outsider in gold stocks was actually the Bank of England, which had barely 300 m.t/9.8 million t.oz in hand at the outbreak of war; less than one-third the French holdings, a quarter of Russia's and one-seventh those of the United States. This was justified in a complacent Treasury memorandum three months before the war, which said, "Our position as a lending nation gives us a power of attracting gold from abroad whenever we require it such as no other country ... this is further justification for the smallness of our Gold Reserves ... it is true that the freedom of her market for gold makes London more liable to demands for gold for export than, e.g., Paris, but this is far more than counterbalanced by the advantage which the free gold market ensures in obtaining and retaining gold".[5]

A unique asset for the Bank was that the British Empire produced 60% of the world's gold. When war was declared, arrangements were made to buy up all South African and Australian production at source and dispatch it to Britain. Six times a year warships brought it by a circuitous route, much to the annoyance of the London refiners, who received no consignments for months and then a shipload to be refined in days.[6] The British government also bought gold in New York and transferred it to Ottawa, the Canadian capital, for safe-keeping. The strategy doubled the Bank of England's reserves by 1915.

Germany, by contrast, had no direct links to newly-mined gold and resorted to subterfuge to get gold from London via Portugal or Spain. A Lisbon newspaper uncovered one scheme whereby the Bank of Portugal bought bar gold in London, but arranged delivery to Spain, where German agents picked it up and spirited it to Berlin. A consignment of over 600 kg/20,000 t.oz even went to Lisbon on the Royal Mail steamer *Avon*.[7]

Such shipments were rare, for the threat of German submarines made international movements of gold dangerous, and war risk insurance did not cover gold, so it was moved only rarely on warships (as with the South African production). In practical terms, gold flows eventually ground to a halt. As Mocatta and Goldsmid's annual circular remarked, "There was no business in gold".

In Britain, the minting of *sovereigns* declined from thirteen million in 1913 to scarcely two million in 1916. Over 115 million *sovereigns* had been in circulation when war broke out, but the Bank of England encouraged trading in for small denomination notes, so that 100 million stacked up in its vaults. The Bank of France called in over 160 million *Napoléons* and the private export of gold was banned, so that France ended the war with high reserves, but little circulating gold coin. Germany's reserves were seriously eroded, being reduced to one-quarter those of France and half those of Britain, quite apart from impossible claims for reparations. The beneficiary was the United States, emerging with one-third of all central bank stocks, heralding her supremacy in gold holdings for the rest of the century.

The United States cut back drastically on the minting of coin, even before she entered the war in 1917, to husband reserves. Once she was engaged in hostilities, exports were controlled, being permitted only with the express approval of the Federal Reserve Board and the Secretary of the Treasury. Domestically, she remained on the gold standard throughout the war, with notes redeemable in gold. The war saw the passing of the torch as the world's leading economic power from Britain to the United States, not least in gold.

Seeking a return to gold

World War I tested the total resources of every combatant nation, requiring them to be mobilised and controlled in a way never previously conceived. The war was a watershed, bringing an abrupt end to the whole *laissez faire* pattern of 19th century economic life. In Europe, infrastructure and industries were shattered. Each country had to focus on trying to rebuild its own economy, facing the social costs among their people when a whole generation of young men had been wiped out and unemployment and inflation were rampant. National self-interest was the priority. The previous tight discipline of the gold standard was not possible. "There was no room in the world of 1919 for so finely balanced a device as the international gold standard of pre-war days," wrote William Brown in an analysis of the way ahead.[8] The matrix of fixed exchange rates based on gold parities could not be swiftly revived. Moreover, the fulcrum was no longer sterling, but the dollar. "The single great source of monetary demand for gold was in the US," Professor Brown added, "so the value of gold became identified with the value of the money of the United States."[9]

Yet many bankers and economists failed to grasp, or at least were in denial, that the strain of war finance had wrecked the old fiscal system. In London, the

Treasury yearned for a general resumption of the gold standard, which had been such a symbol of the might of the British Empire. Just before the war ended, a Committee under Lord Cunliffe, Governor of the Bank of England, was set up to look at post-war currency and foreign exchange arrangements. The Cunliffe Committee was clear. "In our opinion," said their report, "it is imperative that after the war the conditions necessary to the maintenance of an effective gold standard should be restored without delay."[10] The trouble was the 'conditions' had changed totally. Keynes understood that domestic dislocation across Europe required years of patient reconstruction before any general return to gold was feasible, while Russia had succumbed to revolution. But he did tell his students, somewhat wryly, in a lecture in 1920, "The advantage of the gold standard is the convention behind it that it is ... disgraceful to tamper with gold".[11]

Launching the fix

Gold standard or not, some semblance of an international gold market had to be restored. The business was still frozen. Britain even put a complete ban on gold exports in March 1919, when the sterling-dollar exchange rate, which had been pegged at £1 to $4.76 during the war, was allowed to float. Sterling promptly fell against the dollar to £1 to $4.17. That did not please the South African gold producers, who were still tied to the wartime agreement of selling all output to the Bank of England at £3.89 per standard ounce, for they were losing a good premium their gold could have secured in New York. Wartime inflation had also put up their production costs. South Africa's annual output had risen to 260 m.t/8.4 million t.oz by 1919, half of world production, and its disposal was a matter of priority.

The US made the first step in June 1919 by lifting its embargo on the export of gold, allowing gold flows to Japan, South America and India to recommence. The major breakthrough came on 25th July when an agreement was reached between the Bank of England, the South African government and the mining finance houses. All South African output (save a small amount for domestic fabrication) would be shipped to the Bank of England, who undertook to deliver it to the refiners. The Bank also advanced £3.85 per standard ounce on advice of shipment. Once the metal was refined, it was to be sold through the bullion brokers or "such other channel as the producers and their agents may arrange". Crucially, the Bank also undertook to issue export licences once the gold was sold. The sales responsibility was initially offered to Johnson Matthey, as the largest refiners, but they declined, not having the financial resources of a bank.[12] The mining houses turned instead to Rothschilds, being both refiners and bankers. The contract specified that Rothschilds would sell the gold, "at the best price obtainable, giving the London market and the Bullion Brokers an opportunity to bid. Rothschilds advanced £3.89 per standard ounce to the producers on receipt of the refined gold, thus enabling them to reimburse the Bank of England for the initial advance".[13] Any premium obtained (due to sterling's weakness against the dollar) was to be pooled and shared between the mining houses according to the quantity of gold each contributed. Thus, on the morning of 12th September 1919, the London market was back in business with its first gold 'fixing'. The procedure was outlined in a contemporary memorandum:

"All fine gold available for sale on any day will be delivered by the refiners to Rothschilds. Rothschilds decided at 11 o'clock each morning, having regard to the various exchanges, what was the best sterling price of gold which could be obtained by realisation in any part of the world. The four bullion brokers, Mocatta & Goldsmid, Pixley and Abell, Sharps and Wilkins, and Samuel Montagu & Co., were given the opportunity of bidding and would obtain their requirements if the price they bid equalled or exceeded the realisation price fixed by Rothschilds".[14]

The first price 'fixed' on 12th September 1919 was £4 18.9d (£4.94) per ounce, equal to the New York price of $20.67. This reflected not just the depreciation of sterling, but that the price was now quoted for 995 'good delivery' gold, instead of the traditional 916 fine standard gold. Where the standard price had long been £3.89, the price for 995 'good delivery' would have been £4.25 at the old exchange rate. Thus, the new price of £4.94 revealed how sterling had weakened. During the winter of 1919–20, as sterling fell further, the fix went as high as £6.37, giving the South African miners the equivalent of the New York dollar premium.

At the initial fixes the brokers bid by telephone, but it was soon decided it was more practical to hold a formal meeting at Rothschilds' offices at New Court, attended by a representative of each broker. Thus began the daily ceremony, presided over by the head of Rothschilds' bullion department, with each market member at a little desk. At first, they arrived with their orders and had no communication with their offices or clients while the price was settled. This was later amended so that each broker had an open line to his office. A representative of the refiners Johnson Matthey was also invited to attend. And it was George Matthey of Johnson Matthey who suggested each participant should have a small Union Jack flag before him, so he could cry 'Flag Up' to halt proceedings while he conferred with his trading room.[15]

The ritual that evolved began with Rothschilds' chairman suggesting an opening price, to which each broker indicated if he was a seller, buyer or had no interest. A seller specified how many 'good delivery' bars he offered, a buyer merely indicated interest, without specifying how many bars he needed. If no buyer appeared, the price was notched down. Once both sellers and buyers had declared themselves, the chairman asked, 'figures, please' and buyers spoke up, perhaps 'Mocatta 60 bars', 'Montagu 30', each bar being 400 ounces. If the sellers could meet that requirement, the price was 'fixed'.[16] The fixing price quickly became the benchmark that day for gold around the world.

London enjoyed two advantages. First, that it marketed South Africa's growing production, which immediately placed at its disposal half the world's output. Other gold producing nations, to say nothing of central banks, then took advantage of the fixing, which could handle large volumes at a single, clearly-posted price. The second advantage was the close alliance with the Bank of England. The Bank had already been an integral player in the market for two centuries (indeed, its Bullion Office had been the cross-roads for all gold and silver until the 1850s) and it remained in close touch with each fixing. From 1931 it even had its own direct telephone line to the ceremony. The Bank's support for the market was always envied by the Swiss banks in later years when they came to challenge London for supremacy in disseminating supply. A Swiss banker once lamented to me that they did not have "The Old Lady" in their corner. The Swiss, incidentally, were among the first to participate at the 'fix'; Swiss Bank Corporation was a buyer at the third fixing in September 1919. By the 1960s the three main Swiss banks were often the major buyers on the fix.

A classic example of how a considerable quantity of gold could be discreetly acquired at the fixing began in the very first week. The Indian government urgently needed gold to replenish its Gold Standard Reserve by which the rupee was linked to sterling. During the war they had been unable to secure gold, and had borrowed gold from the Bank of England. The borrowed metal now had to be returned. The India Office in London turned to Mocatta & Goldsmid, with whom they already had experience in large silver buying operations. During the first five weeks of the gold fix, Mocatta picked up 10.3 m.t/330,000 t.oz through steady daily buying.[17] The India Office then came back for more, and Mocatta asked Rothschilds if they would reserve 50% of all gold arrivals for them until the end of the year. Rothschilds proposed a two-penny premium per ounce for the privilege. The India Office refused, so Mocatta told Rothschilds they had decided "they would do better to take a chance in the open market like any other". Mocatta remained a stealthy buyer at the fix for two years, acquiring over 110 m.t/3.5 million t.oz for the Indian Gold Standard Reserve.[18] That experience set the pattern for countless future operations on the fix.

The only cloud to threaten London's supremacy in the early years was the South African producers' determination to have their own refinery. The Transvaal Chamber of Mines, acting for them, established the Rand Refinery, which became fully operational in 1922, much to the chagrin of London's refineries who even offered to drop their charges by three pence an ounce if the plans were cancelled. The refined gold, however, was still sold through Rothschilds, with the added advantage that it could now be bought loco *Durban* for immediate shipment to India, saving time and freight. As the sterling gold price had fallen from a high of £6.75 in 1920 to £4.42 by 1922 (little above the historic price of £4.25 for 'good delivery' gold), the Indian private market now came back strongly, encouraged, too, by persistent weakness in the price of silver. In the first three months of 1923 almost 70 m.t /2.25 million t.oz in good delivery bars was sent direct from *Durban* to Bombay. India was asserting itself as one of the major buyers of gold in the 20th century, increasingly forsaking silver which had so long been the staple of the India trade. A reminder of this burgeoning traffic came fifty years later, when

Indian Customs & Excise officers, raiding the palace of the Maharajah of Jaipur in search of undeclared wealth, came across a stack of Rand Refinery bars with serial numbers for 1923 and 1924.[19]

Gold standard, 'mark two'

With the international flows of gold restarted, the debate on the restoration of the gold standard itself gathered pace. In spite of the sea change in the monetary economy wrought by the war, an abiding faith that all would be well after its revival persisted. In Britain, the assumption was that the country could return to gold at the pre-war sterling-dollar parity of £1 to $4.86, regardless of the fact that the exchange rate was close to £1 to $4.30. The Governor of the Bank of England, Montagu Norman, ever mindful of the City's international financial status, argued that could eventually be engineered.

Meanwhile, only the United States was truly back on the gold standard, having lifted export restrictions and struck over 540 m.t/17.4 million t.oz in coin between 1920 and 1924. Plenty of gold was in American pockets. Elsewhere, however, constraint persisted. France minted precisely 3.8 m.t/122,170 t.oz in the early 1920s, while Britain and Germany struck no gold coin at all. Moreover, the US Treasury now held 45% of all central bank gold, compared to a mere 8.6% in France, 7% in Britain and 3% in Germany. Such imbalance hardly boded well for a return to an international standard.

A compromise had been proposed at a League of Nations conference in Genoa in 1922, which underlined that prices had risen so sharply in the war, that existing gold reserves and output of new gold, which was stagnating, was not enough to finance world trade. The delegates recommended gold should be 'economised' by limited coin circulation and small nations keeping most of their reserves in dollars or sterling, which could be readily exchanged for gold if needed.

However, by 1924, the outlook had brightened. The British economy had come through a post-war slump and sterling was stable against the dollar, although not yet at the old parity. The German inflation of 1923 had been contained and a new currency, the *rentenmark*, was underwritten by an American loan through the Dawes plan (an early form of Marshal aid). Montagu Norman, at the Bank of England, was confident that the moment was at hand for the return to gold. He planned carefully with Benjamin Strong of the Federal Reserve in New York. Their aim was to re-establish the old £1 to $4.86 rate of pre-war gold standard days through a delicate minuet with their respective bank rates to steer capital and gold flows. Norman's underlying purpose was to restore the City of London as the world's leading banker, and sterling as the world's leading currency. He told a Treasury Committee that, in the absence of a resumption of gold payments, not just the US dollar, but even the German *mark* would become a far more popular currency than the British pound.[20] Norman was in no haste, but the embargo on free gold exports from Britain, which all still had to be licensed, was due to expire at the end of 1925, so a decision was required. Opposing Norman, John Maynard Keynes feared "many difficult and injurious things" for Britain's industry and employment if sterling was deliberately over-valued at £1 to $4.86. The response from the gold standard advocates was that "moderate sacrifice" by the workers might be necessary to get back to stable currencies underwritten by gold.

By early 1925 the international political momentum in favour of gold was building. "Norman argued that the 'rise in the dollar exchange' was the decisive argument for an early return," noted Robert Skidelsky in his biography of Keynes. "Switzerland, the Netherlands, Sweden, South Africa and Australia were anxious to get back to gold. Britain's return to gold was looked upon as an international question and not as national to this country only."[21] The die was cast on 17th March 1925 at a dinner at 11 Downing Street given by Winston Churchill, then Chancellor of the Exchequer. The guests included a former permanent secretary at the Treasury, Sir John Bradbury, the former Chancellor of the Exchequer and Chairman of the Midland Bank, Reginald McKenna, and John Maynard Keynes. Bradbury was the leading advocate of a return to gold, arguing that, "the Gold Standard was knave-proof. It could not be rigged for political or even more unworthy reasons". Keynes and McKenna were worried by the difference between British and American prices, which did not justify a return to the pre-war sterling-dollar parity. But McKenna, challenged by Churchill, conceded the political pressures were overwhelming. "There is no escape," he replied. "You have got to go back, but it will be hell."[22]

In his budget speech of 28th April 1925 Winston Churchill announced that gold and sterling would once again be interchangeable. Yet he had a caveat. "We are not going to issue gold coinage," he explained. "That is quite unnecessary for the purpose of the gold standard … and would be an unwarrantable extravagance."[23] In short, the 'Mark Two' standard left gold largely corralled in the vaults of central banks, as backing for paper money, not in the pockets of the people. After their experiences in the war, governments wanted gold in their own hands. Bank of England and Treasury notes would be converted into gold coin only *at the option* of the Bank of England, but the Bank would be *obliged* to sell gold bars of not less than 400 ounces – that is, the 'good delivery' bar – against legal tender notes at £4.25 per ounce fine. The smallest amount, therefore, for which gold could be bought was £1,700 ($8,262). At least London was a free market with no export control. Justifying his decision, Churchill declared, "If we had not taken this action the whole of the rest of the British Empire would have taken it without us, and it would have come to a gold standard, not on the basis of the pound sterling, but a gold standard on the dollar".[24]

With hindsight, opinion has not been kind. "The 1925 return to the gold standard," John Kenneth Galbraith wrote fifty years later, "was perhaps the most decisively damaging action involving money in modern times."[25] In reality, the United States, the new financial power, sitting on 45% of official gold stocks and with its greenbacks still readily changeable into gold at the fixed price of $20.67, was the arbiter of the new standard. Indeed, over the next five years, the US struck a further 925 m.t/29.7 million t.oz in gold coinage; Britain minted none. Only the French, also coming back on gold in 1926, along with Belgium, Italy and Poland, struck any significant coinage, using 256 m.t/8.2 million t.oz in five years. The French, after their experience with devaluation in World War I, were becoming great gold hoarders, a reputation that would stay with them until the 1970s. The revived standard experienced more rivalry than cross-border co-operation. "One country after another lacked enthusiasm for the gold exchange system," observed the Bank of England's historian, R. S. Sayers, "and high reserves in actual gold became a fashionable object."[26]

Gold standard under threat

France led the rush, with its economy revived by the strong hand of Raymond Poincaré. The Bank of France turned all its surplus foreign exchange into gold, snapping up every last ounce of South African output available through the London market. Almost 150 m.t/4.8 million t.oz was exported from Britain to France in 1928, with even greater amounts over the next three years. The Bank of England sought to check the flow across the Channel by delivering to the London brokers only 916 fine standard gold from traded-in *sovereigns*. The London refineries were booked "on French account several weeks ahead", bringing the gold up to 995 'good delivery' status, Mocatta and Goldsmid's annual circular reported.[27] The Bank of France also secured much South African production through the London brokers by buying forward the moment the gold was shipped from *Durban*. Germany joined in, taking almost 150 m.t/4.8 million t.oz from London in both 1928 and 1929. They continued into 1930, with Mocatta noting "strong competition from Germany for the weekly arrivals from South Africa".[28]

Gold was concentrated increasingly in few hands. Britain, France, Germany and the United States held 70% of central bank stocks by 1930. Moreover, official reserves now accounted for over 90% of all 'monetary' gold, with under 10% remaining as circulating coin, compared to 1900 when 56% of monetary gold circulated. The imbalance of official gold alarmed the economist Paul Einzig, who wrote, "Other countries have been unable to replenish their gold stocks … Several countries with an excessive stock, such as … Germany, are reluctant to part with their surplus, and though their currency is still unconvertible, are, in fact, endeavouring to increase their gold holdings".[29] The pre-war ebb and flow of gold had vanished. Instead, 'hot money', as it was dubbed, was switched by *arbitrageurs* between London, Paris or New York on the most favourable exchange of the day.

The debate on supply and demand

The pressures on the revived standard led to intense research and debate during the late 1920s and early 1930s on the world-wide supply and demand balance of gold. Foremost in the research was Joseph Kitchen, the manager in London for Union Corporation, the South African mining finance house. The South Africans, as the leading producers, naturally had a vested interest in promoting the gold standard and in monitoring the flows. The broad pattern of statistics that Kitchen knitted together form a valuable record of gold in the late 19th and early 20th centuries. He pointed out that gold output had slumped from a record 700 m.t/22.5 million t.oz in 1915 to scarcely 600 m.t/19.3 million t.oz by 1929, with South Africa ever more predominant. She accounted for 53% of production in 1929, while the United States contributed 11%, Canada under 10% and Australia, a hero in the 19th century, a mere 3%. The output in the latter three countries had fallen precipitously since pre-war days. The British Empire, however, still yielded 71% of world output, as befitted the original founder of the gold standard.

Kitchen pointed out the shifting balance of monetary gold, from central banks holding 65% of 'monetary gold' in 1914 (with the rest being circulating coin) to 92% by 1929. "The monetary condition has been greatly changed by the transference of gold from circulation," he told an evening gathering of the Royal Institute of International Affairs in February 1930. He urged a 'correction of the present maldistribution' of central banks' stocks, pointing out that the Bank of France held rather more gold than all the countries of the British Empire, and more than Britain and Germany together.[30]

Kitchen then set out all components of gold demand. The primary absorption in the 1920s was in monetary gold, which took up 54% of all new mine production each year; the balance was made up by 21% consumed in jewellery and industrial fabrication, and a hefty 25% in Indian private demand for hoarding (which included *sovereigns*). Indian demand, Kitchen calculated, had averaged over 140 m.t/4.5 million t.oz annually during the 1920s. India soon proved pivotal in the gold equation, for within the next two or three years, as the gold price rose, it became a massive dishoarder. Meanwhile, Kitchen revealed that during the economic difficulties of the 1920s, fabrication in jewellery had tumbled everywhere except the United States. Prior to World War I jewellery fabrication ('industrial arts', as it was called in those days) had grown from around 30 m.t/1 million t.oz in 1850 when the gold rushes began, to almost 200 m.t/6.4 million t.oz in 1913.[31] During the 1920s, due to what Kitchen called "the impoverished condition of the world outside the United States", annual fabrication had fallen to about 108 m.t/3.5 million t.oz, of which the United States took about half of new output, excluding recycled scrap. In Britain and France, fabrication slumped by 50% in the 1920s, in Germany it shrank by 90%.

Monetary gold, therefore, was the mainstay of gold demand. Kitchen's statistics are important to the evolution of gold demand in the 20th century, for although he and most others at that time were concerned about gold supplies to the monetary sector, the real longer-term future for gold within another two generations was in fabrication. The trend was already there in the growth of jewellery demand from

1850 in a more prosperous world, but it had been knocked sideways by World War I and the economic aftermath. It would be impeded further by the depression of the 1930s and World War II, but by the 1960s, with a much stronger world economy, the requirements of jewellery and industry would take up most newly-mined gold. In 1930, however, the focus was on the workings, or rather the deficiencies, of the Mark Two gold standard, which was about to be tested to destruction.

Goodbye gold standard

Forty-three countries subscribed to the gold standard in 1930, at least in having a fixed price for gold in their own currency. After that they chose from an *à la carte* menu what best suited their needs. Twelve nations, as diverse as the United States, the Netherlands, Japan, Mexico and Thailand (Siam) were purists with their notes redeemable in gold coin. Several followed the Bank of England's example with the right to redeem notes in 400 ounce (or 12 kg) bars; an option chosen by Belgium, Denmark and India. The Bank of France usually cashed notes in bullion, retaining an option of supplying coin, but subject to a minimum of 215,000 francs. The majority of subscribers opted for a gold exchange standard in which their notes were redeemable in the foreign exchange of countries whose currencies were repayable in gold (coin or bullion), with sterling and the dollar as the prime examples. In effect, there was a gold coin standard, a gold bullion standard and a gold exchange standard.[32] This *mélange* was vulnerable. "The strongest criticism of the return to gold in 1925," wrote Keynes' biographer Robert Skidelsky, "is that it was not part of a concerted move back to a fixed-exchange system, with the parities and the 'rules of the game' agreed in advance."[33]

The fragility of these standards was exposed by the financial instability unleashed by the Wall Street crash of 1929, ushering in the widespread deflation and unemployment of the depression. World trade was cut by one-third in 1930, prices fell by 30%, unemployment soared reaching 21% in Britain, 25% in the United States and 34% in Germany in 1931. A chain-reaction of economic setbacks fed the instability. The collapse of agricultural and commodity prices forced many exporting countries to suspend external debt service to preserve precious foreign exchange for essential imports, bringing, in turn, turmoil to the international bond market. Scrambling for cover, overseas investors and companies withdrew deposits from London, precipitating the very devaluation they feared. In May 1931 Austria's largest commercial bank, Credit Anstalt, failed. In July, Germany's Darmstadter Bank suspended payments.

The run for cover was instantly reflected in gold. The immediate loser was Germany, its gold reserves plummeting 40% between May and June alone (and halving by year-end). The first buyers were the central banks of the Netherlands and Switzerland reacting instantly in May to the Credit Anstalt crash; Belgium and France joined in by June. By July, Britain was the target, losing over 220 m.t/7.3 million t.oz, 20% of its stock (the world's third largest) in the last two weeks of the month. The strain on the Bank's governor, Montagu Norman, who was effectively the architect of the revived gold standard, was such that he collapsed from exhaustion in a meeting at the Bank on 29th July and was absent convalescing over the next two crucial months. His deputy, Ernest Harvey, was meanwhile seeking to prop up the reserves, but could raise only modest foreign exchange credits from the Bank of France (too busy buying gold) and the Federal Reserve in New York, but they amounted to less than the gold lost in July. An additional line for $200 million was sought through J. P. Morgan in New York. The pre-war spirit of co-operation was not available. The fledgling Bank for International Settlements, founded in 1930 as the central bankers' bank, lacked the experience or clout to knock heads together. Countries were too preoccupied with their own internal crises.

In Britain, Ramsey MacDonald's Labour government collapsed on 23rd August 1931, to be replaced by a coalition National government. They faced an over-valued pound sterling, rampant unemployment (with high benefit costs), a weak balance of payments and reserves that might last three or four weeks. A rise in the Bank rate to try to defend sterling and the reserves was politically impossible. The first move came on Thursday 17th September, when the Bank of England exercised its right to refuse to issue *sovereigns*, which it had occasionally supplied in the restoration of the gold standard as 'an act of grace'. Four days later, after a hectic Sunday cabinet meeting, an announcement of the suspension of the Bank's "obligation to sell gold at a fixed price … for the time being" was issued. The necessary legislation went through Parliament as the Gold Standard (Amendment) Act, the next day. The Bank of England was no longer required to sell gold to all comers at the statutory price of £3.89 per standard ounce (£4.25 fine). It never would be again, although the suspension was seen as temporary. *The Times* forecast it would last only six months.

Thus the gold standard, born by mistake in 1717 with Sir Isaac Newton setting that price, and fully suspended only during the Napoleonic wars, and in limbo from 1914–1925, had collapsed. "Britain's suspension of the gold standard … was one of the turning points in the monetary history of the 20th century," wrote R. S. Sayers.[34] Montagu Norman, incidentally, was advised of the suspension on a liner in mid-Atlantic on his way back from convalescence in a somewhat ambiguous cable from his deputy, Ernest Harvey, saying, "Sorry we have to go off tomorrow and cannot wait to see you before doing so". Norman later turned it into a good story that he had assumed at first his deputy was off on holiday, not that Britain was going off the gold standard.[35]

Its demise prompted an even greater rush into gold, both by central banks and private hoarders. European central banks, fearing the dollar might face the same fate as sterling, traded their dollar holdings for gold at the Federal Reserve in New York. Between August and October, the United States sold almost 1,100 m.t/35.4 million t.oz, 17% of its entire reserves, to the central banks of Belgium, France, the Netherlands and Switzerland. In all, from May to December 1931, Britain,

Germany and the United States lost over 1,800 m.t/58 million t.oz, almost 90% of it to those four countries.[36]   Two of them, Belgium and the Netherlands, were reacting to a bitter lesson they had learned by holding large positions in sterling with the Bank of England, which they believed were 'as good as gold', but found overnight they were holding a devalued currency, as sterling fell from its previous pegged rate of £1 to $4.86 to £1 to $3.25.

While gold could still be purchased from the Federal Reserve at the usual fixed price of $20.67, countries trading in their sterling balances had to pay between £5.00 and £6.34 per ounce fine, as the London gold price floated following suspension. The role of London as the world's bullion market, however, was not affected. "The suspension of the gold standard only means that the Bank of England is no longer bound to part with gold at its statutory selling price", *The Economist* pointed out. "Gold may still be imported and exported freely, and foreign backers and private individuals are free to lodge gold for safe custody in London."[37]   South Africa's gold was still sold through the 'fixing', although the Bank of England now became the principal for South Africa, instead of Rothschilds, and gained a direct telephone line into the fixing, an inside track it enjoyed for decades. The London market itself entered a period of great activity, for not only were central banks eager for gold, but the era of the private hoarder had arrived.

The demand came from across Europe. Commercial banks, businesses and individuals, wary of paper money, took refuge in gold. The French hid *Napoléons* and kilo bars (*savonettes*/cakes of toilet soap) in their mattresses or cellars, and as Nazi power grew in Austria and Germany, many people bought a little gold in case they had to run away. The Bank for International Settlements calculated that in the five years after Britain went off the gold standard, almost 3,110 m.t/100 million t.oz, equal to 70% of all gold mined in the period, was hoarded in undisclosed holdings by banks and private individuals.[38]   Much of the gold came from India, where the devaluation of the rupee in line with sterling made it profitable to dishoard gold and send it to London.   India shipped back nearly 1,250 m.t/40 million t.oz of gold between 1931 and 1938, the first dishoarding since 1812–14 during the cash suspension of the Napoleonic wars.[39]

Meanwhile, there was a hiatus in the international monetary system. Along with Britain, Austria, Canada, Finland, Germany, Japan, Norway, Sweden and Portugal had all deserted the gold standard by the end of 1931. That left Belgium, France, Italy, the Netherlands, Switzerland and the United States as the main nations wedded to gold. This gold 'club' held over 77% of all central bank stocks, which enabled them to fight a rearguard action for several years, hoping for a general return to an international standard. The National Bank of Belgium was one of the most aggressive, turning all its foreign exchange holdings into gold, with the Bank of France also eliminating all foreign exchange holdings. Yet it was among the non-members of the club, who had devalued, that economies began to revive because their exports were cheaper and thus more competitive. Gold standard nations, however, still locked into old fixed exchange rates, did not recover and world trade fell another 16% in 1932.[40] With economic conditions still deteriorating in the United States and Europe early in 1933, a World Economic Conference was proposed to seek agreement on exchange rates and, hopefully, stimulate economic recovery. But the fractious gold-versus-non-gold nations would scarcely agree an agenda and, anyway, the event was eclipsed by the inauguration of Franklin Delano Roosevelt as President of the United States, who would create quite a new age of gold.

CHAPTER 23

1934-1968:
The Age of $35 Gold

The inauguration of President Roosevelt at the beginning of March 1933 came at a critical moment. He faced a demoralised nation, with high unemployment, a tidal wave of domestic bank failures (almost half the banks in the United States disappeared between 1929 and 1933) and a flight from the dollar into gold by European speculators. On the very day of Roosevelt's inauguration, an estimated $109 million in gold (164 m.t/5.3 million t.oz) was 'earmarked' in New York for the account of foreign speculators. At his first press conference the new President boldly declared the gold standard was safe. Yet, the next day, he rushed through both Houses of Congress legislation empowering him to regulate or prohibit the export, hoarding, or earmarking of gold or silver, and authorising the Secretary of the Treasury to order US citizens to hand in all gold coin, bullion and gold certificates (some of them issued in the Civil War).[1] Over the next few months almost 500 m.t/16 million t.oz of gold was exchanged by the American people for greenbacks. They were not to be permitted to hold gold again until after midnight on 31st December 1974. Briefly, export licences were granted to central banks and governments, who could still buy gold at $20.67 an ounce, but when exports to France and The Netherlands quickly escalated, Roosevelt took the final step of taking gold off the standard. The link between the dollar and gold was severed on 20th April 1933. The dollar immediately dropped over 28%, taking the New York gold price close to $27.00 per ounce.

The devaluation of the dollar bought breathing space. With American exports cheaper and thus competitive, factory employment and working hours improved within a few months. On the gold front, however, important decisions remained. Was the gold price to be left free to float? What was to happen to the output of American gold mines now that ownership of gold was forbidden, and what should be done about jewellery and industrial fabricators? Roosevelt and his Acting Secretary of the Treasury, Henry Morganthau, decided on 22nd October 1933 that they would buy all US gold production (60 m.t/2 million t.oz annually) at a stated price, and license fabricators to buy gold at that price. A week later the Treasury undertook to buy *imported* gold delivered to the US Assay Office at that same price. The price itself was raised by a few cents daily, with the aim of enhancing the value of existing stocks and so the money supply.

Roosevelt himself decided the gold price over breakfast each day, on the advice of Morganthau. "While Roosevelt ate his eggs and drank his coffee, the group decided what the day's price should be," wrote Arthur Schlesinger Jnr. "The precise figure each day was less important than the encouragement of a general upward trend. One day Morganthau came in more worried than usual and suggested an increase from 19 to 22 cents. Roosevelt took one look at Morganthau's anxious face and proposed 21 cents. 'It's a lucky number,' he said with a laugh, 'because it is three times seven.'"[2]   The breakfast 'fixing' got the price to $33.65 by mid-November, by which time the market was on to the game and anticipated the daily slippage of the dollar.

So Roosevelt and Morganthau abandoned the daily price and made small *ad hoc* adjustments occasionally. These lifted the price to $34.06 by mid-January 1934, approaching a 40% fall in the dollar over nine months. The moment had come to stabilise. A new Gold Reserve Act was passed requiring the future equivalent of the dollar to be not more than 60% and not less than 50% of the previous gold standard level. On 31st January 1934 Roosevelt issued a Proclamation which fixed the gold price at $35 per ounce fine. This official price was to last until 1968 for the open market and until 1971 for inter-central bank dealings. Crucially, the United States stood ready to buy gold from all comers at that clearly posted price, effectively putting it back on a gold standard, with the dollar re-linked to gold. But it would sell gold only to central banks or governments.[3]

The decision dictated the pattern for the gold business for a generation. At the London fix the morning after the Proclamation there was little business; few could believe that the US government would really buy every ounce offered them. Once New York opened in the afternoon and word spread that the US Assay Office indeed bought at $35, everyone wanted gold for New York. The Bank of France was besieged by *arbitrageurs* asking for gold at their old fixed French price. "The Bank of France … determined to maintain the old gold standard parity," Mocatta and Goldsmid's circular noted, "the French authorities nevertheless did everything in their power to discourage the gold exports."[4] They refused to give out bars that were 'good delivery' on the London market, but dealers took any bars since they could be quickly remelted, and refined if necessary, and given a London 'good delivery' chop. In the first month of $35 gold, the Bank of France lost over 180 m.t/5.8 million ounces.

That set the trend of gold flows for the next fifteen years – essentially a one-way traffic across the Atlantic to the United States. Not only French stocks, but those of Belgium, the Netherlands, Switzerland and Italy were eroded over the next two or three years, as they clung to out-dated fixed gold prices. Their domestic economies, struggling with over-valued currencies, suffered from deflationary policies that cut wages and pensions and stirred social unrest. The Belgians did devalue their currency by 28% early in 1935, but stayed on the gold standard, making a market in gold at a higher fixed price until 1938. France held out until September 1936, when the incoming Popular Front government, voted in on promises of increased public expenditure and wage rises, devalued the franc and took the country off the gold standard. An embargo was placed on all gold transactions and people were given one month to declare their holdings or surrender the gold at the pre-devaluation price. Few did. The Netherlands, Switzerland and Italy followed suit. Between them these European central banks lost over 2,000 m.t/64.3 million t.oz of gold by the end of 1936. In turn, the United States reserves rose by 50% to almost 9,000 m.t/290 million t.oz, with much of the gold consigned to the new depository at Fort Knox constructed beneath the blue grasses of Kentucky. The Americans even got a bonus from the devaluations, because many European hoarders, presented with higher domestic gold prices, took a quick profit in the late autumn and winter of 1936–37. The profit-taking was enhanced by fears the Americans might stop buying or even reduce the $35 price. A "golden avalanche" of 933 m.t/30 million t.oz was sold back through the London market, most of it dispatched to bolster American reserves.

The United States was becoming the great reservoir of gold, for while it bought gold from all comers, be they miners, central banks or profit-taking hoarders, the Treasury sold only to central banks, the Bank for International Settlements or governments – and few of them had any spare dollars to pay. 'The gold *guichet*' (ticket window) at the Federal Reserve Bank in New York which handled any sales had little business before the 1950s. So the US stock rose relentlessly to 15,679 m.t/504 million t.oz by 1939 on the eve of World War II. The increase since 1930 exceeded all new mine production during the decade, implying not only that the United States had taken it all up, but absorbed some dishoarding as well.

Despite the one-way trans-Atlantic flow of gold, it was still widely regarded as an international monetary vehicle. Indeed, there was little demand for it in jewellery or industry; Union Corporation estimates for the 1930s show net selling from the 'industrial arts' as much jewellery from distress sales was melted. At the time, Ralph Hawtrey at the Treasury in London, one of the closest observers of the gold standard era, reflected, "Of the annual output of gold … very little is needed for other than monetary purposes … Gold (had) retained its function as a medium for the settlement of international balances even when it was largely deprived of its fixed valuation in terms of currencies".[5] He added a pertinent afterthought, "there is a very real convenience in using … metallic reserves. Other assets take the form of debts, and every debt depends for its value on the person and local situation of the debtor. Gold is an *anonymous* asset, and is capable of transportation from one place to another without retaining any link with the place of its origin".[6] Thus, in 1939, a Treasury mandarin summed up gold's special appeal. The pure gold standard had gone, but not the perception of the metal as a unique asset for governments or their people, which remains to this day.

Gold at $35 – mining booms

The devaluation, first of sterling then the dollar, kick-started a mining boom that doubled world gold production in the 1930s. The mining industry had been languishing for two decades; output in 1930 was on a par with 1910. Australian output was one-sixth that of 1910, American production had halved, even South Africa was down over 10%. No major discoveries had been made, capital and wage costs had soared. The rise in the sterling price from the traditional £4.25 per ounce fine to highs around £6.50 in 1932 galvanised miners in the sterling area. In South Africa, still providing half the world's gold, an attempt to stay on the gold standard after Britain had departed was challenged by the mining industry. Anglo American's Sir Ernest Oppenheimer told a South African parliamentary committee, "I am convinced that the interest of this country will be best served by leaving the gold standard".[7] The South African government yielded in December 1932, devaluing the rand. Output rose 22% in three years just because lower grade ores could be processed.

It is ironic that during the harsh years of the depression gold mining boomed, creating jobs around the world. In California, once $35 gold came in, thousands of the unemployed became gold prospectors, scouring the streams of the High Sierras for gold overlooked by the '49ers nearly a century earlier. At the Homestake Mine in South Dakota output rose over 20% in two years as deeper shafts and better pumps could be afforded. The company even hired college students to 'pan' its waste dumps in their summer vacation.[8] United States' production doubled, reaching 155 m.t/5 million t.oz in 1940, a record not surpassed until 1988. Across the border, Canadian output from 146 mines peaked at 172 m.t/5.5 million t.oz in 1941, a total beaten only in a single subsequent year, 1991. Famous names such as Kerr Addison at Larder Lake and the Hollinger Mine at Timmins each achieved annual outputs close to 20 m.t/640,000 t.oz.

In Western Australia the Golden Mile in that boisterous town Kalgoorlie blossomed again. "People came to Kalgoorlie to escape the depression," remembered Geoffrey Blainey. "At night within a radius of 50 miles the lights of prospectors and miners camped at hundreds of points in the scrub could be seen – men looking for new lodes or re-opening mines."[9] The Lake View and Star mine became the new champion of the Golden Mile itself. Australia's annual output virtually quadrupled in the thirties to over 50 m.t/1.6 million t.oz by 1939, a total not exceeded until 1985.

The search for Soviet gold

The dark horse in this renaissance was the Soviet Union. In the 19th century Russia had been the leading producer until California eclipsed it after 1849, but output had progressed slowly towards 60 m.t/1.9 million t.oz annually by 1914. The Revolution in 1917 disrupted mining, but by the mid-1920s Joseph Stalin was eager to revive it. He had been inspired, apparently, by the writings of Bret Harte, chronicler of the American West, on the California gold rush. He envisaged a similar migration to open up the mineral wealth of Siberia. In 1927 he set up Glavzoloto (Gold Trust) to foster gold mining and told its director, A. P. Serebrovsky, "This process must be applied to our outlying regions … at the beginning we will mine gold, then gradually change over to other minerals such as coal and iron".

Serebrovsky set off under the guise of a professor from the Moscow School of Mines to study US gold mining and recruited an American mining engineer, John D. Littlepage, to mastermind the Russian gold rush. Littlepage worked in the Soviet Union from 1928 until 1937, supervising the creation of a fleet of ninety steam and electric dredges in the alluvial gold fields that accounted for most output. Powerhouses, mechanical hoists, crushers and cyanide plants were also installed in the few underground mines. With Stalin's approval, prospectors who found new deposits were richly rewarded, while special stores were set up supplied with food, clothing and luxury goods, which had to be paid for in gold, as a way of siphoning off unofficial output. Stalin's purges provided plenty of cheap labour for the new gold fields. Production surged ahead. By the mid-1930s it was 155 m.t/5 million t.oz annually, putting the Soviet Union in second place in the world league, where it remained until 1990. John Littlepage himself, in a book written on his return to the United States, declined to reveal precise production figures, but suggested the Soviet Union had the potential to overtake South Africa.[10]

That target was never achieved, but the clear evidence of the potential was seen in 1937, when the Soviet Union sold 187 m.t/6 million t.oz through the London market. Thereafter Soviet output and sales were cloaked in mystery for over fifty years, although the market always recognised the Soviet Union as second only to South Africa. Indeed, between them South Africa and Russia accounted for 80% of world output between the 1940s and 1980s. Soviet reserves were a respectable 2,050 m.t/66 million t.oz in 1952, when a twelve-year sales programme through the London and Paris markets disposed of at least 2,900 m.t/93 million t.oz, (including new output) leaving the reserves well below 1,000 m.t/32 million t.oz.[11] Those Soviet sales, especially between 1963 and 1965, helped keep the gold price pegged at $35.

South Africa; in a league of its own

Initially the world-wide mining boom of the 1930s dented South Africa's share of global output because it was dependent on deep mines which took several years to bring on stream. In 1930 South Africa accounted for 51% of output, in 1938 for only 32.5, and she was not back over 50% until 1944. Geological detective work in that period, however, revealed a series of deep new reefs, that would provide a rich harvest for fifty years.

The initiative came from Gold Fields of South Africa, born of the partnership between Cecil Rhodes and Charles Rudd in the 1880s. Early in the 1930s their consulting engineer, Guy Carleton Jones, was approached by a young German geologist, Rudolf Krahmann, who had just emigrated to South Africa. He proposed Gold Fields should try out a newly developed magnetometer to locate the elusive reefs. The magnetometer, he hastened to explain, would not locate the gold reefs themselves, but could pick up the pattern of magnetic shales of the lower Witwatersrand system. Since the position of gold reefs in relation to the shales was known, they could be charted quickly. Carleton Jones himself had never been satisfied with borehole results from an area known as the Far West Rand eighty miles west of Johannesburg, where surface formations suggested reefs far below. He decided to give Krahmann and his magnetometer a three-month trial for a fee of $840, plus $560 expenses.

It was the best, and cheapest, investment in prospecting ever made in South Africa. The magnetometer at once revealed the pattern of reefs. Carleton Jones then staked his professional reputation on persuading the board of Gold Fields to invest in the new gold field that became known as the 'West Wits Line'. The first two mines, Venterspost and Libanon, were floated in the mid-1930s, and came on stream in 1939 (though Libanon was not fully developed until 1951). Later came the great mines of West Driefontein in 1952 and Anglo American's Western Deep Levels in 1962, and their smaller neighbours, Blyvooruitzicht (Rand Mines) and Doornfontein. West Driefontein became the world's largest producer, yielding over 70 m.t/2.25 million t.oz annually with grades up to 27 grams per tonne, twice the industry average. The bonus of the West Wits Line was that not only did the Main Reef Series of gold-bearing conglomerates underlie the new field, but two hitherto unknown formations, the Ventersdorp Contact Reef and the rich Carbon Leader were also hidden deep within it.[12] The West Wits Line was just a start. Geologists drilling at Geduld Farm in the Orange Free State, two hundred miles south-west of Johannesburg, came up with a borehole result in a newly located Basal Reef in April 1946 of 5,430 g/t (168.876 t.oz/t). A shock wave went through an industry accustomed to grates of 10–30 grams at best. A few months later an even higher grade of over 8,000 g/t turned up.[13] Gold mines are usually floated on scores, even hundreds, or borehole results, never on one or two. But these two, along with others less dramatic, convinced Sir Ernest Oppenheimer at Anglo American that Orange Free State was home to a great gold field. He argued it was "the most significant in South Africa since the finding of diamonds at Kimberley and gold on the Witwatersrand". The decision to develop was taken immediately and the original four mines, Free State Geduld, President Brand, President Steyn and Western Holdings, came on stream in the mid-1950s. Forty years on these mines had yielded over 6,000 m.t/193 million t.oz at an average grade of close to 10 g/t, not quite what the boreholes promised but a fine return over the long haul. When I first went down Free State Geduld in 1967 the grade was still an outstanding 35 g/t, over one ounce per tonne. The speckles of gold between the pebbles of the reef could be clearly seen. Sir Ernest's gamble paid off. "No one would start a mine today on the basis of the information that was available on Free State in 1946," Adriaan Louw, chairman of rival Gold Fields, admitted to me.[14]

The surge in Orange Free State output was astonishing, soaring from a mere 13 m.t/420,000 t.oz in 1953 to 174 m.t/5.6 million t.oz by 1960. With the West Wits Line also in its stride and the opening of the Klerksdorp gold field to its west in the late 1950s, South Africa's overall total output virtually doubled in those same seven years from 317 m.t/11.9 million t.oz to 624 m.t/20 million t.oz. The momentum was maintained during the 1960s, with the help of the small Evander field, south-east of Johannesburg. Evander was the eastern tip of the crescent of gold reefs that swing round Johannesburg to end in the Orange Free State. All told, output in 1970 reached a peak of precisely 1,000 m.t/32.15m t.oz, accounting for 77.6% of all non-communist production in that year. The nearest rivals were Canada with 75 m.t/2.4 million t.oz and the United States with 56 m.t/1.8 million t.oz. This mushrooming South African production was still sold by the South African Reserve Bank through the London gold market, using the Bank of England as its selling agent at the 'fixing'. Every Saturday morning the Reserve Bank cabled the Bank of England telling them how much gold to sell on its behalf the following week; if the Bank was instructed to sell 500,000 ounces it would normally dispose of roughly 100,000 ounces at the fix each day. In turn, each Saturday the Bank of England cabled the Reserve Bank with the exact details, accurate to five decimal places, of the weight of gold sold and the price received on each day. On the Monday, the Reserve Bank paid the Chamber of Mines for distribution to the mining houses. Most of the world's gold came to market between 1954 and 1968 in this unique operation.[15]

Enter the International Monetary Fund

When the world went to war in 1939 the official gold standard had been abandoned, yet gold remained a monetary metal, albeit most of it held by the US Treasury who would buy from all comers and sell to approved customers (the central banks) at $35 an ounce. For the next decade it continued as a buyer, even after World War II ended in 1945, as European central banks sold what little gold they had left to the Treasury for badly needed dollars to rebuild their shattered economies. France disposed of almost 800 m.t/25.7 million t.oz between 1945 and 1949, leaving it a reserve of under 600 m.t/19.3 million t.oz, compared with over 3,900 m.t/125 million t.oz in 1935. The high watermark of US gold reserves came in 1949, when its 22,000 m.t/707 million t.oz of gold represented 75% of all monetary stocks (excluding the Soviet Union) and perhaps half of all gold ever mined. That was a reflection of American economic power, but it was scarcely a balanced international monetary system.

The framework for a new system had been set, however, by the Bretton Woods Agreement in 1944, which created the International Monetary Fund (IMF). The Fund was to oversee a new monetary system based on fixed exchange rates. Fund members agreed to maintain their exchange rates, with only a 1% margin either way, against a benchmark of their relationship to gold or the dollar on 1st

July 1944. The dollar and gold were interchangeable because the US Treasury stood ready to buy or sell gold at $35 to recognised central banks. In effect, this was a dollar exchange standard, in which IMF members agreed not to deal in gold at prices differing from its par value against currencies. This did not mean central banks were barred from buying gold in the market, merely that it should be at the $35 price. Over the next two decades much effort went into trying to keep that price capped in a world which had changed totally from January 1934 when it was arbitrarily set by President Roosevelt.

Initially that was not an issue, for there was little spare purchasing power in the immediate post-war years and the London gold market itself remained in suspension. The market had been closed in September 1939; the final fix, still made in sterling, was £8.05. All gold business thereafter went through the Bank of England. A profitable little loophole was opened shortly after the war, when the Bank of England agreed to small allocations for 'manufactured' gold to be exported. A lively trade in 22 carat (916 fine) gold sheet, pen nibs, ashtrays and even statuettes developed to profit from premiums of $3 an ounce abroad as the gold articles were then melted and the bars dispatched to markets in the Middle East and Far East. This new sideline was immortalised in the film The Lavender Hill Mob, featuring solid gold models of the Eiffel Tower.[16]

Serious business resumed in 1954, when the London market was permitted to re-open. The first fix, on 22nd March 1954, was £12.42, the rise reflecting the devaluation of sterling against the dollar in 1949. The market held a strong hand. Besides the growing South African production, sold on the fix by the Bank of England, the Soviet Union had just begun its twelve year sales programme, mainly through Samuel Montagu, one of the fixing members. Thus London was the prime supplier for allcomers, save for the modest Canadian and American mine output which was easily absorbed in North America. Fabricators elsewhere had to reply on London, as did European central banks, who found purchases on the fix cheaper than the Federal Reserve's *guichet*, because of the added costs of shipping the metal back across the Atlantic. To these appetites were added the nascent nibbles of a new breed of investors, worried about the long-term outlook for the dollar.

The challenge from private demand

This mix of buyers soon changed the dynamics of the market. First, as economies in Europe revived in the 1950s, central banks returned as buyers. Central banks bought 45% of all new mine supply between 1948 and 1964. In 1950 the central banks of Western Europe (excluding Britain) held only 3,334 m.t/107 million t.oz of gold; ten years on, those stocks had tripled and, by 1965, were up to 16,930 m.t/544 million t.oz. Germany, which had no gold in 1950, then held almost 4,000 m.t/129 million t.oz, while France had improved from 558 m.t/17.9 million t.oz to 4,182 m.t/134 million t.oz. US Treasury reserves, meanwhile, had been drained of 9,500 m.t/305 million t.oz, down 40% from their 1949 high.[17]

Not only were gold reserves more equitably divided, reflecting the new era of European prosperity, but governments and central bankers were showing continued devotion to gold as their core monetary reserve. The great advocate was President Charles de Gaulle in France, who declared in a memorable press conference in 1965, "There can be no other criterion, no other standard than gold. Yes, gold which never changes, which can be shaped into ingots, bars, coins, which has no nationality and which is eternally and universally accepted as the unalterable fiduciary value par excellence". The strain of maintaining a fixed price at $35, however, was beginning to tell as private buying by investors and fabricators mounted. In 1960 they took up three-quarters of all newly mined gold and thereafter private demand exceeded central bank purchases every year (excluding gold acquired by central banks trading in dollars to the US Treasury). In October that year, fears that the winner of the forthcoming US Presidential election (won by John Kennedy) would devalue the dollar to solve the US balance of payments deficit pushed the London price to $40. The buyers were European investors, including large companies, who kept part of their reserves in gold with Swiss banks, and added to them because of dollar nervousness. After quick consultation by the Bank of England with the Federal Reserve in New York (whose officials always got hauled out of bed as the 'fixing' was at 10.30 am), it was agreed the Bank should make substantial gold sales to defuse the price. The experience led to discussions on safeguards to hold the line at $35. The trick was to contain the gold price at the London fix between the sterling equivalent of $35.00 and $35.20. Once it topped $35.1675 (the so-called 'gold export point') it became cheaper for European central banks to take gold from the Fed's *guichet* in New York, putting an unwelcome drain on US reserves.

The 'pool' defends $35; India finds it cheap

The outcome, a year later, was the creation of the international 'gold pool' of the US, Britain, Belgium, France, the Netherlands, Switzerland and West Germany to 'stabilise' the price. The Bank of England was assigned the role of operating agent at the London fixing. "It's like a Greyhound bus – we leave the driving to them," a Federal Reserve official once told me. Before long, it was agreed that the 'pool' would not only sell to cool the price, but buy when it fell below the 'export' point of $35.1675. The scheme worked well until 1965, with the pool being a net buyer in occasional years. In 1963, when the Soviet Union made large sales, the Bank bought 500 m.t/16 million ounces for its member central banks.

The scenario changed in 1965. Soviet sales ceased in the autumn because they had few reserves left after twelve years of sales. Demand, however, rose as speculators hedged their positions for a sterling devaluation after the election of a Labour government in Britain; even China switched its sterling balances held in London to gold.[18] President de Gaulle was also at his most aggressive, ignoring the 'pool', to turn French dollar and sterling balances into gold. The 'pool' became a substantial net seller and remained so for the rest of its short life.

A new era was opening in which the private demand for gold regularly took up all mine production (even though South Africa was sprinting towards its 1,000 tonnes record output in 1970). Yet central bankers still focused on maintaining $35 gold, not realising how fast the world of gold was changing. Its role for over two centuries had been as a monetary metal and, as late as the 1930s, virtually all newly mined gold had gone into their stocks. But the British Prime Minister, Harold Macmillan, had signalled a sea change in 1959 when he told electors, "You've never had it so good". The trials of two world wars and the depression between them were over.

The new mood was apparent when I first investigated the gold market in 1966, prompted by a member of the London gold market who thought it was time to report changing gold demand. Two experiences drove that home to me. "Gold is cheap now in terms of work," an official at the Bank for International Settlements in Basle told me, gazing out of his window at the bustling streets. "Take a tram driver here. On his wages, he can buy his wife a gold wedding ring and a gold bracelet once in a while. One central bank is even rebuilding its offices with windows laced with gold thread."[19] For the first time in history gold was not just a symbol of wealth and power for rulers or the rich, but affordable by millions everywhere. In Dubai on the Arabian Gulf I met traders busy filling 'jackets' with small ten tola bars to be smuggled to India on the fleet of dhows moored in the creek.[20] More gold went from London to Dubai in 1966 than to any other country except France and Switzerland – 125 m.t/4 million t.oz, one-tenth of all non-communist mine output. Within a few years Dubai was spiriting double that amount to India's bazaars.[21] In Bombay, the President of the Bombay Bullion Association told me, "The peasant … is always faced with fear of famine, his crops depend on the whim of the monsoon, he knows nothing of banking and credit. Now what is the one thing to tide him and his village over in an emergency? When famine comes they must have something tangible to convert – gold".[22] While it remained pegged at $35 an ounce, they could afford it. From Basle to Bombay, gold was seen as cheap. Yet William McChesney Martin of the US Federal Reserve Board rashly said he would defend the $35 price 'to the last ingot'. His bluff was called.

Goodbye $35 gold

The first test came after the devaluation of sterling in November 1967 brought a new wave of speculators. In a month the London market handled more orders than was normal in nine months; demand was up to 100 m.t/3.2 million t.oz in a day. In an effort to stem the offtake, all forward buying was banned, as was the purchase of gold on credit. Even so, the pool lost over 1,400 m.t/45 million t.oz in 1967, more than a whole year's mine supply. The French, seeing the way the tide ran, had already opted out of the pool. The crunch came in March 1968, following a speech in the US Senate by Senator Javits urging the Treasury to cease support for the gold pool. The same week the ferocious Tet offensive in Vietnam, causing urgent calls for more US troops to be deployed there, brought an onslaught on the dollar. An emergency meeting of 'pool' central bankers in Basle over the weekend still vowed to support "the fixed price of $35 per ounce". Special flights by US military aircraft were laid on to fly ever more gold to London. Every night heavily guarded convoys of military vehicles sped the gold from Lakenheath Air Force base to the back entrance of the Bank of England. So much gold was moved in that the floor of the weighing room collapsed.[23] So did the $35 price. At 3.30 am on 15th March 1968 Roy Jenkins, the Chancellor of the Exchequer, rose in the House of Commons to declare a 'bank holiday' and the closure of the London gold market. Zurich also closed that day; only Paris remained open with gold trading at the equivalent of $44.00 per ounce. On the last four days that the pool operated, 778 m.t/25 million t.oz of gold was supplied to the market. In all, over the final fifteen months, they had put in over 3,000 m.t/96.5 million t.oz in an effort to sustain a price of $35.[24] The market had won.

Two days later, in a hastily cobbled together Washington Agreement, governors of the gold pool banks declared the official price would still be maintained at $35, but that "officially held gold should be used only to effect transfers among monetary authorities and, therefore, they decided no longer to supply gold to the London gold market or any other gold market". In short, central banks would live in a world of gold of their own with an outdated price of $35, while the 'free' market price floated.

The London market remained closed for two weeks. When it re-opened on 1st April 1968, all dealings were in dollars and an extra afternoon fixing at 3 pm was introduced to suit American hours. The first fix was at $38.00. In the interim the three major Swiss banks – Credit Suisse, Swiss Bank Corporation and Union Bank of Switzerland – pulled off a neat coup by persuading the South African Reserve Bank to market its gold in future through them, even setting up their own informal 'pool' to handle it. After almost a century, London had lost exclusive marketing of South Africa's gold. That was almost a detail. The world of gold would never be the same again. After centuries of a fixed price, that was now a moving target.

CHAPTER 24

The View from 2000:
High Technology Gold

The dramatic days of March 1968 were a watershed for gold. So much has changed since that the market in 1968 had more in common with that of 1868 than with the world of gold after 2000. This has become the age of high technology in mining, markets and metallurgy. Gold's unique ductility and conductivity have made it unrivalled as the spidery web at the heart of today's electronics, as versatile here on earth as in space. Equally, the perception of its price changed once it was no longer fixed, but fluctuated literally from moment to moment.

Its destiny was determined by a heady cocktail of forces. The underlying price was founded on the solid foundations of jewellery and industrial demand, but the mix was stirred by central banks (often as sellers), private investors and speculators. The latter whipped up a nice froth from time to time to catch the political or economic mood, while traders, sitting down before their computer screens each morning, were duty-bound to 'make a price'. The purchase was usually made with an eye on profit, rather than to secure a benchmark or safe haven as it has been through centuries of a fixed price. True, many still seek refuge in gold when their currency or country are under siege, but that, in turn, shakes up the cocktail.

So the central issue on everyone's mind was always the price. The miner meeting his bullion bankers, the jewellery fabricator ordering his gold sheet, the investor scanning the *Financial Times*, *Wall Street Journal* or a myriad web sites, all have one question, "What is the price going to do?". It greeted me around the globe for thirty years in the *souks* of Saudi Arabia or the Gulf, in the Javeri Bazaar of Bombay, in Senen Market in Jakarta, around the table with earnest Japanese dealers in Tokyo, at the People's Bank of China in Beijing, and up the Amazon in Manaus from gold diggers in from the rainforest. Given that the price was $35 in 1968, $850 for a brief afternoon in 1980, down at $253 in 1999 and back over $700 in 2006, the preoccupation was understandable.

The game changed and so did the players. In the London market traditional brokers, always off to the country for the weekend, gave way to high-flying traders getting to their computer screens by 7 am to start making prices in what became a round-the-world, round-the-clock forum. London and Zurich bullion dealers opened offices in Hong Kong, Singapore and New York (once Americans could buy and sell gold freely after midnight on 31st December 1974). The American banks and commodities exchanges then joined the international fraternity. New delicacies were offered – futures contracts and a multiplicity of options or derivative instruments that avoided the embarrassment of actually having to take delivery of gold and store it in a vault or under the mattress. Options spawned a new language. Take your pick from 'exotic' and 'naked' to 'look-back' and 'knock-out' options, not forgetting the dangerous 'out-of-the-money'. As for the mysteries of 'delta heading' derivatives, Jessica Cross recalled in her definitive book, "I have witnessed around the world ... utter confusion, eyes that glaze over and people shaking their heads in what can only be described as dismay".[1] Once it had been so simple; a sterling pound note was exchanged for a *sovereign*, ten greenbacks for a golden *eagle*, or a few francs for a *Napoléon d'or*.

These new frontiers for gold were fast moving, bursting with energy. So much was happening on the mines, in the markets, in jewellery factories where machines 'knitted' miles of gold chain to adorn the neck, wrist, or ankle of millions of pretty women, and at electronics manufacturers where fragile patterns in gold on billions of semi-conductors and connectors became the arteries powering washing machines, televisions, DVDs, mobile phones and, of course, spacecraft.[2]

In the process, gold completed what could have been a traumatic transition from being principally a monetary metal in the 19th and early 20th centuries to one sought for jewellery and industrial fabrication. Modern electronics could scarcely function without gold's electrical conductivity, its ductility and its total freedom from tarnishing or corrosion at either high or low temperatures. Gold is uncorrupted underwater or in space. Such credentials enabled gold, much better than silver a century earlier, to bridge the tricky gap between serving primarily as money to use by fabricators, while still fascinating investors. Gold's price may have become a roller-coaster at times, but its price did not wilt, like that of silver in the late 19th century as gold superseded silver coin. The simple fact is that between 1968 and 2006 the mines produced over 70,000 m.t/2,250 million t.oz of gold, while total demand for fabrication in jewellery, industry, dentistry and investment coin was over 80,000 m.t/2,572 million t.oz, with the balance being met by central bank sales and recycled scrap. Jewellery manufacture alone, excluding recycling, took 80% of all newly mined gold. In short, there was a genuine physical demand for gold; it was price-sensitive if the price ran up too fast, but year-in, year-out, it was the heart of the business.

In mining – a technical revolution

Gold miners found this hard to comprehend in the early days of the floating price. The publication in 1969 of the first Consolidated Gold Fields *Gold Survey*, which revealed that fabrication marginally exceeded mine output, was greeted with incredulity.[3] A Swiss gold dealer told me it could not be so. But we were soon bumping into each other up back streets in Jakarta or Vientiane in Laos as he pursued new customers (one of whom had a cycle repair shop as a front) and I tracked the demand, and he came to agree with the strength of physical offtake as it started to surge in Asia. The pattern was not transparent in those days since up to 30% of all newly mined gold was smuggled at some point on the way to its eventual destination. Some miners took longer to accept the real 'bread and butter' applications for gold. The chief executive of one North American company told me in 1987, "Investors in gold will always keep us going". On the contrary, I suggested to him, the only justification for developing a new mine was because of the long-term demand for fabrication. True investors and speculators provided a bonus from time to time, but the viability of a mine should not be dependent on their whim. The miners eventually got the message; leading producers formed The World Gold Council in 1987 to promote both fabrication and investment in gold world-wide.

Miners were slow, however, to enjoy the benefits of a free gold price. The long years of $35 gold left the industry run down and demoralised. South Africa and the Soviet Union accounted for over 80% of all new gold in 1968. Only Australia, Canada (where the industry was subsidised), Ghana and the United States contributed over 20 m.t/64,300 t.oz each, a trifle set against South Africa climbing towards 1,000 m.t/32.15 million t.oz. The geographical spread of gold production was as much imbalanced as central bank stocks had been when the United States held 75% of all official gold in 1949.

Miners, nervous of a capricious floating price, did not hasten to invest in new projects. The output of gold actually fell for over a decade because South Africa peaked in 1970 and declined by one-third by 1980. Little came on stream elsewhere. Remarkably, the lowest output came in 1980, just as gold momentarily hit $850 and averaged a substantial $612 for the whole year. The price then maintained $420 through the next three years, giving the confidence that finally built a world-wide boom, almost doubling production by the year 2000.

The miners gained by waiting. New technology available by the mid-1980s simplified their task and cut costs. Advances in geochemistry and geophysics speeded up the detection of new orebodies, whose composition could be illustrated by a coloured three-dimensional mine plan on a computer screen that could be updated constantly on rock types, zones of mineralisation and the shifting metallurgy of the ores. Geologists and mining engineers could journey visually on screen through the core of a deposit far underground. The extraction of gold from low-grade oxidised ores was speeded up by heap-leaching, in which roughly crushed ore from open-pit operations was piled up on a leach 'pad' and sprayed with a solution of dilute cyanide which absorbed the gold as it percolated down through the pad. The resulting solution, 'pregnant' with gold, then passed through carbon adsorption tanks, where carbon, for which gold has a natural affinity, soaked it up like a sponge taking water. A sophisticated variation was the bio-leaching or bio-oxidation of refractory sulphide ores softened up with bacterial cultures that acted as a catalyst in the oxidation of the ore. Such techniques enabled gold to be recovered profitably from ores with grades as low as 1 g/t or 0.032/t.oz, compared with a minimum of 5–6 g/t in older mines.[4]   This revolution in gold extraction was as significant as the breakthrough of the MacArthur Forrest process in the late 1880s that made South Africa's early mines viable.[5]

On the back of these breakthroughs, output in the United States rose ten-fold and in Australia fourteen-fold within a few years. The United States produced 366 m.t/11.8 million t.oz by 1998, not far short of South Africa's diminished 464 m.t/14.9 million t.oz. Australia was also challenging with over 300 m.t/9.64 million t.oz in 1997 and 1998. The striking change was that gold mining became global. In 1968 only sixteen nations were listed with any notable production; by 2000 fifty-seven countries had output over 1 m.t/32,150 t.oz, twenty managed over 20 m.t/643,000 t.oz, and eight boasted over 100 m.t/3.2 million t.oz annual yield. South Africa and the former Soviet Union accounted between them for just 27% of the gold. The new champions included Peru, which had once spawned those wonderful Precolumbian artefacts (*see chapter 17*); Brazil, whose first gold rush in 1700 provided the metal for Britain's fledgling gold standard (*see chapter 19*); and China, getting back as a serious player two thousand years after the Han dynasty (*see chapter 12*). Ghana, Mali, Guinea and Côte d'Ivoire, the original sources for the trans-Sahara gold trade dating back over two thousand years, all boast modern mines. The roll call must include Spain, the largest (though modest) producer in Europe, where the deposits first tapped by the Romans in the 1st century AD for their coinage (*see chapter 13*) are being revisited.

Gold miners are often gloomy, complaining that deposits are 'exhausted', like a runner at the end of a marathon, or that the 'glory days' in South Africa are over. The evidence of the last twenty years has been to the contrary. Gold mines have been bursting out all over. Exploration fever has certainly cooled since the early 1990s, but the price surge of 2005/6 revived energies. Across Africa and the vast spread of Central Asia and Siberia, it can be argued that resources have hardly been tapped (though political risk may be considerable). The Russian mining specialist, Dr Natalia Zubareva, told me, "The geology is fabulous, but there has been little investment for twenty years although eventually the potential is huge". The exploration budgets of western companies in Russia rose ten-fold between 2000 and 2004, with a notable shift from the traditional placer operations to the search for hard-rock deposits, which house up to 80% of the gold.[6]   Globally, the magazine *World Gold Analyst* listed, beside the major groups, over seventy 'Intermediate Producers' and 'Junior Miners and Producers' in 2006, all eager to find gold.[7] A call came in to me from a geologist just back from the Red Sea coast of Eritrea, as I wrote this conclusion. "We're drilling, drilling, drilling for gold," he cried. "It's just across the desert from where the ancient Egyptians got gold – same geology." Shares are also quoted on the Australian Stock Exchange for an Egyptian mine, Centamin Gold. The historical continuity is matched in Greece, where a new mine is being developed at Skouries near Thessoloniki, tapping resources that first underwrote Philip of Macedon in 350 BC. An entire new generation of gold prospectors has grown up since the 1980s. With all manner of technical wizardry at their disposal, they might strike it rich. In an era of environmental awareness, however, mining is often not assured an easy ride. In Peru, Yanacocha, the world's largest gold mine, has occasionally been blockaded by local farmers, while in Argentina, where three-quarters of the potential mining land is still unexplored, laws prohibiting mining have been passed in some provinces.

The gold market, meanwhile, has evolved out of all recognition. In the early days of the floating price many nations still controlled or limited gold transactions, not least, of course, the United States where private buying had been forbidden since 1933. India, Japan, Hong Kong and Singapore, all key trading centres today, were tightly regulated. So unofficial markets grew up on their doorsteps; above all, Dubai for India, while Vientiane in Laos served Thailand, Vietnam and Cambodia and the Portuguese colony of Macao supplied Hong Kong just across the Pearl River (the gold initially arrived officially at Hong Kong's airport, was transferred to Macao quite openly on a hydrofoil on which I once accompanied it, and then was smuggled back to the British colony). Beirut also provided the conduit to Turkey, Syria, Jordan and Saudi Arabia until its own civil war in 1974 abruptly cut the traffic. Liberalisation was not long coming. Singapore led the way in 1969 as part of Prime Minister Lee Kwan Yu's strategy to make his city-state a financial centre. From the first moment the Monetary Authority of Singapore took a close interest in the gold market, building their own, still undisclosed, reserve and becoming one of the more knowledgeable central banks on gold. Hong Kong and Japan opened up in 1974, with the United States finally relaxing its ban at the end of that year. India was the only major market to remain controlled until the 1990s, with Dubai the chief supplier to its unofficial pipelines, although Singapore and Hong Kong also opened 'lines'. With good sources it was possible to monitor quite closely how much gold ended up in India each year.

The skills of these regional markets were quickly honed by the arrival of dealers from London, Zurich, Frankfurt and New York who grafted themselves on by opening trading rooms. In Hong Kong the Chinese Gold and Silver Exchange (*Kam Ngan*) operated in parallel with a dozen overseas bullion houses; a similar cast jockeyed with the local Chinese banks in Singapore. In New York the commodity exchange COMEX became the hub of futures and options trading. As these instruments caught on, the whole world of gold stayed awake to catch COMEX. Traders in Dubai, Singapore and Hong Kong would excuse themselves from dinner a few minutes before the COMEX opening. In Jakarta trading dens, like speak-easys, operated in back street garages through the night on open lines to New York.

Enter the bullion banks, the miners' minders

In this new twenty-four-hour gold market, bullion banks took on a comprehensive role. The gold brokers, often small family partnerships, matured into or were taken over by banks. Mocatta and Goldsmid, the oldest house in London, celebrated their tercentenary under the wing of Standard Chartered Bank, later being taken over by the Bank of Nova Scotia. The bullion banks soon offered complete packages in mining finance, from gold loans to provide cheap start-up capital and innovative hedging programmes to ease the pain of price fluctuations. They became the miners' minders. A Swiss banker once confided that the challenge of mining finance was the most satisfying part of his work.

Such alliances spawned, in turn, business between bullion and central banks, which proved vital in providing the latter with a way of getting back into the market. The 1968 Washington Agreement had effectively divorced central banks from the hurley-burley of the daily gold market. They were left cocooned with their own price of $35 at which they could still trade in dollars for gold at the Federal Reserve Bank of New York's *guichet*, although increasing delays were imposed by the Fed to discourage such transactions. Convertibility was finally suspended in August 1971 by President Nixon in an attempt to stem the persistent American balance of payments deficit. The final fixed link between gold and currency was snapped. Yet central banks and monetary institutions, sitting on 36,500 m.t/1,173 million t.oz of gold, were uncertain what to do with it. The US Treasury and the International Monetary Fund flirted with gold sales in the late 1970s, aimed at curbing the price, which stood at $200 when they began and was breasting $800 when disposals finished. Thereafter, central bank gold activity was sporadic. Iran's gold reserves at the Federal Reserve in New York were frozen during the 1979 hostage crisis, encouraging Iraq and Libya to buy gold and take it home. Saudi Arabia and the Gulf States, notably Abu Dhabi, turned some oil revenue into gold (all long since sold).

The return of the central banks

Ultimately, it was bullion banks, eager to borrow gold to underwrite miners' projects, that tempted central banks to test the waters of the gold market and gain an education of this new world. The procedure was simple; central banks loaned gold to the bullion bank at a modest one to 3%, which was cheaper than a miner borrowing money. The gold was sold forward by the bullion bank, thus providing the miner with his capital for development. During the late 1980s and 1990s over sixty central banks dabbled in this new game, loaning over 4,650 m.t/150 million t.oz (almost 15% of all official holdings) to the market. From earning a little income through loans, it was a short step to central banks selling their reserves. The loans got central bankers talking to bullion bankers, who explained that a little gold could be sold discreetly over several months, or even years, without the market being aware of what was going on, or, at least, knowing who was selling. By the early 1990s Canada (which was open about it), along with Belgium and the Netherlands (who kept much quieter), were selling gold through bullion banks or that long-term gold market insider, the Bank of England. "What are you going to say about the 'new producers'?", an alert Reuters commodity reporter asked me in 1993 when I was researching a new book. The central banks' arrival as regular sellers just as the gold mining boom was delivering more output every year changed the dynamics of the market.

The erosion of the gold price during the late 1990s owed much to steady, but uncoordinated, central bank selling. The final blow was the Bank of England's public announcement in 1999 that it would be selling half of Britain's gold reserves at a series of auctions. The decision was that of Gordon Brown, the Chancellor of the Exchequer, not of the Bank itself, for the Treasury owns the gold. In the event, it sent a terrible signal to the market. The Bank of England had set Britain on the gold standard in the 18th century; it had nursed the gold market for three hundred years. A former head of its foreign exchange and gold division, Terry Smeeton, had set out a few years earlier his three principal reasons for a central bank holding gold. "First, the war chest argument – that gold is the ultimate store of value in a volatile and uncertain world," said Mr Smeeton. "Secondly, that gold may be seen as a credit-risk-free alternative investment to holdings of currencies in reserves; and, thirdly, as security for loans." He concluded that these pragmatic motives would lead central banks to continue to hold gold or newly wealthy ones to buy.[8] Times change, and he had retired before the Bank's auctions were announced. Not surprisingly, the news knocked the gold price down to $253, a twenty-year low.

The nerves of a jittery gold market were steadied only by the rapid drawing up in September 1999 of a Central Bank Gold Agreement, essentially between European central banks, that sales would be co-ordinated and limited to around 400 m.t/12.86 million t.oz annually for five years. The Swiss, once the disciples of gold, were the biggest sellers, followed by Britain and the Netherlands. The agreement was renewed for five more years in 2004, with potential sales at 500 m.t annually, coupled with a bland statement by the fifteen signatory banks that "Gold will remain an important element of global monetary reserves". At least they have learned to live with the new world of gold, although the question of the stock of over 8,000 m.t/257 million t.oz still held by the United States has not been addressed. The Europeans, with over 13,000 m.t/418 million t.oz in their vaults, can now be regarded as stakeholders in the future of the gold market, even if it will be primarily as sellers. "The most positive message to come out of the European Agreement is that it showed central banks were not indifferent to the gold price and that they would structure their sales and lending accordingly", observed Philip Klapwijk of GFMS. "There is little doubt that the prospect of sub-$250 gold was a major factor behind the Europeans' unprecedented announcement on 26th September. On the other hand, the agreement confirmed the official sector's preference for reducing its bullion holdings. (In this regard, the UK Treasury announcement and the European Agreement were both milestones along the road to gold demonetisation)."[9]

At the present rate it will take sixty years to dispose of the remaining central bank stocks, if it remains a one-way street. Few have turned buyers. China, with close to $1,000 billion in reserves, is often cited as a potential bidder, but the People's Bank shows little interest in such diversification. A scattering of politically isolated states, including Iran, have bought gold and taken it home. In a dangerous world that strategy may continue, but not in the quantities to match other official sales. Gold has to look elsewhere for its buyers.

Shakers of the price cocktail

In the cocktail constantly shaken to stir the price, central banks are modest team players. Most potent is the galaxy of hedge funds and day traders operating through exchange traded futures and options or in the over-the-counter derivative markets. They have no interest in physical gold, but have the financial muscle to move the price up and down, going long or short. Price movement is what they crave. At the other end of the spectrum is the mainstay of jewellery and industrial demand, which seeks a stable price. In between is a modest physical investment demand, chiefly for bullion coins, such as the *Krugerrand*, *Maple Leaf*, *Eagle* and *Nugget*, trading at around 6% over the gold price, along with the *sovereign* still minted in small quantities for collectors or investors. They have been joined by the half-way house of Exchange Traded Funds (ETFs), which are listed on the stock exchange, like a stock, but backed by physical gold. Since 2006 some high net worth investors have also returned to physical buying of allocated gold. Although these elements overlap, they are not neatly packed in a definable compartment. As the gold analyst Robert Weinberg once wrote in a prize-winning essay, "Gold fills many different roles simultaneously. It can be adornment and an industrial metal, a means of displaying wealth and an *anonymous* form of saving, an insurance policy and a gambling chip; it is an international reserve asset yet officially it is not money. In short, it represents different things to different people and they will be driven by different motives at different times".[10]

The joker in this pack is the ability of the physical market to turn around literally overnight on sharp price increases, dumping back gold to defuse the rise. In the Middle East and Asia, where high carat 22, 23 or 24 carat gold ornaments are bought on low mark-ups as much for savings as adornment, the price surges of 1974, 1980 and 2005–6 put local markets in reverse. This 'mood of the *souks*', as I first called it back in the 1980s, is a weather vane of the gold price. 'Investment jewellery', bought on low prices, is simply traded back over the counter of hundreds of jewellery shops in the *souks*, melted down and the gold air-freighted back to international refineries. In the Kuwait *souk* in January 1980, as gold headed for $800, families clutching plastic bags and biscuit tins crammed with ornaments, queued for hours to profit from them. Local exchange houses ran out of cash to supply jewellery shops overwhelmed by the sell-off. Similarly, on price lows in the early 1990s, shops were just as crowded as buyers sensed a bargain. In a world of technical charting and computer tracking, it was wonderful to observe this visible evidence of a market high or low.

It was a stern reminder, too, that, for all the attractions of 'paper' gold, of futures on futures or a basket brimming with the latest options confections, the bread-and-butter business for the metal itself is the long-term future of gold. In fact, demand has been strong. In 2006, miners produced 2,471 m.t/93.8 million t.oz, leaving a shortfall of almost 450 m.t/14.5 million t.oz, to be made up by central bank sales or scrap. Buying pressure also came from physical hoarding of gold bars, the needs of producer de-hedging and rising private investment (notably in the relative newcomers, Exchange Traded Funds). The swirl of ingredients making the price cocktail pushed the price to an average $603.77, the best since 1980. This cooled jewellery fabrication, but it still commanded almost 80% of the newly-mined metal, with another 9% fabricated into coins, dental alloys and decorative applications. The rising star, however, continued to be electronics setting a new record of 304 m.t/9.8 million t.oz, four times what it was in 1968. Electronics offtake now exceeds South African mine output or absorbs up to 60% of current central bank net sales.[11]

Away to the stars

Gold is ubiquitous in this technological era. The appliances in our homes, the IT installations of governments and great corporations, along with spacecraft and space stations all depend on gold. The modern world could hardly function without it. Just to repeat its unique credentials: gold offers superb electrical conductivity, ductility (gold bonding wires of 999.99 fine gold are less than 25 microns thick), and total freedom from corrosion or tarnishing at either high or low temperatures. Gold's corrosion resistance means it provides an atomically clean metal surface which has an electrical contact resistance close to zero, while its high thermal conductivity ensures rapid dissipation of heat when gold is used for contacts.[12] Moreover, fresh applications are on the horizon. "The properties of gold on the nanoscale and its chemical properties are important for the future," argues Dr Chris Corti, director of COReGold Technology. "These include catalysts for pollution control and energy generation, along with use of gold chemical compounds and nanotechnology for medical diagnostics and treatment. Gold is a 'green' metal for the 21st century."

Such virtues, combined with the sheer glowing beauty that first drew people's attention to it gleaming in the tumbling streams of Asia over six thousand years ago, make gold as relevant today as it was in those masterpieces of early goldsmithing found in the tombs of Ur and Egypt.

In January 2006 a piano-sized space probe, weighing almost 500 kg, was lifted into space from Cape Canaveral, Florida, by an Atlas 5 rocket on a nine-year, three billion mile journey to Pluto. The probe will fly close by that icy planet in 2015, before swinging out into deeper space on an endless voyage of discovery. It is shrouded in thin gold foil acting as a shield against radiation and heat build-up; its delicate instruments depend on gold bonding wire for their transistors and integrated circuits, while thin films of gold potassium cyanide speed electrical currents. The Pluto space vehicle marks another new frontier for which gold is uniquely qualified. To ancient people gold was a symbol of the sun, now the metal itself is bound in that direction.

Notes to Chapters

Chapter 1

1. Guido Gregorietti, *Jewellery Through the Ages*, Hamlyn, London 1970, p.41.

2. Sir Leonard Woolley, *Excavations at Ur,* Ernest Benn, London 1954, pp.58–9.

3. Max Mallowan, *Dawn of Civilisation*, Thames and Hudson, London 1961, p.83.

4. Dr Joan Oates, *The Albert Reckitt Archaeological Lecture*, British Academy, London 2004.

5. P. R. S. Moorey, *Ancient Mesopotamian Materials and Industries*, Clarendon Press, Oxford 1994, p.221.

6. K. R. Maxwell-Hyslop, Sources of Sumerian Gold, *Iraq*, Vol.39, 1977, pp.84–85.

7. P. R. S. Moorey, op.cit., p.231.

8. Otar Lordkipanidze, *Oxford Journal of Archaeology*, Vol.20, No.1, Feb 2001.

9. Maxwell-Hyslop, op.cit., pp.73–6.

10. A. L. Oppenheim, The Seafaring Merchants of Ur, *Journal of the American Oriental Society*, Vol.74, 1954, pp.6–17.

11. M. Heltzer, The Metal Trade of Ugarit, *Iraq*, Vol.39, 1977, p.205.

12. S. M. Kramer, Commerce and Trade: Gleanings from Sumerian Literature, *Iraq*, Vol.39, 1977, p.61.

13. Moorey, op.cit., p.237.

14. Joan and David Oates, *Nimrud*, British School of Archaeology in Iraq, London 2001, p.57.

15. Woolley, op.cit., pp.64–6.

16. Ibid., p.66. Woolley described the leaves as 'beech', but later research identified them as willow; beech did not grow in Mesopotamia then.

17. K. R. Maxwell-Hyslop, op.cit., pp.4–13.

18. Marjorie Caygill, *A–Z Companion*, the British Museum, British Museum Press, 1999, pp.340–1. The treasures from the Royal Cemetery at Ur were divided between the Iraq Museum, The British Museum and the University of Pennsylvania Museum in Philadelphia.

19. Sir Leonard Woolley, op.cit., p.90.

20. K. R. Maxwell-Hyslop, op.cit., pp.lxii–lxiv: see also Henri Limet, *Le Travail du Métal au Pays de Sumer au Temps de la IIIe Dynastie d'Ur*, Paris, 1960.

21. Moorey, op.cit., pp.218–19, quoting research by G. D. Young.

22. S. La Niece, *Iraq*, Vol.57, 1995, pp.41–9.

23. Moorey, op.cit., p.226.

24. S. La Niece, op.cit., 1995, pp.41–9.

25. C. S. Smith, *Metallurgical Footnotes to the History of Art*, Proceedings of the American Philosophical Society, 116(2), p.124.

26. Moorey, op.cit., pp.228–9.

27. Maxwell-Hyslop, op.cit., p.65.

28. Moorey, op.cit., pp.230–1; Maxwell-Hyslop, op.cit.,pp.36–7; and K. R. Maxwell-Hyslop, *Iraq*, Vol.39, 1977, p.83.

29. Moorey, op.cit., p.221.

30. Benjamin R. Foster, Commercial Activity in Sargonic Mesopotamia, *Iraq*, Vol.39, 1977, pp.31–43.

31. Mogens Trolle Larsen, Partnerships in the Old Assyrian Trade, *Iraq*, Vol.39, 1977, pp.119–45.

32. Joan Oates, *Babylon*, Thames and Hudson, London 1979, p.9.

33. *A History of Money*, ed. Jonathan Williams, British Museum Press, 1998, p.19.

34. Joan Oates, *Babylon*, op. cit., p.101.

35. J. A. Brinkman, *American Journal of Archaeology*, Vol.76, 1972, pp.271–9.

36. *Cambridge Ancient History*, Vol.II, Part 1, 1978, p.486.

37. J. Knudtzon, *Die el-Amarna Tafeln* (the Tell el-Amarna Tablets), Vol.1, Leipzig 1915. Trs. from Akkadian by M. Kanawaty.

38. Brinkman, op. cit., p.278.

39. A. K. Grayson, *Assyrian Rulers of the Early First Millennium BC*, University of Toronto Press, 1991, p.291. Translation from the Banquet Stele.

40. Caygill, *A–Z Companion*, British Museum, p.57.

41. Joan and David Oates, *Nimrud*, British School of Archaeology in Iraq, London 2001, pp.78–87. This is an excellent account of Nimrud and the treasure, by two archaeologists who each devoted almost fifty years to Mesopotamian research.

42. Ibid., pp.81–7.

43. *Sunday Telegraph*, London 11th January 2004, Review, p.5.

44. Moorey, op. cit., p.223.

45. Oates, *Babylon*, op.cit., p.128.

46. *Herodotus*, Book One, pp.70–1, Penguin Classics, *The Histories*, trs Aubrey de Selincourt, revised John Marincola, London 1972.

47. Ibid., p.72.

48. Donald Wiseman, *Nebuchadrezzer and Babylon*, British Academy, Oxford University Press, 1985, p.67.

Chapter 2

1. Carol Andrews, *Ancient Egyptian Jewellery*, British Museum Press, 1990, p.7.

2. Alix Wilkinson, *Ancient Egyptian Jewellery*, Methuen, London 1971, p.58.

3. Maurice Vierya, *Les Assyriens*, Paris, 1961.

4. Fernand Braudel, *The Mediterranean in the Ancient World*, Allen Lane, London 2001, p.120.

5. B. G. Trigger, B. J. Kemp, D. O'Connor, A. B. Lloyd, *Ancient Egypt*, *A Social History*, Cambridge University Press, 1983, p.260 (D. O'Connor).

6. N. W. Gale & S. A. Stos-Gale, *Journal of Egyptian Antiquities*, Vol.67, 1981, p.113.

7. The chronology and spelling of many names often differs from book to book; for instance, Tutankhamun used to be dated 1361–1352 BC, but 1336–1327 BC is now preferred and the great pharaoh Cheops is billed as Khufu. Here, dates and spellings are those accepted by the Department of Ancient Egypt and Sudan at the British Museum and as used in the British Museum's *Dictionary of Ancient Egypt* by Ian Shaw and Paul Nicholson, British Museum Press, 2002.

8. C. Aldred, *Jewels of the Pharaohs*, Thames and Hudson, London 1971, p.115.

9. British Museum, Sudan: Ancient Treasures exhibition, 2004.

10. Leonard Cottrell, *Lost Worlds*, American Heritage Publishing Co., New York, 1962, p.38.

11. H. W. Müller, *The Royal Gold of Ancient Egypt*, I. B. Taurus, London 1999, p.41.

12. J. Vercoutter, The Gold of Kush, *Sudan Antiquities Service*, 1959, vol.7, pp.120–153.

13. Modern mining exploration east of Koptos has turned up several gold deposits with very high silver content. Australia's *Paydirt*, March 2003, p.19.

14. Aldred, op.cit., p.8.

15. Ibid., p.46.

16. C. Desroches-Nobelcourt, *Tutankhamun*, Penguin, London 1965, p.38.

17. Aldred, op.cit., p.46.

18. Alix Wilkinson, op.cit., p.3 and C. Andrews, op.cit., p.71.

19. S. Hassan, *Excavations at Giza*, Cairo 1932.

20. Andrews, op.cit., pp.76–7 & 83–5.

21. Ibid., p.99.

22. Aldred, op.cit., p.45.

23. Ibid., p.14.

24. Wilkinson, op.cit., pp.24 & 29. Sekhemket's treasure is in the Cairo Museum.

25. Aldred, op.cit., p.175. Queen Hetepheres' bracelets are in the Museum of Fine Arts, Boston.

26. Ibid., p.176. Headband and necklace in Cairo Museum.

27. Wilkinson, op.cit., p.46.

28. L. Cottrell, op.cit., p.72.

29. J. H. F. Notton, Ancient Egyptian Gold Refining, *Gold Bulletin*, Vol.7(2), 1974, pp.50–6.

30. Alix Wilkinson, op.cit., p.71.

31. H. E. Winlock, *The Treasure of el-Lahun*, New York, 1934.

32. C. Andrews, op.cit., pp.171–8.

33. Vercoutter, op.cit., pp.128–133.

34. Agatharchides' account was retold c. 60 BC by Diodorus Siculus in his *Bibliotheca Historica*. This translation is from the C. H. Oldfather version, Loeb Classical History, 1935, pp.115–123.

35. Vercoutter, op.cit., p.130.

36. W. R. Moran, *The Amarna Letters*, London 1992.

37. Aldred, op.cit., p.199.

38. Ibid., p.203.

39. Howard Carter, *Tutankhamun*, Barrie & Jenkins, London 1972, p.49.

40. Ibid., p.129.

41. C. Desroches-Nobelcourt, op.cit., p.164.

42. Ibid., p.10.

43. C. Desroches-Nobelcourt, op.cit., p.149.

44. H. Carter, op.cit., p.50.

45. Ibid., p.157.

46. C. Desroches-Nobelcourt, op.cit., p.70.

47. Müller, op.cit., p.199.

48. P. Montet, *La nécropole royale de Tanis I: Les constructions et le tombeau de Psoussennes à Tanis*, Paris, 1951.

49. Aldred, op.cit., pp.236–7.

Chapter 3

1. The Treasures of Troy, catalogue, Pushkin Museum with Leonardo Arte, Milan, 1996. This detailed catalogue has colour photographs and detailed descriptions of every item, plus essays on Troy.

2. H. Schliemann, *Troy and its Remains: a Narrative of Researches and Discoveries Made on the Site of Ilium and the Trojan Plain*, London 1875.

3. Donald Easton, *Antiquity*, Vol.58, 1984, p.197.

4. Fernand Braudel, *The Mediterranean in the Ancient World*, Allen Lane, London 2001, p.130.

5. G. F. Bass, *American Journal of Archaeology*, 2nd series, Vol.74, 1970, p.335.

6. K. R. Maxwell-Hyslop, *Western Asiatic Jewellery c. 3000–612 BC*, Methuen, London 1971, p.59.

7. Stetch & Pigott, *Iraq*, Vol.48, 1986, pp.39–64, 57.

8. Strabo, XIII.1.23.

9. Prentiss S. de Jesus, The Development of Prehistorical Mining and Metallurgy in Anatolia, *BAR International Series*, 74, Oxford, 1980, Appendix IV.

10. C. W. Blegen, Troy Excavations, conducted by the University of Cincinnati, 1932–38, Parts I–IV, Princeton 1950–58.

11. Prentiss de Jesus, op.cit., pp.88–9.

12. Treasures of Troy, op.cit., pp.182–4.

13. Ibid., pp.200–2

14. Ibid., pp.32–3, 218.

15. Ibid., pp.225–9.

16. Ibid., pp.38–45, 198–200.

17. Ibid., p.230.

Chapter 4
1. J. Lesley Fitton, *The Discovery of the Greek Bronze Age*, British Museum Press, 1995, p.115.

2. Leonard Cottrell, *Lost Worlds*, American Heritage Publishing Co., New York, 1962, p.257.

3. J. Lesley Fitton, *Minoans*, The British Museum Press, London 2002, p.17.

4. Adonis Vasilakis, *The Civilisations of Ancient Crete*, Herakleion Archaeological Museum Guide, Adam Editions, Athens, p.27.

5. John Chadwick, *The Mycenæan World*, Cambridge University Press, 1976, pp.144–5. John Chadwick was the collaborator of Michael Ventris.

6. Lesley Fitton, *The Minoans*, op.cit., p.134.

7. Reynold Higgins, *Greek and Roman Jewellery*, Methuen, London 1980, p.66

8. Marjorie Caygill, *British Museum A–Z Companion*, British Museum Press, 1999, p.14.

9. Dr Arthur Evans, Journal of Hellenic Studies 1892–3. Quoted in Reynold Higgins, *The Aigina Treasure; An Archaeological Mystery*, British Museum Publications, 1979, p.12.

10. Ibid., p.21.

11. Reynold Higgins, ibid., p.21.

12. J. Lesley Fitton, op.cit., .94.

13. Ilias Lalaounis, *Metamorphoses*, privately printed, Athens, 1984.

14. Joan Evans, *Time and Chance: the story of Arthur Evans and his Forbears*, Longman's Green & Co, London 1943, p.350.

Chapter 5
1. Pausanias wrote a guide book to Greece in the 1st century AD.

2. John Chadwick, *The Mycenæan World*, Cambridge University Press, 1976, p.4.

3. Alan Wace, *Mycenæ, An Archaeological History and Guide*, Princeton University Press, 1949, p.v.

4. G. F. Bass, *The Bronze Age Shipwreck at Ulu Burun, American Journal of Archaeology*, vols. 90, 92 & 93.

5. F. Braudel, op. cit., p.142.

6. Basil Petrakos, Sculpture-Bronzes-Vases, National Archaeological Museum, Athens, Cleo Editions, Athens, 1981, p.27.

7. www.culture.gr (has websites for all major Greek museums). The Mycenæan gold displays in the museum were all splendidly refurbished before the Olympic Games in Athens in 2004.

8. J. Lesley Fitton, Discovery of the Greek Bronze Age, op. cit. pp.71–2.

9. R. A. Higgins, Greek and Roman Jewellery, op. cit., p.61.

10. John Chadwick, op. cit., p.147.

11. Ibid., p.145.

12. Greek Jewellery from the Benaki Museum Collections, Adam Editions, Athens, 1999.

13. Alan Wace, op. cit., p.107

14. R. A. Higgins, op. cit., p.75.

15. Ibid., p.77.

16. Alan Wace, op. cit., p.111.

17. R. A. Higgins, op. cit., p.74.

18. J. Brown, *The Voyage of the Argonauts*, Methuen, London 1925.

19. Tim Severin, *The Jason Voyage*, Hutchinson, London 1985, p.223.

20. Otar Lordkipanidze, The Golden Fleece, *Oxford Journal of Archaeology*, Vol.20, No.1, Feb 2001, pp.1–38.

21. John Chadwick, op. cit., p.193.

Chapter 6

1. Maria Eugenia Aubet, *The Phoenicians and the West*, Cambridge University Press, 2nd edition, 2001, p.9.

2. I Kings, 10, v.22–23.

3. *Queen of Sheba*, ed. St John Simpson, British Museum Press, 2002, p.120.

4. Aubet, op.cit., pp.44–5.

5. Herodotus, *The Histories*, Penguin Classics, London 1972. Trs. Aubrey de Selincourt, revised John Marincola, Book Six, pp.46–48.

6. Sabatino Moscati (ed.), *The Phoenicians*, Bompiani, Milan, 1988, p.228. This is the 750-page catalogue of the definitive Phoenician exhibition assembled at the Palazzo Grassi in Venice, which contains articles by several authorities on Phoenicia.

7. M. E. Aubet, op.cit., p.281.

8. Ibid., p.284.

9. M. H. Fantar in *The Phoenicians*, ed. S. Moscati, op.cit., p.168.

10. Donald Harden, *The Phoenicians*, Thames & Hudson, London 1962, p.178.

11. Herodotus, op.cit., Book Four, p.195.

12. Ibid., Book Four, p.196.

13. Thucydides, *History of the Peloponnesian War*, trs. Rex Warner, Penguin Classics, London 1954.

14. Braudel, op.cit., p.220.

15. Enrico Acquaro, *The Phoenicians*, ed. S. Moscati, op.cit., pp.464–6.

16. Homer, *The Iliad*, Bk XXIII, pp.860–65, trs. Lord Derby, J. M. Dent, London 1864.

17. M. E. Aubet, op.cit., pp.136–7.

18. Musée du Bardo, Tunis, and Musée de Carthage, Carthage, Tunisia have a fine collection of these ornaments.

19. Giovanna Pisano, *The Phoenicians*, ed. S. Moscati, op.cit., p.374. The best examples are in Museo Archeologico Nazionale, Caligari, Sardinia.

20. The gold plates are in Museo Archeologico di Villa Giulia, Rome.

21. M. E. Aubet, *The Phoenicians*, ed. S. Moscati, op.cit., pp.228–9.

22. Ibid., p.384.

23. D. Harden, *The Phoenicians*, op.cit., p.213, quoting A. Blanco in Archivo Español de Arquelo, XXIX (1956), 3ff.

Chapter 7

1. Raymond Bloch, *Horizon*, Vol.II, number 5, 1960, p.77.

2. Guido Gregorietti, *Jewellery Through the Ages*, Hamlyn, London 1969, p.52.

3. *The Etruscans*, ed. Mario Torelli, Thames & Hudson, London 2001, p.464.

4. Graham Hughes, *The Art of Jewellery*, Peerage Books, London 1972.

5. D. H. Lawrence, *Etruscan Places*, Martin Secker, London 1932, p.28.

6. Ibid., pp.74 & 77.

7. Michael Grant, *The Etruscans*, Weidenfeld & Nicolson, London 1980, p.10.

8. Etruscan jewellery can be seen in: Museo Archeologico, Florence; Museo di Villa Giulia, Rome; Museo Poldo Pezzoli, Milan; Museo Archeologico, Chianchiano Terme; British Museum, London; Louvre, Paris.

9. Christiane Eluère, A 'Gold Connection' between the Etruscans and Early Celts?, *Gold Bulletin*, Vol.22, No.2, 1989, pp.48–55.

10. S. Moscati (ed.), *The Phoenicians*, Bompiani, Milan, 1988, p.57.

11. The Etruscans, ed. Torelli, op.cit., p.465.

12. Werner Keller, *The Etruscans*, Jonathan Cape, London 1975, p.32

13. George Dennis, *The Cities and Cemeteries of Etruria*, John Murray, London 1883, Vol.II, p.500.

14. Graham Hughes, op.cit., p.178.

15. D. L. Carroll, "A classification for granulation in ancient metalwork", AJA 78 (1974), pp.33–39; P. Parrini, E. Formigli, E. Mello, "Etruscan granulation", AJA 86 (1982), pp.118–121; D. L. Carroll, "On granulation in ancient metalwork", AJA 87 (1983), pp.551–554.

16. G. Hughes, op.cit., p.180.

17. R. A. Higgins, *Greek and Roman Jewellery*, Methuen, London 1980, p.136.

18. J. A. Donaldson, "The use of gold in dentistry", *Gold Bulletin*, Vol.13, No.3, July 1980.

19. Raymond Bloch, *Horizon*, op.cit., p.74.

20. Timothy Green, *The World of Gold*, Rosendale Press, London 1993, p.333.

Chapter 8

1. Amelia Kuhrt, *The Ancient Near East*, Routledge, London 1995, Vol.II, p.567.

2. Herodotus, *The Histories*, Book I:14, trs. Aubrey de Selincourt, revised John Marincola, 1996, pp.6–7. The weight of gold as translated in most versions of Herodotus appears much too great; weights are discussed later in this chapter.

3. A. Kuhrt, op.cit., p.569.

4. Andrew Ramage and Paul Craddock, *King Croesus' Gold*, British Museum Press, 2001. This book has been indispensable in the preparation of this chapter.

5. Ibid., p.21.

6. Herodotus, op.cit., VI:125, p.365.

7. Ibid., p.12.

8. Herodotus, op.cit., I:73.

9. *Money, A History*, ed. Jonathon Williams, British Museum Press, 1997, p.24.

10. Ramage, Craddock, op.cit., p.11.

11. Ibid., p.213.

12. Herodotus, op.cit. I:94.

13. Aristotle, *Politics*, 1257a.

14. Charles Seltman, *Greek Coins*, Methuen, London 1955, pp.5 & 72.

15. Ramage, Craddock, op.cit., chapter on Scientific Examination of the Lydian Precious Metal Coinages by M. R. Cowell and K. Hyne, pp.169–173.

16. Ibid., p.171.

17. Regal Coinage of the Persian Empire, *in Coinage and Administration in the Athenian and Persian Empires*, ed. Ian Carradice, BAR International Series, 343, 1987, pp.73–4.

18. Seltman, op.cit., pp.21–22.

19. Herodotus, op.cit., I:46–51.

20. Ibid., I.76.

21. Ibid., I.86.

22. The anecdote about Solon, reported by Herodotus, must be apocryphal, because he was not an exact contemporary of Croesus, but it made the point that gold was not a panacea.

23. Regal Coinage of the Persian Empire, *Coinage and Administration in the Athenian and Persian Empires*, ed. Ian Carradice, Bar International Series 343, 1987, pp.74–5.

24. Herodotus, op.cit., III.94. Herodotus specifically mentions gold to the value 360 talents, which he multiplies on a gold:silver ratio of 1:13, as being worth 4,860 talents of silver. On this basis, each gold talent weighed c. 2.3kgs/74 t.oz; this is an entirely reasonable bar size, essentially double the modern kilo bar and easy to transport.

25. *Coinage and Administration*, op. cit., p.92.

26. Ibid., p.78.

27. Ibid., p.76, quoting Plutarch, *Artaxerxes* 20.

28. Herodotus, op.cit., VII: 28–29.

29. Xenophon, *The Persian Expedition (Anabasis)*, trs. Rex Warner, Penguin Books, 1949.

30. Seltman, op.cit. p.62.

31. Xenophon, op.cit. p.25.

32. John Curtis, *Ancient Persia*, British Museum Press, 2000, p.62.

33. Ibid., cover and p.64.

34. Forgotten Empire: the World of Ancient Persia, British Museum, 9 Sept 2005–8 Jan 2006. British Museum in association with the Iran Heritage Foundation.

35. Graham Hughes, *The Art of Jewellery*, Peerage Books, 1972, p.23.

Chapter 9

1. Aubrey de Sélincourt, *World of Herodotus*, Sekker & Warburg, London 1962, p.8.

2. M. D. Higgins & R. Higgins, *A Geological Companion to Greece and the Aegean*, Duckworth, 1996, pp.33–4.

3. Herodotus, op.cit., IX.80.

4. Ibid., III.57.

5. Today there is little evidence of the mines, which were in the hills above the resort of Platys Gialos, and no mention of them in the local museum in Kastro.

6. Higgins & Higgins, op.cit., p.120.

7. Herodotus, op.cit. VI.46. Herodotus is referring to the value, not weight, of the metal. The value was in *talents of silver*; one silver talent weighed 26.2 kgs. On a gold-silver ratio of 1:13, one talent of gold would have weighed a shade over 2 kgs. These statistics from the Numismatic Museum, Athens.

8. Thomas Figueira, *The Power of Money, Coinage and Politics in the Athenian Empire*, University of Pennsylvania Press, 1998, p.513.

9. Thucydides, *History of the Peloponnesian War*, trs. Rex Warner, Penguin Classics, 1972, pp.132–3.

10. Figueira, op.cit., p.517.

11. Charles Seltman, *Greek Coins*, op.cit, p.138, and *The Frogs of Aristophanes*, trs. B. B. Rogers, lines 719–722.

12. Manolis Andronicos, *Vergina, The Royal Tombs*, Ekdotike Athenon SA, Athens, 1997, pp.69-73.

13. The Royal Tombs at Vergina are open daily, times vary with the season. They are located 75km west of Thessaloniki.

14. N. G. L. Hammond, *The Genius of Alexander the Great*, University of North Carolina Press, 1997, p.53.

15. Higgins & Higgins, op.cit., pp.108–117.

16. G. Marinos 'Greece' in the *Mineral Deposits of Europe*, ed. S. H. U. Bowie, Institute for Mining and Metallurgy, London 1982.

17. N. G. L. Hammond, op.cit., p.54.

18. Ibid., p.54.

19. Otto Mørkholm, *Early Hellenistic Coinage*, Cambridge University Press, 1991, p.43.

20. C. Seltman, op.cit., p.207.

21. N. G. L. Hammond, *Alexander the Great*, Chatto & Windus, London 1981, p.156.

22. D. Williams & J. Ogden, *Greek Gold*, British Museum Press, 1994, p.13.

23. Didolus Siculus, *Bibliotheca Historica*, trs. C. H. Oldfather, Loeb Classical History, 1935.

24. Indirect evidence that the treasure was largely silver is that up to 10,000 baggage animals and 5,000 camels were required to move the Persepolis treasure north to the town of Ecbatana (modern Hamadan), where it was guarded by a select Macedonian force. If it had been all gold, under 3,000 animals would have been required.

25. Otto Mørkholm, op.cit., p.5.

26. Cambridge Ancient History, Vol.VI, p.383 and C. Seltman, op.cit., p.211.

27. Iannis Touratsoglou in *The Art of Greek Jewellery*, ed. D. Williams, British Museum Press, 1998, pp.35–6.

28. N. G. L. Hammond, *The Genius of Alexander*, op.cit. p.187.

29. Otto Mørkholm, op.cit., p.50.

30. Ibid., p.65.

31. Ibid., p.5.

32. Assuming close to 100 m.t./3.2 million t.oz. of gold had been available from mines and the Persians' stockpile.

33. Mørkholm, op.cit., p.36.

34. D. Williams & J. Ogden, *Greek Gold*, British Museum Press, London 1994.

35. Ibid. pp.49–50.

36. R. A. Higgins, *Greek and Roman Jewellery*, Methuen, London 1980, pp.154–5.

37. *Art of the Greek Goldsmith*, ed. D. Williams, op.cit., p.102

38. Williams & Ogden, *Greek Gold*, op.cit., Kyme Treasure pp.92–104.

39. *Art of Greek Jewellery*, ed. Williams, op.cit: Nigel Meek's essay pp.132–5.

40. Higgins, op.cit., pp.155–6.

Chapter 10

1. E. Jacobson, *The Art of the Scythians*, E. J. Brill, New York 1995, p.6.

2. K. Akishev and A. Akishev, *Ancient Gold of Kazakstan*, trs. O. Belyayeva, Alma-Ata 1983, pp.38–9.

3. Herodotus, op.cit., IV.47, IV.64, IV.71.

4. R. Rolle, *The World of the Scythians*, trs. Gayna Walls, Batsford, London 1989 p.123 *(Die Welt der Skythen, Verlag C. J. Bucher, 1980)*.

5. Rolle, op.cit., pp.53–4.

6. *Art of Greek Jewellery*, ed. D. Williams, op.cit.; Nigel Meeks, pp.132–5.

7. While the Hermitage has most of the earlier discoveries, many items found since 1970 are in the Museum of Historical Treasures of the Ukraine and the Institute of Archaeology in Kiev.

8. L. Galanina & N. Grach, *Scythian Art*, Aurora Art Publishers, Leningrad 1986, trs. V. Sobelev, p.17. This is perhaps the best visual catalogue of Scythian art. All the items mentioned above, except for the stag plaque, are from the Kalermes *kurgan* on the Kuban river, dating c.600 BC.

9. E. Jacobson, op.cit., pp.1 & 6.

10. *Scythian Gold, Treasures from the Ancient Ukraine*, ed. Ellen Reader, Harold N. Abrams, New York, 1999, p.274, plate 135. The necklace is in the Institute of Archaeology, Kiev.

11. *Scythian Art*, op.cit., pp.61–2.

12. Ibid., p.90.

13. *Scythian Art*, op.cit., plates 130, 133, 134, 164, 165. All items in The Hermitage.

14. D. Williams, J. Ogden, *Greek Gold*, op.cit., pp.140–1. The bracelets are in The Hermitage.

15. Esther Jacobson, op.cit., p.51.

16. R. Rolle, op.cit., pp.120–1.

17. *Scythian Gold* op.cit., Mikhail Treister essay, "The Workshop of the Gorytos", pp.71–81.

18. E. Jacobson, op.cit., pp.225–8. *Scythian Gold*, op.cit., plate 105 and *Scythian Art*, op.cit., plates 224 & 225. The *gorytos* cover is in The Hermitage.

19. *Scythian Gold*, op.cit., Mikhail Treister essay, p.77.

20. Ibid., p.79.

21. Ibid. Dr Ellen Reader essay, p.51 & plate 124. The helmet is in the Museum of Historical Treasures of Ukraine.

22. *Scythian Art*, op.cit., p.91 & plates 184–7. Also E. Jacobson, op.cit., pp.203–5.

23. *L'or des Scythes*, Royal Museum of Art, Brussels 1991, pp.96–97.

24. Esther Jacobson, op.cit., pp.115–9. Also, *Scythian Art*, op.cit., plates 118, 119, 120 & 121.

25. *Scythian Art*, op.cit., p.92.

26. Esther Jacobson, op.cit., p.78.

27. *Scythian Gold*, op.cit., p.56.

28. Herodotus, op.cit., V.3–4.

29. Homer, *Iliad* X, 433–441.

30. *Ancient Gold: The Wealth of the Thracians*, ed. Ivan Mazarov, H. Abrams, New York, 1998, p34. This extensive catalogue of a major exhibition of Thracian gold and silver has been invaluable in preparing this section.

31. Ibid., p.35.

32. *Ancient Gold*, op.cit., p.14 and plates 134, 142, 143, 156, 157. The Varna treasure is in the Archaeological Museum, Varna, Bulgaria.

33. Ibid. The Vulchitrun treasure, text and plates, pp.228–32. The treasure is in the Archaeological Institute and Museum in Sofia, Bulgaria.

34. *Financial Times*, London 22nd January 2005.

35. *Ancient Gold*, op.cit., pp.118–21. This harness set is in the History Museum, Turgovishte, Bulgaria.

36. Ibid., pp.160–71 The Letnitsa treasure is in the Museum of History, Lovech, Bulgaria.

37. *Ancient Gold*, op.cit., pp.142–8. The treasure is in the Archaeological Museum, Plovdiv in central Bulgaria.

38. Otto Mørkholm, *Early Hellenistic Coinage*, op.cit., pp.81–2.

39. *Ancient Gold*, op.cit., p.36.

Chapter 11

1. *The Celtic World*, ed. Miranda J. Green, Routledge, London & New York, 1995, essay by P. Northover, 'The Technology of Metalwork', p.296.

2. Ibid., Miranda Green essay, 'Who were the Celts?', p.3.

3. Christiane Eluère, *The Celts, First Masters of Europe*, Thames and Hudson, London 1993, p.51. Christiane Eluère is one of the great authorities on Celtic gold.

4. *The Celts: The Origins of Europe*, ed. Sabatino Moscati, Thames and Hudson, London 1991. Catalogue of exhibition at Palazzo Grassi, Venice. Essay by Paul-Marie Duval, p.27.

5. Virgil, *Aeneid VIII*, 659–62.

6. Polybius, *Histories*, II, 17.

7. Christiane Eluère, 'Prehistoric Goldwork in Western Europe', *Gold Bulletin*, 1983, 16 (3).

8. Joan T. Taylor, *Bronze Age Goldwork of the British Isles*, Cambridge University Press, 1980, p.28.

9. The best collection of *lunulae* is in the National Museum of Ireland, Dublin.

10. Interview with the author in 2003, as he worked on the cape.

11. *Gold Bulletin*, 1983, 16(3), op.cit.

12. Taylor, *Bronze Age Goldwork*, op.cit., p.57.

13. *Gold Bulletin*, 1983, 16(3), op.cit.

14. Christiane Eluère, *The Celts, First Masters of Europe*, op.cit., pp.22–30.

15. *The Celts*, ed. Sabatino Moscati, op.cit., essay: 'The Celtic Princes of Hohenasperg' by Jorg Biel, pp.108–113.

16. The ornaments from all these tombs are in Stuttgart Württembergisches Landesmuseum.

17. *The Celts*, ed. Moscati, op.cit., C. Eluère essay, p.350.

18. *The Celtic World*, ed. Miranda Green, op.cit., p.299.

19. *The Celts*, ed. Moscati, op.cit., C. Eluère essay, p.353.

20. Ibid., Otto Hermann Frey essay on 'Formation of the La Tène Culture', pp.127–144.

21. Beatrice Cauuet, *L'or dans l'Antiquité*, Aquitana, Supplement 9, 1999, pp.24–70. This section is largely based on her paper.

22. *The Celts*, ed. Moscati, op.cit., José Gomez de Soto essay, p.292. The helmet is in Musée de la Société Archéologique de Charente, Angoulême.

23. *Celtic World*, ed. Miranda Green, op.cit., D. N. Briggs essay, p.246.

24. Livy, *History of Rome*, XLIV, 26.

25. Polybius, *Histories*, II, 22ff.

26. *The Celts*, ed. Moscati, op.cit. Hans-Jörg Kellner, 'Coinage', pp.451–9.

27. Ibid., Bernhard Overbeck, p.533.

28. Ibid., Ludwig Pauli, p.218.

29. *The Celtic World*, ed. Miranda Green, op.cit., Peter Northover, p.301.

30. *The Celts*, ed. Moscati, Barry Raferty, 'The Island Celts' pp.555–71.

31. Ibid., R. B. Warner, p.617, and *A New History of Ireland*, Vol.1, ed. Daibhi O Croinin, Oxford University Press, 2005, p.152. The Broighter Treasure is in The National Museum of Ireland, Dublin.

32. Marjorie Caygill, *The British Museum A–Z Companion*, British Museum Press, 1999, p.330.

33. *The Celtic World*, ed. Miranda Green, op.cit. Peter Northover, p.304.

34. Miranda Green, *The Celtic World*, op.cit., p.6.

Chapter 12

1. Statistics from Gold Survey 2007, GFMS Ltd, London 2007.

2. Han Schu 24: *Food & Money in Ancient China*, trs. Nancy Lee Swann, Princeton University Press, 1950, p.228.

3. Peter J. Golas: Joseph Needham, *Science and Civilisation in China*, Vol.5, Part XIII, Mining, Cambridge University Press, 1999, pp.120–1. This monumental series, first launched in 1954 and directly supervised by Joseph Needham until his death in 1995, now encompasses 25 volumes on all aspects of the evolution of science in China, including the mining and uses of gold and the parallel role of alchemy. It has been invaluable in preparing this chapter. The Needham series uses – to indicate BC and + for AD, while also using some slightly different dates and earlier spellings for Chinese dynasties, such as Chou for Zhou and Chhin for Qin, than appear in most modern texts. I have used modern dates/spellings, to be consistent with British Museum style used elsewhere in this book.

4. Emma Bunker, *Nomadic Art of the Eastern Eurasian Steppes*, Yale University Press, New Haven & London 2002, p.33.

5. Ibid., p.26.

6. Emma Bunker, *Artibus Asiae*, Gold in the Ancient Chinese World, AA58, 1993, pp.27–50.

7. Ibid., p.33.

8. Ibid., p.46.

9. Bunker, *Nomadic Art*, op.cit., pp.29–30.

10. Ibid., p.112.

11. Bunker, *Artibus Asiae*, op.cit., p.47.

12. Ibid., p.45.

13. Anton Checkhov, *A Life in Letters*, trs Rosamund Bartlett and Antony Phillips, Penguin Books, London 2004, p.242.

14. Timothy Green, *The World of Gold*, Rosendale Press, London 1993, p.211.

15. *Needham*, Vol.5, Part II, 1974, pp.49–50; and *Needham*, Vol.V, Part XIII, 1999, p.122.

16. Han Schu 24, op.cit., Part Two, Money, pp.219–221.

17. Ibid., pp.228–9.

18. Homer H. Dubs, an Ancient Chinese Stock of Gold, *Journal of Economic History*, Vol.I, 1941, pp.36–39. This widely quoted paper has been partly overtaken by subsequent research.

19. Peter Golas, *Needham*, Vol.5, Part XIII, pp.32–3.

20. Ibid., p.242.

21. Ibid., p.111.

22. Timothy Green, *The World of Gold*, op.cit., pp.206–10.

23. Peter Golas, *Needham*, Vol.5, Part XIII, p.123.

24. *Needham*, Vol.5, Part II, Section 33, p.58. Taken from *Huang Ti Chiu Ting Shen Tan Ching Chueh* (Explanation of the Yellow Emperor's Canon of the Nine-Vessel Spiritual Elixir).

25. Susan Whitfield, *Life Along the Silk Road*, John Murray, London 1999, pp.9–10.

26. Ibid., pp.21–2.

27. Han Schu 24, op.cit., p.229.

28. Ibid., p.377.

29. *Needham*, Vol.5, Part II, CUP, 1974, p.49.

30. Ibid., p.56.

31. Han Schu 24: p.251.

32. Ibid., p.253.

33. Ibid., p.381.

34. Homer H. Dubs, *Journal of Economic History*, 1941, op.cit., p.36.

35. Han Schu 24, op.cit., p.66.

36. Dubs, op.cit., p.36.

37. Ibid., p.37, footnote 2.

38. Richard Duncan-Jones, *Money and Government in the Roman Empire*, Cambridge University Press, 1994, p.167.

39. *Needham*, Vol.5, Part XIII, p.123.

40. *Needham*, Vol.5, Part II, Section 33, p.13 & *Needham*, Vol.5, Part III, Section 33, pp.1–2.

41. *Needham*, Vol.5, Part III, Section 33, p.27.

42. *Needham*, Vol.5, Part II, Section 33, p.188.

43. Ibid., pp.195–9.

44. Ibid., p.209. Note: – 2 is the *Needham* style for BC.

45. *Needham*, Vol.5, Part III, Section 33, pp.91–4.

46. Ibid., p.120.

47. *Needham*, Vol.5, Part II, Section 33, p.144.

48. Helen Wang, *Money on the Silk Road*, British Museum Press, 2004, p.14.

49. *Needham*, Vol.5, Part XIII, 1999, p.241.

50. Bo Gyllensvärd, *Chinese Gold and Silver in the Carle Kempe Collection*, Stockholm, 1953, p.21.

51. John Kieschnick, *the Impact of Buddhism on Chinese Material Culture*, Princeton University Press, 2003, p.7.

52. Ibid., p.11.

53. Ibid., p.68.

54. Ibid., p.11.

55. Ibid., p.10.

Chapter 13

1. Christopher Howgego, *The Journal of Roman Studies*, Vol.LXXXII, 1992, "The Supply and Use of Money in the Roman World 200 BC–AD 300", pp.1–31.

2. *Money, a History*, ed. Jonathan Williams, British Museum Press, 1998, p.51.

3. R. Duncan-Jones, *Money and Government in the Roman Empire*, Cambridge University Press, 1994, p.170. This is not based on mint records, which do not exist, but on studying gold coins from hoards and seeing how many different dies were used, and then estimating how many coins may have been struck by each die.

4. F. Braudel, *The Mediterranean in the Ancient World*, op.cit., p.311.

5. Livy listed Roman pounds; one pound weighed 324 grams/10.4 t.oz.

6. Michael Crawford, *Coinage and Money Under the Roman Republic*, Methuen, 1985, p.250.

7. Ibid., p.279.

8. A. Orejas & F. J. Sánchez-Palencia, "Mines, Territorial Organisation and Social Structure in Roman Iberia", *American Journal of Archaeology*, Vol.104, No.4, Oct 2002.

9. P. R. Lewis & G. D. B. Jones, "Roman Gold-Mining in North-West Spain, *Journal of Roman Studies* LX (1970), pp.169–85. Dr Lewis and Professor Jones not only undertook extensive fieldwork in the region, but made their own unique translation, using modern mining terminology, of the comments of the Elder Pliny in his *Natural History* on the Roman operations in Spain. Their translation is used in this section.

10. Ibid., Pliny, *Natural History*, XXXIII, 67, trs. Lewis & Jones. Gaius Plinius Secundus (AD 23–79) compiled a unique report on all aspects of the natural world in his Natural History and actually died observing the eruption of Vesuvius that destroyed Pompeii.

11. Ibid., Pliny, *Natural History*, XXXIII, 74–75. trs. Lewis & Jones.

12. Ibid., pp.170–5.

13. Ibid., p.184, Pliny, *Natural History*, XXXIII, pp.76–7, trs. Lewis & Jones.

14. R. F. J. Jones & D. G. Bird, "Roman Gold-mining in North-West Spain, II; workings on the Rio Duerna, *Journal of Roman Studies*, LXII (1972), pp.61–74. This is the second paper based on extensive fieldwork in the region by the University of Manchester.

15. C. Domergue & G. Herail, *Mines d'or romaines d'Espagne; la district de la Valduerna*, 1978.

16. Lewis & Jones, op.cit., p.179.

17. Ibid., Pliny, *Natural History*, XXXIII, 68–74, trs. Lewis & Jones.

18. Beatrice Cauuet, *L'Or dans l'Antiquité*, op.cit.

19. A. H. M. Jones, *The Later Roman Empire*, Blackwell, 1964, Vol.II, pp.838–9.

20. Duncan-Jones, op.cit., p.216, Table 15.2.

21. Ibid., p.3.

22. Ibid., p.167. Richard Duncan-Jones concedes, "All estimates are very approximate, and depend on output figures per die".

23. Timothy Green, *The Millennium in Gold*, Rosendale Press, London 1999, pp.19 & 21.

24. Duncan-Jones, op.cit., pp.170–208.

25. E. H. Warmington, *Commerce Between the Roman Empire and India*, Curzon Press, London 1974.

26. C. Howgego, op.cit., p.55.

27. R. Duncan-Jones, op.cit., pp.248–9.

28. Catherine Johns, *The Jewellery of Roman Britain*, UCL Press, London 1996, p.103.

29. Graham Hughes, *The Art of Jewellery*, Peerage Books, London 1972, p.34.

30. The lamp is in Museo Nazionale Archeologico, Naples, along with many items of jewellery from Pompeii. Other fine collections of Roman jewellery are in the British Museum, London Musée Royal de Mariemont, Belgium, and Musée du Louvre, Paris.

31. G. Gregorietti, *Jewellery Through the Ages*, Paul Hamlyn, London 1970, p.120.

32. Gaius Petronius, *Petronii Arbitri Satyricon*, c. AD 65.

33. Catherine Johns, op.cit., p.117.

34. Ibid., p.166.

35. Ibid., pp.215–6. The Thetford treasure, like the Hoxne treasure above, is in the British Museum.

36. R. Duncan-Jones, op.cit., p.34.

37. C. Howgego, op.cit., p.9.

38. R. A. G. Carson, *Coins of the Roman Empire*, Routledge, London 1990, pp.233–6.

39. Ibid., p.237.

40. Michael Hendy, *Studies in the Byzantine Monetary Economy c. 300–1450*, Cambridge University Press, 1985, pp.285–6.

41. Emperor Constantine Augustus to Leontius, Praetorian Prefect, AD 317. Quoted: Hendy, op.cit., p.364.

42. G. Depeyrot, *Crises et Inflation entre Antiquité et Moyen Age*, Paris, 1991, p.212.

43. R. A. G. Carson, op.cit., pp.242–3.

44. Ibid., p.267.

45. T. W. Potter, *Roman Britain*, British Museum Press, 1997, p.91.

Chapter 14

1. Philip Grierson, *Byzantine Coins*, Methuen, London 1982, p.1.

2. Ibid., p.1.

3. *Money*, ed. Jonathan Williams, British Museum Press, 1997, p.62.

4. *The Economic History of Byzantium*, ed. A. E. Laiou, Dumbarton Oaks, Washington DC, 2002, Vol.3, p.241.

5. Michael Hendy, *Studies in the Byzantine Monetary Economy c.300–1450*, Cambridge University Press, 1985, pp.476–8.

6.   John Chrysostom, quoted by S. J. B. Barnish, "The Wealth of Julianus Argentarius", *Byzantion 55* (1985), p.37.

7.   C. W. Previté-Orton, *Shorter Cambridge Medieval History*, Cambridge University Press, 1952, Vol.1, pp.185–8.

8.   *Economic History of Byzantium*, op.cit., p.116.

9.   Gold, Granite and Water: the Bir Umm Fawakir Survey Project, AASOR 52 (1994), pp.37–92.

10. W. Wolska-Conus, *Cosmos Indicopleustes, Topographie Chrétienne*, Paris, 1968, Vol.1, pp.361–3.

11. *Economic History of Byzantium*, op.cit., p.345. Justinian Edict XI, of 559.

12. Ibid., p.492.

13. Grierson, op.cit., p.52.

14. Hendy, op.cit., p.346.

15. Grierson, op.cit., p.341.

16. Hendy, op.cit., pp.332–3.

17. Ibid., p.24.

18. *Economic History of Byzantium,* op.cit., p.188, citing E. Stein, Bas-Empire, 2: 459–6.

19. M. M. Mango in *Ecclesiastical Silver Plate in Sixth Century Byzantium*, ed. S. A. Boyd and M. M. Mango, Washington DC, 1992, pp.125–6. Marlia Mango has calculated both the quantities of gold and silver used in the internal adornments of the church.

20. André Grabar, *Byzantium*, Thames and Hudson, 1966, p.298.

21. André Grabar, *Byzantium*, op.cit., p.102

22. Gianfranco Bustacchini, Gold in Mosaic Art and Technique, *Gold Bulletin*, 1973, 6(2), pp.52–56.

23. *Gold Bulletin*, ibid.

24. André Grabar, *Byzantium*, op.cit. p.102.

25. *Gold Bulletin*, op.cit.

26. A. Grabar, op.cit., p.153.

27. *Gold Bulletin*, op.cit.

28. C. W. Previté-Orton, op.cit., p.200.

29. M. Hendy, op.cit., p.408.

30. *Economic History of Byzantium*, op.cit., p.937. The statistics are rough estimates, and output could have varied considerably from year to year.

31. Ibid., p.937. An exceptional collection of Byzantine gold coins struck at the Syracuse mint may be visited at the Cabinetta Numismatica in Piazza Duomo in Syracuse by appointment.

32. Ibid., p.698–9.

33. Ibid., p.1146.

34. Grierson, op.cit., p.182.

35. *Economic History of Byzantium*, p.1017. Original source: Theophanes Continuatus, 172.

36. The Byzantine pound had declined in weight to 320 grams by 900, compared to the 324 grams of the original Roman and early Byzantine periods.

37. Ibid., p.717.

38. C. W. Previté-Orton, op.cit., p.273.

39. P. Grierson, op.cit., pp.191 & 197.

40. *Economic History of Byzantium*, op.cit., p.738.

41. M. Hendy, op.cit., p.513.

42. Grierson, op.cit., p.10.

43. D. M. Metcalf, *Coinage in the Balkans 820–1355*, Thessaloniki 1965, pp.82–3.

Chapter 15

1. Bernard Lewis, *The Middle East*, Weidenfeld, London 1995, p.55.

2. M. Lombard, *L'Islam dans sa première grandeur*, Flammarion, Paris (trs: Joan Spencer, North-Holland Publishing, Amsterdam, 1971, p.98.

3. Philip Grierson, *Numismatics*, Oxford University Press, 1975, p.39.

4. Bernard Lewis, op.cit., pp.56–8.

5. *Money: a history*, ed. J. Williams, British Museum Press, 1997, p.91.

6. *Economic History of Byzantium*, Vol.II, op.cit., pp.693, 698–9 & 716.

7. *Money*, op.cit., p.97.

8. Lombard, op.cit., p.113.

9. Ibid., pp.59 & 113.

10. E. W. Bovill, *Caravans of the Old Sahara*, International Institute of African Languages and Cultures, Oxford University Press, 1933, pp.43–4.

11. See chapters 6 and 14.

12. Lombard, op.cit., p.60.

13. Ibid.

14. Lombard, op.cit., p.61.

15. Grierson, *Numismatics*, op.cit., p.43.

16. Lombard, op.cit., pp.10–11.

17. Andrew M. Watson, "Back to Gold – and Silver", *Economic History Review*, 2nd series, Vol.XX, No.1, 1967, pp.1–35.

18. Ibid., pp.5, 6, 23 & 27.

19. Ibid., p.9.

20. Ibid., p.11, quoting Al-Makrizi, *Traité des monnaies musulmanes*, ed. Silvestre de Sacy, Paris, 1797, p.43.

21. Maurice Lombard, op.cit., p.237.

22. E. H. Gombrich, *The Story of Art*, Phaidon, 1951, p.101.

23. Marjorie Caygill, *British Museum A–Z Companion*, British Museum Press, 1999, pp.162–3.

24. Barbara Bend, *Islamic Art*, British Museum Press, 1991, pp.36 & 92. The ewer is in the Freer Gallery of Art, Washington DC; the gold bowl in the British Museum.

25. The necklace is in the Israel Museum, Jerusalem.

26. The pair of earrings are in the Al Sabah collection in Kuwait.

27. B. Bend, op.cit., p.20.

28. Ibid., p.54.

Chapter 16

1. Frederic C. Lane & Reinhold Mueller, *Money and Banking in Medieval and Renaissance Venice*, 2 vols., John Hopkins University Press, Baltimore and London 1985 & 1995. vol.1, p.285. Volume 1 of this work is a unique account of the inside workings of Venice's bullion market and invaluable in writing this chapter.

2. James Morris, *Venice*, Faber & Faber, London 1960.

3. Lane & Mueller, op.cit., pp.91–2.

4. Ibid., p.105.

5. Ibid., p.90.

6. Ibid., p.150, quoting Venice State Archives, ASV, Senato, Misti, reg.50, fols. 97–98.

7. Ibid., p.284.

8. Francesco Balducci Pegolotti, *La Practica della Mercatura*, ed. Allan Evans, The Medieval Academy of America, 1936, pp.331–3.

9. Lane & Mueller, op.cit., pp.176–9.

10. Peter Spufford, *Money and its Use in Medieval Europe*, Cambridge University Press, 1988, pp.280–8.

11. E. W. Bovill, *Caravans of the Old Sahara*, 1933, and *The Gold Trade of the Moors*, Oxford University Press, 1969, chapter 8.

12. Oszkar Paulinyi, "The Crown Monopoly of the Refining Metallurgy of Precious Metals … in Hungary and Transylvania (1325–1700)", in *Precious Metals in the Age of Expansion*, ed. Herman Kellenbenz & Jürgen Schneider, Stuttgart, 1981, pp.27–39.

13. Peter Spufford, *Power and Profit: The Merchant in Medieval Europe*, Thames & Hudson, London 2002, p.15.

14. Spufford, *Money and Its Uses in Medieval Europe*, op.cit., pp.277–8, and J. B. Henneman, *Royal Taxation in Fourteenth-century France*, Princeton University Press, 1971, p.233.

15. Lane & Mueller, op.cit., p.214.

16. Paulinyi, op.cit., pp.37–8.

17. Lane & Mueller, op.cit., p.368.

18. Pegolotti, op.cit., pp.287–9.

19. Lane & Mueller, op.cit., pp.374–9.

20. Ibid., p.465.

21. John Day, "The Great Bullion Famine", Past & Present, No.79, 1978; reprinted in *The Medieval Market Economy*, Blackwell, 1987, pp.25–7.

22. Peter Spufford, *Money and Its Use in Medieval Europe*, op.cit., Appendix III.

23. Lane & Mueller, op.cit., p.545.

24. John Day, op.cit., pp.25–7.

25. Eliyahu Ashtor, "The Venetian Supremacy in Levantine Trade", *Journal of European Economic History*, III, Rome, 1974, pp.5–53.

26. Ibid., p.38. Archives of the Venetian firm Antonio Zane.

27. Eliyahu Ashtor, "The Volume of Levantine Trade in the Middle Ages (1370–1498)", *Journal of European Economic History*, VI, Rome, 1975, pp.573–612.

28. Ibid., pp.606–7.

29. Lane & Mueller, op.cit., Vol.II, pp.231–4.

30. Ashtor, *The Venetian Supremacy in Levantine Trade*, op.cit., p.49.

31. Eliyahu Ashtor, *La découverte de la voie maritime aux Indes et les prix des épices; Mélange en l'honneur de Fernand Braudel*, Toulouse, 1973, p.31.

32. Fernand Braudel, *Capitalism and the Material Life*, 1400–1800, Harper Row, New York, 1973 (trs. Miriam Kochan), p.154.

33. E. H. Gombrich, *The Story of Art*, The Phaidon Press, London 1950, pp.267–8.

34. Lane and Mueller, op.cit., pp.156–7.

35. J. F. Hayward, *Virtuoso Goldsmiths*, Sotheby Parke Bernet, New York, 1976, p.32.

36. Patricia Lee Rubin and Alison Wright, *Renaissance Florence, The Art of the 1470s*, National Gallery Publications, London 1999, p.86.

37. Ibid., p.79.

38. John Pope-Hennessy, *Italian Renaissance Sculpture*, Phaidon, London 1958, p.316.

39. Rubin & Wright,, op. cit., p.81.

40. Ibid., pp.238–41. The St John the Baptist panel is in Museo dell'Opera del Duomo, Florence.

41. J. F. Hayward, op.cit., p.32.

42. *The Life of Benvenuto Cellini, Written by Himself*, trs. John Addington Smith, Phaidon Press, London 1949, pp.9–10.

43. Giorgio Vasari, *Vite*, Lives of the most excellent painters, sculptors and architects, 1550, revised 1568, 4 vols, trs A. B. Hinds, J. M. Dent, London E. P. Dutton, New York, 1927.

44. Cellini, *Life*, op.cit., pp.29–30.

45. Ibid., p.40.

46. Ibid., p.105.

47. Ibid., p.274.

48. Ibid., pp.275–6.

49. Ibid., p.305.

50. Ibid., p.306.

51. Graham Hughes, *the Art of Jewellery*, Peerage Books, London 1972, p.175.

52. J. F. Hayward, op.cit., *Introduction*.

53. Graham Hughes, op.cit., p.191.

Chapter 17

1. *Precolumbian Gold*, ed. Colin McEwan, "Diversity of Goldsmithing Traditions in the Americas and the Old World", Susan La Niece and Nigel Meeks, British Museum Press, 2000, p.236. The essays in this book provide a unique insight into Precolumbian gold. The authors include most of the foremost archaeologists and metallurgists working on the subject. The editor, Colin McEwan, is Curator of Latin American Collections at the British Museum.

2. *Precolumbian Gold*, ed. Colin McEwan, "The Technology, Iconography and Social Significance of Metal" by Izumi Shimada, Jo Ann Griffin and Adon Gordus, British Museum Press, 2000, p.51.

3. *The Coming of the Iron Age*, ed. T. Wertime and J. D. Muhly, "The Central Andes: Metallurgy without Iron", Heather Lechtman, Yale, 1980, p.267.

4. Lechtman, op.cit., p.277.

5. Richard L. Burger, *Chavín and the Origins of Andean Civilisation*, Thames & Hudson, London 1995, p.202.

6. Michael E. Moseley, *The Incas and their Ancestors, the Archaeology of Peru*, Thames & Hudson, London 1992, p.180.

7. Lechtman, op.cit., pp.288 & 295.

8. *Precolumbian Gold*, op.cit., p.235.

9. Lechtman, op.cit., p.294.

10. Moseley, op. Cit., fig.66, facing p.177.

11. Ibid., pp.166–7.

12. *Moche Art and Archaeology in Ancient Peru*, ed. J. Pillsbury, "Late Moche Urban Craft Production" by Izumi Shimada, Yale, 2001, p.177.

13. Moseley, op.cit., p.251.

14. *Precolumbian Gold*, op.cit, "A multi-dimensional analysis of Middle Sicán objects", I. Shimada, J. A. Griffin and Adon Gordus, pp.29 and 35.

15. Ibid., pp.40–2.

16. Ibid., p.53.

17. Ibid., p.54.

18. Moseley, op.cit., pp.255–6.

19. *Precolumbian gold*, op. cit., Karen O'Day, "The Goldwork of Chimor", p.67.

20. Ibid., p.62.

21. Ibid., p.62.

22. Moseley, op. cit., p.7.

23. Lechtman, op. cit., p.322.

24. Cieza de León, *La Cronica del Peru*, Madrid, 1947.

25. Garcilasco de la Vega, El Inca (original 1609). *Royal Commentaries of the Incas and General History of Peru*, trs. H. V. Livermore, University of Texas Press, Austin, 1989, p.188.

26. www.banrep.gov.co/museo/

27. Museo de America does not have a website but is reachable on e-mail: mamerica@mail.ddnet.es.

28. "Technology of Ancient Colombian Gold", Clemencia Plazas and Ana María Falchetti, *Natural History*, 1979, Vol.88(9), pp37–46.

29. *Precolumbian Gold*, op. cit., Warwick Bray, "Malagana and the Goldworking Tradition of Southwest Colombia", p.96.

30. *The Art of Precolumbian Gold*, the Jan Mitchell Collection, ed. Julia Jones, Ana Maria Falchetti essay, p.48, Weidenfeld & Nicolson, London 1985.

31. J. Bird, "Legacy of the Stingless Bee", *Natural History*, 1979, vol.88(9), pp.49–51.

32. *Precolumbian Gold*, op. cit., p.103.

33. Ibid., pp.100–102.

34. E. Arcin, C. Plazas, J. Echeverri, *Secrets of El Dorado*, El Sello Editorial, Bogota, 1990, p.15.

35. *Precolumbian Gold*, op. cit., pp.233–4.

36. *The Art of Precolumbian Gold,* op. cit., p.49.

37. *Precolumbian Gold*, op. cit., Roberto Lleras-Pérez, "The Iconography and Symbolism of Metallic Votive Offerings in the Eastern *Cordillera*, Colombia", pp.112–29.

38. The story of the gilded man first came from the conquistador Gonzalo Fernández de Oviedo, in 1535, but the most detailed account was given by the Spanish chronicler, Juan Rodriguez Freyle, in 1636. He had talked to a nephew of the last ruler of the region.

39. Timothy Green, *The World of Gold*, Michael Joseph, London 1968, pp.90–2.

40. *Precolumbian Gold*, op. cit., Ana Maria Falchetti, "The Gold of Greater Zenú", p.137.

41. Ibid., pp.223–5.

42. Ibid., p.144.

43. Ibid. p.145.

44. Warwick Bray, *The Gold of El Dorado*, op. cit., p.39.

45. *Precolumbian Gold*, op. cit., Jeffrey Quilter, "Gold Objects from Southwest Costa Rica", p.192.

46. Ibid., pp.178–9.

47. www.bccr.fi.cr/museos/oro.htm

48. *Precolumbian Gold*, op. cit., p.180. Keith's collection is now divided between the American Museum of Natural History and the Brooklyn Museum.

49. *Precolumbian Gold,* op. cit., José R. Oliver, "Gold Symbolism Among Caribbean Chiefdoms", pp.198–202.

Chapter 18

1. Earl J. Hamilton, *American Treasure and the Price Revolution in Spain 1501–1650*, Harvard University Press, 1934.

2. Having spent almost thirty years myself assessing modern gold flows, many of them unofficial, Hamilton's work to me has 'street credibility'; if you get close to the gold trade, where up to 25% of all gold was smuggled at some stage on its journey from mine to eventual owner in the 1960s and 70s, you know what is and is not realistic, even if you do not always know the precise quantities smuggled.

3. Henry Kamen, *Spain's Road to Empire: the Making of a World Power*, Allen Lane, London 2002.

4. Hamilton, op.cit., p.13 n.1

5. J. H. Hemming, *The Conquest of the Incas*, Macmillan, London 1970, quoted on p.135.

6. Kamen, op.cit. p.501.

7. Felipe Gauman Poma de Ayala, *The First New Chronicle and Good Government*, 1614, quoted in Kamen, op.cit., p.501.

8. Hamilton, op.cit., p.42, Table 3.

9. Hamilton, op.cit. p.22.

10. Hamilton op.cit., p.44.

11. Mathias de Saint Jean, 1646, quoted in F. Braudel, *The Mediterranean and the Mediterranean World in the Age of Philip II*, William Collins, London and Harper & Row, New York, 1972, p.462.

12. Ibid., p.462.

13. Hamilton, op.cit., p.46.

14. Braudel, op.cit., p.478.

15. Ibid., p.503.

16. Ibid., p.499.

17. Warwick Bray, *The Gold of Eldorado*, Rainbird, London 1978, pp.20–3.

Chapter 19

1. A. Kobata, Production and Uses of Gold and Silver in 16th and 17th Century Japan, *Economic History Review* (2nd series), Vol.18, 1965.

2. Sir John Craig, *The Mint*, Cambridge University Press, 1953.

3. Sir John Craig, *Newton at the Mint*, Cambridge University Press, 1946, p.5.

4. Ming-Hsun Li, *The Great Recoinage*, Weidenfeld & Nicolson, London 1963, p.75.

5. Ibid., p.136.

6. Ibid., p.138.

7. K. N. Chaudhuri, *The Trading World of Asia and the East India Company 1660–1760*, Cambridge University Press, 1978.

8. Craig, op.cit.

9. J. Sperling, "The International Payments Mechanism in the 17th & 18th Centuries", EHR, (2nd series), Vol. XIX, 1961.

10. C. R. Boxer, "Brazilian gold & British traders in the first half of the 18th century", *Hispanic American Historical Review* XLIX (1969) pp 454–72.

11. C. R. Boxer, *The Golden Age of Brazil*, *1695–1750*, University of California Press, Berkeley & Los Angeles, 1962. This is perhaps the best account in English of Brazil's gold rush.

12. Ibid., pp.41–2.

13. When I visited the gold diggings in the Brazilian interior in 1981 the grades were much the same; one dealer showed me samples of *ouro bruto* he had bought from a river deposit that varied between 867–950 fine.

14. John Mawe, "Travels in the Interior of Brazil", London 1812, pp 422–3, quoted in C. R. Boxer, op.cit., pp 182–3.

15. V. Magalhaes Godinho, "Le Portugal, les flottes du sucre et les flottes de l'or, 1670–1770", *Annales* (Feb–March 1951), pp 184–197.

16. C. R. Boxer, op.cit. p.53.

17. C. R. Boxer, "Brazilian gold & British traders", op.cit, p.460.

18. Ibid., p.459.

19. The *moeda* weighed 10.8 grams/0.33 t.oz. in 916 gold.

20. Ibid., p.469.

21. Sir Isaac Newton, "State of the Gold and Silver Coin, 25th September 1717", Treasury Papers, Vol.ccviii, p.43.

22. John Conduitt, "Observations upon the present state of our gold and silver coins, 1730", reprinted in W. A. Shaw, *Select Tracts Illustrative of English Monetary History, 1626–1730*, George Harding, 1935.

23. Sir John Clapham, *The Bank of England*, Cambridge University Press, 1944, Vol.1, p.132.

24. Bank of England, Court Book A, 16 Feb 1695.

25. Clapham, op.cit. p.134.

26. Ibid., p.136.

27. Timothy Green, *Precious Heritage, Three Hundred Years of Mocatta & Goldsmid*, Rosendale Press, London 1984.

28. Clapham, op.cit. p.140.

29. Ibid., p.237.

30. Simao Ferreira Machado, *Triunfo Eucharistico*, Lisbon, 1734, pp.24–5.

31. Francisco Tavares de Brito, *Itinerario Geographico do Rio de Janeiro até as Minas do Ouro,* Seville, 1732, p.19.

32. Noya Pinto, *O Ouro Brasileiro e o Comércio Anglo-Portugués*, p.114, Cia Ed. Nacional, Brasília, Instituto Nacional do Livro, 1979.

33. Boxer, *The Golden Age of Brazil*, op.cit. pp.255–7.

34. Ibid., p.269.

35. C. R. Boxer, *Golden Age of Brazil*, p.351.

36. Ibid., p.469.

37. Ibid., p.467.

38. H. E. S. Fisher, *The Portugal Trade, A Study of Anglo-Portuguese Commerce 1700–1770*, Methuen, London 1971, p.100.

39. H. E. S. Fisher, "Anglo-Portuguese Trade 1700–1770", *Economic History Review* (1963), 2nd series, vol.16, p.230.

40. Ibid., p.233.

41. R. Duncan-Jones, *Money and Government in the Roman Empire*, Cambridge University Press, 1994, p.167 (see Chapter 13).

42. Charles Jenkinson, *A Treatise on the Coin of the Realm in a Letter to the King*, p.141.

Chapter 20

1. J. K. Galbraith, *Money, Whence it Came, Where it Went*, Andre Deutsch, London 1975, p.36.

2. This chapter draws on research I undertook in the 1970s for Mocatta and Goldsmid, the oldest members of the London market, for the tercentenary of their founding, originally thought to be in 1684, but actually in 1671. The summary of this research appeared as *Precious Heritage,* Rosendale Press, London 1984.

3. Committee of Treasury Minute Book, 16th October 1792, Bank of England Archives.

4. House of Commons, Third Report from the Committee of Secrecy on the Suspension of Cash Payments, 1797. Evidence of William Boyd, MP, p.35.

5. Sir John Clapham, *The Bank of England, A History*, Cambridge University Press, 1944, Vol.I, p.271. Source: B of E Committee of Treasury, 21st February 1797.

6. *The Times*, 28th February 1797 and 3rd March 1797.

7. Sir William Forbes, *The Memoirs of a Banking House*, Edinburgh, 1803.

8. *The Times*, 2nd March 1797.

9. Select Committee on the High Price of Gold Bullion, 1810, *Accounts*, p.26, Table XIX, An Account of all Gold imported into His Majesty's Mint.

10. *The Picture of London* for 1815, (sixteenth edition), p.101.

11. David Kynaston, *The City of London* Chatto and Windus, 1994, p.9.

12. Ibid., p.23.

13. Timothy Green, *The Millennium in Gold and The Millennium in Silver*, Rosendale Press, London 1999, p.20 in each report.

14. Select Committee on the High Price of Gold Bullion, Evidence of John Humble, pp.225–6.

15. Ibid., pp.225–6.

16. Ibid., *Accounts*, VIII, p.13.

17. Ibid., *Accounts*, VI, p.12.

18. Ibid., Humble Evidence, p.225.

19. Ibid., Minutes of Evidence, p.5. Aaron Goldsmid was not correct in claiming Mocatta had been the Bank's broker since 1694. The original firm, founded by Moses Mocatta in 1671, did not get a licensed broker's medal on the Royal Exchange until 1710 and only began regular dealings with the Bank around 1715. Not until 1721 does the Account of Bullion at the Bank record 'pd Mocatta his brokerage'. Mocatta was also paid annual brokerage by the East India Company in the same year.

20. Ibid., Abraham Goldsmid, Minutes of Evidence, pp.114–121.

21. Ibid., pp.1–3.

22. Ibid., p.7.

23. Ibid., pp.41–2.

24. Ibid., pp.42–3.

25. Ibid., pp.12–17.

26. Ibid., Evidence of William Merle, pp.24–41.

27. Ibid., Evidence of A. A. Goldsmid, p.46.

28. Ibid., Evidence of A. A. Goldsmid, p.17.

29. Ibid., Evidence of Abraham Goldsmid, p.119.

30. Ibid., Minutes of Evidence, John Whitmore and John Pearse, pp.110–4, 121–9, 152, 159, 173–7, 184–9.

31. David Kynaston, op.cit., pp.13–4.

32. 1810 Bullion Committee, Minutes of Evidence, Sir Francis Baring, pp.194–9.

33. Piero Sraffa, ed. *The Works and Correspondence of David Ricardo*, Vol.III, Cambridge University Press, for the Royal Economic Society, 1951, Appendix 'Mr ————' of the Bullion Report, pp.427–435. Sraffa discovered that Parish had worked closely with a British secret agent on the Continent, J. M. Johnson. Early in 1810 Johnson was dispatched by the Austrian statesman, Prince Metternich, to London with new requests for precious metal subsidies. Johnson could get only as far as Hamburg, where he appears to have handed over

the diplomatic note to Parish to deliver, as he had better cover as a merchant moving on business. Sraffa ruled out N. M. Rothschild as the anonymous witness, for his style and opinions before other Parliamentary enquiries in the next few years were entirely different from those of the 'Continental Merchant'.

34. 1810 Bullion Committee, Minutes of Evidence, 'Continental Merchant', pp.77–90, 96–110.

35. Ibid., Report, p.32.

36. Ibid., p.73.

37. Ibid., p.76.

38. P. Sraffa, ed. *The Works and Correspondence of David Ricardo*, Cambridge University Press, Vols.III & IV.

39. Ibid., Vol.IV, pp.52.

40. Bank of England, Letter Book No.2, 1813.

41. Napoleon had issued the *Napoléon d'Or* of 6.45 grams/0.1867 t.oz at 900 fine in 1803 and it would become the French equivalent of the *sovereign* for generations. The Paris Mint used over 37 m.t/1.2 million t.oz of gold for the coins between 1803–7.

42. India Office Records, L/AG/9.5.2, p.39.

43. Secret Committee of the House of Commons on the Expediency of the Bank Resuming Cash Payments, 1819, p.204.

44. *Memoir of John Charles Herries*, John Murray, London 1880, p.86. In this book J. C. Herries recounted his grandfather's account of the events.

45. Bank of England, General Ledger, Vol.19, ffo 807–121.

46. A. Feaveryear, *The Pound Sterling*, Clarendon Press, Oxford, 1963, p.213.

47. Clapham, op.cit., Vol.II, p.71.

48. Secret Committee of the House of Commons on the Expediency of the Bank Resuming Cash Payments, 1819, Minutes of Evidence, p.182.

49. Ibid., p.26.

50. Ibid., p.157.

51. Secret Committee of the House of Lords on the Expediency of the Bank Resuming Cash Payments, 1819, Report, p.16.

52. David Kynaston, *City of London* op.cit., Vol.1., p.40.

53. Hansard, 24th May 1819.

54. Clapham, op.cit., Vol.II, p.71.

Chapter 21

1. J. S. Holliday, *The World Rushed In*, Simon & Schuster, New York, and Gollanz, London 1983, p.50. This book, based on thirty years' research through the letters and diaries of the diggers, is an evocative anthology of their experiences en route to and at the gold fields.

2. R. W. Paul, *The California Gold Discovery*, Sources, Documents, Accounts and Memoirs, Georgetown, Calif. 1967. This is a fine collection of contemporary reports.

3. Colonel Richard B. Mason, Military Governor of California, Monterey, 17th August 1848, to the Adjutant General, Washington DC.

4. *New York Herald*, 11th January 1849.

5. J. S. Holliday, op.cit., p.50.

6. Ibid., p.126.

7. Ibid., p.59.

8. Ibid., p.306.

9. William Swain, 6th January 1850, South Fork of Feather River, in J. S. Holliday.

10. John A. Johnson, "Letters", 20th November 1849.

11. Letters of Edwin Hall, 1849, California Historical Society, San Francisco.

12. House of Commons, Select Committee on Depreciation of Silver, London July 1876. The Committee was presented with estimates from three different sources, including the San Francisco Journal of Commerce and the US Commissioner of Mining Statistics, but a consensus only emerged for 1851 onwards.

13. Although hopeful prospectors continue to this day. I once spent a weekend on the American river with Sacramento 'Nugget Nudgers', patiently scooping sand out of shallow pools and twirling their pans or poking vacuum cleaner nozzles under small rocks hoping to suck out a fleck or two of gold. Some were lucky, a few even made a meagre living. Tiny nuggets and 'nugget' jewellery could be bought nearby.

14. *Pacific News*, 6th January 1851.

15. Dr Isaac Lord, *Diary*, 26th December 1849. Henry E. Huntington Library, San Marino, California.

16. Holliday, op.cit., p.331, footnote.

17. Don Taxay, *The US Mint & Coinage*, Arco Publishing, New York, 1966, p.209.

18. E. Ludwig, *Schliemann of Troy*, G. Putnam, London & New York, 1931. The advertisement is reproduced on page 90.

19. Heinrich Schliemann, *Diaries*, March 1851–April 1852.

20.   Edward Hammond Hargraves, *Australia and Its Gold Fields*, H. Ingram & Co., London 1855, pp.73–4.

21. Ibid., p.96.

22. Ibid., pp.115–16.

23. W. P. Morrell, *The Gold Rushes*, A. & C. Black, London 1968, p.209. This book, by a New Zealand professor of history, is one of the most reliable accounts of the Australian and New Zealand explorations.

24. R. F. Holder, *Bank of New South Wales*, Angus and Robertson, Sydney, 1970, Vol.1, pp.183–5.

25. G. C. Mundy, *Our Antipodes*, London 1852, Vol.III, pp.346–7.

26. G. H. Wathen, *The Golden Colony*, London 1855, p.71.

27. Morrell, op.cit., pp.249–50.

28. W. Howitt, *Land, Labour and Gold*, London 1855, Vol.II, p.139. Howitt worked on most of the gold fields.

29. V. Pyke, *History of the Early Gold Discoveries in Otago, Dunedin*, 1887, Gabriel Read's Narrative, p.127.

30. W. P. Morrell, op.cit., p.274.

31. Sir John Clapham, *Bank of England*, op.cit., Vol.II, p.218.

32. Economist, 21st December 1850.

33. Michel Chevalier, *On the Probable Fall in the Value of Gold*, trs Richard Cobden, 1859, pp.96–9.

34. J. Laurence Laughlin, *The History of Bimetallism in the United States*, D. Appleton & Co., New York, 1895, pp.170–1.

35. Don Taxay, *The US Mint and Coinage*, Arco Publishing, New York, 1966, p.215.

36. J. L. Laughlin, op.cit., p.82, footnote 2.

37. The Bullion Business of the Bank of England, private paper for the Governor, Robert Crawford, December 1869, printed and circulated only in the Bank. Bank of England Library.

38. Select (Secret) Committee on the Banks Acts 1857, Minutes of Evidence, p.3.

39. Ibid., p.4.

40. J. H. Clapham, *Economic Development of France and Germany*, 1815–1914, Cambridge University Press, 1928.

41. Tooke & Newmarch, *History of Prices and State of the Circulation*, 1792–1856, Longman Brown, London 1856, Vol.6, pp.81–3.

42. Bank of England, Court Book Lb, 30 Jan. 1840.

43. Mocatta & Goldsmid, General Expenses Book; Sharps Nominal Ledgers, Archive of Kleinwort, Benson Ltd.

44. Memoirs of Col. Edward Matthey, dictated 1912, never published. Colonel Matthey started work for Johnson Matthey in 1850 at the age of 14. Copy in the author's possession.

45. Archive of N. M. Rothschild & Sons, Royal Mint Refinery statistics.

46. The Bullion Business of the Bank of England, op.cit., pp.9–11.

47. In 1890 Rothschilds' Royal Mint refinery took over the venerable Browne & Wingrove refinery which, as Browne & Brind, had been the first to get its bars 'approved' by the Bank of England in the 18th century. Sharps and Pixley merged in 1957. The only casualty was Raphael's refinery, which shut down in 1921 when South Africa was about to open the Rand refinery.

48. Sir John Clapham, op.cit., Vol.II, p.300.

49. J. K. Galbraith, op.cit., p.97.

50. First Report of the Royal Commission on Gold and Silver 1887, evidence of Stewart Pixley, paras 138–286, and Sir Hector Hay, paras 287–436.

51. D. Taxay, op.cit., p.261, quoting John C. Henderson in *Silver & Gold Money*, 1893.

52. Royal Commission on Gold and Silver, Final Report 1888, Part III, para 29.

53. Ibid., paras 128–9.

54. Timothy Green, Central Bank Gold Reserves, World Gold Council, London 1999, Table 3, p.20. Statistics compiled from: *Bank of England Weekly Returns, 1844–1914*: Dr Adolph Soetbeer, *Materialen*, Hamburg, 1886; *Reports of the Director of the US Mint* 1886–88m 1896, 1906; *Royal Commission on Indian Finance and Currency*, cd 7238, 1913, Appendix XXX; *Royal Commission on Indian Finance and Currency*, London 1926, Appendix 82, *Evidence of Joseph Kitchin.*

55. Timothy Green, *The World of Gold*, Michael Joseph, London 1968, pp.45–6.

56. A. P. Cartwright, *The Gold Miners*, Purnell & Sons, Capetown and Johannesburg, 1962, p.39

57. Timothy Green, *The World of Diamonds*, Weidenfeld & Nicolson, London 1981, pp.14–16.

58. Sir Theodore Gregory, *Ernest Oppenheimer and the Economic Development of Southern Africa*, Oxford University Press, 1962, p.14.

59. A. P. Cartwright, op.cit., pp.51–2.

60. Gardner F. Williams, *The Diamond Mines of South Africa,* Macmillan, London 1902, p.576.

61. Ibid., p.578.

62. W. P. Morrell, op.cit., p.343.

63. Archives of N. M. Rothschild & Sons and Donald McDonald, *The History of Johnson Matthey*, unpublished, Vol.II.

64. Timothy Green, *World of Gold*, Rosendale Press, London 1993, pp.163–4.

65. John McIlwraith and Anthea Harris, *100 Years of the Perth Mint*, Gold Corporation, Perth, 1999.

66. Pierre Berton, *The Golden Trail*, Macmillan, Toronto, 1954.

67. Barry Eichengreen, *Golden Fetters, the Gold Standard and the Great Depression 1919–1939*, Oxford University Press, 1992, p.1.

68. US National Monetary Commission, Senate doc. No.405, Interviews on the banking and currency systems, p.26. Quoted in R. S. Sayers, *The Bank of England 1891–1944*, Cambridge University Press, 1976, Vol.1, p.29.

69. Eichengreen, op.cit., p.31.

Chapter 22

1. John Maynard Keynes, Collected Writings, Vol.XVI, Royal Economic Society, Macmillan/ Cambridge University Press, pp.10–11.

2. D. E. Moggridge, *Maynard Keynes: An Economist's Biography*, 1992, p.238.

3. Timothy Green, *Central Bank Gold Reserves*, op.cit., Table 3, Monetary Gold.

4. Clapham, *Bank of England*, op.cit., Vol.II, p.415.

5. R. S. Sayers, *The Bank of England*, op.cit., Vol.III, Appendix 2, Treasury Memorandum on the Gold Reserves, 22nd May 1914, p.9.

6. McDonald, *History of Johnson Matthey*, op.cit., Vol.II, p.9.

7. *Daily Express*, 3rd August 1916.

8. William A. Brown, *England and the New Gold Standard*, 1919 to 1926, P. S. King, London 1929, p.8.

9. Ibid., p.11.

10. Committee on Currency and Foreign Exchanges after the War, 9182, August 1918. First Interim Report, para 47.

11. Robert Skidelsky, *John Maynard Keynes*, Macmillan, London 1992, Vol.II, p.45.

12. McDonald, *History of Johnson Matthey*, op.cit., Vol.II, p.41.

13. Archives of N. M. Rothschild & Sons; the paragraphs are taken from a short history of the early days of the 'fix', prepared for their internal use.

14. Ibid.

15. Ibid.

16. Timothy Green, *The World of Gold,* Michael Joseph, London 1968, p.105.

17. India Office Records, F. collection, 44/8.

18. Ibid., and Archives of N. M. Rothschild & Sons.

19. The author was asked the progeny of the bars on a visit to India and, with the aid of the Rand Refinery, the date was confirmed.

20. Treasury Papers, T. 160/197, file 7528. Montagu Norman evidence to the Chamberlain Committee, 27th June 1924, p.6.

21. Robert Skidelsky, op.cit., Vol.II, p.197.

22. James Grigg, Prejudice and Judgement, London 1948, pp.182–4. Grigg was Churchill's private secretary, who recorded the only eyewitness account of the dinner.

23. Hansard, 28th April 1925.

24. Ibid.

25. J. K. Galbraith, *Money, Whence It Came, Where It Went*, Andre Deutsch, London 1975, p.168.

26. R. S. Sayers, op.cit., Vol.1, p.347.

27. Mocatta and Goldsmid, Annual Circular, 1930.

28. Ibid.

29. Paul Einzig, *International Gold Movements*, Macmillan, London 1929, pp.3–4.

30. Joseph Kitchen's initial research was published as Appendix 82 of the Royal Commission on Indian Currency and Finance, in 1926. This was updated and published in The *International Gold Problem, Collected Papers, A Record of the Discussions of a Study Group of Members of The Royal Institute of International Affairs, 1929–31*, Oxford University Press, 1931, pp.48–83, from which these paragraphs are drawn. Kitchen's world-wide review of gold supply and demand continued to be made by Union Corporation until the 1960s, when

it was replaced by the Consolidated Gold Fields annual gold survey, on which this author was a consultant for almost thirty years.

31. Ibid., *International Gold Problem*, pp.62–3.

32. B. Eichengreen, op.cit., pp.188–9.

33. Skidelsky, op.cit., Vo.II, p.207.

34. Sayers, *Bank of England*, op.cit., Vol.II, p.387.

35. Ibid., p.415.

36. Board of Governors of the Federal Reserve System, Banking and Monetary Statistics, 1913–1941, Washington DC, 1943.

37. The Economist, 26th August 1933.

38. Bank for International Settlements, 8th Annual Report, 1938, p.45.

39. Timothy Green, *The World of Gold*, Rosendale Press, London 1993, p.47.

40. Eichengreen, op.cit., p.289.

Chapter 23

1. Eichengreen, op.cit., pp.328–331

2. Arthur M. Schlesinger Jr, *The Coming of the New Deal: The Age of Roosevelt*, Vol.2, Houghton Mifflin, Boston, 1960.

3. R. C. Hawtrey, *The Gold Standard in Theory and Practice*, Longmans Green & Co., London and New York, 4th edition, 1939, pp.194–8. Ralph Hawtrey was the 'in-house' economist at the Treasury in London from 1904–45 and monitored the daily operations in gold.

4. Mocatta and Goldsmid, *Annual Bullion Review 1934*.

5. Hawtrey, *Gold Standard*, op.cit., pp.246–259.

6. Ibid., pp.256–7.

7. Theodore Gregory, *Ernest Oppenheimer and the Economic Development of Southern Africa*, op.cit., p.506.

8. Mildred Fielder, *The Treasure of Homestake Gold*, North Plains Press, Aberdeen, South Dakota, 1970, p.313.

9. Geoffrey Blainey, *The Golden Mile,* Allen & Unwin, St Leonards, NSW, 1993, p.128.

10. J. D. Littlepage and D. Bess, *In Search of Soviet Gold*, Harcourt Brace, New York, 1938.

11. Unpublished private estimates.

12. Timothy Green, *World of Gold*, Michael Joseph, London 1968, pp.53–5. Based on interviews at GFSA in Johannesburg in 1967.

13. A. P. Cartwright, *The Goldminers*, Purbell, Johannesburg, 1962, pp.298 and 300.

14. Timothy Green, *World of Gold*, 1968, op.cit., p.51.

15. Timothy Green, *World of Gold*, 1968, op.cit., pp.97–8. The precise details of these sales arrangements were revealed for the first time in this book, based on an interview with Dr Gerard Rissik, Governor of the Reserve Bank, in Pretoria.

16. Timothy Green, *World of Gold*, 1993, op.cit., p.50.

17. IMF, International Financial Statistics.

18. Timothy Green, *The World of Gold*, 1968, op.cit., pp.109–111. These contemporary accounts were based on interviews at the Bank of England, with the London market members and the Federal Reserve in New York.

19. Ibid., p.203.

20. Ten tola bars of 111 grams/3.75 t.oz at 999 fine were the most popular bars on the Indian sub-continent for many years.

21. Timothy Green, op.cit., 1968, p.168.

22. Ibid., p.175

23. Timothy Green, *World of Gold*, 1993, pp.51–2.

24. Samuel Montagu, Annual Bullion Review, 1968, p.4

Chapter 24

1. Jessica Cross, *New Frontiers in Gold: The Derivatives Revolution*, Rosendale Press, London 1994, p.41.

2. The full story of this era is told in the several editions, from 1968 to 1993, of my book *The World of Gold, and in The Prospect for Gold: the view to the year 2000*. See Bibliography.

3. Gold, 1969, D. O. Lloyd-Jacob and P. D. Fells, Consolidated Gold Fields, London. This annual survey continued until 1989, when it was taken over by GFMS, which continues it. An early version of the survey was undertaken in 1967, but not published, although the main findings were leaked to *The Economist*. This writer was a consultant on the survey from 1969–1996.

4. Timothy Green, *World of Gold*, 1993, op.cit., pp.58–60.

5. John Marsden & Iain House, *The Chemistry of Gold Extraction*, Simon & Schuster, New York and London 1992.

6. *World Gold Analyst*, Vol.8, No.10, October 2005, Russian, Special Focus, pp.11–15.

7. *World Gold Analyst*, Vol.9, No.4, April 2006, p.9.

8. T. R. Smeeton, Central Bank Attitudes to the Future of Gold, *Financial Times World Gold Conference,* Montreux, June 1992.

9. Philip Klapwijk, interview

10. Robert Weinberg, Autograph Award Essay, London 1992.

11. Statistics from *Gold Survey 2007*, GFMS Ltd, London 2007.

12. Timothy Green, *The Gold Companion: the A–Z of Mining, Marketing, Trading & Technology*, Rosendale Press, London 1991 and 1997, p.51 Electronics.

Bibliography

Ancient Sources

Han Schu 24, *Food and Money in Ancient China*, trs Nancy Lee Swann, Princeton University Press, 1950.

Herodotus, *The Histories, trs Aubrey de Selincourt*, revised John Maricola, Penguin Classics, London 1972.

Homer, *The Iliad*, Bk XXIII, trs Lord Derby, J. M. Dent, London 1864.

Livy, *The Early History of Rome*, trs Aubrey de Selincourt, Penguin Classics, 1960.

Pliny, *Natural History*, XXXIII, trs P. R. Lewis and G. D. B. Jones in "Roman Gold Mining in North-West Spain", Journal of Roman Studies, LX, 1970, pp.1169–185.

Diodorus Siculus, *Bibliotheca Historica*, c.60 BC, trs. C. H. Oldfather, Loeb Classical History, 1935.

Thucydides, *History of the Peloponnesian Wars*, trs Rex Warner, Penguin Classics, 1972.

Xenophon, *The Persian Expedition*, (Anabasis) trs Rex Warner, Penguin Classics, London 1972.

Primary Sources

UK Parliamentary Reports and Government Papers

Sir Isaac Newton, State of the Gold and Silver Coin, 25th September 1717, Treasury Papers, Vol.ccviii.

Report together with Minutes of Evidence and Accounts from the Select Committee on the High Price of Gold Bullion, House of Commons, 8th June 1810.

Secret Committee of the House of Commons on the Expediency of the Bank Resuming Cash Payments, 1819.

Secret Committee of the House of Lords on the Expediency of the Bank Resuming Cash Payments, 1819.

Select (Secret) Committee on the Bank Acts, 1857.

Select Committee of the House of Commons on the Depreciation of Silver, 1876.

Royal Commission on Gold and Silver, First Report, 1887.

Royal Commission on Gold and Silver, Final Report, 1888.

Committee on Currency and Foreign Exchange (The Cunliffe Report), First Interim Report, August 1918.

Montagu Norman, Evidence to the Chamberlain Committee, 27th June 1924, Treasury Papers, T 160/197, file 7528.

Bank of England Archives

Court Book A, 16th February 1695.

Committee of Treasury Minute Book, 16th October 1792.

Letter Book No.2, 1813.

General Ledger, Vol.19, ff.807/121, 1816.

Court Book, LG, 30th June 1840.

The Bullion Business of the Bank of England, by Robert Crawford, private paper for the Governor, December 1869.

India Office Records

L/AG/9, 5, 2.

F. Collection 44/8.

Other Bank Records

Bank for International Settlements, 8th Annual Report, 1938.

Board of Governors of the Federal Reserve System, Banking and Monetary Statistics, 1913–1941, Washington DC, 1943.

Gold Market Records and Reports

Mocatta and Goldsmid Day Book for 1803, MS 10, 399 and Letter Book, 1800–1812, MS 10, 400, Guildhall Library, London.

Mocatta and Goldsmid, Annual Circulars, 1877–1938.

N. M. Rothschild & Sons Archives: First Gold Fixings 1919.

Samuel Montagu, Annual Bullion Reviews, 1968–1989.

Consolidated Gold Fields, Annual *Gold Surveys*, 1969–1989.

Gold Fields Mineral Services (GFMS), Annual *Gold Survey* 1990–2006.

World Gold Analyst, 1997–2006.

Secondary Sources

K. Akishev & A. Akishev, *Ancient Gold of Kazakstan*, trs. O. Belyayeva, Alma-Ata, 1983.

Cyril Aldred, *Jewels of the Pharaohs*, Thames & Hudson, London 1971.

Carol Andrews, *Ancient Egyptian Jewellery*, British Museum Press, 1990.

Manolo Andronicus, *Vergina, The Royal Tombs*, Ekdotike SA, Athens, 1997.

E. Arcin, C. Plazas, J. Echeverri, *Secrets of El Dorado*, El Sello Editorial, Bogota, 1990.

Eliyatu Ashtor, The Venetian Supremacy in Levantine Trade, *Journal of European Economic History*, III, Rome 1974.

Eliyatu Ashtor, The Volume of Levantine Trade in the Middle Ages (1370–1498), *Journal of European Economic History*, VII, Rome 1975.

Maria Eugenia Aubet, *The Phoenicians and the West*, Cambridge University Press, 2nd edition, 2001.

S. J. B. Barnish, The Wealth of Julianus Argentarius, *Byzantion 55*, 1985.

G. F. Bass, The Bronze Age Shipwreck at Ulu Burun, *American Journal of Archaeology*, Vols. 90, 92 and 93.

G. F. Bass, A Hoard of Trojan and Sumerian Jewellery, *American Journal of Archaeology*, 2nd series, Vol.74, 1970.

Benaki Museum, *Great Jewellery from the Benaki Collections*, Adam Editions, Athens, 1999.

Barbara Bend, *Islamic Art*, British Museum Press, 1991.

Pierre Berton, *The Golden Trail*, Macmillan, Toronto, 1954.

J. Bird, The Legacy of the Stingless Bee, *Natural History*, 1979, Vol.88 (9).

Geoffrey Blainey, *The Golden Mile*, Allen & Unwin, St Leonards, New South Wales, 1993.

C. W. Blegen, *Troy Excavations*, conducted by the University of Cincinnati, 1932–38, Parts I to IV, Princeton, 1950–58.

Raymond Bloch, The Etruscans, *Horizon*, Vol.II, No.5, 1960.

E. W. Bovill, *Caravans of the Old Sahara*, International Institute of African Languages & Culture, Oxford University Press, 1933.

E. W. Bovill, *The Gold Trade of the Moors*, Oxford University Press, 1969.

C. R. Boxer, *The Golden Age of Brazil*, 1695–1750, University of California Press, Berkeley & Los Angeles, 1962.

C. R. Boxer, Brazilian Gold and British Traders in the First Half of the 18th Century, *Hispanic-American Historical Review*, XLIV, 1969.

Fernand Braudel, *The Mediterranean World in the Age of Philip II*, Collins, London 1972.

Fernand Braudel, *Capitalism and the Material Life 1400–1800*, trs. Miriam Kochan, Harper Row, New York, 1973.

Fernand Braudel, *The Mediterranean in the Ancient World*, Allen Lane, London 2001.

Warwick Bray, *The Gold of Eldorado*, Rainbird, London 1978.

Warwick Bray, Malagana and the gold-working tradition of south-west Colombia, in *Precolumbian Gold*, ed. C. McEwan, British Museum Press, 2000.

J. A. Brinkman, Foreign Relations of Babylonia from 1600–25 BC, *American Journal of Archaeology*, Vol.76, 1972.

Janet Brown, *The Voyage of the Argonauts*, Methuen, London 1925.

William A. Brown, *England and the New Gold Standard*, 1919–1926, P. S. King, London 1929.

Emma Bunker, Artibus Asïae, *Gold in the Ancient Chinese World*, AA58, 1993.

Emma Bunker, *Nomadic Art of the Eastern Eurasian Steppes*, Yale University Press, New Haven and London 2002.

Richard L. Burger, *Chavin and the Origin of Andean Civilisation*, Thames & Hudson, London 1995.

Giofranco Bustacchini, Gold in Mosaic Art and Techniques, *Gold Bulletin*, 1973, 6(2).

Ian Carradice (ed.), Royal Coinage of the Persian Empire, *Coinage and Administration in the Athenian and Persian Empires*, BAR International Series, 343, 1987.

D. L. Carroll, A classification of granulation in ancient metalwork, *American Journal of Archaeology*, 78, 1974.

D. L. Carroll, On granulation in ancient metalwork, *American Journal of Archaeology*, 87, 1983.

R. A. G. Carson, *Coins of the Roman Empire*, Routledge, London 1990.

Howard Carter, *Tutankhamun*, Barrie & Jenkins, London 1972.

A. P. Cartwright, *The Gold Miners*, Purnell & Sons, Cape Town, 1962.

Beatrice Cauuet, L'or dans l'Antiquité, *Aquitana*, Supplement 9, 1999.

Marjorie Caygill, *A–Z Companion, The British Museum*, British Museum Press, 1999.

Benvenuto Cellini, *The Life of Benvenuto Cellini*, written by himself, trs. John Addington Smith, Phaidon, London 1949.

John Chadwick, *The Mycenean World*, Cambridge University Press, 1976.

C. E. Challis (ed.), *A New History of the Royal Mint*, Cambridge University Press, 1992.

Michel Chevalier, *On the Probable Fall in the Value of Gold*, trs. Richard Cobden, 1859.

Anton Chekhov, *A Life in Letters*, trs. R. Bartlett & A. Phillips, Penguin, London 2004.

John Clapham, *Economic Development of France and Germany 1815–1914*, Cambridge University Press, 1928.

Sir John Clapham, *Bank of England*, 2 Vols., Cambridge University Press, 1944.

K. N. Chaudhuri, *The Trading World of Asia and the East India Company 1660–1760*, Cambridge University Press, 1978.

John Conduitt, Observations upon the present state of our gold and silver coins 1730; reprinted in W. A. Shaw, *Select Tracts Illustrative of Monetary History 1626–1730*, Clement Wilson, London 1896.

Consolidated Gold Fields, Annual *Gold Surveys* 1969–1989.

Leonard Cottrell, *Lost Worlds*, American Heritage Publishing, New York, 1962.

Sir John Craig, *Newton at the Mint*, Cambridge University Press, 1946.

Sir John Craig, *The Mint*, Cambridge University Press, 1953.

Michael Crawford, *Coinage and Money Under the Roman Republic*, Methuen, 1985.

Robert Crawford, *The Bullion Business of the Bank of England*, Bank of England, 1869.

Jessica Cross, *New Frontiers in Gold: The Derivatives Revolution, Rosendale Press*, London 1994

John Curtis, *Ancient Persia*, British Museum Press, 2000.

John Curtis (ed.), *Forgotten Empire: The World of Ancient Persia*, British Museum Press, 2005.

John Day, The Great Bullion Famine, Past and Present, No.79, 1978; reprinted in *The Medieval Market Economy*, Blackwell, Oxford, 1987.

George Dennis, *The Cities and Cemeteries of Etruria*, John Murray, London 1883.

G. Depeyrot, *Crises et Inflation entre Antiquité et Moyen Age*, Paris, 1991.

C. Desroches-Nobelcourt, *Tutankhamun*, Penguin, London 1965.

C. Domergue & G. Herail, *Mines d'or Romaines d'Espagne: la district de la Valduerna*, Paris, 1978.

J. A. Donaldson, The use of gold in dentistry, *Gold Bulletin*, Vol.13, No.3, July 1980.

Homer H. Dubs, An Ancient Chinese Stock of Gold, *Journal of Economic History*, Vol.1, 1941, pp.36–39.

Richard Duncan-Jones, *Money and Government in the Roman Empire*, Cambridge University Press, 1994.

Paul-Marie Duval in: Celtic Art in *The Celts: The Origins of Europe*, ed. Sabatino Moscati, Thames & Hudson, London 1991.

Donald Easton, Schliemann's Discovery of Priam's Treasure; two enigmas, *Antiquity*, Vol.55, 1981, pp,179–83.

Barry Eichengreen, *Golden Fetters, the Gold Standard and the Great Depression 1919–1939*, Oxford University Press, 1992.

Paul Einzig, *International Gold Movements*, Macmillan, London 1929.

Christiane Eluère, Prehistorical Goldwork in Western Europe, *Gold Bulletin*, 1983.

Christiane Eluère, A Gold Connection between the Etruscans and Early Celts?, *Gold Bulletin*, Vol.22, No.2, 1989, pp.48–55.

Christiane Eluère in *The Celts and Their Gold, in The Celts, The Origins of Europe*, ed. S. Moscati, Thames & Hudson, London 1991.

Christiane Eluère, *The Celts, First Masters of Europe*, Thames & Hudson, London 1993.

Arthur Evans, Aigina Treasure, *Journal of Hellenic Studies*, 1892–3.

Arthur Evans, *The Palace of Minos*, Vols.I–IV, London 1921–36.

Joan Evans, *Time and Chance; the Story of Arthur Evans and his Forbears*, Longman's Green, London 1943.

Ana Maria Falchetti, The Gold of Greater Zenu, in *Precolumbian Gold*, ed. C. McEwan, British Museum Press, 2000.

A. Feaveryear, *The Pound Sterling*, Clarendon Press, Oxford, 1963.

Thomas Figueira, *The Power of Money; Coinage and Politics in the Athenian Empire*, University of Pennsylvania Press, 1998.

Mildred Fielder, *The Treasure of Homestake Gold*, North Plains Press, Aberdeen, S. Dakota, 1970.

J. Lesley Fitton, *The Discovery of the Greek Bronze Age*, British Museum Press, 1995.

J. Lesley Fitton, *The Minoans*, British Museum Press, London 2002.

H. E. S. Fisher, Anglo-Portuguese Trade 1700–1770, *Economic History Review*, 1963, 2nd series, Vol.16.

H. E. S. Fisher, *The Portugal Trade, A Study of Anglo-Portuguese Commerce 1700–1770*, Methuen, London 1971.

Sir William Forbes, *The Memoirs of a Banking House*, Edinburgh, 1803.

B. R. Foster, Commercial Activity in Sargonic Mesopotamia, *Iraq*, Vol.39, 1977.

Otto Herman Frey, *Formation of the La Tène Culture*, in *The Celts*, ed. Moscati, Thames & Hudson, London 1991.

L. Galanina & N. Grach, *Scythian Art*, Aurora Publishers, Leningrad, 1986.

J. K. Galbraith, *Money, Whence it Came, Where it Went*, Andre Deutsch, London 1975.

N. W. Gale & S. A. Stos-Gale, *Journal of Egyptian Antiquities*, Vol.67, 1981.

V. Magalhaes Godinho, "Le Portugal, les flottes du sucre et les flottes de l'or, 1670–1770", *Annales*, février/mars 1951.

P. J. Golas, Joseph Needham, Science and Civilisation in China, Vol.5, part xiii, *Mining*, Cambridge University Press, 1999.

Gold Fields Mineral Services (GFMS), Annual *Gold Surveys*, 1990–2005.

Gold, Granite and Water, the Bir Umm Fawakir Survey Project, AASOR 52, 1994.

R. Goldsmith, *Pre-modern Financial Systems*, Cambridge University Press, 1987.

E. W. Gombrich, *The Story of Art*, Phaidon, London 1951.

Andre Grabar, *Byzantium*, Thames & Hudson, 1966.

Michael Grant, *The Etruscans*, Weidenfeld & Nicolson, London 1980.

A. K. Grayson, *Assyrian Rulers of the First Millennium BC*, University of Toronto Press, 1991.

Miranda J. Green (ed.), *The Celtic World*, Routledge, London & New York, 1995.

Timothy Green, *The World of Gold*, Michael Joseph, London; Walker & Co., New York, 1968.

-- *The World of Gold Today*, Walker & Co., New York, 1973.

-- *The New World of Gold*, Weidenfeld & Nicolson, London; Walker & Co., New York, 1981.

-- *The World of Diamonds*, Weidenfeld & Nicolson, London 1981.

-- *The Prospect for Gold: the View to the Year 2000*, Rosendale Press, London 1987.

-- *The World of Gold* (completely revised), Rosendale Press, London 1993.

-- *The Gold Companion: The A–Z of Mining, Marketing, Trading and Technology*, Rosendale Press, London 1991 (revised 1997).

-- *The Millennium in Gold*, Rosendale Press, London 1999.

-- *Central Bank Gold Reserves*, World Gold Council, London 1999.

Guido Gregorietti, *Jewellery Through the Ages*, Hamlyn, London 1970.

Sir Theodore Gregory, *Ernest Oppenheimer and the Economic Development of Southern Africa*, Oxford University Press, 1962.

Philip Grierson, *Numismatics*, Oxford University Press, 1975.

Philip Grierson, *Byzantine Coins*, Methuen, London 1982.

James Grigg, *Prejudice and Judgement*, London 1948.

Bo Gyllensvärd, *Chinese Gold and Silver in the Carle Kempe Collection*, Stockholm, 1953.

Edward Hall, *Letters 1849*, California Historical Society, San Francisco.

Earl J. Hamilton, *American Treasure and the Price Revolution in Spain 1501–1650*, Harvard University Press, 1936.

N. G. L. Hammond, *Alexander the Great*, Chatto & Windus, London 1981.

N. G. L. Hammond, *The Genius of Alexander the Great*, University of North Carolina Press, 1997.

Edward Hammond Hargraves, *Australia and Its Gold Fields*, H. Ingram & Co., London 1855.

Donald Harden, *The Phoenicians*, Thames & Hudson, London 1962.

S. Hassan, *Excavations in Gaza*, Cairo, 1932.

R. C. Hawtrey, *The Gold Standard in Theory and Practice*, Longmans Green & Co., London & New York, 4th edition, 1939.

J. H. Hayward, *Virtuoso Goldsmiths*, Sotheby Parke Bernet, New York, 1976.

J. F. Healy, *Mining and Metallurgy in the Greek and Roman World*, Thames & Hudson, London 1978.

M. Heltzer, *The Metal Trade of Ugarit*, Iraq, Vol.39, 1977.

J. H. Hemming, *The Conquest of the Incas*, Macmillan, London 1970.

Michael Hendy, *Studies in the Byzantine Monetary Economy c.300–1450*, Cambridge University Press, 1985.

J. B. Henneman, *Royal Taxation in 14th Century France*, Princeton University Press, 1971.

John Charles Herries, *Memoir*, John Murray, London 1880.

M. G. Higgins & R. Higgins, *A Geological Companion to Greece and the Aegean*, Duckworth, London 1996.

Reynold Higgins, *Greek and Roman Jewellery*, Methuen, London 1980.

R. F. Holder, *Bank of New South Wales*, Angus & Robertson, Sydney, 1970.

J. S. Halliday, *The World Rushed In*, Simon & Schuster, New York, 1983.

W. Howitt, *Land, Labour and Gold* (2 Vols.), London 1855.

Graham Hughes, *The Art of Jewellery*, Peerage Books, London 1972.

Esther Jacobson, *The Art of the Scythians*, E. J. Brill, New York, 1995.

Saad Al-Jadir, *Arab and Islamic Silver*, Stacey International, 1981.

Prentiss S. de Jesus, *The Development of Prehistoric Mining and Metallurgy in Anatolia*, BAR International Series, 74, Oxford, 1980.

Catherine Johns, *The Jewellery of Roman Britain*, UCC Press, London 1996.

A. H. M. Jones, *The Later Roman Empire*, Vol.II, Blackwell, 1964.

R. D. F. Jones & D. G. Bird, Roman Gold-mining in North-West Spain, II; Workings on the Rio Duerna, *Journal of Roman Studies*, LXII (1972), pp.61–74.

Julia Jones & Ana Maria Falchetti, *The Art of Precolumbian Gold: The Jan Mitchell Collection*, Weidenfeld & Nicolson, London 1985.

Henry Kamen, *Spain's Road to Empire: the Making of a World Power*, Allen Lane, London 2002.

H. Kellenbenz & J. Schneider, *Precious Metals in the Age of Expansion*, Stuttgart, 1981.

Werner Keller, *The Etruscans*, Jonathan Cape, London 1975.

Hans-Jörg Kellner, Coinage, in *The Celts, The Origins of Europe*, ed. Moscati, Thames & Hudson, London 1991.

E. M. Kelly, *Spanish Dollars and Silver Tokens*, Spink & Son, London 1976.

John Maynard Keynes, *Collected Writings*, Vol.XVI, Royal Economic Society, Macmillan/Cambridge University Press.

John Kieschnick, *The Impact of Buddhism on Chinese Material Culture*, Princeton University Press, 2003.

Joseph Kitchen, *The International Gold Problem*, Oxford University Press, 1931.

J. Knudtzon, *Die el Amarn-Tafeln* (The Tell-Amarna Tablets), Vol.1, Leipzig, 1915.

A. Kobata, Production and Uses of Gold and Silver in 16th and 17th Century Japan, *Economic History Review* (2nd series), Vol.18, 1967.

S. M. Kramer, Commerce and Trade: Gleanings from Sumerian Literature, *Iraq*, Vol.39, 1977.

Amelia Kurt, *The Ancient Near East*, Routledge, London 1995.

David Kynaston, *The City of London*, 2 Vols., Chatto & Windus, 1994 and 1995.

A. E. Laiou (ed.), *The Economic History of Byzantium*, 3 Vols., Dumbarton Oaks, Washington DC, 2002.

I. Lalaounis, *Metamorphoses*, privately printed, Athens, 1984.

Serge Lancel, *Carthage*, Blackwell, Oxford, 1995.

Frederic Lane & Reinhold Mueller, *Money and Banking in Medieval and Renaissance Venice*, 2 Vols., John Hopkins University Press, Baltimore & London 1985 & 1995.

M. T. Larsen, Partnerships in the Old Assyrian Trade, *Iraq*, Vol.39, 1977.

J. Laurence Laughlin, *The History of Bimetallism in the United States*, D. Appleton, New York, 1895.

D. H. Lawrence, *Etruscan Places*, Martin Secker, London 1932.

Heather Lechtman, The Central Andes without Iron, in *The Coming of the Iron Age*, (eds.) T. Wertime & J. D. Muhly, Yale, 1980.

Cieza de Léon, *Cronica del Peru*, Madrid, 1947.

Bernard Lewis, *The Middle East*, Weidenfeld & Nicolson, London 1995.

P. R. Lewis & G. D. B. Jones, Roman Gold-mining in North-West Spain, *Journal of Roman Studies*, LX, 1970.

Ming-Hsun Li, *The Great Recoinage*, Weidenfeld, London 1963.

J. D. Littlepage and D. Bess, *In Search of Soviet Gold*, Harcourt Brace, New York, 1938.

Roberto Lleras-Pérez, The Iconography and Symbolism of Metallic Votive Offerings in the Eastern Cordillera of Colombia, in *Precolumbian Gold*, ed. C. McEwan, British Museum Press, 2000.

M. Lombard, *L'Islam dans sa Première Grandeur*, Flammation, Paris, trs. Joan Spencer, North Holland Publishing, Amsterdam, 1971.

Otar Lordkipanidze, *Oxford Journal of Archaeology*, Vol.20, No.1, Feb 2001.

E. Ludwig, *Schliemann of Troy*, Putnam, New York, 1931.

Max Mallowan. *Dawn of Civilisation*, Thames & Hudson, London 1961.

M. M. Mango, *Ecclesiastical Silver Plate in 6th Century Byzantium*, ed. S. A. Boyd and M. M. Mango, Washington DC, 1992.

John Marden & Iain House, *The Chemistry of Gold Extraction*, Simon & Schuster, New York & London 1992.

G. Marinos, *Greece in the Mineral Deposits of Europe*, ed. S. H. V. Bowie, Institute for Mining & Metallurgy, London 1982.

Edward Matthey, *Memoirs*, unpublished, 1912.

John Mawe, *Travels in the Interior of Brazil*, London 1812.

K. R. Maxwell-Hyslop, *Western Asiatic Jewellery c.3000–612 BC*, Methuen, London 1971.

K. R. Maxwell-Hyslop, Sources of Sumerian Gold, *Iraq*, Vol.39, 1977.

Ivan Mazarov (ed.), Ancient Gold: *The Wealth of the Thracians*, H. Abrams, New York, 1998.

Donald McDonald, *The History of Johnson Matthey*, 2 Vols., unpublished, 1974.

John McIlwraith & Anthea Harris, *100 Years of the Perth Mint*, Gold Corporation, Perth, WA, 1999.

D. M. Metcalf, *Coinage in the Balkans 820–1355*, Thessaloniki, 1965.

D. E. Moggridge, Maynard Keynes, *An Economist's Biography*, Routledge, 1992.

C. Moorhead, *The Lost Treasures of Troy*, Weidenfeld & Nicolson, London 1994.

P. R. S. Moorey, *Ancient Mesopotamian Minerals and Industries*, Clarendon Press, Oxford, 1994.

W. R. Moran, *The Amarna Letters*, London 1992.

W. P. Morell, *The Gold Rushes*, A. & C. Black, London 1968.

Otto Mørkholm, *Early Hellenistic Coinage*, Cambridge University Press, 1991.

James Morris, *Venice*, Faber & Faber, London 1960.

Cecile Morrisson, *L'or monnaié*, 2 Vols., Cahiers Ernest-Babelon, Paris, 1985.

Cecile Morrisson, in *Economic History of Byzantium*, ed. A. E. Laiou, Dumbarton Oaks, Washington DC, 2002.

Sabatino Moscati, *The World of the Phoenicians*, Weidenfeld & Nicolson, London 1968.

Sabatino Moscati (ed.), *The Phoenicians*, Bompiani, Milan, 1988.

Michael E. Moseley, The Incas and Their Ancestors, *The Archaeology of Peru*, Thames 7 Hudson, London 1992.

C. C. Mundy, *Our Antipodes*, London 1852.

Joseph Needham & others, *Science and Civilisation in China*, 25 Vols., Cambridge University Press, 1954–2001.

S. La Niece, *Iraq*, Vol.57,1995, pp.41–49.

P. Northover, "The Technology of Metalwork" in *The Celtic World* (ed.) Miranda Green, Routledge, London & New York, 1995.

J. H. F. Notton, Ancient Egyptian Gold Refining, *Gold Bulletin*, Vol.7 (2), 1974.

Joan Oates, *Babylon*, Thames & Hudson, London 1979.

Joan Oates, *The Albert Reckitt Archaeological Lecture*, British Academy, London 2004.

Joan and David Oates, *Nimrud*, British School of Archaeology in Iraq, London 2001.

Karen O'Day, The Goldwork of Chimor, in *Precolumbian Gold*, ed. C. McEwan, British Museum Press, 2000.

José R. Oliver, Gold Symbolism Among Caribbean Chiefdoms, in *Precolumbian Gold*, ed. C. McEwan, British Museum Press, 2000.

A. L. Oppenheim, The Seafaring Merchants of Ur, *Journal of the American Oriental Society*, Vol.74, 1954.

A. Orejas & F. J. Sánchez-Palencia, Mines, Territorial Organisation and Social Structures in Roman Iberia, *American Journal of Archaeology*, Vol.104, No.4, Oct 2002.

Bernard Overbeck, Celtic Coin, in *The Celts, The Origins of Europe*, ed. Moscati, Thames & Hudson, London 1991.

P. Pacrini, Etruscan Granulation, *American Journal of Archaeology*, 86 (1982), pp.118–121.

R. W. Paul, *The California Gold Discovery, Sources documents and Memoirs*, Georgetown, California, 1967.

Ludwig Pauli, The Erstfold Hoard, in *the Celts, The Origins of Europe*, ed. Moscati, Thames & Hudson, London 1991.

Francesco Balducci Pegolotti, *La Practica della Mercatura*, ed. Allan Evans, The Medieval Academy of America, 1936.

Oskar Paulinyi, "The Crown Monopoly of Refining Metallurgy of Precious Metals in Hungary and Transylvania (1325–1700)", in *Precious Metals in the Age of Expansion*, ed. H. Kellenbenz & Jürgen Schneider, Stuttgart, 1981.

Basil Petrakos, *Sculpture – Bronzes – Vases*, National Archaeological Museum, Athens, Cleo Editions, 1981.

W. M. F. Petrie, *The Pyramids and Temples of Gizeh*, London 1883.

J. Pillsbury (ed.), *Moche Art and Archaeology in Ancient Peru*, Yale, 2001.

Noya Pinto, *O Ouro Brasiliero e o Comercio Anglo-Portugués*, Csa.Ed. Nacional, Brasilia, Instituto Nacional do Livvo, 1979.

C. Plazas & Ana Maria Falchetti, The Technology of Ancient Colombian Gold, *Natural History 1979*, Vol.88 (9).

John Pope Hennessy, *Italian Renaissance Sculpture*, Phaidon, London 1958.

C. W. Previté-Orton, *Shorter Cambridge Medieval History*, Cambridge University Press, 2 Vols., 1952.

V. Pyke, *History of the Early Gold Discoveries in Otago*, Dunedin, 1887.

Jeffrey Quilter, Gold Objects from Southwest Costa Rica, in *Precolumbian Gold*, ed. C. McEwan, British Museum Press, 2000.

Barry Raferty, The Island Celts, in *The Celts, The Origins of Europe*, ed. Moscati, Thames & Hudson, London 1991.

Andrew Ramage & Paul Craddock, *King Croesus' Gold*, British Museum Press, 2001.

Ellen Reader (ed.), *Scythian Gold, Treasures from the Ancient Ukraine*, Harold N. Abrams, New York, 1999.

G. A. Reisner & A. Mace, *The Early Dynastic Cemeteries of Naya-ed-Der*, 2 Vols., Boston, 1908–09.

R. Rolle, *The World of the Scythians*, trs. Gayna Walls, Batsford, London 1989.

Patricia Lea Rubin & Alison Wright, *Renaissance Florence, The Art of the 1470s*, National Gallery Publications, London 1999.

R. S. Sayers, *The Bank of England 1891–1944*, 3 Vols., Cambridge University Press, 1976.

Arthur M. Schlesinger Jr, *The Coming of the New Deal, The Age of Roosevelt*, Vol.2, Houghton Mifflin, Boston, 1960.

Heinrich Schliemann, *Diaries March 1851–April 1852*.

Heinrich Schliemann, *Troy and Its Remains*, London 1875.

Heinrich Schliemann, *Troja*, John Murray, London 1884.

Aubrey de Sélincourt, *World of Herodotus*, Sekker & Warburg, London 1962.

Charles Seltman, *Greek Coins*, Methuen, London 1955.

Tim Severin, *The Jason Voyage*, Hutchinson, London 1985.

Ernest Seyd, *Bullion and Foreign Exchange*, London 1868.

Ian Shaw & Paul Nicholson, *Dictionary of Ancient Egypt*, British Museum Press, 2002.

Izumi Shimada, Jo Ann Griffin & Adon Gordus, The Technology, Iconography and Social Significance of Metals, in *Precolumbia Gold*, ed. C. McEwan, British Museum Press, 2000.

St John Simpson (ed.), *Queen of Sheba*, British Museum Press, 2002.

Robert Skidelsky, *John Maynard Keynes*, Vol.II, Macmillan, London 1992.

C. S. Smith, Metallurgical Footnotes to the History of Art, *Proceedings of the American Philosophical Society*, 116 (2).

José Gomex de Soto, The Agric Helmet, in *The Celts*, ed. S. Moscati, Thames & Hudson, 1991.

J. Sperling, The International Payments Mechanism in the 17th and 18th Centuries, *Economic History Review*, 2nd series, Vol.XIX, 1961.

Peter Spufford, *Money and Its Use in Medieval Europe*, Cambridge University Press, 1988.

Peter Spufford, *Power and Profit: The Merchant in Medieval Europe*, Thames & Hudson, London 2002.

Piero Sraffa, ed., *The Works of David Ricardo*, Vols. II & IV, Cambridge University Press, for the Royal Economic Society, 1950.

Stetch & Piggott, The Metals Trade in Southwest Asia in the 3rd Millennium BC, *Iraq*, Vol.48, 1986.

C. H. V. Sutherland, *Gold, Its Beauty, Power and Allure*, revised edition, Thames & Hudson, London 1969.

Don Texay, *The US Mint and Coinage*, Arco Publishing, New York, 1966.

Joan T. Taylor, *Bronze Goldwork of the British Isles*, Cambridge University Press, 1980.

Tooke & Newmark, *History of Prices and State of the Circulation 1792–1856*, Vol.6, Longman Brown, 1856.

Mario Torelli (ed.), *The Etruscans*, Thames & Hudson, London 2001.

W. T. Treadgold, *Byzantium and Its Army*, Stamford University Press, 1995.

Mikhail Treister, *The Treasures of Troy*, Catalogue, Pushkin Museum, Moscow, with Leonardo Arte, Milan, 1996.

Mikhail Treister, *Scythian Gold, Treasures from the Ancient Ukraine*, (ed.) E. Reeder, Harold Abrams, New York, 1999.

B. G. Trigger, B. J. Kemp, D. O'Connor & A. B. Lloyd, *Ancient Egypt, A Social History*, Cambridge University Press, 1983.

Giorgio Vasari, *Vite, Lives of the Most Excellent Painters, Sculptors and Architects 1568*, 4 Vols., trs. A. B. Hinds, J. M. Dent, London, E. P. Dutton, New York, 1927.

A. Vasilakis, *The Civilisations of Ancient Crete*, Herakleion Archaeological Museum Guide, Adam Editions, Athens.

Garcilasco de la Vega, El Inca (original 1609), *Royal Commentaries of the Incas and General History of Peru*, trs. H. V. Livermore, University of Texas Press, Austin, 1989.

J. Vercoutter, *The Gold of Kush*, Sudan Antiquities Service, 1959, Vol.7, pp.120–153.

Maurice Vierya, *Les Assyriens*, Paris, 1961.

Alan Wace, *Mycenae, An Archaeological History and Guide*, Princeton University Press, 1949.

Helen Wang, *Money on the Silk Road*, British Museum Press, 2004.

E. H. Warmington, *Commerce Between the Roman Empire and India*, Curzon Press, London 1974.

R. B. Warner, The Broighter Hoard, in The Celts, The Origins of Europe, ed. Moscati, Thames & Hudson, London 1991.

G. H. Watcham, *The Golden Colony*, London 1855.

Andrew M. Watson, Back to Gold – and Silver, *Economic History Review*, 2nd series, Vol.XX, No. 1, 1967.

Robert Weinberg, *Autograph Award Essays*, London 1992.

T. Wertime & J. D. Muhly (eds.), *The Coming of the Iron Age*, Yale, 1980.

Susan Whitfield, *Life Along the Silk Road*, British Museum Press, 2004.

D. Williams & J. Ogden, *Greek Gold*, British Museum Press, 1994.

D. Williams (ed.), *The Art of Greek Jewellery*, British Museum Press, 1998.

Garder F. Williams, *The Diamond Mines of South Africa*, Macmillan, London 1902.

Jonathan Williams (ed.), *A History of Money*, British Museum Press, London 1998.

Donald Wiseman, *Nebuchdrezzer and Babylon*, British Academy, Oxford University Press, 1985.

W. Wolska-Conus, *Cosmos Indicopleustes, Topographic Chrétienne*, Vol.1, Paris, 1968.

Sir Leonard Woolley, Excavations at Ur, E. Benn, London 1954.

Index

A

Abd ar-Rahman I and III, Caliphs 232
Abdul al-Malik, Caliph 228, 235
Abu Bakr 226
Abydos (Anatolia) 138
Abydos (Egypt) 39, 45
Achaemenids dynasty 131-2, 146
Adams & Co. 331
Agamemnon 153
Agatharchides geographer 51, 58
Ahhotep, Egyptian Queen 48, 53
Ahmose I, King of Egypt 49, 53
Aigina Treasure 73-4
Akishev, K. and A. 142
Akrotiri 75
Alali battle of 93
Albu, Leopold and George 345-6
alchemy, Chinese 171, 179, 182-3
Alcmaeon 111-2
Aldred, Cyril 38, 42
Aleppo 217, 234
Alexander the Great, 93, 126-36, 139, 154, 187
Alexander IV, Macedonia 135
Alexander, Mount (Australia) 333-4
Alexius I, Byzantine Emperor 222
Alexius IV of Constantinople 223
al-Hajjaj Baladuri 228
al-Hajjaj bin Yousuf, Wasit governor 228
alik Telmun 19
Alluvial 18-24, 192, 210, 230, 297, 303
Altai mountains 143, 172
Alyattes, King of Lydia 110, 113
Amarna/el-Amarna 52-53, 55-6
amber 61, 104
Amenemhat II, Pharaoh 35, 45, 46
Amenemhat III, Pharaoh 48
Amenhotep I, Pharaoh 49
Amenhotep III, Pharaoh 35, 42-3, 50
Amenophis III, King of Egypt 29
American Museum of Natural History 273
American River 326, 329
Amiens 200
Amorium (Anatolia) 229
Amphipolis 129, 135, 155
amphora of Panagyurishte 155
Amsterdam 241, 252, 289, 301, 304, 315
    decline as financial centre 310
amulets 97

Amun (god) 58
Amun-pnufer (tomb robber) 42
Amur river 172, 175-6
Amur-Istar, naruqqam of 26-7
Anastasius, Roman Emperor 208
Anatolia Turkey 65, 118, 135, 137
Andrews, Carol 35
Andronicos, Manolis 126
angel (coin) 287, 289
Angitis river 128
Anglo American Corporation 346
Ankhesenamun, Tutankhamun's wife 54, 56
anonymity of gold 367
Antioch 203-4, 210, 216, 220
    and Crusades 234-5
Antiochus I, Bactrian ruler 120, 135
antoninianus 202
Antonil (Jesuit priest) 297
Antonius Pius, Roman Emperor 196
Antwerp 252, 287
Apollo 155
Aquileia 203
Arabs/Arabia 90, 226
Aradus 87-8
Arameans 88
Archivo General de Indias (Seville) 281
Arezzo 101, 107
argenteus 203
Aristophanes 125, 126
Aristotle 113, 128
Armenia 131, 247
arsenic 183
Arte della Seta (Florence) 255
ashab al-matalib (tomb-robbers) 228
Ashmolean Museum (Oxford) 73, 113, 164, 187
Ashtor, Eliyahu 250, 251-2
Assay Office (US) 365
assaying 23, 243
Assur 16, 23, 31
Assurnasirpal II, King of Assyria 30
Assyria/Assyrian Empire 16, 79
Aswan 38, 45
Atahualpa of Incas 282, 284
Athena (goddess) 125-6, 129, 138, 147, 155
Athens/Athenians 77, 123-39, 138
Aubet, Maria Eugenia 88, 90, 92, 98
Augustus, Roman Emperor 190, 196-8, 203

Aurelian, Roman Emperor 202
aureus 195-8, 202-3, 241, 306
   Nero recoinage 306
Australia (gold rush) x, 30, 84, 187, 196, 296, 306, 381

B

Babylon 17, 21, 23, 33-4
Bactria (Afghanistan) 16, 20, 116, 118, 135
Baladhuri, al-Hajjaj 228
Ballarat 333-4
Baltimore: Walters Art Gallery 149
Bamako, Mali 230
Bambouk, Mali (Wangera) 230
Banco Central de Costa Rica: Museo del Oro 279-80
Bank of England x, 338, 339
   see also Bullion Office
Bank of France 338, 343, 359-61, 366
Bank for International Settlements 362-3, 367, 374
Barcelona Mint 286
Bardi Bank (Venice) 243-5, 247, 249, 253
Baring, Alexander 322-3
Baring, Sir Francis 316-17
Barnato, Barney 345-6
Basil I, Byzantine Emperor 219-21
Basil II, Byzantine Emperor 220, 232-3
Bass, G. F. 63
battiloro 254-5
Bavaria 165
Beaurains treasure 200
Beirut 68, 250, 381
Beit, Alfred 345
Belgium 341, 382
Benaki Museum (Athens) 82, 136
Bendigo 333, 334
Berbers 227, 229-30, 237
Berenice 40-1
Berlin Royal Ethnological Museum 279
Bernard the German 242
Bernardini tomb 104
Berton, Pierre 348
billon 202, 222
Bir Umm Farakir 210
Bird, Junius 273
Black Death 247, 249
Black Obelisk of Shalmaneser III 31
Blainey, Geoffrey 368
Bland Allison Act (USA, 1878) 342
Blegen, Carl 64, 66, 78, 81
Bloch, Raymond 101, 107
Blondeau, Pierre 294
Boer War 346
Bohemia 165, 167, 242, 287
Bolivia 252, 268, 282, 285, 289, 293
Bombay (Mumbai) x, 374, 377
Book of the Dead (Egypt) 55

Botticelli, Sandro 253-4
bowls, golden 31
Bradbury, Sir John 358
Brannan, Sam 326
brass 182-3, 236
Bray, Warwick 273, 278
Brazil 52, 84, 111, 268, 290
Bretton Woods Agreement 371
British Museum
   Scientific Research Department viii, x
Broighter hoard (Ireland) 166
bronze 16, 36, 71
Brown, Gordon 383
Brown, Janet 4
Brown, William 353
Brown & Wingrove 339
Bruges 243, 246, 249
Brunelleschi, Filippo 255
Bryan, William Jennings 336, 343
Buhen 45-6, 50
bull dancing 72
bulla 199
Bullion Committee (1810) in London 307-24
Bullion Office (Bank of England) 311-13, 339, 355-6
Bullion Warehouse, Bank of England 301-2
Bunker, Emma 172-4
Burger, Richard 264
Buritica (Colombia) 271, 276-7, 285
Bustacchini, Gianfranco 214-5
Buyids 236
Byblos 16, 25, 28, 69
Byzantium/Byzantine empire vii, ix, 205, 207-24

C

Caere (Cerveteri) and Etruscans 101-2, 104-6
Cairo viii, 38
Cajamarca 268, 284, 285
Californian gold rush 30, 84, 187, 196, 296, 306, 325-32, 336, 338
Caligari 91
Calima culture (Peru) 270-2
Callao 285
calligraphy 236
Cambyses, King of Lydia 116
Canakkala 63
Canning, George 319
Cantabrica Cordillera 193-4
carats/carati 211, 246, 248
caravans 18, 26
Carle Kempe Collection (Stockholm) 184
Carleton Jones, Guy 369-70
Carradice, Ian 116-17
Carroll, Diane Lee 106
Carson City Mint 337
Carson, Robert 203, 205
Cartagena (New Carthage) 93, 188, 190

Carter, Howard vii, 35, 55-7
Cartwright, A. P. 344
Casa de la Contratación (Seville) 281-2, 286-7
Casa de la Moneda (Seville) 281
Casa de Moeda (Lisbon) 298, 304
Castile 232
catty (Chinese weight) 179-1
Cauca river (Colombia) 198, 270-1, 274-8, 285
Caucasus (now Georgia) 25, 63-4, 84, 144, 229
Cauuet, Beatrice 163
Cellini, Benvenuto viii, 253, 256-8
    salt cellar 257-9
Celts x, 34, 103, 107, 156-68
cementation 23, 41, 51, 112, 113
Centamin Gold mine 380
Chadwick, John 72, 77, 81, 85
Champagne 243
Charles V, Holy Roman Emperor 284, 286-7
Charles IX, King of France 258
chasing 43
Châtillon sur Seine museum 168
Chavin Culture (Peru) 262-4
Chekhov, Anton 175
Chertomlyk *kurgan* 148
Chevalier, Michel 336
Chile 262, 282, 303
Chimor/Chimú empire of Peru 264, 267-9, 284
China ix, 171-85, 209, 293, 299, 338
Chrysostom, John 208
Churchill, Sir Winston 358
Cimmerians 142
cire perdue see lost-wax casting
Clapham, Sir John 300-2, 322, 324, 336, 340, 352
Claudius, Roman Emperor 197
Clement VI, Pope 247
Clement VII, Pope 257
cloisonné 25, 43, 47, 184
Coclé culture 278
Codex Justinianus 209, 211
Colchis 84, 144
Cologne 105
Colombus 270-90
Columbus, Christopher 252, 279, 282
COMEX (commodity exchange) 381
Comstoke Lode 332
Conduitt, John 300
Consolidated Gold Fields viii, x, 378
Constantine I, the Great, Roman Emperor 201, 203, 207, 208, 214
    and *solidus* 204
Constantine V, Byzantine Emperor 217
Constantine VIII, Byzantine Emperor 221
Constantine IX, Byzantine Emperor 222, 229
Constantinople
    and Byzantium 210-1, 215-9, 221
Cordoba, Spain 226, 228, 230, 232, 234, 236, 237-8
Corinth 77, 132
Coronets 61
Corsica 93, 107

Cortés, Hernán 282
Corti Chris 10, 385
Cortona (Curtun) 101
Cosmos Indicopleustes 210, 212, 231
Costa Rica 279
Côte d'Ivoire 380
Craddock, Paul vii, x, 111, 113
Craig, Sir John 294
Crawford, Michael 190
Credit Anstalt (Austria) 361
Credit Suisse 375
Crimea 137
Croatia 194
croesids 114, 116-7
crown (coin)
    see *escudo*
Crusades 223, 233-4, 235, 242
cruzado 251
Cuba 279, 282
cuneiform script 17, 52
Cunliffe, Lord 354
cupellation 23, 41, 92, 112
currency bars 67
Curtis, John 119-20
Cuzco 264, 268-9, 279, 284-5
cyanide 345-6
Cyprus 69, 217, 223
Cyrus the Great 34, 109, 114, 123, 132
Cyrus the Younger 118

D

Da Gama, Vasco 251
Dabeida 276
Dacia 191, 195-7, 201
Dahshur 46-7
Dalmatia 194, 196
Damascus 31, 131, 216
Dandolo, Doge of Venice 223, 241-2, 244
Dardenelles 62, 64
darics 116-18, 120, 130, 132
Darius, the Great, 131-2
Darius III, King of Persia 109, 129, 130-1
Darmstadter Bank (Germany) 361
Darwin, Charles 261
Davene hoard 151
Dawes plan 357
Day, John 249
de Beer, Johannes and Diedrich 345
de Gaulle, Charles 373
Delphi 158
denarius 196-7, 202, 225
Denmark 341, 361
dentistry 378
Denver Mint 337
depletion gilding 24, 274, 278
Desroches-Nobelcourt, Christiane 42, 55, 57

Deutsche Bank 341
Diadorus Siculus 93
diamonds 344-5
Dilmun (Bahrain) 19, 27-8
dinar
    Byzantium 218, 220
    Islam 225, 228-34
    Rome 203
Diocletian, Roman Emperor 202-3, 208
dirhem 225, 233-4, 235
Djeb, Mountain of 50
Djerid 230, 232
Dnieper river 141, 147, 149-50
Dolaucothi (Wales) 190, 194
Dolfin, Lorenzo 251
Domergue, C. 192, 194
Domitian, Roman Emperor 196
Donatello 253
Douala (Cameroon) 94
Dubai 28, 68, 374, 381
Dubrovnik (Ragusa) 242
Dubs, Homer H. 176, 180-1
ducat (Venetian) 203, 241, 246-52
Dumbarton Oaks collection 278
Duncan-Jones, Richard x, 195, 306
Dutch East India Company 289, 293
Duval, Paul-Marie 157

E

eagle 336, 378, 384
Easton, Donald 62
Ebora, El Tresore de 99
Ecbatana 135
Eckstein, Hermann 345, 346
ecu 247
Ecuador 261-2, 268
Egypt vii, 34, 35-59, 63, 69, 80, 210, 381
Eichengreen, Barry 348, 349
Einzig, Paul 359
el-Amarna see Amarna
electrochemical replacement gilding 265
electronics vii, 378, 385
electrum 18, 64, 145
Elizabeth I, Queen of England 287-9
el-Lahun 46-7
elm-pod-coins 179
Eluère, Christiane 103, 157, 161-2
embroidery, gold 255-6
Eritrea 36, 380
Eros 138
    medallion 136
escudo (crown) 252, 287, 288, 289
Etruscans/Etruria 101-8
Euboea 63, 117
Euphrates, River 16, 18, 28, 52, 118, 131, 220
Euthydemus I, Bactrian ruler 120

Evander gold field 346, 371
Evans, Sir Arthur 70, 73, 75
Evans, Joan 75
Exchange Traded Funds, (ETFs) 385

F

Falchetti, Ana Maria 274, 277
Falmouth packet 305
Fatimid dynasty 221, 229, 233-8
Feather river 326
Feaveryear, Sir Alfred 322
Federal Reserve Bank, New york (US) 353, 357, 362, 367, 372, 373, 374, 382
Ferdinand V of Castille and Isabella 282
Fernández Enciso, Martin 271
Fez x, 237
fibulae (crossbow brooches) 105, 200
Figueira, Thomas 126
filigree 15, 25, 65, 72, 138, 160, 162, 172, 237, 277
Finland 363
Finzenú 276, 277
Fire Assaying, see assaying
Fisher, H. E. S. 305
Fitton, Lesley 70, 72, 81
Five Brothers kurgan 148
Flanders 235, 245, 289
Florence 242, 245, 248, 250-8
follis 208, 219
Fondaco dei Tedeschi (Venice) 242, 243, 252
Forbes, Sir William 309
Fort Knox 367
Foster, Benjamin 26
Francis (François) I, France 257
Frankfurt 381
Franks, Sir Augustus 118
Free State Geduld mine 370
frescoes 21, 28, 72
Frontino mine 276
Fugger banking house 288
fur trade/fur Route 141, 172
Fustat (Cairo) 226, 228

G

Gadir (Cadiz) 87, 91-2, 98
Gagarin, Prince Mikhail 144
Galanina, Liudmila 145-6, 149-50
Galassi, Vicenzo 104
Galbraith, John Kenneth 307, 340, 358
Gambia 251
Gaugamela, Battle of 131
General Mining and Finance Corporation 346
Genoa 243, 245-6, 252-3, 304
genovino 243, 249

George I, King of Great Britain 300
George III, King of Great Britain 309-10
George, Dennis 102
Georgia 153, 210
Germany 198
GFMS Limited viii, x
Ghana (country) 94, 379, 380
Ghana (town) 230-1
Ghiberti, Lorenzo 253, 255-6
Ghirlandaio, Domenico 213, 254
gilding 24
    see also depletion gilding 265, 274, 278, 336
Giovanni Dei, Antonio de 254
Giza 43
Goerz, Adolf 346
Goethe, Johann W. von 259
Golas, Peter J. 171, 176-7
Gold Alloys
    See electrum, red gold, tumbaga, white gold
gold coinage
    boom 247
    and Britain's Bullion Committee 309-11, 314-15, 319-20
    Byzantium 207, 211-12, 216-18, 220, 222
    China 180
    decline 249
    France 308, 319, 337-8
    and gold rushes 325, 336-7
    Rome 195-8, 201, 202, 203-5
    Scythia 146
    Spain 251, 252, 281, 287-8, 289
    stocks, table of (1850-1913) 344
    gold coins
    see *angels, aureus, croesid, crown, daric, dinar, double eagle, ducat, ecu, eagle, florin, genovino d'oro, guinea, hyperpyron, louis d'or, mark, moedas de oro, moydores, Napoléon, noble, nomisma, perpero, solidus, sovereign, stater, tanghi d'oro*
gold coin recoinages
    Rome/Nero 181, 306
    Britan/George 294-6, 305-6
Gold fixings
    See London, Venice
Gold hoarding 351, 362-3
Gold mining
    See Altai mts, Australia, Bolivia, Brazil, Canada, Caucasus (Georgia), China, Colombia, Dacia, Dalmatia, Egypt, Kazakhstan, Macedonia, Mali, Nubia, Peru, Russia/Soviet Union, South Africa, United States
Gold 'ports'
    See Djerid, nul Lamta, Sijilmasa, Wurgla
Gold Reserve Act (US, 1934) 365
gold rushes
    see Australia, Brazil, California, Hungary, Klondike, New Zealand, South Africa
gold scrap 20-1, 68-9, 80, 201
gold: silver 'parting' 109, 112-13

gold: silver ratio
    China 221
    Colombia 338
    Egypt 37-8
    Greece 133
    Lydia/Persia 135
    Mesopotamia 20, 23
    Rome 234, 246, 251
    Spain 289
Gold Standard 291-363
Gold Standard Act (US, 1900) 343
Gold Standard Reserve (India) 356
Gold wire 25, 44, 53, 64, 237
Golden Fleece mining technique 19, 84, 163, 176-7
'golden man' of Issyk 142-3
Goldsmid family (Aaron, Abraham, Benjamin, George and Isaac) 309, 311, 313-16, 320
Goldsmid and Eliason 309, 313, 316
Goldsmiths' Techniques and technology
    See casting, cementation, chasing, chisels, *cire perdue*, cloisonné, cupellation, depletion gilding, filigree, gilding, granulation, hammers, moulds, *repoussé, opus interassile*, sintering
Gombrich, E. H. 217, 236, 253
Gori, Vittorio 107
gorytos 147-8, 149
Grabar, André 213-5
Granicus, battle of 130
Grant, Michael 102
granulation
    China 171, 174
    Egypt 43-4, 47-8
    Etruscan 97, 103-6
    Islam 237
    Latin America 264
    Mesopotamia 15, 25
    Minoan Crete 72, 74
    Mycenæ 83
    research and debate on techniques 105-6
    Troy 65, 67, 74
Greece/Greeks 24, 30, 63, 123-39, 203, 381
Green, Miranda 157, 168
Greffuhle, John 318
Gregorietti, Guido 101
Gregory, Sir Theodore 345
Grierson, Philip 207, 219, 222, 225, 232
Grossman, Joel 262
Guadalquivir river see Seville
guanin 279
Guatavita, Lake 276, 290
guild, goldsmiths' 219
Guinea 294, 380
guineas 304, 306
gulden 246-8
Gyges, King of Lydia 109

H

Hadrian, Roman Emperor 197
Haggard, William 339
Haghia Sophia 209, 212-13, 216
hair-rings 64
Haiti (Hispaniola) 279, 282
    al-Hakim II, Caliph 232, 237
Hall, Edwin 329
Hallstatt culture (Austria), 161-2
Halys river 110, 114, 115
Hamadan 121, 236
Hamburg 304, 317
Hamilton, Earl J. ix, 282, 286, 287, 288, 289
Hammond, N.G.L. 127, 128, 129, 134
Hammurapi, King of Babylon: and Code 17, 28, 29
Han dynasty 174
Han Schu 24 (Chinese economic history) 175, 176, 179, 180
Hannan, Paddy 347
Hanno (Phoenician navigator) 94-5
Hanseatic trade 243
Hapsburg 287
Harden, Donald 95
Hargraves, Edward Hammond 332, 334
Harrison, George 345
Hartmann, Axel 158
Harun al-Rashid, Caliph 229, 236
Harvard-Cornell Sardis expeditions 111, 114
Harvey, Ernest 362
Hawtrey, Ralph 367
Hayward, J. F. 254, 258
Hendy, Michael 211, 222
Herakleion Archaeological Museum Crete viii, 69, 71, 72
Herat 236
Heredia, Pedro de 279, 284
Hermitage (St Petersburg) vii, ix
    Scythian collection viii, 144-6, 149
Hermus river 111
Hernández, Luis 286
Herodotus ix, 33, 111, 123
Herries, John 320-1
Hervey, Captain Augustus 305
Heuneburg 161, 162
Higgins, Raymond 139
Higgins, Reynold 106, 200
Hijaz (Arabia) 229
Hinduism 249
Hiram I, King of Tyre 89
Hispaniola (Haiti) 279, 282
Hissarlik 61-63, 65
Hittites 88
hoarding 351, 363
Holland see Netherlands
Holliday, J. S. 325, 329
Holy Land 88, 223, 234, 235, 236
Homestake mine (South Dakota) 332, 368

Honorius, Western Roman Emperor 205, 207
Hong Kong 377, 381
Horner, Francis 307, 318, 321
horses price of 173-4
Howgego, Christopher 187, 188, 197, 202
Hoxne treasure 200
Hsiung-nu 180
Huaca del Sol/de la Lune (Moche) 266
Huancevalina 285
huang-chin 175
Huelva 92
Hughes, Graham 101, 105, 106, 121, 198, 259
Humble, John 311-13
Hungary 30, 52, 296
Huskisson, William 307
Huy, Viceroy of Kush 50-1, 56
hydraulic mining 330
hyperpyron ('*perpero*') 203, 222-3, 241, 242, 244-5, 248

I

Illirtsi *kurgan* 148
Imperial Bank of Russia 343
Incas 264, 268-9, 283
India x, 16, 178, 197, 381
Indonesia 52, 111, 293
Indus river 20
Inner Mongolia 177
Instanbul Archaeological Museum 61
International Monetary Conference (1881) 341
International Monetary Fund 371-2, 382
Irene, Empress 218, 229
Irsching hoard 165
Isaac II of Constantinople 223
Isfahan 228, 236
Isidorus of Miletus (architect) 212
Iskenderun 131
Islam 217, 225-38
Israel 31, 87, 88
Issus, Battle of 130, 131
Issyk, `golden man' of 142
Italy 103, 137, 235, 241-59, 341
ivory 70, 80, 87, 89, 104
Izmir see Smyrna

J

Jacobson, Esther 142, 145, 147, 150
jade 172, 173, 174
Jagersfontein 345
Jakarta 377, 378, 381
Jao-Yuan mine 184
Japan 183, 293, 299
    high technology gold 377, 381

Jason see Golden Fleece
Jenkins, Roy 375
Jenkinson, Charles, 1ˢᵗ Earl of Liverpool 305, 306
Jenkinson, Robert Banks, 2ⁿᵈ Earl of Liverpool 322
Jerusalem and Holy Land 88, 223, 234, 235, 236
jewellery 367, 378
    Celts 161, 164-6
    see also gold ornaments & goldsmiths' techniques
Jing, Prince, tomb of 173
Johannesburg 370-1
    Consolidated Investment Company 346
John II and V, Byzantine Emperors 222-3
Johns, Catherine 198, 200
Johnson Matthey 340, 347, 354-5
Jones, G. D. B. 191, 193
Julius Caesar 167, 188, 195-6, 202
Justinian I, Byzantine Emperor 209-216
Justinian II, Byzantine Emperor 228, 237
Justinian II, Emperor 218

K

Kairouan 230, 233
Kalgoorlie x, 347-8, 368
Kam Ngan (Chinese Gold and Silver Exchange) 381
Kanes (Kültepe) 26, 27, 63
kantar 246
Kazakhstan 143, 172
Kazanluk (Seuthopolis) 154
Kerma 46, 49
Kerr Addison 368
Keynes, John Maynard 351, 354, 358
Khalid, General 226
Kieschnick, John 185
Kiev Museum 148
Kimberley diamond mines 345
Kitchen, Joseph 360
Kition (Larnaca) 87, 90, 96
Klapwijk, Philip x, 10, 383
Klerksdorp gold field 371
Klondike gold rush 347-8
Knights Templar 223, 234
Knossos xi, 68, 69
Koptos 39, 41, 50, 58
Krahmann, Rudolf: magnetometer 370
Kravelo treasure 154
Kremnica 246
Krenides (later Philippi) 127
krugerrand 113, 384
Kuban river 46
Kufic script 236, 238
Kuhrt, Amelia 110
Kul Oba kurgan 147-8, 149
Kültepe (Kanes) 26-7, 63
Kunsthistorisches Museum (Vienna) viii, 258
Kurigulzu I, King of Babylon 29
Kush 40, 41, 46, 49, 50-52
Kutna Hora mines 244
Kuwait 32, 384
Kyme treasure 138
Kynaston, David 310, 316, 323

L

La Niece, Susan x, 24, 261, 277
La Tène 162-3, 166, 167
Lailou, Angeliki 219
Lalaounis, Ilias 75
Lambayeque river 262, 264, 268
Lampsacus (Lapseki) 63, 130, 135, 155
Lane, Frederick ix, 241, 242, 244, 245, 249
Langlaagte farm 345
Laos 381
Larnaca (Kition) 87, 90, 96
Larsa 16, 23, 27
Las Huacas 278
Las Medulas 191-2
Lassois, Mount 161, 162
Latin Monetary Union (1865) 341
Laughlin, J. Laurence 336
Laurion 123-4, 188
Lavrio 123
Lawrence, D. H. 101
League of Nations 357
Lebanon 49, 88
Lechtman, Heather 262, 265, 269
Lee Kwan Yu 381
Lemnos (Poliochini) 63-65
Leo III, Byzantine Emperor 217
Leo VI, Byzantine Emperor 219
León 190, 191
León, Cieza de 269
Leonardo da Vinci 253
Lepidus 188
Letnitsa treasure 154
Lewis IV, King of Bavaria 247
Lewis, Bernard 225
Lewis, P. R. 191-3
Lewis Pond Creek 332
Libya 48, 116, 382
Licinius, emperor of Eastern Empire 204
Lima 285
lime-flasks 272-5
Limoges 163, 196
Linear A 71, 75
Linear B 71-2, 74, 78, 81, 85
Lion Gate of Mycenæ 77-8, 85
Lisbon 252, 352
Littlepage, John D. 369
Liv Sheng, Emperor of China and wife 174
Livy 95, 164, 188
Lixus 87, 91
Lleras-Pérez, Roberto 276
LLoyd George, David 351

Lombard, Maurice 225, 232, 233, 235
Lombards 216, 217
Lord, Isaac 331
lost-wax casting 278
Louis d'Or 308, 319
Louvre (Paris) 96
Louw, Adriaan 371
Lucagnolo (goldsmith) 256
Lugdunum (Lyon/s) 196, 208, 288
Lukovit treasure 154
lunulae 158-9
Lusitano, Viera 304
Lydia, 19, 30, 92, 96, 102, 103, 109-21
Lyon/Lyons (Lugdunum) 196, 208, 288

M

Macarthur-Forrest process/MacArthur, John 346, 380
MacDonald, Ramsay 362
Macedonia 156, 210, 220
McIntyre, Ian x, 159-60
McKay, James 337
McKenna, Reginald 358
Macmillan, Harold 374
Magan 19
Magdalena river (Colombia) 270-1, 275, 278, 285
Magreb 229
Magyar Nemzeti Muzeum (Budapest) 168
Malagana Treasure 271-3, 275
Mali 94, 230-1, 246, 250, 380
Mallia 71, 73-4
Mallowan, Max 21
Mamluks 249
    al-Mamun, Caliph 229
Manaus 377
Mannerism 258
Manning, William 319
Mansa Musa, ruler of Mali 246, 249
Manuel I, Byzantine Emperor 222
Manzikert, battle of 222
maple leaf 384
maps
    Alexander the Great's campaigns and mints 125
    Troy, Minoan Crete, Mycenea 79
    California gold rush 327
    China: Han Empire 173
    Mesopotamia 17
    Precolombian and Peruvian cultures 263, 283
    Roman mines and mints 189
    Scythia and Central Asian Steppe 143
    West Africa 227
Marathon, battle of 116
Marco Polo 184
Marcone, Antonio 256
Marcos, Rodriguez 286
Marcus Aurelius, Roman Emperor 197
mark 341, 357

Mark Antony 188
Marlborough, Duke of 301
Marrakech 237
Marshall, James 325, 326
Martel, Charles 230
Martin, William McChesney 374
Matienzo, Sancho de 282
Matthey, Edward 339
Matthey, George 355
Matto Grosso 297, 303
Mauritania 94
Mawe, John 297
Maxwell-Hyslop, Kathleen 25, 63
Mazarov, Ivan 151, 155-6
Mecca 226
Medes 110, 114
Medici family 253-5
Medina 226, 229
Meeks, Nigel x, 105, 261, 277
Melbourne 333-4
Melitopol kurgans 148
Meluhha 19-0
Memphis 38, 43-4
Mentuhotep II, Pharaoh 45
mercury 172, 174, 182-3
Mereret, Egyptian Queen 48
Mererula, Saqqara vizier 43
Merle, William 315
Mes-kalam-dug, Prince of Ur 15, 21, 25, 31
Mesopotamia ii, 15-34, 49, 69, 79, 81, 90
Mesquita and mihrab in Cordoba 237-8
Metropolitan Museum of Art (New York) 28, 48, 53
Mexico 361
Michael III, Byzantine Emperor 219
Michael IV, Byzantine Emperor 221
Michelangelo 253-4
Midas 110
Milan 101, 164
Miletus 109, 114, 135
Minas Gerais 290, 296-7, 302, 303
mining, salt 161
mining, silver
    Bolivia 293
    Egypt 38
    Latin America 293
    Minoan Crete ix, 69-76, 77, 79, 88
    agriculture 70-2
    Aigina Treasure 73-4
    diaspora 74-5
    economy 70-2
    and Egypt 47, 57-8, 70, 74, 80-1
    jewellery 69, 71, 73-5
    and Mesopotamia 21, 25, 34
Minotaur 76
Mint, primitive 114
Mints
    See Abydos, Alexandria, Bactria, Baghdad,
    Barcelona, Carson City, Constantinople,
    Damascus, Lampsacus, Lisbon, London (Royal

Mint), Lugdunam (Lyon), Paris, Pella, Perth (Western Australia), Philadelphia, Rio de Janeiro, Rome, San Francisco, Sardis, Seville, Sydney, Thessalonika, Venice
mithqal 228
Mithradates 188
Mittani 52
Mocatta, Abraham 299, 301
Mocatta, Edward `Jock' 340
Mocatta, Moses 301
Mocatta and Goldsmid ix, 308, 338-40, 353, 355-6, 359, 366, 382
   and Bullion Committee 308-9, 311-16, 319, 320, 322
mocenighi 251
Mocenigo, Tommaso, Doge of Venice 250, 251
Moche/Mochica people of Peru 264-7, 285
Mochlos 63, 71
moedas 304
Mohammed Fantar 93
Mold Cape, Celtic x, 159-60
Montagu, Samuel 339, 342, 355, 372
Montefurado tunnel 193
Montet, Pierre 59
Moorey, P. R. S. 20, 25, 33
Morgan, J.P. (bank) 362
Morganthau, Henry 365-6
Morrell, W. P. 336, 346
Morris, James 242
Morrison, Cécile 211
mosaics 213-5
Moscati, Sabatino 92, 104
Moseley, Michael 265, 266, 268
Morkholm, Otto 133, 135, 136
Mosul 30, 131, 236
Motya 91
moydore 304
Mozolovsky, B. N. 150
Mueller, Reinhold ix, 241-2, 244, 245, 249
Muhammed, Prophet 216, 225-6
Muisca culture 271, 275-8, 279, 290, 344
   al-Mu'izz, Caliph 233
Müller, Hans 40, 58
Mumbai (Bombay) x, 374, 377
Museo Arqueológico Nacional (Madrid) 98
Museo Arqueológico (Seville) 99
Museo Egizio (Turin) 41
Museo del Oro (Banco Central de Costa Rica) 279
Museo del Oro (Bogotá) viii, 270, 271-2, 274, 276
Museo Poldi-Pezzoli (Milan) 101
Museo di Villa Giulia (Rome) 105
Museum of Historical Treasures of Ukraine (Kiev) 148, 150
Muzahim Mahmud Hussein 31
Mycenæ 34, 68, 69, 77-85, 88, 89, 123
Myriandrus (Iskenderun) 131

N

Nabopolassar, King of Babylon 33
Nag el-Deir 39
Napata 49
Naples 287
Napoleon I 253, 307-8, 310, 319, 320, 321
napoléon d'or 319, 325, 337, 338, 353, 363, 378
Napoleonic Wars 307, 308-11, 314, 319-21
Naqada (Nubt) 39-41
Narmer, Pharaoh 38
naruqqum (gold contracts) 25-7, 30
Nash Briggs, Daphne 164
National Archaeological Museum (Athens) viii, 61, 80
National Museum of Costa Rica 279
National Museum of Iran 120
National Museum of Ireland viii, 168
Nauplia, Gulf of 78
Nebuchadrezzer II, King of Babylon 33
Nechi river 271, 276
Necho, Pharaoh 87
necklaces 21-22, 32
Needham, Joseph 182-3
Nefertiti, Egyptian Queen 55-6, 80
Nekcsei, Demetrius 246
Nekhbet 56
Nekheb 40
Nelson, Horatio 310
Nero, Roman Emperor 181, 194-7, 218, 306
Netherlands/Holland 252, 382
New Kingdom (Egypt) 36, 38, 43, 49-54, 57-8
New South Wales, Bank of 333-4
New Zealand: gold rush 335
Newton, Sir Isaac 324, 362
   and Britain and Brazil 293-6, 299-300, 306
Nicephorus I, Byzantine Emperor 218
Nicephorus II, Byzantine Emperor 220, 237
Niger river 230
Nihavand treasure 236
Nike (goddess) 124, 126, 128, 129, 138, 147, 155
Nile, River vii, 35-6, 38, 45-6, 51, 74, 229, 233
Nimrud 16, 21, 30-3
Ninevah 16, 216
Nippur 16
Nixon, Richard 382
noble 247
nomads see Scythians
nomisma (earlier solidus) 203, 241
Norman, Montagu 357, 362
North America see Canada; United States
`North Pontic cities' 141
Northover, Peter 157, 162, 166, 167
North-West Palace (Nimrud) 31
Novia Scotia, Bank of 382
Nubia vii, 29, 45-6, 74, 84, 188

nué embroidery 255-6
nugget 384
Nul Lamta 230, 232
Numidia 188
Numismatic Museum (Athens) 132
nummi 208
Nuñez de Balboa, Vasco 271

O

Oates, Joan viii, 18, 29, 33
O'Day, Karen 268
O'Hara, James, 2nd Baron Tyrawly 304
Olbia 141, 143
Old Kingdom (Egypt) 36, 37, 38, 39-41, 45
Ophir 87, 89-90
Oppenheimer, Sir Ernest 346, 368, 370
Ouargla (Wurgla) 230
Ouro Preto 296, 304
Oxford see Ashmolean Museum
Oxus river 114, 118, 129
Oxus Treasure ix, 118-21

P

Pactolus river 63-4, 111, 113, 117, 130
`paddocking' 335
paglola (gold dust) 243
Pampa Grande 266
Pan Gu (historian) 181
Panagyurishte treasure 154-5
Panama 279, 283, 285, 331
Pangaion, Mount 129, 137, 154
Pantikapaion 144-8
Paracas people of Peru 264
Parish, John 317, 320
Paulinyi, Oszkar 247
Pearse, John 316
Peel, Sir Robert: Act of 1819 323
Pegolotti, Francesco Balducci 245, 248
Pella mint 128, 129
Perceval, Spencer 307
perpero see *hyperpyron*
Perruzzi (Florence) 249
Persepolis 121, 132
Persia/Persians 109-121, 129-136
Perth Mint 347
Peru 68, 262-70, 272, 273, 381
Peruzzi family 243, 247, 253
Peter I, the Great, Tsar 144
Petrakis, Basil 80
Petrie, Sir W. M. Flinders 39, 47
Philadelphia Mint 336
Philip II, King of Spain 287, 288
Philip VI, King of France 247

Philip of Macedon viii, 120, 132, 135, 137, 143, 154, 381
Philippeioi (coins) 128, 129
Philippines 52, 111, 184, 289
Phocaea 109, 114
Phoenicians 34, 38, 87-99
Phokaia 138
Phrygians 110
pins 160
Pisano, Giovanna 97-8
Pitt, William 308
Pixley, Stewart 339-40
Pixley and Abell 355
Pizarro, Francisco 268, 279, 282-4
placer gold see alluvial
platinum 160
Pliny the Elder iii, 63, 84, 176, 178
Poincaré, Raymond 359
Poliochini (Lemnos) 63-5
Polk, President James 328, 336
Pollaiuolo, Antonio del 255, 256
Polybius 158, 164
Poma de Ayala, Felipe Guaman 284
Pompeii 187, 195, 198-9, 201
Populonia 101
Portugal 319
Porzia, Madonna 256-7
Potosi mine (Bolivia) 252, 282, 285, 293
pottery 17, 53, 71, 80, 103, 141
Praeneste (Palestrina) 96, 97, 101, 104
President Brand/President Steyn mines 370
Previté-Orton, C. 216
Psusennes I, Pharaoh 38, 59
Ptolemy I of Egypt 131, 135
Pu-abi, Queen of Ur 21-2, 24, 25
Puerto Rico 279, 282
Punic wars 99
Pushkin Museum (Moscow) ix, 61-2, 65, 67-8
Pylos 72, 75, 77, 81-2, 84

Q

Quesada, Gonzalo Jimene de 279
Quilter, Jeffrey 278
Quimbaya people and Treasure (Colombia) ix, 184, 270-1, 274-5, 277
Qur'an 225, 236

R

Ra (sun god) 36
Raferty, Barry 166
Ragusa (Dubrovnik) 242
Ramage, Andrew 111, 113
Rameses II, Pharaoh 49, 58

Rameses III, Pharaoh 35, 58, 84
Rand Refinery 347, 356
Raphael, Henry Lewis 339
Ravenna 201, 207, 215
    mosaics 209, 212-17, 237
Read, Gabriel 335
Reader, Ellen 149, 150
real 288
red gold (with copper) 19, 23
Red Sea 50, 87
Reisner, George 39
Renaissance goldsmiths in Florence 253-9
repoussé 264, 277
Rhesos Eionides 151
Rhodes, Cecil 345, 346, 369
Rhodope mountains 127, 151, 153
rhytons 155
Rialto see Mint under Venice
Rialto (Venice) 244, 253
Ricardo, David 307, 311, 315, 319, 321, 324
Rio de Janeiro 297, 298, 304
Rio Narcea Gold 194
Rio Tinto (Andalucia) 92, 201
Rivas-Panteon de la Reina 279
`river mining' 330
Robinson, J. B. 345, 346
rock crystal 61, 68
Romani see also Dacia
Romanus IV, Byzantine Emperor 222
Rome/Romans 30, 107, 187-205, 207, 241, 256, 380
Romulus 207
Roosevelt, Franklin Delano 364, 365-6, 372
Rothschild, Nathan Mayer 317, 320, 323, 339
Rothschilds banking house 331-2, 339, 347, 354, 355, 363
Royal Cemetery (Ur) viii, 15, 19, 21-2, 24, 25
Royal Commission on Gold and Silver in Britain (1886) 342
Royal Ethnological Museum (Berlin) 279
Royal Mint London, 293-5, 310-11, 315, 320, 322, 332, 337, 347
Royal Numismatic Cabinet (Munich) 165
`royal road' (Susa to Sardis) 116
Rubin, Patricia Lee 254
Rud, Charles 346
Rudd, Charles 369
Russia/Soviet Union 175, 221, 225, 311, 380

S

Sacramento (town and river) 326, 330-1
Sahara 91, 103, 210, 250
Saka people 142
Saladin 235
Saldana river 271, 275
Samarkand 178-9, 234
Samos 93

Samsi-ilu, golden bowl of 31
San Agustin 271, 273
San Bartolome 92
San Francisco 326, 329, 330
San Jorge river 276
San José (Costa Rica) 279
San Lucar de Barrameda 286
San Marco mint 242
San Vitale 209, 213, 215
Sánchez-Palencia, F. Javier 190
Sant'Apollinaire Nuovo (Ravenna) 213-16
São Paulo 297
Saqqara 44
Sardinia 102, 104, 234, 287
Sardis x, 63, 109, 112, 115, 117, 130, 134, 155
Sargon II, King of Nimrud 20, 26
Sarmatians 150
Saudi Arabia 20, 68, 377, 381, 382
Sauromatians 142
Säve-Söderbergh, T. 52
Sayers, R. S. 359, 362
Schlesinger Jnr, Arthur 366
Schliemann, Heinrich viii, 127, 153, 339
    Californian gold rush 331
    Mycenæ 70, 73, 77, 78, 81
    Troy 61-2, 65-8
Schliemann, Louis 331
Schroder & Co. 331
Scythia and Central Asian Steppe, map 143
Scythians ix, 109, 123, 137, 141-56, 174
Scythians 141-56
    and China 172
Sekhemket, Pharaoh 44
Seleucid dynasty 135
Sélincourt, Aubrey de 123
Seltman, Charles 114, 118-40
semissis 211, 219
Senegal 94, 230, 251,
Senusret I, Pharaoh 35, 45
Senusret II, Pharaoh 47-8
Senusret III, Pharaoh 35, 45, 48
Serbia 242
Serebrovsky, A. P. 369
Seti I, Pharaoh 50, 58
Seuthopolis (Kazanluk) 154
Seven Brothers kurgan 146
Severus Alexander, Roman Emperor 199, 202
Seville 92, 228, 243, 250, 252, 298
Seyhan River 19
Shalmaneser III, 31
Shamans Colombia 275
Shangdong peninsula 184
Sharps & Wilkins 339-40, 355
Sheba, Queen of 90
Sherman Silver Purchase Act (1890) 343
Siberia 172, 176, 380
Sicán (Lambayeque) people (Peru) 265, 266-7
Sicily 70, 87, 91, 93, 95, 123, 137, 209, 211, 217, 218, 220, 231, 233, 243, 287

Sierra de Teleno 192
Sierra Nevada de Santa Marta 278
sigloi 117, 132
Siguas people of Peru 264
Sijilmasa (Morocco) 230-2, 250
Silk Road 172, 178-9, 184, 209
silk trade 178
silver 289
    Bolivia 262
    Britain 326
    Byzantium 212-13
    Carthage 96
    Celts 163, 167
    China 181, 182, 184, 248
    Crusades 228
    Egyptian 37-8, 44, 59
    Etruscan 102, 103
    `fixing' 244
    Florence 255, 256
    Greece 124, 125, 129-30, 131
    India 248
    Islam 225, 228-1, 233-4
    Latin America 262, 264, 266
    Laurion 123, 188
    Macedonia 128, 188
    Mesopotamia 16-20, 24, 26-7, 28
    Minoan Crete 70
    Mycenæ 80
    `parting' from gold 109, 112-13
    Phoenicia 87, 88-7, 90, 91-2, 93, 96
    Romans 93
    Spain 285-8
    Troy 61, 63, 64
    United States 342-3
    Venice 242, 247, 248
    see also gold: silver ratio
silver coinage
    Britain 309-10, 311
    Byzantium 208-9, 211, 218, 219, 221
    Greece 124, 125, 126-7, 128-33, 132, 134, 135
    increased (20th century) 351
    Islam 225, 228-1, 233-4
    Lydia/Persia 121
    Netherlands 338
    Rome 16, 20, 63, 96, 195, 196, 197, 202
    United States 326, 336-7, 341-3
    Venice 242, 251
Singapore 378, 381
`sintering' 106
Siphnos gold 123
Skidelsky, Robert 358, 361
Skookum, Jim 348
Slovakia 246
Smeeton, Terry 383
Smith, C. S. 24
Smyrna (Izmir) 109, 110, 138, 155
Snettisham Treasure 157, 167
Sobkemsaf II, Pharaoh 42
sodium chloride, salt 112

Sogida (Tajikistan) 116
Sogliane, Giovanbattista 256
solidus 203-5, 207, 208, 211, 217-18, 222
Soloka kurgan 149
Solomon, King of Israel 89
Solon 115
Soto, José Gomez de 163
Sounion, Cape 123
South Africa Gold Mining 190, 296, 342, 342-7, 352, 354-9, 369-71, 372-4, 379, 380, 385
South African Reserve Bank 347, 371, 375
sovereign 304, 378, 384
space exploration 378, 385
Spain ix, 90, 168, 184, 243, 252, 281-90, 352
Sparta 77, 117-8, 126
spice trade 250-1
Spufford, Peter 245, 247, 249
Stalin, Joseph 368-9
Standard Chartered Bank 382
star pagodas 319-20
stater 113, 120, 128-30, 132, 134-5, 165
statues, gold 126
stingless bee and lost-wax casting 261, 270, 272-4
Stockholm 184
Stos-Gale, Z. A. 37
Strabo 63, 84, 91, 157
Stradonice 165
Strong, Benjamin 357
Stuttgart 161
Sucio river 276
Sudan (country) 36, 40
`Sudan' (West Africa) 229, 231
Sulla 188
Sumer/Sumerians 15, 16, 18-20, 45
Susa 116, 121, 129, 131, 132
Sutter, John 325, 326
Swain, William 328, 329
Swann, Nancy Lee 179
Sweden 341, 358, 363
Switzerland 103, 157-8, 161-2, 361-3
Swiss Bank Corporation 356, 375
Sydney 332, 333
    Mint 334
Syracuse (Sicily) 95, 210, 218

T

Taino people Haiti 279
Tairona people Colombia 271
Tairona river and people 277, 278
Tajikistan (Sogida) 116, 118
tanghi d'oro 248
Tanis 38, 58-9
tapputu contracts 27
Tarquinii Tombs of the Feast/Leopard 101-2
Tarsus 118, 130
Tartessus 91-2

Tashkent 234
Taurus mountains 19, 210, 217
Taxay, Don 337, 341
Taylor, Joan 159
Tbilisi 19
Ténès 200-1
tesserae mosaics 214, 237
tetarteron 220
tetradrachms 126, 128-32, 134
Thailand (Siam) 361, 381
Thai-shan mountains 177
Thao-Hung Ching (alchemist) 183
Thasos 124, 127
Thassos (Sardinia) 87, 90, 91, 96, 97, 102, 103
Thebes 56
Thebes (Boetian city) 75, 77, 81, 84, 126, 127
Thebes (Egypt) 42, 43, 45, 49, 50
Theodora (daughter of Constantine VIII) 221
Theodora (wife of Justinian) 209, 215
Theodora (wife of Theophilus) 219
Theodosius I, Roman Emperor 205, 207
Theodosius II, Roman Emperor 208
Theophilus, Byzantine Emperor 219, 229
Thessaloniki 128, 203, 207, 210, 221
Thetford treasure 200-1
Thornton, Henry 307, 310
Thrace 90, 127-8, 134, 151-5
Thucydides 95, 123, 126
Thutmose I, Pharaoh 49
Thutmose/Thutmosis III, Pharaoh 29, 35, 49, 51-2
    `minor' wives of 53-4
Tiberius 195
Tiberius II, Roman Emperor 216
Tiglath-Pileser I, King of Assyria 30, 32
Tigris, River 16, 18, 30, 131, 228
Timbukto 230
Tiryns 75, 77, 84
Tmolus, Mount 111, 112
Tokyo 377
Tolfa, Mount 102
Tolima culture (Colombia) 271, 273, 275
Tolstaya Mogila *kurgan* 150
Tooke and Newmarch 338
torcs, Celtic 160-2, 166, 167
Torre del Oro (Seville) 281, 284
touchstones 23, 179
Trajan, Roman Emperor 194, 196-7, 201
Transcaucasia 19
Transvaal Chamber of Mines 356
Transylvania 158, 194
Treasury (US) 382
Trebizond 210, 221
Treister, Mikhail 68, 147-8
tremissis 205, 211, 219
Trialeti 19
Trier 203
Tripoli 233, 235
Troy viii, 34, 61-70, 78
Trujillo 265

Tulunids 229
Tumaca people 272
Tumaco culture Colombia 273
Tumaco-La Tolita 271
tumbaga (gold-copper alloys in Latin America) 262, 265, 267, 268, 270, 274, 277, 278, 279
Tunis 230, 250
tunjos (votive offerings) 275-6
Turkey 92
turquoise, Egyptian 44, 45, 47
Tushratta (Mittani ruler) 52
Tutankhamun, King of Egypt 29, 42, 44, 49, 275
Tyre 131, 233
Tyrol 242, 251
Tyrrhenian Sea 101, 102, 104, 107

U

Uëtliberg 161
Ugarit 20, 47, 69, 80, 88, 89, 96
Ukraine 141, 143, 148, 150
Umayyad dynasty 226, 230, 231, 232
Umma 16, 26, 226
Union Bank of Switzerland 375
Union Corporation 360, 367
United States 325-32, 336, 340-3, 352-3, 361, 365-7, 371, 381,
Ur 15-16, 18, 21, 23, 27-8, 31, 63, 65, 74
Urartu 109
Uruk 16, 18, 19, 25, 27
Uzbekistan 118

V

Van, Lake 18, 30, 222
Van Rijn, Michel 265
Varna treasure 152
Vasari, Giorgia 254
Vasilakis, Adonis 71
Vega, Garcilaso de la, El Inca 269
Venice ix, x, 30, 101, 184, 241-53, 372-6, 289
Ventris, Michael 71-2, 78, 81, 85
Vercingetorix 167
Vercoutter, J. 40, 46, 52
Vergina (Aegae) 126
Verocchio 253
Vetulonia and Etruscans 101, 102, 105-6
Vienna: Kunsthistorisches Museum 258
Vientiane 381
Vietnam 374, 381
Virgil 158
Visigoths 209, 216
Vix princess 162
Vulchitrum treasure 151, 153

W

Wace, Alan 78, 82-3
Wadi Allaqi 38, 46, 50, 51
Wadi Elei 38, 41
Wadi Gabgaba 46
Wadi Hammamat 40, 41, 210
Wales 190, 194
Walker, George 345
Walters Art Gallery, Baltimore 150
Wang, Helen 184
Wang Mang, Emperor of China 171, 180-1
Wangera (Bambouk) 230
Wargla 232
Washington Agreement 375, 382
Watson, Andrew 233
Wawat 40, 41, 46, 50-1
Waywaka 262, 268
weaving 264
Weguelin, Thomas 337
Wei Ch'ing, General 180
Wei-Yang Palace 181
Weinberg, Robert x, 111, 384
Wellington, Duke of: army 319
Wells Fargo 331
Wên Ti, Emperor of China 182
`Wessex' culture 160
West Africa 91, 94, 103, 210, 225, 227-31, 243, 249-51, 294, 301
West Wits Line gold field 370
Western Holdings mine 370
white gold 23
Whitmore, John 316
Wilkinson, Alix 47
Williams, Dyfri 130, 137, 147
Williams, Gardner 345
Williams, Tim x, 40, 191
Winlock, Herbert 48
wire, gold 45, 53, 64, 237
`Women, Grave of' (Mycenæ) 81
Woolley, Sir Leonard 15, 22
World Gold Analyst 380
World Gold Council 379
World War I 347-9, 353, 359, 360-1
World War II 361, 367, 371
Wright, Alison 254
Wu Ti, Emperor of China 183
Wu Tshang Shan Ching 176
Wurgla (Ouargla) 230
Wuzong, Emperor of China 185

X

Xerxes I, King of Persia 117, 132, 151
Xionghu tribe (China) 174, 181

Y

Yaba, Assyrian Queen 32
Yancocha mine 263, 266
Yaqut 231
Yellow river 173, 175
Yemen 90, 228
Ying 175
Yuba river 330

Z

Zab rivers, Great and Lesser 18-21
Zacatecas 285, 300
Zanata family 230
Zeng, Marquis of 173
Zhang Qian, Chinese emissary 178
Zhi Daolin 185
Zoe (daughter of Constantine VIII) 221
Zubaida 236
Zubareva, Natalia v, 380
Zucchi, Antonio 107
Zurich 168, 375, 377, 381